IFIP – The International Federation for Information Processing

IFIP was founded in 1960 under the auspices of UNESCO, following the First World Computer Congress held in Paris the previous year. An umbrella organization for societies working in information processing, IFIP's aim is two-fold: to support information processing within its member countries and to encourage technology transfer to developing nations. As its mission statement clearly states,

> IFIP's mission is to be the leading, truly international, apolitical organization which encourages and assists in the development, exploitation and application of information technology for the benefit of all people.

IFIP is a non-profitmaking organization, run almost solely by 2500 volunteers. It operates through a number of technical committees, which organize events and publications. IFIP's events range from an international congress to local seminars, but the most important are:

- The IFIP World Computer Congress, held every second year;
- Open conferences;
- Working conferences.

The flagship event is the IFIP World Computer Congress, at which both invited and contributed papers are presented. Contributed papers are rigorously refereed and the rejection rate is high.

As with the Congress, participation in the open conferences is open to all and papers may be invited or submitted. Again, submitted papers are stringently refereed.

The working conferences are structured differently. They are usually run by a working group and attendance is small and by invitation only. Their purpose is to create an atmosphere conducive to innovation and development. Refereeing is less rigorous and papers are subjected to extensive group discussion.

Publications arising from IFIP events vary. The papers presented at the IFIP World Computer Congress and at open conferences are published as conference proceedings, while the results of the working conferences are often published as collections of selected and edited papers.

Any national society whose primary activity is in information may apply to become a full member of IFIP, although full membership is restricted to one society per country. Full members are entitled to vote at the annual General Assembly, National societies preferring a less committed involvement may apply for associate or corresponding membership. Associate members enjoy the same benefits as full members, but without voting rights. Corresponding members are not represented in IFIP bodies. Affiliated membership is open to non-national societies, and individual and honorary membership schemes are also offered.

Claude Godart   Norbert Gronau
Sushil Sharma   Gérôme Canals (Eds.)

Software Services
for e-Business
and e-Society

9th IFIP WG 6.1 Conference
on e-Business, e-Services and e-Society, I3E 2009
Nancy, France, September 23-25, 2009
Proceedings

 Springer

Volume Editors

Claude Godart
Gérôme Canals
LORIA, Campus Scientifique
54506 Vandœuvre-les-Nancy Cedex, France
E-mail: {claude.godart, gerome.canals}@loria.fr

Norbert Gronau
University of Potsdam
Business Information Systems and Electronic Government
Am Neuen Palais 10, 14496 Potsdam, Germany
E-mail: norbert.gronau@wi.uni-potsdam.de

Sushil Sharma
Ball State University
Department of Information Systems and Operations Management
Whitinger Business Building, 2000 W. University Ave., Muncie, IN 47306, USA
E-mail: ssharma@bsu.edu

CR Subject Classification (1998): J.1, K.4.4, K.6.5, D.4.6, J.1

ISSN   1868-4238
ISBN-13   978-3-642-26026-1 Springer Berlin Heidelberg New York

springer.com

© IFIP International Federation for Information Processing 2009
Softcover reprint of the hardcover 1st edition 2009

Typesetting: Camera-ready by author, data conversion by Scientific Publishing Services, Chennai, India
Printed on acid-free paper   SPIN: 12755790   06/3180   5 4 3 2 1 0

Preface

I3E 2009 was held in Nancy, France, during September 23–25, hosted by Nancy University and INRIA Grand-Est at LORIA. The conference provided scientists and practitioners of academia, industry and government with a forum where they presented their latest findings concerning application of e-business, e-services and e-society, and the underlying technology to support these applications. The 9th IFIP Conference on e-Business, e-Services and e-Society, sponsored by IFIP WG 6.1. of Technical Committees TC6 in cooperation with TC11, and TC8 represents the continuation of previous events held in Zurich (Switzerland) in 2001, Lisbon (Portugal) in 2002, Sao Paulo (Brazil) in 2003, Toulouse (France) in 2004, Poznan (Poland) in 2005, Turku (Finland) in 2006, Wuhan (China) in 2007 and Tokyo (Japan) in 2008.

The call for papers attracted papers from 31 countries from the five continents. As a result, the I3E 2009 program offered 12 sessions of full-paper presentations. The 31 selected papers cover a wide and important variety of issues in e-Business, e-services and e-society, including security, trust, and privacy, ethical and societal issues, business organization, provision of services as software and software as services, and others. Extended versions of selected papers submitted to I3E 2009 will be published in the *International Journal of e-Adoption* and in *AIS Transactions on Enterprise Systems*. In addition, a 500-euros prize was awarded to the authors of the best paper selected by the Program Committee. We thank all authors who submitted their papers, the Program Committee members and external reviewers for their excellent work.

I3E 2009 also included three prestigious keynotes given by Schahram Dustdar, Vienna UT, Dimitrios Georgakopoulos, CSIRO Canberra, and Bill Rosenblatt, Giant Steps. The conference was co-located with the international workshops for "Technical, Economic and Legal Aspects of Business Models for Virtual Goods" and "Open Digital Rights Language."

We would also like to acknowledge the local organization team, in particular Anne-Lise Charbonnier, Nicolas Alcaraz and Nawal Guermouche, Publicity Chair Khalid Benali, and IFIP WG 6.11 Co-chairs Wojciech Cellary, Winfried Lamersdorf and Reima Suomi for their connection with previous events and IFIP.

We hope that these proceedings motivate the different actors to develop new ideas to push the Web toward many innovations for tomorrow's e-Business, e-Society and e-Services.

September 2009

Claude Godart
Norbert Gronau
Sushil Sharma
Gérôme Canals

Organization

General Chair   Claude Godart, France

Program Chairs   Norbert Gronau, Germany
Sushil Sharma, USA

Publicity Chair   Khalid Benali, France

Publication Chair   Gérôme Canals, France

Liaison Chairs   Motohisha Funabashi, Japan
Khaled Ghedira, Tunisia
Heiko Ludwig, USA
Gustavo Rossi, Argentina
Volker Tschammer, Germany

IFIP TC6 Representatives   Wojciech Cellary, Poland
Winfried Lamersdorf, Germany
Reima Suomi, Finland

Local Organization Chair   Gérôme Canals, France

Local Organization Committee Nicolas Alcaraz, France
Anne-Lise Charbonnier, France
Nawal Guermouche, France

Program Committee

Esma Aïmeur, Canada
Masanori Akiyoshi, Japan
Joao Paulo Almeida, Brazil
Americo Nobre Amorim, Brazil
Katja Andresen, Germany
Achraf Ayadi, France
Khalid Benali, France
Boualem Benatallah, Australia
Salima Benbernou, France
Djamel Benslimane, France
Sami Bhiri, Ireland
Markus Bick, Germany
Melanie Bicking, Germany

Olivier Boissier, France
Omar Boucelma, France
Jerzy Brzezinski, Poland
Regis Cabral, Sweden
Gérôme Canals, France
François Charoy, France
Jen-Yao Chung, China
Christine Collet, France
Bruno Defude, France
Dirk Deschoolmeester, Belgium
Marie Dominique Devignes, France
Alicia Diaz, Argentina
Marie-Christine Fauvet, France

Sponsoring Institutions

Table of Contents

Session 5: e-Government 2

Session 6: Security 2

Session 7: e-Commerce 2

Session 8: Modelling 2

Session 9: User Interactions

Session 10: Simulation

Session 11: Security 3

Session 12: Modelling 3

Electronic Voting Using Identity Domain Separation and Hardware Security Modules

Thomas Rössler

Secure Information Technology Center Austria (A-SIT)
thomas.roessler@a-sit.at

Abstract. E-voting increasingly gains interest in e-Democracy and e-Government movements. Not only the technical security issues of electronic voting systems are of paramount importance, but also the necessity of following an all-embracing approach is challenging and needs to be addressed. This paper discusses e-voting as being a supreme discipline of e-Government. It introduces an innovative e-voting concept using the Internet as the voting channel. The concept introduced is based on Austrian e-Government elements and the Austrian identity management concept in particular. As a result, this paper presents a novel approach of building an e-voting system relying on two core principles: strong end-to-end encryption and stringent identity domain separation.

1 Introduction

Voting is the most important tool in democratic decision making. Therefore, elections and referenda should be accessible to as many people as possible. It is especially difficult for citizens living abroad to participate in elections.

The word e-voting is a general term that refers to any type of voting in electronic form. This work introduces a remote Internet e-voting concept that suits the needs of international election fundamentals—as formulated by the Venice Commission [1] and the Council of Europe in [2] and [3]—and the needs of Austrian elections [4] in particular[1].

Today, the e-Government infrastructure is highly developed in many member states of the European Union. Austria in particular has actively pursued its e-Government strategy since the beginning and thus is today one of leading countries in Europe with respect to e-Government.

E-voting, seen as a special application of e-Government technologies, can be considered as being the supreme discipline of all e-Government applications due to its conflicting priorities of unique identification and perfect anonymity.

The proposed e-voting concept draws upon two principles in order to protect the election secrecy. On the one hand, the proposed e-voting system makes use of strong

---

[1] In preceding work [5] we worked out an exhaustive and all-embracing set of security requirements by following a standardised methodology (i.e. Common Criteria methodology). The security requirements have been created based on (legal) election fundamentals [1], [2], [3], [4], [6] and existing security considerations [7], [8]. These achievements serve the basis for the e-voting concept presented here.

C. Godart et al. (Eds.): I3E 2009, IFIP AICT 305, pp. 1–12, 2009.
© IFIP International Federation for Information Processing 2009

end-to-end encryption between the voter casting her vote and the electronic device responsible for counting. Thus, the cast vote is immediately encrypted by the voter after she has filled in her decision and is only decrypted for the single moment of counting. On the other hand, the proposed e-voting concept introduces a stringent domain separation model that has to ensure unique identification of voters during registration, but also guarantee perfect anonymity of cast votes. A special case in the introduced e-voting concept is that although votes are cast anonymously it is still possible to determine whether a given voter has cast her vote already or not. This mechanism is available during the election event only. This is important and a big advantage of the proposed scheme as it enables a voter to cast her vote conventionally at a polling station although she has decided to vote electronically. This characteristic of the proposed e-voting concept faces problems in connection with the Internet and the voter's local infrastructure as raised by the SERVE-report [9] for instance.

From a technical perspective, the proposed e-voting concept makes use of Austrian e-Government components such as the Citizen Card [10]. Although the core principles of this e-voting concept are versatile, the resulting e-voting concept is tailored to a certain degree for Austrian elections. Thus, the proposed e-voting concept has been named "EVITA" (Electronic Voting over the Internet - Tailored for Austria). The EVITA voting model aims to follow the process model of conventional postal elections which has two phases. In phase one, voters have to register and in phase two the voting process is carried out. Also from a technical perspective EVITA follows tight the model of postal elections. The EVITA scheme requires to encrypt the voter's decision without any identifying information and to attach additional voter related information to the encrypted vote. This corresponds to scenario of postal election scenarios where the vote is put into an inner envelope which itself is wrapped by an outer envelope that contains additional identifying information about the voter.

This paper introduces the core elements of the proposed EVITA-voting concept. The rest of this paper is organised as follows. The next section explains the core principles of the EVITA concept and introduces the dual approach of using strong end-to-end encryption and stringent identity domain separation. Section 3 and 4 further elaborate these core aspects—the creation of the identifiers following the Austrian electronic identity management in particular—in several sub-sections in detail. Section 5 briefly sketches the counting phase. Finally conclusions are drawn.

2   Core Elements of the EVITA Schema

First of all, an e-voting schema (EVS) must guarantee that a voter's decision remains an inviolable secret. To do so, most of them use cryptographic mechanisms and principles. Existing e-voting schemes can be grouped as follows:

- EVS based on Homomorphic Encryption, e.g. [11][12][12]
- EVS based on Mixing Nets, e.g. [14][15][16]
- EVS based on Blind Signatures, e.g. [14][17][18]

To guarantee that a voter's decision remains an inviolable secret, two distinct general approaches seem to be promising. One approach is to have a voting scheme that prevents the vote from being spied on by applying cryptographic methods. Another approach for protecting the secrecy of the ballots is by removing any form of identifying information from the cast vote thus breaking any link between the voter and her cast vote. Both approaches have drawbacks and advantages. Furthermore, regarding the requirements given by the targeted use-cases neither approach by itself would be satisfactory.

In the first approach, the use of encryption algorithms seems to be adequate. Various strong encryption algorithms exist, so question that remains is how and where to hold the decryption keys needed to decrypt votes. There are several schemes which do not need to decrypt votes in order to count them (e.g. schemes based on homomorphic encryption), but those approaches have limitations regarding write-in votes or they are too complex.

However, the use of strong encryption algorithms in order to protect the secrecy of ballots is no guarantee that these algorithms will be able to resist attack in the future. Due to the ever-increasing power of new computer systems it could become quite easy to crack a given encrypted vote by a brute force attack (e.g. by trying all encryption keys possible).

Therefore, using strong encryption mechanisms in combination with a comprehensive identity management concept in order to keep cast votes anonymous throughout the election and beyond are the key elements of the EVITA e-voting schema. Due to a sophisticated identification and authentication model that is based on the Austrian identity management concept[2], it can be ensured that the identity of a voter cannot be determined based on her cast vote, especially after the election. This eliminates the progressive weakness inherent to encryption algorithms.

3 Encryption Using a Hardware Security Module

From the moment the voter makes her decision there is no more need to reveal it except for the reason of counting. There is no need to uncover the voter's decision, her vote respectively, at any other time. The aim is to achieve an end-to-end encryption of the cast vote between the voter and the counting device. At this point two questions arise. How to provide the voter with the encryption key and how to ensure that only the counting device is able to decrypt the vote. An obvious answer to the first question is to use an asymmetric encryption algorithm and a public key infrastructure. The latter question is more difficult to address as both technical and organisational measurements have to be put in place.

One technical solution for protecting the confidentiality of the private decryption key is to build the counting device on the basis of a hardware security module. Due to this, the private key used for decrypting of cast votes is solely stored in the hardware security module in a very secure way. However, additional organisational and technical measures are required in order to address the process of key generation and distribution. The private key—or any copy of it—must not exist outside the hardware security module without any technical or non-technical security measure.

In order to export, backup and (re-)import the private key of the hardware security module—which is necessary in real election scenarios—an adequate and sophisticated

---

[2] For further details about the Austrian electronic identity management system see 19 and 10.

key management must be put in place. It would be a desirable to require the hardware security module to provide a key export and import mechanism following a defined shared key schema. If a shared key schema is provided, a dedicated organisational framework has to be defined that states how to distribute the key shares and to whom. The organisational framework as well as the legal framework of an election must state clearly how many shares are required at a minimum to import or reset the decryption key of the hardware security module. Furthermore, it must describe which organisations—or more generally which entities of the election process—are eligible to hold a key share. From an organisational and legal perspective, a shared key schema would be perfect for replicating the legal responsibilities of the participating political parties regarding the election.

The EVITA approach is to decrypt the vote only at the very single moment of counting; a cast vote remains encrypted at any time before and after counting. This contrasts with other e-voting approaches where votes are decrypted before counting. However, the counting device holds the decryption key for decrypting the votes within the counting process. It must meet the requirements of a hardware security module in order ensure that the key cannot be exported or stolen. Furthermore, the counting device must ensure that votes are decrypted only for the purpose of counting. There must not be any chance to learn decrypted votes by accessing the counting device by any means. It is not sufficient to use a hardware security module only for the purpose of securely holding the keys. Additional critical components of the counting device—critical with respect to revealing encrypted votes unintentionally—are the counters used to compute the result. The counting device must not offer any possibility of finding out intermediate results or to observe the current status of the counting process. However, logs for recording information might be put in place throughout the counting process by the counting device in order to collect additional information that confirm the correctness of the count, e.g. for an election audit.

4 Domain Separation and Identification Model

On the one hand, the process requires unique identification of the voter in the course of the registration procedure in order to record who has cast her vote. On the other hand, the cast vote must not be linkable to the voter. Although these requirements seem to be contradictory, the EVITA voting schema meets both requirements by introducing a sophisticated identification concept and domain separation schema (domain separation with respect to identity domains).

The concept of domain separation is based on the need-to-know principle since neither of the involved authorities—usually we have two authorities: a Registration Authority dealing with registration issues and an Election Authority dealing with the election itself—need to know the voter's unique identity (identifier). Usually it is sufficient to identify the voter within a dedicated context. This principle is also the underlying idea of the whole identity management of Austrian e-Government and the Citizen Card concept.

The Austrian identity management concept introduces a unique identifier for each citizen, called Source Personal Identification Number (sPIN), as well as identifiers for sectors of applications, called Sector Specific Personal Identification Numbers (ssPIN), in order to uniquely identify a citizen within a given sector of applications. It is important to note that a person's sPIN is only stored in her Citizen Card. There exists neither a register of sPINs nor is any authority or application allowed to handle or store them. Applications and authorities are only allowed to work with sector-specific identifiers which are derived from a person's sPIN by applying cryptographic one-way functions (section 0 describes this derivation process in detail).

Since it was the aim to develop an e-voting schema that is fully compliant with Austrian e-Government elements, the EVITA voting schema adopts and extends the concept of sector-specific identifiers.

The EVITA voting schema follows a two phase approach, which differs between registration phase and election phase. Therefore, the identification schema needs to be discussed and developed in two levels. On the first level, the identification schema must handle registration issues. On the second level, the identification schema must offer the possibility to determine whether or not a voter has cast her vote already.

To clarify the requirements for the identification schema, here is a list of scenarios and phases where identification is necessary:

1. **During the registration phase:** The voter requests to vote electronically using her Citizen Card.
2. **During the election phase:** In the event the voter is unable to vote electronically—due to technical problems within the voter's technical environment etc.—the voter should have the possibility to visit a polling station in order to vote conventionally (this is a design requirement for the EVITA concept). At the polling station, the election officials must (electronically) identify the voter in order to determine whether she has already cast her vote via e-voting or not.
3. **During the election phase:** In the course of casting a vote electronically, the voting system should determine whether the voter has already cast a vote or not, in order to prevent double votes.

Although the second and the third scenarios appear to contradict the election secrecy at first glance, the proposed domain separation model is able to solve the problem. Thus EVITA proposes an identification schema that is built on the established identity management concept of Austrian e-Government and makes use of two different identifiers which are loosely bound to each other using cryptographic technologies.

From an organisational point of view, there are two different domains. The registration system has to identify the voter in existing registers and databases, such as the register of voters, the Central Resident Register, etc. The representation of a voter's identity must match existing records of registers and authorities, therefore, the first form of identity is taken directly from the conventional identity management system of the Austrian e-Government, i.e. a conventional sector-specific personal identification number (ssPIN). Since these registers are used for conventional elections as well, they usually contain additional information about the voter, such as her given name, name, date of birth, etc.

The information attached to the encrypted vote must contain some identification information in order to determine whether a voter has already cast her vote and thus prevent double votes. The latter question is important when conducting a conventional election in parallel and allowing e-voters to cast their votes by conventional means as well (in the event of technical problems, etc.).

So, two different domains and two different representations of a voter's identity appear necessary:

1. The first domain is denoted as Registration Domain and it deals with identifiers taken from the conventional Austrian e-Government (such as ssPIN).
2. The second domain is denoted as Election Domain and it deals with identifiers distinct from those of the Registration Domain.

A bidirectional link must not be allowed to exist between the identity representations of both domains. Nevertheless, it must be possible to prove whether or not a given voter has already cast a vote by checking the voter's identity representation in the Registration Domain.

Only in the event that an e-voter is not able to cast her vote electronically for some reason and thus shows up at a conventional polling station to cast her vote it is legitimate to search for the existence of the voter's vote. It must be noted that this is a strict uni-directional query from a given (conventional) identity to the appropriate cast vote. In terms of identity representations, it means that a corresponding identity representation in the Election Domain should be derivable from a given identity representation in the Registration Domain but not vice versa.

The requirement is to define two identity domains and two respective identity representations in which a corresponding identity representation in the Election Domain can be derived from a given identity representation in the Registration Domain. This requirement leads to having a link between identity representations from the Registration Domain and the corresponding personal identifiers of the Election Domain. Creating this link using simple derivation mechanisms—following the mechanism used for deriving a ssPIN from a given sPIN—is not satisfactory since the identity representations of the Registration Domain are conventional e-governmental identifiers and are based more or less on conventional identification information (such as name, date of birth, etc.). Without additional measures it would be too easy to find out a citizen's identity representation in the Registration Domain, and with this information find the corresponding identity representation in the Election Domain.

The EVITA voting schema suggests creating the link between the personal identifiers in the Registration Domain and the corresponding identifiers in the Election Domain as depicted in figure 1. This sketch outlines both domains and the different forms of identifiers.

The Registration Domain deals with conventional electronic identifiers; i.e. sPIN and a sector-specific identifier which is specific to the election event (ssPIN(v)). In the course of crossing domains, the EVITA schema requires that a special personal identification number be derived that is only to be used within the Election Domain—referred to as a vPIN—from a given ssPIN(v). By applying a mathematical one-way function (HASH function), the link between the ssPIN(v) and the derived vPIN is uni-directional, pointing from the Registration Domain to the Election Domain. Furthermore, in order to have no permanent direct link between both identifiers, the derivation procedure applies secret keys.

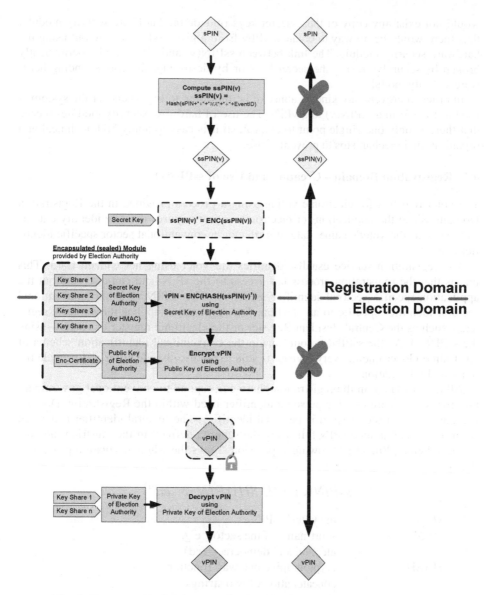

Fig. 1. Cryptographic link between Registration Domain and Election Domain

Since the link between both domains is only necessary during the election event (after election there is usually no need to search for a voter's cast vote after polling stations have been closed), the secret keys that are used to create a vPIN from a given ssPIN(v) are needed during the term of the election event only and have to be destroyed immediately after the election event. This can be ensured on a technical level by using hardware security modules for generating and holding the keys. If the hardware security modules do not provide functionality for exporting the keys, there would not exist any copy of these secret keys outside the hardware security module, thus there would be no way to create a vPIN from a given ssPIN(v) without using the hardware security module. The link between ssPIN(v) and vPIN can be permanently broken by securely erasing the secret keys or by destroying the corresponding hardware security modules.

In order to prevent any kind of abuse, it is important to log whenever the system is used to transform a ssPIN(v) to a vPIN. The use of hardware security modules means that there is only one single point to control, so it is easy to apply both technical and organisational mechanisms to prevent abuse.

4.1 Registration Domain – Creation and Use of ssPIN(v)

The voter registers for electronic voting using a process provided in the Registration Domain. Since the application for electronic voting requires discrete identity data as well, such as the voter's name, date of birth etc., a conventional sector specific identifier is used.

The registration service usually identifies the voter using her Citizen Card. This means that the registration process has access to the sPIN, and can also find out the application-specific sectoral identifier ssPIN(v). The ssPIN(v) is the conventional sectoral identifier specific to an election. The registration application contacts registers—such as the Central Resident Register or the electronic register of voters—using the ssPIN(v). As the ssPIN(v) conforms to the conventional identification schema of Austrian e-Government, every register is able to resolve the identifier and provide the requested information.

All actions taken in the registration phase correspond to conventional governmental processes. Therefore, the personal identifier used within the Registration Domain is a conventional sector-specific personal identifier. The sectoral identifier is derived from the voter's unique sPIN following the schema defined in the Austrian identification schema [20]. The following expression shows the whole derivation process in detail:

$$ssPIN(v) = HASH(sPIN \oplus "ed")$$

sPIN	the voter's sPIN
'ed'	short-name of the sector, e.g. election and democracy (ed)
HASH	cryptographic one way function
$\oplus$	concatenation of two strings

4.2 Election Domain – Creation and Use of vPIN

In contrast to the Registration Domain, the Election Domain does not require any discrete identity information about the voter. It is not even necessary to identify the voter in person within the Election Domain since the processes of the Election Domain do not deal with identification but rather with authorisation. The election process is not interested in the unique identity of the voter. The only thing the voter has to prove is that she is eligible to vote.

There needs to be a way to track which voter has already cast a vote. This is necessary when running a conventional election process in parallel and considering the conventional election process as a fallback scenario for the electronic election. This implies that the officials at the polling station must be able to prove whether or not the voter has already cast a vote. It must be kept in mind that the voter at the polling station might only be carrying a conventional identity card, e.g. a passport, which leads to the requirement of having a link from a voter's conventional identity information through a sectoral identifier (ssPIN(v)) to her corresponding identifier of the Election Domain (vPIN).

The creation of a ssPIN(v) from a set of discrete identity information which is sufficient enough to identify the person uniquely is only possible with the help of the so called Source PIN Register Authority. Thus it is possible to determine a voter's ssPIN(v) based on the information given on her conventional identity card. As a consequence, the algorithm for creating the vPIN has to take the ssPIN(v) as input. Moreover, this creation algorithm must always yield the same vPIN for a given ssPIN(v). Since the link between ssPIN(v) and vPIN is only needed temporarily, there must be a way to remove the link relation permanently, for example, immediately after the election event. The algorithm given in the following equation achieves both requirements:

$$vPIN = HMAC\big(ENC\big(ssPIN(v)\big)_{SK_{RA}}\big)_{SK_{EA}}$$

SK_{EA}	secret key of the Election Authority
SK_{RA}	secret key of the Registration Authority
HMAC	keyed hash function; e.g. realized through ENC(HASH(x))
ENC	symmetric encryption algorithm

The algorithm for creating vPINs is a logical continuation of the ssPIN(v) algorithm. Here again the algorithm makes use of a one-way function (HASH function) in order to ensure uni-directionality. Contrary to the creation of the ssPIN(v), the algorithm for creating vPINs requires a secret security measure for both the Registration Domain and the Election Domain. This measure may be implemented in several ways, for instance by adding secret phrases or by applying cryptographic algorithms such as encryption algorithms or keyed HASH functions.

The proposed algorithm for creating a vPIN takes the previously created ssPIN(v) as input. First, the algorithm adds the secret of the Registration Domain to the ssPIN(v) by applying a symmetric encryption algorithm (e.g. 3DES, AES). Here the encryption algorithm makes use of a secret key which is under the sole control of the Registration Authority (i.e. the authority controlling the Registration Domain/Process). The resulting encrypted ssPIN(v) is further derived by applying a keyed HASH function as a one-way function. This keyed HASH function (HMAC) not only creates the HASH value for the given input but also combines it with a secret by applying a secret key provided by the Election Authority (i.e. the authority controlling the Election Domain/Process).

As a result, the link between a vPIN and the underlying ssPIN(v) cannot be created without knowing both secret keys. Thus both secret keys are important elements of the vPIN-creation algorithm, which leads to a temporary link between the personal identifiers of both domains. In other words, both authorities have to cooperate to uncover a voter's identifier. Therefore, Registration Authority and Election Authority have to be separated by organisational means, which is common in elections.

Just involving secret keys in the derivation process as a technical measure is not sufficient. Additional organisational measures are required. The management of the secret keys is of crucial importance since possession of both secret keys enables the owner to create vPINs. Therefore, each secret key has to be provided and handled within the respective domain by the according authority and has to be handled appropriately. The use of a hardware security module is not only strongly recommended, but rather should be treated as a requirement for creating and holding the keys securely.

Figure 1 shows the proposed approach for handling both secret keys. This proposal suggests using a shared key schema for the handling of the Election Authority's secret key. The key shares should be held by the members and representatives of the election commission. In order to permanently break the link between the identifiers of both domains, it is sufficient to destroy at least one of both secret keys.

Figure 1 also highlights a second but very important issue in the vPIN creation process. Since a vPIN is created by using a specific ssPIN(v) as input, the creation process should be located within the Registration Domain. The process has to ensure that the vPIN that is created cannot be accessed by any entity in the Registration Domain. Therefore, the schema requires encryption of the vPIN for the Election Authority (Election Domain) immediately after it has been created.

Any technical implementation of the vPIN-creation process must follow the requirements stated above. In addition to all technical measures there is a strong need for organisational measures. Thus it is recommended that the Election Authority provide the technical implementation for dealing with its secret keys for the vPIN creation process by means of a sealed module (e.g. sealed hardware and electronically signed software) that contains a hardware security module holding all keys of the Election Authority (see ``Encapsulated (sealed) Module'' in figure 1).

5 Sketch of the Cast Vote and Counting Phase

For a complete understanding it is important to sketch the cast vote and counting process briefly. In order to cast a vote, the voter has simply to contact a server of the Election Authority which takes the voter's encrypted vote. As mentioned before, a cast vote consists of two parts: the inner part holding the encrypted vote which solely contains the voter's decision; the outer part holding at least the voter's vPIN in order to detect double votes and to mark which voter has cast a vote. During counting—which might take place any time later—the counting module removes the outer part of votes and just takes the encrypted inner part as input for counting. All encrypted parts become mixed up and fed into the counting device (i.e. a hardware security module) which decrypts votes and prepares the final result. The hardware security module of the counting device solely holds the private key to decrypt votes.

The EVITA approach is to decrypt the vote only at the very single moment of counting; a cast vote remains encrypted at any time before and after counting. This contrasts with other e-voting approaches where votes are decrypted before counting. However, when re-counts are considered, keeping votes encrypted is more advantageous. The counting device holds the decryption key for decrypting the votes within the counting process. It must meet the requirements of a hardware security module in order ensure that the key cannot be exported or stolen. Furthermore, the counting device must ensure that votes are decrypted only for the purpose of counting. There must not be any chance to learn decrypted votes by accessing the counting device by any means. It is not sufficient to use a hardware security module only for the purpose of securely holding the keys. Additional critical components of the counting device—critical with respect to revealing encrypted votes unintentionally—are the counters used to compute the result. The counting device must not offer any possibility of finding out intermediate results or to observe the current status of the counting process. However, logs for recording information might be put in place throughout the counting process by the counting device in order to collect additional information that confirm the correctness of the count, e.g. for an election audit. This information also must not be disclosed to anybody during counting as it can be used to reveal cast votes.

This sketch of the counting phase is very simplified. Important details, such as an additional signature on votes (before casting) to prevent manipulation of cast votes or the mechanism of indirect voter authentication, have been omitted due to length restriction.

6 Conclusions

The proposed e-voting solution relies on two core principles: strong end-to-end encryption and stringent domain separation. Both principles are closely coupled to Austrian e-Government solutions. The latter principle especially is an extension of the Austrian identity management concept. Due to the domain separation concept introduced, the e-voting concept is able to handle unique identification of voters while protecting the anonymity of cast votes with the simultaneous possibility of gaining knowledge about whether a given voter had cast a vote already (during the election event). Thus, the proposed e-voting scenario allows voters to cast their vote conventionally at a polling station on election day even though the voter might have registered for e-voting. Allowing e-voters to cast their vote at the polling station as well—under extenuating circumstances—is an important element of the EVITA's embracing security concept which makes the EVITA concept different from other e-voting schemes. The use of the Internet inherently brings with it some risks that cannot be addressed by technical measures (i.e. network security elements, redundancy, etc.) alone, however they can be tackled by having a comprehensive technical, organisational, and legal security concept. So, allowing e-voters to cast their vote at the polling station is an organisational measure facing a possible break-down of the e-voting channel (e.g. due to DoS, etc).

References

1. European Commission for Democracy through Law (Venice Commission). Code of Good Practice in Electoral Matters (October 2002)
2. Council of Europe Committee of Ministers. Recommendation Rec(2004)11 of the Committee of Ministers to member states on legal, operational and technical standards for e-voting. Council of Europe (September 2004)

3. Multidisciplinary Ad Hoc Group of Specialists (IP1-S-EE). Explanatory Memorandum to the Draft Recommendation Rec(2004) of the Committee of Ministers to member states on legal, operational and technical standards for e-voting. Council of Europe (September 2004)
4. Working-Group "E-Voting". Abschlussbericht zur Vorlage an Dr. Ernst Strasser, Bundesminister für Inneres (November 2004)
5. Rössler, T.: Electronic Voting over the Internet – an E-Government Speciality. PHD-Thesis, Institute for Applied Information Processing and Communications (IAIK), Graz University of Technology, Austria (September 2007)
6. Council of Europe. Convention for the Protection of Human Rights and Fundamental Freedoms (November 1950)
7. Bundesamt für Sicherheit in der Informationstechnik. Basissatz von Sicherheitsanforderungen an Onlinewahlprodukte (Version 0.18) (May 2007)
8. Gesellschaft für Informatik e.V (GI). GI-Anforderungen an Internetbasierte Vereinswahlen (August 2005)
9. Jefferson, D., Rubin, A.D., Simons, B., Wagner, D.: A security analysis of the secure electronic registration and voting experiment (serve) (January 2004)
10. Rössler, T., Hayat, A., Posch, R., Leitold, H.: Giving an interoperable solution for incorporating foreign eids in austrian e-government. In: Proceedings of IDABC Conference 2005, March 2005, pp. 147–156. European Commission (2005)
11. Cohen, J., Fischer, M.: A robust and verifiable cryptographically secure election scheme. In: Proceedings of the 26th IEEE Symposium on the Foundations of Computer Science (FOCS), pp. 372–382. IEEE, Los Alamitos (1985)
12. Cohen, J., Yung, M.: Distributing the power of government to enhance the privacy of voters. In: Proceedings of 5th ACM Symposium on Principles of Distributed Computing (PODC), pp. 52–62. ACM, New York (1986)
13. Cramer, R., Gennaro, R., Schoenmakers, B.: A secure and optimally efficient multiauthority election scheme. In: Fumy, W. (ed.) EUROCRYPT 1997. LNCS, vol. 1233, pp. 103–118. Springer, Heidelberg (1997)
14. Chaum, D.: Untraceable electronic mail, return adresses, and digital pseudonyms. Communications of the ACM 24(2), 84–86 (1981)
15. Juang, W.-S., Lei, C.-L.: A collision free secret ballot protocol for computerized general elections. Computers and Security 15(4), 339–348 (1996)
16. Hirt, M., Sako, K.: Efficient receipt-free voting based on homomorphic encryption. In: Preneel, B. (ed.) EUROCRYPT 2000. LNCS, vol. 1807, p. 539. Springer, Heidelberg (2000)
17. Fujioka, A., Okamoto, T., Ohta, K.: A practical secret voting scheme for large scale elections. In: Zheng, Y., Seberry, J. (eds.) AUSCRYPT 1992. LNCS, vol. 718, pp. 244–251. Springer, Heidelberg (1993)
18. Okamoto, T.: Receipt free electronic voting schemes for large scale elections. In: Christianson, B., Lomas, M. (eds.) Security Protocols 1997. LNCS, vol. 1361, pp. 25–35. Springer, Heidelberg (1998)
19. Leitold, H., Hollosi, A., Posch, R.: Security architecture of the austrian citizen card concept. In: Proceedings of ACSAC 2002, Las Vegas, December 9-13, pp. 391–400. IEEE Computer Society, Los Alamitos (2002)
20. Hollosi, A., Hörbe, R.: Bildung von Stammzahl und bereichsspezifischem Personenkennzeichen (SZ-bPK-Algo -1.1.1). Platform Digital Austria, AG Bürgerkarte (January 2006), http://www.ref.gv.at (as seen on May 12, 2007)

Electronic Voting by Means of Digital Terrestrial Television: The Infrastructure, Security Issues and a Real Test-Bed

Roberto Caldelli, Rudy Becarelli, Francesco Filippini, Francesco Picchioni,
and Riccardo Giorgetti

MICC, University of Florence, Florence, Italy
{roberto.caldelli,rudy.becarelli,francesco.filippini,
francesco.picchioni}@unifi.it, giorgetti@lci.det.unifi.it
http://lci.micc.unif.it/index.php

Abstract. Electronic voting has been largely studied in different forms and applications. Typical objectives of electronic voting are to enhance security and to grant easy accessibility. Security can be pursued by means of several strategies oriented to secrete the vote, to check the voter identity, to decouple the voter from his choice and to allow the ballot to be audited. On the other hand, accessibility too can be greatly improved by providing the opportunity to vote remotely or by using voting machines, located at polling stations, equipped with appropriate interfaces for disabled people.
In this paper a Digital Terrestrial Television (DTT) based voting system is presented. This kind of electronic voting technology allows disabled users (especially people with mobility problems), but not only, to cast their vote from home and, above all, by using common well-known devices. In fact, the needed basic equipment are a TV set, a Set Top Box (STB) with its remote control and a telephone line. The complete infrastructure consists of an MHP (Multimedia Home Platform) application that acts as a client application; a server application that acts as a network/counting server for e-voting; and a security protocol based on asymmetric key encryption to ensure authentication and secrecy of the vote. The MHP application is broadcasted by a certified (e.g. national) TV channel that grants its originality. The user needs a smart card issued by a national authority (e.g. the electronic identity card) to authenticate himself to the application and to sign the encrypted ballot to send to the server application. The voter can simply browse the application, displayed on his TV screen, by acting on the STB remote control. The server application is in charge to verify user identity, to gather and store user's encrypted ballots and finally to count votes. The communication between the client application and the server takes place by means of a secured channel (using HTTPS), established over the common telephone line, while the voting operations are secured with the help of asymmetric keys encryption. The whole infrastructure has been proven in laboratory tests and also in a public demonstration for USA Presidential Election on 2008 November 4th.

Keywords: DTT, MHP, e-voting, e-democracy, digital divide, disabled people accessibility.

C. Godart et al. (Eds.): I3E 2009, IFIP AICT 305, pp. 13–25, 2009.
© IFIP International Federation for Information Processing 2009

1 Introduction

Electronic, mechanical, or electromechanical voting are nowadays form of voting commonly accepted in various countries worldwide. Despite of this diffusion, these voting techniques have been always criticized for many reasons. Typical critics are related to the possibility, for the voter, to audit his vote or have some kind of control on the underlying mechanism during the polling phase that is when the vote is cast. This kind of frights arise naturally from the intrinsic complexity and/or from the opacity of the mechanism itself and can be amplified by a justified sense of caution. These critics highlight that one of the most important open issues is security and in particular how to achieve or, eventually, increase it with respect to a traditional voting scenario. Electronic voting can, besides, enhance the accessibility to vote even for people living outside the country of origin or for disabled persons. Electronic voting, that is widely exploited, offers mainly two different approaches to solve both security and accessibility issues. The first approach aims to substitute traditional voting form in the polling stations with electronic machines trying to match the requirements for accessibility and security. The second tries to solve the accessibility issue by making people vote through web based or broadcasted applications, not disregarding the security of the communication channel that must be used in this case. Electronic voting machines in polling stations, named DRE (Direct Recording Electronic) voting systems [1][2], have been widely used especially after US presidential elections in 2000 when mechanical punching machines led to a large number of invalid ballots. Actually, despite of the confidence given by citizens to such a solution, DRE machines are very sensitive to various kind of attacks, as detailed in [11][6]. In order to improve the security of DREs in terms of capability of performing an audit by the user, secrecy of vote, and relative independence from technical flaws the *receipt* approach has been proposed. As explained in [3][4][7][9], the central idea is to give the user an encrypted receipt which can be used to audit the vote as an evidence that the vote has been cast and that can be seen like the ballot itself, since the user's choice is encrypted. Typically these systems, implemented as electronic or manual, give as a result of the voting operation two distinct ballots. After the voting phase (this is part of the security mechanism) the user is asked to destroy one of these ballot, chosen by himself, and scan the other one. The scanned ballots are sent to a server that acts like a ballot repository. Since both the ballots are encrypted and only the combination of the two can give some chance of recovering the vote, at the end of the operation the voter owns an *encrypted receipt*. The actual ballot is readable only with the help of some codes owned by the trusted authority that controls the voting operation (e.g. the Ministry of Internal Affairs). To allow the user to audit his vote, every encrypted ballot is identified by a readable unique number. The number, that is decoupled from the user's identity, can be used to audit the ballot via web with the help of a specific web application.

Recently electronic voting has proposed a new approach based on web applications allowing user to vote from worldwide. One of the first experiment in this direction has been SERVE (Secure Electronic Registration and Voting

Experiment) [12], a web based application developed for military personnel deployed overseas. Its security is mostly based upon asymmetric key encryption and HTTPS connection. An analysis of possible security flaws can be read in [5]. Other similar systems have been developed starting from the SERVE experience, as for the Estonian e-voting system used during political elections in 2005 [10]. The SERVE security architecture and the Estonian experiment have been used as a reference for the implementation described in the proposed work. This paper is not aimed at presenting a new technology for voting security, but a new architecture whose purpose is to provide an usable voting system in order to allow, in particular, people with mobility problems to vote.

The architecture presented is based on the DTT (Digital Terrestrial Television) infrastructure and on the use of Java interactive applications running on a common television by means of a simple decoder (Set-Top-Box, STB). DTT is worldwide spread as a family of different standards for digital TV (DVB in Europe, Australia and Asia [13]; ATSC in North America [15]; ISDB in Japan and Brazil [16]). Specifically the proposed architecture is built upon DVB-T/MHP (Multimedia Home Platform) [14] technology but it could be extended to the other standards. MHP applications, named Xlets, are similar to Applets for the web, both in structure and life-cycle; they are broadcasted by multiplexing them with the digital TV transport stream and can be accessed on the television screen. Such application, through the STB and a return channel (e.g. the telephone line), can allow a *one-to-one* interaction between the user and the server side.

The proposed system is based on two applications: an MHP application running on the client side and a server application running on the server side. The first, broadcasted by the authorized TV channel (trusted authority), when downloaded on the STB, permits to authenticate the user, and to send the digital ballot to the server application. On the other side the server application is in charge to check the user ID and eventually allows the user to vote. Then the server application manages the secret ballot and decouple the vote from the voter.

The whole system has been tested in laboratory emulating a real world situation by broadcasting the TV signal and checking the functionalities provided by various kinds of STBs present on the market.

During the phase of development an usability study has been performed to make on interface easy to use and understand even for users subject to "digital divide". Also the entire architecture, in an ad-hoc setup, has been presented and tested, as a demonstration, on 4th of November 2008 during the latest USA Presidential Election. A convention, organized by the TAA (Tuscan American Association [20]), was held in Florence (Italy) to wait for the actual result of the elections.

The paper is organized as follows: an exhaustive description of the system is given in section 2. Security issues are debated in section 3, while usability aspects are discussed in section 4. The experience faced during the "Election Night Event" is presented in section 5 and section 6 concludes the paper.

2 System Description

This architecture for electronic voting was basically designed as an aid to people with mobility problems and not only. The idea behind this infrastructure is to provide the chance to vote remotely by using very *well-known* devices, like a television and a remote control, in a domestic environment. In addition to that, the simplicity of the required equipment (i.e. a STB for DTT, a telephone line connection and a TV screen) allows to easy access to vote not only persons with computer science skills but also people without a personal computer, living in needy areas of the country.

The infrastructure is based on the DTT (Digital Terrestrial Television) platform and on the use of Java interactive applications called Xlets. Such applications run on common television through the use of a simple decoder called Set-Top-Box (STB). The standard that in Europe rules this architecture is based on DVB-T/MHP (Multimedia Home Platform) technology. DVB-T defines the caracteristics of the signal transmission, while MHP covers the part related to the interactive applications. MHP applications in DTT are similar to Java Applet for the web; they are broadcasted by multiplexing them with the digital TV transport stream and loaded in the STB where runs a Java Virtual Machine with MHP stack.

The whole platform is reported in Figure 1 . The MHP application certified by the authority which is responsible for voting operations (e.g. the Ministry of Internal Affairs) is broadcasted by the TV channel/channels authorized to distribute the service (e.g. the national TV broadcaster like RAI in Italy, BBC in UK, CNN in USA, etc.). The user by selecting the channel can download the application and watch it on the television screen. Being equipped with the appropriate smart card (e.g.Electronic Identity Card - EIC), he can proceed to the authentication phase and then to the vote by using the return channel on the PSTN connection. It is easy to understand that the structure for this kind of electronic vote is basically composed by two main parts: the "Client" (MHP application) and the "Server" (Server-side application) which communicate each other through an HTTPS connection over the Return Channel. Decoders on the market have to types of network interface: modem 56k or Ethernet.

The Client application is a Xlet (Java Application) broadcasted together with TV transport stream that a voting user can launch from the remote control of STB. STBs have a slot for electronic cards, typically used for pay TV or other interactive services, where user can insert his EIC to be authenticated by the system. Each smartcard has a secret numerical PIN that the user must enter by using the Remote Control. Through the remote control it is possible to easily navigate the application; instructions are provided on the screen too. When the user sends his vote, the application activates the Return Channel and establishes a secure connection with the server via HTTPS protocol.

The Server application has two principal roles: user authentication and vote registration. Authentication is done by receiving the identifying data contained in the Smart-Card by the return channel, validating the public certificate (X.509) and verifying if the user has already voted. When the user has been authenticated,

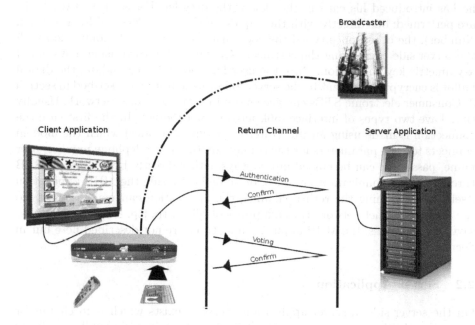

Fig. 1. System infrastructure

he can select his favorite candidate or party and his vote is sent to the server that records user's preference.

The following paragraphs illustrate in detail each part of the proposed system.

2.1 Set-Top-Box, Smart Card and Client Application

The client side is essentially composed by four parts: STB (Set-Top-Box) and its remote control, Smart Card (like Electronic Identity Card), Return Channel and MHP application (Java Xlet). Let's see in detail these components. STB is a decoder that transcodes the broadcasted digital television signal into a classical analog one by following the standard DVB-T (Digital Video Broadcasting - Terrestrial). It is essential that these devices implement the MHP stack with the appropriate Java virtual machine, without that Java applications can not be executed (common STBs on the market satisfy that). The user can launch the application by the remote control, generally clicking on the *APP* button (it depends on models). Another prerequisite is that the STBs are equipped with the SATSA (Security And Trust Services API) [17] libraries to interact with this type of smart card (again common STBs on the market satisfy that). Once launched, the application needs to authenticate the user and at this stage the smart card plays an essential role. There are many types of cards used for pay-TV such as Irdeto® [18] and Nagravision® [19]. This application supports all SmartCards that refers to ISO 7816 standard [21] like EIC (Electronic Identity Card) and NCS (National Services Card). Application is able to authenticate the user after he has introduced his card in the slot of the decoder. For security two checks are performed: one directly with the request of the PIN (Personal Identification Number), the other, once typed the code, using a secure cable connection with the server side exchanging the certificate (X.509) of the card using a system of asymmetric key encryption. Once the user has chosen his candidate, the digital ballot is encrypted and sent to the server following a protocol described in section 3. Consumer electronic STBs can access the Internet or a local network. Usually they have two types of interface: 56k modem or Ethernet. In the first case the connection is made using an ISP (Internet Service Provider) which the modem connects to. The parameters for the connection (i.e. ISP telephone number, user name, password) can be passed in two ways: either directly by setting the STB through its communication interface, or embedded inside the MHP application itself. After opening the return channel, the application can make requests to the normal internet network through protocols like http, ftp, https, pop etc. For save of conciseness, the MHP application features are not described here but in Section 4.

2.2   Server Application

On the server side, a server application (Servlet) exists which is in charge for the authentication phase and for vote storaging. It receives the public certificate of the smart card, extracts the personal data (i.e. an unique Revenue Service Code) and verifies that the user has not already voted. If the user has already voted the server returns a message stating that the session is going to be closed. On the contrary if voting is admitted it gets and records the user's encrypted ballot decoupling it from the voter. As previously mentioned, all transactions between client and server are made using the return channel within a HTTPS connection (Hypertext Transfer Protocol over Secure Socket Layer).

3   Security Issues

In this section an implementation of the security protocol used to hide sensible data and authenticate the user is drawn. The architecture presented in the section 2 consists of two applications (a client-side and a server-side one) that exchange data along a secure channel using HTTPS and asymmetrical key encryption. In this scenario two main security issues arise: application security and communication security.

   Application security is easily achievable by trusting two main authorities: the broadcaster of the MHP application and the server side application warrantor. The broadcaster must ensure that the application, acting like a client, is the original one. The server application instead must ensure that votes coming from the client are sent by a certain person and that, above all, the vote is decoupled from the voter. The adopted model of communication security, instead, makes use of an encrypted channel and two pairs of asymmetrical keys, one for the server and one for the client. The first necessary step is to build a secure channel between the client and the server. In order to do that an encrypted HTTPS connection is established adopting SSL (Secure Socket Layer) and TLS (Transport Layer Security) technologies. Typical attacks to the secure channel (e.g. Man-In-The-Middle attacks operated by poisoning the ARP - Address Resolution Protocol etc.) can be neutralized with an appropriate *double check* of the SSL certificate. Once the secure connection is established, the protocol makes use of the client and the server keys to encrypt the user's vote. The *Server* pair of keys are PK_S (public) and SK_S (secret). This pair is used to encrypt and make anonymous the vote of the user. The *Client* instead has a pair of keys addressed as PK_C and SK_C. These keys are used to authenticate the user and sign the data exchanged along the secure channel. The exchange of public keys is done as follows: PK_S is broadcasted directly with the MHP application, PK_C is sent from the client through the SmartCard certificate.

The encryption mechanism used in a voting session is pictured in Figure 2 and detailed hereafter. The user logs into the client application by inserting his smartcard into the slot and by entering the secure PIN code to unlock the card. After this client side authentication, the user digital certificate is sent via HTTPS to the server that checks whether the user is allowed to cast the vote or not by extracting from the digital certificate the unique public data for identifying the voter (e.g. the Revenue Service Code). If the user is allowed to vote, the PK_C key is extracted from the digital certificate and stored in a session object ready to be used for further operations. A message, containing the positive or negative acknowledgement, is sent back to the client through the established HTTPS channel. The message is signed with PK_S in order to ensure the user that the message sender is the server. If a positive acknowledgement is sent, the user is invited by the client application to cast his vote. Once his choice has been expressed, the client application generates a random number r, encrypts the message with the server public key (PK_S) and signs it with the private user key (SK_C) as follows: $SIGN_{SK_C}(ENC_{PK_S}(v, r))$, where v is a unique identifier for the user's choice and r is the random number. Random number r is concatenated with the vote in order to generate each time a different encrypted ballot to improve security, otherwise the types of encrypted ballots would be as much as the number of eligible candidates/parties. $ENC_{PK_S}(v, r)$, the encrypted ballot, is also stored as a *receipt* for checking back the server answer while the entire message is sent to the server. The client application stands by for a positive acknowledgement that will close the transaction. When the server gets the message it is confident that the message comes from the user (that is granted by the signature) and that none but its own is able to read the content of the inner envelope; not even the user who does not hold the necessary server private key SK_S. The server, verified the sender identity, obtains an encrypted ballot $ENC_{PK_S}(v, r)$ containing the user's choice. The encrypted ballot is then stored in a database, ready to be balloted. In this phase the voter's identity is decoupled from the ballot as it happens in mail voting systems. The security model implemented is then, at least, the one granted with mail voting. If all these phases terminate with success, the server sends back to

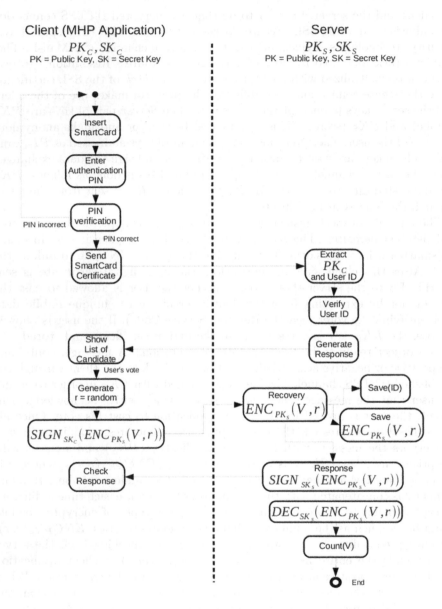

Fig. 2. Security mechanism

the client a signed answer containing the encrypted ballot. The answer is signed with the server secret key SK_S. Once the client receives this message is able to recover the anonymous envelope and compares it with the previously stored copy. If the comparison is positive the transaction closes. Once the whole voting operations are closed, the server side authority, who is responsible to manage the votes, can disclose every single encrypted ballot using the private server key and taking into account the r random number, since r is separated from vote by a sequence of known characters. Then votes are computed and the final results are published.

4   System Characteristics: An Analysis

In this section an usability analysis and an explanation of some of the advantages and drawbacks of the presented system is carried out.

4.1   Usability

During the phase of client application development an usability study has been performed. It is important to underline that this system uses a structure and devices well-known to everybody. The application is accessed through a common TV and the remote control of STB, devices already used by millions of people.

To simplify as much as possible the operations which the user must perform, the use of buttons on the remote control was limited. The application can be used only by resorting at the arrow keys (*UP/DOWN* and *LEFT/RIGHT*) and by pressing *OK* button. Usually MHP applications exploit the four *coloured* buttons (red, green, yellow and blue), making more complicated the use of the interfaces. The interface consists of a sequence of screens thought to be easy to use and understand even for users subject to "digital divide". The application however fully comes in help of people by using a written guide (see Figure 3(a)) to give the user some basic hint for interacting with the interface in a correct way (audio-guide messages have also been implemented). The most difficult step for the user can be the typing of the *PIN*, but because it is simply numerical the operation is reduced to just press the code on the numeric keypad on the remote control, typically used to change TV channels, and then confirm with the *OK* button. It is important to highlight that at each step, in case of an error by the user, it is possible to go back. Both for the *PIN* and for any selection of the candidate, the pressure of the *OK* button displays a *confirmation dialog* (see Figure 3(b)). Without this check is not possible to proceed to the next step. It was also used a very specific criterion in the choice of using the arrow keys. Vertical arrows (*UP* and *DOWN* buttons) are used only for the selection of candidates/parties (see Figure 3(a)). These have the role to move the focus on the respective boxes of the candidates/parties. While the horizontal arrows (*LEFT* and *RIGHT* button) are used only in the *confirmation dialog* to move the focus on *YES* (confirm) or *NO* (cancel) buttons (see Figure 3(b)).

4.2   Advantages and Drawbacks

In this subsection advantages and drawbacks of the system are outlined and comparisons with classical voting systems and other electronic voting forms are carried out. Basically the proposed system allows the user to vote from home like the classical mail voting. Additionally the system encrypts the digital ballot and

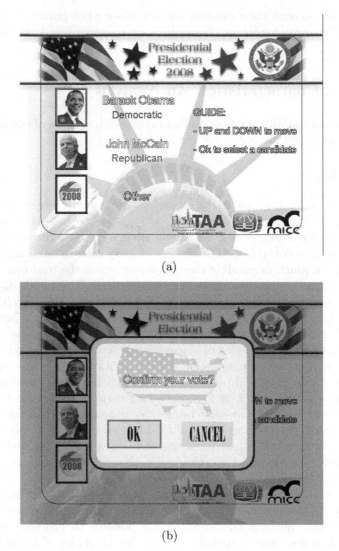

(a)

(b)

Fig. 3. MHP application screenshots

the communication towards the server with asymmetric key encryption. Besides the use of a smart card and a Personal Identification Number simplifies the authentication phase increasing at the same time the security level. A possible critic relies on the fact that such a system is not able to recognize whether a voter has actually cast his vote, because it's possible that the smart card and the PIN are used by someone else but the owner. It can be noted that the same critic can be arisen to a well known and accepted system like the mail voting. Another advantage of this system is the fact that the MHP application is broadcasted (i.e. with a *push* technology) to everyone making the Man In

The Middle attack almost impossible. This kind of intrinsic security is given by the nature of the on-the-air broadcasting that can be modelled as a *one-to-many* scheme. Other possible drawbacks can come out from the structure of the system based on the client-server paradigm. The most attackable part of the system is the return channel that is exposed to MITM attacks. Similar attacks can be minimized by using HTTPS and performing a double security check from the client as requested by the protocol itself. Another clear advantage is the fact that the digital ballot can not be repudiated and the secrecy of the ballot itself ensured by the use of asymmetric cryptography properly implemented within the system. Besides, the use of the application does not affect the user in any way by demanding some particular cost. No extra hardware is needed to make the application run. The only things needed is a commercial STB and at least a PSTN connection.

5 A Real Test Bed (*Election Night*)

The entire architecture, in an ad-hoc setup, has been presented and tested, as a demonstration, on 4th of November 2008 during the latest USA Presidential Elections. A convention named "Election Night", organized by the TAA (Tuscan American Association, http://www.toscanausa.org/Election_EN.asp) and sponsored by Tuscany Region (http://www.regione.toscana.it), was held in Florence (Italy) to wait for the actual result of the elections.

The architecture previously presented has been modified in order to simplify the voting phase during the *Election Night*. These changes have been necessary since a large number of people (about one thousand persons) were expected to cast their vote in few polling booths. The polling booths were equipped with a STB receiving the digital signal directly from a PC running a DVB-T/MHP object carousel and acting as a broadcaster. This PC used an appropriate hardware interface to modulate the digital signal to RF (Radio-Frequency) and sent it, via coaxial cable, to all STBs. These configuration has been adopted since no real broadcaster were available that night. Besides, since the STBs in use were fitted with the necessary connectors and interfaces, another PC were connected via Ethernet to each STBs to act like the server side machine as described above.

People who wanted to try the system, had to ask a hostess a smartcard with an associated dummy identity used during the tests. The voter, then, had to enter the polling booth and insert the card into the STB slot. The authentication phase, in this scenario, has been skipped since the smart card available were few and in order to speed up all the operations. In particular, the voter was not asked to unlock the card by entering the PIN code. The only security operation performed by the application was to check the presence of the card inside the slot to authorize the voter to go on. The following phases of voting took place as described in the previous chapters. During the night some exit polls has been simulated by projecting partial votes to a wall screen. People who took part in the convention expressed their appreciation for the initiative. The large number of voters clearly demonstrates that such a system matches the minimal usability requirements and that is easily comprehensible. A photograph of some tests can be seen at http://www.toscanausa.org/gallery/images/dnvye__C0B1305.jpg

6 Conclusions

The system presented in this paper is mainly aimed to reduce the "digital divide" in e-voting by exploiting DTT technology. People having mobility problems or leaving in weedy areas can vote by means of a STB and a PSTN connection even from their home. The security is ensured using HTTPS connection and an appropriate encryption of sensible data; in this case the user's vote. The encryption is operated by means of two pairs of asymmetrical keys owned respectively by the server and by the user's smartcard. The security protocol is similar to the ones designed for web based e-voting applications like SERVE [12] and the estonian e-voting system [10]. The architecture is composed by a client application running on a STB and broadcasted by a trusted TV channel that is responsible to preserve its integrity. This application is able to communicate, via PSTN or digital connection, with a server that authenticates the user and eventually authorizes him to vote. The server stores his cyphered ballot, decoupling it from the user identity, until the scrutiny phase. The scrutiny takes place using a secret key used to decypher the encrypted ballots. This system is easily extending to other platform describe in the section 1 and not only. For the characteristics of the MHP standard, it is possible to reproduce this architecture in other system like: DVB-S (Satellite), DVB-C (Cable) or DVB-H (Handheld).

Acknowledgements

The authors would like to thank Tuscany Region for supporting the project and RTV38, Italian TV broadcaster, for the technical effort during testing phases and for contributing to the "Election Night"event.

References

1. Federal Election Commission, Voting system Standards, Performance Standards, Introduction,
   http://www.fec.gov/agenda/agendas2001/mtgdoc01-62/v1/v1s1.htm
2. Federal Election Commission, Voting System Standard,
   http://www.fec.gov/agenda/agendas2001/mtgdoc01-62/overview.htm
3. Chaum, D., Essex, A., Carback, R., Clark, J., Popoveniuc, S., Sherman, A., Vora, P.: Scantegrity: End-to-End Voter-Verifiable Optical- Scan Voting. IEEE Security & Privacy 6(3), 40–46 (2008)
4. Chaum, D.: Secret-ballot receipts: True voter-verifiable elections. IEEE Security & Privacy 2(1), 38–47 (2004)
5. Jefferson, D., Rubin, A.D., Simons, B., Wagner, D.: A Security Analysis of the Secure Electronic Registration and Voting Experiment (SERVE) (2004),
   http://www.servesecurityreport.org/ (21.01.2007)

6. Kohno, T., Stubblefield, A., Rubin, A.D., Wallach, D.S.: Analysis of an Electronic Voting System (2004),
   http://avirubin.com/vote.pdf (21.01.2007)
7. Essex et al.: The Punchscan Voting System: Vo-Comp Competition Submission. In: Proc. 1st Univ. Voting Systems Competition, VoComp (2007),
   http://punchscan.org/vocomp/PunchscanVocompSubmission.pdf
8. Garera, S., Rubin, A.D.: An Independent Audit Framework for Software Dependent Voting Systems. In: Proc. 14th ACM Conf. Computer and Comm. Security (CCS 2007), pp. 256–265. ACM Press, New York (2007)
9. Chaum, D., Carback, R., Clark, J., Essex, A., Popoveniuc, S., Rivest, R., Ryan, P., Shen, E., Sherman, A.: Scantegrity II: End-to-End Verifiability for Optical Scan Election Systems Using Invisible Ink Confirmation Codes. IEEE Security & Privacy (May/June 2008)
10. Mägi, T.: Practical Security Analysis of E-voting Systems. Master Thesis Tallinn University of Technology, Faculty of Information Technology, Department of Informatics, Chair of Information Security, Tallinn (2007)
11. Fisher, E.A., Coleman, K.J.: The Direct Recording Electronic Voting Machine (DRE) Controversy: FAQs and Misperceptions, Congressional Research Service, The Library of Congress (2005)
12. Jefferson, D., Rubin, A.D., Simons, B., Wagner, D.: A Security Analysis of the Secure Electronic Registration and Voting Experiment (SERVE),
   http://www.servesecurityreport.org/
13. DVB Project, http://www.dvb.org
14. MHP-DVB Project, http://www.mhp.org
15. The Advanced Television Systems Committee, Inc., http://www.atsc.org
16. Integrated Services Digital Broadcasting, Japanese standard,
   http://www.dibeg.org
17. Security and Trust Services API for J2ME (SATSA),
   http://java.sun.com/products/satsa
18. Irdeto Access B.V., http://www.irdeto.com
19. Nagravision SA, http://www.nagravision.com
20. TAA, Tuscan American Association,
   http://www.toscanausa.org/Election_EN.asp
21. ISO/IEC 7816,
   http://www.iso.org/iso/search.htm?qt=7816&searchSubmit=Search&sort=rel&type=simple&published=on

Towards User Acceptance of Biometric Technology in E-Government: A Survey Study in the Kingdom of Saudi Arabia

Thamer Alhussain[1] and Steve Drew[2]

[1] School of ICT, Griffith University, Parklands Drive, Southport, Qld, Australia
t.alhussain@griffith.edu.au
[2] School of ICT, Griffith University, Parklands Drive, Southport, Qld, Australia
s.drew@Griffith.edu.au

Abstract. The paper discussed an exploratory study of government employees' perceptions of the introduction of biometric authentication at the workplace in the Kingdom of Saudi Arabia. We suggest that studying the factors affecting employees' acceptance of new technology will help ease the adoption of biometric technology in other e-government applications. A combination of survey and interviews was used to collect the required data. Interviews were conducted with managers and questionnaires were given to employees from two different government organisations in the Kingdom of Saudi Arabia to investigate the employees' perceptions of using biometrics. The results of this study indicate a significant digital and cultural gap between the technological awareness of employees and the preferred authentication solutions promoted by management. A lack of trust in technology, its potential for misuse and management motives reflect the managers' need to consider their responsibilities for narrowing these gaps. It was apparent that overcoming employees' resistance is an essential issue facing biometric implementation. Based on the research we recommend that an awareness and orientation process about biometrics should take place before the technology is introduced into the organisation.

Keywords: E-government, Biometric technology, Users' perceptions, Kingdom of Saudi Arabia.

1 Introduction

New technologies constantly evolve new dimensions to daily life. They can be used to provide interactions between users and their governments through electronic services. Governments are looking for more efficient and effective uses of technology in order to electronically deliver their services [1, 22]. Electronic government (e-government) has therefore become an important world-wide application area.

With e-government applications, users are required to provide governments with personal information which necessitates an efficient, secure technology to provide reliable methods, particularly for users' identification as well as secure information systems. Thus, the implementation of e-government is facing important issues such as information security, user authentication and privacy in which biometric authentication

C. Godart et al. (Eds.): I3E 2009, IFIP AICT 305, pp. 26–38, 2009.

is a potential solution to deal with such concerns [13]. It can provide reliable identification of individuals as well as the ability for controlling and protecting the integrity of sensitive data stored in information systems [20]. As a result, several governments have implemented biometric authentication systems in order to efficiently and securely provide their services.

However, the adoption of biometrics in e-government has become a major component of political planning for several governments. In particular, user acceptance can be an essential factor for the successful implementation of biometrics [6, 18, 22]. Moreover, users can have a direct impact on the operational performance of biometric systems, so their concerns need careful consideration, even if their concerns are fairly rough and ill defined [6].

This paper discusses a study conducted in the Kingdom of Saudi Arabia of government employees' perceptions of the introduction of biometric authentication at the workplace in 2008. The aim is gain an understanding of factors affecting the employees' acceptance of biometrics and to advise on how to successfully adopt biometrics in e-government applications. The paper is structured as follows. The relevant literature is reviewed followed by the description of the empirical study that involved a descriptive survey and interviews of the managers and employees in two organisations.

2 Background

To introduce the context in which this study was undertaken it is necessary to consider the concepts of e-government and biometric authentication and how they relate to the technological sophistication of the major users. Saudi Arabia presents a unique set of cultural and technology uptake circumstances that have implications for management of a digital divide. We discuss the background to this enquiry in the following sections.

2.1 E-government

Electronic government involves the citizens of that country in certain government activities in order to help solve problems. E-government provides unparalleled opportunities to streamline and improve internal governmental processes, enhance the interactions between users and government, and enable efficiencies in service delivery [22]. It refers to the use of information technology by government agencies in order to enhance the interaction and service delivery to citizens, businesses, and other government agencies [1, 4]. Thus, there are four categories of e-government applications which are: Government-to-Citizen (G2C); Government-to-Business (G2B); Government-to-Government (G2G); and Government-to-Employee (G2E) [4].

2.2 Saudi Arabia and Its Adoption of Technology

The Kingdom of Saudi Arabia is located in the Southern-Eastern part of the Asian continent. It occupies 2,240,000 sq km (about 865,000 sq mi) [25]. The total population reached 26,417,599 in mid-2005, compared with 24.06 million in mid-2004, reflecting an annual growth rate of 2.9 percent; however, 5,576,076 million of the population is non-Saudis [10].

Regarding Information Technology in the Kingdom of Saudi Arabia, national e-government program has been launched, early 2005, under the name Yesser, an Arabic word meaning "simplify" or "make easy". It plays the role of the enabler / facilitator of the implementation of e-government in the public sector. Its objectives include raising the public sector's efficiency and effectiveness; providing better and faster government services, and ensuring availability of the required information in a timely and accurate fashion. Yesser vision is that by the end of 2010, everyone in the Kingdom will be able to enjoy world class government services offered in a seamless, user friendly and secure way by utilizing a variety of electronic means [14].

2.3 Digital and Cultural Gap

Digital divide refers to the gap between the group of people that are very familiar and have good access to high technology and those who do not [7]. It can be a result of several reasons such as a lack of financial resources, great education, and computer literacy. However, the digital divide makes the successful of e-government applications challenging [3].

In the case of Saudi Arabia, a digital divide can be caused by the lack of knowledge and experience with technology, for instance, people in rural areas and inner city neighbourhoods may have less internet access than others, while those who have never used computers may simply be reluctant to use the new technology [1]. Moreover, Al-Shehry and others [3] indicated that there is a significant risk of a digital divide in Saudi society and even among employees in public sector since there are a large number of people and employees that are still not computer-literate. Evidence of digital and cultural gap between the technological awareness of government employees and increasing need to deal with new technology can be realized in the result section.

2.4 Biometric Authentication Technology

Biometric technology provides a range of automated methods which can used to measure and analyze a person's physiological and behavioral characteristics [27]. Physiological biometrics includes fingerprint recognition, iris recognition, facial recognition, and hand recognition. Behavioral biometrics contains voice patterns and signatures, which are usually taken for identification and verification purposes. Basic authentication is usually based on something somebody knows, like a pin or a password, or something somebody has, like a key, passport or driver's license. The limitations of these authentication measures in some application areas have led to the development and adoption of biometric technology which is now used to identify individual behaviors and characteristics [27].

Biometric technology usually involves a scanning device and related software which can be used to gather information that has been recorded in digital form [8]. Having digitally collected the information, a database is used to store this information for comparison with the previous records. When converting the biometric input, namely the already collected data in digital form, this software can now be used to identify the specific inputs into a value that can be used to match any data previously collected. By using an algorithm, the data points are then processed into a value that can be compared with biometric data in the database [8].

2.5   Examples of Biometric Technology in E-government Applications

By using biometric technology, e-government aims to give its citizens improved services with efficient and secure access to information by providing reliable identification of individuals as well as the ability for controlling and protecting the integrity of sensitive data stored in information systems. Most researchers such as Ashbourn [6], Bonsor and Johnson [9], Scott [22], and Wayman et al. [27] argue that a wider use of biometric technology can be applied to e-government projects. Currently biometric technology is used for applications like e-voting to ensure that voters do not vote twice. With biometric technology, governments are better able to prevent fraud during elections and other transaction types. Moreover, biometric technology has most recently been used to ensure correct working times are recorded and that only authorized personnel have access to government property and resources.

Biometric technology can also be used by e-governments for business. For instance, banks frequently adopt a facial feature recognition system to ensure that there is a reduced potential for theft. For example, photos are taken on the bank slips which are stored on computer software. As a result, this has avoided the issue of fraudulent bank slips when withdrawing money at ATMs. These technological advances in authenticating dealings with business have helped the government to conduct its activities more effectively and more securely [9].

In business transactions there is frequently the need for full authentication of employees to ensure that, in case of any problem, management is in a position to identify the person responsible for that act. Commercial applications may also require full identification capability, digital certificates, human interface, and one or more authentication devices to ensure that the business can run safely and effectively. People are also in a position to do their business with increased trust. Digital trust through public key cryptography, strong authentication and certification allows greater transaction confidence as long as that organisation has a certified identity as an effective and trustworthy company [6].

Biometric technology is also used in the identification of citizens by e-government applications. Every nation could ethically be able to identify its citizens and differentiate non-citizens by using variations of national identification cards, visas, and passports with biometric data encoded within. Prior to the use of biometric data with such documents they were too easily forged or altered to allow unauthorized access to resources and facilities. As a result many nations have avoided the use of mechanisms such as a national identity card in the past.

Effective e-government biometric applications to authenticate and identify citizens have effectively been used in reducing the issues of illegal immigration, access bottlenecks in busy facilities and high costs of employing security personnel. A good example is the United States whereby, since "September 11", it has widely adopted biometric technology. Two laws were made in the United States as a first mass deployment of biometrics. Seven million transportation employees in the United States incorporate biometrics in their ID cards. Moreover, in order to closely control visitors who enter and leave the country, all foreign visitors are required to present valid passports with biometric data; consequently, over 500 million U.S. visitors have to carry border-crossing documents which incorporate biometrics [6].

Several European governments have also started to implement the use of biometrics. The U.K. government has established issuing asylum seekers with identification smart cards storing two fingerprints. General plans have also been made to extend the use of biometrics throughout the visa system in the U.K. as well as in France, Germany and Italy [22].

The Australian Customs established an automated passenger processing system, that is, the e-passport SmartGate at Sydney and Melbourne airports, and it aims to introduce self-processing by employing facial recognition systems to confirm identities and streamline the travelers'' facilitation procedures [24].

E-government facilities use the various types of biometric identification in order to control certain illegal behavior. For example, the Japanese government plans to use biometric technology in passports to tackle illegal immigration and to enable tighter controls on terrorists. This will be applied within a computer chip which can store biometric features like fingerprints and facial recognition [22].

Other e-government applications are using the biometrics for certain defense bases for secure areas. For instance, hand recognition has been used at the Scott Air Force Base to save more than $400,000 in manpower costs through their metro-link biometric access gate [17].

2.6 Concerns about the Use of Biometric Technology

While biometrics can provide a high level of authentication through identifying people by their physiological and behavioural characteristics, there are also several negative aspects. Biometrics can sometimes be ineffective when using the various styles of identification. For instance, fingerprints can be saturated, faint, or hard to be processed with some of devices, particularly if the skin is wet or dry. Hand recognition can sometimes be ineffective when the hand is damaged, thereby no results will be obtained to match with the images already in the database. Few facilities have databases or hardware to employ iris recognition, which makes the upfront investment too high to initiate a worldwide iris ID system. Biometric technology has also been criticized for its potential harm to civil liberties. This is because people have been denied access to the various regions and countries simply because they do not have the correct identities for those places. Moreover, there is potential for people's privacy to be violated with this new technology [8].

3   Methodology

The review of the current literature on biometric applications guided our research and the literature on methods available for an exploratory study. Given the exploratory nature of the study the two research questions were aimed at providing descriptive information on the perceptions of current and potential users of biometric application. The research was designed to answer the following questions.

1. What are the managers' perceptions regarding the use of biometric authentication in e-government applications?
2. What are the employees' perceptions regarding the use of biometric authentication in e-government applications?

Given the two distinctive groups of people – managers and employees - involved the research was carried out in two distinct stages.

Method of sampling was purposive. This method of sampling [19] is a strategy in which "particular settings, persons, or activities are selected deliberately in order to provide information that can't be gotten as well from other choices" (p.88). A selection of knowledgeable interviewees was approached.

The literature on user acceptance of new technology was used to design the questionnaire. The interviews were to discuss the questions in more detail and to gain further understanding on the factors that influence the use of biometric application, such as authentication.

Two distinct stages were designed in this research, each using a different method and each with a particular focus. A mix of qualitative methods and user groups provides rigor through triangulation and quantitative techniques provide useful trend analysis. Thus the use of the multiple or mixed methodology with both qualitative and quantitative aspects compensates for the weakness of one method via the strengths of the other method [21]. A combination of qualitative and quantitative methods in the research "may provide complementary data sets which together give a more complete picture than can be obtained using either method singly" [26, p.197]. Additionally, the use of multiple qualitative methods enhances the richness and validity of the research [21]. In particular, interviews were conducted with managers and questionnaires were given to employees in order to investigate their perceptions regarding the use of biometrics.

3.1 Interviews

Interviews with knowledgeable individuals are recommended as an appropriate method to narrow down the scope of the research and investigate the range of issues [23]. In this research, face-to-face interviews were conducted in the Kingdom of Saudi Arabia with eleven managers of the General Organisation for Technical Education and Vocational Training and the Royal Commission for Jubail and Yanbu. However, the participants were selected at different management levels. In order to obtain personally meaningful information from the participants, open-ended questions were used for the interviews [21].

3.2 Questionnaire

The questionnaire was used for data collection for this research as it is an efficient means to gain data from a large participant group, it is an appropriate method to answer the research questions, and it is an effective method to investigate people's attitudes and opinions regarding particular issues [16]. In this research, a total 101 participants completed the questionnaire, and they are all employees in one of these two organisations: the General Organisation for Technical Education and Vocational Training and the Royal Commission for Jubail and Yanbu.

3.3 Data Collection and Analysis

As mentioned, the data of this research were collected through face-to-face interviews and questionnaires as well as the literature review. The justification for using different techniques for collecting the data is triangulation to provide verification. Triangulation refers to the use of several different methods or sources in the same study in order to confirm and verify the data gathered [21].

In the interview, all participants were asked if the interview could be recorded, and none of them objected. The expected maximum time for each interview was 60 minutes; however, the actual time for each recording was about 25 to 40 minutes. Notes were taken during each interview as a safeguard against recording failure. Afterwards, all interviewees' answers were categorized according to each question of the interview and they are presented in the results section.

In the questionnaire, permission from the surveyed organisations as well as all the managers of the participating employees is gained to distribute the questionnaire to the employees. However, all responses were stored in the SPSS (Statistical Package for the Social Science) software which was used for the analyses. Statistical analysis includes the frequency and the percentage of each category of the responses for each answer, the Chi square value and its level of significance.

4 Results

It is noteworthy that the two investigated organisations implemented fingerprint scanners for proving employees' attendance. Previously, manual signature recording was the official process for proving employees' attendance in most agencies in the Kingdom of Saudi Arabia. In this process, the employee has to sign and record attendance twice a day, at the beginning of the work day and at the end as well. This process has several negatives, because the employees may sign for others and may not write the correct time of signing. Therefore, this was not an effective or efficient process for recording attendance, and was considered a good reason for implementing biometric technology.

However, in this section we will present just a number of our survey questions which are relevant to detecting problems in this context and seeking solutions to reducing the digital and cultural gap.

4.1 Interview Results of Managers

A question by question analysis is presented as follows:

4.1.1 What Cultural Gap Do You Perceive between the Employees' Level of Technological Experience and the Level of Biometric Technology That Is Being Deployed?

This question investigates the cultural gap between the employees' level of technological experience and the level of biometric technology that is being deployed in their organisation. Nine of the respondents to this study agreed that there is a cultural gap between the employees' technical cultural levels and the level of technology being used, but they attributed this gap to different reasons, as follows:

- Four respondents attributed the technical cultural gap of the staff to their levels of technological literacy.
- Two respondents attributed the technical cultural gap to the employees' age; that is, the older the employee, the wider the gap.

- One respondent attributed the cultural gap to a perception that use of this technology indicates a level of mistrust of employees by management causing them not to want to use the technology
- Two respondents did not attribute the cultural gap to a particular reason.
- Two other respondents did not agree that there is a cultural gap at all.

4.1.2 Do You Accept a Level of Responsibility for Narrowing This Cultural Gap?

This question investigates the managers' perceived responsibility for narrowing the cultural gap between their employees' level of technological experience and the level of biometric technology.

- Five of the interviewed managers felt that they are responsible for narrowing the cultural gap; they proposed procedures concentrating on enhancing employee awareness of technology and its utilities.
- Four respondents did not consider that it was their responsibility to narrow the cultural gap.

4.1.3 Have You Experienced Any Difficulties in Dealing with This Technology? If So, What Were They?

This question investigates the managers' points of view regarding the difficulties in dealing with biometric technology in their workplace. Regarding the difficulties being experienced, 11 responses were presented by the interviewees, distributed among the following categories:

- Employee resistance (11 respondents);
- Disabling and breaking the fingerprint device by some employees (4 respondents);
- System failures (5 respondents); and,
- System unable to take fingerprints from some users (7 respondents).

4.1.4 What Are the Main Barriers (Inconveniences) of Applying Biometric Technology in Your Organisation?

This question investigates the managers' point of view regarding the main barriers of applying biometric technology in their organisations.

- All responses to this issue were related to digital and technological culture as well as resistance to change that was evidenced by the employees at the beginning of the deployment.

4.1.5 How Do You Think the Use of Biometric Technology Affects Self Perceived Social Level of Your Employees?

This question investigates the social impact of the use of biometric technology on the employees themselves and among their society. A wide range of responses were provided regarding the social impact of the fingerprint technology; these responses showed contradictions regarding the effects on hardworking employees.

- Six respondents said that there were positive effects as regulation became stricter.
- Five respondents highlighted the negative effects of using this technology.

However, they attributed the positive and negative effects to the following:

- Three respondents raised the issue of mistrust concerns that the employees may feel. They feel the perception that their managers do not trust them and that this may reflect badly on them in their society as other people may mistrust them as well.
- Four respondents commented that this type of regulative technology has reported positive effects on all types of employees, especially when comparing with other employees who do not use this technology. For example, one response said that I feel proud with my friends that I use this new technology while they do not.

To sum up, managers' responses to all questions indicated that there is a digital and cultural gap evidenced by the technological awareness of employees and the preferred authentication solutions promoted by management. This digital and cultural gap creates a resistance to change by the employees which reflects on the acceptance and adoption of new technologies such as these.

4.2 Questionnaire Results of Government Employees

As mentioned before the questionnaire was distributed to 101 government employees and a question by question analysis is presented in this section. Questions were presented as a five point Likert scale (1 to 5) where 1 is the lowest level of importance and five is the highest. There was an "opt out" option if the respondent did not know the importance or relevance of the question's concept. Likert responses have been generalised to provide a preliminary analysis view.

4.2.1 How Important Do You Think the Use of Biometric Technology Is to the Organisation?

Responses to this question examine the users' points of view regarding the level of importance that the employees think the organisation places on the use of biometric technology. The responses were as the following:

- No one of the respondents think that it is not important.
- 23.8% feel that it is important.
- 13.9% feel that it is very important.
- A minority (45.5%) of the respondents have no idea of the importance of using fingerprint technology in their workplace.

4.2.2 How Important Do You Think It Is That There Should Be an Awareness of This Technology before Its Implementation?

Responses to this question examine the users' points of view regarding the importance of awareness before implementation of the used biometric technology. The concept of awareness includes aspects of notification, information and education of employees. All respondents classified the level of importance as follows.

- Only 5% of the respondents feel that it is not necessary to promote employee awareness of the technology before the implementation.
- 15.8% think that it is important.

- A majority (52.56%) of the respondents perceived that it is very important to have awareness before using fingerprint technology.

4.2.3 Do You Think That the Use of This Technology in Your Workplace Means That Employers Mistrust Employees?

Responses to this question examine the users' points of view regarding the perception of employer mistrust created by introducing and using biometric technology. There is a significant difference among employees' responses as follows.

- 33.7% of the respondents state that it does not mean mistrust.
- 11.9% think that it means mistrust.
- 22.8% think that it certainly means mistrust.
- 33.7% of the respondents are unsure if it means mistrust or not.

5 Discussion

The results indicate that nine of the interview respondents agreed that there is a digital/cultural gap created by the employees' low familiarity with technology and the organisation's adoption of biometrics. This has been supported by several studies; for instance, Ashbourn [6] stated that education is an essential phase that users need. The organisation that is going to implement such biometric technology has to communicate with users in order to provide them with a good understanding and overview about biometrics, how this technology works, and the reasons for its implementation. Moreover, if this information is presented in an attractive and truly informative manner, the organisation will achieve much in warming users towards the project and raising their confidence regarding the implementation of this technology.

In addition, this result reflects some of the literature findings regarding the challenges in the implementation of e-government in the Kingdom of Saudi Arabia. These might be summarized as the weakness due to the lack of social and cultural awareness of the concepts and applications of e-government, the extent of computer illiteracy, as well as the deficiency of the official education curricula in addressing the information age. However, the result of this study supports the finding which reveals that there is a need programs related to the application of e-government [2, 5].

Only five of the interviewed managers felt that they are responsible for narrowing the technological cultural gap. This result concurs with Ashbourn's [6] finding that managers need some in-depth training in order to understand the various issues regarding the introduction and use of such technology. In particular there is a need to be able to fulfill their roles regarding the ongoing running of the application and user acceptance and understanding. Therefore, such training may lead managers to narrow the technical cultural gap.

It is important to note that employee resistance is an essential issue facing organisations, as mentioned by all respondents through their answers to several questions. Several employees have tried to prevent the use of this technology in many ways. Four interviewees clarified that some employees had tried to break down the device which meant that some managers had to install cameras in order to catch the person and prevent this from happening. Furthermore, some employees tried to distort their fingers by injuring them or rubbing them on wood in order to make the system unable to read their fingerprints in an attempt to prove this technology to be ineffective. In addition, this result relates with the literature finding where Alsuwail [5] and Al-shareef [2] confirmed resistance by employees to change as one of the challenges of implementing e-government in the Kingdom of Saudi Arabia. This has been supported by Feng [15] who stated that one of the main barriers to implementing e-government is the need for change in individual attitudes and organisational culture. Furthermore, user acceptance and perception problems relating to the implementation of the new technology have been clarified by Giesing [18] as factors that would prevent an organisation from implementing or adopting biometric technology.

Furthermore, the interviews provided a wide range of responses regarding the social impact of the fingerprint technology. Six respondents said that there were positive effects through the regulation of attendance and working hours. On the other hand, five respondents highlighted the negative effects of using this technology, which relate to the literature finding by Coventry [12] who highlighted the weakness of the social and cultural awareness of the concepts and applications of e-government. Coventry continued that the usability and acceptance of biometric services can be affected by the context of use as well as the social issues, such as the perceived benefits to the user and the perceived privacy risks. Application contexts with obvious, apparent benefits and low risks may lead to greater perceptions of usability and higher acceptance opinions of biometrics than contexts where there are little obvious benefits and high risks.

On the other hand, a minority (45.5%) of the employees had no idea of the importance of using fingerprint technology, which may relate to the shortage of any awareness program that the employees could undertake before using such technology. This supports the challenges of implementing e-government in the Kingdom of Saudi Arabia which indicate a scarcity of information programs related to the application of e-government, the deficiency of the official education curricula in addressing the information age, and the lack of computer literacy among citizens [1, 2, 5].

A small majority (52.56%) of the respondents perceived that it is very important to have an awareness of the introduction and implications of the technology through information and education programs before using fingerprint technology. Change resistance might also be a key factor here. In fingerprint technology contexts in Saudi Arabia, many people raise the issue of radiation risks that they think are associated with using these systems, as well as the disease transfer by every employee touching the same point, which was also illustrated in other responses to the interviews. These concerns will simply be reduced as the levels of awareness increase, and as the usual habits continue after adaptation to this technology takes place. As stated, a weakness of the social and cultural awareness of the concepts and applications of e-government has been noted in the literature by Alshareef [2] and Alsuwail [5] as well as a scarcity of education programs related to the application of e-government. Moreover, Alharbi [1] clarified that society lacks awareness about e-government advantages and benefits. However, a study by Giesing [18] noted that the employees expressed the need for more information about biometric technology in general and for more detailed information on the specific biometrics that will be used, as they only had basic knowledge of biometrics. Giesing's study shows that employees would like to know more regarding biometric technology, such as background information, advantages and disadvantages, user guides on the use of the biometrics, technical specifications, the storage of biometric data, as well as the security and privacy issues. Furthermore, Ashbourn [6] stated that the education phase of implementing technology is very important for users in order to provide them with a good understanding and to make them more confident in its use.

A significant 33.7% of the respondents to the survey section of this study do not know whether introduction of this technology indicates mistrust and 22.8% of them think the use of this technology certainly means employers mistrust employees. This may be attributed to various factors including a lack of awareness through consultation, notification, information, and general levels of computer literacy. The scarcity of programs related to the application of e-government may also explain these some of the results. As 33.7% of respondents do not feel that it signifies mistrust of employees and these may relate to the proportion of the user population with higher levels of the familiarity with technology, its adoption, convenience and usefulness which they may have experienced elsewhere.

6 Conclusion

A study was undertaken to investigate government employees' perceptions of factors relating to the introduction of biometric authentication at the workplace. This was undertaken to determine how best to gain employees' acceptance of biometric in order to successfully adopt biometrics in e-government applications. Results supported a number of findings reported in literature regarding user acceptance and adoption of biometrics and e-government technology. Analysis of results shows that an awareness and orientation process about biometrics should take place before the technology is introduced into the organisation. This is highlighted as all managers expressed employees' resistance to the technology's installation at the beginning of its implementation. The employees should be made aware about the use of the new technology, the purpose of its implementation and the benefits. Since about half of the managers had not considered their responsibilities for narrowing the digital and cultural gap regarding the fingerprint technology, it is recommended that managers should be made aware of their responsibilities in this issue. They should recognize that digital and cultural gap in technological awareness exists and that they have to act as leaders and role models for their employees. Finally, as the managers have a big part of the responsibility to successfully implement biometric technology in their organisations, they need to gain a detailed understanding of this technology and preferably have a basic background about Information Technology as well.

References

1. Alharbi, S.: Perceptions of Faculty and Students toward the Obstacles of Implementing E-Government in Educational Institutions in Saudi Arabia. West Virginia University (2006)
2. Alshareef, T.: E-Government in the Kingdom of Saudi Arabia, Applicational Study on the governmental mainframes in Riyadh City. King Saud University, Saudi Arabia (2003)
3. Al-shehry, A., Rogerson, S., Fairweather, N., Prior, M.: The Motivations for Change towards E-government Adoption: Saudi Arabia as a case Study, eGovernment Workshop. Brunel University, West London (2006)

4. AlShihi, H.: Critical Factors in the Adoption and Diffusion of E-government Initiatives in Oman. PhD thesis, Victoria University, Australia (2006)
5. Alsuwail, M.: Directions and local experiences, Foundations and Requirements of E-Government. E-Government Conference, Institute of Public Administration, the Kingdom of Saudi Arabia (2001)
6. Ashbourn, J.: Practical biometric from aspiration to implementation. Springer, London (2004)
7. Blau, A.: Access isn't enough: Merely connecting people and computers won't close the digital divide. American Libraries 33(6), 50–52 (2002)
8. Bolle, R., Connell, J., Pankanti, S., Ratha, N., Senior, A.: Guide to Biometrics. Springer, New York (2004)
9. Bonsor, K., Johnson, R.: How Facial Recognition Systems Work, How Stuff Works, http://computer.howstuffworks.com/facialrecognition.htm (viewed on October 1, 2007)
10. Central Department of Statistics & Information (CDSI), The Kingdom of Saudi Arabia (2009), http://www.cdsi.gov.sa
11. Central Intelligence Agency (CIA): The Word Fact Book (2009), https://www.cia.gov/library/publications/the-world-factbook/
12. Coventry, L.: Usable Biometrics, Security and usability, ch. 10, pp. 181–204. Human Centred Systems Group, University College London (2005)
13. Dearstyne, B.: E-business, e-government and information proficiency. Information Management Journal 34(4) (2001)
14. E-government Program (Yesser). The Ministry of Communications and Information Technology (2009), http://www.yesser.gov.sa
15. Feng, L.: Implementing E-government Strategy is Scotland: Current Situation and Emerging Issues. Journal of Electronic Commerce in Organizations 1(2), 44–65 (2003)
16. Fraenkel, J., Wallen, N.: How to design & evaluate research in education. McGraw-Hill, United States (2000)
17. Frees, R.: Biometric technology improves identification security. U.S. Air Force (2008), http://www.af.mil/news/story.asp?id=123084564 (Viewed on March 3, 2008)
18. Giesing, I.: User response to biometric, pp. 95–135. University of Pretoria (2003)
19. Maxwell, J.A.: Qualitative Research Design: An Interactive Approach, 2nd edn. Sage Publication, Thousand Oaks (2005)
20. McLindin, B.: Improving the Performance of Two Dimensional Facial Recognition Systems. University of South Australia (2005)
21. McMurray, A., Pace, R., Scott, D.: Research: a commonsense approach. Thomson Social Science Press, Melbourne (2004)
22. Scott, M.: An assessment of biometric identities as a standard for e-government services. Services and Standards 1(3), 271–286 (2005)
23. Sekaran, U.: Research Methods for Business: A Skill Building Approach, 4th edn. John Wiley & Sons Inc., New York (2003)
24. The Annual Report of the Australian Customs Service (ACS) (2005), http://www.customs.gov.au/webdata/resources/files/ACSannualReport0405.pdf
25. The Saudi Network, http://www.the-saudi.net/ (viewed on January 14, 2009)
26. Tripp-Reimer, T.: Combining qualitative and quantitative methodologies. In: Leininger, M.M. (ed.) Qualitative research methods in nursing, pp. 179–194. Grune & Stratton, Orlando (1985)
27. Wayman, J., Jain, D., Maltoni, H., Maio, D.: Biometric Systems: Technology, Design and Performance Evaluation. Springer, New York (2005)

Biovault: Biometrically Based Encryption

B.L. Tait[1] and S.H. von Solms[2]

[1] University of Johannesburg, Kingsway Avenue, Auckland Park, Gauteng, South Africa
Btait@uj.ac.za
[2] University of Johannesburg, Kingsway Avenue, Auckland Park, Gauteng, South Africa
basievs@uj.ac.za

Abstract. Biometric based characteristic authentication is an asymmetric [1] authentication technology. This means that the reference biometric data generated during the enrolment process and stored in the biometric database, will never match any freshly offered biometric data exactly (100%). This is commonly accepted due to the nature of the biometric algorithm [2] central to the biometric environment.

A password or pin on the other hand, is a symmetric authentication mechanism. This means that an exact match is expected, and if the offered password deviates ever so slightly from the password stored in the password database file, authenticity is rejected.

Encryption technologies rely on symmetric authentication to function, as the password or pin is often used as the seed for a random number that will assist in the generation of the cipher. If the password used to encrypt the cipher is not 100% the same as the password supplied to decrypt, the cipher will not unlock.

The asymmetric nature of biometrics traditionally renders biometric data unfit to be used as the secret key for an encryption algorithm.

This paper introduces a system that allows biometric data to be used as the secret key in an encryption algorithm. This method relies on the BioVault infrastructure. For this reason BioVault will briefly be discussed, followed by a discussion of biometrically based encryption.

Keywords: Encryption, Biometrics, BioVault, security, secure transaction, data protection, key management, privacy-enhancing technology, data security.

1 Introduction

To date, it was not possible to use a biometric data directly as the secret key for an encryption algorithm or for a MAC algorithm. The reason for this resides in the fact that a biometric authentication process is always asymmetric. In order for an encryption algorithm to function, the secret key provided to encrypt a message must be exactly the same (symmetrical) as the secret key used to decrypt the message.

If a secret key is used to generate a MAC, this exact same secret key must be provided to test the MAC.

The possibility that a person would repeatedly be able to provide biometric data that would be 100% the same as earlier provided biometric data is highly unlikely. This makes biometric data useless as the secret keys for hashing or encryption.

C. Godart et al. (Eds.): I3E 2009, IFIP AICT 305, pp. 39–50, 2009.

Digital signatures use encryption and hashing as its underlying, primary technology.

The paper is based on the BioVault protocol. Because of the length restriction on this paper, the BioVault protocol cannot be discussed in detail. However a short discussion of the protocol will be given, followed by a detailed discussion of how the protocol can be used to create biometrically based digital signatures.

For a detailed discussion of the BioVault protocol see [6], [7].

In the sections to follow it will be demonstrated how the BioVault infrastructure allows biometric data to be used for encryption.

2   Encryption Using a Secret Key or Biometric Data

2.1   Secret Key Encryption

If a user wishes to send a message to another user over an unsecured network, the message must be encrypted in one or other way. $C = E*k(M)$ [3] where:

C = Cipher message
M = Original message
k = secret key
E = Encryption algorithm

The typical encryption process using a secret key is illustrated in figure 1

As illustrated in figure 1, John wishes to send a secret message to Sam. In order to secure the message during the transmission, John encrypts the message using an encryption algorithm. In order for the encryption algorithm to yield cipher text that is absolutely random, a secret key must be provided. This secret key is shared between Sam and John as illustrated in figure 1. The secret key provided by John to encrypt the message is exactly the same as the secret key that Sam will provide to decrypt the message.

Step 1
John generates the message that he wishes to send to Sam.

Step 2
John provides a secret key to the encryption algorithm, and the encryption algorithm uses this secret key to generate the cipher text.

Step 3
The message in cipher text is sent over the internet to Sam. If a hacker should intercept this message, the hacker must be in possession of the secret key shared between Sam and John, in order to decrypt the message.

Step 4
Sam receives the message sent by John and uses the same encryption algorithm and the secret key that is shared between the two of them. If the secret key that Sam supplied to the encryption algorithm is exactly the same as the secret key used by John, Sam will retrieve the original, unencrypted message that John created.

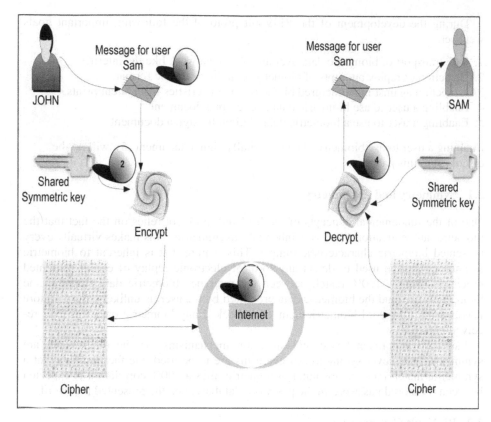

Fig. 1. Typical encryption process

From the above mentioned example it becomes clear that biometric data can not be used for secure encrypted communication between two people.

If John used his biometric characteristic as the secret key for encrypting a message destined for Sam, Sam would not be able to provide the same biometric characteristic to decrypt the message (as this was John's biometric characteristic that Sam does not possess).

In this paper it is illustrated in what way the BioVault infrastructure is a solution in allowing John to send an encrypted message to Sam, by using his biometric characteristic. This method relies on the fact that both John and Sam are part of the BioVault infrastructure – very much as EBay [4] relies on the fact that buyers and sellers are both part of the PayPal [5] environment. The BioVault infrastructure is a new development, and subsequently not commonly known. For this reason the following section will give a brief outline of the BioVault infrastructure, followed by an explanation of biometrically based encryption. For a detailed discussion of the BioVault infrastructure see [6], [7].

3 Brief Introduction to BioVault Version 3.0

BioVault does not rely on any specific biometric technology to function, however certain technologies are inherently stronger technologies and would obviously be preferred by industry.

During the development of the BioVault protocol the following important goals were set:

1. Safe transport of biometric data over an un-safe network like the internet.
2. Detection of replay attempts of biometric data in electronic format.
3. Protection against manufactured biometric characteristics from latent prints.
4. Enabling a user to use biometric data to encrypt a document
5. Enabling a user to use a biometric data to digitally sign a document.

Enabling a user to use biometric data to digitally sign a document (5), will not be discussed in this paper.

3.1 Symmetry and Asymmetry

One of the fundamental concepts of the BioVault protocol relies on the fact that the biometric authentication process is inherently asymmetric. This makes virtually every presented biometric characteristic unique. This feature that is inherent to biometric technology can be used to detect any form of electronic replay of earlier presented biometric data. A 100% match between the reference biometric data stored in the biometric store, and the biometric data presented by the user, is unlikely. Furthermore it is possible to record biometric data, and check if any biometric data was ever received before.

Password and token based authentication mechanisms, on the other hand, are symmetric. Whenever symmetric mechanisms are to be used, the fact remains that a symmetric match must be absolutely symmetric, thus a 100% correlation is expected between the stored password in the password database, and the presented password.

3.2 BioVault Components

The following components are part of the BioVault infrastructure:

3.2.1 The Bio-Archives (BA)
Two Bio-archives (BA) are created; one bio-archive on the authentication server known as the Server bio-Archive (SBA) and one Client side bio- Archive known as the CBA. The SBA will store all biometric data used by the user that was successfully authenticated by the biometric matching algorithm. The SBA will assist in the identification of possible replay attacks. For this reason access to the biometric data stored in the SBA must be very fast. To ensure that specific biometric data inside the SBA can be found very fast, the SBA will be sorted. Considering that SBA is sorted, a binary search algorithm can be used to find biometric data in the SBA efficiently.

The CBA will assist in biometric data protection during transmission.

Initially the CBA will consist of a limited number of previously used biometric data of the specific user (to be discussed in more detail later). The larger this bio-archive the stronger the system will be.

The biometric data inside this CBA are totally random and provided to the user by the authentication server. The authentication server will populate the CBA from time to time with different previously offered biometric data of the given user.

Whenever a secure connection is established between the user and the authentication server, the server can update the CBA. However it is recommended that the CBA is updated under strictly controlled environments. This means that CBA can be updated by the authentication server, whenever a user visits a bank or ATM machine, as an example.

CBA storage.
The Bio-Archive that the user will use, will store previously offered biometric data. The following are possible options that can be used to store the CBA.

1. A USB flash memory – These tiny appliances like the Micro SD memory, presently offer surprisingly large   storage space with storage sizes reaching 64Gb [114], furthermore, no additional equipment will be needed to integrate this technology into the environment.
2. A Smart card –These devices however need additional equipment and storage capacity on smartcards is limited.
3. A subcutaneous microchip – This technology ensures that a person cannot forget or misplace his CBA, but workable and acceptable solutions are still in development. Storage capacity is limited and technology is controversial. [8], [9].

3.2.2 The Bio- parcel Used during the Authentication Process

The Bio- parcel will always include freshly offered biometric data and old biometric data that is obtained from the CBA as requested by the Authentication server. The contents of the bio-parcel will be joined using a XOR operator. This is illustrated in figure 2. The aim of the XOR operator is to secure the bio-parcel while transmitted over a public network, without using encryption systems. Encryption systems using for example shared symmetric keys, introduces a lot of system overhead.

For the example as illustrated in figure 2 the CBA would include 50 randomly picked biometric tokens from the SBA of this specific user. The SBA on the server will still include each and every biometric data ever used by the user in his lifetime. As will soon be discussed, these randomly selected biometric data of the user, will serve as a special key, and can be compared to the working of a one time pad.

3.3 BioVault Mechanism

Step 1 (As in figure 2)
When a user needs to be authenticated the user attaches the appliance containing the CBA with the previously offered biometric data to the terminal (for example the user's computer or ATM machine), where he intends to do the transaction.

Step 2
The user provides a fresh biometric characteristic as shown, directly to the biometric scanner. The scanner will digitize the biometric characteristic and forward the biometric data to the driver software of the biometric device.

Step 3
During the previous encounter with the authentication server, the server sent a challenge to the. This challenge demanded specific biometric data from the CBA that had to be included at the time of the next contact with the authentication server.

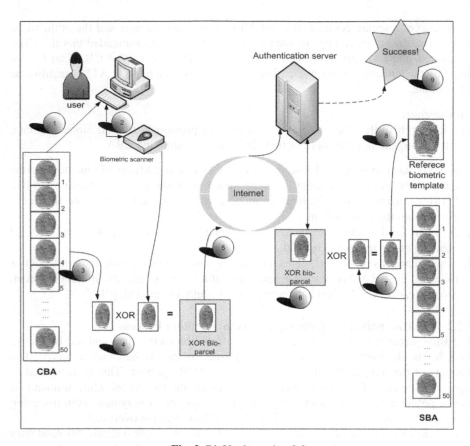

Fig. 2. BioVault version 3.0

In figure 2, the server requested the 4th biometric data in the CBA. The system will thus automatically obtain the 4th biometric data from the user's CBA.

Step 4
The BioVault client side software will take the electronic representation of the freshly offered biometric data and XOR it with the electronic representation of the 4th biometric data obtained in step 3 from the CBA. For example:

Electronic representation of fresh biometric data from scanner:

10101110111011010

Electronic representation of challenged (4th) data from CBA: <u>10110101111011110</u>

New bio-archive after XOR process: 00011011000000100

This result in a smaller bio-parcel than proposed in BioVault version 2.0, as only the result of the XOR process will be submitted to the authentication server as the XOR bio-parcel.

Step 5
The XOR bio-parcel is submitted via the internet or any networked environment to the authentication server.

Step 6
The server receives the XOR bio-parcel as shown in step 6, and prepares to run the XOR operator on the bio-parcel.

Step 7
The server requested previously that the client XOR the fresh biometric data with the fourth biometric data in the CBA. The server obtains the biometric data in the SBA that corresponds with the expected biometric data received from the user in the XOR bio-parcel.

The server must then XOR the received XOR bio-archive with the 4th biometric data from the SBA, corresponding with the 4th biometric data in the CBA, in order to get the fresh biometric data of the user. For example:

XOR bio-archive received from user:	00011011000000100
Expected 4th biometric data from SBA:	10110101111011110
Result of XOR process = the fresh biometric data:	10101110111011010

Step 8
The fresh biometric data extracted from the XOR bio-archive during step 7, is now asymmetrically matched to the reference biometric template found in the database. The authentication server compares the freshly offered biometric data with the reference biometric template. If the offered biometric data falls within the tolerances defined in the matching algorithm, the system declares the biometric data as authentic and adds this biometric data to the SBA, after checking the SBA for an exact match.

Step 9
As the bio-parcel passed all the requirements, authentication is pronounced successful. The server will proceed to the generation of a new challenge destined for the user.

4 Biometric Encryption Using BioVault

The whole encryption method using the BioVault infrastructure is a 4-phased process.

4.1 Biometric Encryption Overview

In phase 1, John identifies himself to the authentication server, and indicates that he wants to send an encrypted message to Sam. In order to send an encrypted message to Sam, John requests a "biometric key" of Sam from the server.

In phase 2, the authentication server retrieves a biometric key from Sam's STA also found in Sam's CTA, and sends it to John.

In phase 3, John uses this biometric key of Sam, as an encryption key to create the encrypted message, and sends this encrypted message to Sam over the network.

In phase 4, Sam receives the message sent by John, and decrypts the message by testing all the biometric keys in her CTA, against the received cipher text. In essence, Sam will the 'brute force' the decryption of the cipher.

4.2 Biometric Encryption Discussion

Figure 3 illustrates the first phase that John would follow in order to send an encrypted message to Sam.

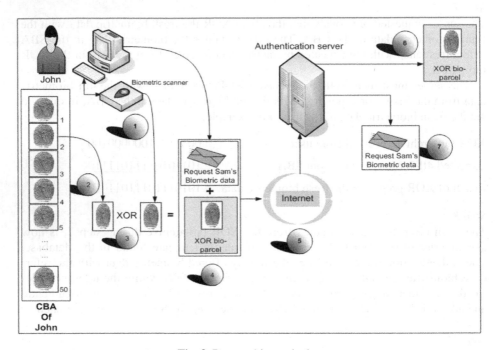

Fig. 3. Request biometric data

4.2.1 Request of Biometric Data

At this stage John sent a request to the server, stating that he wished to communicate with Sam. The server authenticated John, based on the fact that the fresh biometric data supplied by John was accepted and the expected biometric data from John's CBA was correctly supplied.

Subsequently the server ensured that Sam is a user on the BioVault system, allowing the second phase to commence. Phase two is illustrated in figure 4.

4.2.2 Phase 2: Submission of Biometric Data of Sam to John

During the second phase the server sends stored biometric data from the SBA of Sam, back to John. The server is aware that this biometric data exists inside Sam's CBA. The steps below explain this process:

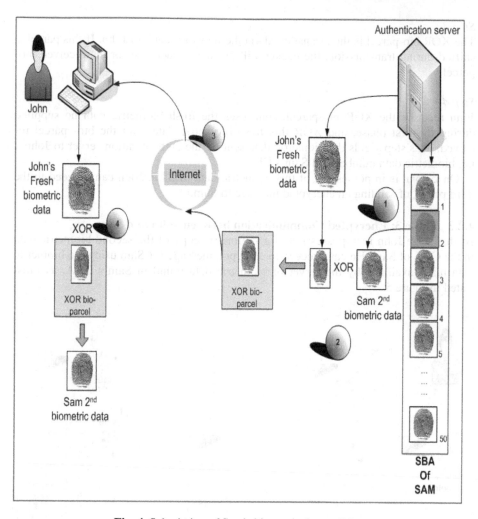

Fig. 4. Submission of Sam's biometric data to John

Step 1
The server obtains biometric data, in this particular illustration the second biometric data, from the SBA of the user Sam. This biometric data is also present in the CBA of user Sam.

The server marks this biometric data as "used for encryption" to prevent this particular biometric data ever again rendered for encryption or authentication. This guarantees that Sam and John are the only people in possession of this biometric data.

Step 2
The server will XOR the biometric data from Sam's SBA, in this case the 2nd one, with the fresh biometric data received in phase 1 from John, creating a new XOR bioparcel.

Step 3
The XOR bio-parcel is then transmitted via the network, back to John. If this parcel is sniffed during transmission, the hacker will not have much use for the received bio-parcel.

Step 4
John receives the XOR bio-parcel. John uses the fresh biometric data he supplied during the first phase, and XOR this fresh biometric data with the bio- parcel received. This step yields the biometric data sent by the authentication server to John – i.e. biometric data number 2 in Sam's CBA.

Once John is in possession of this biometric data of Sam, John can proceed to the third phase, of sending an encrypted message to Sam.

4.2.3 Phase 3: Encrypted Communication between John and Sam

At this stage John is in possession of a symmetric copy of the second biometric data in the CBA of Sam. He can proceed to encrypt a message for Sam using the biometric data made available by the server of biometric data found in Sam's CBA, as illustrated in figure 5.

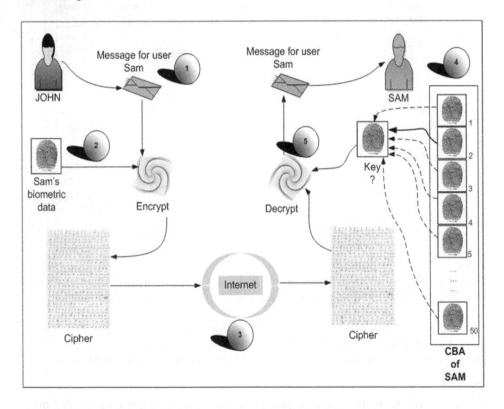

Fig. 5. Encrypted communication between John and Sam

It is illustrated in figure 5 the following steps indicates how John will send an encrypted message to Sam.

Step 1
John generates the message that he intends to send to Sam.

Step 2
John provides the received biometric data of Sam to the encryption algorithm, and the encryption algorithm uses this biometric data as a secret key to generate the cipher text.

Step 3
The message in cipher text is sent via the internet to Sam. If a hacker should intercept this message, the hacker must be in possession of the correct biometric data of Sam, in order to decrypt the message. Considering the working of BioVault version 3.0, this is highly unlikely.

In the final phase Sam will need to decrypt this message sent by John to her, using the biometric data inside her CBA. This process is illustrated in step 4 and step 5 of figure 5.

Step 4
Sam receives the message sent by John and accesses her own CBA. The client software on Sam's machine uses all the biometric data in her CBA to brute force the cipher. As there are only a limited number of biometric data in the CBA, this process will unlock the cipher rapidly.

Step 5
As the biometric data Sam used to decrypt the message is the same as the biometric data used by John, Sam will retrieve the original, unencrypted message created from the cipher created by John.

5 Conclusion

This paper demonstrated that the BioVault infrastructure makes it absolutely possible to encrypt a message using biometric data.

Biometric data relates directly to the users. If a user used a person's biometric characteristic to encrypt a message (similar to using a person's public key in the PKI system) only the receiving party with the correct biometric data will be able to decrypt the message- however unlike the PKI system, biometric data is directly related to the user. If tokens and passwords are used, only the token or password are authenticated, the user offering the token or password are not necessary authentic. Biometrics authenticates the user directly.

If it is considered that a user generates a number of biometric tokens every day, each one unique, this method of encryption is closely related to one time pad technology – the keys used, are very long and do not form any pattern. As each key are used, this biometric key is marked as used for encryption by the server in the SBA, and will not be used ever again.

References

[1] Tait, B.L., von Solms, S.H.: Solving the problem of replay in Biometrics- An electronic commerce Example. In: Proceedings of 5th IFIP Conference on Challenges of expanding internet: E-commerce, E-business, and E-government (I3E 2005), October 28-30, pp. 468–479. Springer, Boston (2005)

[2] Wayman, J., Jain, A., Maltoni, D., Maio, D.: BiometricSystems: Technology, Design and Performance Evaluation, 1st edn. Springer, Heidelberg (2004)

[3] Pfleeger, C.P., Pfleeger, S.L.: Security in Computing, 3rd edn. Prentice Hall, Englewood Cliffs, ISBN 0-13-035548-8

[4] Ebay online Auction, http://www.ebay.com/, http://www.ebay.co.uk

[5] PayPal online payment environment, http://www.paypal.com

[6] Tait, B.L., von Solms, S.H.: BioVault: a Secure Networked Biometric protocol, D.Com Dissertation, University of Johannesburg (2008)

[7] Tait, B.L., von Solms, S.H.: Secure Biometrically Based Authentication Protocol for a Public Network Environment. In: Proceedings for the 4th International Conference on Global E-Security, University of East-London, Docklands, United Kingdom, June 23-25, pp. 238–246 (2008)

[8] Wolinsky, H.: Tagging products and people. Despite much controversy, radiofrequency identification chips have great potential. EGE. Ethical Aspects of ICT Implants in the Human Body MEMO/05/97, Brussels, Belgium, March 17 (2005b)

[9] EGE. Ethical Aspects of ICT Implants in the Human Body: Opinion Presented to the Commission by the European Group on Ethics. MEMO/05/97. European Group on Ethics in Science and New Technologies, Brussels, Belgium, March 17 (2005b)

Value Encounters – Modeling and Analyzing Co-creation of Value

Hans Weigand

Tilburg University, Dept. Information Systems and Management, P.O. Box 90153,
5000 LE Tilburg, The Netherlands
H.Weigand@uvt.nl

Abstract. Recent marketing and management literature has introduced the concept of co-creation of value. Current value modeling approaches such as e3-value focus on the exchange of value rather than co-creation. In this paper, an extension to e3-value is proposed in the form of a "value encounter". Value encounters are defined as interaction spaces where a group of actors meet and derive value by each one bringing in some of its own resources. They can be analyzed from multiple strategic perspectives, including knowledge management, social network management and operational management. Value encounter modeling can be instrumental in the context of service analysis and design.

Keywords: Service-Dominant logic, value modeling, business ontology.

1 Introduction

In recent years, Vargo and colleagues [27, 16, 1] have contributed to the development of service science [23] by introducing the concept of "service-dominant (S-D) logic". As the name suggests, S-D logic focuses on service provision in contrast to goods production (G-D logic). S-D logic can be seen as an attempt to view services not as a particular kind of (intangible) good that should be produced and marketed in the same way as traditional goods. Service provisioning is doing something before and with another party. In this perspective, what the company provides is not an output, but an input for a continuing value-creation process. The shift from G-D to S-D logic is one from a value proposition consisting of operand (passive) resources to one consisting of operant (active) resources. Instead of seeing value being created *within* companies that exchange the means for this value creation from one to another, it sees the value being created *between* companies (or companies and consumers). In its focus on co-creation of value, it builds forth on already existing management theory work of Norman [18] and Prahalad [21] and the marketing literature [12]. The notion of S-D logic still needs to be worked out further and gain more empirical validation [5], but in this article, we take it as a starting-point, and address the question how to support this logic using current value modeling and business ontology approaches [3].

Current value modeling approaches can deal well with services and have provided several conceptual tools to support service design [15, 30, 13]. However, they fall short at the moment in supporting an S-D analysis of value creation. In particular, when focusing on e3-value (see section 2), we note the following limitations:

C. Godart et al. (Eds.): I3E 2009, IFIP AICT 305, pp. 51–64, 2009.
© IFIP International Federation for Information Processing 2009

- To assess the sustainable value of network collaboration, the analysis must look beyond economic transactions. The dynamics of intangible benefits, in particular the effects on knowledge development and the social network, need to be taken into account as well.
- Collaborations often involve more than two actors. Although an e3-value analysis helps to clarify the value that each actor draws from other parties in terms of value that they receive, the model does not identify the value that the stakeholders draw from the collaboration as such. The same holds for the resources that they bring in. The e3-value model breaks up the collaboration into binary value exchanges. This approach is fitting from a purely economic perspective, as contracts are most often made between two parties, but it can obstruct a holistic understanding of the collaboration and the value that is created in the collaboration.

In order to overcome these limitations, this paper introduces an extension of the e3-value approach in which collaborations are treated as first-class citizens. To assess the viability and sustainability of the collaboration, we take a holistic approach. We introduce the notion of value encounters in which the collaboration becomes concrete. The validity of this construct is put to the test in two ways: first, by a fictive but realistic business scenario from the health care domain that we model (section 4) and analyze (section 5). Secondly, by developing a formal ontology of the value encounter (section 6). In section 7, we draw some conclusions and relate to other work in business economics.

2 Background: Value Modeling

There exist a number of approaches, languages, and ontologies for business modeling in literature. In [3] the e3-value [9] and the REA ontologies [17] were compared (together with a third business ontology – the BMO [Os04]) in order to establish a common reference business ontology. One result of that comparison was a set of mappings between e3-value and REA indicating strong similarities between the concepts of the two. Both REA and e3-value were originally designed for capturing tangible exchanges of economic resources between actors. Allee [2] complements this view by proposing to include intangible exchanges as well. Examples of resources transferred through intangible exchanges are knowledge or status.

The *Resource-Event-Agent (REA) ontology* was formulated originally in [17] and has been developed further, e.g. in [8] and [26]. REA was originally intended as a basis for accounting information systems and focused on representing increases and decreases of value in an organization. REA has been extended to form a foundation for enterprise information systems architectures [14], and it has also been applied to e-commerce frameworks [26]. The core concepts in the REA ontology are Resource, Event, and Agent. The intuition behind the ontology is that every business transaction can be described as an event where two actors exchange resources. To acquire a resource an agent has to give up some other resource. For example, in a goods purchase a buying agent has to give up money in order to receive some goods. The amount of money available to the agent is decreased, while the amount of goods is increased. Conceptually, two events are taking place: one where the amount of money is decreased and another where the amount of goods is increased. This combination of events is called a duality and is an expression of economic reciprocity - an event increasing some resource is always accompanied by an event decreasing another resource. A corresponding change of availability of resources takes place at the seller's side. Here the amount of money is increased while the amount of goods is decreased.

There are two types of events: exchanges and conversions [14]. An exchange occurs when an agent receives economic resources from another agent and gives resources back to that agent. A conversion occurs when an agent consumes resources to produce other resources. Events often occur as consequences of existing obligations of an actor; in other words, events fulfill the commitments of actors.

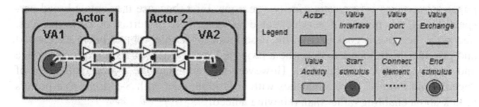

Fig. 1. Basic e3-value constructs

The *e3-value value ontology* [9] aims at identifying exchanges of resources between actors in a business case. It also supports profitability analyses of business cases. The ontology was designed to contain a minimal set of concepts and relations to make it easy to grasp for its intended users. e3-value includes a graphical notation for business models. The basic concepts in e3-value are actors, resources, value ports, value interfaces, value activities and value transfers (see Fig. 1).

An *actor* is an economically independent entity. An actor is often, but not necessarily, a legal entity, such as an enterprise or end-consumer or even a software agent. A set of actors can be grouped into a market segment. A resource (also called *value object*) is something that is of economic value for at least one actor, e.g., a car, Internet access, or a stream of music. A *value port* is used by an actor to provide or receive resources to or from other actors. A value port has a direction: in (e.g., receive goods) or out (e.g., make a payment), indicating whether a resource flows in to or out from the actor. A *value interface* consists of in and out ports that belong to the same actor. Value interfaces are used to model economic reciprocity and bundling. A *value exchange* represents one or more potential trades of resources between these value ports. A *value activity* is an operation that can be carried out in an economically profitable way for at least one actor.

According to Allee's approach to value network modeling [2], a distinction must be made between tangible and intangible exchanges of resources. Tangible exchanges are established and explicitly regulated in contracts. They correspond to exchanges of economic resources in the REA ontology and e3-value. Intangible exchanges are established informally and their terms are not present in contracts. As stated in [2], "Intangible knowledge and information exchanges flow around and support the core product and service value chain, but are not contractual. Intangibles include those "little extras" people do that help keep things running smoothly and build relationships. These include exchanges of strategic information, planning knowledge, process knowledge, technical know-how, collaborative design work, joint planning activities, and policy development." There is no formal correspondence between an intangible exchange and any concept in REA or traditional e3-value.

E3-services [15] is an extension of e3-value that is aimed at identifying bundles of services. E3-services introduces the concepts of needs, consequences and wants. The *consequence* of a service is anything that results from consuming valuable service properties. A *need* is a solution-independent goal, whereas a *want* is defined as a service implementing a specific solution. A want matches a need when the consequences of the want satisfy the need. Consequences are viewed in a broad sense. Both functional properties and quality properties are taken into account. For the purpose of this paper, e3-services is interesting for two reasons. First, because it adopts a broad perspective on the notion of service value as described in terms of consequences. Secondly, because it goes beyond the description of a value object being exchanged and provides instruments to describe a proposed service as well as a required service and how these two are matched. However, we note that the conceptualization of "needs" and "wants" betters matches with G-D logic than with S-D logic that prefers to talk about enabling rather than relieving a need.

3 Motivating Example

For illustrative purposes and as a running example we use the fictive but realistic business scenario from the health care domain, including actors such as hospitals, patients, and medical equipment providers, as described in [4]. It is constructed to highlight some problems related to exchanges of resources that a business analyst or modeler may encounter. The verbal description as given below is intentionally underspecified and imprecise, as this is always the case in practice. Therefore, it should be analyzed, for instance, using the value object analysis introduced in [28].

The Hospital purchases medical equipment from the Medical equipment providers by placing Orders and paying Cash. Furthermore, the Hospital acquires Product knowledge through their interactions with the Medical equipment providers.

The Sales agents assist the Medical equipment providers to acquire new customers, i.e. they market the products of the Medical equipment providers, negotiate with potential customers and deliver valid Customer orders to the providers. Through participating in this interaction, the Sales agents will get Product knowledge from the providers, while the latter will get Market knowledge from the Sales agents.

The Patients receive Health care services from the Hospitals such as examinations and treatments. These services will improve the Health state of Patients but also their Knowledge about their health conditions as well as their Feeling of safety. The Hospitals will get paid by the Insurance Company of the Patient. They also get improved Medical knowledge by examining and treating complex cases. The Government collects tax from citizens in order to provide health care for all. The Hospitals interact with the Government providing Health care services and receiving Cash in return. Furthermore, the Government gives the Hospitals access to the market by providing Authorization. The Hospitals may participate in Professional communities with which they exchange Knowledge. A Professional community will also get the Attention of the Hospital. Through its participation the Hospital will earn Status.

4 Value Encounter Modeling

When addressing a certain value network, the value encounter analysis postpones the question of who is exchanging value to whom, but focuses on the value encounters first. A value encounter is an interaction space between multiple actors where each actor brings in certain resources; these resources are combined then in such a way that value is created to all of them. Value encounters can be connected by means of a causal relationship ("+"), when activity in one encounter reinforces the activity in another encounter. In this way, the dynamics of the system become apparent.

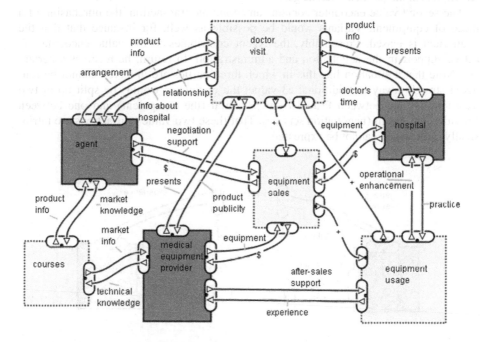

Fig. 2. Value encounters medical equipment agent

In the hospital example, several independent groups of value encounters can be distinguished:

- Between Hospital, Equipment Provider and Agent having to do with the purchasing of medical equipment.
- Between Hospital and other Hospitals, having to do with knowledge sharing and legitimization.
- Between Hospital, Patient and Insurance Company having to do with health care provisioning.
- Between Hospital and Government (not worked out in this paper)

We start with the first group, depicted in Fig. 2. The value encounters are rendered graphically as dotted light (yellow) rectangles. We have distinguished four encounters.

Each of them creates certain value independently of the other, but they mutually reinforce each other, so they are put together in one group. The doctor visit is an encounter. This is an interaction that does not involve an economic transaction and hence would not be included in a traditional e3-value model. Nevertheless, it is of crucial importance for the business model of the Agent, and has also value for the other actors. For the Agent, the primary goal is to build a relationship with doctors and be kept informed about possible needs of the hospital. For the doctor, the value is that he receives information about new products and possibly also some give-away from the Provider. However, it does cost him some time investment. For the Provider, the value of the interaction is in the publicity that he gets.

The second value encounter contains an economic transaction, the purchasing of a piece of equipment. Variants would be possible as well, for instance that that the equipment is leased. Presumably, the Agent contributes to the value encounter by active support in the negotiation and administration. In return, he receives a certain fee. Note that a situation like this in which three parties are involved cannot be rendered straight-away in traditional e3-value; the encounter would be split up in two transactions, one between Provider and Hospital (the equipment) and one between Provider and Agent (negotiation service). That these two value transactions are intrinsically intertwined cannot be expressed.

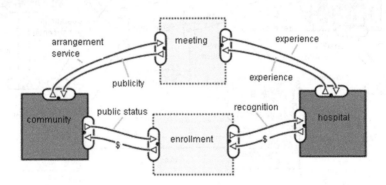

Fig. 3. Value encounters hospital community

The third value encounter is about the actual usage of the equipment. Here the Provider brings in technical support and perhaps spare parts. The Hospital gains operational enhancement (support for its medical work). However, the usage of the equipment also brings in practical experience from which the Provider can gain.

The fourth encounter is between Provider and Agent only, and involves an exchange of knowledge, e.g. in the form of a course. The Provider brings in his technical expertise, from which the Agent gains product knowledge.

The *second group* of value encounters (Fig. 3) concerns the participation of the hospital in the professional community. The bottom line would be that hospitals interact in a peer-to-peer fashion. However, on the basis of the description we assume that there is an institutionalized community that facilitates these interactions.

A distinction is made here between two encounters: the first creates and maintains enrollment. From this encounter, the hospital can claim recognition. The resource that the community brings in is nothing more or less than its public status. The second value encounter consists of the meetings organized by the community in order to facilitate the sharing of experience. Evidently, there are typically more supporting actors involved, like catering, or could be involved, such as equipment providers sponsoring the meeting in return for some publicity. The goal of the value model is to express what is deemed relevant at some point in time, not to be complete.

The *third value encounter group* (Fig. 4) is about the health care itself.

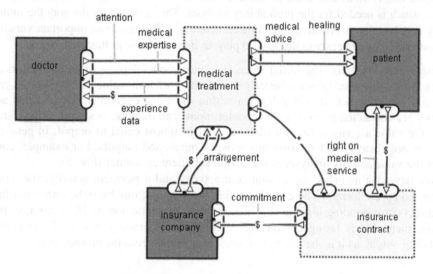

Fig. 4. Value encounters doctor-patient

The medical treatment is modeled here as a single value encounter. This is a simplification of course, as many different kinds of encounters – doctor visit, surgery, hospital care, etc. – could be distinguished. Basically, the Patient receives medical advice and healing. The Doctor brings in his medical expertise and his attention. On the other hand, he gains experience data from the encounter itself. The Insurance Company is paying the treatment and is therefore a stakeholder as well. In certain cases, the Insurance Company is the one that can arrange a medical treatment for its customers, so we have included this service as well. The value encounter between Insurance Company and Patient is about the contract. The patient pays for a right on medical service in return. The company brings in a commitment (we will guarantee your medical care). There is a relationship identified between the value encounters: the more contracts the insurance company has acquired, the more medical treatments it has to arrange.

5 Value Encounter Analysis

Once the value encounters have been modeled, the next step is to analyze them. Analysis always focuses on one aspect at a time. Which aspects are relevant differs from case to case. Complementing the profitability analysis provided by traditional e3-value, we propose the following:

- value activity analysis
- knowledge management
- social network (social capital) management
- operational management

Although profitability analysis is not worked out here, it should be noted that starting from value encounters, profitability analysis and contract design need to be performed in combination. A value encounter model does not show how the money is distributed exactly, which is needed for the profitability analysis. This depends on the way the multi-party collaboration is broken up into bilateral contracts. Fairness is an important variable in sustainable value networks that should play an important role in this breaking up.

Value activity analysis. The initial value encounter model depicts value encounters as black boxes. In order to get a better understanding of how value is created, we can identify the value activities that happen within the value encounter. These value activities are connected to the value encounter inputs and outputs. In simple value transfers, the value activity is low profile and input is almost equal to output. In general, there is not always a 1-1 relationship between inputs and outputs. For example, consider the value activity analysis of the Hospital-Patient encounter (Fig. 5).

We have distinguished an appointment activity and a payment activity, the latter being fed by the former. The experience that the Doctor gains from the encounter has no direct corresponding input as it is gained from the interaction itself. In contrast, the arrangement that is brought about by the Insurance Company has no direct corresponding output, as it is the interaction itself that profits from the arrangement.

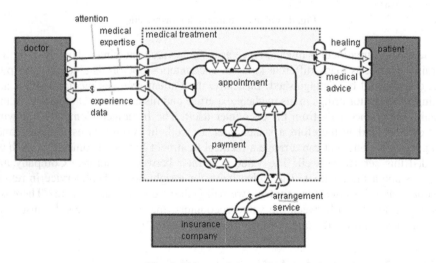

Fig. 5. Value activity analysis

Knowledge Management. From the KM perspective, the question is: how do actors maintain their knowledge resources [7, 2]? The assumption is that for actors to survive in the long run, their knowledge – both explicit and implicit in routines – is the core competency [6].

Some sub questions are:

- Is there a healthy mix of explicit and implicit knowledge transfers? In the case of the Hospital, we see in fact instances of both.
- If certain data is available, is it possible to gain more value from it, e.g. by Business Intelligence techniques? For example, the experience data that the doctor gets from patient consults. If some of these data are encoded digitally, the hospital could integrate the information from different sources and mine for certain patterns.
- Is the knowledge acquired also explored? For example, if medical equipment is to be purchased, are all doctors with relevant knowledge involved in the process?
- Is the knowledge making up core competencies actively maintained and increased? In the example, we see that the Hospital maintains its knowledge in various ways: from contacts with Agents, from dealing with Patients (complex cases) as well as from interaction with other Hospitals in the community.

Social network management. Over time, individual actors will change their value proposition. To enable evolution of the value network drawing on the same partner base, the social network underlying the collaboration should be kept healthy [16, 25]. So the main question here is: how do actors maintain their social network?

Some sub questions are:

- Is there a healthy mix of informal (face-to-face) and formal contact? In the example, most of the value encounters are based on face-to-face meetings in which social relationships are maintained in a natural way. However, more attention could be given to the formal part, e.g. by the use of evaluation forms regarding the doctor-patient encounter (on some regular basis).
- Is information about the social networks maintained in a systematic way? In the hospital case, this is particularly important for the Agents who are very much dependent on good relationships with the doctors. The hospital itself could consider the opportunity to integrate the multiple social networks that its doctors maintain individually. Although such integration is not something that can be imposed, it can be stimulated by providing facilities such as a professional social network platform.
- Is the social network actively explored? For example, the hospital can explore the social network it maintains within the community when job vacancies have to be filled.
- Is the social network actively developed? Actual participation in a hospital community and its meetings is a point in case.

Operational management. For a value encounter to be satisfactory in the long run, it must be run efficiently for all participants. Treacy and Wiersema [24] mention operational excellence as one of the three critical value disciplines. The question is: how to optimize the efficiency of the value encounter?

Some sub questions:

- How is the value encounter to be characterized? To answer this question, the analyst can make use of encounter patterns. Examples of patterns are "group meeting", "single service counter", "sequential service counter", "1-1 meeting" and "sales".

In some cases, the pattern needs to be decided on carefully. For instance, is the doctor visit in the hospital organized as a single service counter (each doctor viewed independently) or a sequential one? The choice has consequences for the way the encounter is to be supported.

- How is the value encounter supported? Continuing the example from above: in the former case, a simple agenda planning system per doctor is sufficient. In the latter case, if the patient will have to visit several service points, one should try to minimize waiting time and a global planning system is needed. For value encounters characterized as "group meeting", a registration system is needed.
- How is the optimization of the encounter ensured? To optimize the efficiency of the value encounter, it needs to be monitored, and the responsibility of this task should be allocated. Different stakeholders in a value encounter will have different optimization goals, so there is a risk of Prisoner Dilemma phenomena. In some cases, there is a natural "leader" and the allocation is easy; e.g. when there is a binary collaboration between a provider and a customer segment. In complex cases, the monitoring can be allocated to a partner that is involved for this function. Or the parties can agree on collaborative monitoring.

6 Value Encounter Ontology

In the above, we have introduced the value encounter concept in an informal way. In order to apply the technique in a consistent way, we need a more formal definition as well.

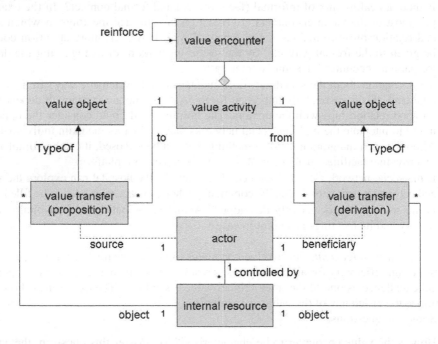

Fig. 6. Value encounter ontology (as a UML class diagram – the dotted lines represent derived relationships)

The value encounter ontology (Fig. 6) is intended to be a generalization of the e3-value value ontology. Value activities within value encounters get input from value propositions and provide output to value derivations – both are value transfers in e3-value terminology. A value proposition says what the actor brings in (in terms of "resourcing" [16]). A value derivation says what the actor gets out of the value encounter. These connections are viewed as instantiations of a value object, e.g. "negotiation service". The value encounter ontology is a generalization of e3-value: a value encounter can involve more than two actors, whereas a value exchange in e3-value includes only two. The generalization also makes it possible to distinguish between value propositions and value derivations. A value derivation type corresponds to what [15] calls a need, that is, a requested service and a value proposition type to a provided service. A value encounter is an aggregation of value activities. By default (as in the examples in section 4), the value encounter contains one holistic value activity not explicitly rendered in the diagram.

The question what exactly is brought in by an actor, that is, the question of resourcing, is not that simple, as there are many possible business model types and the modeling should not be restricted or biased to a particular kind only. In fact, we can distinguish a whole spectrum of business model types ranging from a typical G-D kind of exchange on the one hand to an advanced S-D kind of value co-creation at the other. Resourcing can be in the form of a good or product that is sold by the Provider, acquired by the Customer, and used internally in some value adding process. In such a case, the value encounter is almost reduced to an object exchange. We say "almost", as even in this case, the encounter involves a service contact between the actors in which secondary values and benefits do play a role. In the case of face-to-face meetings, there is always a social aspect. Somewhere at the middle of the spectrum, resourcing takes the form of services (economically, these are resources as well, cf. [30, 20]). An example is the arrangement service in Fig. 3 or the after-sales service provided by the Equipment Provider. Such a service draws on internal resources but it is not the internal resource itself. The service can be used *within* the value encounter (a meeting being organized) or be consumed by some other actor (the patient taking benefit from the advice and improving his health). At the other (S-D) side of the spectrum, the actors provide access to their internal resources – e.g., their knowledge, and these resources are explored by collaborative value activities *within* the value encounter in order to create something of value. Whether there is indeed a shift from G-D logic to S-D logic remains an empirical question [5], as is the question of the benefits and costs of such a shift.

7 Discussion

According to a recent paper by Jim Spohrer and colleagues [Sp08], "formalizing the notion of value-cocreation interactions and further developing the types of value propositions is a challenge for service science". This paper takes up the challenge and has introduced and formalized the notion of value encounter as an extension to current value modeling approaches. It encourages a service-dominant logic view of value networks where value is not viewed as exchanged but as created when different actors come together each bringing in their resources in order to create something of value to all. However, it does not exclude G-D based models or hybrid forms. A value encounter model can be subject to various kinds of analysis in order to support strategic management and business redesign [We07]. These, in turn, can be a starting-point for IS design. In a co-design approach, IS design and value encounter modeling can be pursued in parallel [10]. The use of IT may enable innovative extensions of existing value encounters or generate completely new ones.

The introduction of the notion of value encounters draws attention to something not considered yet in value modeling, as far as we know, that is, the relevance of the value exchange *context*. A value encounter is explicates the context. Sometimes value exchanges can only be realized in the right context, for example, a certain governmental regime. The contribution of this regime is like a catalyst in chemical reactions: it does not participate actively, but without it, the reaction would not take place. The relevance of context has been recognized in economics before, in particular in the theory of *country-specific resources* (CSRs) and *clusters* [5]. These theories go back to the work of the early trade theorists who focused their analyses on basic factor inputs such as land, labour and capital. Attention was also paid to the role of geographic location as a country-specific resource. More recent work has broadened the discussion of CSRs to include not only inherited resources but also those that are created by a country. In all these cases, the resource in question is a product of investments made over a long period of time in any given country [11]. Examples are the education system, technological and organizational capabilities, communications and marketing infrastructures, labour productivity and research facilities. *Clusters* share many characteristics of networks but are differentiated by co-location and active efficiencies. The notion of value encounter allows us to model a geographical unit or cluster not so much as a resource but as a space in which resources are put on the table in order to co-create value. This is relevant to business modeling and strategy analysis. In traditional value modeling, the actors are located in an abstract space. Why a certain value network does grow and prosper in one environment and not in another, remains unexplained. It makes sense to view strategy design as an attempt either to *develop completely new value encounters* (which typically needs a long line of investment) or to *build on and extend* already existing value encounters. In the course of time, these value encounters grow and adapt and as such they represent a long history of economic as well as social investments. Such an approach is not only interesting in view of physical environments but also of virtual environments. For example, a social network site as Facebook facilitates value encounters on which companies can capitalize in order to build new business models [31]. The notion of value encounter is a starting-point for developing this way of thinking, but many questions are still open. For instance, how do we delineate and relate contexts? Can we use the reinforcement relationship introduced above for that purpose?

References

[1] Alter, S.: Service system fundamentals: Work system, value chain, and life cycle. IBM Systems Journal 47/1, 71–86 (2008)
[2] Allee, V.: A Value Network Approach for Modeling and Measuring Intangibles. White paper presented at Transparent Enterprise, Madrid (November 2002)

[3] Andersson, B., Bergholtz, M., Edirisuriya, A., Ilayperuma, T., Johannesson, P., Gordijn, J., Grégoire, B., Schmitt, M., Dubois, E., Abels, S., Hahn, A., Wangler, B., Weigand, H.: Towards a Reference Ontology for Business Models. In: Embley, D.W., Olivé, A., Ram, S. (eds.) ER 2006. LNCS, vol. 4215, pp. 482–496. Springer, Heidelberg (2006)

[4] Andersson, B., Johannesson, P., Bergholtz, M.: Purpose Driven Value Model Design. In: Proc. CAiSE workshop BUSITAL 2009, CEUR (2009)

[5] Arnould, E.J.: Service-dominant logic and resource theory. J. of the Academy of Marketing Science 36, 21–24 (2008)

[6] Barney, J.: Firm resources and sustained competitive advantage. Journal of Management 17(1), 99–120 (1991)

[7] Blecker, T., Neumann, R.: Interorganizational knowledge management— Some perspectives for knowledge oriented strategic management in virtual organizations. In: Malhotra, Y. (ed.) Knowledge management and virtual organizations, pp. 63–83. Idea Group Publishing, Hershey (2000)

[8] Geerts, G., McCarthy, W.E.: An Accounting Object Infrastructure For Knowledge-Based Enterprise Models. IEEE Int. Systems & Their Applications, 89–94 (1999)

[9] Gordijn, J., Akkermans, J.M., van Vliet, J.C.: Business modeling is not process modeling. In: Mayr, H.C., Liddle, S.W., Thalheim, B. (eds.) ER Workshops 2000. LNCS, vol. 1921, p. 40. Springer, Heidelberg (2000)

[10] Goldkuhl, G.: Action and media in interorganizational interaction. Comm. ACM 49(5), 53–57 (2006)

[11] Gray, H.P.: Macroeconomic theories of foreign direct investment: An assessment. In: Rugman, A.M. (ed.) New Theories of the Multinational Enterprise, pp. 172–195. Croom-Helm, London (1982)

[12] Grönroos, C.: Service Logic Revisited: Who Creates Value? And Who Co-Creates? European Management Review 20(4), 298–314 (2008)

[13] Henkel, M., Johannesson, P., Perjons, E., Zdravkovic, J.: Value and Goal Driven Design of E-Services. In: Proc. of the IEEE Int. Conference on E-Business Engineering (Icebe 2007). IEEE Computer Society, Washington (2007)

[14] Hruby, P.: Model-Driven Design of Software Applications with Business Patterns. Springer, Heidelberg (2006)

[15] de Kinderen, S., Gordijn, J.: E3service: A model-based approach for generating needs-driven e-service bundles in a networked enterprise. In: Proceedings of 16th European Conference on Information Systems (2008)

[16] Koka, B.R., Prescott, J.E.: Strategic alliances as social capital: a multidimensional view. Strateg. Manage. Journal 23, 795–816 (2002)

[17] Lusch, R.F., Vargo, S., Wessels, G.: Toward a conceptual foundation for service science: contributions from service-dominant logic. IBM Systems J. 47(1), 5–14 (2008)

[18] McCarthy, W.E.: The REA Accounting Model: A Generalized Framework for Accounting Systems in a Shared Data Environment. The Accounting Review (1982)

[19] Norman, R., Ramirez, R.: From value chain to value constellation: Designing interactive strategy. Harvard Business Review, 65–77 (July–August 1993)

[20] OASIS. Reference Model for Service Oriented Architecture 1.0 (2006), http://www.oasis-open.org/committees/download.php/19679/soa-rm-cs.pdf

[21] Osterwalder, A.: The Business Model Ontology, Ph.D. thesis (2004), HEC Lausanne, http://www.hec.unil.ch/aosterwa/ (last accessed 007-07-01)

[22] Prahalad, C.K., Krishnan, M.S.: The New Age of Innovation: Driving Cocreated Value Through Global Networks. McGraw Hill, New York (2008)

[23] Spohrer, J., Anderson, L., Pass, N., Ager, T.: Service-science and service-dominant logic. Otaga Forum 2 (2008), http://marketing.otago.ac.nz/events/OtagoForum/

[24] Treacy, M., Wiersema, F.: The Discipline of Market Leaders: Choose Your Customers, Narrow Your Focus, Dominate Your Market. Addison-Wesley, Reading (1995)

[25] Tsai, W., Ghosha, S.: Social Capital and Value Creation: The Role of Intrafirm Networks. The Academy of Management Journal 41(4), 464–476 (1998)

[26] UN/CEFACT Modelling Methodology (UMM) User Guide (2003), http://www.unece.org/cefact/umm/UMM_userguide_220606.pdf (2008-02-19)

[27] Vargo, S.L., Lusch, R.F.: Evolving To a New Dominant Logic for Marketing. Journal of Marketing 68, 1–17 (2004)

[28] Weigand, H., Johannesson, P., Andersson, B., Bergholtz, M., Edirisuriya, A., Ilayperuma, T.: On the Notion of Value Object. In: Dubois, E., Pohl, K. (eds.) CAiSE 2006. LNCS, vol. 4001, pp. 321–335. Springer, Heidelberg (2006)

[29] Weigand, H., et al.: Strategic Analysis Using Value Modeling–The c3-Value Approach. In: Proc. HICSS 2007, p. 175 (2007)

[30] Weigand, H., Johannesson, P., Andersson, B.: Bergholtz Value-based Service Modeling and Design: Toward a Unified View of Services. In: Proc. CAiSE 2009, pp. 410–424. Springer, Heidelberg (2009)

[31] Weigand, H.: Value Modeling for the Pragmatic Web – the Case of Social Advertising. In: Proc. I-Semantics, Graz, Austria (September 2009)

A Model for Value-Added E-Marketplace Provisioning: Case Study from Alibaba.com

Hong Hong Qing[1] and Zi Shan Xue[2]

[1,2] College of Computer Science and Information Engineering, Chongqing Technology & Business University, Chongqing, P.R. China, 400067
Qing.lily@163.com, xzs@ctbu.edu.cn

Abstract. Alibaba.com is one of the leading B2B e-Commerce companies in China. It provides an e-Marketplace connecting small and medium-sized buyers and suppliers both in China and around the world. Alibaba.com has grown admirably from its initial beginning as a general e-Market to a giant e Marketplace. During its rapid growth, it has incurred challenges and became more exposed to greater competition. Currently the quality of its services and achieving profitability remain Alibaba's greatest challenges. In this paper we examine the key factors of the strategies of Alibaba.com, including trust, market, search, payment and tools. Alibaba's strategies led to its success: strong brand, providing customers with outstanding value and a superior shopping experience, massive sales volume and realizing economies of scale.

Key words: e-Marketplace, e-Commerce, Strategies.

1 Introduction

Alibaba.com, a member of the Alibaba Group of companies, is the world's leading B2B e-commerce company. Alibaba.com runs an international marketplace (www.alibaba.com) focusing on global importers and exporters, and a Chinese marketplace (www.alibaba.com.cn) focusing on suppliers and buyers trading domestically in China. Together, its marketplaces form a community of around 30 million registered users from over 240 countries and regions. In China, Alibaba.com runs a C2C and B2C marketplace (www.taobao.com), with over 62 million registered users.

Since launching in 1999 the marketplaces have built up a community of more than 24 million registered users and over 255,000 paying members by November 2007, Alibaba launched on the Hong Kong stock exchange and raised HK$13.1 billion (US$1.7 billion) in gross proceeds before offering expenses, making it the largest Internet IPO in Asia and the second largest globally.

Jack Ma, the founder of Alibaba, was first introduced to the Internet in 1995 when he went to Seattle as an interpreter for a trade delegation and a friend showed him the Internet. They searched for the key word "beer" on Yahoo and discovered that there were no data about China. He decided to launch a website and registered the name China Pages.

He borrowed $2,000 to set up his first company and at the time knew nothing about personal computers or e-mails, and had never touched a keyboard before. He described the experience as "a blind man riding on the back of a blind tiger."

C. Godart et al. (Eds.): I3E 2009, IFIP AICT 305, pp. 65–72, 2009.

Initially, the business did not fare well, since it was a part of China Telecom and Jack Ma reflects that: "everything we suggested, they turned us down, it was like an elephant and an ant."

He resigned, but in 1999, he gathered 18 people in his apartment and spoke to them for two hours about his vision. Everyone put their money on the table, and he got $60,000 to start Alibaba.

He chose Alibaba as the name since the name was easy to spell and associated with "Open, Sesame," the command that Ali Baba used to open doors to hidden treasures in One Thousand and One Nights.

During the dot-com bubble, there were layoffs, such that by 2002 there was only enough cash to survive for 18 months. Alibaba had a lot of free members using alibaba.com, and Alibaba didn't know how they would make money. But they then developed a product for China exporters to meet U.S. buyers online, which saved the company. Alibaba made only $1 in profits in 2002. By the end of 2004, Alibaba made $1 million a day profit. Each year since it has improved in profitability to the position where it was launched on the stock market.

Today, Jack Ma's vision is to build an e-commerce ecosystem that allows consumers and businesses to do all aspects of business online. They are partnering with Yahoo and have launched online auction and payment businesses. His vision is expansive, he says: "I want to create one million jobs, change China's social and economic environment, and make it the largest Internet market in the world" [1].

Building a model for value-added e-Marketplace provision is one of the key elements of successful e-Marketplace. The speed and strategy of the customer frontline change have placed the focus on the process and a possible need for a closer integration between e-Marketplace and customer-close activities.

The present study considers the strategies of the model of Alibaba's e-Marketplace, focusing on the e-Marketplace development processes and effective operation. The target groups are the companies within the Alibaba e-Marketplace, mainly SMEs. Most SMEs use new technology and multiple channels extensively to do business with customers, and are in general, Alibaba.com with new business models. Thus they can provide an interesting comparison with other models.

The purpose of the present study is to find Alibaba.com success factors, best-practice example and areas of improvement for the coordination of the business and e-Marketplace development processes, by investigating:

1. The development process, with a focus on the strategic stages of e-Marketplace.
2. Problems with, and solutions for, across product lines and services,
3. Problems, solutions and co-ordination of purchaser-supplier relations, and
4. The possible effects of customer front-line changes with reference to the co-ordination of processes between the business and management

This paper is only an initial presentation of the results, with analysis and categorization of key success factors.

2 Overview of the Online Marketplace

The population of Internet and World Wide Web users has risen fast since 1990s with the development and advancement of computer technologies. Many firms have launched their businesses through the Internet because of these technological innovations. This resulted in a wide variety of product offerings from Internet Businesses online. Online purchasing has grown at an amazing rate. Therefore, companies that carry out online business have great opportunities to achieve success. Conversely, there are great competition and threats as well when a company chooses to enter online business [2].

E-Business is one of the flourishing industries. Barriers to entry into this industry are quite high, and suppliers have modest influence over suppliers. The introduction of the Internet has brought about many changes to this industry because it has increased rivalry, purchasing capability of buyers and substitutes.

The Chinese suppliers offer the largest products market. Chinese suppliers on the Internet are fragmented; most of Chinese suppliers conduct their business through traditional exporters. With the development of the Internet, buyers and sellers now have a quick and timely communication channel, and switch to conduct business online. Thus, more and more business companies favor to do business on an e-Marketplace.

From the mid-1990s, The Chinese government has advocated formation of industry focused websites. There are some websites that offer B2B for import and export companies. e.g. http://www.iexportcn.com/, http://www.gjtrade.net/ etc. Since these e-Marketplaces can reduce intermediates like wholesalers, business companies can sell their products at a discounted price. Because of this strategy, the volume of B2B transactions reached RMB ¥ 1.25 trillion in 2007, a growth rate increase of 25.5% from 2006. In addition, according to their self-report, they are growing almost 25 to 35 percent a month. Many independent stores have gone out of business because of this trend. Such scenarios set the stage for the success of Alibaba.com [3]. The real opportunity created by Alibaba.com is its own unique Web site management methods. Jack Ma led his team to implement their e-Marketing strategies to meet the needs of a group of SMEs, and they have got great benefits from its e-Marketplace [4].

It is necessary to understand the e-Marketplace industry as a whole and the competitors in the e-Marketplace as well in order to remain competitive in the market. One of Alibaba.com's largest competitors is vertical e-Marketplaces, i.e. industry enterprise website, which obviates the fact that Alibaba should build an e-Commerce ecosystem that allows consumers and businesses to do all aspects of business online.

3 Research Method

The present study is based on the study of a series of reports from Alibaba. The paper aims at understanding the experience of using alibaba.com processes and their strategies. A qualitative research method has been employed in this study.

In each report, personal interviews were carried out with persons from the SMEs as well as those from business organizations, which helps to enable exploration and comparison of the internal processes and capabilities from two different viewpoints, including the customer view (e-Marketing) and the management view (e-Marketplace). The analysis is based on the results which are obtained from interviews with SMEs and Alibaba.com.

4 Alibaba.com Strategies Analysis

E-Business has been expanding at a phenomenal rate during 2000's. New on-line business were opening and growing into firms on e-Marketplaces previously not served by any website. The number of new products each year grew because new suppliers increasingly found their way into export and import markets. Similarly, the profit for sellers rose by robust percentages, and B2B industry began evolving into the maturity stage of the industry life cycle in the mid of 2000s. Jack Ma, CEO of Alibaba Group, predicts that Internet product purchases will grow exponentially over the next few years, and he proposes the strategic framework to enhance the competitiveness of Alibaba (figure1).

Alibaba's five forces of strategy framework is a valuable way in analyzing the industry, and the five forces are competition from trust, market, search, payment and tools.

Fig. 1. Alibaba.com Company Strategies

4.1 Trust

For E-Marketplaces to win customers credibility is required, rather than purely financial or technological benefits. Due to the lack of Internet laws, web-based transactions have to face a serious credibility crisis. Alibaba announced the establishment of an online credit integrity system for the business community in 2002; it is a credibility-scheme, based on confidence-building mechanisms. It is called "China TrustPass membership".

Similar to the corporate version, entrepreneurs need to pass a third-party authentication and verification process before they become a China TrustPass member. As part of this process applicants need to provide their identity card and bank information. Once they become an authorized China TrustPass member, Alibaba.com will maintain an online trust rating for individuals to build confidence and credibility with potential buyers.

Alibaba.com launched its original China TrustPass membership in 2002 and as of March 31, 2008 had more than 280,000 paying members. Alibaba.com's China marketplace has close to 25 million registered users and is growing at over 36% year-on-year. The price of the new service is RMB 2,300 per year, slightly lower than the corporate version which currently sells at RMB 2,800.

June 10, 2008, Alibaba.com announced the launch of a new service called "China TrustPass for Individuals" on its Chinese-language online marketplace, which connects suppliers and buyers trading domestically in China. Until now, Alibaba.com's China TrustPass membership had only been available to corporate users [5] [6].

4.2 Market

Avoiding the most popular portal model, Alibaba adhered to B2B and C2C for SMEs and help them to quickly find business opportunities in a global market. Three websites were launched from 1999 to 2003: Global import and export enterprises and enterprises in the e-Marketplace (www.alibaba.com, 1999), Domestic trade enterprises and enterprises in the e-Marketplace (www.alibaba.com.cn, 2000) Terminal between consumers and retailers of the e-Marketplace (www.taobao.com, 2003). SMEs have gained huge profits from Alibaba e-Marketplaces.

As of June 30, 2008, Alibaba.com's international marketplace had 29,766 Gold Supplier members, a net increase of 7,748 from 22,018 as of June 30, 2007. The number of International TrustPass members reached 13,912 as of June 30, 2008, a net increase of 2,953 from 10,959 as of June 30, 2007.

Alibaba.com's China marketplace had 324,328 China TrustPass members as of June 30, 2008, a net increase of 101,752 from 222,576 as of June 30, 2007. The strong growth in China TrustPass members is due to both external and internal factors. Externally, the increased Internet penetration in China and a continued strong domestic economy is benefiting Alibaba.com's business. Internally, it is seen that improvements in customer acquisitions through Alibaba's sales force and their network of resellers. The sales of value-added services such as keyword bidding and premium placements also recorded healthy growth. In addition, the launch of China TrustPass for Individuals' in the second quarter added over 10,000 paying members as of June 30, 2008 [7][8].

4.3 Search

August 2005, a strategic partnership between Alibaba and China Yahoo, Alibaba has therefore become China's largest Internet company. Similarly, Yahoo Alibaba in the future of industrial layout also has important significance. While most people have never viewed eBay as a search engine, but in fact it approximately deal with 130 million searches every day from all over the world, equivalent to Google's search volume. Many of the businessmen who sell on eBay, every year on Google bid for ads to fight for PPC. At present, Alibaba have made a series of adjustments to yahoo.com.cn with powerful search technology, E-mail, IM tools, and PPC advertising business, though its future business model has not yet been determined, but no doubt it will be the practice of the theory of Jack Ma "e-Commerce search is the electronic search business".

4.4 Payment

A lack of payment confidence is a sensitive issue. Alibaba.com created the third-party payment platform (www.alipay.com). It is responsible for the funds between parties to the transaction. October 2003, Alipay.com partnered with the Industrial and Commercial Bank of China, China Construction Bank, Agricultural Bank and China Merchants Bank,

China Construction Bank, the International Organization of VISA International. This means that since the International Organization of VISA International, and other major financial institutions established a strategic partnership with Alipay.com, it has become the country's largest independent third-party electronic payment platform. As of December 2005, the daily average transaction volume through Alipay.com has been more than ¥ 20 million, and still growing rapidly.

4.5 Tools

January 2007, Alibaba.com established Alisoft.com in order to improve the levels of SMEs management. Alisoft.com offer new SaaS (software as a service) model for the majority of SMEs to provide full life cycle of software services, and at the same time meet their e-Commerce and enterprise management needs.

August 2, 2008, Alibaba.com announced the beta launch of Export-to-China, a new service which will enable international entrepreneurs and small and medium-size enterprises (SMEs) to sell direct to China's growing number of buyers [9].

5 Alibaba.com Industry Analysis and Discussion

Alibaba.com identifies the key success factors in its business model such as a strong brand, providing customers with outstanding value and a superior shopping experience, massive sales volume and realizing economies of scale.

Alibaba.com is the only e-Marketplace which includes B2B, B2C, and C2C. Alibaba is the world's No.1 international trade and domestic trade e-Marketplace in China according to Forbes Statistics. Additionally, according to Chinese Academy of Social Sciences "2005 Report on the e-Commerce Analyst Report", Alibaba.com is estimated to have over 72 percent of the C2C market and 50 percent of the B2B market in China [10].

However, Jack Ma's vision, has evolved much further than just being the world's largest e-Marketplace. The vision is to be the world's largest single e-Marketplace for online shoppers and to become a premier all-purpose e-Business by leveraging its existing brand and business model.

Alibaba.com has several core values which play a crucial part in the success of the company. The first one is excellent customer service based on extraordinary technology. The company provides various services such as product search and safe payment. In addition, the company also provided business information containing descriptions, snippets of reviews and testimonials posted by sellers and buyers.

Convenience and price is the second core value of the company. It manages the e-Marketplace over the Internet and has its own distribution system. Similarly, Alibaba does not have to spend too much money on real estate and other operation costs because it is pursuing Internet-based business. Thus, it can reduce SMEs' inventory expenses.

On one hand, the company has several key resources and capabilities to meet the challenges presented by opportunities and threats. These resources and capabilities have thus far allowed the company to be the world leader in the special e-Marketplace of B2B and C2C industry. Jack Ma, founder and chairman of Alibaba since 1999, is the driving force behind the company. He is a valuable resource that gives the company the competitive advantage with above-average return.

Alibaba.com has also a very strong brand name presence in the e-Marketplace of B2B, B2C and C2C which is primarily due to their successful exploitation of their "first-mover" advantage. It would be able to leverage this brand name as it realizes its plans for expansion in the future.

In addition, the technological infrastructure of Alibaba also gives its competitive advantage against the other rivals. It can open a new e-Marketplace with different products offerings very easily because its core search technologies are easily re-usable.

Its website is elegantly designed, easy to navigate and quick to load. It also has numerous proprietary inventions like the click shopping, personalized recommendations and user rating which make shopping more pleasurable [11].

Alibaba's strategies, such as trust, market, search, payment and tools, strategic partnership, compelling value, and active advertising implemented by the company have contributed to its success in sales growth and cost efficiency.

However, transitioning the company culture is one of the problems and weaknesses encountered by Alibaba.com. A lot of changes have to be made in order for Alibaba to adjust to different situations especially since the rules of business keep changing rapidly. Alibaba was only a start-up few years ago but it grew rapidly and successfully in the e-Business. Thus, Alibaba should no longer be considered a start-up but a company moving from one culture to another because of its expansion and time in the industry [12].

Another problem and weakness is the financial difficulties brought about by its international exposure. The fluctuation of exchange rates from different currencies into RMB may affect Alibaba's money market. The success of Alibaba's international expansion also depends on local economic and political conditions.

6 Conclusion

Alibaba.com has grown admirably from its initial beginnings as a small e-Marketplace into a giant e-Marketplace. During this process of rapid growth, it has becomes more exposed to greater competition. China's role in the global market is evolving from a top manufacturing hub and exporter into a powerful global buyer as well. China's growing demand for imported goods is being fueled by a booming economy, an emerging middle class, the rising Chinese Yuan and favorable government measures promoting imports. Cutting costs and achieving profitability remain Alibaba's greatest challenges. However, there are key factors such as a strong brand, providing customers with value-added e-Marketplace, outstanding value and a superior shopping experience, massive sales volume and realizing economies of scale that all contributes a lot to the success of this company. These factors and the people around the company enable Alibaba.com to face the threats presented by competitor e-Marketplaces. Essentially, the company should aim to maintain its gross margins in its existing business and in future product lines such as the TrustPass system, the AliPay system, powerful search technology, E-mail, IM tools, and PPC advertising etc. In order to do this, Alibaba.com should develop strategic partnerships with all of its main suppliers and its customers to build an e-commerce ecosystem that allows consumers and businesses to do all aspects of business online.

References

1. Chaffey, D.: Alibaba case study - E-commerce marketplace in China, http://www.davechaffey.com/
2. Zeng, M.: The Future Internet will be e-Commerce (February 29, 2008), http://aliresearch.com/
3. The E-Businessmen Conference Organizing Committee, 2008 Report on the Development of e-Market in China, pp. 1–18 (July 2008)
4. Fang, D.X.: The Arrival of Third Wave of China's Internet, Peking University Business Review. Peking University Press (April 25, 2008), http://aliresearch.com/
5. Alibaba.com Launches New China TrustPass Product for Individuals (June 10, 2008), http://www.ir.alibaba.com/
6. Xiao, Y.: Alibaba.com Announces 2008 Interim Results (July 16, 2008), http://www.aliresearch.com
7. Liang, C.X., Song, F.: Businessmen on the Internet will Win the World, June 2008, pp. 43–59. China Citic Press (2008)
8. Alibaba.com Announces 2008 Interim Results (August 27, 2008), http://ir.alibaba.com/
9. Alibaba.com Helps Small and Medium Businesses Sell Direct To China (August 2, 2008), http://ir.alibaba.com/
10. China's Social Science Research Institute, 2005 Report on the e-Commerce, 184-265 (December 2005)
11. Liang, C.X., Song, F.: Businessmen on the Internet will Win the World, June 2008, pp. 15–23. China Citic Press (2008)
12. Jing, L.B.: Alibaba further expansion of the value chain (June 6, 2008), http://aliresearch.com

Networked Virtual Organizations:
A Chance for Small and Medium Sized Enterprises
on Global Markets

Wojciech Cellary[*]

Poznan University of Economics
Department of Information Technology
Mansfelda 4, 60-854 Poznan, Poland
cellary@kti.ue.poznan.pl

Abstract. Networked Virtual Organizations (NVOs) are a right answer to challenges of globalized, diversified, and dynamic contemporary economy. NVOs need more than e-trade and outsourcing, namely, they need out-tasking and e-collaboration. To out-task, but retain control on the way a task is performed by an external partner, two integrations are required: (1) integration of computer management systems of enterprises cooperating within an NVO; and (2) integration of cooperating representatives of NVO member enterprises into a virtual team. NVOs provide a particular chance to Small and Medium size Enterprises (SMEs) to find their place on global markets and to play a significant role on them. Requirements for SMEs to be able to successfully join an NVO are analyzed in the paper.

Keywords: virtual organizations, small and medium size enterprises, core competences, context competences, virtual teams.

1 Introduction

Computer science and engineering has been developing faster than any other discipline in the history of human civilization. Also, current spread of computer applications has no precedence [6]. Computer science revolutionized business management providing a possibility to store arbitrarily detailed information about an enterprise and every kind of its activity in databases, as well as providing a possibility to process this information for managerial reasons. Due to computer science and engineering, it was possible to abandon uniformization of business processes and to shift to mass personalization on a global scale. As a consequence, it was possible to better serve diversified clients, and better exploit business opportunities arising on dynamically changing markets.

Development and mass deployment of information and communication technologies followed by organizational changes of businesses, as well as increased customer

[*] This work has been partially supported by the Polish Ministry of Science and Higher Education within the European Regional Development Fund, Grant No. POIG.01.03.01-00-008/08.

C. Godart et al. (Eds.): I3E 2009, IFIP AICT 305, pp. 73–81, 2009.

expectations and market globalization challenge enterprises. This challenge is particularly important for Small and Medium sized Enterprises (SMEs) that up to date worked mostly at local markets in relatively stable environments [5].

In this paper we argue that to face the challenges of today economy, Networked Virtual Organizations are the proper business structure. Big, hierarchical corporations should flatten to become Networked Virtual Organizations, while SMEs should integrate in Networked Virtual Organizations.

In Section 2 we briefly characterize contemporary business environment showing the impact of information and communication deployment on businesses. In Section 3 we present the concept of networked virtual organizations. Section 4 is devoted to features of networked virtual organizations, while Section 5 to the requirements an SME has to satisfy to be able to participate in an NVO. In Section 6 two integrations are discussed: that of computer management systems and that of representatives of NVO member enterprises into virtual teams. In Section 7 ongoing research on Virtual Breeding Environments, as an intermediary between a universe of enterprises and NVOs, is described. Finally, Section 8 concludes the paper.

2 Business Environment

Due to features of electronic information and communication, contemporary enterprises and their employees are available all the time in a space without geographical constraints. Computers make it possible to acquire information from everywhere in real time and to contact anybody in every moment. Of course, words: "everywhere", "everybody", and "any moment" concern mostly the advanced part of the world and advanced parts of developing countries, but this part of the world sets the ton of global economy.

Constant availability in a space without geographical constraints is followed by dynamism and diversity of business activities. Contemporary economy is characterized by permanent changes. Markets are changing, both from the macroeconomic and microeconomic perspectives. From the macroeconomic perspective – because competitive conditions are changing. From the microeconomic perspective – because enterprises are permanently trying to enter new markets with innovative products and services. Customers, suppliers and business partners of an enterprise are changing, because finding and contacting them is easy due to electronic communication. Technologies of production and service delivery are changing due to innovations following from research and development. Innovation is considered to be the main driver of competitiveness. Innovations are spreading faster than ever again due to electronic information and communication. Many changes are following from permanent improvement of computer software used in production and service delivery. Also methods of work are changing, which requires news skills from employees. These new skills are mostly related to the use of software supporting employees in their work. Organization of work is changing as well, in particular workplaces based on information and communication. A good example of organizational changes is teleworking. Finally, technological and organizational changes are followed by indispensable changes of law.

Differentiation of enterprise activities may be perceived on both macro- and microeconomic level. On the macroeconomic level, increasing number of enterprises, including SMEs, are present on global markets. They have to deal with different economical conditions and law systems in different countries. Even in such integrated multinational organizations as European Union, law requirements and administrative procedures in different countries are far not the same. This requires from enterprises a lot of specific knowledge. More subtle and therefore more difficult to manage are cultural differences. Knowledge of cultural nuances is often a necessary condition for business success. Culture is often a determining factor for acceptance or non-acceptance of a given product or service on a particular market.

On the microeconomic scale, a contemporary tendency is realization of holistic needs of a customer. From an enterprise point of view, a motivation for such approach is conviction that the most costly and difficult part of any business process is, first, to win a customer, and then to retain him/her. Therefore, a won customer has to be provided with the largest possible offer of complementary products and services. This means that an enterprise needs to have a wide offer of such products and services at customer's disposal.

3 Concept of Networked Virtual Organizations

A right answer to challenges of globalized, diversified, and dynamic business environment presented in Section 2 are Networked Virtual Organizations. A Networked Virtual Organization (NVO) is a set of business and/or administrative units mutually cooperating through a computer network, perceived on the market as if they were a single enterprise [1], [3], [4].

There are two possible processes of transforming enterprises to NVOs: decomposition of traditional, hierarchical organizations, and integration of small and medium sized enterprises. In the paper era, when information and documents flow was slow, costly and geographically dependent, hierarchical organizations were efficient. To minimize costs of information flow, it was reasonable and justified to assume rigid roles and functions of organization component units, as well as their hierarchical structure. When rigid roles of units were assumed, the units knew what and when to do even in case of reduced, costly and inefficient communication. It is worth to add that not long ago, when the use of computers in the production processes and the amount of computer supported services was low, the enterprises were not able to rapidly change the production and provided services. Therefore, the market was not dynamic, so also the need for fast communication was not so important.

In contemporary economy, where electronic information and communication is dominating (though often replicated on paper) the hierarchical organization based on fixed functions and roles is not efficient any more. In the electronic information era, business decisions should be based on instant communication instead of rigid rules and functions fixed in advance in the hierarchical organization. Since the employees of any enterprise may capture information all the time, from everywhere, in real time, and contact each other at every moment, their creativity and entrepreneurship should not be limited by the fixed structure of the organization, especially as modern technology offers possibility to rapidly change production and services provided. In the electronic information and communication era, a flat network organization provides more opportunities for dynamic business process optimization and better possibilities to adapt businesses to rapid changes on the markets.

A parallel phenomenon to decomposition and flattening of big, hierarchical organizations is integration of SMEs into larger networked virtual organizations. The main driver for SME integration is the conviction that a single, small or medium sized enterprise is not able to face challenges of the dynamic and diversified global markets. Therefore, such an SME should join a bigger economic organization. A self-organization of SMEs into NVOs is a good solution, because it allows SMEs to retain their identity and independence that is very important to SME owners. In the integration process, SMEs can join NVOs coming from decomposition of the big, hierarchical organizations opening their structures for independent SMEs, or self-organize into NVOs in order to offer more complex products and services on the market and to improve their competitive position on the global market.

4   Features of Networked Virtual Organizations

There are three main features of NVOs [1]. First, business culture and way of functioning is focused on constantly evolving customer needs. Second, focusing of each NVO component unit on improvement of its own core competences and entrusting of all other functions to partners from the NVO. Third, standardization of data, software systems, and business processes within the whole NVO to achieve higher economic effectiveness.

The first feature meets modern market requirements, where, as mentioned in Section 2, competitiveness is – first of all – achieved through ability to accommodate fast changes. Business culture focused on following the changes on the market demands promotion of creativity and innovation. An enterprise has to be organized in such a way that innovative ideas are driven to deployment.

The second feature of NVO component units – improvement of their own core competences – demands from enterprises to reject the conviction that they are self-sufficient and to entrust non-core functions to partners from the NVO, for which these functions are core competences. Only breaking distrust between partners permits an enterprise to focus on developing and improving its own core competences. A core competence is defined as the one that directly contributes to the competitive advantage of an enterprise on the future market.

To focus on its core competences, an enterprise has to transform its functioning and operation. Functional transformation consists of outsourcing and out-tasking. In case of outsourcing, an enterprise entrusts control over the entire business process to an NVO partner enterprise. The outsourcing enterprise is interested only in the results of the entrusted business process. In case of out-tasking, the enterprise retains control over the way a process is performed by an NVO partner enterprise. Outsourcing of enterprise non-mission critical activities is a method well known and widely used to reduce enterprise operating costs. On the contrary, out-tasking is a relatively new method characteristic for networked virtual organizations. Out-tasking concerns enterprise non core but mission critical activities, such as research and development of products and services. This kind of activities demands very close cooperation between partners, under control of the out-tasking enterprise.

The third main feature of NVOs members is standardization of data, software systems and business processes within the whole organization. Standardization is required to provide an NVO with high economic effectiveness. Standardization is far the best method of integration from the operational point of view. It reduces costs, because it eliminates translation of one partner enterprise standard to another, facilitates software systems integration, and enables common realization of complex, computer supported business processes. It should be emphasized that in contemporary economy, a computer system providing tools just to manage internal enterprise resources and processes is not sufficient anymore. An enterprise system must provide external integration, i.e., it must be able to serve and control cross-enterprise processes within an NVO.

Standardization is a key condition enabling fast external integration. Speed of external integration is essential, because a need of immediate cooperation between partners can appear suddenly, as a result of an unexpected business opportunity. Capacity to take up such cooperation depends on the ability of computer systems of business partners to externally integrate.

5 NVO Requirements for SMEs

In contemporary economy, small and medium sized enterprises can play an important role, but only under condition that they are able to cooperate within networked virtual organizations. NVOs are required to quickly provide holistic solutions in response to changing customer needs arising in dynamic and diversified environments. This requirement goes beyond traditional expectation that an enterprise possesses competences sufficient to gain competitive advantage in a sector of production or services. Of course, this traditional requirement remains valid, but it is not anymore sufficient to achieve success on the market. A key competence that determines success in modern economy is the ability to cooperate with different business partners via network using information and communication technologies. To develop these competences, an enterprise has to collect and update information resources in formats that are standard within the networked virtual organization. Otherwise, this information is not ready for fast integration and thus useless.

An enterprise has to gain adequate knowledge that is wider than the professional knowledge of its economical sector. Wider knowledge is necessary to correctly interpret information coming from different partners from other parts of the world, other economical sectors, other professions, etc. This information is necessary to discover new business opportunities and to join promising business ventures emerging on evolving markets.

An enterprise has to know about capabilities of its NVO partners. Then, in case of a business opportunity, an enterprise is able to quickly organize an executive team, or at least to notify the NVO about the business opportunity not to be missed.

Employees of an enterprise must be skilled in communication and negotiation via network. Such skills are not very common among SMEs working in traditional sectors of production and services. Without such skills cooperation within an NVO is impossible.

Further requirements for SMEs to successfully join a networked virtual organization are the following: activity, multiculturalism, interdisciplinarity, creativity and innovation.

Activity is indispensable in a dynamic economy without fixed roles and functions. In such economy, a passive enterprise risks to be excluded from the market.

Multiculturalism is necessary to face challenges of globalization. Ignorance of cultural requirements prevailing on remote markets makes expansion on them impossible. Cooperation within a networked virtual organization with partners from different regions and cultures requires at least basic knowledge of those cultures.

Interdisciplinarity is necessary to meet holistic customer requirements, instead of only partial ones. To face holistic customer needs, professionals from different fields have to cooperate, e.g., economists, lawyers, engineers and artists. Without basic mutual comprehension of other fields, such cooperation is at least difficult, if not impossible.

Finally, creativity and innovativeness are the best strategy for maintaining and improving competitive position on dynamically evolving markets. Creativity and innovativeness can be achieved only in favorable business culture, which is quite rare due to natural conservative attitudes. Four kinds of innovations are distinguished [8].

- Product innovation that means providing the market with a new product or service, or significant improvement of previously offered products or services with reference to their characteristics or destination. Improvement can concern technical characteristics, components, materials, implemented software, more friendly interfaces, or other functional features.
- Process innovation consists of deployment of a new or an improved way a given product or service is produced or delivered.
- Marketing innovation means a new marketing method that encompasses significant changes in product appearance, packaging, positioning, advertising, business model or pricing policy.
- Organizational innovation consists of restructuring an enterprise, or reengineering enterprise business processes, new organization of workplace or external relationships.

The above kinds of innovation cannot be ranked by their importance for an enterprise. Each of them may contribute to improvement of the competitive position of an enterprise or the whole NVO on the market. Therefore, each of them should be carefully developed.

6   Two Integrations: Computer Management Systems and Virtual Teams

An SME that wants to be a member of an NVO has to integrate its computer management system with the systems of the remaining NVO members, and to integrate some of its employees with the representatives of NVO member enterprises into a virtual team.

Integration of computer management systems of different enterprises is a costly process. A candidate for an NVO member needs to trust that benefits of the integration are higher than costs of integration. The cheaper is the integration, the shorter coopera-tion within an NVO can be, i.e., more dynamic an NVOs can be built.

There are two main approaches to integration of computer management systems: standardization and intermediation. As mentioned in Section 4, standardization is a very efficient method of integration, because it eliminates incompatibilities and makes direct cross-operations possible. Usually, in an NVO a standard middleware is de-ployed. All member enterprises may contact one another adapting their own computer management system just to the middleware standard.

If standards used in an NVO are widely accepted, standardization provides only-limited risk to an enterprise aiming at joining the NVO. On the contrary, if the re-quired standards are internal de-facto standards of the dominating partner within an NVO, the risk for a partner enterprise related with the acceptance of these standards is much higher, because internal de-facto standards create dependence. Also, standards accepted within an NVO are not necessarily optimal for activities outside the NVO performed by a member enterprise. Widely accepted standard solutions reduce costs, but do not provide competitive advantage. In general, standardization is a good method of integration for tightly coupled NVOs aiming at long lasting cooperation.

An alternative method of integration of computer management systems is interme-diation by software agents. Intermediation is recommended for loosely coupled NVOs, cooperating only temporarily. Intermediation conserves autonomy of a partner enterprise and permits to gain competitive advantage following from its non-standard solutions.

A software agent is an autonomous program that independently performs given tasks at a given place and a given time according to the pre-programmed orders of its owner. In case of intermediation within an NVO, a software agent observes selected data of the partner enterprise, which reflect the current status of its business processes, and reports to the NVO management system all interesting events. Every partner enterprise may have a different software system and different data. For every partner enterprise an "interesting event" means something different. What is interesting, what is not, may be easily redefined in runtime. Every interesting event may happen in an arbitrary moment. Software agents permit extremely dynamic ad-hoc NVOs.

The second integration required by an NVO concerns representatives of partner en-terprises who mutually cooperate via network to achieve NVO goals. They have to become a virtual team. It is relatively easy to provide the members of a virtual team with appropriate information, knowledge, and cooperation tools, which are mostly the same as in the case of computer supported collocated teams. These tools include: cooperation tools, project management tools, time management tools, document man-agement tools, change management tools and tools to access to NVO databases and knowledgebases. Difficulties come from the fact that partner enterprises are by defini-tion heterogeneous in order to achieve complementarities. While managing virtual teams, it is necessary to consider different business and national cultures, because they may determine important business factors.

The ultimate goal of a virtual team is common understanding of arising problems by all virtual team members to cooperatively provide a right solution. To correctly interpret information (about problems, opportunities, and solutions) knowledge is required. Knowledge is divided into: explicit knowledge (codified) and tacit knowl-edge (uncodified). To provide explicit knowledge, e-learning methods are used.

Provision of common tacit knowledge is much more difficult, because tacit knowledge is acquired mostly by experience. To manage a virtual team, it is necessary to create a common business culture and to stimulate knowledge sharing. The measure of spread of tacit knowledge within a virtual team is the ability to solve problems, which may be tested in simulated environments.

7 Ongoing Research

Current research are focused on Virtual Breeding Environment, as an intermediary between a universe of enterprises and NVOs. The concept of Virtual Breeding Environment has been proposed within the framework of the ECOLEAD project as "an association of organizations and their related supporting institutions, adhering to a base long term cooperation agreement, and adoption of common operating principles and infrastructures, with the main goal of increasing their preparedness towards collaboration in potential Virtual Organizations" [2]. A very important research problem are methods aiming at facilitation of creation of Virtual Breeding Environments. Their creation requires strategic and management decision-making processes substantially different from those met in traditional organizations. Various aspects have to be addressed: from technological, organizational, and economic, to legislative, psychological, and cultural ones. Aspects related with business and knowledge has been already considered, while social aspects need to be more deeply investigated. In [11] social network analysis is applied to this end. Metrics are proposed as a way for a planner of a Virtual Breeding Environment to express social requirements.

In [9] methods are proposed that equip Virtual Breeding Environment with possibilities of NVO modeling aiming at NVO partners search and selection, definition of partner roles and finally NVO composition. A possibility of modeling an NVO before its composition and running is a very important factor of its success.

When an NVO is running, an important problem is its performance measurement. Basing on measurement results it is possible to early detect friction points, improve collaboration between partners, and adapt the NVO to business needs. However, measuring performance of a distributed organization as a whole is not an easy task. In [10] a Reference Model for NVO performance measurement is presented. This model comprises a set of common terms that are used to describe key performance indicators.

8 Conclusions

As follows from the above, NVOs provide a chance for SMEs to successfully play a significant role on global markets. It is, however, difficult for traditional SMEs to meet requirements of NVOs, which concern skills of SME employees and external integration of SME software systems.

To help Polish SMEs, a special priority axis has been included to the Operational Programme Innovative Economy financed by European Commission in 2007-2013 [7]. 460 million Euro has been allocated to this priority axis. An SME that obtains a grant from this priority axis may finance both adaptation of software systems and business process reengineering, aiming at cooperation with business partners via network. This programme brings hope of upgrading Polish SMEs to increase their potential of cooperation and as a consequence to extend markets on which they operate to the whole European Union, and beyond.

A social consequence of this program is creation of knowledge based workplaces related to international cooperation mostly for young, well-educated Polish people.

As this programme have just started, it is too early to report its detailed results.

References

1. Brunett, K., Fishman, G. (eds.): The NVO Way of Doing Business. The Bridge: Connecting Business and Technology Strategies. Cisco Systems Internet Business Solution Group (2003)
2. Camarinha-Matos, L.M., Afarmanesh, H., Galeano, N.: Characterization of Key Components, Features, and Operating Principles of the Virtual Breeding Environment. Deliverable 21.1. ECOLEAD (2004)
3. Camarinha-Matos, L.M., Afsarmanesh, H., Ollus, M. (eds.): Virtual Organizations: Systems and Practices. Springer, Heidelberg (2005)
4. Camarinha-Matos, L.M., Afsarmanesh, H., Ortiz, A. (eds.): Collaborative Networks and their Breeding Environments. Springer, Heidelberg (2005)
5. Cellary, W.: Globalization from the Information and Communication Perspective. In: Janowski, T., Mohanty, H. (eds.) ICDCIT 2007. LNCS, vol. 4882, pp. 283–292. Springer, Heidelberg (2007)
6. Cellary, W.: People and Software in a Knowledge-Based Economy. Computer 38(1), 114–116 (2005)
7. Innovative Economy Operational Programme 2007-2013, Polish Ministry of Regional Development (2007), http://www.mrr.gov.pl/
8. Oslo Manual, Guidelines for Collecting and Interpreting Innovation Data, OECD (Organization for Economic Co-Operation and Development) and Eurostat (Statistical Office of the European Communities) (2005)
9. Paszkiewicz, Z., Picard, W.: Modeling Virtual Organization Architecture with the Virtual Organization Breeding Methodology. In: 10th IFIP Working Conference on Virtual Enterprises PRO-VE 2009, Thessaloniki (Grece), October 7-9. Springer, Heidelberg (to appear, 2009)
10. Paszkiewicz, Z., Picard, W.: Reference Model for Performance Management in Service-Oriented Virtual Organization Breeding Environments. In: 10th IFIP Working Conference on Virtual Enterprises PRO-VE 2009, Thessaloniki (Grece), October 7-9. Springer, Heidelberg (to appear, 2009)
11. Świerzowicz, J., Picard, W.: Social Requirements for Virtual Organization Breeding Environments. In: 10th IFIP Working Conference on Virtual Enterprises PRO-VE 2009, Thessaloniki (Grece), October 7-9. Springer, Heidelberg (to appear, 2009)

A Rule-Based Approach of Creating and Executing Mashups

Emilian Pascalau[1] and Adrian Giurca[2]

[1] Hasso Plattner Institute, Germany
emilian.pascalau@hpi.uni-potsdam.de
[2] Brandenburg University of Technology, Germany
giurca@tu-cottbus.de

Abstract. This paper shows how business rules and particularly how JSON Rules can be used to model mashups together with underlining the advantages of this solution compared to traditional techniques. To achieve this, a concrete use case combining Monster Job Search and Google Maps is developed. In addition, we study the similarities between the conceptual models of *mashup* and *Software as Service* and argue towards a common sense by using their common root: the services choreography.

Keywords: Mashup, Software as Service, Web 2.0 applications, Business rules, JSON Rules.

1 Introduction

A common perception regarding Future Internet is that of an Internet of Services and Internet of Things. As described by SAP co-CEO Henning Kagermann [1], *"The Internet of Services is largely based on a service-oriented architecture (SOA), which is a flexible, standardized architecture that facilitates the combination of various applications into inter-operable services. The Internet of Services also uses semantic tools technologies that understand the meaning of information and facilitate the accessibility of content (video, audio, print). Thus, data from various sources and different formats can easily be combined and processed toward a wealth of innovative Web-based services."*

In this context several major paradigms get mixed: Software as a Service (SaaS) [2], Web 2.0 [3], and Enterprise 2.0 [4].

We are witnessing a continuous growth in interest for the services that embraces different shapes such as SaaS, mashups, combined with Semantic Web technologies, all of them towards improving interactivity and collaboration on the Web.

According to Gartner's study Market Trends: Software as a Service, Worldwide, the worldwide market for software as a service will grow from 4.25 billion in 2006 to 13.02 billions in 2011. Major players such as Salesforce and Google already experiment and provide services that meet the requirements of SaaS applications.

C. Godart et al. (Eds.): I3E 2009, IFIP AICT 305, pp. 82–95, 2009.

They provide several APIs and interconnectivity technologies either between their services or between other services (such as Facebook for example).

Despite open APIs, another perspective of services aggregation on the Web is offered by mashups. In its early stage this concept has been seen more like a tool approach, but in the last time it started to receive attention also from the academia's side (see for example, [5], [6], [7]). Looking to both SaaS and mashups paradigms we can see a common root: both of them deal with the same major concept - *service aggregation*.

This paper strives to bring to a common sense several paradigms that have already been enumerated here, in particular SaaS and Mashups. We introduce a rule modeling and execution approach to build up mashups. Rules already attract the interest of some players such as Google (i.e. in Google Spreadsheet the user is allowed to change colors using rules) or Adobe (interested in emulating a rule parser in Adobe Flex) simply because, using rules, offers to both mashup creators and mashup users the ability to dynamically change according to their taste their experience on the Web.

In the area of rule modeling there are different developer communities like UML modelers and ontology architects. The former uses rules in business modeling and in software development, while the latter uses rules in collaborative Web applications. The main reason is that rules can be easily captured and modified, and they empower applications with grater flexibility. Therefore, using rules to model and to execute mashups seems to be an appealing solution that could: (1) offer another solution for service aggregation (the main focus is on SOAP/REST based services) and (2) provide a simple way to understand, model and define behavior/interaction between services.

In overall, this work proposes a rule-based approach of modeling and creating mashups. This approach uses JSON Rules, a JavaScript-based rule language and rule engine. This language was introduced in one of our previous work ([8]) with the goal to empower Web 2.0 applications with rule-based inference capabilities.

2   Introduction to JSON Rules

JSON Rules language [8] was built by following two requirements: (1) The "Working Memory" is the Document Object Model (DOM) [9] of the page i.e. the main effect of rules execution is the DOM update, and (2) Rules are executed in the browser. The reason of these requirements is that the content displayed in a web page, besides multimedia content, is mainly a DOM tree. Therefore the main constructs of the language are strongly influenced by this particular environment where the rules are going to be executed.

The language uses a condition language similar with other rule systems (for example Drools, [10]) and employs any JavaScript function call as actions. The syntax was influenced by the JSON Notation [11] a well known notation to express JavaScript objects. In addition to the classical production systems, JSON Rules deals with *Event-Condition-Action (ECA) rules* triggered by DOM Events [12].

A condensed version of the rule metamodel is depicted in Figure 1.

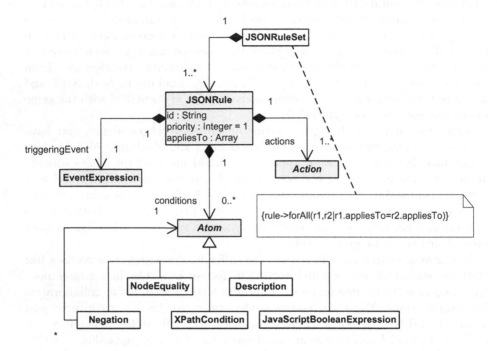

Fig. 1. An excerpt of JSON Rules language metamodel

In brief we identify the following properties, many of them found in all classical production systems:

- A JSON Rule is uniquely identified by an `id`.
- A `priority` optional attribute is used to express the order in which rules get ordered in the activation queue (1 by default). The execution order for rules with the same priority is irrelevant.
- The required `appliesTo` attribute holds a list of URL's on which the rule can be executed.
- An EventExpression is used to match any DOM Event. Therefore it contains a number of standard DOM Events properties such as: `type`, `target`, `timeStamp` and `phaseType`.
- The rule may contain a list of conditions (logically interpreted as a conjunction of atoms). There are four types of conditions that can be actually expressed using JSON Rules:
  (1) `JavaScriptBooleanCondition` - the simplest atom allowing JavaScript boolean, (2) `Descriptions` - a simplified version of Drools description pattern, (3) `==` - DOM Node equality, (4) `XPathCondition` - evaluates the membership of a DOM Node against the nodelist obtained by evaluating

an XPath [13] expression and (5) **not** - negation of conditions. Further extensions of the language may envision other types of conditionals.

- The rule must contain a nonempty array of actions, all of them being executed sequentially. Any JavaScript function call is allowed as an action. If the function is not available, no call is performed.

3   Creating Mashups with JSON Rules

There are several concrete use cases on which this approach could be illustrated. We picked a simple one interesting and practical in the same time. In a world were speed is one of the most important decision factors and were businesses changes also at a great speed, people are required to relocate all the time, and change jobs, especially for those working in the IT field. There are several important aspects that usually are taken into account when looking for job, especially if you have family and kids including where is the job located - and you would like to see that on a map. Based on the job location you would like to see the quality of family environment, for example, if there are any schools/universities in the area and their quality facts. The neighborhood is also important and you may want to see some photos in the area.

There are many helpful public services such as Monster Job Search Service, Google Maps, Wikipedia or Flicker which can be used to reach the goal.

One may use these services in a separate way collecting the data he needs. However this process is time consuming and not always with out difficulties, because you have to run between several open tabs, you have to remember and manually insert again and again data from different services. A nice approach would be to have all these services *interacting each other* in the same page.

A programmer may choose one of the available mashup editors but, in this case, he will not be able to run the mashup on an arbitrary server. Usually they run on the tools provider's server. Using JSON Rules, this shortcoming is removed since the engine can be packed in different ways: either as a stand alone JavaScript application that can be imported and used in any page or as a browser add-on. In addition, the service interaction is difficult to be expressed using mashup editors and ends into large and complex code to be written.

For simplicity our example mashup will only use the Monster Job Search Engine and Google Maps.

Lets consider the following case:

We are looking for a job using the Monster Job Search Service. Once the job is obtained the location is shown on a Google Maps and if it is possible, some supplementary information is provided.

The following requirements were considered:

- All these services must interact in one page. This page is called *choreographer*.
- The search term must be inserted manually in a form invoking the Monster Job Search Service. The other services must react on the returned data.

- When the mouse is over a job, the job should be visually indicated on Google Maps.
- When the mouse is over a job, the information regarding the job, if any, should be retrieved from another service (such as Wikipedia).
- Involved services should be personalized.

To be able to define rules that will power our use case we must know how involved services look like, how they can be interrogated and how does their response look like.

3.1   Monster Job Search

The Monster start page provides a number of components that may not be necessary in our mashup, as, for example the Sign Up!/Sign In component.

Figure 2 shows an excerpt of the HTML output of the Monster search and it is necessary to understand the rules related to the usage of Monster inside of our mashup.

3.2   Google Maps

The maps service from Google is well known probably to everyone reading this paper, so we will present here only the DOM tree view (Figure 3) of the search field which is necessary to understand the rules that will implement the search.

3.3   Modeling the Mashup Rules

Having presented the input and output of the involved services we can now present the rules that power up our mashup. To be able to define rules that will make the several involved services work together, they must be available to the Choreographer.

Rule: *Load services so that the Choreographer can use them*

```
{ "id":"loadServices",
   "appliesTo":["http://www.jsonrules.org/examples/i3e/"],
   "eventExpression":{
                     "type":"load"
                     },
   "condition":true,
   "actions":["load('http://jobsearch.monster.ca')",
            "load('http://maps.google.com')"]
}
```

The above rule applies to the choreographer URL and states that whenever a DOM event of type load occurs then two load action are executed. The side effect is the loading of the services we need in the mashup.

```
1   <div class="jobSearchResultDiv" id="jobSearchresult">
2     <div id="sortOptions" class="sortOptions">
3       ...
4     </div>
5     <div class="stackedView">
6       <div class="stackedRowPurple">
7         <div class="jobInfo" style="width: 673px;">
8           <div class="stackedViewJobViewLink"
9             id="stackedViewJobViewLink0">
10            <div id="joblink_0" class="joblink">
11              <a onclick="jobViewOnClickSaveCookie(0);"
12                href="..." onmouseover="ctlMouseOverRender(0);"
13                id="jobviewlink_0" class="joblinks">
14                Technical Solution Architect – IT
15              </a>
16            </div>
17          </div>
18          <div class="stackedViewWidth1" style="width: 224.333px;">
19            <div class="stackedViewCompanyLogo"
20              id="stackedViewCompanyLogo0"/>
21          </div>
22          <div class="stackedViewWidth2" style="width: 224.333px;">
23            <div class="stackedViewCompany">
24              Lockheed Martin Canada
25            </div>
26            <div class="stackedViewDate">
27              Posted:March 23
28            </div>
29          </div>
30          <div class="stackedViewWidth3" style="width: 224.333px;">
31            <div class="stackedViewJobPlace">
32              <div class="jobPlace">
33                Ottawa, ON
34              </div>
35            </div>
36            <div class="stackedViewMiles">
37              <div class="distanceTextMsg">
38                Distance:
39              </div>
40            </div>
41          </div>
42        </div>
43        <div class="jobIcons" style="width: 92px;">
44          ...
45        </div>
46      </div>
47      ...
48    </div>
49  </div>
```

Fig. 2. Monster Job Search Service - excerpt of search output

```
1   <form id="q_form" action="/maps" ...>
2     <div class="srchcol controls">
3       <input type="text"
4         value="" autocomplete="off"
5         maxlength="2048" tabindex="1"
6         title="Search the map" name="q" id="q_d"
7         style="width: 33em;"/>
8       ....
9     </div>
10  </form>
```

Fig. 3. Google Maps - search field

Filtering the DOM to eliminate undesired elements can be easily performed by using XPathConditions. For example, the below rule identifies the Sign Up!/Sign In component of Monster by using the XPath expression: /html/body/form/div[3]/div[2]/div and remove all elements:

Rule : *Remove Sign Up!/Sign In component rule*

```
{"id":"ruleDeleteMonsterLoginComponent",
   "appliesTo": ["http://www.jsonrules.org/examples/i3e/",
                  "http://jobsearch.monster.ca/"],
   "eventExpression":{"type":"load"},
   "condition": ["$X in '/html/body/form/div[3]/div[2]/div'"],
   "actions":["document.removeChild($X)"]
}
```

On event of type load, remove all nodes returned by evaluating the XPathCondition.

Having data received from Monster (as in Figure 2) we find the results in a specific div element (having id="jobSearchresult" and class="jobSearchResultDiv"). Although such a div has several children we are particulary interested in those div children having class="jobInfo". The children of this div provide us with all the information needed further for the Google Maps service.

To find out the location of a job identified as stated above we must retrieve the company name and the location and provide this information as input value for the Google Maps input field (See Figure 3). In addition, our requirements impose that the location of a job should be displayed when a mouseover event occurs on the element containing the specific job.

Rule: *Find a job location on a Google Map*

```
{"id":"findJobLocation",
   "appliesTo": ["http://www.jsonrules.org/examples/i3e/",
                  "http://jobsearch.monster.ca/"],
   "eventExpression":{"type":"mouseover",
```

```
                        "target":"$X"
                    },
  "condition":
        [
        "$X:HTMLElement(
          tagName=='div',
          className=='jobInfo'
          )",
        "$Y in 'child::$X'",
        "$Y:HTMLElement(
          tagName=='div',
          className=='stackedViewCompany'
          )",
        "$Z in 'child::$X'",
        "$Z:HTMLElement(
          tagName=='div',
          className=='jobPlace'
          )",
        "not($Y==$Z)",
        "$T:HTMLElement(
          tagName=='input',
          id=='q_d'
          )",
        "$companyName == $Y.nodeValue",
        "$jobLocation == $Z.nodeValue",
        "$form:HTMLElement(
          tagName=='form',
          id=='q_form'
          )"
        ],
  "actions":
        [
        "update($T,'nodeValue',
              '$companyName+' '+$jobLocation')",
        "autoSubmitForm($form)"
        ]
}
```

The findJobLocation rule is triggered by a mouseover event. However as already stated the required information needed to be able to find the location of the job using Google Maps is provided by the children of a div element having class='jobInfo'. In accordance with this the rule verifies if the mouseover event has been raised from a div element having class='jobInfo' and among the children of this particular div element there are other different div elements having class='stackedViewCompany' (bounded to $Y variable) and class='jobPlace' (bounded to $Z variable). If the DOM contains an input

element having id='q_d' and a form element having id='q_form' validates
the availability of the Google Maps Service. To be able to search the location for
the current job the employer name is needed and it's location. This information
is bound to $companyName and $jobLocation variables. If all the above conditions hold then the update and autoSubmitForm actions can be executed. The
update action performs an update of the nodeValue property of the element
$T with the value ($companyName+' '+$jobLocation). The autoSubmitForm
action performs an automatic submission of the form provided as parameter.

4   Towards a Common Sense for Mashup and Software as Service

[14] analyzes terms such as *software as a service, software on demand, adaptive
enterprise* and *mashups* and concludes that they are overlapping to many ex-
tents. This section tries to argue towards a common sense, to create a bridge
between *software as a service* and *mashups*.

It is well known that in the nowadays business environment there is a strong
need and a general request of being capable to change software easily to meet
the fast evolving business requirements.

As stated in [2], "*the term software as a service is beginning to gain acceptance
in the market-place; however the notion of service-based software extends beyond
these emerging concepts*".

In such an approach a service conforms with the much accepted definition
stating that a service is "*an act or performance offered by one party to another.
Although the process may be tied to a physical product, the performance is essentially intangible and does not normally result in ownership of any of the factors
of production*" ([15]).

In addition, [2] argued that the "*service-based model of software is one in
which services are configured to meet a specific set of requirements at a point in
time*". Components may be bound instantly, based on the needs and discarded
afterwards.

There are some key points that characterize *software as a service* (see for
example, [16]):

- network-based access and management of commercially available software
- activities managed from central locations rather than at each customer's site,
- enabling customers to access applications remotely via the Web
- application delivery typically closer to a *one-to-many model* (single instance,
  multi-tenant architecture) rather than to a *one-to-one model*, including architecture, pricing, partnering, and management characteristics
- centralized feature updating, which obviates the need for end-users to download patches and upgrades
- frequent integration into a larger network of communicating software - either
  as part of a mashup or as a plugin to a platform as a service.

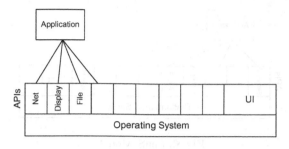

Fig. 4. Computer Model (David Berlind, ZDNet)

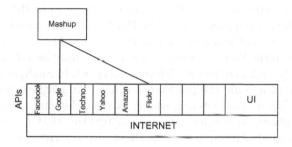

Fig. 5. Mashup Model, (David Berlind, ZDNet)

Mashups are hybrid web applications, usually found out under the association of SOA plus REST principles. Mash-up content is usually accessed through APIs from third party providers, (sites, services), processed and then presented to the user in a different format and with new insights. In such way new value is provided. One simple way to explain mashups was introduced by ZDNet Executive Editor David Berlind in a video presentation, What is a mashup?, where, among other issues, he claims that mashups are the fastest growing ecosystem on the Web.

Berlind introduced the mashup model by comparing it with the well known software stack on the traditional computers. In traditional computer systems we have an operating system, and, on top of this, a number of application programming interfaces (APIs) to access different services (i.e. the network, the display, the file system) and UIs to get to different applications (i.e. the mouse, the keyboard) as in Figure 4. Developers use these APIs to access different necessary services to create their applications.

Somehow mashups follow the same model but with a different infrastructure. The Operating System is replaced by the Internet, and the old APIs are replaced with APIs offered by different service providers such as Yahoo, Google, Technorati, Amazon etc. as depicted in the Figure 5. In the same way developers use these APIs to get access the available services. These services reside in the Internet, or we may also say on top of the infrastructure offered by the Internet. In this way new applications are created from old ones.

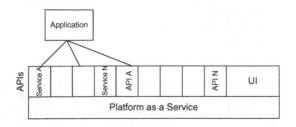

Fig. 6. SaaS Model

The *software as a service* approach uses a very similar model (see Figure 6). Salesforce is a concrete example of this approach. However in this case the Operating System/Internet is represented by the Platform as a Service (i.e. Force.com).

Therefore, we see that while mashups are generally based on various service sources available on the Web, software as service is mainly based on a proprietary centric platform (which may handle different services). In SaaS, new applications are generated by using only the platform services (i.e. *platform as a service*).

Due to their *"open"* character, mashups besides the characteristics that define SaaS applications have some other characteristics that arise from the way they are implemented. Although some of these characteristics might overlap we present them here:

– Mashups are usually created with a mashup editor such as: Google Mashup Editor, JackBe,Lotus Mashups, Microsoft Popfly, Mozilla Ubiquity, Yahoo Pipes.
– Mashups use APIs from different platforms to aggregate and reuse the content.
– Usually mashups operate on XML based content such as Atom [17], [18], RSS 2.0 [19], and RDF [20], sometimes directly on the HTML level, strictly for presentation
– "Melting Pot" style such that content is aggregated arbitrarily
– Create, read, update and delete (CRUD) operations are preferred to be based on REST principles

However, an important restriction of actual mashup editors is that they allow users to build and run mashups on specific platforms.

The rule based approach presented here removes the specific platform level and works directly on the content that any user has access to through a Web browser. In this way a simple model of mashups can be imagined as in the Figure 7.

Because DOM and JavaScript are the fundamental assets that power the content that we see every day in browsers, it is natural to use an approach that uses exactly the same assets because in this way you get finer granularity, and avoid learning of different APIs.

There are several features that the presented approach offers:

– Mashups can be executed on any browser allowing JavaScript.
– Services can be accessed directly without intermediary parties such as APIs.

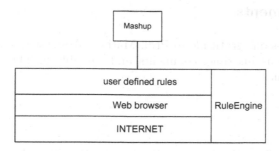

Fig. 7. Our Model

- Flows can be defined on top of any component that is available in the service answer (i.e. any DOM entity can be used)
- The behavior is defined declaratively.
- Data can be accessed as usual (Atom, RSS , RDF) but also in raw format.
- Concerns that are very actual, regarding creation of UI's based on the service are overcome because the UI provided as default by the server in the form of a web page can be used, and modified as desired; Look and aspect can be managed with rules too.
- Data mapping can be very easy implemented (such as data from Monster to be submitted to the Google Maps service)

Recall that in our use case there is a service called Choreographer since it corresponds to the application that puts together data from different services and defines the way they interact. According to [21] process choreography is used to define cooperation between process orchestrations. Moreover this collaboration is specified by collaboration rules. With respect to our approach, rule-based modeling and execution of mashups are nothing else but collaboration rules and the mashup itself is a *browser-based service choreography.*

5   Conclusions and Future Work

We have presented how business rules and in particular JSON Rules can be used to model mashups together with underlining the advantages of this solution compared to traditional techniques. To achieve this a concrete use has been presented together with the rules modeling it.

In addition, we studied the similarities between the conceptual models of SaaS and Mashups and observed that both of them have a common root: service choreography.

Future work concerns the study of how choreography principles can be related to JSON rule modeling of mashups towards a methodology of creation and maintenance of rule-based mashups. Another topic is related to application of visual modeling techniques for rules as well as building an infrastructure allowing sharing and reusing.

Acknowledgements

We want to express our gratitude to Prof. Mathias Weske who shared his ideas with us and gave us his time, comments and valuable insights on SaaS and choreographies issues.

References

1. Kagermann, H.: Toward a European Strategy for the Future Internet A Call for Action. White paper, SAP AG (2008),
   http://www.sap.com/about/company/research/fields/internet_services/index.epx
2. Bennett, K., Layzell, P., Budgen, D., Brereton, P., Macaulay, L., Munro, M.: Service-Based Software: The Future for Flexible Software. In: Proceedings of the Seventh Asia-Pacific Software Engineering Conference (APSEC 2000), pp. 214–221. IEEE Computer Society, Los Alamitos (2000), http://www.bds.ie/Pdf/ServiceOriented1.pdf
3. O'Reilly, T.: What is web 2.0. design patterns and business models for the next generation of software. Oreillynet.com (September 2005),
   http://www.oreillynet.com/pub/a/oreilly/tim/news/2005/09/30/what-is-web-20.html
4. McAfee, A.P.: Enterprise 2.0: The Dawn of Emergent Collaboration. MIT Sloan Management Review 47(3), 21–28 (2006)
5. Abiteboul, S., Greenshpan, O., Milo, T.: Modeling the mashup space. In: WIDM 2008: Proceeding of the 10th ACM workshop on Web information and data management, pp. 87–94 (2008)
6. Jarrar, M., Dikaiakos, M.D.: Mashql: a query-by-diagram topping sparql. In: ONISW 2008: Proceeding of the 2nd international workshop on Ontologies and nformation systems for the semantic web, pp. 89–96. ACM, New York (2008)
7. Phuoc, D.L., Polleres, A., Morbidoni, C., Hauswirth, M., Tummarello, G.: Rapid semantic web mashup development through semantic web pipes. In: Proceedings of the 18th World Wide Web Conference (WWW 2009) (April 2009),
   http://pipes.deri.org/attachments/004_fp160-lephuoc.pdf
8. Giurca, A., Pascalau, E.: JSON Rules. In: Proceedings of the 4th Knowledge Engineering and Software Engineering, KESE 2008, collocated with KI 2008, vol. 425, pp. 7–18. CEUR Workshop Proceedings (2008)
9. Hors, A.L., Hegaret, P.L., Wood, L., Nicol, G., Robie, J., Champion, M., Byrne, S.: Document Object Model (DOM) Level 3 Core Specification. W3C Recommendation (April 2004), http://www.w3.org/TR/DOM-Level-3-Core/
10. Proctor, M., Neale, M., Frandsen, M., Griffith Jr., S., Tirelli, E., Meyer, F., Verlaenen, K.: Drools 4.0.7,
    http://downloads.jboss.com/drools/docs/4.0.7.19894.GA/html_single/index.html (May 2008)
11. Crockford, D.: The application/json Media Type for JavaScript Object Notation (JSON) (July 2006), http://tools.ietf.org/html/rfc4627
12. Pixley, T.: Document Object Model (DOM) Level 2 Events Specification. W3C Recommendation (November 2000),
    http://www.w3.org/TR/DOM-Level-2-Events/

13. Berglund, A., Boag, S., Chamberlin, D., Fernandez, M.F., Kay, M., Robie, J., Simeon, J.: XML Path Language (XPath) 2.0. W3C Recommendation (November 2007), http://www.w3.org/TR/xpath20/
14. Foster, I., Tuecke, S.: Describing the Elephant: The Different Faces of IT as Service. Enterprise Distributed Computing 3(6), 26–34 (2005)
15. Lovelock, C., Vandermerwe, S., Lewis, B.: Services Marketing. Prentice Hall Europe, Englewood Cliffs (1996)
16. Traudt, E., Konary, A.: Software as a Service Taxonomy and Research Guide. Technical report, IDC.com (2005)
17. Nottingham, M., Sayre, R.: Atom Publishing Format (RFC4287) (2005), http://tools.ietf.org/html/rfc4287
18. Gregorio, J., de hOra, B.: Atom Publishing Format (RFC5023) (2007), http://tools.ietf.org/html/rfc5023
19. RSS: RSS 2.0 Specification, version 2.0.11 (March 2009), http://www.rssboard.org/rss-specification
20. Klyne, G., Caroll, J.: Resource Description Framework (RDF): Concepts and Abstract Syntax. W3C Recommendation (February 2004), http://www.w3.org/TR/rdf-concepts/
21. Weske, M.: Business Process Management: Concepts, Languages, Architectures. Springer, Heidelberg (2007)

Implementing a Rule-Based Contract Compliance Checker

Massimo Strano, Carlos Molina-Jimenez, and Santosh Shrivastava

Newcastle University, Newcastle upon Tyne, UK
{massimo.strano,carlos.molina,santosh.shrivastava}@ncl.ac.uk

Abstract. The paper describes the design and implementation of an independent, third party contract monitoring service called Contract Compliance Checker (CCC). The CCC is provided with the specification of the contract in force, and is capable of observing and logging the relevant business-to-business (B2B) interaction events, in order to determine whether the actions of the business partners are consistent with the contract. A contract specification language called EROP (for Events, Rights, Obligations and Prohibitions) for the CCC has been developed based on business rules, that provides constructs to specify what rights, obligation and prohibitions become active and inactive after the occurrence of events related to the execution of business operations. The system has been designed to work with B2B industry standards such as ebXML and RosettaNet.

1 Introduction

There is a growing interest - both within industry and academia - in exploring innovative ways of automating the management and regulation of business interactions using electronic contracting systems. By regulation we mean monitoring and/or enforcement of business–to–business (B2B) interactions to ensure that they comply with the rights (permissions), obligations and prohibitions stipulated in contract clauses. A well designed electronic contracting system can play a central role in ensuring that the business processes of partners perform actions that comply with the contract in force, detecting violations, facilitating dispute resolution and determining liability by providing an audit trail of business interactions. Within this context, we consider the design and implementation of an independent, third party contract monitoring service called *Contract Compliance Checker* (CCC). The CCC is provided with the specification of the contract in force, and is capable of observing and logging the relevant B2B interaction events, as well as determining whether the actions of the business partners are consistent with the contract. We consider here the basic functionality of the CCC, that of a passive observer. It is possible to extend this functionality to make the CCC into a *contract enforcer* that ensures that business partners execute only those operations that are permitted by the contract; however, this aspect is not considered in this paper.

To realise the third party service, the computer infrastructure of business partners concerned with B2B messaging must be instrumented to create a monitoring channel to the CCC for it to observe the relevant B2B events accurately. More precisely, we assume the existence of a *monitoring channel* with the properties: (i) transmission and processing delays of events originating at business partners to the CCC are bounded and

C. Godart et al. (Eds.): I3E 2009, IFIP AICT 305, pp. 96–111, 2009.
© IFIP International Federation for Information Processing 2009

known; and (ii) events are delivered exactly once to the CCC in temporal order. We also assume that all clocks within the system are synchronised to a known accuracy. Given the above assumptions, we concentrate in this paper on how an appropriately structured contract can be used to analyse the events collected at the CCC for compliance checking. Subsequently we explain compliance checking in more detail as well as what B2B events need to be collected at the CCC.

We have developed a contract specification language called *EROP* (for Events, Rights, Obligations and Prohibitions) for the CCC, based on business rules, that provides constructs to specify what rights, obligation and prohibitions become active and inactive after the occurrence of events related to the execution of business operations [1,2]. Our language is particularly suited to the specification of *exceptional* (or *contingency*) clauses that come in force when the delivery obligation stated in the 'primary clause' is not fulfilled (breach or violation of the contract). As we argue in [2], in electronic contracts it is important to distinguish violations caused by infrastructure level problems, arising primarily because of the inherently distributed nature of the underlying computations (e.g., clock skews, unpredictable transmission delays, message loss, incorrect messages, node crashes etc.) from those that are not and are mostly human/organisation related. Our language takes this factor into account and provides intuitive ways of specifying the consequences of the above problems.

In this paper we describe the design and implementation of a CCC service for contracts written in the EROP language. The service relies on the JBoss Rules [3], commonly known as Drools, for rule management. For each partner, the current set of business operations that the partner can execute are classified into *Rightful*, *Obligatory* and *Prohibited* and are explicitly stored in the current ROP set and available for consultation and update. Additional Java components for Drools implement the functionality required for the manipulation of ROP sets, historical queries and timer management.

To be effective, a third party service must be able to work with standards compliant B2B messaging systems. Our system has been designed to work with industry standards such as ebXML [4] and RosettaNet [5]. Thus, we require that business interactions between partners are based on the model presented in the next Section, that preserves the essential aspects of these standards, abstracting away low level protocol details.

The rest of this paper is organized as follows. The next Section defines the basic concepts of this work and presents a sample contract used further on to provide an example; Section 3 introduces the architecture of the CCC. Section 4 focuses on the implementation of the CCC itself. Section 5 elaborates on the translation of the EROP language to Drools rule files; Section 6 discusses related work, and finally Section 7 presents concluding remarks.

2 Contracts and Business Operations

Contract clauses state what business operations the partners are permitted (equivalently, have the right), obliged and prohibited to execute. Informally, a right is something that a business partner is allowed to do; an obligation is something that a business partner is expected to do unless they wish to take the risk of being penalised; finally, a prohibition is something that a business partner is not expected to do unless they are prepared to be penalised. The clauses also stipulate when, in what order and by whom the operations are to be executed. For instance, for a buyer-seller business partnership, the contract would stipulate when purchase orders are to be submitted, within how many days of receiving payment the goods have to be delivered, and so on.

As an example, a hypothetical contract between a buyer and seller is shown below. In this example, clause C1 grants the buyer a right; similarly, clause C2 imposes an obligation on the seller. Of particular interest is C7, which illustrates a clause that takes into account problems caused by infrastructure level problems; our study of messaging standards such as eBXML [4], RosettaNet [5] suggests that at the highest level of specification (e.g., legal English), such problems can be referred to as business problems (problems caused by semantic errors in business messages, preventing their processing) and technical problems (problems caused by faults in networks and hardware/software components). This aspect is discussed further below.

C1: The Buyer has the right to submit a Purchase Order, as long as the submission happens from Monday to Friday and from 9am to 5pm.

C2: The Seller has the obligation to either accept or refuse the Purchase Order within 24 hours. Failure to satisfy this obligation will abort the business transaction for an offline resolution.

C3: If the Order is accepted, the Seller has the obligation to submit an invoice within 24 hours. If the order is rejected, the business transaction is considered concluded.

C4: After receiving an invoice, the Buyer has the obligation to pay the due amount within 7 days.

C5: Cancellation of a Purchase Order by the Buyer eliminates all obligations imposed on the Seller and the Buyer and concludes the business transaction. If a payment had been received before a cancellation, it will be refunded.

C6: Once payment is received, the Seller has the obligation to ship the goods within 7 days. The shipment of goods will conclude the business transaction.

C7: If the payment fails for technical or business reasons, the Buyer's deadline to respond to the invoice is extended by seven days, but the Seller gains the right to cancel the Purchase Order.

C8: The buyer and the Seller are obliged to stop the execution of the business transaction upon the detection of three consecutive failures to execute a given business operation. Possible disputes shall be sorted offline.

We assume that interaction between partners takes place through a well defined set of primitive *business operations* $B = \{bo_1, \ldots, bo_n\}$ such as *purchase order submission, invoice notification*, and so on; each operation typically involves the transfer of one or two business documents. A bo_i is supported by a *business conversation*: a well defined message interaction protocol with stringent message timing and validity constraints (normally, a business message is accepted for processing only if it is timely and satisfies specific syntactic and semantic validity constraints). RosettaNet Partner Interface Processes and ebXML industry standards serve as good examples of such conversations.

We assume that the execution of a bo_i generates an *initiation outcome* event, one from the set $\{InitSucc, InitFail\}$, and if the initiation succeeds (the event is *InitSucc*), an execution outcome event, one from the set {*Success, BizFail, TecFail*}. These are the events (together with their attributes described subsequently) that are sent to the CCC. The rationale is as follows.

B2B messaging is typically implemented using Message oriented Middleware (MoM) that permits loose coupling between partners (e.g., the partners need not be online at the same time), we assume what follows. To guarantee that a bo_i conversation protocol is started only when both business partners are ready for the execution of a business operation, they execute an initiation protocol; the actual conversation protocol is executed if initiation succeeds. We then assume that an initiation protocol for the execution of a bo_i generates an *initiation outcome* event from the set {*InitSucc, InitFail*} respectively for initiation success or failure. Following ebXML specification [4], we assume that once a conversation is started, it always completes to produce an *execution outcome* event from the set {*Success, BizFail, TecFail*} which represent respectively a successful conclusion, a business failure or a technical failure. *BizFail* and *TecFail* events model the (hopefully rare) execution outcomes when, after a successful initiation, a party is unable to reach the normal end of a conversation due to exceptional situations. *TecFail* models protocol related failures detected at the middleware level, such as a late, syntactically incorrect or missing message. *BizFail* models semantic errors in a message detected at the business level, e.g., the goods-delivery address extracted from the business document is invalid. For additional details, see [6,7], that also describes the details of synchronization required to ensure that the above events are mutually agreed outcome events between the partners.

The contract stipulates how and when rights, obligations and prohibitions are granted or revoked to business partners. We call *ROP sets* the sets of rights, obligations and prohibitions currently in force for a participant. A business operation is said to be *contract compliant* if it matches the ROP set of the participant that executes it, while also matching the constraints set by the contract clauses for its execution. A $bo_i \in B$ is said to be *out of context* if it does not. *Unknown* business operations, not present in B, are taken to be non-contract compliant. The task of the CCC during the execution of a contract consists in verifying that the operations executed by the participants are contract compliant by matching them with their ROP sets and verifying their contractual constraints, and in modifying those ROP sets as specified by the contract clauses.

2.1   The EROP Language

The EROP language describes business contracts with ECA rules that explicitly manipulate the partners' ROP sets, which are then used to monitor contract compliance. This section will present a brief tutorial for the language.

We use the keywords *roleplayer*, *businessoperation* and *compoblig* as follows. *Roleplayer* declares a list of role players involved in the contract; for example, *roleplayer buyer, seller* declares the two role players of our example.

businessoperation declares a list of known business operations, for example, *businessoperation PurchaseOrderSubmission, InvoicePayment*.

A composite obligation is a tuple of obligations with a single deadline, to be executed OR–exclusively to satisfy the composite obligation. We use *compoblig* to specify and name composite obligations; for example, the composite obligation from clause C2 of our contract example that stipulates that upon receiving a purchase order, a seller is obliged to either accept or refuse it, can be specified as **compoblig** *RespondTo-Order(POAcceptance, PORejection)*, where *RespondToOrder* is the name of the composite obligation.

Structure of Rules and Trigger Blocks. A rule follows the syntax **rule** *ruleName* **when** *triggerBlock* **then** *actionBlock* **end**. The expression *triggerBlock* contains an event match and a list (possibly empty) of conditions; a rule is *relevant* only when the event match and the conditions are satisfied. The event match takes the form *e* **matches** *(field operator value [, field operator value]*)*, where *e* is a placeholder for the event object being currently processed, and *field* is any of *botype* (the business operation type), *outcome* (the outcome of the operation), *originator* and *responder* (the role players initiating and responding to the operation), and *timestamp*. An *operator* is a boolean comparison operator: ==, !=, <, >, and so on. A *value* is a legitimate constant expression for that comparison.

Conditions are Boolean expressions that restrict the cases where a rule triggers. They verify the compliance of a business operation with a participant's ROP set and can also evaluate historical queries. Historical queries search for events in the historical log that match certain constraint, and can be *boolean* or *numeric*, respectively if they verify their presence or if they count the number of occurrences. Boolean queries take the form **happened**(*businessOp, originator, responder, outcome, timeConstraint*), where "***" can be used as a wildcard. Numeric queries have the **counthappened** keyword in place of **happened**.

The compliance of a business operation with the ROP set of a participant can be tested with *businessOperation* **in** *roleplayer*. The keyword **in** can also be employed to test the presence of composite obligations in a participant's obligation set.

The Action Block. The *actionBlock* is a list of actions where each action is + =, − =, *pass* or *terminate*. Actions + = and − = respectively add and remove business operations or composite obligations from the ROP sets; *pass* has no effect, while *terminate* concludes the execution of a contract. The use of + = and − = to add or remove rights, prohibitions and obligations (simple or composite) is demonstrated in the following statements:

```
roleplayer.rights += BusinessOper(expiry);      roleplayer.rights -= BusinessOper;
roleplayer.prohibs += BusinessOper(expiry);     roleplayer.prohibs -= BusinessOper;
roleplayer.obligs += BusinessOper(expiry);      roleplayer.obligs -= BusinessOper;
roleplayer.obligs += Obligation(expiry);        roleplayer.obligs -= Obligation;
```

expiry is a deadline constraint imposed on a role player to honour his contractual right, obligations and prohibitions; the absence of a deadline indicates a duration up until the contract terminates. Notice that obligations with no deadlines are pointless as their fulfillment cannot be verified.

Conditional statements can also appear in the *actionBlock* of a rule, using the syntax **if** *conditions* **then** *actionBlock* *[else actionBlock]* **endif**. Conditions of *if*-statements are the same ones used in a trigger block.

In an *actionBlock* the *status guards* **Success, InitFail, BizFail, TecFail, Otherwise** can be used to group actions for conditional execution according to the outcome of a business operation, with **Otherwise** used as a catchall case.

2.2   Language Example

In order to showcase the EROP language, we will present in this Section some significative rules of the EROP version of the sample contract given earlier. First of all, the declaration section:

```
roleplayer buyer, seller;
businessoperation POSubmission, Invoice, Payment, POCancellation, Refund;
businessoperation GoodsDelivery, POAcceptance, PORejection;
compoblig RespondToPO (POAcceptance, PORejection);
```

Here follow the rules derived from clauses C3, C4, C6 and C7 of the sample contract in Section 2. Note that in general the mapping between rules and clauses is N to N; in some cases, several clauses are mapped into a single rule, while in others many rules derive from a single clause. In the simplest case the mapping is one to one.

Rules R3, R4 and R8 presented below could also be written using status guards in the action block and removing the constraint on the outcome from the event matches. Both forms are equivalent, and choosing one over the other comes down to style preferences. Rule 3 below derives from clause C3, while Rule 4 derives from clause C4.

```
rule "R3"
  when
    e matches (botype == "POAcceptance",
    outcome == "Success"
    originator == "seller",
    responder == "buyer")
  RespondToPO in seller.obligs
  then
    seller.obligs -= RespondToPO;
    seller.obligs += Invoice("24h");
end
```

```
rule "R4"
  when
    e matches (botype == "Invoice",
    outcome == "Success",
    originator == "seller",
    responder == "buyer")
    Invoice in seller.obligs
  then
    seller.obligs -= Invoice;
    buyer.obligs += Payment("7d");
end
```

Rule 6 derives from clauses C6 and C7, while Rule 8 derives from clause C8.

```
rule "R6"
  when e matches (botype == "Payment",
    originator == "buyer",
    responder == "seller")
    Payment in buyer.obligs
  then
  Success:
    buyer.obligs -= Payment;
    seller.obligs += GoodsDelivery("7d");
  TecFail:
  BizFail:
    buyer.obligs -= Payment;
    buyer.obligs += Payment("7d");
    seller.rights += POCancellation();
  Otherwise:
    pass;
end
```

```
rule "R8"
  when
    e matches (botype == "Payment,
    "originator == "buyer",
    responder == "seller")
    e.outcome != "Success"
    counthappened("Payment", "buyer",
      "seller", "InitFail", "*")
    + counthappened("Payment", "buyer",
      "seller", "TecFail", "*")
    + counthappened("Payment", "buyer",
      "seller", "BizFail", "*") >= 3
  then
    terminate("TecFail");
end
```

3   Architecture of the CCC

The events supplied by the business partners to the CCC (shown in Fig. 1) carry information on undertaken business operations: the outcome, one of *InitSucc* or *InitFail* for initiation outcomes, and, if initiation succeeds, one from the set {*Success, BizFail,*

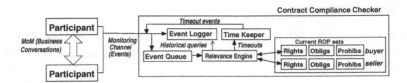

Fig. 1. The Contract Compliance Checker

TecFail}, the operation's originator and responder, and a timestamp. Events are forwarded to the **Event Logger**, that keeps a history of the business interaction as seen by the CCC, to be queried when evaluating rules with historical constraints. The **Event Queue** holds all events awaiting to be processed. The current **ROP sets** are the sets of rights, obligations and prohibitions currently assigned to the role players (to the buyer and seller in our example). The **Time Keeper** keeps track of the deadlines of rights, obligations and prohibitions. When a timeout expires (e.g. obligation deadline expiration), the Time Keeper generates a *timeout event* and forwards it to the Event Logger and the Event Queue. The **Relevance Engine** analyses queued events and triggers any relevant rules among those it holds in its working memory, following this algorithm:

1. Fetch the first event e from the Event Queue;
2. Identify the relevant rules for e;
3. For each relevant rule r, execute the actions listed in its right hand side, either ROP set manipulation or termination of a contract instance.

4   Implementation of the CCC

Figure 2 presents a diagram of the implementation of the CCC. Its main components were identified in Section 3 as the Event Queue, the Time Keeper, the Event Logger and the Relevance Engine. The Event Queue, defined in the class *EventQueue*, is a First In, First Out queue of incoming Event objects, owned by the Relevance Engine. The Event Queue offers two operations: adding an Event to the end of the queue, and taking an Event out of the head of the queue. Events are added by the participants (simulated in our prototype), and by the Time Keeper (timeout events). Only the Relevance Engine removes Events from the Event Queue.

The Time Keeper, defined in the class *TimeKeeper*, manages the deadlines for the expiry of ROP Entities, and offers two operations: adding and removing a deadline. Deadlines are internally represented using Java Timers, stored in a hash table indexed by the name and type of the ROP Entity they refer to, and the involved role players. Whenever a deadline expires, its corresponding Java Timer notifies the Time Keeper, passing as parameters the relevant data - Business Operation type, relevant Role Players, and so on. The Time Keeper then instantiates a new Event of the relevant type, appending *Timeout* to the name. The outcome of the new Event object is set to *timeout*.

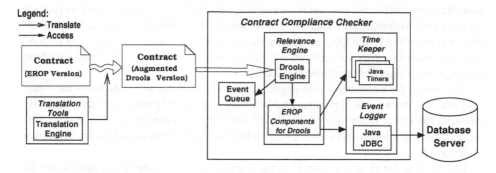

Fig. 2. Implementation Details for the Contract Compliance Checker

The Event Logger maintains the historical database and offers three operations: logging events in the database, submitting boolean queries and submitting numerical queries. The Relevance Engine (RE) relies on an instance of the Drools rule engine [3] to power its decision making capability. It offers four operations: adding an Event for processing, initializing a contract instantiation to start a new business interaction, processing the Event queue and verifying that the Event queue is empty. As anticipated earlier on, the RE's algorithm presented in Section 3 to trigger relevant rules is implemented using the recognize-act cycle of the Drools engine: the RE inserts the events retrieved from the Event Queue in Drools' working memory, to trigger a recognize-act cycle to identify any relevant rule and executes their right-hand-side actions.

4.1 Implementation of the Relevance Engine

Drools powers the decision making capability of the Relevance Engine. A rule engine is a software system that uses a set of rules to define and direct its own activity, instead of relying on static, hardcoded knowledge like a conventional system. Knowledge is therefore separated from the rest of the execution environment, and segregated in a *rule base*, or *knowledge base*, so as to be altered by users when needed without having to alter the execution environment. Drools is a *forward chaining* [8] rule engine, where *facts*, items of knowledge that are atomic from the perspective of the system, are brought in and stored for evaluation in the *working memory*, a buffer area separated from the rule base. Every time the working memory is altered by adding, removing or modifying facts, the rule engine starts a *recognise-act cycle*, examining all rules to find those for which the left hand side conditions match the current state of the working memory (*triggered* rules). The actions in the right hand side of these rules are then executed, and the facts that triggered any rules are removed from the working memory. This generally alters the working memory, so the recognise-act cycle is restarted, until no rule is triggered.

Drools also allows the definition of *globals*, objects that reside in a special area of the working memory and persist between recognise-act cycles, not triggering new ones even if they are altered. Globals usually act as hooks to external services, and are therefore the only channel to the outside world that a running Drools system has. To implement our system, we have a global for a reference to the running RE, used for housekeeping purposes, and one for a reference to the Event Logger, used to provide access to the historical log. There also is a global for each Role Player and their ROP Sets. Events in the Event Queue awaiting processing are inserted one by one in Drools' working memory to start a recognise-act cycle, which implements the rule matching and triggering algorithm described in Section 3.

The reason for choosing a rule engine to power the Relevance Engine is the small semantic gap between EROP rules and business rules; EROP rules are fundamentally business rules that make use of the EROP ontology introduced in Section 4.2. This makes the translation process from EROP to Drools relatively straightforward, as shown in Section 5.

The reasons for choosing Drools as the particular rule engine in our system are its availability with an Open Source license, and a number of useful features, notably its use of Forgy's Rete algorithm [9], a relatively efficient algorithm to search the knowledge base for relevant rules, which is the most computationally intensive task in a rule engine. Another notable feature is the possibility to write the right hand sides of rules directly in a programming language (specifically Java, Python or Groovy). This last feature allows a more direct, simpler mapping to the implementation of the EROP ontology.

4.2   The EROP Ontology

The *EROP ontology* is a set of the concepts and relationships within the domain of B2B interaction employed to model the execution of business operations between partners, to reason about the compliance of their actions with their stated objectives in their agreements. The EROP ontology includes the following classes:

Role Player: an agent, not necessarily human, employed by one of the interacting parties, that takes on and plays a role defined in the contract.

Business Operation: a specific activity defined in the contract for the purpose of producing value.

Right: A Business Operation that a Role Player is allowed to execute.

Obligation (Simple): A Business Operation that a Role Player must execute.

Prohibition: A Business Operation that a Role Player must not execute.

Composite Obligation: A set of Obligations with a single deadline; a Role Player must execute exactly one of the set to satisfy the Composite Obligation.

ROP Entity: A right, obligation or prohibition.

Deadline: A time constraint that can be imposed on rights, and prohibitions and is always imposed on both simple and composite obligations.

ROP Set: A set (possibly empty) of rights, obligations and prohibitions belonging to a Role Player. Each Role Player has exactly one ROP Set.

Event: A message carrying a record about the occurrence of a business activity, such as initiating or concluding a business operation, the expiry of a deadline, and so on.

The classes of the EROP ontology are implemented by the Java classes *RolePlayer, BusinessOperation, Right, Obligation, Prohibition, CompositeObligation, ROPEntity, Deadline, ROPSet* and *Event*. The class *ROPEntity* is the parent of classes *Right, Obligation* and *Prohibition*, and the ancestor of *CompositeObligation*, as shown in the UML diagram presented in Figure 3.

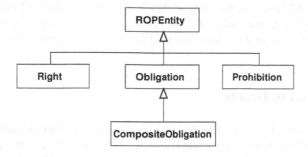

Fig. 3. Descendants of the class ROPEntity

The remaining classes, *Event, BusinessOperation, RolePlayer* and *ROPSet*, do not belong to an inheritance hierarchy.

4.3   The Historical Database

The Historical Database contains four tables: one for the Role Players, one for the relevant Event types, one for the possible status outcomes, and one for the Event history proper. The first three tables remain unaltered by the CCC for all its lifetime, and are supposed to be prepared in advance by an ancillary application. The fourth table, the actual Event history, is created empty before the first run of the system, and is filled during the contract's lifetime. Whether it has to be emptied between successive runs of the same contract depends on the conditions in the contract itself; it makes sense to allow for the possibility of writing clauses that refer to past iterations of the same contract to alter the ROP sets of the participants, e.g., a clause providing a 10% discount to buyers with at least three successfully completed purchase orders that were paid on time. Therefore there is no special provision to erase the the Event history, in order to leave the choice to do this to the involved parties.

As explained in Section 2, historical queries can be classified into two main categories: *boolean* queries, verifying whether an Event matching a given set of constraints is logged in the historical database, and *numeric* queries that count the number of occurrences of such logged Events.

In either case, the set of constraints is the same: the business operation type, the originating and responding Role Players, the Event's outcome, and a temporal constraint. An example of an acceptable set of historical constraints would be *originator = "buyer", responder = "seller", type = "PurchaseOrder", status = "Success", timeConstraint = "timestamp < 15/12/2009 10:00:00 "*. The given set of constraints is used to build a SQL query, and the answer of the database server is then analysed to generate the appropriate response. Rule R8, presented in Section 2 includes a numeric query; this maps to the method *countHappened()* of the class *EventLogger* after translation. Similarly, a boolean query would map to *happened()*. These methods build the SQL statements for the historical database from the received parameters, submit them to the database server, then parse the results and return them. So the numerical query in R8 is translated into the SQL statement SELECT COUNT(*) FROM *eventhistory* WHERE *type*='Payment' AND *originator*='buyer' AND *responder*='seller' AND *timestamp* >= '1 Jan 2008' AND *outcome*='success'. The result of the query, as per the SQL standard, is the number of rows in the *eventhistory* table that record events within the desired constraints.

5   Translation to Drools

The Java implementation of the EROP ontology presented earlier extends the rule language offered by Drools to reason about contract compliance; we call this extended language *Augmented Drools* (AD). Because of its origin, Augmented Drools is more verbose and Java-like than the EROP language, as well as less abstract and human-readable. It also needs to have additional code for housekeeping purposes, necessary to manipulate the EROP ontology, such as lines to instantiate and assign objects and arrays.

The EROP language maps completely into Augmented Drools; it is possible to write contracts in AD with the same expressive power of EROP, but, as mentioned above, the resulting code is more implementation-aware yet less declarative in style and less readable. Most importantly, however, AD can run on available software - the Drools rule engine. The problem of creating a compiler for the EROP language therefore reduces to the translation of EROP to AD. Such a translator has not yet been implemented, however it is seen to be a straightforward task that we are planning to complete in the future. The rest of this section will show how EROP statements map into AD statements.

5.1   Declarations in Augmented Drools and EROP

A rule file in Augmented Drools starts, like in EROP, with the declaration of the objects and entities used in the file: Role Players, Business Operations and Composite Obligations, together with be declarations of the Role Players' ROP Sets, and of the currently running Relevance Engine and Event Logger for reference in the rules. The definition of global indentifiers is done with the **global** Drools keyword, followed by the class of the object to declare, its name and a semicolon. As an example, here is the part of a sample contract where identifiers are declared:

```
global RelevanceEngine engine;        global BusinessOperation purchaseOrder;
global EventLogger logger;            global BusinessOperation finePayment;
global RolePlayer buyer;              global BusinessOperation payment;
global RolePlayer seller;             global BusinessOperation poAcceptance;
global ROPSet ropBuyer;               global BusinessOperation poRejection;
global ROPSet ropSeller;              global BusinessOperation goodsDelivery;
```

Here we declare the instances of the Relevance Engine and Event Logger to use, two Role Players, *buyer* and *seller*, their two ROP Sets, and the Business operations used in subsequent rules. Business Operation names begin in lowercase here as they are Java objects and follow Java style rules; *po* stands for *Purchase Order*.

The syntax to define rules is the same in Drools and EROP, as the second is derived from the first: **rule** *RuleName* **when** *triggerBlock* **then** *actionBlock* **end**. Rule names must be unique within a rule file. Comments in AD, like in Drools, are preceded by a hash sign (#), and continue until the end of the line.

Event matching, done in EROP with the syntax *e **matches** (attribute == value, [attribute == value]*)* (see Section 2), translates to the AD syntax *$e: Event (attribute == value, [attribute == value]*)*, where *$e* is an event placeholder variable.

Other conditions outside the event match are written using the Drools construct *eval*, that evaluates boolean expressions in the left hand side of rules. Therefore, historical queries of the form *happened(businessOperation, originator, responder, status, time-Constraint)* would map to ***eval** (eventLogger.happened (businessOperation, originator, responder, status, timeConstraint))*, where *eventLogger* is the running instance of the class *EventLogger*. Numerical queries would similarly translate in a similar fashion to calls to the *countHappened()* method using *eval*.

The test for the presence of a ROP Entity in a Role Player's ROP Set, expressed in EROP with *ROPEntity **in** rolePlayer.rop* where *rop* is one of *rights, obligs* or *prohibs*, maps to AD as a method call of the class *ROPSet*; ***eval**(playersROPSet.matchesRights (BOType))* for rights, and so on. *Eval* is here used again to evaluate a boolean method call.

5.2 Actions in EROP and Augmented Drools

ROP sets are manipulated in EROP with the += and -= operators, e.g. *seller.obligs += Invoice("24h")*. This maps in AD to a method call of the class *ROPSet*, such as *ropSeller.addObligation("Invoice", "24h")*.

The EROP keyword *terminate* maps to the AD statement *engine.terminate()*, where *engine* is the current instance of the RE; the argument of *terminate* is passed to this method. Executing *engine.terminate()* concludes the current contract instance and notifies its participants of the termination and of its outcome.

5.3 Conditional Structures

In general, EROP rules using *if-then-else* statements or status guards generally map to more than one rule in AD. So an EROP rule with status guards maps to as many AD rules as the number of guards used in it; each of those AD rules will have a constraint on the outcome of the event under scrutiny added to its trigger block matching the corresponding status guard. So a rule of the form

```
rule "RuleForManyOutcomes"
  when e matches (botype == SomeBO)
  then
    Success:
      actionBlock1
    TecFail:
      actionBlock2
    Otherwise:
      actionBlock3
end
```

would be mapped to the following rules:

```
rule "RuleForSuccess"                rule "RuleForTechnicalFail"
  when                                 when
    e matches (botype == SomeBO,         e matches (botype == SomeBO,
    outcome == "success")                outcome == "tecfail")
  then actionBlock1                    then actionBlock2
  end                                  end
```

```
rule "RuleForOther"
  when e matches (botype == SomeBO)
    ((e.outcome != "success")||(e.outcome != "tecfail"))
    then actionBlock3
end
```

A rule with an *if-then-else* statement would be similarly mapped to two AD rules, one with the *then*-block and one with the *else*-block.

5.4   Examples of Translation to Augmented Drools

To offer a translation example from EROP to Augmented Drools, we will now show how rules R3 and R8 from the sample contract fragment discussed in Section 2 are mapped to Augmented Drools.

```
rule "R3"
  when
    $e: Event(type=="POAcceptance", originator=="seller",
      responder=="buyer", outcome=="Success")
    eval(ropSeller.matchesObligations("RespondToPO"));
  then
    ropSeller.removeObligation("ReactToPO");
    ropBuyer.addObligation(payment, "24h");
end

rule "R8"
  when
    $e:  Event (type=="Payment", originator=="buyer",
      responder=="seller", outcome=="success")
    eval(ropBuyer.matchesObligations(payment))
    eval(eventLogger.countHappened("Payment", "buyer", "*", "InitFail", "*")
      +eventLogger.countHappened("Payment", "buyer", "*", "TecFail", "*")
      +eventLogger.countHappened("Payment", "buyer", "*", "BizFail", "*")
      >= 3 )
  then
    engine.terminate("BizFail");
end
```

5.5   Performance Considerations

The CCC depends on the Drools rule engine to perform the most computationally intensive task, the selection of the relevant rules for incoming events. This is accomplished by the recognize-act cycle of the rule engine, using the Rete algorithm presented in [9]. The performance of the Rete algorithm depends on the number of facts in the working memory and in the characteristics of the rule base; in our system, only one fact is evaluated at a time, and so the number of facts in the working memory is not an issue. Performance is therefore determined by the characteristics of the rule base; specifically, by its size, and by how much overlap there is between the conditions on the left hand sides of rules. In general, the time needed for a recognize-act cycle grows as the size of a rule base grows; the effects of the size of a rule base on performance are discussed in [10].

The Rete algorithm uses a dataflow network to represent the left hand side conditions of the rules. Rules with common conditions share nodes in this network; the more conditions are shared, the more nodes are shared, and the more efficient a recognize-act cycle is. In our system rules are written taking a contract in natural language as a starting point. While it is reasonable to expect a certain amount of overlap between rule conditions (e.g., all rules about operations initiated by a given role player are going to share a condition asserting that role player's identity as the initiator), our experiments did not readily suggest criteria to predict the exact amount of overlap. Much depends on the definition of business operations and on writing style; equivalent contracts can be written with strongly diverging rule bases. Future work on EROP will include an investigation on the best practices of contract writing in order to achieve more efficient dataflow networks for the Rete algorithm.

Our experiments showed, however, that the code for the CCC only adds a very small constant factor to the time needed for recognize-act cycles, and so its impact on efficiency can be neglected. The overall time needed to process an event remained of the order of magnitude of milliseconds; considering that time scales in business relationships are of the order of magnitude of hours, days, or even longer, efficiency does not appear to be a limiting factor for our system.

6 Related Work

The implementation of languages for specification and monitoring of electronic contracts is an active research topic; however formal treatments and abstract models have received greater attention. In [11], a mediating entity, the Synchronization Point (SP), has a similar role to our CCC, hosting a knowledge base of contract clauses, consulted whenever the participants send an event at the conclusion of a business operation. The knowledge base is written as ECA rules using Protege [12], and interrogated using its query language PAL. The authors describe a method to generate ECA rules from an abstract model of a contract; however, the semantic distance between the model and the business rules in a natural language contract appears to be greater than the distance between our EROP rules and natural language rules.

Heimdahl [13] is another ECA-based work comparable to ours. It employs a policy monitor similar to our CCC to decide which actions are legal, and to enforce the contractual clauses. Enforcement involves asserting the presence of certain events in the future if certain events occur in the present; the monitor executes compensatory actions if the expected future events do not occur. Heimdahl's focus is on the monitoring and enforcing of SLA, so there is not much scope for the concepts of business operations and mechanisms for exception handling as offered by EROP.

Law-Governed Interaction [14,15] is an early work in the implementation of an architecture for contract monitoring and enforcement. The Moses middleware presented in [14] has Controllers located between the interacting parties, receiving events and taking actions based on a knowledge base of rules; rules are stored by Law Servers and can be written in customized versions of Prolog or Java. Moses is an integrated system that requires Moses components to be installed within all the participants; this is in contrast to the CCC that has been designed to act as a third party service.

Compliance monitoring is investigated in [16] within the context of service based systems – systems composed dynamically from autonomous web services and coordinated by a composition process. A framework is proposed for the monitoring of compliance of such composite systems with a set of behavioural properties extracted from a BPEL specification of the composition process. At runtime, the events exchanged between the interacting parties are intercepted and processed similarly to what our CCC does, watching for violations of specified behaviour in a non-intrusive manner. Currently the specification of requirements to monitor are expressed in an abstract event calculus language that is not suitable for use by non technical people in a business environment.

Non intrusive monitoring for agent-based contract systems is investigated in [17], as part of the EU Contract Project [18]. In this work, a group of observers monitor the messages exchanged by the interacting agents, and the observed communications patterns are then matched with expected patterns derived from running contracts to detect violations. It is assumed that all messages relevant to the ongoing business transactions are visible and comprehensible to the observers.

Work on contract monitoring from the perspective of a model-driven approach is presented in [19]. The paper presents a metamodel level discussion on a variety of topics, including sub-contracting, simultaneous execution of several interleaving contract instances, nested executions, multiple monitoring and so on. Our work can be considered a concrete instance of some of the metamodels of the paper, that takes into consideration a number of practical issues not touched upon there, such as the treatment of deadlines, and of technical and business failures.

7   Conclusion and Future Work

In this paper we have presented the implementation of a prototype for a Contract Compliance Checker supporting contracts written in the EROP language. Our system is designed as a third party service monitoring B2B interactions for compliance. Our current design operates under the assumption that the business partners operate in good faith: they do not knowingly generate malicious events. Enhancements required to prevent abuse of the service is a topic for further investigation. Future work will also include completing a translator for EROP into Augmented Drools, an evaluation of the system in realistic settings, an investigation into the impact of contract writing style on efficiency and validation of the rule bases for consistency.

Acknowledgements

We would like to thank Davide Sottara of the Engineering Department of the University of Bologna for fruitful discussions on the inner workings of Drools and on its performance.

This work has been funded in part by UK Engineering and Physical Sciences Research Council (EPSRC), Platform Grant No. EP/D037743/1, "Networked Computing in Inter-organisation Settings".

References

1. Strano, M., Molina-Jimenez, C., Shrivastava, S.: A Rule-based Notation to Specify Executable Electronic Contracts. In: Bassiliades, N., Governatori, G., Paschke, A. (eds.) RuleML 2008. LNCS, vol. 5321, pp. 81–88. Springer, Heidelberg (2008)

2. Molina-Jimenez, C., Shrivastava, S., Strano, S.: Exception Handling in Electronic Contracting. In: Proc. 11th IEEE Conf. on Commerce and Enterprise Computing (CEC 2009), Vienna, Austria, July 20-23. IEEE Computer Society, Los Alamitos (2009)
3. JBoss Rules (2009), http://www.jboss.org/drools/
4. ebXML: Business Process Spec. Schema Tech. Spec. v2.0.4 (2006), http://docs.oasisopen.org/ebxml-bp/2.0.4/OS/spec/ebxmlbp-v2.0.4-Spec-os-en.pdf
5. Implementation Framework - Core specification, Version V02.00.01 (March 2002), http://www.rosettanet.org/
6. Molina-Jimenez, C., Shrivastava, S.: Maintaining Consistency Between Loosely Coupled Services in the Presence of Timing Constraints and Validation Errors. In: Proc. 4th IEEE European Conf. on Web Services (ECOWS 2006), pp. 148–157. IEEE CS Press, Los Alamitos (2006)
7. Molina-Jimenez, C., Shrivastava, S., Cook, N.: Implementing Business Conversations with Consistency Guarantees Using Message-Oriented Middleware. In: Proc. 11th IEEE Int'l Conf. (EDOC 2007), pp. 51–62. IEEE CS Press, Los Alamitos (2007)
8. Cawsey, A.: Forward Chaining Systems (1994), http://www.macs.hw.ac.uk/~alison/ai3notes/subsection2_4_4_1.html
9. Forgy, C.L.: Rete: a fast algorithm for the many pattern/many object pattern match problem. IEEE Computer Society Reprint Collection, 324–341 (1991)
10. Brant, D., Grose, T., Lofaso, B., Miranker, D.: Effects of Database Size on Rule System Performance: Five Case Studies. In: VLDB 1991: Proceedings of the 17th International Conference on Very Large Data Bases, pp. 287–296. Kaufmann Publishers Inc., San Francisco (1991)
11. Perrin, O., Godart, C.: An Approach to Implement Contracts as Trusted Intermediaries. In: Proc. of the 1st IEEE Int'l Workshop on Electronic Contracting (2004)
12. Noy, N.F., Crubezy, M., Fergerson, R.W., Knublauch, H., Tu, S.W., Vendetti, J., Musen, M.A.: Protege-2000: an Open-Source Ontology-Development and Knowledge-Acquisition Environment. In: AMIA Annual Symposium Proceedings, p. 953 (2003)
13. Gama, P., Ribeiro, C., Ferreira, P.: Heimdhal: A History-Based Policy Engine for Grids. In: Proc. of the 6th IEEE Int'l Symposium on Cluster Computing and the Grid (CCGRID 2006), pp. 481–488 (2006)
14. Minsky, N.H., Ungureanu, V.: Law-governed Interaction: a Coordination and Control Mechanism for Heterogeneous Distributed Systems. ACM Trans. Softw. Eng. Methodol. 9(3), 273–305 (2000)
15. Minsky, N.H., Ungureanu, V.: Scalable Regulation of Inter-enterprise Electronic Commerce. In: Electronic Commerce: 2nd Int'l Workshop (November 2001)
16. Spanoudakis, G., Mahbub, K.: Non Intrusive Monitoring of Service Based Systems. Int'l Journal of Cooperative Information Systems 15(3), 325–358 (2006)
17. Faci, N., Modgil, S., Oren, N., Meneguzzi, F., Miles, S., Luck, M.: Towards a Monitoring Framework for Agent-Based Contract Systems. In: Klusch, M., Pechouœek, M., Polleres, A. (eds.) CIA 2008. LNCS (LNAI), vol. 5180, pp. 292–305. Springer, Heidelberg (2008)
18. The IST Contract Project, http://www.ist-contract.org/
19. Linington, P.F.: Automating Support for E-Business Contracts. Int'l Journal of Cooperative Information Systems 14(2-3), 77–98 (2005)

Modeling Medical Ethics through Intelligent Agents

José Machado[1], Miguel Miranda[1], António Abelha[1], José Neves[1],
and João Neves[2]

[1] Universidade do Minho
Departamento de Informática Braga,
Portugal
{miranda,jmac,abelha,jneves}@di.uminho.pt
[2] Centro Hospitalar de Vila Nova de Gaia e Espinho, Portugal
j_neves@hotmail.com

Abstract. The amount of research using health information has increased dramatically over the last past years. Indeed, a significative number of healthcare institutions have extensive Electronic Health Records (EHR), collected over several years for clinical and teaching purposes, but are uncertain as to the proper circumstances in which to use them to improve the delivery of care to the ones in need. Research Ethics Boards in Portugal and elsewhere in the world are grappling with these issues, but lack clear guidance regarding their role in the creation of and access to EHRs. However, we feel we have an effective way to handle Medical Ethics if we look to the problem under a structured and more rational way. Indeed, we felt that physicians were not aware of the relevance of the subject in their pre-clinical years, but their interest increase when they were exposed to patients. On the other hand, once EHRs are stored in machines, we also felt that we had to find a way to ensure that the behavior of machines toward human users, and perhaps other machines as well, is ethically acceptable. Therefore, in this article we discuss the importance of machine ethics and the need for machines that represent ethical principles explicitly. It is also shown how a machine may abstract an ethical principle from a logical representation of ethical judgments and use that principle to guide its own behavior.

Keywords: Morality, intelligent agents, medical ethics.

1 Introduction

Ethics is focused on moral goods rather than natural goods. However, both moral and natural goods are equally relevant and have to be taken under consideration. Morals are created by and define society, philosophy, religion or individual conscience, usually associated with the fundamental questions concerning the complexities of the human soul [1]. Several forms of ethics have been approached, namely the ones:

C. Godart et al. (Eds.): I3E 2009, IFIP AICT 305, pp. 112–122, 2009.

- Applied ethics, i.e. ethics seeks to address questions such as how a moral outcome can be achieved in a specific situation;
- Normative ethics, i.e. how moral values should be determined;
- Descriptive ethics, i.e. what morals people actually abide by;
- meta-ethics, i.e. what the fundamental nature of ethics or morality is, including whether it has any objective justification; and
- Moral psychology, i.e. how moral capacity or moral agency develops and what its nature is.

The role of computers is rapidly evolving from that of passive cipher to that of active participants in the trading process, which lead us to an imperious need of analysing the questions of morality. In Philosophy, morality has different meanings, namely [2]:

- A code of conduct which is held to be authoritative in matters of right and wrong;
- An ideal code of conduct, one which would be espoused in preference to alternatives by all rational people, under specified conditions; and
- A synonymous of ethics, the systematic philosophical study of the moral domain.

On the other hand, interoperabiliy in healthcare units is defined as the ability to move clinical data from place to place. Bringing interoperabity to these facilities it is possible to reduce costs and give to clinical and medical staff more powerful tools for patient assistance, in particular in the decision support and problem solving procedures. In Medicine, physicians and nurses have daily to deal with incomplete information, which in association with moral judgements and emotivism, turn decisions sometimes wrong, slow, expensive or unacceptable. This leads us to the need of defining formalisms to identify and evaluate morality and ethics in Medicine.

Medical ethics is primarily a field of applied ethics, the study of moral values and judgments as they apply to Medicine, in particular the examination of particular issues that are matters of moral judgments and morally correct behavior in various fields. Medical ethics encompasses its practical application in clinical settings as well as work on the fields of History, Philosophy, Theology, and Sociology. Medical ethics tends to be understood narrowly as an applied professional ethics, whereas bioethics appears to have worked more expansive concerns, touching upon the philosophy of science and the critique of biotechnology. The two fields often overlap and the distinction is more a matter of style than professional consensus. Medical ethics shares many principles with other branches of healthcare ethics, such as nursing ethics.

Some attributes that may apply to Medical Ethics are depicted below [2]:

- Autonomy,i.e. the patient has the right to refuse or choose their treatment;
- Beneficence, i.e. a practitioner should act in the best interest of the patient;
- Non-maleficence, i.e. "first, do no harm";

- Justice, i.e. concerns the distribution of scarce health resources, and the decision of who gets what treatment;
- Dignity, i.e. the patient (and the person treating the patient) have the right to dignity; and
- Truthfulness and honesty, i.e. the concept of informed consent has increased in importance in the last few years.

Those parameters must be quantified and its importance can not be subestimated in the decision making process. All the ethical questions around virtual entities or agents, have to be taken under a practical perspective and are related with the embedded environment. This study has been performed before in terms of electronic commerce, considering the case of the legal and ethical context of contract made by means of intelligent agents [3] [4]. Nonetheless, there exists the need to undergo a particular approach when considering morally dubious areas, where every little may have great moral consequences. This is the case of Medicine, where interoperability and decision support are presently in continuous analysis and development. Following this thread of thought and taking in consideration the state of the art of the Agent Oriented Paradigm, it will be analyzed in this study the moral context of agents, discussing the possibility of an agent at a given state of development, have the moral capacity and legal responsibility for actions.

2   Intelligent Agents and Medical Ethics

In a healthcare unit, intelligent agents can be used as a mean towards the integration of different services and the software being used. Within this system, different intelligent agents, autonomously and adaptively, defend individually or by means of cooperation their interests and objectives. They concentrate vital functions of the healthcare unit, improving the quality-of-service and the people quality-of-life. As part of this system there exists different agents which, by different forms, support the medical research, having the capacity to interact with its environment and evolve, acquiring new methodologies and information to improve their own qualities and competence, i.e. to solve different problems according to its duties.

For example, a physician, when analyzing an exam received from a computerized tomography, is presented instead of thousand of pictures, a smaller number of pictures selected by intelligent agents. In light of the selected images, it was not possible to detect any anomaly. Meanwhile, in the group of selected images missed a small set of pictures which evidentiated the existence of small metastasis which might have changed the diagnose. This case was misdiagnosed by influence of the agents. The physician taked a decision which ultimately had moral and legal consequences. This decision revealed itself as a bad help to the diagnose, placing at stake a human life.

Another important topic in medical ethics is the concept of futility. What should be done if there is no chance that a patient will survive but the family members insist on advanced care? And what should be made if a patient is in a Intensive Care Unit, using a bed that is necessary to save another patient with more chance to survive? Rational decisions can be taken to solve this particular problem, following legal or practical rules, either by physicians or by intelligent agents. But who will be responsible for taking such moral decisions?

Facing such situations, several questions and doubts arise, namely: What is or defines a Moral Agent? Is an intelligent agent a Moral Agent? Will these agents have at any point in time either the capacity and ability to take moral decisions or being capable to handle with decisions which carry a great ethical dilemma? Which are the legal and moral responsibilities in an agent based system?

The present period, or step in a process or development in Artificial Intelligence (AI) is still far from the usual scenarios imagined by science fiction. However, it is becoming an embedded characteristic in aplications of different areas, from Commerce to Medicine. Indeed, AI techniques which imbue software systems with a considerable degree of intelligence, autonomy and proactivity, and the ability to adapt to the environment being populated are growing, being essential to attain a superior level of utility and interactivity. Infact, it urges the necessity to evaluate and regulate the scope of the capacities of this software systems, either when they are called to execute different tasks or to take decision which may have any arguable moral value. The field of ethics associated to non-organic entities, Machine Ethics, thereby lacks of a more practical oriented and cautious reflexion, that will analyse the state of the art of AI in all its vast extension. It will be then possible to defined moral competences and restrictions to its use in any environment, where morality and reputation are to be questionable.

3   Intelligent Agents in Medicine

The requirements of software applications for the healthcare arena, although being rather similar to those of other areas, develops in a completely different dimension due to the value inherent to the moral good, i.e. the health condition of a human being. All agents, either human beings or software agents need to be aware of the immeasurable value of an human life and the ethical complexity existing when dealing with this specific good. As information systems continue to disseminate and strengthen in the healthcare sector, the significance of their use increases and so does their moral responsibilities, i.e. a great part of the scope of intervention of agents in this area carries a moral context and ethical responsibility, which it is made aware, even in software artifacts that inevitably will be designed to automatize and manage the larger loading of information generated by medical practices and underlying activities. In fact, this amount of information is so huge that it becomes impracticable to store and extract any sort of knowledge, without the use of computational methods and AI based techniques.

From the different computational paradigms in use in AI, Agent Oriented Programing has pursued a sheer growth considering the level and number of the available systems, being capable of integrating other technologies and techniques for problem solving such as Neural Networks or Case Based Reasoning. An individual agent or a network of agents based on different communities of agent possess a class of characteristics that allows them to be independent from the will, desires and objectives of other virtual agents or human beings, granting a certain degree, although limited, of individuality [5]. On the other hand, an agent method cannot be invoked by other than the entity itself, being determined by its will and degree of responsibility. Only the agent is in charge of its own behavior. Regardless, the use of learning techniques from AI, enable the agent to contextualize and evolve dynamically, making the underlying behaviors dependent of the environment, as well as from other circumstances, which may go out of the scope of its initial parameterization. This possibility rises issues concerning the ethical and legal responsibility of the agent owner, in line with the characterization of intelligent agents as autonomous, self-learning and dynamic entities.

The distributed and heterogeneous nature of this environment, makes the best use of this technology [6], which is being applied to different services and situations, going from heterogeneous system integration to decision support systems [7]. A great effort of academic and corporate synergies allowed the use of intelligent agents in several medical centers which aggregate several hospitals and health units, which use an Agency for Integration, Archive and Diffusion of Medical Information (AIDA), an agent based software artifact, that intends to integrate and agregate information from different systems and locations [8].

On the other hand, the use of intelligent agents for integration of systems may not seem to hold a great deal of ethical significance. However,although these tools improve the security and functionality of the medical information as a whole, the consequences of the loss or adulteration of clinical information or the permissiveness towards this sort of actions, carries a unmeasurable ethical and moral value. A lot more can be said about the decision support systems whose action, although being in support of a decision, contributes indirectly to the diagnose and the treatment of patients. Taken these situations into consideration, it becomes essential an objective discussion about the capacities and characteristics of these systems, in order to define the moral competences of an intelligent agent. This characterization is vital as weell as the need of practical guidelines and rules or ethical conduct for the development and behavior of this sort of systems, so that the quality of the services provided may improve.

4   Moral Capacity

A moral agency is defined by the moral requisites that drive its behavior. In this way, the underlaying concept of a Moral Agent (MA), relies on the existence of moral premises that rule its behavior, differentiating good from evil. It is important not to misunderstand the concept of MA with Moral Patient (MP). While the first has moral obligations, a MP is an entity in which moral rights speak for themselves. Moral agents are in most of the cases moral patients, however this relation is non-reciprocal, as the discussion on delimitating the grounds of MA considers that only a part of MP are in fact capable of being MA. An adult is a MA although a recently born child is solely a MP, being capable, however, of becoming one during his/her life time [9]. This statement that an entity may become during its life time a MA, is indeed very important, once it allows, in an analogous way, to state that an agent, at a given moment, acquire such a property. It is necessary to understand what is a intelligent software agent and which are the characteristics that will allow it to become a MA.

According to Wooldridge, an agent embodies a computational system capable of revealing an autonomous and flexible action, developed in a determined universe of discourse. The flexibility of the agent is related with its capacity of reaction, initiative, learning and socialization [10]. Although the definition may not be considered an universal one, for an organic or software based entity, there exits two levels of intrinsic characteristics, which define in a weak or strong form, whether or not that entity is an intelligent agent. On the one hand, the weak notion of agent represents the minima characteristics of an agent, centering in its capacities of autonomy, reactivity, pro-activity and sociability. On the other hand, in the strong notion of agent, are defined imminently cognitive characteristics, that can result in the development of a self-consciousness by part of the agent and in the enablement of other valuable properties such as perception, sentimentality and emotions [11]. The establishment of this characteristics is an important factor in the contextualization of the designation of intelligent agents in a way to normalize what is in fact and object, and any other form of software based intelligent entities.

The comprehension of these characteristics has to be a analyzed relatively to a Level of Abstraction (LoA) that uniforms them and limit the possibility of relativism on their analysis. Turing first used the notion of LoA to, according to a level established by him, to define intelligence. This concept was used by Floridi and Sander to analyze, according to different LoA the characteristics of intelligent agents before their capacity to undertake moral decisions. Although LoA is a concept derived from Computer Science, more concretely from the disciplines of Formal Methods, that uses discrete mathematics to specify and analyze the behavior of information systems. A LoA consists in a collection of observable, being each one defined by a group of values and results. In other words, before the same entity there exists different LoA that characterize it in a distinct way without adding any type of relativity in the resulting observation. Given a set of values of X well defined, an observable of the type X is the variable which response values are contained in X. A LoA consists then in a collection of observable that are considered on the observation. In a less abstract level, in the case of a car, there can be defined different LoA such as of the buyer, mechanic, insurance officer, all of which present different points and characteristics that, even being distinct, do not present relativity[12].

Depending on the LoA, just as an entity can be considered an object or an intelligent agent, defining the proper LoA the properties that defined a MA can be be of use, being for this reason the notion of LoA used by Floridy and Sanders to define the criteria which must be included in the LoA of a moral agent. The three criteria considered in this LoA are interactivity (a), autonomy (b) and adaptability (c), being the synchronous existence of these characteristics what enables an intelligent agent to become a MA [12]. In order to better analyze these characteristics, one must specify and adequate them with the definition of an agent and, as well, with the state of the art of the development of intelligent agents, namely:

(a) The base for interaction underlaying this study is related with the capacity of the agent to identify and comunicate with other agents, nevertheless their nature, i.e. wether they might be MA or AM, software based or human beings. It can be related with the reactivity described by Wooldridge, before different stimulus provided by the environment where the agent is based. Comparing with the string definition of agent, one can perceive this as the ability to socialize and relate with another.Taking into consideration this property there are norms developed by the Foundation for Intelligent Physical Agents (FIPA) in order to normalize the communication among agents in different systems and based on different technologies [13] [11].

(b) The autonomy of an agent is a function of its grasp on the universe of discourse and must be in line with its own objectives. A moral agent has the capability to change its state without any external intervention that will force it into a particular line of action. Contrary to an object in Object Oriented Programming, a moral agent is not invoked and in a certain way "forced" to execute a determined action; the agent only performs actions according to its own directives. This characteristic is already considered so essential that exists middleware based on Object Oriented Programming, like the Java Agent DEvelopment Framework (JADE), that protect their agents from remote evocation [13].

(c) The adaptability of an agent is linked to its capacity to learn and adapt its own behaviors according to the surrounding environment, without external intervention.

Modeling moral agent behavior is in line with the procedures being used to simulate human moral behavior. Although this simulation may provide a better understanding of human ethical choices and give a new perspective on moral in general, the lines under which an agent evolves its moral codes are yet to be set in order to be used as a mean towards building moral agents [14].

5   Moral Decisions

Considering the LoA used in the previous section, let us consider an Intensive Care Unity (ICU) with 2 (two) monitoring agents. Both agents interact with the environment reading the patients monitoring data, either it comes from cameras, oxygenation level reading devices or electrocardiograms. In a similar way, both agents can alter their procedures, such as altering oxygenation and temperature levels in the room or warning the medical team of the existence of any abnormality. They are also capable to predict future situations, extracting rules from past situations for future use, and to integrate them in the depths of their soul. These agents are ruled by a set of ethic norms, having as their ultimate objective the provision of the best possible service to the patient. Presenting a scenario in this way, are these agents moral agents? According to the LoA of moral agent, one may conclude that yes, they are. Both of them are moral agents, however, one is a human agent, while the other is a software one. In fact, both will be able and probably will commit os ethically dubious, if not incorrect; however, it is clear that contrary to the second case, the responsibility of their actions reflect only upon themselves. In other words, the responsibility in the case of the agent is not so clear to be defined concerning the entity it should reflect, if the agent itself, or its owner, or even other environment input. Its certain that from the developers LoA, an agent is not as independent, pro-active, or interactive as it resembles, once he/she set the rules that the agent has to follow. However, taking into consideration its capacity of adaptation, it is expectable that in the short term it may remodel itself into a version completely distinct from the former one. It acts in the same way as a father that educates a son and transmits to him/her his moral code. However, there is always the question: to whom should be inputted the responsibility of their future actions.

Although the enlargement of the moral agent class in order to include the existence of virtual agents which are also moral agents, is not consensual, i.e. it is valid and advisable considering the inevitability of, during one of its learning cycles, a moral decision presents itself to the agent. It is thereby essential to define a set of principles that will allow an improvement of the agent development process, delimitating the frontier of action and principles that ensure, not only in the future, but as well as in the present, that these systems will work in synergies with society.

Although norms and regulations have been made for standardization of agent argumentation and communication, no similar approach has yet to be successful in the definition of properties that are essential for agents to have when taking actions in an areas such as medicine where sometimes little decision may have humungous ethical drawbacks. While a general ethics code was in fact developed by the Association for Computing Machinery (ACM), this code, though comprised of essential points which are essential for any area and technology, is by this reason not specific enough for the needs of agents developer in the healthcare area [15] A set of guidelines and rules must be defined to clearly state the characteristics an intelligent agent must have to be considered moral agent as well as the division of the developers responsibility, and the major role taken by the environment through machine learning techniques.

6   Modelling Morality with Extended Logic Programming

With respect to the computational paradigm it were considered extended logic programs with two kinds of negation, classical negation, $\neg$, and default negation, *not*. Intuitively, *not p* is true whenever there is no reason to believe p (close world assumption), whereas $\neg p$ requires a proof of the negated literal. An extended logic program (program, for short) is a finite collection of rules and integrity constraints, standing for all their ground instances, and is given in the form:

$$p \leftarrow p_1 \wedge \ldots \wedge p_n \wedge \text{ not } q_1 \wedge \ldots \wedge \text{ not } q_m; \text{ and}$$

$$?p_1 \wedge \ldots \wedge p_n \wedge \text{ not } q_1 \wedge \ldots \wedge \text{ not } q_m, (n, m \geq 0)$$

where ? is a domain atom denoting falsity, the p_i, q_j, and p are classical ground literals, i.e. either positive atoms or atoms preceded by the classical negation sign $\neg$ [16]. Every program is associated with a set of abducibles. Abducibles may be seen as hypotheses that provide possible solutions or explanations of given queries, being given here in the form of exceptions to the extensions of the predicates that make the program.

For example, let us suppose that in the KB (Knowledge Base) of the AgR (agent R) the information related to the areas of expertise of the AgP_i identified as Peter, is represented by the following program:

$area\_of\_expertise("Peter", pediatrics).$
$\neg area\_of\_expertise("Peter", oncologist).$

If the KB is questioned if the area of expertise of Peter is *pharmacy* the answer should be unknown, because there is no information related to that. On other hand, situations of incomplete information may involve different kinds of nulls. The ELP language will be used for the purpose of knowledge representation. One of the null types to be considered stands for an unknown value, a countable one (i.e. it is able to form a one-to-one correspondence with the positive integers). As an example, let us suppose that one of the agents that belong to the agent community AgP, at the registration phase, does not specify its interest topics; it just informs that it has interest topics. This means that the interest topics of the agent are unknown:

$\neg skill(A, B) \leftarrow \text{ not } skill(A, B) \wedge \text{ not } exception(skill(A, B)).$
$exception(skill(A, B)) \leftarrow skill(A, something).$
$skill("John", something).$

Another type of null value denotes information of an enumerated set. Following the previous example, suppose that an agent does not give information related to its availability, but its state of affairs is one of the three: uncommitted, committed or in-action:

$\neg availability(A, B) \leftarrow \text{ not } availability(A, B)$
$\quad \wedge \text{ not } exception(availability(A, B)).$
$exception(availability("John", committed)).$
$exception(availability("John", uncommitted)).$
$exception(availability("John", in\text{-}action)).$

$((exception(availability("John", A)) \vee exception(availability(John, B)))$
$\wedge \neg(exception(availability("John", A))$
$\wedge exception(availability("John", B))).$

The last statement stands for an invariant that denotes that the agent states of committed, uncommitted and in-action are disjointed.

Therefore, being Γ a program in ELP and $g(X)$ a question where X contains variables $X_1 \wedge \ldots \wedge X_n (n \geq 0)$, one gets as an answer:

The answer of Γ to $g(X)$ is *true* iff
$g(X) \rightarrow demo(\Gamma, g(X), true).$
The answer of Γ to $g(X)$ is *false* iff
$\neg g(X) \rightarrow demo(\Gamma, g(X), false).$
The answer of Γ to $g(X)$ is *unknown* iff
not $\neg g(X) \wedge$ not $g(X) \rightarrow demo(\Gamma, g(X), unknown).$

where *unknown* stands for a truth value in the interval 0...1. Being Γ a Program it is possible to define the Minimal Answer Set of Γ ($MAS(\Gamma)$):

$$\Gamma \vdash s \text{ iff } s \in MAS(\Gamma)$$

where $\Gamma \vdash s$ denotes that s is a logical consequence or conclusion for Γ.

Being now AS_i and AS_j two different answer sets of Γ, being E_{ASi} and E_{ASj}, respectively, the extensions of predicates p in AS_i and AS_j, it is defined that AS_i is morally preferable to AS_j ($AS_i \prec AS_j$) where $\prec$ denotes the morally preferable symbol, if for each predicate p_1 it exists a predicate p_2 such that $p_1 < p_2$ and $E_{ASi} \setminus E_{ASj}$ is not empty ($\setminus$ denotes the difference set operator).

7 Conclusions

It is believed that this work is a step in the direction of the final goal of machine ethics, i.e. to create a machine that by itself will follow an ideal ethical principle or set of principles making decisions about possible courses of action it could take. Indeed, it was shown how a machine might abstract an ethical principle from a logical representation of ethical judgments and use that principle to guide its own behavior. A machine that is an explicit ethical agent will be able to calculate the best action in ethical dilemmas using ethical principles. It may represent ethics explicitly and then operate effectively on the basis of this knowledge, here given in terms of logical formulae, understood as productions in a Multi-value Extended Logic Programming Language, as referred to above. On the other hand, and for those that populated the Artificial Intelligence and Logic Programming arenas, it may sanction support for work leading to the development of autonomous intelligent machines that may contribute to improve the lives of human beings. A machine that is an explicit ethical agent will be able to calculate the best action in ethical dilemmas using ethical principles. It will represent ethics explicitly and then operate effectively on the basis of this knowledge.

References

1. Deigh, J. (ed.): Ethics and Personality: Essays in Moral Psychology. Chicago University Press (1992)
2. Deigh, J.: The Sources of Moral Agency: Essays in Moral Psychology and Freudian Theory. Cambridge University Press, Cambridge (1996)
3. Andrade, F., Neves, J., Novais, P., Machado, J.: Software agents as legal persons. Virtual Enterprises and Collaborative Networks 149, 123–132 (2004); CamarinhaMatos, LM 18th World Computer Congress, Toulouse, France, August 22-27 (2004)
4. Andrade, F., Neves, J., Novais, P., Machado, J., Abelha, A.: Legal security and credibility in agent based virtual enterprises. Collaborative Networks and Their Breeding Environments 186, 503–512 (2005); CamarinhaMatos, LM 6th Working Conference on Virtual Enterprises SEP 26-28, Valencia, Spain (2005)
5. Machado, J., Alves, V., Abelha, A., Neves, J.: Ambient intelligence via multiagent systems in medical arena. International Journal of Engineering Intelligent Systems, Special issue on Decision Support Systems 15(3), 167–173 (2007)
6. Nwana, H.S.: Software agents: An overview. In: Knowledge Engineering Review, vol. 11, pp. 1–40. Cambridge University Press, Cambridge (1996)
7. Machado, J., Abelha, A., Novais, P., Neves, J., Neves, J.: Improving patient assistance and medical practices through intelligent agents. In: Workshop on Health Informatics, AAMAS 2008 (2008)
8. Miranda, M., Abelha, A., Santos, M., Machado, J., Neves, J.: A group decision support system for staging of cancer. In: Weerasinghe, D. (ed.) Electronic Healthcare, Springer-Verlag, Series Institute for Computer Sciences, Social Informatics and Telecommunications Engineering (2009)
9. Himma, K.E.: Artificial agency, consciousness, and the criteria for moral agency: what properties must an artificial agent have to be a moral agent? In: Ethics and Information Technology. Springer, Heidelberg (2008)
10. Wooldridge, M.J.: Multiagent Systems – A Modern Approach to Distributed Artificial Intelligence. MIT Press, Cambridge (1999)
11. Wooldridge, M., Jennings, N.R.: Intelligent agents: Theory and practice, vol. 10, pp. 115–152. Cambridge University Press, Cambridge (1995)
12. Floridi, L., Sanders, J.W.: On the morality of artificial agents, Hingham, MA, USA, vol. 4, pp. 349–679. Kluwer Academic Publishers, Dordrecht (2004)
13. Bellifemine, F., Caire, G., Greenwood, D.: Developing Multi-Agent Systems with JADE. John Wiley & Sons, Chichester (2007)
14. Pereira, L.M., Saptawijaya, A.: Modelling morality with prospective logic. In: Neves, J., Santos, M.F., Machado, J.M. (eds.) EPIA 2007. LNCS (LNAI), vol. 4874, pp. 99–111. Springer, Heidelberg (2007)
15. ACM: Code of ethics and professional conduct (January 2009)
16. Analide, C., Abelha, A., Machado, J., Neves, J.: An agent based approach to the selection dilemma in cbr. In: Badica, C., Mangioni, G., Carchiolo, V., Burdescu, D. (eds.) Intelligent Distributed Computing, Systems and Applications. Studies in Computer Science, vol. 162, Springer, Heidelberg (2008)

Requirements for Electronic Delivery Systems in eGovernment – An Austrian Experience

Arne Tauber

IAIK, Graz University of Technology
Arne.Tauber@iaik.tugraz.at

Abstract. Electronic mailing systems are the dominant communication systems in private and business matters. Public administrations deliver documents to citizens and businesses – subpoenas, legal verdicts, notifications, administrative penalties etc. However, official activities are more strongly linked to legal regulations than in civil law. Delivery of crucial and strictly personal documents raises the demand for qualified identification and non-repudiation services as featured by registered mail in the paper world. Legal requirements for electronic delivery carried-out by public administrations (eDelivery) cannot be fulfilled by standard certified mailing systems. Although the requirements for eDelivery systems may differ due to national legal regulations, this paper discusses common requirements and challenges on an abstract level. Moreover, we show how these requirements have been addressed by introducing the Austrian eDelivery system for eGovernment applications.

Keywords: eGovernment, Registered Mail, Certified Mail, Electronic Delivery.

1 Introduction

Electronic mail (e-mail) has become the most popular communication method in our daily life – we are used to write and receive e-mails when communicating with friends, families, relatives or even in business matters when submitting contracts or invoices. This has been confirmed by a survey [1] reporting that about 90% of active internet users in Austria are using the internet for communication purposes.

Electronic communication is of great importance not only in the private and business sector. The delivery of documents such as notifications, administrative penalties, permits or laws, is a fundamental and resource-intensive task for governments and public administrations. For instance, the Austrian Treasury and Ministry of Justice deliver more than 44 million documents each year. The transition to electronic delivery systems (further denoted as eDelivery systems) is a key requirement towards service-oriented architectures in eGovernment. Electronic delivery has still to be considered as a value-added service and will not replace paper-based delivery at least for the next decades. Reduced costs associated with delays and saving paper, 7 x 24 availability and improved accessibility are the promises. Delivery is one of the last steps in public proceedings and raises the demand for an electronic counterpart in order to avoid media-breaks for processes carried-out fully electronically.

C. Godart et al. (Eds.): I3E 2009, IFIP AICT 305, pp. 123–133, 2009.

Due to the high penetration rate e-mail seems to be the first choice when looking for communication media serving different kind of transactions – from citizens to administrations (C2A), administrations to citizens (A2C), businesses to administrations (B2A), administrations to businesses (A2B) as well as administrations to administrations (A2A). However, official activities are more strongly bound to legal regulations than in civil law and applied tools and technologies have to be almost legally regulated. Especially the justice sector requires a receiver to prove her identity in a qualified way when delivering crucial documents. A typical example is a subpoena, a written command to a person to testify before a court. A signed proof of receipt further guarantees that a receiver has picked-up the delivery at a certain point of time and thus are a valid evidence in public proceedings.

Several EU member states have already recognized the need for legal regulations concerning administrative deliveries. A number of domestic laws and regulations have been enacted in the last years providing the basis for qualified eDelivery systems. Austria has introduced its eDelivery system early in 2004. Looking at the national level of other EU member states there are similar initiatives such as DE-Mail [2] in Germany, Posta Elettronica Certificata (PEC) [3] in Italy or Secure Mailbox in Slovenia. From a local point of view, several Austrian ministries have launched a closed mailing system, e.g. the Austrian eDelivery system for legal relations (ERV) [4] provided by the Ministry of Justice or the eDelivery system for communications with tax authorities (FinanzOnline[1] - DataBox) provided by the Austrian Treasury.

Although the mentioned eDelivery systems are based on different national legal regulations and thus are implemented in different ways, this paper discusses common requirements on an abstract level. In the remainder of this paper we identify these requirements, discuss technologies backing qualified eDelivery systems and practical experiences gained in the Austrian case. In section 2 requirements and challenges to eDelivery systems are discussed. Although these requirements and challenges are specific to the public sector, some can be found in the private sector as well. In section 3 we discuss the common eDelivery architecture and addressing approaches from an abstract point of view. We continue in section 4 with discussing the Austrian electronic delivery system for eGovernment applications to show how requirements, challenges and security technologies have been implemented nationwide on the large scale. Synergies with the private sector to make eDelivery systems economic and initiatives towards cross-border delivery reducing barriers to EU member states are briefly discussed in section 5. Finally, conclusions are drawn.

2   Requirements and Challenges to eDelivery Systems

Registered mail is a fundamental vehicle in traditional means of carrying out public administration. In many cases subpoenas, legal verdicts, notifications, permits or administrative penalties are served by registered mail. In the private sector we are used to serve submits for bidding processes, contracts, dismissals etc. by registered mail. Registered mail gives the sender the guarantee of having sent a delivery at a certain point of time. Depending on the case, public authorities may require a qualified proof of

---

[1] https://finanzonline.bmf.gv.at

receipt to have legal evidence that a receiver picked-up a delivery at a certain point of time. This is determinant, e.g. for the commencement of the period for appeal. Deliveries may further be strictly personal meaning only the receiver herself can pick-up the delivery. Standard deliveries can usually be picked-up by families, relatives or neighbors as well. Qualified identification and a signed proof of delivery give evidence to public authorities on who has picked-up a delivery.

Based on the considerations made so far we can sketch the basic requirements for qualified eDelivery systems:

1. *Qualified identification:* qualified identification is a fundamental requirement for public administrations when delivering documents strictly personal. Usually receivers prove their identity by showing their passport, identity card, driver's license or another official ID. EDelivery systems must therefore guarantee that receiver registration is based on a reliable identification procedure. Most certified mail systems provide non-repudiation concerning a particular address or mail-box. This does not apply to eDelivery systems where qualified identification is a fundamental requirement.

2. *Non-repudiation services:* legal provisions may force an eDelivery system to provide a delivery confirmation and/or a qualified proof of delivery. The former gives evidence to public authorities of having sent the delivery at a certain point of time. The latter gives evidence to public authorities that a receiver has picked-up the delivery at a certain point of time. EDelivery systems must thus provide non-repudiation services offering protection against false denial of involvement as described in RFC 2828 [5]. These services must include "non-repudiation with proof of origin" and "non-repudiation with proof of receipt" to provide an electronic delivery confirmation and/or a digital proof of receipt containing a timestamp and an electronic signature of the receiving unit (either the receiver herself or her service provider). Implementation guidelines concerning non-repudiation protocols are given in [6][7].

3. *Trust:* citizens shall innately trust the eDelivery system they are using. Therefore, entities acting as trusted third party (TTP) must be approved by governmental controlling institutions.

Standard communication systems such as e-mail have their limitations and cannot provide qualified identification or qualified proofs of receipt. Even in most certified mailing systems there is a lack of qualified identification. In the remainder of this section we discuss further requirements that may be part of eDelivery systems depending on legal regulations. Several requirements can already be partially handled by standard or certified mailing systems:

4. *Privacy, integrity, confidentiality and authenticity:* analogous to the privacy of correspondence in the paper world, eDelivery systems must ensure that the content of deliveries cannot be altered and can be solely disclosed to the receiver. It should be evident that the delivery origin is authentic backed by security technologies on the transport or application layer.

5. *Delivery quality:* legal regulations may provide different quality levels concerning administrative deliveries. These levels could range from standard deliveries with no further requirements to qualified deliveries offering non-repudiation services. Delivery qualities may further define dedicated receiver groups, e.g. that a delivery can only be picked-up by the receiver herself or even by an authorized representative.

6. *Representation:* an eDelivery system must support communications between citizens and administrations (C2A, A2C) as well as communications between businesses and administrations (B2A, A2B). It must be ensured in a technical or organizational way that deliveries to businesses can only be picked-up by authorized representatives, e.g. the registered manager of a company or other authorized business employees.

7. *Look-up service:* if allowed by legal regulations, a look-up service could facilitate the search for a particular receiver. Such a service could be useful in heterogeneous or federated delivery systems featuring a broad range of delivery service providers.

8. *Interoperability:* service architectures and protocols must be standardized to ensure interoperability between all entities of the eDelivery system. Open standards should be used for transparency, freedom of choice and to facilitate interoperability, also in terms of cross-border on the large scale.

9. *Absence:* citizens may not be able to pick-up deliveries, e.g. when being on vacation or being hospitalized. EDelivery systems should therefore allow the absence of receivers concerning commencements of the period for appeal.

10. *Accessibility:* eDelivery systems should be designed for ease of access by enabling participants to use commodity products such as e-mail clients or web browser. The installation of additional software on the client side should be minimized wherever applicable.

3 Architectural and Technical Considerations

In this section we discuss architectural and technical issues of eDelivery systems on an abstract level. We aim to identify the main entities of such a system and to address requirements for a qualified identification. From an abstract point of view qualified eDelivery systems can be seen as a closed communication system providing different services for its participants. Technical, organizational and legal policies are usually defined by legal regulations on a local, regional or national level.

The common architecture of eDelivery systems for eGovernment applications is illustrated in fig. 1. This architecture has been sketched on a very high abstraction level and identifies four types of entities: service providers, receivers, senders and an optional look-up service.

Similar to standard mail providers, *service providers* run communication services allowing the transmission of qualified deliveries. It is practically impossible to provide a qualified delivery system on the large scale without trusted third parties (TTP). TTPs must follow legal provisions and are usually approved by governmental controlling institutions. *Receivers* have to register with at least one service provider and can receive deliveries depending on their identification quality. This means that receivers should only be able to pick-up "strictly personal" deliveries if and only if they are registered based on an official ID. Standard deliveries could even be picked up using a pretended identity like in standard mailing systems. Following the EU Signature Directive [8], many EU member states have already introduced electronic IDs (eID) based on qualified signature certificates. Such eIDs have the same legal impact as traditional official IDs in the context of public services. It is obvious that eDelivery systems for eGovernment applications are supposed to enable eIDs in order to be carried-out fully electronically. This applies to registration processes as well as the qualified identification of receivers when picking-up of deliveries.

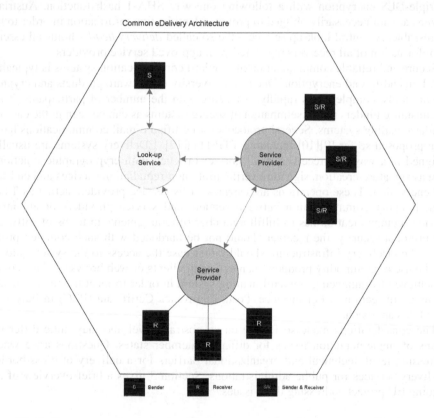

Fig. 1. Common architecture of an eDelivery system for eGovernment applications

Depending on legal provisions *senders* must not necessarily register with a service provider. However, authenticity of senders should be ensured in some way. Digital Signatures or SSL/TLS client authentication are e.g. technologies backing an adequate authentication on the transport layer. On the application layer electronic signatures could guarantee authenticity of senders. If a service provider supports the feature of sending deliveries, receivers could act as senders and vice versa.

There are a number of approaches ensuring a reliable addressing of receivers. Unique identifiers are a common way to address entities in communication systems. DE-Mail in Germany and PEC in Italy make use of identifiers based on the common e-mail address format, e.g. givenname.familyname@systemprovider.it. In this way citizens can provide their eDelivery address when applying for public services. Another approach is to use a unique national ID as a basis for reliable addressing a receiver. Austria introduced a so called delivery specific personal identification number – a derivation of a citizen's assigned unique identification number held in the base registers – the Central Residents Register (CRR) and the Supplementary Register for persons who do not have a registered address in Austria. For data protection reasons public authorities are not allowed to use the CRR number in public proceedings. The delivery specific PIN is therefore a derivation using strong cryptography by applying a Triple-DES encryption with a following one-way SHA-1 hash function. Austrian citizens are not necessarily obliged to provide identification information in order to be addressable. A central look-up service – the so called *delivery head* – holds all essential information of all receivers registered with approved service providers.

Secure and reliable communication in standard communication systems is typically based on end-to-end encryption. Due to the diversity of software products and cryptographic tools, complexity is rapidly increasing with the number of participants. This circumstance hinders the dissemination of secure systems as can be seen in the case of standard mailing systems. Several protocols for certified e-mail communications have been proposed so far [9][10] including TTPs[11][12]. EDelivery systems are usually designed in a way that receivers shall not get in touch with cryptographic functions such as signature creation, signature verification, non-repudiation services and end-to-end encryption. These operations are carried-out by service providers acting as TTP. Even if entity communication between senders and service providers or an intra-provider communication has to fulfill a number of requirements in terms of software and protocol security, the receiver should not be burdened with such complex processes. An eDelivery infrastructure should rather ease the access to the system allowing the use of commodity products such as e-mail clients or web browsers. This could be achieved by enhancing standard mailing system in order to meet the requirements discussed in section 2. For instance, Posta Elettronica Certificata (PEC) in Italy followed this approach.

The considerations made so far are on an abstract level and may quite differ by means of implementation issues for different member states. Questions arise when addressing legal, technical and organizational barriers for a delivery of cross-border eDelivery services for public administrations. Section 5 gives a brief overview of an ongoing EU project addressing these issues.

4   The Austrian Delivery System for eGovernment Applications

In this section we discuss how the considerations made so far have been implemented on a national level by introducing the Austrian eDelivery system for eGovernment applications. Policies and general requirements are laid down by the Austrian eGovernment Act – enacted on 1st March 2004 – which provides the legal basis to facilitate electronic communications with public bodies. In the remainder of this section we discuss architectures, main process building blocks, open standards and security technologies backing the Austrian eDelivery system.

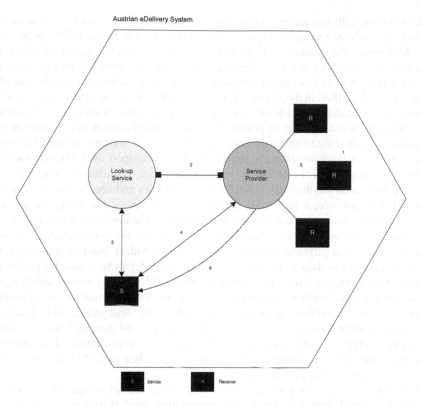

Fig. 2. Architecture of the Austrian eDelivery system

Fig. 2 shows the architecture of the Austrian eDelivery system for eGovernment applications. From an abstract point of view the main entities are as follows:

1. **Service providers:** as long as legal, technical and organizational provisions are fulfilled, any public body or business can operate as service provider. A service provider can only be approved by the Federal Chancellor and must offer a number of basic services such as the receipt of administrative deliveries and several non-repudiation services.
2. **Receivers:** all Austrian citizens and businesses can register with any service provider. Once the citizen or business is registered, all public administrations can address the receiver by electronic means. Electronic delivery is free of charge for receivers.
3. **Senders:** all Austrian public bodies are allowed to deliver documents to registered receivers.
4. **Look-up service:** the main look-up service (so called *delivery head*) can be seen as a register holding the data of all receivers. Service providers are therefore required to communicate all registered receivers to the look-up service.

(1) Registration with service providers can only be carried-out with the Austrian citizen card, the official electronic identification (eID) of citizens for online public services. Moreover, the citizen card offers the option of creating qualified electronic signatures. As stated by the EU Signature Directive, qualified signatures have the same legal impact as handwritten signatures. The security architecture of the Austrian citizen card is described in detail in [13]. Registration with service providers is explicitly voluntary as electronic delivery can be seen as an add-on service to traditional means of carrying-out delivery of printed documents. Registration of corporate bodies is based on so called electronic mandates. As citizen cards are only issued to physical persons, the Austrian eGovernment movement has developed an XML-scheme [14] for electronic mandates, the technical vehicle for acting on someone else's behalf. Electronic mandates are digitally signed XML structures and can be stored on a citizen's eID. For instance, a registered manager of a company can apply for an electronic postal mandate and accordingly act on behalf of the company when registering with a service provider. Postal mandates are available for representation of both corporate bodies and physical persons. (2) Service providers must communicate the receiver's registration data to the look-up service in order to be found by public authorities. Among personal data like delivery specific PIN, given name, family name, date of birth, e-mail address, a service provider has to communicate an optionally supplied X.509 encryption certificate for end-to-end encryption, the receiver's preferred document formats - e.g. PDF or MS-Office - and declared absence times. End-to-end encryption between senders and receivers is only applied if the receiver explicitly wishes this additional security layer by providing an X.509 encryption certificate in order to receive encrypted e-mails.

(3) In order to search for particular receivers, public authorities are forced to register with the central look-up service. The registration process is based on SSL/TLS X.509 client certificates having an appropriate attribute (Austrian eGovernment OID [15]) to assure that only public authorities can register with the look-up service. Using object identifiers to define appropriate attributes (OID) is a common practice in public key infrastructure (PKI). The supplied certificate must be used for searching receivers at the look-up service as well as for transmission of deliveries to a service provider. Public authorities are allowed to search for receivers using particular parameters such as given name, family name, date of birth and the e-mail address. Public authorities are not always aware of the citizen's e-mail address, e.g. in the case of traffic offence penalties. They are therefore recommended to use the encrypted unique delivery specific PIN for searching receivers that can be obtained by querying a frontend service of the Central Residents Register (CRR). For data protection reasons public authorities are never in the possession of the plain delivery specific PIN, it is rather protected using strong cryptography (RSA 1024bit) and can only be decrypted by the look-up service. Requests to the look-up service are sent using a HTTPs GET request based on SSL client authentication. Search parameters are passed as HTTP GET encoded parameters. Returned search results are based on an XML structure containing all service providers a receiver is registered with. For data protection reasons the look-up service must provide a limited result set only - the web service location of the service provider, preferred document formats and an optional encryption certificate, if the receiver has supplied one. In case of absence or a receiver has never registered with a service provider, a *not found* answer will be returned by the look-up service.

(4) If a receiver could be found, the public authority transmits the delivery to the web service location of the service provider returned by the look-up service. SSL client certificates with a public authority OID assure authenticity of senders on the transport layer. Public authorities are advised to electronically sign documents before delivery to assure authenticity on application layer. By 2011 all administrative processes bound to the General Administrative Process Law [16] are obliged to digitally sign official copies. The transmission of electronic deliveries is based on the Soap with Attachments (SwA) protocol supplying a MIME container. The SOAP part contains particular data to identify the receiver's delivery account such as the encrypted delivery specific PIN as well as additional metadata concerning unique reference numbers or delivery qualities. Attached binary documents are supplied within the MIME part of the SwA message. If a receiver has supplied a certificate for end-to-end encryption, a SMIME container is supplied respectively. The use of (S) MIME containers ensures the interoperability with standard e-mail clients. Service providers can either provide the MIME container in a well structured form through a web-interface or forward the container to the receiver's standard e-mail account.

(5) After having accepted a delivery, service providers must notify the receiver by electronic means, e.g. e-mail or SMS that a delivery is ready to be picked-up. If the delivery will not be picked-up within 48 hours, a second notification is sent-out. The receiver can pick-up the delivery logging in at the web interface of the service provider with her citizen card and sign a delivery confirmation with her qualified signature certificate. The delivery confirmation is as an XML document and must be signed following the XMLDSIG [17] standard. Receivers can optionally login using a standard mail client based on SSL client authentication. In this case the delivery confirmation must be signed by the service provider. The Austrian eDelivery system distinguishes between two delivery qualities - qualified deliveries (RSa) and standard deliveries.

(6) RSa requires a service provider to return the signed confirmation back to the sending public authority either by e-mail or a SOAP based web service. If a receiver does not pick-up the delivery in time an appropriate non-delivery confirmation is returned as well.

So far not all Austrian citizens are registered for electronic delivery and printed documents are still dominating the world of delivery. In order to encourage public authorities to integrate their services into the eDelivery system, the Austrian eGovernment movement has developed the concept of *dual delivery*. This concept follows the *fire-and-forget* pattern allowing all kinds of deliveries to be carried-out over one single interface. If a receiver cannot be found querying the look-up service, the document will be printed out and delivered using conventional channels, e.g. by post.

5 Ongoing and Future Work

The low frequency of electronic deliveries a year raises the demand for synergies with the private sector to make systems deployed on the large scale economic. Registered mail is a fundamental vehicle in the private sector when delivery of crucial documents asks for a qualified proof of receipt. Legal provisions allow businesses to make use of the Austrian eDelivery system with limitations. By using national and international standards a specification meeting the requirements for shared use of both governmental and business processes has been published this year. A service following this specification has recently been put into practice by an approved service provider and other providers are encouraged to follow suit.

With the introduction of the EU Service Directive [18] cross-border eGovernment gets on the agenda of all EU member states. The ongoing EU Large Scale Pilot "STORK" [19] aims to achieve interoperability by bridging public services based on different legislations. Austria has the lead of Pilot 4, the so called eDelivery pilot[2] focused on coupling eDelivery systems of different Member states.

6 Conclusions

Registered mail is a fundamental vehicle in the paper world. With respect to electronic communications, standard mailing systems do not meet the requirements for an adequate qualified delivery. Several EU member states have already delivered eDelivery services based on domestic legal regulations. Even if at first sight these systems seem to quite differ from each other, common requirements such as qualified identification and non-repudiation services can be identified. Furthermore, this paper discusses common architectural characteristics of eDelivery systems on an abstract level by identifying the main entities and requirements. Considerations regarding reliable identification, authentication and confidentiality are made and discussed.

As an example the Austrian eDelivery system facilitating electronic communications with public bodies is discussed. This use case demonstrates how requirements stated so far have been implemented on basis of Austrian legal regulations. Open standards and security technologies backing the Austrian eDelivery system are discussed as well. Ongoing work regarding the demand for synergies with the private sector in order to make such a system deployed on the large scale economic is briefly noted. Finally, a short outlook to the EU large scale pilot STORK is given, addressing cross-border interoperability by coupling eDelivery domains of different member states.

References

1. STATISTIK Austria, ICT Usage in Households (2008) (in German)
2. DE-Mail: Richtlinie für Bürgerportale, Version 0.98 (03.02.2009) (in German)
3. PEC: Regole tecniche del servizio di trasmissione di documenti informatici mediante posta elettronica certificata (in Italian)
4. Ornetsmueller, G.: WEB-ERV – ERVService, Version 1.1 (March 15, 2007)
5. Shirey, R.: RFC 2828, Internet Security Glossary (May 2000)
6. ISO/IEC 13888, Information technology - Security techniques - Non-repudiation
7. ISO/IEC DIS 10181, Information technology - Open systems innterconnection - Security framework in open systems
8. European Parliament and Council, Directive 1999/93/EC on a Community framework for electronic signatures

---

[2] The author of this paper is involved in this pilot.

9. Schneider, B., Riordan, J.: A Certified E-Mail Protocol. In: Proceedings, of 14th Annual Computer Security Applications Conference (1998)
10. Al-Hammadi, B., Shahsavari, M.: Certified exchange of electronic mail (CEEM). In: Southeastcon 1999. Proceedings. IEEE, Los Alamitos (1999)
11. Oppliger, R., Stadlin, P.: A certified mail system (CMS) for the Internet. Computer Communications 27 (2004)
12. Puigserver, M.M., Gomila, J.L.F., Rotger, L.H.: Certified e-mail protocol with verifiable third party. In: EEE 2005. Proceedings (2005)
13. Leitold, H., Hollosi, A., Posch, R.: Security Architecture of the Austrian Citizen Card Concept. In: Proceedings of 18th Annual Computer Security Applications Conference (2002)
14. Rössler, T., Hollosi, A.: Elektronische Vollmachten Spezifikation 1.0.0 (2006) (in German)
15. Hollosi, A., Leitold, H., Rössler, T.: Object Identifier der öffentlichen Verwaltung (2007) (in German)
16. General Administrative Process Law 1991 – AVG. BGBl. 1991/51 idF BGBl. 2004/10 (in German)
17. Eastlake, D., Reagle, J., Solo, D.: XML Signature Syntax and Processing, W3C Recommendation (2002)
18. Directive 2006/123/EC of the European Parliament and of the Council, of 12 December 2006 on services in the internal market
19. STORK: STORK – An overview (March 12, 2009)

Facilitating Business to Government Interaction Using a Citizen-Centric Web 2.0 Model

Alexandros Dais, Mara Nikolaidou, and Dimosthenis Anagnostopoulos

Harokopio University of Athens, Department of Informatics and Telematics,
El. Venizelou 70, 17671, Athens
{adais,mara,dimosthe}@hua.gr

Abstract. Modelling Business to Government (B2G) interaction is considered to be more complex than Citizen to Government (C2G) interaction, since the concept of authorized citizens, representing the Business while interacting with specific governmental organizations should be explored. Novel interaction models should be introduced, transforming the way Governmental services are delivered to Businesses. To this end, we propose a Web 2.0 citizen-centric model facilitating Business to Government interaction by establishing a social network between citizens and public agencies. All kinds of interactions (B2G, G2G) are expressed as C2G interactions establishing the citizen-centric nature of the proposed interaction model. The architecture of a Web 2.0 platform, named MyCCP, based on the suggested interaction model is also presented, along with a case study illustrating business-to-government interaction to indicate the potential of the suggested model.

Keywords: Business to Government interaction model, Citizen Centric Model, Web 2.0, T- Gov.

1 Introduction

Whole-of-government approach is the current trend in providing complex cross-organizational e-services to citizens by supporting a "central portal" acting as a "single access point" for all services, either cross-organizational or not [1]. The integration and coordination of existing services, provided by independent public agencies, in an automated and transparent fashion is explored in the case of "active life event portal" [2]. Life events constitute a grouping mechanism of public e-services according to citizen needs. In particular, each life event corresponds to a workflow pre-composed by existing e-services and executed by the citizen as a single application. Such services are currently provided through a "central portal" acting as a "single access point" for all governmental services either cross-organizational or not.

Modelling Business to Government (B2G) interaction is considered to be more complex than Citizen to Government (C2G) interaction, since the concept of an authorized citizen, that represent the Business while interacting with a specific governmental organization should be introduced. Similar to the real world, in the digital world, a business should be considered as a legal entity represented by authorized

C. Godart et al. (Eds.): I3E 2009, IFIP AICT 305, pp. 134–147, 2009.
© IFIP International Federation for Information Processing 2009

citizens when interaction with the state. Thus, new requirements are imposed when modelling B2G interaction, not effectively handled in case of complex cross-organizational services, where the Business is represented by different citizens when interacting with different governmental agencies. In such case, relations between businesses, citizens, as well as among government agencies, should be established and managed. Furthermore more effective interaction models are needed for cross organizational integration, while innovative service delivery and enforcement of privacy and confidentiality should also be considered.

The adoption of the Web 2.0 paradigm to effectively model B2G interaction is a challenge resulting in the transformation of B2G service delivery. B2G service delivery transformation can be regarded as part of the Transformational Government (T-Gov) concept [3]. T-Gov requirements, as expressed in terms of citizen-centric delivery of public services and effective cross-organizational interoperability, could be fulfilled utilizing Web 2.0 concepts. Though Web 2.0 can not be perceived as a single new technology or standard, it can be outlined by its key features which revolve around the notions of a user built, user-centred and user-run Internet [4]. The most prominent example of the Web 2.0 paradigm is social computing. A new generation of web-based communities are rapidly becoming popular among people worldwide. In fact, an entire generation of young people has come of age using Internet as the dominant medium for socializing. These virtual communities are familiar with the interaction mechanisms provided by the social networking platforms. Eventually, Web 2.0 environment, emphasizing on collaboration and communication, will gradually affect citizens' perception of electronic government and will contribute to the transformation of government structures and services. A corresponding interaction model should take into consideration every kind of relationship between the constituents of T-Gov, namely citizens, business and government agencies, and allow them to communicate in a seamless, simple fashion, similar to one they are used to in real life.

In the following, we introduce a citizen-centric model for B2G interaction by adopting the Web 2.0 perspective. Basic characteristics of B2G service delivery are defined in section 2. The proposed interaction model is described in section 3. The architecture of a Web 2.0 platform, named MyCCP, based on the suggested interaction model is briefly presented in section 4. In section 5 a case study is described, illustrating business-to-government interaction to indicate the potential of the suggested model, while conclusions reside in section 6.

2 Transforming B2G Service Delivery

Business to Government (B2G) interaction is considered to be more complex to handle than Citizen to Government (C2G), as businesses are often represented by authorized employees that actually interact with the government to complete a specific task. Those employees are actually intermediates between the Business and the Government. Elaborating the model, we argue that authorized employees are actual citizens performing authorized tasks inside the context of a specific B2G service. So any B2G service should be decomposed to corresponding C2G services forming it. Such decomposition poses new requirements.

First of all citizens should be authorized to act as intermediates for a business. The authorization process should be formal and legally correct. Non repudiation methods should be enforced to bind citizens to their actions. Furthermore, the authorization mechanism should be agile. Relations between the citizens the business should be handled in a proper way.

Additionally, intermediates should only view the information that is required to accomplish their task and certainly not every kind of business information. Confidentiality and privacy issues should be addressed to prevent unauthorized access to business information. So, data handling is considered a major requirement to be fulfilled.

The distributed nature of B2G service decomposition requires some sort of central control. In the real word, there is always someone that is liable to governmental laws, acts and regulations as far as the business is concerned.

Last but not least, cross organizational tasks often requires the involvement of many intermediates. So there is a need for the intermediates to collaborate in an asynchronous and distributed way to accomplish a common goal. So, a reliable interaction mechanism between the intermediates should exist.

Furthermore, issues related to Authentication, Data Integrity and Availability should be addressed. While confidentiality deals with the unintentional disclosure of information outside the authorized parameters, data integrity assures the trustworthiness of the information and availability ensures that the information is made available to authorized intermediates.

Taking into account the requirements mentioned before, we propose a Citizen-Centric Model for Business to Government interaction utilizing most of Web 2.0 conceptual and technical characteristics. Technical Web 2.0 characteristics refer, among other things, to rich application interfaces, syndication and micro content delivery. The conceptual features of the Web 2.0 paradigm emphasise on the collaboration and communication, providing great opportunities for citizen-centric service delivery, improved citizen participation and rich citizen connection between the citizen and the public sector. The adoption of the web 2.0 features in electronic Governance is discussed in [5] [6].

3   B2G Interaction Modeling Based on a Web 2.0 Citizen-Centric Model

A thorough governance model should take into account all types of governmental interaction (C2G, B2G, G2G). The proposed model is focused on B2G interaction, which is consecutively decomposed to multiple C2G interactions. In fact, every interaction (B2G, G2G) is decomposed to C2G interactions revealing a true citizen-centric model. The interaction model has been implemented as a social network with two kinds of relations: between citizens and between citizen and the government.

Government is an abstract term. The government sector consists of Public Agencies (PA) which are represented in the model through the Applications they provide. The design, the implementation, the development and the maintenance of the application is performed by the PA's IT sectors. PA Applications reside and executed in the corresponding PA IT infrastructure.

Citizens are represented in the model through the Citizen's Profiles, which are considered as the fundamental components of the model. The importance of the citizen's profiles arises from the fact that every interaction with the governmental services has to pass through them. The Citizen Profile entity consists of three sections, namely Citizen, Business and Views as illustrated in figure 1.

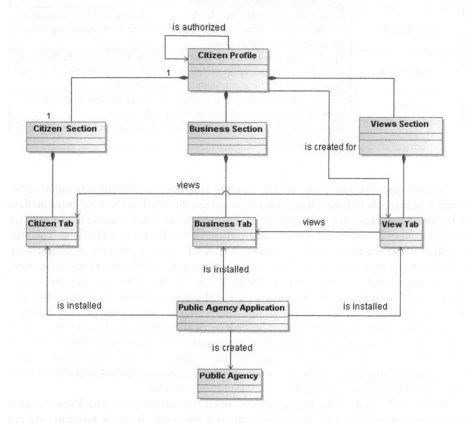

Fig. 1. A meta-model for Web 2.0 citizen-centric interaction

Figure 1 depicts the basic entities used to describe all types of interaction in a Web 2.0 citizen-centric fashion. Table 1, associated to the figure 1, further elaborates associations among the model's entities.

The Citizen Section of the Profile models Citizen to Government interaction. For consistency reasons the citizen section includes one and only Citizen Tab. The citizen tab can be considered as the personal data vault where the citizen can add information (by installing specific public agency applications) concerning his/her interaction with the government. For example, the citizen section could contain information about his/her studies, his tax status and so on. Cross organizational tasks can be accomplished by installing several applications from different public agencies and sharing the information that resides into the citizen tab among them. The installation of the applications into the citizen tab is depicted by the "is installed" association between the citizen tab and the public agency application.

Table 1. Description of the association among Web 2.0 citizen-centric model entities

Association	Description
is authorized	A citizen profile can authorize another citizen profile. A formal authorization scheme is adopted.
is created for	A view tab is created inside the views section of the intermediate for the specific citizen profile (either citizen or business tag) when the authorization takes place.
is installed	Applications can be installed in the citizen tab and in the business tab. They can also be installed on behalf of the citizen tab or the business tab and be administered in the view tab.
views	A view tab remotely administers some applications that consist a view of the business tab or the citizen tab.
is created	Applications are created by the Public Agencies and are uploaded in the platform registry.

The Business Section of the profile models Business to Government interaction. When a business is initiated, there must be a citizen declared as the legal intermediate of the business. This citizen is liable to governmental laws, acts and regulations as far as the business is concerned. Upon initialization of the business a Business Tab will be added inside the Business Section of the Citizen Profile. A citizen can administrate multiple businesses, so multiple business tabs can exist inside the business section. The citizen should be able to add applications on "his/her" business tab, to accomplished tasks on behalf of the business. This is the most simplified Business to Government interaction. In the real world, this interaction is more complex, as a business (or more accurately the citizen that is in charge of the business) often declares other citizens to accomplish tasks on behalf of the business. The interaction becomes even more complex when a business declares another business to represent it and accomplish governmental tasks. Thus, the notion of the Business or even Citizen Representative, as an intermediate, should be supported by the model.

The Views Section of the profile is introduced for that purpose. The Views section is decomposed to View Tabs that are instantiated when the citizen is asked to perform a task on behalf of another business or citizen, as an intermediate. An authorization procedure among citizen profiles is followed, the outcome of which is the creation of customized view tabs ("is created for" association of Table 1). The authorization scheme which is adopted requires a notification of the citizen profile and the explicit consent of the citizen to that request ("is authorized" association of Table 1). Consequently, the authorized citizen can install applications in the view tab that administers. Conceptually, the application is installed and executed in the business tab of the citizen that triggered the authorization. The authorized citizen remotely administers some applications that consists a view of the business tab ("views" association of Table 1). The output of the application is loaded on the business tab, which acts as a reference point for the coordination, the information extraction and the control of the applications, and is viewed or accessed by the view tab. The decomposition of business tab to views is also necessary to preserve sensitive business data and to enforce control over business processes. When cross organizational tasks are involved coordination of all the citizens that administer the business tab of the business should be supported.

Citizen to Citizen interactions to accomplish governmental tasks are also modeled. A citizen can authorize another citizen or business (more accurately a citizen that administers a business). The authorized citizen will act, on behalf on the citizen, by adding applications into the view tab of the citizen. The authorization process can involve more than one step. A citizen can authorize another citizen which authorizes another citizen to accomplish the same or part of the initial task and so on. The model is working, as the reference point for the coordination remains the business and the citizen tab.

To conclude, citizens may have multiple properties, as in the real world. They are mainly citizens with their attributes (Citizen Section), they can also administer a business that requires interaction with the Government (Business Section) and finally can accomplish a task on behalf of another citizen or business as a properly authorized intermediate (Views Section). Conceptually, a social network is created. Special effort was placed so as the model to be simple, accurate and consistent. Citizens provide the content to the platform, using the necessary applications. It is up to them to decide whether they will share their private content with other citizens or public agencies to accomplish complex or cross organizational tasks.

Simplicity can be considered as another key feature of the model. As, it is mentioned in the "Laws of Simplicity" book the "the simplest way to achieve simplicity is through thoughtful reduction" [7]. The model was intentionally designed without complex Government to Government integration schemas leaving the interaction workflow to the citizens

4   MyCPP Platform

To support the suggested Web 2.0 citizen-centric interaction model, a corresponding platform, named MyCCP, is proposed. Its purpose is to provide an easy to use interface for citizens to built and manage their profiles, using Web 2.0 technology, while at the same time it provides for PA application registration and integration in a concise manner.

Applications are developed and deployed by public agencies, integrated in MyCCP platform and finally delivered to citizens, operating as MyCCP users. From the technological perspective, key technical features of the Web 2.0 paradigm such as rich application interfaces, syndication and micro content delivery should be integrated within MyCCP to enhance service delivery to citizens. From the public agencies point of view, applications are running on their IT infrastructure and invoked as web services based on the concepts of Web Oriented Architectures (WOA) [8]. Representational state transfer protocol (REST) [9] has been adopted as the architectural style of API development. Applications should be authenticated by the platform and registered in an application registry. Both citizens and PA IT personnel, uploading applications, should be properly authenticated using the necessary certificates to enhance privacy and trust.

4. 1 Architecture

MyCCP platform architecture is depicted in figure 2. It consists of three layers: integration, interaction and application layer. The integration layer provides the necessary low level functionality for the Public Agencies to develop and integrate applications within the platform. The interaction layer provides built-in services for the citizens to interact with the applications in a safe and easy to use environment. It also consists of the internal management modules that facilitate the profile, the applications, the relations and the trust mechanisms. The application layer is used, in conjunction with the integration and interaction layer to provide applications to the citizens.

4.2 Integration Layer

This layer enables applications to be easily integrated into the platform, in a seamless fashion. It also addresses issues related to Authentication, Data Integrity and Availability. While confidentiality deals with the unintentional disclosure of information outside the authorized parameters, data integrity assures the trustworthiness of the information and availability ensures that the information is made available to requesting authenticated clients. The integration layer is based on a platform-specific *API* and a mark up language (*MyCCP ML*). Specific client libraries provide a functional wrapper for the Platform's API REST interface. The main concern of the API is to facilitate a secure pull and push mechanism for the data process. The mark-up language (*MyCCP ML*) contains the required tags to implement citizen's profile. Thus, it contains presentation and semantic tags facilitating citizen-related data presentation and exchange between public agency applications. The special tags are used for the accurate acquisition of the profile information.

4.3 Interaction Layer

The interaction layer is in the core of the platform. It provides built–in functionalities for the citizens to interact with the platform and consequently PA applications. The interaction layer consists of two sub layers: The *built- in citizen services* sub-layer provides the necessary functionality for the citizen to interact with the platform. Based on the citizen requirements five services have been identified.

The *log-in and authentication* module provides citizen authentication. Only citizens can log-in in the platform. Alternative interaction models usually provide a username and a password to a business thus permitting a "business" to log-in and interact with the government. We argue that this concept is inappropriate. Businesses should be decomposed to the citizens that work for that business, so the citizen interaction with the government should be modelled. Upon log-in, citizen can access the citizen the business and views section of their profile. Certain policies can be adopted based on the technological background of the citizens including smart cards and certificates issued by a certification authority. HTTP/SSL mechanism provides the appropriate log-in security.

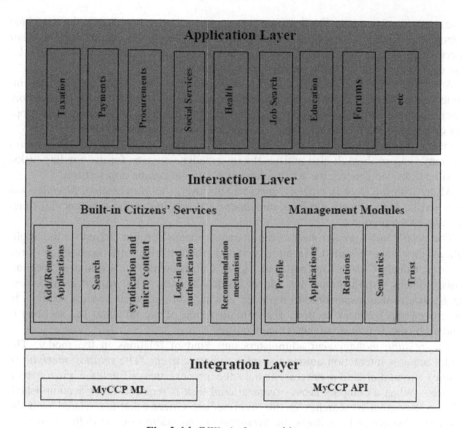

Fig. 2. MyCCP platform architecture

The *add and remove applications* module provides the necessary functionality for an application to be installed and uninstalled in the citizens profile in a seamless way. A citizen can add an application in the citizen and in the business section of his profile. Additionally, can remotely add and execute an application on behalf of another citizen or business. This sort of interaction takes place in the Views section. It is noteworthy to mention that, restrictions regarding the addition and the execution of the applications are handled solely by the applications. For instance, if an application is required to be added only by accountants, it is the application task to check the appropriate accountant registries and allow or not the addition of the application. The *add and remove applications* service is used complementary to the *Recommendation mechanism service*.

The *Recommendation mechanism* is part of the personalization features provided by the platform. The recommendation mechanism assists the citizen to arrange his/her profile, for example install the necessary applications to accomplish a task. Upon removal of an application, this module notifies the citizen for the possible implications on the execution of the depended applications. The recommendation mechanism is a complex service. It requires semantic information to identify the prerequisite applications. The decomposition of the business to the intermediate citizens also poses new requirements. For instance, an application executed by an intermediate citizen may require a prerequisite application that should be executed by another intermediate citizen. The recommendation mechanism, in conjunction with the *relation module* should handle the interaction between them.

A *search module* enables citizens to search for the appropriate applications included in application registry. Semantic information is stored for each application, providing the documentation for the citizens to find the right applications and properly combine them so as to complete a complex cross organizational task.

Syndication and micro content delivery module alerts citizens for particular issues that may concern them. It also notifies the intermediate citizens for the pending tasks. Pending tasks can concern the addition and execution of certain applications.

Along with the *Built in citizens' services* sub layer, the *Management Modules* sub layer exists. Management modules implement and administer the fundamental functionality of the platform.

The *profile management mechanism* updates citizens' profiles based on the applications they have installed. As already stated, the citizen profile consists of three sections, namely Citizen, Business and Views. Consequently, the sections are decomposed to tabs. Applications are added inside the tabs. The *profile management mechanism* is also responsible to replicate information contained in view sections to the citizen and business section. The administration of the tabs and the sections is handled by the *profile management mechanism.*

The *relation management* administers any kind of relations in the model. The model requires interaction among the intermediate citizens. The *relation mechanism* handles the authorization process, that is the process that affiliates a citizen to a business. When a complex cross organizational task is required to be accomplished, *relation management* searches for the intermediate citizens that are related with the business. Consequently, utilizes the *Syndication and micro content delivery* module and notifies the citizen about the pending jobs.

Trust mechanism facilitates rating of public services and provides feedback to other citizens and the public sector.

Application management mechanism is responsible for ensuring the registration, the authentication and the availability of the applications. An application registry will be utilized for that purpose. Applications are developed by the public agencies to provide specific services to the platform. The distributed nature of the model requires that applications are implemented unaware of the existence of the other applications that may have been implemented. Application registry requires some necessary information for the application to be uploaded such as the public agency, the category of the application (e.g finance), the date that was added to the registry, a description of the application, some tags to identify the use, the preconditions (input) that are required for the application to execute and finally the output information that the application will add to the citizen profile. Some additional information may also be required by the registry, e.g. for security reasons.

The output information that is posted from an application should be discovered and used, upon citizens' explicit consent, as prerequisite information for another application. Thus, the output information should be semantically tagged in a proper and coherent way.

The *semantics module* is responsible for the semantic tagging, which is not performed in an automated manner. Semantic annotation in a decentralized Web 2.0 environment is hampered by the vocabulary problem and the language gap [10]: an application requires some preconditions as input information, but is unable to use the right terms to search for it and there is a lack of common semantic descriptions of available output information. To this end, a collaborative recommendation tagging system is proposed to implement semantics module. When registering an application, the corresponding Public Agency is forced to provide tags upon output usage and functionality forming tag-clouds per Public Agency or Category. Tag clouds refer to aggregated tag information in which a taxonomy or "tagsonomy" emerges through repeated collective usage of the same tags.

When the output information of the application is about to be semantically described, the collaborative recommendation system will recommend the most frequently used tags that have been added by Pubic Agencies included in the same category. For example, when the majority of the Universities have tagged the output of their "Degree Certificate" application as "degree rate", the collaborative recommendation system will recommend that tag instead of the "grade rate" used by a specific University, leading to more consistent semantic tagging. The tag cloud mechanism will also facilitate Public Agencies to select the proper preconditions for their applications from those already included in the registry, by minimize tag range. For example, the collaborative recommendation system will notify the public agencies involved that the most frequently used tags in the category "universities" are the "degree rate" and the "grade rate". Consequently, it is up to the public agencies to decide whether they will require as precondition the "degree rate", the "grade rate" or both, it they have similar meaning. In the conceptual level, Public Agencies formulate a social sub-network where collaborative tagging provides a collective intelligence to the platform.

4.4 Application Layer

The Application Layer provides a set of interface specifications to support various types of applications in every administrative level (Local, Federal, European). Public Agencies' databases and business logic will remain intact. However, a front end interface will have to be implemented using the platform's API and platform's markup language. Then, the application will have to be tagged with semantic information and be uploaded in the registry. Applications can be considered as the main execution component of the platform. They act as gateways between the citizens and the public agencies, providing a fundamental engagement mechanism. Applications can provide governmental services from the whole public sector spectrum including taxation and payment, procurements, social services, health, job and education.

5 Case Study

To demonstrate the potential of the proposed interaction model a cross-organizational business-to-government example is discussed in the following. Let's assume a mid-scale software company, called *Synapses* and a Public Agency making a call for proposals to purchase software. According to EU legislation, any proposal should be accompanied with certifications proving that the company's tax and insurance status is clear. The founder and the CEO of the company, named *Jason*, has a *business tab* with the name of the company added inside the *business section* of his profile. So, Jason's *Citizen Profile* currently consists of the Citizen Section that includes his Citizen Tab and the Business Section that includes Synapses Business Tab. Jason wishes to authorize *Alice* as the accountant and *Bob* as the lawyer, while both work as freelancers representing potential client when interaction with the government. Jason also wishes to authorize *Charlie,* an employer, as a intermediate to place offers for public calls. When Alice, Bob and Charlie accept their roles, a *view tab,* named Synapses, is added to their citizen profile inside the *Views Section.*

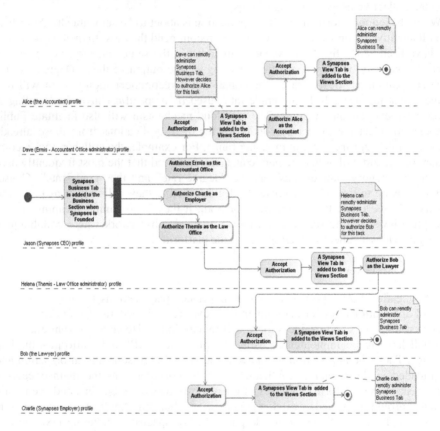

Fig. 3. Authentication Procedure

A more complex interaction takes place when the Jason authorizes, instead of citizens, another business. Let's suppose that Jason authorizes an accountant office called *Ermis* to take care of the accountant and financial tasks of "his" business. He also authorizes *Themis* as the law office to accomplish tasks for Synapses. Ermis, is administered by a citizen called *Dave* and *Themis* is administered by a citizen called *Helena.* They both accept the authorizations and a view tab, named Synapses, is added to their citizen's profile. Suppose that Alice the accountant is working for

Ermis and Dave authorizes her to elaborate on Synapses' tax issues. Alice will accept Dave's authorization on Synapses, which means that Alice is able to administer Synapses Business Tab. A Synapses View Tab will be added in her profile. In the exact same way, Bob, who is working for Themis, is authorized as the lawyer for Synapses. The authorization procedure is depicted in figure 3.

The public Agency has created an application that requires a clearance certification from both the tax office (Ministry of Economy and Finance) and the National Insurance Company (Ministry of Labor) and consequently processes the proposals. Charlie installs that application and the recommendation mechanism informs him about the prerequisites. Charlie does not know who is responsible to install and run the necessary applications, so the platform searches *Synapses business tab* and alerts every citizen that views some part of it for the pending tasks. This is actually performed by the relation module of MyCCP.

Practically, relation module will check the Synapses business tab on Jason's profile to find the corresponding authorized citizens, which are Dave and Helena (as the accountant and law office administrators) and consequently Alice and Bob. The information that was posted in Synapses business tab located on Jason's citizen profile will be replicated to Synapses' view tab located on the Dave's citizen profile and

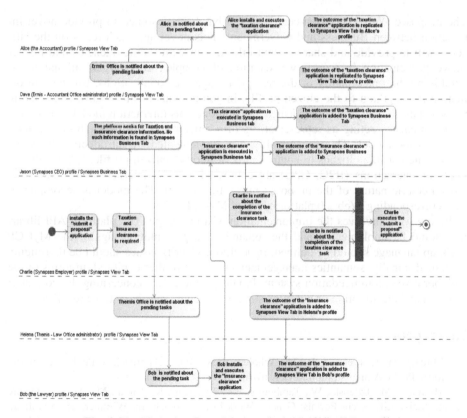

Fig. 4. The "Submit proposal for purchasing software" Procedure

consequently to Synapses view tab located in the Alice's citizen profile. Alice will be notified about the pending task and will add in Synapses business tab in the views section of her profile the appropriate application from the Ministry of Economy and Finance that will verify that Jason's company has paid the necessary taxes.

In a similar fashion, Bob the Lawyer will be notified by Themis, which will be notified by Synapses. The information will be posted to Synapses business tab located on Jason profile, will be replicated to Synapses view tab located on Helena's profile and finally be replicated to Synapses view tab located on Bob's profile.

Both applications will be actually executed in the Synapses business tab of Jason's profile and will be ultimately replicated in Alice's and Bob's corresponding tabs in the views section of their profile. Note, that Bob is unaware of Alice's application and so does Alice for Bob's. Only Jason, as the business tab owner, has a full report of the information that was posted in the view tabs. Charlie is notified that the pending tasks are completed and accomplishes the proposal submission. Synapses business tab in the Business Section of Jason's profile is the reference point for every interaction. Corresponding profile interaction is illustrated in figure 4.

6 Conclusions

The proposed Web 2.0 citizen-centric model has been designed to provide novel interaction between Business and Government. This novel approach relies on the citizens' will to provide and share certain information with public agencies and his/her active participation in workflow execution of complex cross-organisational tasks, combining the functionality of discrete public agencies applications. Business information is integrated to the citizen profile, in autonomous business tabs, contributing to the establishment of a sophisticated and homogenous interaction model. The notion of intermediates acting as representatives of a citizen or a business tab is also integrated in the model. This functionality was implemented by introducing the View Tabs, which enable citizens to control parts of another citizen profile. Ultimately, all kinds of interactions (B2G, G2G) are expressed as C2G interactions revealing the citizen-centric nature of the proposed interaction model. The model is accompanied by a corresponding Web 2.0 platform, called MyCCP.

Future work involves the implementation of a prototype. The platform API libraries should be implemented and the semantic and presentation tags of the MyCCP mark up language should be defined. In addition, security issues should be thoroughly examined. Finally, semantics management should be further explored, in terms of the collaborative recommendation system. Finally, some issues concerning the cold start problem and the adoption or not of existing e-gov ontologies have to be resolved.

References

1. Christensen, T., Lægreid, P.: The Whole-of-Government Approach to Public Sector Reform. Public Administration Review 67(6), 1059–1066 (2007)
2. Momotko, M., Izdebski, W., Tambouris, E.s., Tarabanis, K., Vintar, M.: An Architecture of Active Life Event Portals: Generic Workflow Approach. In: Wimmer, M., Scholl, J., Grønlund, E. (eds.) EGOV 2007. LNCS, vol. 4656, pp. 104–115. Springer, Heidelberg (2007)

3. Sahraoui, S., Ghoneim, A., Irani, Z., Ozkan, S.: T-Government for benefit realisation: A research agenda. In: Evaluating information Systems. Public and Private Sector, pp. 359–373. Butterworth-Heinemann/Elsevier (2008)
4. Oreilly, T.: What is Web 2.0: Design Patterns and Business Models for the Next Generation of Software, http://oreilly.com/web2/archive/what-is-web-20.html
5. Maio, A.: Government and Web 2.0: The Emerging Midoffice. Gartner (2007)
6. Maio, A.: The E-Government Hype Cycle Meets Web 2.0. Gartner (2007)
7. Maeda, J.: The Laws of Simplicity (Simplicity: Design, Technology, Business, Life), pp. 73–81. MIT Press, Cambridge (2006)
8. Sholler, D.: Reference Architecture for Web-Oriented Architecture. Gartner (2008)
9. Fielding, R., Taylor, R.: Principled Design of the Modern Web Architecture. ACM Transactions on Internet Technology (TOIT), 115–150 (2002)
10. Fernandez, A., Hayes, C., Loutas, N., Peristeras, V., Polleres, A., Tarabanis, K.: Closing the Service Discovery Gap by Collaborative Tagging and Clustering Techniques. In: ISCW 2007, Workshop on Service Discovery and Resource Retrieval in the Semantic Web (2008)

Empowerment through Electronic Mandates – Best Practice Austria

Thomas Rössler

Secure Information Technology Center Austria (A-SIT)
thomas.roessler@a-sit.at

Abstract. For dealing with electronic identities—especially in the area of e-Government—several approaches have been developed and successfully deployed already. However, most of them lack of an adequate vehicle to express exhaustively all kinds of representation and authorization types with which we are faced in every day's life. This is even more unsatisfying as, for instance, the European Union undertakes tremendous efforts to enforce the support of e-services for businesses and service providers, e.g. through the EU Service Directive. Especially businesses and service providers have an urgent need for being able to express all the various kinds of representations by electronic means. This paper firstly addresses the issue of representation from a general perspective in order to analyze the requirements. Finally, it introduces a concrete approach to solution—the concept of electronic mandates—which is successfully used by the Austrian e-Government initiative. This concept provides an exhaustive and all-embracing vehicle for building any kind of representation by electronic means.

1 Introduction

Empowering a person to act for another person or to conduct a certain transaction are important legal elements in everyday business. Empowering is almost always implicitly accepted in various situation, e.g. if a parent acts for her minor child or if a businessman acts on behalf of his company. Both scenarios are examples of authorisation because a person becomes authorised to act under delegated power. In the former example, the law empowers parents to represent their child in business. If a parent wants to act for her child in a conventional business, it is almost always sufficient to claim to be the parent. In the "worst" case, the adult would have to prove her identity and if the surname of both the adult and the child are the same, then parenthood is usually deemed to be proved. In the latter example, when "claiming" that a businessman acts in the name of some company it is often sufficient just to present a business card. Often no further proof is required, depending of course on the intended action.

Both examples demonstrate that authorisation and representation are elements of daily life that are taken for granted implicitly. In everyday life, proof of authorisation is not usually required, but when working with electronic transactions, authorisation has to be expressed explicitly. This creates a need for having an electronic form of empowerment and representation.

Throughout Europe, several Member States of the European Union are using various concepts in order to realize empowerment by electronic means. For instance,

C. Godart et al. (Eds.): I3E 2009, IFIP AICT 305, pp. 148–160, 2009.
© IFIP International Federation for Information Processing 2009

Spain issues special digital certificates to companies with which total empowerment is simply expressed (i.e. the holder of the certificate has absolute power to represent the company by all means). However, introducing special types of certificates or to just add identifiers to digital certificates that express a certain type of representation provides a basis for building only simple scenarios and does not provide flexibility.

Also in literature (e.g. [1][2][3]) representation and empowerment has been discussed from various perspectives whereas most of the existing work focus on role based access control. On the other hand, [4] and [5] proposes using attribute certificate profiles and policies for expressing empowerment and delegation. Although this approach would somehow fit to the targeted scenario—i.e. the introduction of a mechanism for electronic empowerment in the electronic identity (e-ID) system of Austrian e-Government—a solution based on attribute certificates would be of limited flexibility. Thus, this paper introduces XML based electronic mandates as a vehicle for achieving empowerment and representation by electronic means within the Austrian e-ID system.

Electronic mandates were introduced into the Austrian identification schema for two main reasons. On the one hand, electronic mandates are the electronic equivalent of conventional mandates for empowering a person, in which a proxy acts for another person, referred to as the mandatory under certain circumstances. On the other hand, electronic mandates serve to close the gap between private persons and legal entities with respect to the Austrian electronic identity management system. Austrian Citizen Cards, i.e. the vehicle to electronically identify a person in front of Austrian e-Government applications, are issued to natural persons only. So without electronic mandates legal entities cannot actively participate in Austrian e-Government as they do not possess a Citizen Card to do so.

The rest of this paper is organized as follows. The following section shortly introduces the Austrian e-ID system and the Citizen Card concept in particular. Section 3 analysis scenarios where representation may occur and identifies the basic types of representations. In the course of this, the scenario of chained mandates will be discussed. Section 4 describes the Austrian approach to solution, i.e. the Austrian electronic mandates, in detail. After giving a report on the Austrian practical implementation, section 6 shortly touches a specialty of representation, namely how to deal with so called professional representatives. Finally conclusions are drawn.

2   The Austrian E-ID System at a Glance

The Austrian e-ID system is technically realized through the Austrian Citizen Card which serves two purposes: electronic identification and qualified electronic signatures. This section highlights the most important issues of both elements (for further readings refer to [6] and [7]) as electronic mandates extend the existing Austrian e-ID system.

For identification purposes, the Austrian e-ID system provides unique identification on the one hand, but aims to provide a maximum of privacy on the other hand. Every Austrian citizen—i.e. natural person—residing in Austria has to be registered with the so called Central Register of Residents (CRR). As a result, each Austrian citizen got assigned a unique identifier derived from her very unique CRR number.

As the so created unique identifier serves the basis for electronic identification in Austrian e-Government, it is denoted as Source Personal Identification Number (sourcePIN). The concrete derivation algorithm is depicted in figure 1.

SourcePINs are created during the Citizen Card issuing process only. This process and all required secrets, i.e. the secret key used during the creation process, are under the control of the so called Source-PIN Register Authority which is governed by the Austrian Data Protection Commissioner. Due to privacy reasons, it is forbidden by law to use this sourcePIN within e-Government applications directly. Instead, Austrian e-Government applications have been divided into a number of application sectors and for each application sector a different Sector-Specific Personal Identification Number (ssPIN) has to be created (the derivation algorithm is given in figure 1). As a result, an ssPIN of one sector, e.g. sector "SA", cannot be used in another sector, e.g. "GH", to identify the affected citizen and vice-versa.

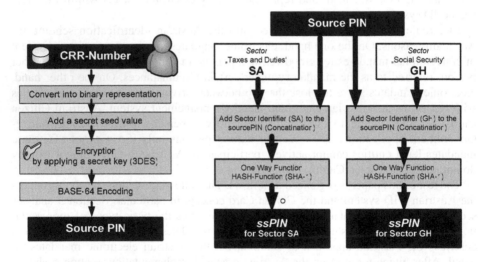

Fig. 1. Left: Creation of sourcePIN; Right: Creation of two ssPINs of different sectors

For authentication purposes the Austrian e-ID system fully relies on qualified electronic signatures according to the Austrian Signature Law [8] and the EU Signature Directive [9]. In other words, the Austrian Citizen Card is a secure signature creation device in terms of the laws mentioned before.

In order to realize person authentication, i.e. proving that a person is really the person she claims to be, the Citizen Card introduces the so called Identity-Link which is an XML structure combining a person's unique identification number—her sourcePIN—and her qualified signature. Very similar to an electronic signature certificate the Identity-Link combines a person's sourcePIN with her public keys required to verify her qualified signatures. The Identity-Link structure itself is electronically signed by the issuing Source PIN Register Authority which is in charge of issuing the identity credentials of the Austrian Citizen Card. In contrast to ordinary public-key certificates, the Identity-Link is solely stored in the person's Citizen Card. Furthermore, the Identity-Link is the only place where a person's sourcePIN is allowed to be stored (note, although the issuing authority is called Source-PIN Register Authority it does not maintain a register of sourcePINs; this authority is only allowed to create sourcePINs on demand during the Citizen Card issuing process by taking a person's base identification number from the CRR and applying the derivation mechanism described above).

Based on the Identity-Link, identification and authentication of a person in front of an e-Government application is easy to achieve by the following steps:

1. The application asks the citizen to provide her Citizen Card. The citizen will usually make use of a middleware that provides communication between the Citizen Card and the e-Government application.

2. Through the middleware, the application reads the person's Identity-Link from her Citizen Card. Next, the e-Government application has to verify the electronic signature on the Identity-Link in order to prove its authenticity. If verification attains success, the application takes the person's sourcePIN in order to create her according ssPIN immediately.

3. In order to authenticate the person, the application asks the citizen to create a qualified electronic signature. Therefore, the middleware presents a given text to be signed (the text is given by the application and usually relates to the application's context or purpose) and asks the citizen to sign it by entering her secret code (the code is used to trigger the signature creation process on the Citizen Card).

4. The application finally verifies the created signature. Furthermore, after signature verification the application tries to match the public-keys given in the Identity-Link with the electronic signature just provided by the citizen. If the match is successful, the application is ensured that the claimed identity (i.e. represented through the sourcePIN/ssPIN provided in step 1) is the one who has created the electronic signature provided (in step 3).

From a technical perspective, the Citizen Card is an open concept which means it is bound neither to a concrete technology nor to a concrete implementation. There just exists a detailed specification defining the interfaces of and the requirements for an Austrian Citizen Card, however, every technical device which provides qualified electronic signatures and fulfills the technical Citizen Card specification can be immediately used as a Citizen Card in Austria. This means that the Citizen Card is not limited to smartcards only.

3 Scenarios and Types of Representations

From a use-case perspective, electronic mandates should serve to describe any kind of representations. Thus it should enable, for example:

a) a natural person to represent a legal person/entity
b) a natural person to represent another natural person
c) a legal person/entity to represent another legal person/entity
d) a legal person/entity to represent a natural person.

By combining multiple mandates of different types, even more complex situations can be created (by chaining multiple mandates).

These four examples roughly sketch the set of possible empowerment scenarios. Instead of discussing empowerment scenarios based on examples, the following sections will introduce generic types of representations from an abstract point of view. Finally, the special scenario of "chained mandates" will be discussed.

3.1 Types of Representations

The basic form of all types of representations is a simple *bilateral representation* where a person empowers another person to act in her name. More generally speaking and as representations are not just focused on natural persons only, a bilateral representation can be established between two entities.

However, the analysis of possible scenarios for representations bears three basic types of representations:

A) Bilateral Type
B) Substitution Type
C) Delegation Type

All three types are depicted in figure 1; this illustration requires three roles:

- Proxy
- Mandator
- Intermediary

The **Proxy** is the entity who becomes empowered to represent the **Mandator**. An **Intermediary** is an entity who may act between the Proxy and the Mandator in the event of indirect representations. As figure 1 deals with entities in general, natural persons and legal persons are used synonymously. According to this terminology, types of representations can be defined as follows (as it is not relevant for this general discussion, the following characterisation does not make assumptions about the scope of empowerment):

Bilateral Type. A bilateral representation is the basic type as mentioned above. In this case an entity—the Mandator—empowers another entity—the Proxy—to act in her name. This type is also denoted as direct representation.

Substitution Type. In contrast to the bilateral type a substitution is a pure indirect representation requiring two relations. Firstly, the Mandator has to empower an Intermediary. Considering this first relation solely, it turns out being a simple bilateral representation. Additionally, the Mandator has to allow the Intermediary to empower a substitute for representing the Mandator. This first relation in addition with the allowance for substitution is the precondition for this type of representation. Secondly, the Intermediary chooses a substitute—the real Proxy—to act in her name. As the Intermediary is empowered to represent the Mandator and as the Mandator gave the allowance that the Intermediary may choose a substitute, the substitute is empowered to represent the Mandator as well. Thus the substitute becomes a Proxy of the Mandator.

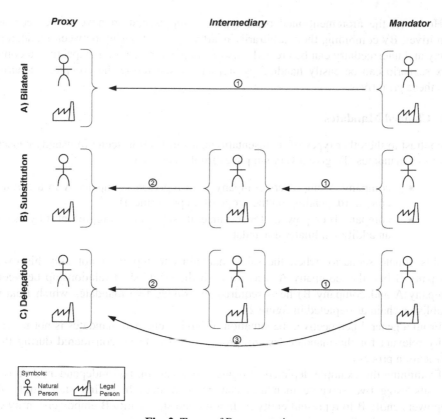

Fig. 2. Types of Representations

Delegation Type. The delegation type is an indirect representation at first sight. In contrast to the Substitution Type, the Delegation Type requires three relations. Firstly, the Mandator empowers an Intermediary to act in her/its name. Secondly, the Intermediary acts in the name of the Mandator and empowers another entity—the Proxy—to act in the name of the Mandator. Of course, the original Mandator has to allow this kind of delegation during the establishment of the relation between Intermediary and Mandator. As a result, the Proxy becomes empowered to act in the name of the original Mandator. In this third relation the Intermediary disappears as this relation exists between the Mandator and the Proxy only. So this third relation is finally a pure bilateral one as it exists between Mandator and Proxy directly. However, the important difference is that not the Mandator but an Intermediary establishes this relation.

Most of the existing empowerment scenarios are either of bilateral or delegation type. From the point of view of verification—i.e. the process of verifying if a given electronic mandate is authentic and establishes the empowerment required by a given application—these two types are rather simple to handle as just one electronic mandate has to be proven. In contrast to this, the substitution type may require to verify not only one but several mandates as it may cause to build a so called chain of mandates. The next subsection discusses the situation of chained mandates briefly.

However, the aforementioned basic types of representation have to be seen as primitives. By combining them arbitrarily nearby any relationship between mandator, proxy and intermediary can be created. Also from the verification perspective, a complex scenario can be easily handled by stepwisely separating the complex scenario into these primitives.

3.2 Chained Mandates

In contrast to the other types of representations, a substitution scenario usually causes chains of mandates. To give a very simple example, consider:

- company A empowers company B to represent company A in a certain context (depending on the scope of empowerment)
- company B empowers, for instance, its sales man to represent it by using an additional bilateral mandate

In this simple scenario, when the sales man aims to represent not only his own company B but also company A (according to the established relationship between company A and company B) he is required to provide two mandates which finally establish a chain as depicted in figure 2.

From a general perspective, the situation of having chained mandates is not necessarily relevant for the mandate issuing process but has to be considered during the verification process.

Examining the example depicted in figure 2 once again, two independent empowerments using two separate mandates can be identified. In a first step, entity A empowers entity B to represent entity A. In a second step, entity B empowers entity C to represent entity B.

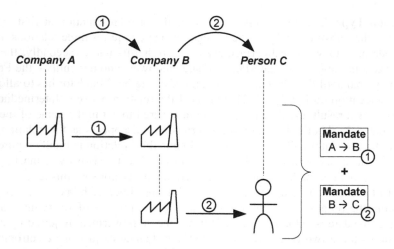

Fig. 3. A simple example of chained mandates

It is important to note that both relations are totally independent from each other. For example, the second empowerment may be established even before the first one. Furthermore, the second one does not necessarily contain any explicit provision or statement relating to the first empowerment and vice versa. However, depending on the national law it may be necessary that at least the first mandate contains the explicit allowance for this kind of substitution. From the point of view of an e-Government application, it will simply ask Person C—e.g. the sales man—to provide both mandates (mandate 1 and 2). In the course of the mandate verification process, the application must prove not only both mandates separately but also whether the mandator given in mandate 2 (i.e. Company B) corresponds to the proxy given in mandate 1.

4   The Concept of Electronic Mandates in Austria

Electronic mandates aim to provide end to end security as the proxy is holding a token (i.e. an electronic mandate) asserting that she is empowered to act in the name of another entity and can prove it in front of any application. So it is not an issue for applications to know about a person's authorisation to represent other entities/persons. Applications just have to verify electronic mandates. This makes it finally easy to manage authorizations from applications' perspective.

Similar to conventional mandates, an electronic mandate should hold:

- identity of the mandator
- identity of the proxy
- date and place of issuing
- content and concern of the mandate
- optional restrictions

The electronic mandate must hold the electronic identity of the mandator (i.e. the person who empowers another person to act in her name). In the event the mandator is a natural person, the identity of the mandator is denoted not only by her first and last name, date of birth, etc. but also by her unique electronic identifier, i.e. her sourcePIN as introduced before. The mandator's unique identifier is important as it is required to uniquely identify the mandator within applications. The identity of the proxy has to be similarly formulated by her full name, date of birth and her unique identifier which is her sourcePIN in the event the proxy is a natural person. In the event of having legal entities, analogous identity attributes are to be used, e.g. the full name of a company and its unique identifier taken from the commercial register.

The main concern of a mandate—i.e. the scope of empowerment—should be formulated in a textual description, more precisely, in arbitrarily combinable textual description blocks. It is expected that standard text blocks will come up for all types of standard mandates, e.g. mandates representing a procuration. In addition to the textual description of a mandate's concern, optional restrictions may be applied.

In order to assert the authenticity of a mandate, it has to be electronically signed, either by the mandator or by an issuing authority.

The concept for electronic mandates should introduce an electronic mechanism for revoking a mandate. The introduction of this technical revocation mechanism would be a great improvement in comparison to conventional mandates and it is especially necessary for electronic mandates. On the one hand, it is sufficient from a legal perspective to revoke a mandate by publicly announcing a revocation. Consider conventional paper-based mandates: if the proxy is still in the possession of a paper that pretends to act as a valid mandate, the proxy would still be able to act illegally in the name of the mandator. Thus, the only effective way to avoid this problem is to request that the proxy destroy the paper mandate, which would prove hard to verify. With electronic mandates, this situation is much more difficult since the proxy could create an arbitrary number of copies of the electronic mandate and the mandator could never be sure whether any illegal copies still exist. An electronic revocation mechanism is therefore very desirable for electronic mandates.

Therefore, the introduction of an electronic revocation mechanism is strongly recommended. To make an electronic mandate electronically defeasible, the mandate needs to be registered with a certain revocation service. As a result, electronic mandates may hold an Internet address that provides revocation information on request. When attempting to verify an electronic mandate, the named revocation service has to be asked about the current revocation status by using the serial number of the electronic mandate. A similar revocation mechanism for digital certificates is already widely used and well-established. Thus, the concept of mandate revocation can be made similar to the revocation mechanism of digital certificates.

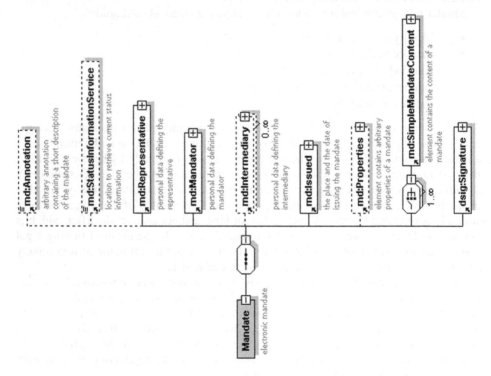

Fig. 4. Basic layout of electronic mandates (XML schema)

Electronic mandates that follow the characteristics described above have been introduced into the Austrian electronic identification schema in 2006. On a technical level, an electronic mandate in Austria is a specific XML structure (figure 4 illustrates the XML-structure of an electronic mandate in Austria) which must be electronically signed by an issuing authority, i.e. the Source-PIN Register Authority. The issuing authority just asserts that the electronic representation bases on an existing and already established authorisation.

The concept of electronic mandates requires that electronic mandates are held by the proxies. Every time a proxy makes use of a mandate, she has firstly to use her e-ID (i.e. Citizen Card) to prove her own identity. Additionally, she has to declare to the e-Government application that she is rightfully acting in the name of the mandator by presenting the electronic mandate.

To summarize and according to the be basic requirements of electronic mandates introduced before, an electronic mandate according to the Austrian specification [10] contains the following mandatory and optional elements (referring to figure 4):

- **Identity of the Proxy (Representative)**:
  - natural person: first name, last-name, date of birth
  - legal person: full name
  - the person's unique identifier (i.e. the sourcePIN in the event of natural persons)
- **Identity of the Mandator**:
  - natural person: first name, last-name, date of birth
  - legal person: full name
  - the person's unique identifier (i.e. the sourcePIN in the event of natural persons)
- **Identity of the Intermediary [optional]**:
  - natural person: first name, last-name, date of birth
  - legal person: full name
  - the person's unique identifier (i.e. the sourcePIN in the event of natural persons)
- **Scope of Empowerment**:
  - One or several text blocks are used to describe the scope of empowerment. Although arbitrary text blocks are possible, typical electronic mandates are built by using standardized text blocks. This eases mandate verification. However, in order to be able to create any kind of mandate, arbitrary text is allowed.
- **Constraints [optional]**:
  - Additional to the scope of empowerment, arbitrary restrictions can be formulated (optionally). Currently, the specification defines three concrete types of restrictions by using specialized XML elements: time constraint (i.e. a mandate is effective within a given time frame only), collective constraint (i.e. a proxy cannot act alone; further proxies are

required) and financial constraint (i.e. actions taken based on the given mandate are limited with a financial transaction limit).

- **Serial Number**
  - o Each electronic mandate gets assigned a unique serial number. This is required for revocation purposes.
- **Link to a Revocation Service [optional]**:
  - o If a link to an electronic mandate revocation service is given, the verifier of a mandate is requested to contact this service in order to verify the revocation status of the mandate. For requesting the revocation status a HTTP-based protocol has been developed [10]. Currently, the Source PIN Register Authority runs a mandate revocation service; currently all existing electronic mandates are registered with this registration service per default.
- **Electronic Signature of the issuing Authority**:
  - o Due to Austrian law, every electronic mandate has to be signed by the issuing Source PIN Register Authority. This also applies to bilateral mandates.

Electronic mandates are issued by the Source PIN Register Authority only. Therefore, this authority provides a web-application with which citizens can apply for electronic mandates based on an existing authorization (empowerment). This means, that the empowerment must be already established, e.g. based on paper mandates or entries in official registers (e.g. the register of commerce). In order to foster the take up of electronic mandates in the field of e-Government applications, the Austrian e-Government initiative provides open-source software modules for providers and developers of e-Government services, which automatically verify electronic mandates—including chain verification—and provide e-Government applications the unique electronic identity of the mandator and the proxy.

To give an example of how electronic mandates influence the process of identification and authentication, the following scenario illustrates a typically identification and authentication process using the Austrian Citizen Card and electronic mandates. In this example a person aims to access an e-Government application in the name of a company. In addition to the four basic steps already introduced in section 2, the following additional steps are required due to the use of electronic mandates:

1. to 4. See workflow given in section 2. As a result, the application has authenticated the person and thus holds her sourcePIN.
2. The e-Government application has to read the person's mandate(s). As her mandate(s) are stored in her Citizen Card, the application requests to read this/these mandate(s) through the Citizen Card middleware.
3. For each mandate provided, the application has to verify the electronic signature.
4. If the mandate is authentic, the application has to verify whether the person defined as proxy by the mandate is the person who accessed the application by using her Citizen Card. This match is easily verifiable thanks to the sourcePINs

given in the electronic mandate and in the person's Identity-Link. If sourcePINs are equal, the person using the service is an empowered proxy.

5. The application has to verify whether the given mandate—or more precisely its scope of empowerment—is sufficient for this particular e-Government application. This could be verified by comparing the textual description given within the electronic mandate against profiles configured in the application. If the given text block can be recognized and is considered being sufficient, the application can succeed.

6. The application finally takes the identity data of the mandator given by the electronic mandate. As the mandator's unique identifier is given as well, the application can use the mandator's e-identity in the same way as the mandator would access the application personally (in the event of natural persons, the mandator's sourcePIN is provided by the mandate; thus, the application is able to create the mandator's ssPIN immediately).

The electronic delivery service was one of the very first e-Government applications in Austria which accepted electronic mandates. Mandates are especially important for the Austrian electronic delivery service since legal entities are only able to register for electronic delivery with the use of electronic mandates (this means that a private person has to act in the name of a legal entity).

5 Specialtiy: Professional Representatives

Mandates as described in this paper are just used for so called explicit and bilateral empowerments. In contrast to this, the so called professional representatives, e.g. lawyers, tax advisors, etc., are not required to provide an explicit mandate if they want to act in the name of their clients. For them it is sufficient to prove that they are professional representatives.

Thus, their Citizen Cards, or to be more precisely their qualified certificates, hold a special object identifier (OID, according to ISO/IEC 9834-1) identifying them being a professional representative. As a result, professional representatives are not required to present explicit electronic mandates; instead e-Government applications just verify whether the digital certificate of the representative contains the OID defined for Austrian professional representatives. This situation is similar to the situation we have in the paper world. In order to "mark" professional representatives using standardized methods, the Austrian Federal Chancellery has reserved an OID-sub tree that defines these OIDs on an international level [11].

6 Conclusions

As mandates are an important element of our everyday's life, mandates—or more generally speaking empowerments or representations—have to be introduced in electronic identification systems as well. Not only the existing e-Government applications raise the need for it but especially the upcoming EU Service Directive that explicitly focuses on processes and applications for service providers, i.e. companies, etc., boosts the demand for a vehicle to express empowerment and representation by electronic means.

Therefore, this paper analyses various types of representations from a general and abstract perspective and identifies three primitive types of representations. By combining these primitives all possible scenarios can be built. Furthermore, this paper introduces a concrete approach for electronic empowerment by introducing the concept of electronic mandates as it is used in Austria. This concept of electronic mandates is used in the Austrian e-Government framework not only to establish empowerment by electronic means but also to close the gap between natural and legal persons.

References

1. Crampton, J., Khambhammettu, H.: Delegation in Role-Based Access Control. In: Gollmann, D., Meier, J., Sabelfeld, A. (eds.) ESORICS 2006. LNCS, vol. 4189, pp. 174–191. Springer, Heidelberg (2006)
2. Zhang, L., Ahn, G.-J., Chu, B.-T.: A rule-based framework for role-based delegation and revocation. ACM Trans. Inf. Syst. Secur. 6(3), 404–441 (2003)
3. Peeters, R., Simoens, K., DeCock, D., Preneel, B.: Cross-Context Delegation through Identity Federation. In: Brömme, A., Busch, C., Hühnlein, D. (eds.) Proceedings of the Special Interest Group on Biometrics and Electronic Signatures. Lecture Notes in Informatics (LNI) P-137, pp. 79–92. Bonner Köllen Verlag (2008)
4. Farrell, S., Housley, R.: An Internet Attribute Certificate Profile for Authorization. RFC 3281 (2002)
5. Francis, C., Pinkas, D.: Attribute Certificate (AC) Policies Extension. RFC 4476 (2006)
6. Leitold, H., Hollosi, A., Posch, R.: Security Architecture of the Austrian Citizen Card Concept. In: Proceedings of ACSAC 2002, pp. 391–400 (2002) ISBN 0-7695-1828-1
7. Rössler, T.: Giving an interoperable e-ID solution: Using foreign e-IDs in Austrian e-Government. Computer law and security report the bi-monthly report on computer security and the law governing information technology and computer use 24 (2008)
8. Austrian Federal Law: Federal Act on Electronic Signatures 2001 (Signature law), Austrian Federal Law Gazette, part I, Nr. 190/1999, 137/2000, 32/2001 (2001)
9. Directive 1999/93/EC of the European Parliament and of the Council of 13 December 1999 on a Community framework for electronic signatures. EC Official Journal, L 013, 12–20 (2000)
10. Rössler, T., Hollosi, A.: Elektronische Vollmachten - Spezifikation 1.0.0 (May 2006)
11. Digital-Austria: OID der öff. Verwaltung, OID-T1 1.0.0. (February 2009)

Not All Adware Is Badware: Towards Privacy-Aware Advertising

Hamed Haddadi, Saikat Guha, and Paul Francis

Max Planck Institute for Software Systems (MPI-SWS), Germany

Abstract. Online advertising is a major economic force in the Internet today. A basic goal of any advertising system is to accurately target the ad to the recipient audience. While Internet technology brings the promise of extremely well-targeted ad placement, there have always been serious privacy concerns surrounding personalization. Today there is a constant battle between privacy advocates and advertisers, where advertisers try to push new personalization technologies, and privacy advocates try to stop them. As long as privacy advocates, however, are unable to propose an alternative personalization system that is private, this is a battle they are destined to lose. This paper presents the framework for such an alternative system, the Private Verifiable Advertising (Privad). We describe the privacy issues associated with today's advertising systems, describe Privad, and discuss its pros and cons and the challenges that remain.

1 Introduction

Online advertising is one of the key economic drivers of the modern Internet economy. It supports many web sites and web services, is the basis for such industry giants as Google and Yahoo!, and helps pay for data centers and ISPs. Online advertising has long been touted as a natural basis for highly targeted and personalized advertising. It is good for advertisers who can avoid losing money by delivering ads to uninterested consumers, and good for consumers, who do not get bombarded with ads that are not in line with their interests. Unfortunately, personalized online advertising, at least so far, comes at a price: individual privacy. In order to deliver ads that individuals are interested in, advertisers learn what individual's interests are. While a number of private advertising systems have been designed, these either exhibit too weak a notion of privacy, or are too expensive to deploy (see Section 4). This paper introduces what we believe can form the first viable strongly private personalized online advertising system.

Online advertising has a long and storied history. Because it has always violated individual privacy, its practice has always been controversial opposed by privacy advocates (where here we use the term broadly to encompass governments and concerned users as well as privacy advocacy groups like the Electronic Frontier Foundation (EFF)). Privacy advocates have had some successes: most adware has been shut down, through a combination of legal (individual and

C. Godart et al. (Eds.): I3E 2009, IFIP AICT 305, pp. 161–172, 2009.

class-action lawsuits) and technical means (virus detection software). More recently, privacy advocates have had some success in stopping or slowing trials of ISP-based advertising technologies such as proposed by the companies NebuAd[1] and Phorm[2].

Privacy advocates have also had some major failures, specifically in the now ubiquitous advertising models deployed by Google, Yahoo!, Microsoft, and others. In spite of the fact that each of these companies, including recently Google, maintain personalization information about users, privacy advocates have so far been pretty much powerless to put a stop to it. Arguably the reason for this is that these and other companies play such a central role in the Internet economy that the deal that privacy advocates offer, privacy OR advertising, is not acceptable to industry, governments, or most individuals. In other words, as long as privacy advocates do not offer up an alternative privacy-preserving approach to personalized advertising, we will be stuck with the status quo or worse.

This paper introduces a framework for that alternative model. Specifically, we propose a Private Verifiable Advertising (Privad), a personalized advertising model based on the following three principles:

1. That all personalization information is kept on the client computer, and all decisions about what ads to show are made *purely local* to the client computer. This is made possible by pushing many or all ads to all client computers in advance of showing each ad.
2. That all reports about which ads are shown provide *zero information* to any given system component that would otherwise allow that component to associate users with ads viewed.
3. That privacy advocates are able to *verify* that the first two principles are indeed maintained in practice by observing all messages that go in and out of the various system components. It is this verification principle in particular that makes Privad powerful and unique.

It is worth pointing out that Privad is, by any reasonable definition, adware: software runs on client computers that monitors user behavior, builds up a profile of some sort, and uses that to present targeted ads to the user. We argue that not all adware is badware, and that in fact a client-based personalization system (i.e. adware) is the only way to achieve privacy in advertising. "Good adware" is not an oxymoron.

The rest of this paper is structured as follows. In Section 2 we introduce the basics of current advertising systems and we discuss user privacy. Section 3 presents the Privad framework. In Section 4 we give an overview of related work on privacy and advertising. Finally in Section 5 we conclude the paper and speculate on potential future avenues for research and for the advertising industry.

---

[1] http://www.nebuad.com
[2] http://www.phorm.com

2 Advertising Basics

For this paper, we define four major components of advertising systems: advertisers, publishers, clients, and brokers. Advertisers wish to sell their products or services through ads. Publishers provider opportunities to view ads, for instance by providing space for ad banners. Clients are the computers that show publisher web pages and ads to users. Brokers bring together advertisers, publishers, and clients. They provide ads to users, gather statistics about what ads were shown on which publisher pages, collect money from the advertisers, and pay the publishers.

Brokers can serve ads with or without user personalization. For instance, Google provides ads that match the topic of the web page with the embedded banner, on the assumption that if the user is interested in the web page, then the user is also likely to be interested in the ad. In this limited case, there is no personalization (Google, until recently, did not profile the user per se). Even in this case, however, there is a potential privacy violation: Google and other brokers see many of the web pages each client visits. This information can easily be used to personalize clients and their users. Even if the broker does not directly obtain Personally Identifying Information (PII) such as names, addresses, social security numbers and so on, PII can often be obtain through tracking cookies or by correlating IP addresses with PII obtained elsewhere [6].

In spite of the fact that some advertising can be done without user personalization, increasingly this personalization is being done by major advertising companies in form of persistent cookies. These cookies store information about user's visits to different websites, the frequency of such visits and the click information. An example of use of such cookies is with Behavioral Targeting in Google AdSense[3] or the Microsoft advertisement program. Although these brokers use some of the collected information in order to personalize the ads shown, they insist the systems select ads based only on non-PII data. For example, they store page views, clicks and search terms used for ad personalization separately from the user contact information or other PII data that directly identifies him or her. They also provide the ability to opt-out of personalized ads. Google has also tried to alleviate the concerns grown over about profiling users by promising not to create sensitive interest categories like race or religion or cross-correlating the data with other information saved in Google accounts. However the consumer can only trust Google to adhere to its word. Similar levels of privacy concerns have grown over commercial software such as the Google Desktop[4], where personal information can be used to effect public search results for targeted advertising[5].

These methods all lead to erosion of user privacy by the historically dominant players in the field such as Google, Microsoft and Yahoo!, as well as by relative newcomers like FaceBook. This leaves those concerned about privacy in a frustrating situation. On one hand, they can not easily modify the

---

[3] http://googleblog.blogspot.com/2009/03/making-ads-more-interesting.html
[4] http://desktop.google.com/
[5] http://www.theregister.co.uk/2004/10/15/google_desktop_privacy/

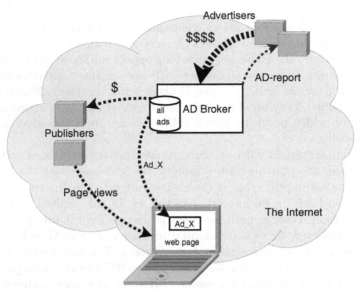

Today's broker-centric advertisement method

Fig. 1. Modern keyword-based advertising

operational behavior of the big players, in part because there is little regulation of the industry, and in part because these players play such an important role in the Internet economy. On the other hand, they spend a great amount of effort trying to impede new players and technologies to enter the market, without offering any viable alternative solutions. Ironically, this only helps solidify the position of the dominant players.

Figure 1 illustrates the current advertising model. The advertiser provides ads and bids (how much the advertiser is willing to pay for views and clicks of its ads) to the broker. When a publisher provides banner space to the client on a web page, a request goes to the broker asking to fill in the banner space with an appropriate ad. The broker makes the decision as to which ads to place based on a number of criteria such as the keywords for the web page, personalization information about the client, the keywords of the ad, and the bid associated with the ad. The broker provides the ad to the client, informs the advertiser of the ad view, and eventually settles the financial bookkeeping with advertisers and publishers. The broker also records user clicks on ads and possibly other events associated with ads (such as a product purchase), and reports to the advertiser. The advertiser uses the received information to run its ad campaign. That is, to decide how much to bid for ads, which keywords to associate ads with, which demographics to target, and so on.

3   The Privad Framework

Figure 2 illustrates the Privad model. The first thing to note here is that it preserves the economic framework of existing advertising systems. There are advertisers, publishers, clients, and a broker. Privad does introduce a fifth component, the untrusted proxy. The proxy is an entity that wishes to ensure that privacy is maintained, but nevertheless is itself not trusted with private information. As such, it could be operated by government agencies or by privacy advocacy groups (though possibly financially supported by the broker).

In Privad, no single entity obtains private information, including the proxy, and can therefore be untrusted. We do require that the proxy and the broker do not collude with each other. Proxy operation, however, can easily be monitored to insure with high probability that no collusion is taking place. Because the proxy is intrinsically interested in maintaining privacy, it should be willing to open itself to such monitoring.

Although Privad preserves the basic economic structure of current advertising systems, there are key differences. The main difference is that ads are served not by the broker, but by the client itself. This is done by providing the client with two things: a database of all or most ads, and a software agent that selects ads from the database to show the user, probably though not necessarily through user profiling.

In this model, when the client receives a webpage with banner space from a publisher, it itself fills in the banner with an appropriate ad. It generates an encrypted report identifying the ad and the publisher. The broker can decrypt the report, but not the proxy. The report is transmitted to the proxy, which now knows that the client viewed or clicked on an ad, but cannot know which ad or which publisher. The proxy forwards the report to the broker, and in so doing hides the IP address of the client. Upon decrypting the report, the broker now

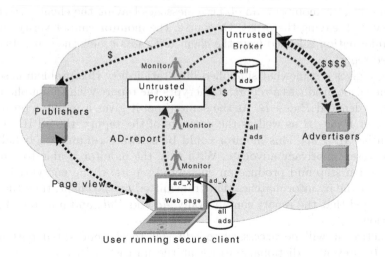

Fig. 2. The Privad architecture

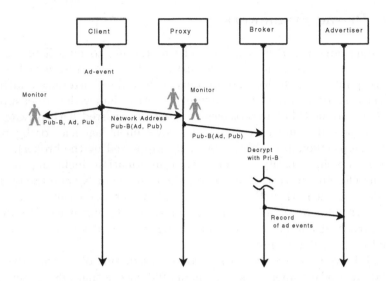

Fig. 3. Inter-party Encryption details

knows that some client viewed a particular ad served by a particular publisher, but does not know which client. What's more, there is no information in the report that allows the broker to associated multiple reports with a given client. The broker then reports to the advertiser as with today's systems. A similar report is produced by the client for other ad events such as clicks, purchases, and so on.

As already stated, a critical feature of Privad is that its privacy attributes can be verified, thus eliminating the need for trust in any single component. This can be done by a monitor positioned in two places: at the client and at the proxy. Specifically, monitors can observe messages leaving the client, arriving at the proxy, and leaving the proxy. Of course, the monitor cannot verify that no private information is leaked from the client if it cannot view the contents of the encrypted report.

Figure 3 gives a somewhat simplified illustration how this problem is solved. When the client produces a report, it encrypts the report with the public key of the broker, denoted $Pub - B$. At the same time, it gives a monitor positioned at the client $Pub - B$ as well as the contents of the report, the ad ID Ad and the publisher ID Pub. This monitor could be software running on behalf of a concerned user or privacy advocate. With this, the monitor is able to replicate the encryption step and produce an encrypted report. If the encrypted report produced by the monitor matches that transmitted by the client, then the monitor is assured that the report contains only Ad and Pub, and not some private information.

In practice, it will be necessary to add salt to the encrypted part of the message to prevent a dictionary attack at the untrusted Proxy. If this salt is produced through a pseudo-random number generator, then the client cannot use the salt as a covert channel (i.e. pick "random" numbers that in fact embed personal user information). If the monitor provides the initial key, and knows the pseudo-random number generator algorithm, then it can validate that the salt is not a covert channel.

Likewise, monitors at the input and output of the proxy can verify that each report going into the proxy is matched by a report going out of the proxy, and that therefore the proxy did not convey the IP address to the broker.

Of course, these reports alone are not the only means by which the client could potentially communicate private information to the broker, or that the proxy could communicate IP addresses to the broker. Legitimate processes within client computers commonly transmit thousands of messages in the background to a wide variety of destinations around the Internet. The software agent could hide its own messages within this background noise. We admit that individual users would not be in a position to detect such messages. Rather, we envision that privacy advocates would install the software agent in clients that they control and carefully monitor all messages going in and out. Privacy advocates could then build up reasonable confidence that no software agents are leaking private information.

Likewise, a proxy intent on colluding with the broker could convey client IP addresses through background channels such as file transfers or even disks sent through physical mail. Proxy operation, however, is relatively simple, and so we would reasonably expect a monitor to be able to audit the operating procedures of a proxy to insure with high confidence that no collusion is taking place.

In the following, we provide additional detail and related challenges.

3.1   Profiling

User profiling has a long established history in the advertising industry. Starting from initial adware and banner advertisements and leading to today's cookie placement strategies and user traffic stream analysis, the brokers and advertisers have been continuously working on improving their penetration levels into more fine-grained groups of users. This has, unfortunately, been all at the expense of gathering a large amount of information from the users who, usually unknowingly, accept the long and complicated terms and conditions used by most providers. This has the effect of hiding the monitoring abilities of such cookies and adware software from users.

With Privad, Users would voluntarily install the software agent, probably bundled with some useful software package as historically done with adware (and, unfortunately, spyware). Because Privad is private, and hopefully has the imprimatur of privacy advocates and government agencies, it will not be necessary to obscure the profiling operation of Privad from users. Users would opt-in with full knowledge. It should go without saying that the software agent would be disabled when users un-install the associated bundled software package.

Of course, it is necessary to keep the profiling information stored locally on the client safe from the prying eyes of other users of the client or other malware that may invade the client. This problem is similar in spirit to the privacy issues created by the browsing histories kept by browsers. The problem is in some respects potentially made worse by Privad, however, because the profile may contain such information as salary and specific shopping habits. To mitigate this, the profile can be encrypted as long as it is on disk, and only kept in the clear while in memory. Another option might be to allow users to flush the profile from time to time, though the ability to do this, or the frequency with which it can be done, has to be weighed against the loss in ad targeting.

3.2   Ad Database Dissemination

A major challenge in Privad is ad dissemination. Not only do potentially hundreds of thousands of ads need to be disseminated, the associated bids and targetting meta-data such as keywords need to be disseminated as well. If all ads are pushed to all clients, then nothing is learned about those clients. If this does not adequately scale, however, the broker must be selective in which ads it gives to which clients. To the extent that this selection requires specific knowledge about client profiles, Privad leaks private information.

Before discussing how we can mitigate these scaling issues, it is worth pointing out that substantial volumes of information can be broadcast to clients with existing broadband installations. For instance, thousands of ads can be downloaded into a client for the equivalent bandwidth of a few minutes of YouTube. To ease load on the proxy server, the download could take place as an ongoing BitTorrent. Existing peer-to-peer video broadcasting systems, for instance, have demonstrated the ability to disseminate many megabytes of video stream to thousands of clients within a few tens of seconds [7]. The client could locally discard any ads that are clearly unlikely to be relevant, thus reducing its memory requirements.

One way to reduce the volume of distribution, while preserving privacy, would be to distribute each ad to a randomly selected fraction of clients. The advertiser only requires that each ad is shown a certain number of times, not that the ad ultimately distributed to all clients. If the budget for an ad is relatively small, then the ad may correspondingly be distributed to a relatively smaller number of clients. Randomness could be achieved by exploiting the randomness inherent in a BitTorrent peer-to-peer style of distribution. For instance, each ad could have attached to it the number of clients that should store the ad. This number could be divided and decremented as the ad is shared with peers and stored, thus limited the distribution of the ad.

If random scoping is not adequate, then scoping based on certain relatively non-sensitive demographic information could be done. For instance, ads could be disseminated based on language or location.

While we have some confidence that the scaling issues associated with ad dissemination can be overcome, measurement and experimentation are ultimately required to support or undermine this confidence.

4 Related Work

In this section we briefly present the related work on user profiling and private advertising. We also cover the case of advertising on online social networks as the amount of detail provided by users in their profiles puts these social networks in a strong position in relation to targeted advertising. For example in the case of FaceBook[6] there were a range of advertisement plans devised by the owners. Using the FaceBook interface, companies would be able to selectively target FaceBook's members in order to research the appeal of new products through a polling system called Engagement Ads and FaceBook Beacons. However in some cases the user's privacy concerns forced changes to such policies[7].

Recently there has been attempts by ISPs to monitor customers' traffic and offer them targeted advertisements. For example information such as web pages viewed and links clicked on, including advertisements, search terms, browsing trends and page click chains, response to advertisements and more importantly demographics such as language, the day of the week, time and domain locations are used by some of these cooperative advertisement business plans[8].

In UK, British Telecommunication initially announced that a controversial online advertisement system would be rolled out, but it stressed that any profiling will be done only with the knowledge and agreement of the customer. This announcement was motivated by the belief that systems such as Phorm[9] are the only way to keep ISPs afloat in the future. In the trial stages, BT had admitted that it secretly used customer data to test Phorm's ad targeting technology, and that it covered it up when customers raised questions over the suspicious redirects. BT faced legal action from customers who were not pleased that their web traffic was compromised.[10] However this has not yet stopped development of business ties between Phorm and a few major UK ISPs in order to monitor user traffic for targeted advertising.

We are not the first to design privacy-preserving advertising, though the academic literature contains surprisingly few examples. There are a number of patents that claim to be privacy preserving[11], but many of these are private only by virtue of claiming not to gather explicit PII per se. They can, however, associate user IP addresses with ad events such as views and clicks, and are therefore only weakly private.

Juels [4] designed a strongly private system as early as 2001. Like Privad, Juels' system assumes an agent running on the client. Unlike Privad, however, Juels made the assumption that pushing ads to the client was not feasible (and indeed in 2001 it certainly was not as feasible). Therefore, Juels proposes a system whereby the client requests a certain type of ad, and the broker supplies

---

[6] http://www.facebook.com

[7] http://www.nytimes.com/external/readwriteweb/2009/02/02/
02readwriteweb-facebook_sells_your_data.html

[8] http://www.nebuad.com/privacy

[9] http://www.phorm.com/

[10] http://www.theregister.co.uk/2008/03/17/bt_phorm_lies/

[11] US patents 6085229, 6182050, and 6370578.

that ad. To preserve privacy, however, Juels places an untrusted mixnet between the client and the broker. Mixnets such as the one that Juels proposes are robust against collusion, and thus go further than Privad, which requires monitoring. However, mixnets are complex and heavyweight, and introduce delays into the ad serving process. As a result, it doesn't strike us as attractive an approach as Privad.

Kazienko and Adamski [5] propose AdROSA, a method for displaying web banners using usage mining based on processing of all user's HTTP request during visits to publisher's website. This method was suggested to solve the problem of automatic personalization of web banner advertisements with respect to user privacy and recent advertising policies. It is based on extracting knowledge from the web page content and historical user sessions as well as the current behavior of the online user, using data-mining techniques. Historical user sessions are stored in the form of vectors in the AdROSA database and they are clustered to obtain typical, aggregated user sessions. The site content of the publisher's web pages is automatically processed in a similar way. The system extracts terms from the HTML content of each page. However passing on such information to the advertisement broker may generate the same privacy concerns experienced by efforts of Phorm and NebuAd.

Similar issues as text advertisement have been seen in banner advertisements. Claessens et al. [2] highlight some of the privacy issues with current advertising model based on banner displays, which over time could be linked to individual users using server-side analysis of the cookies stored on user's system. In addition, there is a security threat from the publisher or users to cooperate in order to increase the click rate, hence claiming more money from the advertiser. They suggest the separation of profile managers from user by use of anonymous networks and web proxies. The profile management side can be done at the user end. They suggest a client-side banner selection solution will not be practical in terms of scalability of updates.

5   Future Directions and Conclusions

In this paper we have highlighted the privacy issues with current advertising schemes and outline a new system, Privad, based on a variant of adware systems. Specifically, Privad runs a software agent at the client that locally profiles the user and serves out ads, thus preserving the privacy of the users. Privad, however, operates within the current economic framework of advertising consisting of advertisers, publishers, and brokers. Ad events like view and clicks are reported to brokers and advertisers in such a way that no single system component needs to be trusted individually, and that the privacy of the system can be verified with high confidence.

Although Privad is promising, there are a number of technical challenges ahead.

We have already mentioned the issue of scalable ad and bid dissemination, and we are continuing research in this area.

We believe that the Privad model engenders a wide range of advertisement selection approaches. At the simple extreme, the agent could simply monitor which search terms the user types into the popular search engines, and later match these with keywords associated with advertisements. On the other extreme, the agent could do sophisticated demographic profiling of the user, and advertisers could bid on fine-grained demographics. Taken to its logical limit, this approach could end up revealing private information in another way. For instance, imagine that profiling was so detailed that an advertiser could target an ad to the demographic "families with two or more children under the age of 10, living in large metropolitan cities, with income between $80,000 and $100,000". In this case, when a user clicks on such an ad, the advertiser immediately knows a great deal about the user. Overall, we need to strike a balance between the granularity of targeting and privacy. This is another ongoing topic of research.

There are claims that augmenting social networks with online markets places improves trust between transactions and increases user satisfaction. The advantages of a social-based system over a reputation-based system have been studied previously, showing that malicious users can still boost their transaction-based reputation, while they can not improve their social-based trustworthiness [1]. An interesting avenue for more targeted profiling is also to perform distributed cluster detection algorithms on profiles based on their interests. Such methods have also been developed in order to present better search results by linking to users' social network group [3]. Ironically, such an approach may overcome the privacy concerns with highly targeted ads. If a private reputation system can be devised, then all that is known by the advertiser is that a user who clicked on an ad has something in common with some other user who also clicked on the ad. The advertiser, however, doesn't know what that something is.

Another major problem in advertising systems today is click fraud. For Privad to be viable, it must be at least no more susceptible to click fraud than existing advertising systems, and ideally it improves in this area. While this is also ongoing research, we observe that since the agent can monitor user behavior, it is potentially in a good position to detect clickfraud. Making this work depends on being able to protect the agent software from being tampered with.

Finally, it is worth mentioning that our approach is not limited to web browsers. The system can serve ads in a variety of ways, for example in virtual reality games, Internet chat conversations, or embedded in other applications. This variety of channels makes our approach well suited for future evolution of advertising systems.

References

1. Bhattacharjee, R., Goel, A.: Avoiding ballot stuffing in ebay-like reputation systems. In: P2PECON 2005: Proceedings of the 2005 ACM SIGCOMM workshop on Economics of peer-to-peer systems, pp. 133–137. ACM, New York (2005)
2. Claessens, J., Diaz, C., Faustinelli, R., Preneel, B.: A secure and privacy-preserving web banner system for targeted advertising (2003)

3. Gummadi, K.P., Mislove, A., Druschel, P.: Exploiting Social Networks for Internet Search. In: Proc. 5th Workshop on Hot Topics in Networks, Irvine, CA, pp. 79–84 (2006)
4. Juels, A.: Targeted advertising.. And privacy too. In: Naccache, D. (ed.) CT-RSA 2001. LNCS, vol. 2020, pp. 408–424. Springer, Heidelberg (2001)
5. Kazienko, P., Adamski, M.: Adrosa–adaptive personalization of web advertising. Information Sciences 177(11), 2269–2295 (2007)
6. Krishnamurthy, B., Wills, C.: On the leakage of personally identifiable information via online social networks. In: WOSN 2009: Proceedings of the second workshop on Online social networks, Barcelona, USA (2009)
7. Zhang, X., Liu, J., Li, B., Yum, T.: Coolstreaming/donet: A data-driven overlay network for efficient live media streaming. In: IEEE Infocom 2005, Miami (2005)

The Step Method – Battling Identity Theft Using E-Retailers' Websites

Marion Schulze and Mahmood H. Shah

University of Central Lancashire, Lancashire Business School, PR1 2HE Preston, UK
MSchulze@uclan.ac.uk, MHShah@uclan.ac.uk

Abstract. Identity theft is the fastest growing crime in the 21st century. This paper investigates firstly what well-known e-commerce organizations are communicating on their websites to address this issue. For this purpose we analyze secondary data (literature and websites of ten organizations). Secondly we investigate the good practice in this area and recommend practical steps. The key findings are that some organizations only publish minimum security information to comply with legal requirements. Others inform consumers on how they actively try to prevent identity theft, how consumers can protect themselves, and about supporting actions when identity theft related fraud actually happens. From these findings we developed the Support – Trust – Empowerment – Prevention (STEP) method. It is aimed at helping to prevent identity theft and dealing with consequences when it occurs. It can help organizations on gaining and keeping consumers' trust which is so essential for e-retailers in a climate of rising fraud.

Keywords: Identity Fraud, Identity Theft, Customers' Behavior, Websites, Security, Privacy, E-retailer.

1 Introduction

This paper aims to investigate how e-retailers in the UK communicate identity theft on their websites, and what can be considered as promising practice. Identity theft related fraud is a growing problem and can be seen as the fastest growing type of fraud in the UK (CIFAS, 2008).

We distinguish between identity theft and identity theft related fraud. Identity theft is "... the misappropriation of the identity (such as the name, date of birth, current address or previous address) of another person, without their knowledge or consent." (CIFAS, 2008) Identity theft is often followed by identity fraud which "... is the use of misappropriated identity in criminal activity, to obtain goods or service by deception." (CIFAS, 2008) e-Retailers become victims of identity fraud when fraudsters take over customer accounts, e.g. after getting hold of user name and password by "phishing" (Myers, 2006). Fraudsters may also set up new accounts with stolen identities and stolen payment card details. Internet fraud clearly damages Internet businesses. (Lindsay, 2005; SOPHOS, 2007) Not only trading goods are lost, also the trust of consumers, damaging the Internet economy as a whole (Tan, 2002; Berkowitz and Hahn, 2003; Sullins, 2006; PITTF, 2007; Acoca, 2008). Therefore it is important for e-retailers to find ways to gain consumers' trust in times of rising fraud.

C. Godart et al. (Eds.): I3E 2009, IFIP AICT 305, pp. 173–183, 2009.

Publishing information on websites is one way of achieving this. Collins (2005) points out that legal requirement about what to publish are merely superficial. She suggests an e-business website that is perceived by customers as secure. In addition, it should offer information on how customers can help secure their own privacy. She recommends that organizations should perform a website security assessment to measure the performance of their website in terms of how security is perceived by customers.

Collins' recommendation how to communicate identity theft on websites focuses on perceived security. Our analysis aims to investigate if this approach is enough and how it is used in practice on websites of well-known e-retailers in the UK. The next section describes our research methodology. The findings section outlines what UK e-retailers are communicating on websites regarding identity theft and related fraud. The discussion section proposes what can be considered as promising practice, we call it the STEP method. The final section concludes with a critical evaluation of the results.

2 Research Methodology

The nature of this research required an analysis of organizations' websites. This paper is an analysis of websites of ten large online retailers in the United Kingdom, shown in appendix one and table one. All of them sell consumer goods online. One of these retailers is the sponsor of this research.

Table 1. Chosen sample of retailers

No	E-retailer	Industry	E-retailer
A	Computer Supermarket.com	Computer	http://www.computersupermarket.com/
B	Bodyshop	Body care	http://www.thebodyshop.co.uk/
C	Laura Ashley	Furniture, Home	http://www.lauraashley.com/
D	Multizoneav.com	Computer	http://www.multizoneav.com/
E	PC World	Computer	http://www.pcworld.co.uk/
F	Amazon.co.uk	Miscellaneous	http://www.amazon.co.uk/
G	Sainsbury's	Supermarket & miscellaneous	http://www.sainsburys.co.uk/home.htm
H	Debenhams	Miscellaneous	http://www.debenhams.com/
I	Marks & Spencer Plc	Cloths & Grocery	http://www.marksandspencer.com/
J	Shop Direct (Littlewoods)	Miscellaneous	http://www.littlewoods.com/

We identified all possible actions companies mention or perform on their websites that are related to identity theft and identity fraud. Based on a first sample we developed an analysis sheet, containing five categories of information that will be presented separately in the findings section: Accreditation, prevention of identity theft, prevention of identity fraud, empowerment of customers, and reaction when fraud occurs.

3 Findings

3.1 Trust-Building Information

It is important to publish security and identity theft related information on websites because consumers have the legal right to be informed. Consumers may also gain trust if they get the impression that a company takes these issues seriously.

We found that e-retailers try to establish trust on websites by letting customers know what they do to battle the crime: accreditation, prevention of identity theft, and prevention of identity fraud. These attempts are described here and evaluated in the discussion section.

3.1.1 Accreditation

One way of gaining trust is demonstrating an accreditation with companies who check the safety of internet pages. Information on different accreditation programs can be followed up by links given in appendix 2. The following table shows how our sample of e-retailers makes use of it.

Table 2. Information given about accreditation of data security

	A	B	C	D	E	F	G	H	I	J
Participant of the Safe Harbor Framework						x				
ISIS accredited by IMRG										x
Certified Tier 1 PCI DSS Compliance				x						
SafeBuy Web Code of Practice	x									
VeriSign SSL certificate					x					
IMRG member (e-retail industry body)										x
Link to accreditation website	x	x								x

When a website links to an accreditation program, it does not always mean that the organization is accredited, e.g. the ISIS link on Laura Ashley's (C) website. Half of the e-retailers of our sample do not mention accreditation at all.

3.1.2 Prevention of Identity Theft

A second way of gaining trust is to demonstrate how much the organization does to prevent identity theft. The statements we found on the analyzed websites are described in following table three.

Most of these points reflect the requirements of the Data Protection Act 1998 (ICO, 2009). Organizations in the UK are legally obliged to protect customers' data from identity theft and publish a security statement on their websites. The security statement should inform consumers about who is collecting their personal information, which data are stored, what the data are used for, their rights of accessing the data and refusing their storage and usage, and finally the use of cookies and other tracking systems. Additionally the Data Protection Act 1998 demands a transcription-based transmission system. Sensitive personal information should be secured by encryption or similar techniques on a website operator's server.

The analysis of organizations' websites in table three reveals that some of the organizations just mention the minimum requirements of the Data Protection Act 1998; others put a lot of effort in to show how serious they are about data security.

Table 3. E-retailers' actions to prevent identity theft

	A	B	C	D	E	F	G	H	I	J
Protect customers' data when they are transferred or stored										
Secure online data transfer										
Secure sockets layer (SSL) software is used	x		x	x	x	x			x	x
E-retailer only accept orders using SSL software					x					
Encryption is used	x	x			x		x		x	
Secure storage of data										
Encrypted sensitive data when stored (e.g. credit card data)								x		
Stored data on separate server / secure server	x		x		x		x			
Payment card data are deleted when account has not been used for a while						x			x	
Secure transfer of data										
Onward transfer of data only to reliable sources or not at all					x	x				
Choice of established delivery firm									x	
Only part of the debit or credit card is revealed when confirming the order					x	x				

Table 4. E-retailers' actions to prevent identity fraud

	A	B	C	D	E	F	G	H	I	J
Fraud-monitoring systems in place										
Data checked with fraud prevention agencies										x
Credit Card checks - details passed to credit reference agencies	x		x		x					
Procedures in place to detect fraud						x	x			x
Automated decision making systems in place when assessing customers										x
Authentication systems in place										
Multi-factor authentication for customers' accounts										
Ask for password and postcode										x
Additional protection for payment cards										
3D Secure Schemes (MasterCard SecureCode, Verified by Visa)	x							x	x	x
Information for customers what happens when identity fraud is detected										x

3.1.3 Prevention of Identity Fraud

There are no legal obligations in the UK about how companies should inform consumers on websites about identity fraud.

The Data Protection Act 1998 (ICO, 2009) only obliges organizations to publish their physical address on their website. This enables consumers who are victims of identity fraud to ask for relevant information. Nevertheless the website analysis, shown in table four, reveals that some organizations describe other means to protect customers from becoming fraud victims.

3.2 Empowering Information – How Customers Can Protect Themselves

Apart from gaining customers' trust as shown above, organizations use websites as well to inform customers how they can secure their own privacy, illustrated in table five. Again, some of the organizations mainly focus on the minimum requirements of the Data Protection Act 1998; others put a lot of effort into providing information for customers.

Table 5. E-retailers' information for customers to deal with data security

	A	B	C	D	E	F	G	H	I	J
Information about legal requirements										
Give notice how data are handled	x	x	x	x	x	x	x	x	x	x
Tell customers that they have the choice of submitting data or not	x		x	x		x	x		x	x
Let customers know how they can access their data	x			x	£10	x	x		£10	£10
Mention that data are used in accordance with legal requirements	x	x	x	x	x	x	x	x	x	
How to protect personal information										
Contribution to secure data transfer										
How to recognize secure websites					x	x		x	x	
Inform customers about secure versions of internet software					x					
Account protection										
How to create safer passwords						x		x		
Remind customers to keep password safe						x		x		
Prompt customers to sign off before leaving the website						x				
Prompt customers to close browser when finished on public computers						x		x		
Protect customers from Spoof/false e-Mails and false phone calls										
Explain the nature of spoof/false e-mails						x		x		
Let customers know how you do not contact them					x	x	x		x	x

Table 5. (*Continued*)

	A	B	C	D	E	F	G	H	I	J
Advise customers never to enter sensitive data into an email						x	x	x	x	x
Let customers know how you contact them						x		x		
Inform customers about data security and secure online shopping in general										
10 Tips of ISIS			x							x
Data transfer via internet is never 100% safe	x								x	
Explain what is identity theft										x
Advice to check security of linked websites before entering data			x			x	x		x	
Advice to ensure that customers' personal details are kept confidential										x
Advice to destroy documents with personal details by using paper shredders										x
Advice to check payment statements regularly for unknown transactions										x
Advice to fully close accounts when customers do not need them anymore										x

3.3 Supporting Information – What Companies Do When Identity Fraud Occurs

Finally we found some information that has not been considered by Collins' (2005). Three e-retailers of our sample communicate on their websites what they do when identity fraud occurs, shown in table six.

3.4 Types of Information Policies on Websites

We can summarize that we found three main approaches in battling identity theft on e-retailers' websites. The minimalist approach just fulfils legal requirements and does not seem to put much emphasis on trust-building, e.g. the website of Bodyshop (B). This finding supports Collins' hypothesis that the minimalist approach is still used by practitioners. The prevention approach aims to gain customers' trust by highlighting how securely data are handled and by informing customers of how they can protect themselves. It has been recommended by Collins (2005) and is used by most e-retailers of our sample. Finally there is a holistic approach, e.g. the website of Shop Direct / Littlewoods (J), which combines the prevention approach alongside giving additional information of what happens after identity fraud occurs. In the following

Table 6. E-Retailers' Information what happens when Identity Fraud occurs

	A	B	C	D	E	F	G	H	I	J
In case of unusual orders, drivers can reserve the right to query the order									x	
Identity theft team - Personal case worker									x	
Inform fraud prevention agencies									x	
Pay for up to £50 of damage if payment card is fraudulently used								x		
Information for customers how to apply for a personal credit report									x	
FAQ - what do I do when my card has been used fraudulently?							x			
Security and identity theft as help topic									x	

section we will discuss the components of these approaches and develop promising practice which we call the STEP method.

4 Discussion

Because of legal requirements all organizations have to follow at least the minimalist approach. Should e-retailers do more on their websites? We are proposing the STEP method which stands for Support – Trust – Empowerment – Prevention (STEP).

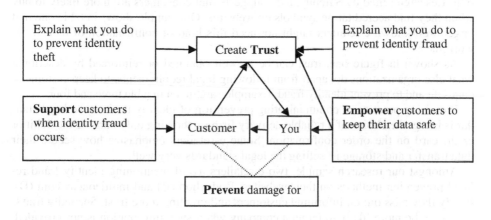

Fig. 1. The STEP Method

This holistic approach is based on the promising practice of the findings' section above.

4.1 "S" for Support

Support means that organizations should provide the best possible support for consumers when the latter become victims of identity fraud. Identity fraud does not only cause financial losses, it can have tremendous impacts on consumers' health. Collins (2005) points out that identity fraud can cause an emotional component comparable to the effects of rape and calls the crime "identity rape". Therefore we suggest E-retailers should not only provide fast support for victims but also make this support visible on their websites. Promising practice is described in table six. We recommend positioning this information in the Help or Customer Services menu and under frequently asked questions. It should contain information about who to contact when identity fraud happens; and provide general information about the first essential steps the consumer needs to take, e.g. how to contact credit reference agencies for credit reports. A fully trained personal case worker seems to be a promising way of dealing with the emotional upset of victims. A good example for this kind of support is the website of Shop Direct / Littlewoods (J) in table six.

We recommend on top of this to inform customers on e-retailers' websites in more detail about the nature of identity fraud, how it usually occurs, and its impact on victims.

Figure one shows that support prevents damage for customers. Victims are not necessarily customers when a fraudster has set up a fraudulent account in their name. E-retailers can see this as an opportunity to win victims of such crimes as new customers by supporting them in a best possible way and winning their trust.

4.2 "T" for Trust

Trust means that consumers should have evidence that they can trust the website. For many well-known companies trust is implicit given their long-standing reputation. Younger and less well-known companies may benefit from some form of accreditation. Research (cited by Safebuy, n.d.) suggests that consumers are more likely to buy when they find accreditation symbols on websites. Our sample shows in table one that larger well-known e-retailers might not need this kind of confirmation of their trustworthiness.

As shown in figure one, trust can be as well obtained or reinforced by describing what else organizations do, apart from following legal requirements, to keep customers' data safe and to prevent identity fraud. Examples are given in table three and four.

Promising practice of communicating prevention of identity theft above legal standards is e.g. the choice of a reliable delivery firm or showing only parts of the debit or credit card on the order confirmation. Some e-retailers emphasize how secure their data transfer and storage is, selling the legal standards very well.

Amongst our research sample, two e-retailers avoid mentioning identity fraud related prevention methods on their websites, Bodyshop (B) and multizoneav.com (D). Firstly they miss out on informing customers and creating more trust. Secondly fraudsters may be more likely to target a company when such information is not provided. Therefore we recommend including it on websites. 3D secure schemes, credit card checks and procedures to detect fraud are the most popular prevention methods mentioned in our sample. We recommend additionally implementing multi-factor authentication and communicating it on websites as this seems to be one of the safest prevention methods.

Finally there is an expected positive effect on trust when e-retailers support victims of identity fraud. Trust is, as shown in figure one, beside prevention one of the two central themes of the STEP method.

4.3 "E" for Empowerment

Empowerment stands for informing the customers of how they can avoid identity theft and fraud. We regard it as good practice to inform consumers about the real risk of identity theft and identity fraud. They need to take it seriously in order to be prepared to actively prevent it. The empowerment of customers to deal with data security has two main advantages, as shown in figure one. Firstly consumers are more likely to protect themselves when they are aware of the risk of identity theft and know how they can minimize it. This reduces the damage for the e-retailer. Secondly consumers will be more interested in the security statement when it applies to them and probably gain the impression that this organization takes their security seriously.

Table five gives an overview what kind of information can be given. We find it especially useful to inform customers about "phishing" and ways how they can avoid becoming a victim of this crime. This includes spoof / false e-mails. The websites of Amazon (F) and Marks & Spencer Plc (I) are good examples. Customers should be made aware how they can protect there payment card details, how important it is to logoff their accounts, and how they should choose their passwords to make them more secure. The more information is given, the better the empowerment. The only exception is the legal requirement that does not seem to be helpful to prevent identity theft.

4.4 "P" for Prevention

As shown in figure one, support, trust, and empowerment ensure that the e-retailer heads for a better level of prevention than with the minimalist approach or the prevention approach that has been proposed be Collins (2005).

The likelihood for the e-retailer of becoming a victim of identity fraud can be reduced. If prevention methods are communicated on websites fraudsters may be less likely to target this company. Customers are more likely to prevent crime when they are empowered and know how. We would expect less account takeovers and cases of application fraud for an e-retailer who provides such information, and therefore less related costs.

The support within the STEP method adds one additional preventative point; as arrows demonstrate in figure one. Negative effects of occurred identity fraud on customers, especially emotional damage, can be better prevented when supportive information is in place. Customers are more likely to stay customers when they are treated with care, and when trust is created through this experience. The advantage for the e-retailer might be the prevention of lost revenues or even a gain of more customers.

Therefore we can summarize that prevention is beside trust-building one of the two strength of the STEP method. It outperforms the prevention method in both aspects.

5 Conclusion

We reached our aim and identified three approaches of communication on websites in practice regarding identity theft and identity fraud, the minimalist approach, the prevention approach, and the holistic approach. We favor the holistic approach and recommend the STEP method that combines different ways of good practice we have found on the reviewed websites. The outcome of this paper can be used by e-retailers to review their current websites and their identity theft risk management approaches. It proposes plenty of options of how to inform customers on websites not only to gain trust, but also to better prevent crime. It is as well a good starting point for further research.

This paper will be followed by primary research testing the pros and cons of the holistic approach compared to the more popular prevention approaches. The result of this paper is based on a limited sample of organizations and needs to be confirmed by extending the sample size. It is also limited by using websites as the only source of gathering information.

References

1. Acoca, B.: Online Identity Theft. OECD Observer 268, 12–13 (2008)
2. Berkowitz, B., Hahn, R.W.: Cyber Security: who's watching the Store. Issues in Science & Technology 19(3), 55–63 (2003)
3. CIFAS: Identity fraud and identity theft. CIFAS Online, http://www.cifas.ork.uk/default.asp?edit_id=561-56
4. Collins, J.M.: Preventing Identity Theft in Your Business: How to Protect Your Business, Customers, and Employees, pp. 156—161, 173–177. John Wiley & Sons, Hoboken (2005)
5. ICO, Data Protection Act 1998 - Data Protection Good Practice Note for collecting personal Information using Websites, Information Commissioner's Office's Data Protection Guide (1998), http://www.ico.gov.uk/home/for_organisations/data_protection_guide.aspx
6. Lindsay, N.: E-Commerce: Boom or Bust? Computer Weekly, 18–19 (January 25, 2005)
7. Myers, S.: Introduction to Phishing. In: Jakobsson, M., Myers, S. (eds.) Phishing and Countermeasures, pp. 1–29. John Wiley & Sons, Hoboken (2006)
8. PITTF: Combating Identity Theft: A strategic Plan. The President's Identity Theft Task Force (2007), http://www.idtheft.gov/reports/StrategicPlan.pdf
9. SOPHOS: Phishing, phaxing, vishing, and other Identity Threats: The Evolution of Online Fraud. A SOPHOS White Paper (2007), http://ithound.vnunet.com/view_abstract/1181?layout=vnunet
10. Sullins, K.L.: "Phishing" for a Solution: Domestic and international Approaches to decreasing Online Identity Theft. Emory International Law Review 20(1), 397–433 (2006)
11. Tan, H.S.K.: E-Fraud: Current Trends and international Developments. Journal of Financial Crime 9(4), 347–354 (2002)

Appendix 1: Websites of the Analyzed Sample

Amazon.co.uk. (March 10, 2009), http://www.amazon.co.uk/
Bodyshop, (March 24, 2009), http://www.thebodyshop.co.uk/
Computer Supermarket.com, (March 24, 2009), http://www.computersupermarket.com/
Debenhams, (March 24, 2009), http://www.debenhams.com/
Laura Ashley, (March 24, 2009), http://www.lauraashley.com/
Marks & Spencer Plc, (March 24, 2009), http://www.marksandspencer.com/
Multizoneav.com, (March 24, 2009), http://www.multizoneav.com/
PC World, (March 11, 2009), http://www.pcworld.co.uk/

Sainsbury's online, (March 10, 2009), http://www.sainsburys.co.uk/home.htm
Shop direct group: Littlewoods, (March 24, 2009), http://www.littlewoods.com/

Appendix 2: Websites for Accreditation

Certified Tier 1 PCI DSS Compliance by venda, (March 24, 2009), http://www.venda.com/
IMRG, (March 24, 2009), http://www.imrg.org/
ISIS, (March 24, 2009), http://isisaccreditation.imrg.org/
Safebuy, (March 24, 2009), http://www.safebuy.org.uk/
US-EU Safe Harbor Framework, (March 10, 2009), http://www.export.gov/safeharbor/
VeriSign SSL, (March 24, 2009), http://www.verisign.co.uk/ssl/

Proposal and Implementation of SSH Client System Using Ajax

Yusuke Kosuda and Ryoichi Sasaki

Tokyo Denki University 2-2, Kanda-Nishiki-Cho, Chiyoda-Ku Tokyo,
101-8457 Japan
kosuda@isl.im.dendai.ac.jp, sasaki@im.dendai.ac.jp

Abstract. Technology called Ajax gives web applications the functionality and operability of desktop applications. In this study, we propose and implement a Secure Shell (SSH) client system using Ajax, independent of the OS or Java execution environment. In this system, SSH packets are generated on a web browser by using JavaScript and a web server works as a proxy in communication with an SSH server to realize end-to-end SSH communication. We implemented a prototype program and confirmed by experiment that it runs on several web browsers and mobile phones. This system has enabled secure SSH communication from a PC at an Internet cafe or any mobile phone. By measuring the processing performance, we verified satisfactory performance for emergency use, although the speed was unsatisfactory in some cases with mobile phone. The system proposed in this study will be effective in various fields of E-Business.

Keywords: Ajax, SSH, security, mobile phone, mobile PC, PDA, Smartphone.

1 Introduction

In recent years, many web applications based on a technology called Ajax (Asynchronous JavaScript and XML: see Section 2.1 for details) have been developed. Ajax applications, represented by Google Map [1], have greatly contributed to the realization of "Web 2.0." Unlike conventional web applications, Ajax applications can provide functionality and operability equal to those of desktop applications. Since the Ajax applications do not depend on the OS or Java execution environment, it is anticipated that they can be used from mobile phones, PDA, or other mobile terminals. Because of the capability of extremely safe access to a remote computer, SSH (Secure Shell: see Section 2.2 for details) is used daily by server and network administrators as an essential tool for work execution.

The current SSH, however, is not free to use in any environments. Even when an Internet-connected terminal is available, SSH communication is not possible without SSH client software installed in the terminal. For emergency SSH communication, a user needs an Internet-connected terminal where a corresponding SSH client is installed or provided for installation.

C. Godart et al. (Eds.): I3E 2009, IFIP AICT 305, pp. 184–196, 2009.
© IFIP International Federation for Information Processing 2009

In this study, therefore, we propose and implement a SSH client system using Ajax. Ajax makes SSH communication available from various kinds of Internet-connected equipment with an installed browser. If widely provided as a service, the proposed system will be very helpful in emergency cases and effective in various fields of E-Business.

The function described previously has already been implemented in programs such as MindTerm using Java [19], [20]. These implementation methods, however, cannot be applied to many existing PCs or mobile terminals (mobile phone, PDA, etc.) without Java execution environment. With the results of this research, we can ensure the safe implementation of the above functions even in environments where it previously was not possible.

2 Elemental Technologies

2.1 Outline of Ajax

Ajax is a technique for web application implementation combined with the existing web development technologies. More specifically, asynchronous HTTP and/or HTTPS (After this, we represent HTTP and/or HTTPS as HTTP(S)) communication is set up by the XMLHttpRequest object of JavaScript and a web page is dynamically rewritten by dynamic HTML, as if a web page read into a web browser rewrites part of itself through communication (Fig. 1). If Ajax is applied to a web search, for example, search results can be displayed on a real-time basis because the search is executed not after the confirmation of input as before, but in the background while the user is inputting the key. By executing communication in the background and using various events and functions of JavaScript, web applications can provide high responsiveness and various functions almost equally as desktop applications.

The XMLHttpRequest object is supported by major web browsers for the PC and its support is successively increased among mobile phones and other mobile terminals. Also, through a working draft at W3C (World Wide Web Consortium) [2], this object is being standardized.

Ajax-applied web applications use such web standard technologies as HTML, JavaScript, and Style Sheets. If only a supporting web browser is available, therefore, the applications can be used independently of the OS or Java environment.

The same origin policy [6] for the security limit is applied to XMLHttpRequest which is one of the Ajax cores. When XMLHttpRequest is directly written on a web page with a script tag, communication can be set up only with the generated-from server (the same protocol port) of the web page. When XMLHttpRequest is written in an external .js file, communication can be set up only with the generated-from server (the same protocol port) of the web page calling the .js file by the script tag.

This limit is a function preferable for safety but disrupts the realization of the target function in this research. To avoid the limit, therefore, the generated-from server becomes a proxy for relaying (mutual conversion is also conducted if the protocols are different).

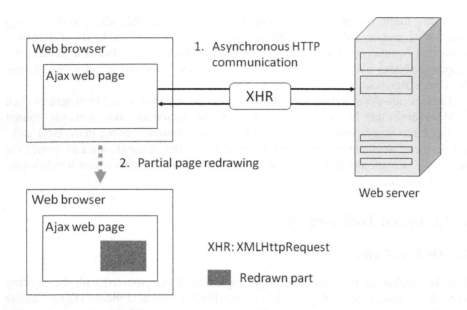

Fig. 1. Image of Ajax web applications

2.2 Outline of SSH

SSH is a communication protocol and program for login to a remote computer and command execution through a network.

Compared with the conventional TELNET and rlogin, SSH has the following safety mechanisms using authentication and encryption technologies:

- Server host authentication for a client to judge whether the connected server is allowed access and also to prevent a man-in-the-middle attack
- User authentication (e.g., password, public key authentication and many other kinds of authentication) for a server to judge whether to accept a connection requested by a user
- Communication channel encryption (e.g., TripleDES, AES, RC4, and other common key encryption) for end-to-end encryption between a client and a server to prevent tapping
- Integrity assurance to prevent tampering and illegal data insertion

For details about SSH, refer to Ref. [4].

3 Existing Systems

3.1 Outline of Existing Systems

There are already Ajax-applied systems using SSH clients [5], [6]. These systems have the configurations shown in Figs. 2 and 3. The existing systems realize SSH communication by operating an SSH client in a web server through HTTP(S) using XMLHttpRequest from an Ajax web page with an I/O function read into the web browser. Therefore, SSH communication is only partial between a web server and a remote computer.

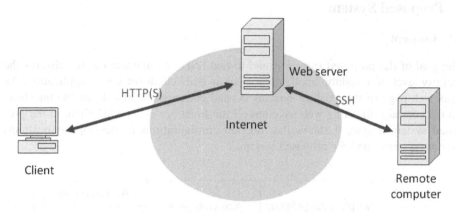

Fig. 2. Network configuration of existing systems

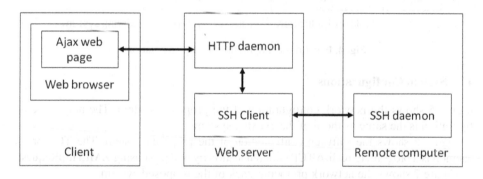

Fig. 3. Software configuration of existing systems

3.2 Problems of Existing Systems

The existing systems are subject to tapping, tampering, or spoofing by a man-in-the-middle attack on a communication channel. This attack may impair the substantially secure function of SSH.

HTTP communication between a web browser and a web server may be attacked by a network attacker because communication data is not encrypted.

Encryption using HTTPS between a web browser and a web server protects communication from an attack on a network. The problem with this method, however, is that processing in the web server is a black box for the user. We cannot deny the possibility of an attack on command input from a web browser or output from a remote computer. In addition, the user cannot verify this possibility.

With a completely reliable web server, the existing systems are suitable for a service using HTTPS in a server at home or at an organization where the user belongs. However, such systems may not be suitable for a service provided to the public.

4 Proposed System

4.1 Concept

The goal of the proposed system is end-to-end SSH communication that ensures the security level of a desktop application using an SSH client for a web application. An Ajax web page of the existing systems is used currently to provide an I/O interface. To the contrary, the Ajax web page has all the functions of an SSH client in the proposed system. Figure 4 shows the function configurations of desktop applications, existing systems, and the proposed system.

I/O	Application program	Ajax web page	Ajax web page
SSH			Web server
TCP/IP	OS	Web server	

Desktop application   Proposed system   Existing system

Fig. 4. Functions configuration of implementations

4.2 System Configurations

Figure 5 shows the network configuration of the proposed system. The network configuration is the same as those of the existing systems.

Figure 6 shows the software configuration of the proposed system. The TCP proxy daemon is a program to realize TCP communication by a request using XMLHttpRequest.

Figure 7 shows the network protocols stack of the proposed system.

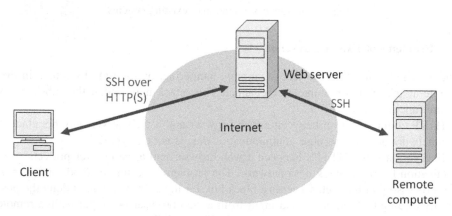

Fig. 5. Network configuration of proposed system

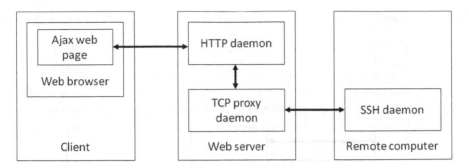

Fig. 6. Software configuration of proposed system

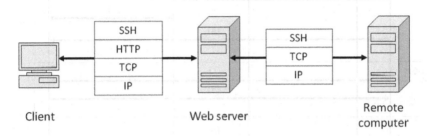

Fig. 7. Protocols stack of proposed system

4.3 Operation Outline

Figure 8 shows the communication sequence of the proposed system.

The proposed system operates in order from (1) to (6), listed as follows.

(1) Web page acquisition

By using the web browser, the user accesses the HTTP daemon of the web server and acquires the Ajax web page. Thus, the software configuration becomes that shown in Fig. 6.

(2) TCP connection request

The user enters the remote computer name, port number, user name, and other information into the Ajax web page for login. With the remote computer name and port number as arguments, the Ajax web page sends a TCP connection request to the TCP proxy daemon through the HTTP daemon by using XMLHttpRequest.

(3) Establishment of TCP connection

By receiving the request of (2), the TCP proxy daemon establishes a TCP connection with the SSH daemon. This establishes a virtual TCP connection from the Ajax web page to the SSH daemon.

(4) Establishment of SSH connection

Through the web server, the Ajax web page establishes an SSH connection with the SSH daemon on the virtual TCP connection established at (3) (SSH over HTTP).

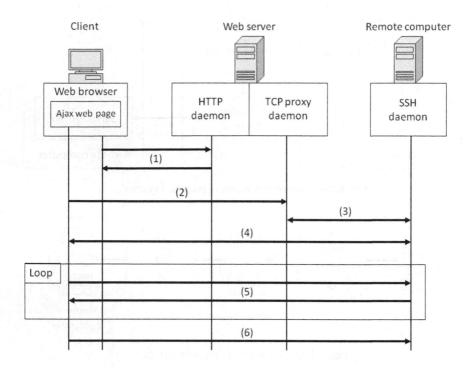

Fig. 8. Communication sequence of proposed system

(5) SSH receive processing
     The Ajax web page receives SSH packets repeatedly from the SSH daemon
     through the web server. For this processing, Comet [7] is used to keep a re-
     quest from the web browser at the web server for a specified time and return a
     response when the receive data is generated. When SSH packets are received,
     they are decrypted and their check bytes are calculated by JavaScript for
     screen refreshing and other processing.

(6) SSH send processing
     Commands entered to the Ajax web page by the user are acquired by
     JavaScript events. The commands are encrypted and their check bytes are
     calculated by JavaScript. Then SSH packets are generated and sent to the
     SSH daemon through the web server.

5 Implementation

A prototype system was implemented (Ajax web page and TCP proxy daemon in Fig. 6).
     The functions listed in Table 1 were mounted. The SSH protocols are SSH1 [8]
and SSH2 [9], [10], [11], [12], [13], [14], [15], [16]. Many vulnerabilities of SSH1
have already been noted and so the use of SSH2 is recommended. Because of easy
development, however, we decided to use SSH1 for implementation.

Table 1. Functions of implemented system

SSH protocol	SSH1
User authentication	Password authentication
Common key encryption	Triple DES
Communication	Each time a key is pressed

5.1 Operation Check

Figures 9 and 10 show screen shots of the implemented prototype. Table 2 gives the IP address configurations of the machines used for the performance check.

Figure 11 shows the communication of (2) and later processes, described in Section 4.3 "Operation Outline," captured on the web server. The communication type is HTTP between the client and the web server and SSH (SSH1) between the web server and the remote computer. Figures 12 and 13 show the packets of No. 176 and 177 in Fig. 11 in detail.

Fig. 9. Screenshot of login dialog

Fig. 10. Screenshot of terminal window

Table 2. IP address configurations

Client	192.168.1.5
Web server	192.168.1.3
Remote computer	192.168.1.2

No. ·	Source	Destination	Protocol	Info
149	192.168.1.5	192.168.1.3	HTTP	POST /work/20080307/ajax_ssh/interface.php
150	192.168.1.3	192.168.1.5	TCP	80 > 1065 [ACK] Seq=1 Ack=539 Win=64997 Le
151	192.168.1.3	192.168.1.2	TCP	1220 > 22 [SYN] Seq=0 Win=65535 Len=0 MSS=
152	192.168.1.2	192.168.1.3	TCP	22 > 1220 [SYN, ACK] Seq=0 Ack=1 Win=5840
153	192.168.1.3	192.168.1.2	TCP	1220 > 22 [ACK] Seq=1 Ack=1 Win=65535 Len=(
154	192.168.1.3	192.168.1.5	HTTP	HTTP/1.1 200 OK
155	192.168.1.5	192.168.1.3	HTTP	POST /work/20080307/ajax_ssh/interface.php
156	192.168.1.2	192.168.1.3	TCP	58054 > 113 [SYN] Seq=0 Win=5840 Len=0 MSS
157	192.168.1.3	192.168.1.2	TCP	113 > 58054 [RST, ACK] Seq=1 Ack=1 Win=0 L
158	192.168.1.2	192.168.1.3	SSHv1	Server Protocol: SSH-1.99-OpenSSH_4.3p2 Del
159	192.168.1.3	192.168.1.5	HTTP	HTTP/1.1 200 OK (text/html)
160	192.168.1.5	192.168.1.3	HTTP	POST /work/20080307/ajax_ssh/interface.php
161	192.168.1.3	192.168.1.2	SSHv1	Client Protocol: SSH-1.5-AJAXSSH0.2
162	192.168.1.2	192.168.1.3	TCP	22 > 1220 [ACK] Seq=33 Ack=20 Win=5840 Len
163	192.168.1.3	192.168.1.5	HTTP	HTTP/1.1 200 OK
164	192.168.1.5	192.168.1.3	HTTP	POST /work/20080307/ajax_ssh/interface.php
165	192.168.1.2	192.168.1.3	SSHv1	Server: Public Key
166	192.168.1.3	192.168.1.5	HTTP	HTTP/1.1 200 OK (text/html)
167	192.168.1.3	192.168.1.2	TCP	1220 > 22 [ACK] Seq=20 Ack=437 Win=65099 L
168	192.168.1.5	192.168.1.3	TCP	1065 > 80 [ACK] Seq=2127 Ack=2297 Win=6553
169	192.168.1.5	192.168.1.3	HTTP	POST /work/20080307/ajax_ssh/interface.php
170	192.168.1.3	192.168.1.2	SSHv1	Client: Session Key
171	192.168.1.3	192.168.1.5	HTTP	HTTP/1.1 200 OK
172	192.168.1.5	192.168.1.3	HTTP	POST /work/20080307/ajax_ssh/interface.php
173	192.168.1.2	192.168.1.3	TCP	22 > 1220 [ACK] Seq=437 Ack=304 Win=6432 L
174	192.168.1.2	192.168.1.3	SSHv1	Server: Encrypted packet len=5
175	192.168.1.3	192.168.1.5	HTTP	HTTP/1.1 200 OK (text/html)
176	192.168.1.5	192.168.1.3	HTTP	POST /work/20080307/ajax_ssh/interface.php
177	192.168.1.3	192.168.1.2	SSHv1	Client: Encrypted packet len=17
178	192.168.1.2	192.168.1.3	TCP	22 > 1220 [ACK] Seq=449 Ack=332 Win=6432 L
179	192.168.1.3	192.168.1.5	HTTP	HTTP/1.1 200 OK

Fig. 11. Packets captured on the web server

```
⊞ Transmission Control Protocol, Src Port: 1065 (1065), Dst Port: 80 (80), Seq: 3550,
⊞ Hypertext Transfer Protocol
⊟ Line-based text data: application/x-www-form-urlencoded
    Session=1213012265687&Method=SEND&Data=AAAAEd5PMOp!sbG8!UIGyPfJd7ziqv5scFNq1Q==
```

Fig. 12. Detail of the HTTP packet (No.176)

```
⊞ Transmission Control Protocol, Src Port: 1220 (1220), Dst Port: 22 (22), Seq: 304,
⊞ SSH Protocol
0000  00 e0 18 22 cb 10 00 13  a9 2a 67 df 08 00 45 00   ..."..... .*g...E.
0010  00 44 0c 33 40 00 80 06  6b 2b c0 a8 01 03 c0 a8   .D.3@... k+......
0020  01 02 04 c4 00 16 4f 7d  28 ce 6f e7 0f ed 50 18   ......O} (.o...P.
0030  fe 3f c5 d5 00 00 00 00  00 11 de 4f 30 ea 7e b1   .?....... ...00.~.
0040  b1 bc f9 42 06 c8 f7 c9  77 bc e2 aa fe 6c 70 53   ...B.... w....lpS
0050  6a 95                                              j.
```

Fig. 13. Detail of the SSH encrypted packet (No.177)

In the line starting from "Session=" of the HTTP packet shown in Fig. 12, the data of "AAAAEd5PMOp" (omitted hereinafter) after "Data=" is encoded into Base64. This corresponds to "00 00 00 11 de 4f " (omitted hereinafter) of the SSH encrypted packet (i.e., TCP payload) shown in Fig. 13. This indicates end-to-end SSH communication from the client to the remote computer.

The implemented system was verified to operate with the following main web browsers (all running on Windows XP Home Edition SP2):

- Internet Explorer 6.0
- Mozilla Firefox 2.0
- Opera 9.26
- Safari 3.1

5.2 Support of Cell Phone

In addition, we separately implemented an Ajax web page for mobile terminals and verified its operation by using the PC site viewer (Opera Mini 3.1) provided with the mobile phone KDDI AU W53S. The web page for the PC is the same as that for PC except for communication at every line feed.

6 Evaluations of Proposed System

6.1 Safety Evaluation

6.1.1 Safety against Illegal Access to Ajax Web Page with SSH Client Function

The proposed system is based on the web server's assumption that the Ajax web page is read normally into a web browser to provide the SSH client function. This assumption consists of two conditions:

(A)   The page in the web server is normal.
(B)   The page is not tampered on a communication channel when being downloaded from the web server to the web browser.

The condition of (B) can be realized by using HTTPS.

The condition of (A) is not easy to satisfy completely. The components (HTML, JavaScript, and Style Sheets) of the page allow the browsing of their source codes on a client. Therefore, a knowledgeable person can analyze them (about 2.5 K steps under the current implementation). A whitelist-type program may also enable automatic judgment. Under these circumstances, a server provider is considered to have psychological resistance against illegal behaviors. This prevention will be easy if Internet Mark [17], proposed separately by the authors, becomes popular. Internet Mark is a mechanism in which a trusted third party guarantees the validity of contents.

6.1.2 Safety against Man-in-the-Middle Attack in the Existing Systems

In the proposed system, an Ajax web page has the SSH client function and directly handles SSH packets, as mentioned in Section 4.1, to allow end-to-end encryption between a client and a remote computer. With the SSH login to a remote computer and later command exchange, this encryption prevents a man-in-the-middle attack that used to be a problem in the existing systems.

6.1.3 Safety of General SSH Client

In SSH, a client generally verifies the public key of a connect-to server to prevent a man-in-the-middle attack. For this verification, the SSH desktop application compares the public key with those on the public key list registered in the known_hosts file. This function is not implemented in the proposed system now but will be realized if a password-based encryption function (see Ref. [18]) is added to an Ajax web page that provides the SSH client function and if the encrypted known hosts file is stored in the web server.

Judging from the above, the proposed system is not inferior to the SSH desktop application in safety against a man-in-the-middle attack.

The proposed system cannot solve a Distributed Denial of Service (DDoS) attack at any layer lower than SSH where the existing SSH cannot secure safety.

6.2 Performance Evaluation

From the user's point of view, the time required for login and the I/O processing performance of the implemented system were measured.

Tables 3 and 4 list the client specifications, and Table 5 lists the average of 10 measurements for each. (A) to (C) describe the measuring methods and outline the client processing at each measuring point.

(A) Login measurement

Time was measured from when the user pressed the login button on the login screen shown in Fig. 8 until the screen shown in Fig. 9 was display for command input.

The login processing includes RSA encryption operation for server host authentication and MD5 hash operation for session ID generation.

(B) Input measurement

Time was measured from when a function (argument: key code) was called 100 times synchronously by a for loop at a key input event until echo-back (the server outputs and sends back input characters) after the exit from the for loop.

The input processing includes Triple DES encryption operation and CRC32 check byte operation.

(C) Output measurement

Time was measured from when a program was called from the remote computer to read random character strings for 100 lines (80 characters/line) and a command was entered from the client until the display was completed.

The output processing includes a Triple DES decryption operation and CRC32 check byte operation.

Table 3. Specification of client PC

OS	Windows XP Home Edition SP2
CPU	AMD Mobile Sempron 3100+ 1.80 GHz
Memory	512 MB
Web browser	Internet Explorer 6.0

Table 4. Specification of client mobile phone

OS	REX OS + KCP
CPU	ARM9E
Memory	—
Web browser	Opera mini 3.1 (8.60)

Table 5. Result of measurement

	Processing Time (second)	
	PC	Mobile Phone
Login	0.82	46.38
Input (100 characters)	4.05	286.04
Output (100 lines)	0.93	73.73

According to calculations from the results, 24.72 characters can be entered from a PC per second and it takes approximately 0.01 second to display one line. These values are considered practical for ordinary usage.

For a mobile phone, however, every processing ended in a severe result for ordinary use. For login, 20 seconds was necessary for the RSA encryption operation executed twice (1024 and 768 bits). The large communication overhead, which can be ignored in a PC, also lowers the performance of a mobile phone. In an emergency, however, the use of SSH may be unavoidable. For example, only one administrator while traveling without a PC may access a server using SSH. In such a case, the proposed system is worth using because it is available for various terminals even though the performance may be low.

We did not measure the time required to load an Ajax web page to a web browser. Since the code set of an Ajax web page is extremely small at approximately 100 KB, the time can be considered negligible.

7 Conclusion

In this study, we proposed a SSH client system using Ajax, independent of the operating environment. Unlike existing systems, the proposed system could greatly increase the substantial safety of SSH by end-to-end SSH communication such as that on a desktop application.

By implementation, we found the proposed system to run at a speed satisfactory for regular use by a PC. The proposed system is not fast enough for regular use by a mobile phone, but can be used in an emergency if there is no alternative.

In the future, we will enhance the proposed system for practical use by supporting SSH Protocol 2 and multi-byte characters, and we will also study its usage to take full advantage of the features.

References

1. Google Map, http://maps.google.com/maps
2. W3C Working Draft, The XMLHttpRequest Object,
   http://www.w3.org/TR/XMLHttpRequest/
3. Mozilla Japan,
   http://www.mozilla-japan.org/projects/security/components/
   ame-origin.html
4. Barrett, D.J., Silverman, R.E., Byrne, R.G.: SSH, the Secure Shell The Definitive Guide,
   2nd edn. O'Reilly, Sebastopol (2005)
5. http://blog.bz2.jp/archives/2005/09/ajax_ssh.html
6. Ajaxterm, http://antony.lesuisse.org/qweb/trac/wiki/AjaxTerm
7. http://itpro.nikkeibp.co.jp/article/COLUMN/20080220/294242/
8. Ylonen, T.: The SSH (Secure Shell) Remote Login Protocol,
   http://www.graco.c.u-tokyo.ac.jp/~nishi/security/ssh/RFC
9. The Secure Shell (SSH) Protocol Assigned Numbers,
   http://www.ietf.org/rfc/rfc4250.txt
10. The Secure Shell (SSH) Protocol Architecture,
    http://www.ietf.org/rfc/rfc4251.txt
11. The Secure Shell (SSH) Authentication Protocol,
    http://www.ietf.org/rfc/rfc4252.txt
12. The Secure Shell (SSH) Transport Layer Protocol,
    http://www.ietf.org/rfc/rfc4253.txt
13. The Secure Shell (SSH) Connection Protocol,
    http://www.ietf.org/rfc/rfc4254.txt
14. Using DNS to Securely Publish Secure Shell (SSH) Key Fingerprints,
    http://www.ietf.org/rfc/rfc4255.txt
15. Generic Message Exchange Authentication for the Secure Shell Protocol (SSH),
    http://www.ietf.org/rfc/rfc4256.txt
16. The Secure Shell (SSH) Transport Layer Encryption Modes,
    http://www.ietf.org/rfc/rfc4344.txt
17. Yoshiura, H., Shigematsu, T., Susaki, S., Saitoh, T., Toyoshima, H., Kurita, C., Tezuka, S.,
    Sasaki, R.: Authenticating Web-Based Virtual Shops Using Signature-Embedded Marks –
    A Practical Analysis. In: The 2000 Cambridge International Workshop on Security Proto-
    cols (2000) (in Cambridge)
18. Burnett, S., Paine, S.: RSA Security's Official Guide to Cryptography. The McGraw- Hills
    Company, New York (2001)
19. MindTerm, http://www.appgate.com/products/80_MindTerm/
20. JTA - Telnet/SSH for the JAVA(tm) platform, http://www.javassh.org/

Smart Order Routing Technology in the New European Equity Trading Landscape

Bartholomäus Ende, Peter Gomber, and Marco Lutat

Goethe University Frankfurt, Chair of e-Finance, Grüneburgweg 1,
60323 Frankfurt, Germany
{Ende,Gomber,Lutat}@wiwi.uni-frankfurt.de

Abstract. In Europe, fragmentation of execution venues has been triggered by increasing competition among markets and a new regulatory environment set up by MiFID. Against this background, IT-based sophisticated order routing systems (Smart Order Routing systems) promise to assure efficiency despite fragmented markets. This raises the question on the relevance and economic value of this technology in European equity trading. Based on order book data for EURO STOXX 50 securities of ten European electronic execution venues, this paper assesses the potential of Smart Order Routing technology by measuring the performance of actual executions in European order book trading relative to a Smart Order Router implementation that detects and accesses best European prices. We identify 6.71% full trade troughs and 6.45% partial trade-throughs in our dataset enabling for significant absolute and relative savings. This indicates that Smart Order Routing technology can provide business value by improving order executions in European cross-tradable equities.

Keywords: e-Finance, Auction, Economics of IS, Empirical Study, Marketplaces.

1 Introduction

In the last two decades, securities markets have undergone massive technological changes, mostly notable by the shift from floor trading to electronic trading systems [1, 2]. The electronification of market venues in Europe, i.e. exchange trading systems like Xetra (Deutsche Börse), SETS (London Stock Exchange) or NSC (Euronext France) took place in the late 1990s and enabled market participants (banks, brokers as well as their institutional and retail customers) to access electronic order books via remote access without the need for physical presence on an exchange floor.

Concerning the order execution by investors and brokers, i.e. the users of the markets, currently another massive technological change can be observed: In the past, orders were delegated to (human) brokers whose core competency is the execution of the investors' order flow. New trading technologies expand the decision set for organisations which seek for more trading control in order to reduce their implicit trading costs. Institutional investors and investment firms can choose to execute their orders via new electronic execution concepts like Direct Market Access, Algorithmic Trading and Smart Order Routing, at exchanges or alternative trading systems (e.g. crossing networks).

C. Godart et al. (Eds.): I3E 2009, IFIP AICT 305, pp. 197–209, 2009.

The technological basis for this development is laid by the broker's business model of a virtual Direct Market Access. With this service orders are not touched by brokers anymore but are instead forwarded directly to markets. Algorithmic Trading and Smart Order Routing are built on the basis of Direct Market Access: Algorithmic Trading is based on mathematical models exploiting historical and real-time market data to determine ex ante or continuously the optimum size of the (next) order slice and its time of submission to the market [3]. Smart Order Routers perform an automated search for trading opportunities across multiple markets and route suborders to the most appropriate combination of markets as depicted in Figure 1.

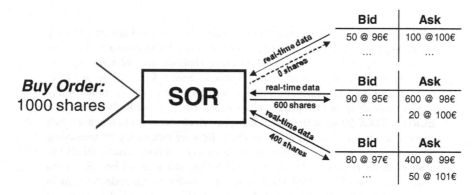

Fig. 1. Operating principle of a Smart Order Router (SOR)

While order execution strategies for securities that are listed exclusively at one stock exchange require only to focus on order timing and order slicing to minimise market impact things are more complicated when one or multiple alternative execution venues prevail. In such fragmented markets, a real-time investigation of order execution venues as well as their available executable orders and quotes can improve execution results and increase portfolio performance for both agent and proprietary trading. In the US, market fragmentation between regulated exchanges and Electronic Communication Networks introduced in the late '90s triggered the need for order routing concepts to assure best execution of orders. In European equity trading, market fragmentation is currently triggered by the emergence of new execution venues like BATS, Chi-X, Turquoise or Equiduct and their relevant market share gains in European blue chip stocks.[1] They are able to provide trading services across Europe based on the Markets in Financial Instruments Directive (MiFID) which has been in effect since November 1st, 2007. While institutional investors benefit from the increasing competition among venues in terms of lowered explicit costs or reduced latency, liquidity fragmentation requires sophisticated technology to achieve an order's completion at the most favourable prices. As MiFID requires investment firms to execute customer orders on terms most favourable to the client (best execution) both discussions within the MiFID regulatory process [4] as well as recent

---

[1] European market fragmentation (in terms of market share) is measured e.g. by Fidessa. For further information, please refer to http://fragmentation.fidessa.com.

competitive forces [5] raise the question on the relevance of IT-based Smart Order Routing systems for European equity trading.

Generally, for IT investments the question arises if these generate a positive business value [6]. Against this background our paper aims at investigating whether Smart Order Routing technology allows generating business value and thus, the related research question can be formulated as:

> *Does Smart Order Routing Technology enable for relevant improvements in order execution and thereby generate positive business value in European equity markets?*

For this purpose, we analyse the existence of suboptimal order executions in ten European securities markets. To simulate a Smart Order Router, for each of more than 8 million trades in European blue chip stocks, we seek better execution conditions, i.e. lower best offers for buy and higher best bids for sell orders. A relevant proportion of suboptimal order executions indicates the relevance and positive economic value of Smart Order Routing technologies and therefore justifies investments into their development.

The remainder of the paper is organised as follows: Section 2 reviews previous literature on Smart Order Routing and on order execution quality. Section 3 elaborates on our instrument and marketplace choice, describes the dataset and explains the assumptions and data adaptations necessary for the analysis. Section 4 presents and discusses our results. A conclusion and an outlook are provided in section 5.

2 Related Literature

Academic work on Smart Order Routing technology and its economic assessment is mainly related to execution quality measurement as well as relative execution performance of concrete trading venues:

With a few exceptions, studies investigating order execution quality across multiple trading venues are related to NYSE trading and brokers routing orders away from that venue for reasons of internalisation, internal crossing or order preferencing. Huang and Stoll [7] measure execution costs for a matched sample of NYSE and Nasdaq stocks and find execution costs for Nasdaq twice the NYSE costs. They conclude that internalisation and preferencing are obstacles for narrower spreads. Bessembinder and Kaufman [8] in a matched pairs study reach similar results with trading costs on the Nasdaq having fallen, but still being substantially higher than on the NYSE. Petersen and Fialkowski [9] find significant differences in midpoint trades between Nasdaq and NYSE and back these results with statistics of 19 percent of all retail brokerage orders in their sample routed to an exchange with an inferior quote. More recent studies on the subject include Battalio et al. [10] who compare NYSE execution prices with those of four regional exchanges and the Nasdaq InterMarket. Consistent with other research they find that overall, NYSE provides the best execution prices but lacks on execution speed. Bacidore et al. [11] point out that previous measures of execution quality might be biased for markets with substantial non-displayed liquidity.

Bakos et al. [12] analysed the law of one price against the background of brokers' execution performance and their different levels of commissions. They found relatively few price improvements, which are a measure of execution quality. The difference among brokers in obtaining price improvements was not statistically significant, but brokers do exhibit statistically significant differences in total trading costs as the rates of price improvement in general do not offset higher commissions charge. As the quality of order executions can vary heavily for different trading venues [13] a reasonable selection of a venue for a particular order appears to be important for the US and findings from Battalio et al. [14] indicate that strategic routing of decisions for orders, e.g. via Smart Order Routing, could help to improve overall order execution quality.

Against the background of new opportunities in order handling Ramistella [15] observed that the demand for reasonable order routing solutions has intensified for investment firms. Foucault and Menkveld [16] analyse the implications of market fragmentation and the rate of price priority violations (i.e. an order was executed in a market providing an inferior price compared to a price available in a different market) of two trading venues for Dutch equities. From their findings they interpret trade-throughs as being due to a lack of automation of routing decisions.

The contribution of this paper to the existent literature is twofold: First, it examines suboptimal order executions in Europe rather than the US and is based on order book data rather than price data. Second, to the knowledge of the authors it is the first paper that analyses execution performance after the MiFID introduction in Europe and assesses the relevance of Smart Order Routing technology in the new European landscape.

3 Methodology, Data and Assumptions

Before we will present our results in section 4, in the following we define important terms for our investigation of suboptimal order executions. Their existence delivers the economic foundation for the application of Smart Order Routing technologies in European equity trading. In this section we introduce the term "trade-throughs", describe the dataset and the data handling/cleaning operations as well as our hypotheses.

To identify suboptimal order executions, in the following we use the definition of trade-throughs according to Schwartz and Francioni [17] stated below.

Definition: Trade-Through
A trade-through in a particular stock is said to take place "...when a transaction occurs at a price that is higher than the best posted offer or lower than the best posted bid and orders at these better prices are not included in the transaction".

Figure 2 shows an example of a trade-through where – although market A shows a best offer of 86.44 € – the buy order is executed on market B at 86.50 € per share.

Moreover, we label a situation where an order could be executed in a different market with its full order size at a better price (better bid or better offer limit) to be a *full trade-through*, whereas a situation in which only a part of an order could be executed in a different market at a better price (better bid or better offer limit) is classified as a *partial trade-through*.

In this paper we focus on the gross perspective, i.e. exclude (explicit) transaction costs that will be incorporated in a next step of the research project.

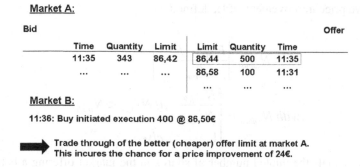

Fig. 2. Example of a trade-through situation

Smart Order Routing technology is intended to avoid trade-throughs as defined above since it allows to automatically detect fragmented liquidity across multiple markets. They continuously gather real-time data from the respective venues concerning their order book situations, i.e. current quoted volumes and prices. Based on this information the routing engine slices incoming orders and decides where to route individual suborders in respect of the best prices available in that logical second. Then, the routing engine receives order confirmations or notes of unfilled orders. In the latter case, the routing process will be repeated or cancelled depending on a customer's instructions.

As our objective is to determine the business value of Smart Order Routing technology we identify full and partial trade-throughs for each order execution in our data set. We compare trade data (trade price and volume, trade direction and time stamp) of the market where the execution actually took place (e.g. market B in figure 2) with the order book situations in all other markets simultaneously at the time of this execution. A trade-through (full or partial) is found if at least one marketplace exists (e.g. market A in figure 2) where a strictly positive amount of savings could be realised. We pick the market with the highest potential overall savings for the trade. Obviously, execution quality can be characterized by a multiple of other determinants like e.g. fill rates, execution likelihood and execution speed, but in the following we will focus only on price difference among trading venues.

3.1 Hypothesis and Statistical Testing

The new competition among trading venues triggered by MiFID raises the question on the business value of Smart Order Routing. Assuming traders' rational behaviour in executing their orders and based on their responsibility to identify the best result for clients' orders, one should expect that the proportion of sub-optimally executed orders will not reach a significant level. For testing this hypothesis two variables have been derived for each stock and each marketplace:

1. Absolute amount of savings (Savings), defined as the maximum savings per trade if executed in a different market. This variable equals zero if an order was executed optimally (placed at best market conditions), but is strictly positive if there is a market offering better execution conditions.

2. Relative price improvements (PI), defined as

$$PI = N_{adjust} \cdot \left| \frac{P_{better} - P_{trade}}{P_{trade}} \right|$$

$$with \ N_{adjust} = \begin{cases} \dfrac{N_{better}}{N_{trade}} & , if \ N_{better} < N_{trade} \\ 1 & , else \end{cases}$$

where N_{better} equals the quoted number of shares in the market offering a better price and N_{trade} is the actual trade's number of shares. P_{better} and P_{trade} are the potential price in the market offering better conditions and the actual trade price respectively. The *PI* variable equals zero if a trade was executed at best conditions and indicates the available relative improvement otherwise. $N_{adjust} = 1$ reflects full trade-throughs, whereas $N_{adjust} < 1$ reflects partial trade-throughs.

Assuming that both test statistics have a *Student's t distribution* under the null hypothesis both variables' means will be tested for

H₀: mean = 0   against   **Hₐ**: mean > 0.

Results will be checked against those from a *Wilcoxon signed-rank test* as the number of observations strongly varies among combinations of stock and marketplace.

3.2 Instrument and Market Choice

The instrument choice is based on the constituents of the Dow Jones EURO STOXX 50 Index as of October 2007 since these represent the actively traded shares on multiple markets in Euro currency. The index covers 50 blue-chip stocks from 12 Eurozone countries: Austria, Belgium, Finland, France, Germany, Greece, Ireland, Italy, Luxembourg, the Netherlands, Portugal and Spain. One EURO STOXX 50 instrument (ARCELORMITTAL) was not available in the dataset, therefore the sample finally consists of 49 instruments of the index.

Concerning the execution venues in our sample, we included the European markets trading in Euro currency that feature a fully-electronic open central limit order book (CLOB) in the period under investigation. Therefore, ten markets have been identified for this study: Bolsa de Madrid, Borsa Italiana Milan, Chi-X, the Euronext markets (Amsterdam, Brussels, Paris, and Lisbon), Helsinki Stock Exchange (NASDAQ OMX Helsinki), SWX Europe (formerly Virt-x) and Xetra (Deutsche Börse).

The trading mechanisms of these execution venues for liquid stocks apply continuous trading and opening and closing prices are set via scheduled (time-triggered) call auction mechanisms (Chi-X opening and prices are established using the opening price of a stock's primary market). To assure price continuity, additional volatility interruptions stop continuous trading in case of potential extreme price movements and trigger an unscheduled (event-triggered) auction. Except for Chi-X (the Chi-X trading system does not accept orders leading to a violation of price continuity), all execution venues in our sample shift from continuous trading to a non-scheduled auction for a minimum of two minutes following a potential violation of price continuity.

3.3 Description of the Data Set

Intraday trade and order book data for each stock (for each market) are sourced from the archives of Reuters that were made available by the Australian Capital Markets Cooperative Research Centre Limited (CMCRC). For the markets in our sample, this database contains each best bid/offer limit and trade price with respective volume and a date and time stamp with a granularity of one second assigned to it. The data set under investigation represents level 1 data, i.e. it does not include depth of order book information, consisting of orders positioned beyond the top of the book (level 2 data). Reuters trade and order book data do not contain an indication of trade direction, which must therefore be inferred. In the ten fully electronic markets these inferences are straightforward. All trades executed at the best offer are categorised as buy-initiated; all trades executed at the best bid quote categorised as sell-initiated (for further information on tick rules see [18]). Total traded value and other aggregated activity figures for each stock were calculated from the Reuters trade and order book data.

Our sample consists of 20 trading days divided into two distinct sample periods with the first from December 10–21, 2007 and the second from January 7–18, 2008. Altogether 8,010,905 executed trades representing an overall trading volume of 262,314 million € are included in the dataset.

3.3 Data Handling and Data Cleaning

For the investigation, our dataset had to be cleaned and prepared in several dimensions. Trade and order book data lacking essential information like e.g. associated volume were eliminated. In the case of order book data, the most recent valid limit orders featuring all information necessary for our analysis were considered for comparison of execution quality. Moreover, trades for which a trade direction could not unambiguously be determined were eliminated from the dataset. Regarding trade sizes no data cleaning measures were required.

As trading hours among the ten electronic markets included in this study vary slightly, for a comparison of markets only the periods of simultaneous trading were taken as a basis. As we focus on continuous trading, auctions times were neglected and additionally, any order book or trading activity within two minutes around scheduled as well as non-scheduled auctions were eliminated from our dataset. As stated before, our dataset contains time stamps for trades and quotes with a granularity of one second. With a quote change in a comparison market arriving within the second of a trade occurrence in our original market this new quote is considered available and thus presents the most recent order book situation to this trade. With more than one quote change within the second of a trade occurrence at one market, the quote resulting in the least savings is taken as a basis for an execution performance comparison in order to retrieve a lower boundary for the possible price improvements.

4 Results

Results for trade-throughs will be presented in this section as follows: First, we will deal with our findings on trade-throughs addressing summarising descriptive statistics. This will be followed by an in-depth analysis for an exemplary instrument with our results broken down into the individual markets where that instrument is tradable.

Consequently, our test statistics for the relative and absolute savings will be presented. For all other instruments results will be summarised while abstracting from individual execution venues. From our total of 8,010,905 trades, 6.71% (absolute: 537,764 trades) could have been executed at better price conditions with their full volume (full trade-throughs), 6.45% (absolute: 516,797 trades) at least with a part of their volume (partial trade-throughs). For our sample period and given our selection of instruments and European trading venues investors could have saved € 9.50 million in total and € 9.01 on average per suboptimal order execution (before explicit execution costs) if they had used a Smart Order Routing system which places orders at the best price. The savings add up to 7.54 basis points (bps; 1 bps = 0.01%) relative to total trade-through value and 0.36 bps relative to total traded value.

TOTAL led the EURO STOXX 50 index in terms of market capitalisation as of December 31st, 2007 [19]. Therefore, in the following TOTAL will be taken as an example to explain our key figures in table 1.

Table 1. Trade-through statistics for TOTAL

	Euronext FR	Chi-X	Euronext BR	Milan	SWX Europe	Overall
Number of trades	293,729	26,263	465	210	18	320,685
Volume [K shares]	183,140	8,061	85	31	211	191,528
Value [K €]	10,300,568	455,751	4,787	1,715	11,860	10,773,682
Avg. volume per trade [shares]	624	307	183	146	11,725	597.2
Avg. value per trade [€]	35,065	17,353	10,295	8,167	658,883	33,595.8
Full trade-throughs [%]	14.58	9.52	53.98	53.33	5.56	14.24
Partial trade-throughs [%]	10.88	5.24	4.95	1.90	5.56	10.40
Number of trade-throughs	74,778	3,875	274	116	2	79,045
Full	42,815	2,499	251	112	1	45,678
Partial	31,963	1,376	23	4	1	33,367
Savings [€]	493,219	16,679	3,360	542	331	514,131
Avg. savings per trade-through [€]	6.60	4.30	12.26	4.67	165.64	6.50
Savings / trade-through value [bps]	4.23	3.33	12.73	8.28	51.19	4.22
Savings / trade value [bps]	0.48	0.37	7.02	3.16	0.28	0.48

Table 1 features the results for the individual execution venues. The "Overall" column summarises over all markets. The table's upper section gives an overview on the markets' activity for TOTAL applying characteristic figures. Trade activity varies heavily among market places with the second in number of trades (here: Chi-X) not even measuring up to one tenth of that of the primary exchange (here: Euronext France (FR)). This is a common observation for most stocks in our sample.

The lower section introduces findings on trade-throughs for each market with relative and absolute figures on full and partial trade-throughs. In the example 14.6% or 42,815 out of the 293,729 trades which occurred in Euronext FR could have been executed in its full size at a better price in (at least) one of the other markets. Potential accumulated savings over all trades are shown along with the absolute and relative average savings per trade-through [Avg. savings per trade-through and Savings/trade-through value respectively]. Finally, the savings are related to the total trade value for each market.

Table 2 presents the mean, standard deviation and t-statistics of the variables price improvement [PI] and absolute savings [Savings] of TOTAL for each market. It should be noted that the mean PI and Savings are unconditional and therefore are not identical to the Savings / trade-through and Avg. savings per trade-through values respectively from table 1. Except for SWX Europe the null hypotheses of no systematic relative price improvement and absolute savings can be statistically rejected.

Table 2. Test statistics for price improvements [PI] and absolute savings [Savings]

		Euronext FR	Chi-x	Euronext BR	Milan	SWX Europe
	N	293,729	26,263	465	210	18
PI (bps)	Mean	0.80	0.37	6.34	4.40	1.41
H_0: PI=0,	Standard deviation	2.85	1.60	10.72	6.06	5.92
H_a: PI>0	t-statistic	152.80***	36.98***	12.74***	10.52***	1.01
Savings (€)	Mean	1.68	0.64	7.23	2.58	18.40
H_0: Savings=0,	Standard deviation	7.91	3.31	22.66	6.30	72.94
H_a: Savings>0	t-statistic	115.04***	31.05***	6.88***	5.93***	1.07

*** .01 level of significance

Descriptive overall results for all other instruments are shown in table 3.

Table 3. Descriptive statistics of trade-throughs for all instruments

Instrument	Number of trades	Value [€ mn]	Value/ trade [€]	% full trade-through	% partial trade-through	Savings [€]	Avg. savings /trade-through [€]	Savings /trade-through value [bps]	Savings /trade value [bps]
AEGON	125,881	2,397.4	19,045	14.30	6.24	287,978	11.14	9.72	1.20
AIR LIQUIDE	137,656	1,960.0	14,238	5.21	3.68	18,804	1.54	2.35	0.10
ALCATEL LUCENT	117,490	1,730.5	14,729	8.05	6.90	113,667	6.47	14.20	0.66
ALLIANZ	190,387	8,673.0	45,555	13.29	14.34	272,392	5.18	3.50	0.31
ASSICURA-ZIONI GEN-ERALI	112,315	2,984.2	26,570	0.21	0.11	3,099	8.80	5.64	0.01
AXA	208,272	5,143.0	24,694	11.61	9.73	881,357	19.83	18.71	1.71
BASF	131,899	5,487.2	41,602	7.43	8.24	84,518	4.09	2.81	0.15
BAYER	135,287	5,912.6	43,704	6.19	8.47	112,074	5.65	4.16	0.19
BCO BILBAO VIZCAYA ARGENT	137,718	6,415.8	46,587	0.56	0.94	20,345	9.82	10.24	0.03

Table 3. (*Continued*)

BCO SANTANDER	165,497	11,024.8	66,616	11.88	22.17	2,034,860	36.11	32.59	1.85
BNP PARIBAS	297,256	6,746.5	22,696	16.70	12.86	337,179	3.84	3.86	0.50
CARREFOUR SUPERMAR.	132,166	2,726.3	20,628	4.07	3.91	22,275	2.11	2.72	0.08
CREDIT AGRICOLE	144,184	2,074.5	14,388	3.73	4.66	29,979	2.48	5.59	0.14
DAIMLER	173,898	8,531.9	49,063	5.94	10.72	170,043	5.87	4.97	0.20
DEUTSCHE BANK	189,235	8,416.7	44,478	11.56	14.13	226,700	4.66	3.20	0.27
DEUTSCHE BOERSE	96,267	3,532.2	36,691	1.06	2.97	14,754	3.80	4.51	0.04
DEUTSCHE TELEKOM	103,617	7,702.1	74,332	9.10	7.13	141,996	8.44	5.09	0.18
E.ON	172,070	8,778.9	51,019	8.24	13.48	466,167	12.47	8.38	0.53
ENEL	133,043	4,158.2	31,254	1.95	1.61	207,925	43.90	54.79	0.50
ENI	171,544	5,969.3	34,798	0.73	0.56	20,379	9.17	6.36	0.03
FORTIS	230,052	5,672.3	24,656	16.51	7.92	488,988	8.70	6.25	0.86
FRANCE TELECOM	210,668	5,190.2	24,637	6.16	4.55	121,109	5.36	5.43	0.23
GRP DANONE	170,115	3,192.2	18,765	0.39	0.31	21,806	18.28	19.59	0.07
GRP SOCIETE GENERALE	246,933	6,323.9	25,610	2.01	1.57	161,869	18.32	14.31	0.26
IBERDROLA	98,281	4,285.8	43,608	0.16	0.39	8,396	15.49	25.67	0.02
ING GROEP	183,835	5,913.2	32,166	3.83	1.76	224,677	21.85	10.60	0.38
INTESA SANPAOLO	119,681	4,805.5	40,153	0.49	0.17	20,275	25.66	11.56	0.04
L'OREAL	137,517	2,327.6	16,926	3.72	4.35	27,480	2.48	4.30	0.12
LVMH MOET HENNESSY	150,690	2,710.5	17,987	3.73	4.44	26,264	2.13	3.60	0.10
MUENCHEN-ER RUECK	120,327	4,607.9	38,295	9.58	8.82	88,364	3.99	2.64	0.19
NOKIA	179,301	9,235.7	51,509	2.39	3.11	167,993	17.05	10.57	0.18
PHILIPS ELECTRON-ICS	202,630	5,368.0	26,492	11.32	6.29	286,566	8.03	5.73	0.53
RENAULT	171,747	3,104.4	18,075	3.75	4.68	38,316	2.65	4.46	0.12
REPSOL YPF	95,611	2,631.3	27,521	0.30	1.05	57,300	44.38	118.40	0.22
RWE	132,587	5,712.3	43,083	5.00	8.56	75,185	4.18	3.99	0.13
SAINT GOBAIN	158,017	2,521.0	15,954	5.25	5.83	73,193	4.18	7.47	0.29
SANOFI-AVENTIS	209,655	6,004.3	28,639	6.10	5.22	95,685	4.03	3.46	0.16
SAP	118,283	4,972.4	42,038	4.81	6.23	115,952	8.88	6.51	0.23
SCHNEIDER ELECTRIC	147,489	2,321.4	15,739	3.84	4.99	24,692	1.90	3.78	0.11
SIEMENS	190,914	10,639.8	55,731	7.43	11.92	478,100	12.94	8.29	0.45
SUEZ	194,471	4,723.2	24,287	8.00	7.06	146,770	5.01	5.14	0.31
TELECOM ITALIA	100,334	3,790.0	37,774	0.60	0.80	16,924	12.08	12.75	0.04
TELEFONICA	171,690	8,535.1	49,712	4.14	8.27	109,178	5.12	7.19	0.13
TOTAL	320,685	10,773.7	33,596	14.24	10.40	514,131	6.50	4.22	0.48

Table 3. (*Continued*)

UNICREDITO ITALIANO	215,043	11,573.4	53,819	1.29	0.85	110,155	23.98	13.14	0.10
UNILEVER NV	184,066	4,809.7	26,130	10.33	5.03	260,660	9.22	5.92	0.54
VINCI	193,968	2,890.0	14,899	5.46	3.90	122,639	6.75	12.18	0.42
VIVENDI	162,783	3,092.6	18,998	4.87	5.32	67,594	4.08	5.21	0.22
VOLKSWAG-EN	117,850	4,221.5	35,821	9.02	9.03	86,120	4.05	2.97	0.20
ALL IN-STRUMENTS	8,010,905	262,313.9	32,745	6.71	6.45	9,502,869	9.01	7.54	0.36

Generally, our findings exhibit a high level of heterogeneity among instruments regarding the trade-through characteristics with the minimum of full trade-through percentage at 0.16 and the maximum at 16.7 percent. Table 4 summarises those results for our sample of 49 instruments.[2]

Table 4. Summary statistics of trade-through key figures over all instruments

	% Trade-throughs		Avg. savings per trade-through [€]	Savings / trade-through value [bps]	Savings / trade value [bps]
$N=49$	Full	Partial			
Mean	6.05	6.03	10.46	11.20	0.32
Standard deviation	4.54	4.58	10.08	18.05	0.38
Minimum	0.16	0.11	1.54	2.35	0.01
1st quartile	2.39	2.97	4.08	4.16	0.11
Median	5.21	5.22	6.50	5.73	0.20
3rd quartile	9.02	8.47	12.47	10.60	0.42
Maximum	16.70	22.17	44.38	118.40	1.85
t-statistic	9.33***	9.22***	7.47***	4.54***	5.98***

*** .01 level of significance

Results show that investors could have realised significant savings on their trades across all instruments resulting from executions at the best prices available based on sophisticated Smart Order Routing technology.

5 Conclusion

In fragmented equity markets, Smart Order Routing systems promise to generate economic value by electronically accessing the best available bid and offer among the execution venues where the respective security is traded. After the introduction of

---

[2] Please notice that the means in table 4 have been computed as un-weighted averages over all 49 instruments and thus differ from the figures for "All Instruments" in table 3 which are averages over all trades.

MiFID, the European trading landscape moved from concentration rules to relevant fragmentation and the best execution rules imposed by MiFID urge investment firms to achieve the best possible result for their customers. Against this background, the paper assesses the economic relevance of Smart Order Routing engines based on a four week data set of EURO STOXX 50 securities consisting of 8 million executed trades with an overall value of € 262 billion. The analysis shows that on a gross basis there is a relevant and statistically significant extent of suboptimal order executions where a different execution venue provides a better executable limit: 6.71% of orders can be executed better in their full size (6.45% of orders partially) enabling for total savings of € 9.5 million, i.e. 7.54 bps relative to total trade-through value and 0.36 bps relative to total traded value. With that evidence on hand we can conclude that Smart Order Routing Technology enables for relevant improvements in order execution and thereby can generate positive business value in European equity markets.

An obvious next step in the research project is the inclusion of trading, clearing and (cross-system) settlement costs. While the execution venues differ in their domestic costs structures, the main driver of explicit costs are the cross-border/cross-system settlement costs.

Based on these net results, further analysis may focus on the one hand on the explanation of the main drivers for both suboptimal order executions and on the other hand on the inclusion of data on the order book depth of the respective markets to extend the concept of full trade-through to all the trades and eliminate the partial trade-through approach. Thereby, the research project both can contribute to the assessment of the economic value of Smart Order Routing technology as well as to its actual design and technical implementation.

References

1. Kempf, A., Korn, O.: Trading System and Market Integration. Journal of Financial Intermediation 7, 220–239 (1998)
2. Theissen, E.: Market structure, informational efficiency and liquidity: An experimental comparison of auction and dealer markets. Journal of Financial Markets 3, 333–363 (2000)
3. Gomber, P., Gsell, M.: Catching up with technology – The impact of regulatory changes on ECNs/MTFs and the trading venue landscape in Europe. Competition and Regulation in Network Industries 1(4), 535–557 (2006)
4. European Commission. Background Notes to Draft Commission Directive implementing Directive 2004/39/EC (February 6, 2006),
   http://ec.europa.eu/internal_market/securities/docs/isd/
   dir-2004-39-implement/dir-backgroundnote_en.pdf
   (last accessed: 15.06.2008)
5. Jeffs, L.: Instinet chief expects boost in volumes (May 2008),
   http://www.efinancialnews.com/index/content/2350621038
   (retrieved 09/25/08)
6. Kohli, R., Grover, V.: Business value of IT: An essay on expanding research directions to keep with the times. Journal of the Association for Information Systems 9(1), 23–39 (2008)
7. Huang, R., Stoll, H.: Dealer vs. auction markets: a paired comparison of execution costs on Nasdaq and the NYSE. Journal of Financial Economics 41, 313–357 (1996)

8. Bessembinder, H., Kaufman, H.M.: A cross-exchange comparison of execution costs and information flow for NYSE-listed stocks. Journal of Financial Economics 46(3), 293–319 (1997)
9. Petersen, M., Fialkowski, D.: Posted versus effective spreads. Journal of Financial Economics 35, 269–292 (1994)
10. Battalio, R., Hatch, B., Jennings, R.: Post-reform Market-order Execution Quality: Multi-dimensional Comparisons Across Market Centers. Financial Review 38, 123–152 (2001)
11. Bacidore, J.M., Battalio, R., Jennings, R.: Depth improvement and adjusted price improvement on the New York stock exchange. Journal of Financial Markets 5, 169–195 (2002)
12. Bakos, Y., Lucas, H.C., Wonseok, O., Viswanathan, S., Simon, G., Weber, B.: Electronic Commerce in the Retail Brokerage Industry: Trading Costs of Internet versus Full Service Firms. Working Paper Series Stern #1S99-014 (1999)
13. Macey, J., O'Hara, M.: The law and economics of best execution. Journal of Financial Intermediation 6, 188–223 (1997)
14. Battalio, R., Greene, J., Hatch, B., Jennings, R.: Does the Limit Order Routing Decision Matter? The Review of Financial Studies 15(1), 159–194 (2002)
15. Ramistella, A.: Crossing Networks: Bringing Back Large Block Trades to Instituional Trading. Technical report, Tower Group Inc. (2006)
16. Foucault, T., Albert, J.M.: Competition for Order Flow and Smart Order Routing Systems. Journal of Finance 63, 119–158 (2008)
17. Schwartz, R.A., Francioni, R.: Equity markets in action: The fundamentals of liquidity, market structure and trading. John Wiley& Sons, Inc., Hoboken (2004)
18. Ellis, K., Michaely, R., O'Hara, M.: The accuracy of trade classification rules: evidence from NASDAQ. Journal of Financial and Quantitative Analysis 35, 529–551 (2000)
19. STOXX Ltd.: Composition Lists of the Blue-chip Indices (2008),
http://www.stoxx.com/data/composition_list/bluechip.html#
(retrieved 9/24/08)

Algorithmic Trading Engines and Liquidity Contribution: The Blurring of "Traditional" Definitions

Sven S. Groth

Goethe University Frankfurt & E-Finance Lab, Grüneburgplatz 1,
60323 Frankfurt am Main, Germany
sgroth@wiwi.uni-frankfurt.de

Abstract. Being provided with a unique high-frequency dataset, we are able to show by means of an empirical analysis that computer-based traders, i.e. Algorithmic Trading (AT) engines, behave significantly different from human traders with regard to their order cancellation behaviour. Furthermore, given exactly this difference we point out that the application of well-established "traditional" liquidity measurement methods may no longer be unequivocally applicable in today's electronic markets. At least those liquidity measures that are based on committed liquidity need to be questioned.

Keywords: Liquidity provision, algorithmic trading, limit order book, option analogy.

1 Introduction

The evolution of electronic order books, such as Deutsche Börse's "Xetra" or London Stock Exchange's "SETS", eased the way for the automation of trading processes. Being able to access electronic markets via "Remote Access", the physical presence at an exchange is no longer necessary. Both brokers (sell side) and – at least – those institutional investors (buy side) that are provided with a direct market access are frequently making use of the "new" opportunities provided by electronic markets. One of the resulting success stories during the last decade deals with the proliferated utilization of so called "Algorithmic Trading" (AT) engines. Today the group of computer-based traders, i.e. AT, generate about one-half of trading activity on major European markets (e.g. Xetra) and the percentage share continues to grow [1].

In a broader sense, algorithmic trading can be defined as "the use of algorithms to manage the trading process" [2, p. 1]. In a narrower sense, it can be defined as "the automated, computer-based execution of equity orders via direct market-access channels, usually with the goal of meeting a particular benchmark" [3, p. 1]. Depending on the respective definition, the investment decision is either exogenous or endogenous to the AT model. If the original investment decision is exogenous to the AT model the task of an algorithm is "limited" to implement a given external trading intention with the goal to minimize market impact (implicit trading costs) and sustain potential alpha. This is the case when for example an investment fund manager makes a strategic investment decision that is large in volume. If this order is routed to the market as one

C. Godart et al. (Eds.): I3E 2009, IFIP AICT 305, pp. 210–224, 2009.
© IFIP International Federation for Information Processing 2009

big order, the potential market impact might jeopardize the investment yield aimed at. Therefore, these investment funds would advise brokers to, for instance, slice the original large order into several small orders. This task is conducted by both humans and AT engines with the difference that computers are usually cheaper to employ than humans. If the investment decision is endogenous to the AT model, the main goal of AT engines is not to sustain potential alpha, but to create alpha, i.e. find and implement profitable (intraday high frequency) investment strategies.

2 Related Work and Derived Hypotheses

Existing research on AT can be grouped into the categories *algorithmic efficiency*, *algorithmic design / selection* and *algorithmic influence* on the market. Literature on *algorithmic efficiency* aims to answer whether or not the use of algorithms, compared to traditional brokerage, creates additional value [3; 4]. Research on *algorithmic design / selection* guides especially practitioners on which kind of algorithm to choose for which kind of task and how to actually evaluate its' success [5; 6]. The increased share of algorithmic trading activity during the last decade called for research on the *algorithmic influence* on the market as a whole. [7] sets up an agent-based simulation and evaluates the influence of AT on price formation and price volatility. [2] investigate whether or not AT improves liquidity and find that algorithmic trading and liquidity are positively related. But their proxy for AT, the normalized measure of "New York Stock Exchange" (NYSE) electronic message traffic, does not necessarily pick up variations in algorithmic liquidity supply though. Moreover, their approach is limited to the observation of a certain event and cannot be applied similarly in other markets. Consequently, having reviewed existing research on AT, we identified the liquidity contribution of AT as an area of research that still lacks sufficient insights.

This paper aims to fill this gap because – among other things – liquidity is an important determinant of market quality [8]. But instead of directly trying to identify relationships between AT activity and associated market liquidity as [2] did, we question whether or not existing liquidity measurement concepts are still applicable and – most importantly – meaningful in today's electronic markets.

The cognition that "no single measure tells the whole story about liquidity" [9, p. 55] has already been present for decades. Our main question, however, is whether or not the electronification of markets (including the increased utilization of AT engines) challenges existing, seemingly accepted, beliefs on the applicability of particular liquidity measures to certain market structures.

For example, the *spread* is one of the most commonly applied liquidity measures. A small difference between best bid and best ask usually indicates that a market is liquid. But as this liquidity measure is not capable to adequately capture all dimensions of liquidity (i.e. breadth, depth, immediacy, and resiliency), further liquidity measures such as the *Cost of Round Trip* (CRT) were proposed [10]. Hereby, CRT is defined as the weighted average price (VWAP) at which an order of a given size (D) can be executed. [10, p. 24] state that CRT will be "particularly useful in any market where a high proportion of available liquidity is *committed* [...][and] as world equity markets increasingly adopt a pure electronic order book architecture, the applications of CRT(D) should increase". The proposal of a similar approach by [11] underpins the increasing importance assigned to information contained in the depth of the order book. It may therefore be concluded that CRT is commonly viewed as an appropriate liquidity measure for today's electronic markets.

It is, however, questionable whether or not the majority of (visible) liquidity in today's electronic markets is in fact *committed*. For example, given their technical abilities, AT engines are able to constantly monitor the market and instantaneously react to market movements by adjusting / cancelling their orders. This expected behaviour lowers the probability of being executed against informed order flow. Thus, compared to human traders, AT engines provide / commit liquidity to the market for a shorter period of time. [12] support this hypothesis because they find that a large amount of (non-marketable) limit orders are cancelled within a very short period of time in a limit order market. They call these rapidly cancelled orders "fleeting orders" and because of their frequent appearance question the "usual framework of patient limit orders and impatient market orders" (p. 2). Hypothesis H1 is expressed accordingly and will be addressed by means of a survival analysis.

Hypothesis H1:   The lifetime of AT orders is significantly shorter than the lifetime of Non-AT orders.

If the behaviour of AT engines is significantly different from humans (see for example H1; or [13]), if AT engines frequently make use of non-marketable – i.e. passive – limit orders, and if their market share is sufficiently large, the application of "traditional" liquidity measures that are based on the *committed liquidity assumption* may no longer be representative of overall market liquidity. Applying "traditional" liquidity measures to electronic markets with a large share of AT activity / trading might understate the liquidity contribution of this group of traders. This is especially true if AT engines commit liquidity only for a short period of time, but simultaneously represent a viable (passive) trading counterparty. In other words, even though AT engines do not commit liquidity to the market in a "traditional" sense these enhance a market's liquidity by increasing the probability of finding a (passive) trading counterparty. We therefore expect the "traditional" liquidity measures that are based on committed liquidity to be (systematically) significantly lower than an alternative trade-based liquidity measure. This, however, does not imply that the applied trade-based liquidity measure is superior to the other ones. It simply gauges a different aspect of liquidity provision that is not grasped by described "traditional" liquidity measures. Hence, Hypothesis H2 is expressed as follows:

Hypothesis H2:   Liquidity measures that are based on committed liquidity exhibit significantly lower liquidity levels than alternative trade-based liquidity measures in markets with a high degree of AT activity.

As the evaluation of overall market liquidity alone does not allow us to evaluate Hypothesis H2, we will assess the liquidity contribution of AT engines. The main reason for this procedure is given by the fact that AT order flow is expected to be significantly different from Non-AT order flow (see H1).

Hypothesis H2 is addressed by means of an empirical analysis. In order to incorporate above identified time component into the liquidity assessment, we will adopt the well known and often cited *limit order option analogy* [14] as one liquidity measurement method. Similar to CRT, it also aggregates the state of the entire limit order book into a single number. Thereby, limit orders are viewed as free trading options. For example, a limit order on the bid side indicates that a trader is willing to buy shares at its limit price. Accordingly, other market participants are given the opportunity to sell shares to the limit order liquidity provider at the respective limit price. In this case, the liquidity provider writes a free put option, i.e. one that "gives the holder [i.e. other market participants] the right to sell the underlying asset [...] for a certain price [limit]" [15, p. 7]. In other words, a market is viewed as more liquid the more volume is available at the top of the order book and the longer the liquidity (i.e. limit orders) is provided to the market.

Finally, in order to discuss the usefulness / applicability of above liquidity measures, we provide the reader with a (liquidity) benchmark that is based on executed volume (by trader group). The benchmark builds upon the notion that markets may also be termed liquid, if a lot of trading activity occurs. The *volume of trading* or the *number of transactions* respectively also serve as input to the liquidity measures proposed by [16] and [17].

The remainder of the paper is organized as follows: First, we introduce the reader to a unique dataset that will allow us to scrutinize above hypotheses. Second, we will separately address above hypotheses by means of an empirical analysis. Third, we will discuss the usefulness of the measurement methods and possible implications for market microstructure, i.e. e-finance, research.

3 Description of the Market and the Dataset

3.1 Xetra Trading System

The Frankfurt Stock Exchange (FWB) is operated by Deutsche Börse AG and offers both floor trading and fully-electronic trading via Xetra. In terms of market share, in 2007, 98.30% of order book turnover in German blue-chip DAX30 equities took place on Xetra. Remaining turnover was generated at FWB floor (1.08%) and at other regional German exchanges (0.62%) [1]. Dependent upon asset classes and corresponding asset liquidity, Xetra exhibits characteristics of a (1) pure order-driven, (2) pure quote-driven and (3) hybrid market model. Below analyses mainly concentrate on the pure-order driven market.

(1) Highly liquid shares, e.g. those included in the DAX30 index, do not need market makers to provide liquidity to the market. Instead, investors post orders into the limit order book. Equities are traded continuously between an opening and a closing call auction, interrupted by one (midday) intraday call auction. Additional intraday call auctions are triggered by so called volatility interruptions, i.e. whenever a potential execution price lies outside a pre-defined static and / or dynamic price range. Matching of orders follows the price-time priority rule.

(2) Xetra Best constitutes a functionality within the Xetra order book that allows for preferred execution of orders with order book consistency.

(3) Analogue to the pure order-driven market, the hybrid market allows for continuous trading interacting with auctions. Investors' orders are, however, complemented by limit orders (quotes) submitted by designated sponsors to improve liquidity.

3.2 Dataset

Deutsche Börse AG provided us with high-frequency order book data for those companies that were member of the German blue-chip DAX30 index during the period under investigation, i.e. between 2007-10-08 and 2007-10-12. The dataset contains all Xetra order book events during continuous trading, (opening-, intraday-, and closing-) auctions, pre-trading, post-trading and volatility interruptions. Each order, which is assigned a unique *order number* by the trading system, should at least trigger two events: First, a submission event and second either a full execution or a cancellation / deletion event. Each order can be partially executed and / or modified more than once. In Xetra, a modification event merely refers to a reduction of order volume. An increase in order volume would negatively affect the priority or execution probability of other orders. In this case, the system automatically generates a deletion event for the modified order and a new order entry event with increased volume. Analogue, technical deletion and insertion events occur due to changing trade restrictions that do not affect the price-time priority of other orders.

For each event, if appropriate, the following additional information is provided: timestamp, ISIN (*International Security Identification Number*), order number, auction trade flag, order type, buy/sell indicator, (hidden) size, price / limit, event code, trade restriction, and *ATflag*. The *auction trade flag* indicates the trading phase, e.g. continuous trading, during which the specific event occurred. One order may reveal different auction trade flags as for example order submission and order execution can take place during different trading phases. *Order type* indicates whether an order is a limit order, market order, iceberg order or market-to-limit order. Orders may also be restricted to be exclusively executed during a certain trading phase (*trade restriction*), e.g. auctions.

The *ATflag* indicates whether (*ATflag* = 1) or not (*ATflag* = 0) a certain event has been triggered by an algorithm. It does not allow the identification and exploitation of activities of single market participants though. The identification of algorithms is made possible because Deutsche Börse AG offers its clients a special pricing model for computer generated trades (*Automated Trading Program*: AT). Participants of the *Automated Trading Program* oblige themselves to exclusively make use of the rebate-relevant AT User-ID whenever transactions have been generated by an electronic system. Thereby "the electronic system has to determine two out of the three following order parameters: price (order type and / or order limit where applicable), timing (time of order entry) and quantity (quantity of the order in number of securities). [...] The electronic system must generate buy or sell orders independently, i.e. without frequent manual intervention, using a specified program or data." [18, p. 1]. Considering both above "electronic system" definition and granted financial incentives (fee rebates), the AT flag can be appreciated as the best proxy for algorithmic trading activity currently available [19, p. 7]. It shall, however, be noted that despite of the strong financial incentives not all "algorithmic traders" may take part in the program.

The above dataset allows for an order book reconstruction of covered DAX30 securities at any time during the period under investigation, including all trading phases. Basically, all orders submitted prior to the time of interest, i.e. order book reconstruction, that are not fully executed, cancelled or deleted (including "deleted" invalid day orders) remain in the order book. The actual order limits are determined by further incorporating partial executions and modifications. The *OrderEntryTimestamp* allows for the consideration of time priority.

4 Evaluation of Order Lifespan

Hypothesis H1 is addressed by means of a survival analysis. Analogue to [12] we apply the life-table method. Thereby, for each order either "time to cancellation" (*ttc*) or "time to execution" (*tte*) are calculated. Results are broken down by levels of factor AT, i.e. has the order been submitted by an algorithm or not. Calculating the probability of cancellation, the execution event is used as (exogenous) censoring event, and vice versa. In this analysis, we merely refer to active cancellation. This does not include orders that are (automatically) deleted due to expiration. Actual (active cancellation) activities shall represent traders' behaviour best. The sample includes all non-marketable DAX30 limit orders without auction-only trade restrictions that were submitted during continuous trading (during the one week sample period). Results can be found in Table 1.

Table 1. Cancellation and execution rates of limit orders

Time	Cumulative proportion surviving at end of interval			
	Cancellation		Execution	
	AT	Non-AT	AT	Non-AT
0.1 second(s)	0.877	0.958	0.986	0.991
1	0.714	0.785	0.952	0.973
2	0.662	0.729	0.941	0.967
10	0.493	0.519	0.875	0.932
1 minute(s)	0.229	0.230	0.713	0.831
2	0.148	0.137	0.633	0.773
10	0.033	0.062	0.470	0.631
1 hour	0.001	0.004	0.148	0.145
Wilcoxon (Gehan) statistic	15,174 ***		56,429 ***	

*** indicates significance at the 1%-level.

Probability of cancellation during the first 100 milliseconds is 12.3% for AT orders and 4.2% for Non-AT orders. Significance values based on the Wilcoxon (Gehan) statistic, which is based upon the differences in group mean scores, provide evidence that the probabilities of cancellation are significantly different across groups AT and Non-AT. The same holds true for the probability of execution. To conclude, Hypothesis H1 can be corroborated as AT engines show a different cancellation behaviour than Non-AT traders, i.e. humans.

5 Evaluation of Order Types

In order to make valid predictions regarding Hypothesis H2, it first of all needs to be scrutinized whether or not AT engines frequently make use of non-marketable – i.e.

passive – limit orders. If this is the case and if their market share is sufficiently large, the application of "traditional" liquidity measures that are based on the *committed liquidity assumption* are expected to be no longer representative of overall market liquidity. A descriptive summary of used order types can be found in Table 2. The respective sample consists of all orders from DAX30 companies without auction-only trade restrictions that were submitted during continuous trading (during the one week sample period).

Table 2. Order types

Order type	No. of orders		% of AT / Non-AT	
	AT	Non-AT	AT	Non-AT
Limit order	2,163,801	1,828,696	99.64 %	94.99 %
(1) non-marketable	*1,911,213*	*1,704,567*	*88.01 %*	*88.55 %*
(2) marketable	*252,588*	*124,129*	*11.63 %*	*6.44 %*
Market order	3,042	40,973	0.14 %	2.13 %
Iceberg order	4,733	54,792	0.22 %	2.85 %
Market-to-Limit order	0	599	0.00 %	0.03 %
SUM	2,171,576	1,925,060		

It can be observed that both groups of traders, i.e. AT and Non-AT, submit comparable number of orders. AT, however, make use of limit orders more frequently. 99.64% of all submitted AT orders are limit orders. This may be due to the fact that Non-AT deploy other order types such as iceberg orders (2.13%) or market-to-limit orders (2.85%) more often. It follows that the potential liquidity provision of algorithms via non-marketable limit orders is huge. 52.86% of all non-marketable limit orders are submitted by algorithms. For a discussion on why limit order trading actually seems viable see for instance [20].

It shall be noted that the average size of AT orders is smaller than the average size of Non-AT orders (not shown here). Systematically smaller AT order sizes may in fact lower the absolute value of below described committed liquidity contribution measures. The relative comparison to the trade-based liquidity measure is, however, not influenced by lower order sizes.

6 Evaluation of Liquidity Measures

In order to address Hypothesis H2, we introduce three different liquidity measures and apply them to the dataset. Potentially differing results will then serve as a basis to discuss the usefulness of each liquidity measure, especially with regard to the application in markets with a large degree of AT activity. The first two liquidity measures will stick to the "traditional" notion and will basically concentrate on the amount of limit orders in the order book. For both calculations, the order book is reconstructed on a minute-by-minute basis and the two liquidity measures are calculated according to below description. The third liquidity measure, however, is totally different in nature. It defines liquidity by means of trading activity.

6.1 Pure Order Volume

The first measure of AT liquidity contribution via non-marketable limit orders is a quite simple one. For each (minute-by-minute) reconstructed limit order book, we know which order has been submitted by an algorithm, i.e. member of the AT-program, or a human trader (see Table 3, AT orders are marked grey). Liquidity contribution by AT engines is then defined as the share of pure submitted volume resting in the order book ($\sum$AT size / $\sum$size).[1] It follows that this liquidity measure is based on committed liquidity, i.e. liquidity provided to the market via non-marketable limit orders.

Table 3. Exemplary order book

BID				ASK			
cVol	C	Size	Limit	Limit	Size	C	cVol
1,218.39	0.2248	5,421	47.14	47.18	225	0.0614	34.20
3.58	0.0996	36	47.14	47.18	1,757	0.1424	250.16
11.87	0.1187	100	47.13	47.18	557	0.1678	37.77
57.89	0.0680	851	47.12	47.19	252	0.2247	56.63
3,359.80	0.3360	10,000	47.11	47.20	500	0.3021	151.05

Relevant inputs to *pure order volume* (see 6.1)

Relevant inputs to *option value* (see 6.2)

6.2 Option Value

The volume measure takes account of the depth of the order book, but obviously does not differentiate between order aggressiveness and the time of liquidity contribution. In order to incorporate these dimensions as well and, especially, to show the impact of above identified lifespan differences (Hypothesis H1), above introduced limit order option analogy is applied by means of the order book option value. [14, p. 1457] were the first to empirically evaluate the option-like characteristics of limit orders "by characterizing the cost of supplying quotes, as writing a put and a call option ['free' straddle option] to an information-motivated trader". Since then the approach has been applied to both non-dealer markets such as the Australian Stock Exchange [21] and hybrid markets such as the New York Stock Exchange [22].

Based on the Black & Scholes [23] option pricing model (see Formula 1, 2, 3 for a call option), option values are calculated for all limit orders in the order book (also see Table 3). These limit order option values C are multiplied with their respective volumes to achieve *cVol*. Afterwards, aggregate option values ($\sum cVol$) for both the bid and the ask side are calculated, including (1) all limit orders and (2) only AT-orders. Respective values for the whole order book (*cAll*) are achieved by equally

---

[1] Example BID side (given that the displayed orders constitute the whole order book): "$\sum$AT size" is equivalent to the sum of those orders that are marked grey, i.e. 36 + 851 = 887. "$\sum$size" is the sum of all orders resting in the order book, i.e. 16,408. The AT liquidity contribution for this particular point in time is then 0.054.

weighting AT liquidity contribution of the bid and the ask side. Inputs to the option pricing model were chosen as described below.

$$C_0 = S_0 N(d_1) - X e^{-rT} N(d_2) \tag{1}$$

where
$$d_1 = \frac{\ln\left(\frac{S_0}{X}\right) + \left(r + \frac{\sigma^2}{2}\right) T}{\sigma \sqrt{T}} \tag{2}$$

$$d_2 = d_1 - \sigma \sqrt{T} \tag{3}$$

C_0 Current call option value
S_0 Current stock price
$N(d)$ Probability that a random draw from a standard normal distribution will be less than d.
X Exercise price
r Risk-free interest rate
T Time to maturity
Σ Standard deviation

6.2.1 Asset Price and Strike Price (S_0, X)

Following the option analogy, asset price S is given by the security's mid-point. Strike price X is the price of the limit order. Options are always out-of-the-money. In the case of bid put options, the asset price is larger than the strike price ($S > X$), and in the case of ask call options, the asset price is smaller than the strike price ($S < X$).

6.2.2 Riskless Rate of Interest (r)

We use the 3-month EURIBOR (Euro Interbank Offered Rate) as of 2007-10-08 for the risk-free interest rate. Analogue to [22, p. 37] we believe that "the assumed interest rate has essentially no impact on the results since the short time intervals [option's maturity] involved ensure that it has little effect on the option values". Moreover, any bias will likely affect both sides of the order book and both AT and Non-AT orders. The riskless rate of return as well as the following figures "volatility" and "maturity" were annualized.

6.2.3 Asset's Volatility (σ)

[21] calculate implied standard deviations using the method proposed by [24]. [22] estimate volatility by its annualized daily return variance and mention that a time-varying volatility model was not expected to change their results. We follow their approach and estimate *end-of day* volatilities. Daily closing data is directly taken from "Reuters Tick History" (University access) for the six month period prior to the observation period.

6.2.4 Option's Maturity (T)

The life of a limit order begins upon submission and ends upon full execution, cancellation or expiration (deletion). [21] arbitrarily allocate lifetimes to the limit orders. Thereby, all limit orders independent of their size or position in the order book are treated alike and are expected to remain in the order book for the same amount of time. In contrast, [22] model limit order lifetimes depending on their prices, sizes and market conditions. We also believe that the expected lifetime of orders is dependent upon both individual order particularities and the order book situation. Therefore, for each security the following linear model is estimated:

$$E(logTtr) = \beta_0 + \beta_1 logAge + \beta_2 queue + \beta_3 middiff + \beta_4 logTimetoClose$$
$$+\beta_5 dummytoday + \beta_6 size + \beta_7 ATflag + \beta_8 queue \tag{4}$$
$$* TimetoClose + \beta_9 middiff * TimeToClose$$

The estimated "time to removal" (*Ttr*) includes execution, cancellation and expiration events. Analogue to [22], we log the dependent variable *Ttr* to control for residual heteroskedasticity. *LogAge* refers to the (log) time the respective order has already rested in the order book. *Queue* represents the cumulated volume (size) of orders with higher price priority and time precedence. Before the respective order can be executed, all orders in the *queue* need to be executed (or cancelled) first. *Middiff* is the absolute difference between the orders limit and the mid-point between best bid and best ask. *TimetoClose* is the (log) minute time until the end of the trading day. *Dummytoday* constitutes a dummy variable that indicates whether (1) or not (0) an order was submitted the same day. *Size* naturally refers to the submitted volume of the respective order. In our case, it includes both visible size and hidden size provided by iceberg orders. Finally, the *ATflag* indicates whether (1) or not (0) the respective order was submitted by an algorithm. Analogue to [22], the two interaction terms model cross-effects among terms *queue* and *TimetoClose* and among terms *middiff* and *TimetoClose*.

For the estimation samples, the order book is reconstructed on a minute-by-minute basis each trading day between 9:00 AM and 5:30 PM. Then *logTtr* is estimated for all (limit) orders in the order book where the time of removal is known. Given the minute-by-minute order book reconstruction approach, the same orders may appear in different estimation samples at different times with different inputs though.

Regression results can be found in Table 4. Analogue to below analyses, calculations are conducted on a sub-sample of five randomly chosen DAX30 companies. Except on the coefficient *queue* (ALV), all coefficients are significant at the 1%-level. It can be observed that AT orders have a shorter lifetime than Non-AT orders, i.e. (negative coefficient). It shall, however, be noted that *Ttr* is influenced by both execution and cancellation events that may act in different directions. For example, regarding *middiff* it might be expected that more aggressively priced orders are executed earlier. This is due to the fact that these rest at the top of the order book. Simultaneously, less aggressively priced orders are presumed to be cancelled more frequently. Less aggressively priced orders, waiting deep in the order book, are less likely to be executed and due to new information arrival might need to be updated. The observation of negative coefficients for *middiff* therefore provides evidence that the "cancellation-effect" outweighs the "execution-effect". Comparatively low fill rates (not shown here in detail), i.e. the percentage of orders that were actually executed, of 11.78% for Non-AT submitted orders and 17.12% for AT submitted orders confirm the importance of the "cancellation-effect".

Table 4. Regression coefficients from linear model

Company*:	ALV	BMW	DTE	MAN	CON
Adjusted R^2	0.553	0.520	0.513	0.595	0.609
Constant	-0.4203	-0.1116	0.2383	-1.4575	-0.6203
logAge	0.6263	0.5063	0.4935	0.6423	0.5848
Queue	1.4 E-06	1.8 E-06	6.0 E-08	4.9 E-06	5.2 E-06
Middiff	-0.0003	-0.0155	-0.0031	0.0022	-0.0041
logTimetoClose	0.3447	0.3919	0.3834	0.5213	0.4065
dummytoday	0.3517	0.2310	0.0603	0.4421	0.2944
Size	-1.4 E-05	-1.2 E-05	-6.8 E-06	-3.7 E-05	-6.5 E-05
ATflag	-0.3631	-0.3966	-0.3476	-0.2081	-0.3663
QueueTimetoClose	6.6 E-11	2.6 E-11	7.5 E-12	2.3 E11	1.7 E-10
middiffTimetoClose	-1.8 E-07	-1.1 E-06	-1.0 E-07	-7.7 E-08	-5.5 E-08

* ALV = Allianz; BMW; DTE = Deutsche Telekom; MAN; CON = Continental

6.3 Passive Trading Counterparty

The last proposed measure evaluates the liquidity of a market by means of trading activity. The liquidity measure is assumed to be especially useful for the assessment of markets where the majority of liquidity is not "committed", but a lot of trading activity occurs. Analogue to previous liquidity measures, the main focus is again laid on those (limit) orders that seemingly provide liquidity by passively sitting in the order book. Looking at actual executions, it is assessed how much volume is executed against passive AT limit orders. In other words, this measure builds upon the notion that a market is more liquid, the higher the probability of finding a "passive" trading counterparty is. This definition, of course, merely refers to the liquidity contribution of AT engines.

6.4 Results

Results for the first two liquidity measures *pure order volume* and *option value* can be found in Table 5. Regarding the first two liquidity contribution figures, two findings are obvious:

First, the liquidity contribution of AT engines suggested by pure submitted volume is consistently larger than the value suggested by option valuation. The most likely reason for this finding may be found with the "time of liquidity contribution" (see Table 1, Table 4). Consequently the free trading option offered to the market is less valuable.

Second, the values provided by both methods are much smaller than the share assumed by the number of non-marketable limit orders submitted by AT engines. In the whole DAX30 sample, 54.20% of all submitted limit orders originate from algorithms. Thereby, 88.01% (1,911,213) of all AT-submitted orders are non-marketable limit orders (see Table 2).

Table 5. AT liquidity contribution

		Share of AT orders, given option values			Share of AT orders, given order volumes		
		BID	ASK	Both	BID	ASK	Both
ALV	Mean (in %)	2.88	3.29	3.08	9.78	6.71	8.24
	Standard Deviation	*0.010*	*0.008*	*0.005*	*0.020*	*0.010*	*0.014*
BMW	Mean (in %)	2.38	6.07	4.23	10.63	12.54	11.58
	Standard Deviation	*0.015*	*0.036*	*0.018*	*0.036*	*0.042*	*0.025*
DTE	Mean (in %)	3.37	3.35	3.36	7.11	3.95	5.53
	Standard Deviation	*0.021*	*0.009*	*0.014*	*0.023*	*0.015*	*0.015*
MAN	Mean (in %)	3.65	1.83	2.74	8.20	3.45	5.83
	Standard Deviation	*0.025*	*0.019*	*0.015*	*0.062*	*0.032*	*0.035*
CON	Mean (in %)	2.54	2.66	2.60	4.74	4.08	4.41
	Standard Deviation	*0.020*	*0.012*	*0.009*	*0.024*	*0.020*	*0.015*

Results for the third liquidity measure *passive trading counterparty* can be found in Table 6. The figure of interest is the one where AT engines constitute the passive counterparty within a trade. In other words, the passive limit orders sit in the order book and are executed because of an incoming market order or marketable limit order. The share of AT being Non-Aggressor is comparatively high. For example, 40.28% of executed volume in BMW is executed against passive AT engines.

Table 6. Volume of executions with AT as Non-Aggressor

	Volume of executions	Aggressor		Non-Aggressor (passive counterparty)	
		AT	Non-AT	AT	Non-AT
ALV	9,129,140	54.83%	45.17%	42.97%	57.03%
BMW	10,760,588	46.85%	53.15%	40.28%	59.72%
DTE	111,047,806	34.18%	65.82%	32.34%	67.66%
MAN	6,811,806	39.52%	60.48%	36.65%	63.35%
CON	5,176,324	39.66%	60.34%	38.67%	61.33%

Even though both the last liquidity measure *passive trading counterparty* and the first two liquidity measures *order volume* and *option value* incorporate passive non-marketable limit orders submitted by AT, the results significantly[2] differ from each other. This is due to the fact that AT engines behave significantly different from humans (Hypothesis H1) and that this behaviour cannot sufficiently be grasped by "traditional" liquidity measures. For example, the *option value* approach implicitly assumes that

---

[2] Liquidity measures *order volume* and *option value* were calculated on a minute-by-minute basis given the reconstructed order books. Based on a simple t-test it can be concluded that these two figures statistically significantly differ from each other. Figures of the liquidity measure *passive trading counterparty* are based on the calculation of the one-minute period prior to the respective order book reconstruction. Based on two t-tests, this measure also statistically significantly differs from the other two measures. Pre-requisites for the t-test are fulfilled.

those orders which seemingly provide liquidity to the market by non-marketable limit orders are also the ones that will finally be executed. But especially for the new trader group, AT engines, this is not necessarily true: AT engines place their limit orders in such a way that these will remain in the order book for only a short period of time which results in a low option value. These might not want to reveal their trading intentions to the market by means of providing free trading options. Analogue to above liquidity definition, this part of liquidity is merely "committed" for a very short period of time. Nonetheless, proven by the volume of executions (Table 6), these do provide (passive) liquidity to the market. This liquidity, however, is merely transient / fleeting and may only reveal itself when an eligible trading counterparty emerges. To conclude, Hypothesis H2 can be corroborated.

7 Conclusion

Having conducted a short literature review on AT, we identified the interaction of algorithmic trading (i.e. technology) and liquidity as an important area of research that still lacks rigorous insights and methodologies. Pursuing to fill this gap, we assess the applicability of liquidity measurement concepts in the presence of frequent AT activity. As liquidity measures, such as the order book option value, are to a certain degree based on a particular market (behaviour) belief, the derived results also provide evidence how AT order flow *blurs traditional definitions*.

Being provided with a unique high frequency dataset that enables us to allocate the origin of each single order in the order book to either "algorithms" or "normal" human traders, we are – to our knowledge – the first to draw valid conclusions on the liquidity contribution of AT engines. To summarize, the empirical analysis provides evidence that AT engines behave significantly different from human traders with regard to their order cancellation behaviour. Furthermore, given exactly these differences, we were able to show that the application of liquidity measures that are based on "traditional" (*liquidity commitment*) market microstructure beliefs do not necessarily represent the "real" liquidity contribution of AT engines. Due to the fact that the share of AT trading is likely to increase in European markets, the potential for liquidity misinterpretation might even increase and should therefore be taken into account by traders, market providers, and researchers. Nonetheless, it shall be noted that we do not want promote the "one" right liquidity measure, but instead we hope to trigger a discussion on the usefulness of certain liquidity measures in today's electronic markets. Overall, we were able to show that the heavy use of technology (i.e. AT engines, computers) changes the way financial markets work and therefore also the way these should be assessed / interpreted.

Future work will include above appraisal on the whole DAX30 dataset. Moreover, the relation between different liquidity measures over a period of time will be investigated. The assessment of intraday patters might also provide an interesting direction of future research.

Acknowledgments

The author gratefully acknowledges the support of the E-Finance Lab, Frankfurt for this work.

References

1. Deutsche Börse AG: Factbook 2007 (2007), http://deutsche-boerse.com
2. Hendershott, T., Jones, C., Menkveld, A.: Does Algorithmic Trading Improve Liquidity? WFA Paper 2008 (2008), http://ssrn.com/abstract=1100635
3. Domowitz, I., Yegerman, H.: The Cost of Algorithmic Trading - A First Look at Comparative Performance. In: Bruce, B. (ed.) Algorithmic Trading: Precision, Control, Execution, pp. 30–40. Institutional Investors Inc. (2005)
4. Chakravarty, S., Kalev, P., Pham, L.T.: Stealth Trading in Volatile Markets. Working Paper, Monash University, Australia (2005)
5. Yang, J., Jiu, B.: Algorithm Selection: A Quantitative Approach. In: Algorithmic Trading II, pp. 26–34. Institutional Investor, New York (2006)
6. Kissel, R., Malamut, R.: Algorithmic Decision-Making Framework. Journal of Trading 1, 12–21 (2006)
7. Gsell, M.: Assessing the Impact of Algorithmic Trading on Markets: A Simulation Approach. In: Proceedings of the 16th European Conference on Information Systems (ECIS), pp. 587–598 (2008)
8. Gomber, P., Schweickert, U., Theissen, E.: Zooming in on Liquidity. In: 9th Symposium on Finance, Banking and Insurance (2004)
9. Bernstein, P.L.: Liquidity, Stock Markets, and Market Makers. Financial Management 16(2), 54–62 (1987)
10. Irvine, P., Benston, G., Kandel, E.: Liquidity beyond the Inside Spread: Measuring and Using Information in the Limit Order Book. Working Paper, Emory University & Hebrew University (2000)
11. Barclay, M., Christie, W.: Effects of Market Reform on the Trading Costs and Depths of Nasdaq Stocks. Journal of Finance 54, 1–34 (1999)
12. Hasbrouck, J., Saar, G.: Technology and Liquidity Provision: The Blurring of Traditional Definitions. Journal of Financial Markets (2008)
13. Gsell, M., Gomber, P.: Algorithmic Trading Engines Versus Human Traders - Do They Behave Different in Securities Markets? In: Proceedings of the 17th European Conference on Information Systems, ECIS (2009)
14. Copeland, T.E., Galai, D.: Information Effects on the Bid-Ask Spread. Journal of Finance 38(5), 1457–1469 (1983)
15. Hull, J.: Options, Futures, and Other Derivative Securities, 2nd edn. Prentice Hall, Englewood Cliffs (1993)
16. Cooper, S.K., Groth, J.C., Avera, W.E.: Liquidity, Exchange Listing, and Common Stock Performance. Journal of Economics and Business, 21–33 (1985)
17. Marsh, T., Rock, K.: Exchange Listing and Liquidity: A Comparison of the American Stock Exchange with the NASDAQ National Market System. American Stock Exchange Transactions Data Research Project No. 2 (1986)
18. Deutsche Börse AG: ATP Agreement for Participation in the "Automated Trading Program" (ATP) via the Electronic Trading System Xetra, http://deutsche-boerse.com
19. Deutsche Börse AG: Xetra: International führende Plafform für den Börsenhandel - Hohe Geschwindigkeit, geringe Latenz, http://deutsche-boerse.com
20. Handa, P., Schwartz, R.A.: How Best to Supply Liquidity to a Securities Market - Investors want three Things from the Markets: Liquidity, Liquidity, and Liquidity. The Journal of Portfolio Management, 44–51 (1996)

21. Jarnecic, E., McInish, T., Zürich, T.H.: An Empirical Investigation of the Option Value of the Limit Order Book on the Australian Stock Exchange. In: Financial Management Association International Conference (1997)
22. Harris, L.E., Lawrence, E., Panchapagesan, V.: The Information Content of the Limit Order Book: Evidence from NYSE Specialist Trading Decisions. Journal of Financial Markets 8(1), 25–67 (2005)
23. Black, F., Scholes, M.: The Pricing of Options and Corporate Liabilities. Journal of Political Economy 81 (1973)
24. Brenner, M., Subrahmanyam, M.G.: A Simple Formula to Compute the Implied Standard Deviation. Financial Analysts Journal, 80–83 (1988)

Anonymous, Yet Trustworthy Auctions

Prasit Bikash Chanda[1], Vincent Naessens[2], and Bart De Decker[1]

[1] K.U. Leuven, Dept. of Computer Science, DistriNet-SecAnon
{Prasit.Chanda,Bart.DeDecker}@cs.kuleuven.be
[2] Katholieke Hogeschool Sint-Lieven, Dept. of Industrial Engineering, Mobility & Security
Vincent.Naessens@kahosl.be

Abstract. An auction is an inevitable market mechanism to setup prices of goods or services in a competitive and dynamic environment. Anonymity of bidders is required to conceal their business strategies from competitors. However, it is also essential to provide the seller guarantees that a bidder is trustworthy and competent enough to perform certain tasks (e.g transports). This paper proposes an auction protocol where bidders will participate anonymously, yet prove to be trustworthy and competent and can be held accountable towards auctioneers and sellers. Moreover, the protocol introduces promises, bonuses and compensations to ensure the best price for the sellers, extra profit for bidders and opportunities for newcomers in the business. It also handles ties, and copes with last minute bidding. Finally, the auction's fair proceedings and outcome can be verified by everyone.

Keywords: Auction, Credential, Anonymity, Trust, Distributed Systems.

1 Introduction

The logistic management of a typical organization is an extension of the Supply Chain Management (SCM). SCM is the complete picture of planning, implementing and controlling of products or services across the business boundary to an extended environment composed of dealers, wholesalers, end-users and suppliers. It also includes management of transportation strategies (e.g. on-time delivery, reducing cost). Currently, organizations face numerous challenges regarding this issue. Hence, they are inclined towards outsourcing their transport activities to a fourth party organization 4PL[1]. These 4PL have short or long term contracts with third party organizations 3PL[2] and independent transport firms. The 4PL has to manage shipments within predefined time periods (e.g. 24 hours) through 3PL organizations or transport firms to meet the customers' demands. However, in a fast-paced dynamic and distributed setting, it is not sufficient to have short or long term contracts. The 4PL will also have to choose transport firms from open markets to cope with the specified scenario. Hence, auctions are needed to hire freelance transport firms from these markets. In such a setting, the anonymity of the transport firm

---

[1] A Fourth Party Logistics provider (4PL) is a supply chain service provider that searches the best transport solutions for its clients, typically without using own assets or resources.

[2] Third Party Logistics (3PL) is the supply chain practice where one or more transport functions of a firm are outsourced to a 3PL provider.

C. Godart et al. (Eds.): I3E 2009, IFIP AICT 305, pp. 225–239, 2009.

is important, both to ensure the best price for the 4PL and to hide its business strategies from its competitors (e.g. increase its market share, open up new routes, keep its workforce busy, ...). However, anonymity may lead to abuse. For instance, an anonymous transport firm may win a deal to transport freights on a certain route in which it has no experience. Hence, the 4PL and the auction houses need guarantees from the transport firms that they are trustworthy and competent enough to perform a certain transport. Besides, these transport firms must be held accountable for carrying out such transports.

This paper is organized as follows. Sections 2 and 3 describe the requirements, assumptions and notations. Then, in section 4, an overview of the building blocks is given. Sections 5 and 6 deal with guarantees, bonuses and compensations. Section 7 gives a detailed design of the auction system. In section 8, the system is evaluated and section 9 describes related work. A conclusion and suggestions for future work can be found in section 10.

2   Requirements

The main goal of this paper is to design an efficient auction system, that allows bidders to remain anonymous, but offers sufficient guarantees to the sellers.

The auction should fulfill several requirements. These are divided into functional requirements and privacy, security and trust requirements.

Functional Requirements

- (F1) *Best price*: An auction should guarantee the seller the best price.
- (F2) *Efficiency*: The auction system should be simple and introduce no extra overhead or delays; therefore, multi-round auctions are not acceptable.
- (F3) *Fairness*: The auction system should be fair. Everybody should be able to verify the auction's proceedings and outcome.
- (F4) *Openness*: Every prospective bidder should be able to register for the auction system. Every registered bidder can participate in an auction if he fulfills the auction's prerequisites.
- (F5) *Generic*: The trust paradigms used by the system should be generic and extensible.

Privacy, Security and Trust Requirements

- (PST1) *Bidder's Anonymity*: Bidders will remain anonymous to hide their business strategies. Only the seller will eventually learn the true identity of the winning bidder.
- (PST2) *Guarantees for Seller and Auctioneer*: The seller or auctioneer should be ensured of the trustworthiness of the bidders. The seller should be able to define prerequisites that must be fulfilled by the bidders. The auctioneer will verify these guarantees when bids are collected.
- (PST3) *Accountability*: Each party within the system can be held liable for its actions.
- (PST4) *Selective Disclosure*: The bidder can decide which attributes (or properties thereof) of his credential will be disclosed during an auction.

3 Assumptions and Notations

In the sequel of this paper, the following **assumptions** are made:

RSA Key Pair and X.509 Certificates. The protocol assumes that each entity in the protocol holds one or more RSA key pairs [21]. RSA key pairs consist of a public key and a private key. The private key is kept secret and the public key will be certified in (X.509) certificates [19] issued by a trusted Certification Authority (CA).

Entity bound credentials. Each credential is bound to its owner. Sharing of credentials can be discouraged by including a valuable secret (e.g. credit card number) in the credential.

In the sequel of this paper, the following **notations** are used:

- $X \rightarrow Y$: *data* (resp. $X \leftarrow Y$: *data*)   denotes that X sends *data* to Y (resp. X receives *data* from Y).
- $X \rightleftharpoons Y$: *(res$_X$; res$_Y$)* $\leftarrow$ protocol(*Common; Input$_X$; Input$_Y$*) is used throughout the paper and represents a generic protocol where *Input$_X$* and *Input$_Y$* are inputs from X resp. Y. *Common* is known to both X and Y. The protocol produces the results *res$_X$* for X and *res$_Y$* for Y.
- $\text{Sig}_X(Data)$ represents the signature on *Data* with X's private signature key Pr_X^s.
- $\lceil X \rceil$ (cloaked X) denotes that entity X is anonymous in a particular interaction.

4 Building Blocks

In this section, the major building blocks used in the auction system will be briefly described. We discuss *TLS/SSL connections, anonymous channels* and *anonymous credentials.*

TLS/SSL Connections. The protocol specifies that TLS connections [15] should be set up prior to any interaction between business entities. The following protocol is relevant:

- $X \rightleftharpoons Y$: *(id$_Y$; id$_X$)* $\leftarrow$ setupTLS(*Cert$_X^a$,Cert$_Y^a$; Pr$_X^a$; Pr$_Y^a$*) represents the establishment of a TLS connection between X and Y. Here, *id$_X$* and *id$_Y$* are the identities of X and Y respectively, which are embedded in the certificates *Cert$_X^a$* and *Cert$_Y^a$*. During the set-up, X and Y mutually authenticate. The TLS connection protects the confidentiality, integrity and authenticity of the exchanged information.

Anonymous Channels. The protocol also uses anonymous channels (e.g. through MIX networks or Onion Routing networks) during some interactions. Anonymous channels [16] basically hide the traffic patterns (*'Who sends to Whom'*). Such channels will ensure confidentiality and integrity as well. The following protocol is relevant:

- $\lceil X \rceil \rightleftharpoons Y$: *(id$_Y$; $\emptyset$)* $\leftarrow$ setupAnonChannel(*Cert$_Y^a$; $\emptyset$; Pr$_Y^a$*) represents the establishment of anonymous channel between X and Y. During the setup, Y authenticates towards X, while X remains anonymous. The Anonymous channel also protects the confidentiality and integrity of the exchanged information.

Anonymous Credentials. Anonymous credential systems [10,11] allow for anonymous yet accountable transactions between users and organizations and allow for selective disclosure by showing only part of the credential attributes or properties thereof (e.g. when the credential contains an attribute numberOfTransactions, it is possible to prove that this number is greater than 70 while hiding its actual value and the values of all the other attributes). In the Idemix system [10], different usages of the same credential are unlinkable, except when unique attribute values are revealed. Credentials can have features such as an expiry date, the allowed number of times it can be shown or the possibility to be revoked. Note that an anonymous channel is required for every credential show to provide anonymity at the network layer. The following protocols are relevant:

- $X \rightleftharpoons I$: *(Cred$_X$;$\emptyset$)* $\leftarrow$ issueCred*(trust values, id$_X$, Cert$_I^c$; $\emptyset$; Pr$_I^c$)* represents the protocol where a trusted credential issuer I issues a credential *Cred$_X$* to a entity X. The anonymous credential *Cred$_X$* contains an expiry date, the identity *(id$_X$)* of the holder and possibly other attributes *(trust values)* and is signed with I's private key *Pr$_I^c$*.

- $\lceil \overline{X} \rceil \rightleftharpoons Y$: *(trans$_X$; trans$_Y$)* $\leftarrow$ showCred*(props, Cert$_I^c$; Cred$_X$; $\emptyset$){data}* represents the protocol where an anonymous entity X proves to the entity Y the possession of a valid credential *Cred$_X$*, issued by I. X will selectively disclose attributes (or properties thereof) of *Cred$_X$* described in *props* (see also section 6). During the credential show, X can sign *data* with its *Cred$_X$* creating a provable link between the proof and *data*. The protocol returns the transcripts *trans$_X$* and *trans$_Y$*.

  Additionally, transcripts resulting from showCred can be deanonymized by a predetermined trusted third party D. In this case, the credential owner (the prover, X) sends during the credential show its identity (verifiably encrypted [14] with the public key of D) to the verifier Y. Since the identity is also embedded in the credential, the owner can prove that the correct value has been encrypted, without actually disclosing the identity to the verifier. Deanonymization is used to determine the identity of the winner of an auction. Also, in case of abuse or disputes, the identity of the credential holder can be recovered.

5   Guarantees

Sellers want some guarantees from bidders: e.g. the seller may want that the bidder is specialized in transporting fragile goods, that the bidder has experience in delivering goods in a particular foreign country, that he is in business for more than 10 years, or that he has carried out already more than 500 transports.

These characteristics of the bidder are embedded in a credential and are proven during the bidding. The values are certified by a trusted third party (TTP) (the credential issuer). We use a simple but realistic trust model: most likely, the TTP will be a transportation association. We do not impose the existence of just one TTP. In fact, there may be several associations, and sellers can specify which TTPs they trust. Depending on the certification procedures used by these TTPs, sellers may have less or more trust in these TTPs and require weaker or stronger guarantees. For simplicity reasons, however, we assume in this paper that only one TTP exists. Extending the protocols to more TTPs is just straightforward.

In this paper, we use characteristics which can be easily verified by the TTP: years in business, total number of transactions, average value of transported goods, total value of transported goods, specialties in handling particular goods, experience in routes, etc. These can be derived from the charter of foundation of the company and from signed contracts. The TTP can use an *aging* mechanism to make sure that some accumulating values remain accurate: $new = \alpha \times old + evidence$, with $\alpha < 1$.

It is also possible to add characteristics that are related to the transporter's *reputation*, such as: reliability (e.g. expressed as the percentage of timely and undamaged deliveries out of the total number of transports) or satisfaction of the seller (e.g. a rating from 0 to 10). However, such values require a feedback system that is foolproof, and may involve trusted arbiters in case of disputes. For instance, the transportation association may play the role of mediator, and if the dispute cannot be solved, a judge may return the final verdict. In this paper, we ignore such disputes and refer to future research.

To boostrap the system, bidders (transporters) have to register themselves with a TTP, the credential issuer R (see also section 7) and receive in return an anonymous credential in which the transporter's characteristics (trust values) are embedded. The relevant simplified functions that apply to guarantees are as follows; both are exclusively used by the registrar R:

- *trust values* ← calcTrustValues(*evidence, certificates, guarantees*) is a function that calculates the trust values based on information provided by a prospective bidder, such as: verifiable evidence, certificates issued by trusted CAs and other guarantees signed by an external trusted party (e.g. Government Institute or a non-governmental organization).
- *new trust values* ← updateTrustValues(*old trust values, new transactions*) is a function that calculates the *new trust values* when $Cred_B$ expires and needs to be re-issued. The function calculates the *new trust values* according to the record(s) received. The records contain information about B's previous transactions signed *anonymously* by the sellers. Hence, the TTP does not learn anything about business relations between the bidders and the sellers.

6 Bonuses and Compensations

Winning bidders can get a **bonus** if they are prepared to prove more than is required (e.g. proving more guarantees than the auction prerequisites) or if they promise additional services (e.g. late night delivery). The seller determines before the auction starts which bonuses can be earned.

If the seller agrees, bidders that do not fulfill the prerequisites may nevertheless be allowed to participate in an auction if they fulfill less stringent requirements. However, they can only participate in exchange for a **compensation**. When the contract is signed the bid will be decreased with that compensation. This way, new participants with low or no guarantee values can participate but at a lower price. For instance, a particular auction prerequisite states that a bidder should have completed at least 50 transports during its business lifetime. However, the seller may allow bidders with only 20 transports to participate but they will have to compensate their lack of experience with a penalty of say 1000 EUR. The latter can be used by the seller to take an extra insurance.

Only the bids are taken into account for determining the winner of the auction. However, when the contract is signed, the bid_B is increased with the bonuses and decremented with the compensations. The relevant simplified functions are as follows:

- *(bid, promises, props)* ← determineBidProps*(description, best bid)* represents the User Interface (UI) where a bidder B prepares a scheme (e.g. bid to offer, promises to bear and properties to prove) based on the auction description (i.e. prerequisites, bonuses, and compensations) and the best bid so far.
- *(bonus, compensation)* ← calcBonusCompensation*(description, props, promises)* is a function (used by the seller) to determine the bonus and compensation based on the description of the auction, the properties (*props*) proved by the bidder and promises made by the bidder.

7   Design of an Anonymous, Yet Trustworthy Auction System

Initially, bidders have to register (once) with the registrar R, a trusted credential issuer. During the registration, bidders have to provide R with certificates and other evidence of experience signed by external trusted parties. Upon verification, the issuer delivers an anonymous credential to the bidders. With these anonymous credentials, bidders can anonymously participate in auctions and prove that they are trustworthy and competent enough to carry out certain transports. The seller defines the auction prerequisites, the bonuses and compensations and forwards this auction description to the auctioneer. The auctioneer publishes the description in the public domain. Bidders may make promises to earn bonuses and/or agree to compensate (when they do not satisfy the auction prerequisites and when this is allowed by the seller). Bidders can bid as many times as they want as long as the auction is not closed. Each bid is signed with the credential. The auctioneer publishes every bid transcript in the public domain so that everyone can verify the fair proceedings of the auction.

After a predefined deadline, the auction is closed and the winner is selected based on the **lowest bid**. The auctioneer requests the trusted deanonymizer to identify the winner (i.e. deanonymize the winning transcript). Note that, the winner's identity is only revealed to the seller. Later, the seller and winner will sign the transport contract.

After completing a transport, the seller will confirm the transport[3], which will be used for updating the trust values in the credential.

7.1   Initial Certification

The auction protocol involves several parties: Bidder(s) denoted by **B** (e.g. Skippers, Charter Truck Companies, 3PL), a Registrar (**R**) (e.g. a transport association), an Auctioneer (**A**) (e.g. an independent auction house), a Seller (**S**) (e.g. 4PL), a Bulletin Board

---

[3] If the credentials contain reputation-based values, the seller may also evaluate the transport. However, in case of disputes, a trusted arbiter may be involved.

(**BB**) and a deanonymizer (**D**). **R**, **A** and **D** are trusted third parties. The winner, which is the bidder with the lowest bid is denoted by **W**. We assume that each entity E has one or more key pairs (Pk_E, Pr_E) of which the public key (Pk_E) is certified in a certificate $(Cert_E)$ by a trusted certification authority (**CA**). (A superscript refers to its usage: e for encryption, a for authentication, s for signing and c for issuing credentials.)

7.2 Registration and Trust Calculation

A prospective bidder B must first register with the registrar R. The bidder presents certificates and other evidence of experience that will be used by the R to calculate guarantees (trust and business parameters). R will issue a credential that includes as attributes these guarantees (*trust values*) and the identity information (id_B). See Table 1 for details.

$B \rightleftharpoons R : (id_R; id_B) \leftarrow \mathsf{setupTLS}(Cert_B^a, Cert_R^a; Pr_B^a; Pr_R^a)$

$B \rightarrow R : \text{guarantees, certificates, evidence, ...}$

$\quad\quad R : \textit{trust values} \leftarrow \mathsf{calcTrustValues}(\text{evidence, certificates, guarantees})$

$B \rightleftharpoons R : (Cred_B; \emptyset) \leftarrow \mathsf{issueCred}(\textit{trust values}, id_B, Cert_R^c; \emptyset; Pr_R^c)$

Table 1. Registration and Trust Calculation

Similarly, a prospective seller S has to register with R and receives as a result an anonymous credential $Cred_S$ with which S can confirm anonymously a transport.

7.3 Auctions

Figure 1 gives an example of a description of an auction, including the prerequisites, bonuses and compensations. The prerequisites specify that the bidder's credential needs to be issued by `TrucAssoc`, and that the bidder should be in business for at least 5 years and be specialized in transporting fragile goods. A bonus of 1000 EUR is awarded if the goods can be delivered within 2 days and an extra bonus of 500 EUR for early delivery (before 6am). A compensation of 2000 EUR is requested for newcomers (between 2 and 5 years in business) or if the bidder not specialized in this kind of transport.

---

auction: transport 10 pallets of crystalware from Leuven to Rome
prerequisites: `certifier` = TrucAssoc, `specialty` = fragile goods AND `YearsInBusiness` > 5
bonus: 1000 EUR **if** `delivery` <= **today** + 2 **days**
bonus: 500 EUR **if** `delivery` < 6 **am**
compensation: 1000 EUR **if** (2 < `YearsInBusiness` < 5) OR **no** specialty

---

Fig. 1. Description, prerequisites, bonus and compensation of an Auction

Creation of a new Auction. A seller S submits a description of a new auction and a certificate[4] $Cert^e_S$ to the auctioneer A. The description of the auction, together with the auction policy and deadline, is posted on the bulletin board BB. See Table 2 for details.

S	: $descr_{auc}$ ← (transport description, prerequisites, bonuses, compensations)
S ⇌ A	: $(id_A; id_S)$ ← setupTLS($Cert^a_S, Cert^a_A; Pr^a_S; Pr^a_A$)
S → A	: $Sig_S(descr_{auc}, Cert^e_S), Cert^s_S$
BB ← A	: $Sig_A(Sig_S(descr_{auc}, Cert^e_S), policy, deadline_{auc}), Cert^s_S, Cert^s_A$
BB	: publish $Sig_A(Sig_S(descr_{auc}, Cert^e_S), policy, deadline_{auc}), Cert^s_S, Cert^s_A$

Table 2. Creation of a new Auction

Anonymous Bidding. A potential bidder B retrieves the description of an open auction from BB and bids anonymously to the auctioneer A. The bidding consists of a credential-show of an anonymous credential ($Cred_B$). During the show, the prerequisites are proven and possibly other properties which give right to bonuses. Besides the bid itself, the bidder can also sign extra promises, with which extra bonuses can be earned. The auctioneer A posts the transcript of the bid on BB and returns a receipt to B. See Table 3 for details. Note that $trans_A$ contains a verifiable encryption of the identity of B with the public key of the deanonymizer D ($VEnc_D(id_B)$).

⌈B⌉ → BB	: request type of transports
⌈B⌉ ← BB	: $Sig_A(Sig_S(descr_{auc}, Cert^e_S), policy, deadline_{auc}), Cert^s_S, Cert^s_A$
For every bid:	
⌈B⌉ ⇌ A	: $(id_A; \emptyset)$ ← setupAnonChannel($Cert^a_A; \emptyset; Pr^a_A$)
⌈B⌉ ← A	: "Hello anonymous bidder", t_s, $descr_{auc}$, Best Bid, $deadline_{auc}$
⌈B⌉	: $(bid_B, props, promises)$ ← determineBidProps($descr_{auc}$, Best Bid)
⌈B⌉ ⇌ A	: $(trans_B; trans_A)$ ← showCred($props, Cert^e_R; Cred_B; \emptyset)\{bid_B, promises, t_s\}$
⌈B⌉ ← A	: $Sig_A(trans_A)$
A → BB	: $Sig_A(trans_A)$
BB	: publish $Sig_A(trans_A)$

Table 3. Anonymous Bidding

Since the auction is multithreaded, simultaneous bids are possible. Therefore, as soon as a new thread is created to handle a new bid, a unique timestamp (t_s) is assigned to that thread. The bidder will sign both t_s and bid_B with his credential. Note that the bid_B, $promises$, $props$ and t_s can be recovered from the transcripts.

The auctioneer will check whether the bid is better than any bid posted on the BB prior to time t_s. In order to avoid that some bidders start a bid, but only finish the bidding at the end of the auction period, each bid must be finished within a predefined time limit. If that time limit expires, the bidding is aborted. In order to avoid that some

---

[4] The certificate will be used later (by the deanonymizer) to encrypt the winner's identity.

bidders do a final bid at the end of the auction period which is only marginally better than the best bid, the auction policy should define minimum deltas to be used in the different time frames.

Example: [00:00–01:00], -5%; [01:00–01:45], -10%; [01:45–End], -15%. This policy specifies that during the first hour of the auction, each bid should be at least 5% better than the previous best bid. Then, during the next 45 minutes, each bid should be at least 10% better than the previous best bid. After that, bids should be 15% better than the last best bid.

Only the best bid published before t_s is taken into account, so it is possible that simultaneous bids do not differ that much (in that case, a later higher bid will be ignored).

Selection of the Winner and Contract Signing. Once the deadline of the auction has expired, the auctioneer A selects the first lowest bid and sends the transcript of the bid to the deanonymizer D. D recovers the identity of W, and returns that identity (encrypted with the public key of the seller S) to the auctioneer who forwards it to S. The seller will calculate the bonus and compensation and contact W to sign a contract. R is also kept informed by D about a W's transport engagement (i.e. anonymized[5] details of the task (such as the route, type of goods, the total transaction value, etc.). The transport has to be confirmed (e.g. done or canceled) before the deadline expires (see Table 4). Note that *reportID* is a unique number used to match a transport report with a transport engagement.

A	: $trans_W \leftarrow$ selectFirstLowestBid(all bids)
$A \rightarrow BB$	: $\text{Sig}_A(trans_W, "winner")$
BB	: post $\text{Sig}_A(trans_W, "winner")$
$A \rightleftharpoons D$	: $(id_D; id_A) \leftarrow$ setupTLS($Cert_A^a, Cert_D^a; Pr_A^a; Pr_D^a$)
$A \rightarrow D$	: $\text{Sig}_A(trans_W, \text{Sig}_S(descr_{auc}, Cert_S^e), "winner"), Cert_S^s, Cert_A^a$
D	: $id_W \leftarrow$ Deanonymize($Pr_D^e, trans_W$)
D	: $(reportID, summary) \leftarrow$ genUniqueReportID($descr_{auc}$)
$A \leftarrow D$	: $\text{Enc}_S(\text{Sig}_D(trans_W, id_W, "winner", reportID)), Cert_D^s$
$A \rightleftharpoons S$	: $(id_S; id_A) \leftarrow$ setupTLS($Cert_A^a, Cert_S^a; Pr_A^a; Pr_S^a$)
$A \rightarrow S$	: $trans_W, \text{Enc}_S(\text{Sig}_D(trans_W, id_W, "winner", reportID)), Cert_D^s$
$S \rightleftharpoons W$	: $(id_W; id_S) \leftarrow$ setupTLS($Cert_S^a, Cert_W^a; Pr_S^a; Pr_W^a$)
S	: $bid_W \leftarrow trans_W.bid$
S	: $(bonus, compensation) \leftarrow$ calcBonusCompensation($descr_{auc}$,
	$\qquad\qquad trans_W.props, trans_W.promises$)
$S \rightarrow W$	: $\text{Sig}_S(contract, bid_W + bonus - compensation)$
$S \leftarrow W$	: $\text{Sig}_W(contract, bid_W + bonus - compensation)$
$D \rightleftharpoons R$	: $(id_R; id_D) \leftarrow$ setupTLS($Cert_D^a, Cert_R^a; Pr_D^a; Pr_R^a$)
$D \rightarrow R$	: $\text{Sig}_D(W, reportID, summary, deadline_{transport})$
R	: append $\text{Sig}_D(W, reportID, summary, deadline_{transport})$ to record[W]

Table 4. Selection of the winner

---

[5] The details are generalized so that they cannot identify a specific auction.

End of Contract. When a transaction between S and W has been completed, S will confirm the transport (e.g. done or canceled). If the bidder's credential also contains reputation-based values, then S and W should also agree on the outcome (late/timely delivery, damaged/undamaged goods, etc.). However, if they cannot agree a trusted arbiter will have to step in.

The result (confirmation and possibly assessment) is signed by W and this signature together with the reportID (provided by D when the winner was announced to S) is signed anonymously by S during a credential show to R, which will –after some checks: signatures, outcome and reportID are valid– add it to the list of reported transports of W. Finally, a receipt (i.e. the signed transcript of the credential show) is sent to W via S. See Table 5 for details.

$S \rightleftharpoons W$	: $(id_W; id_S) \leftarrow$ setupTLS$(Cert^a_S, Cert^a_W; Pr^a_S; Pr^a_W)$	
$S \rightleftharpoons W$	: $result \leftarrow$ agreeOutcome()	
$S \leftarrow W$	: $\text{Sig}_W(W, result)$	
$\lceil S \rceil \rightleftharpoons R$	: $(id_R; \emptyset) \leftarrow$ setupAnonChannel$(Cert^a_R; \emptyset; Pr^a_R)$	
$\lceil S \rceil \rightleftharpoons R$	: $(trans_S; trans_R) \leftarrow$ showCred$(Cert^c_R; Cred_S; \emptyset)\{\text{Sig}_W(W, result), \text{reportID}\}$	
R	: append $trans_R$ to record[W]	
$\lceil S \rceil \leftarrow R$	: $\text{Sig}_R(trans_R, "OK"), Cert^s_R$	
$S \rightarrow W$	: $\text{Sig}_R(trans_R, "OK"), Cert^s_R$	

Table 5. End of Contract

7.4 Updating Credentials

When a bidder's credential expires (typically, a credential will be valid for one or two months), the bidder will request a new credential from the registrar (R). The registrar will verify whether the outcome of all previous expired transactions (i.e. transactions for which the transport deadline has been exceeded) have been reported. If not, an investigation may be started. (See Table 6.)

$B \rightleftharpoons R$	: $(id_R; id_B) \leftarrow$ setupTLS$(Cert^a_B, Cert^a_R; Pr^a_B; Pr^a_R)$
R	: *new trust values* $\leftarrow$ updateTrustValues(old *trust values*,
:	$\forall_i$ record[B].$result_i$)
R	: $\forall_i$ delete record[B].$result_i$
$B \rightleftharpoons R$	: $(Cred_B; \emptyset) \leftarrow$ issueCred(*new trust values*, id_B; $\emptyset$; Pr^c_R)

Table 6. Updating Credential

8 Evaluation

The protocol is evaluated against the requirements of section 2.

(F1) Best price. Since bidders can bid anonymously, it is less likely that they restrain themselves when making a bid (they do not reveal their business strategies). Also, all

bids are posted on a bulletin board. Hence, as long as the auction is open, a bidder can make a lower bid. The auction system has schemes for bonuses and compensations (see section 6). The bonus scheme increases the bidder's profits when the bidder is willing to provide extra services or prove extra guarantees. Similarly, the compensation scheme increases the seller's revenues (or reduces its risks) as it allows an unexperienced bidder (newcomer) to take part in an auction in exchange for a compensation. The winner is finally selected by sorting the bids according to their unique timestamp and considering the earliest lowest bid.

(F2) Efficiency. Sellers have to complete a particular task within a predefined time to satisfy their customers' needs. Repeat or round bid auctions are time consuming and are inappropriate in a distributed environment: distributed agents (auctioneer, bidders) have to exchange a lot of messages during auctions and the execution periods are lengthy. An example can be found in [5]. Similarly, a concurrent or distributed auctioning mechanism [4,18] has the same time complexity and also has to aggregate information about other market demands.

(F3) Fairness. The auctioneer A posts the bids for a particular auction on a bulletin board BB. At the same time, A returns a receipt (the signed transcript) to the bidder. The transcript contains a verifiable encryption of the identity (id_B) of the bidder with the public key (Pk_D^e) of the deanonymizer D. Everyone can verify the transcripts on BB without learning anything meaningful about the identities of the bidders. In case of abuse, the identity of the culprit can be recovered. Also, the winner of an auction will be held accountable for his bids.

(F4) Openness. Every prospective bidder B can register in the system. A bidder can take part in an auction as long as his $Cred_B$ is valid and fulfills the auction prerequisites. The seller may allow bidders that fulfill only a less stringent version of the prerequisites in exchange for a compensation.

(F5) Generic. The guarantees embedded in $Cred_B$ help auctioneers to choose competent bidders based on their business and trust parameters. However, these guarantees are not a part of the auction mechanism itself. It is easy to adopt or extend the set of trust values.

(PST1) Bidder's Anonymity. $Cred_B$ contains the identity of the bidder but it is not revealed during the **showCred**() protocol. The id_B sent to the auctioneer is verifiably encrypted ($\mathsf{VEnc}_D(id_B)$) with the public key of a trusted deanonymizer (D). The identity of the winner will only be disclosed to the seller. Note also that business relations between bidders and sellers are not revealed to the registrar: the seller anonymously reports about a finished transport. Only the trusted deanonymizer D will temporarily learn this relationship. However, D is not required to keep logs or store evidence information.

(PST2) Guarantee for Seller and Auctioneer. It has been discussed earlier that the guarantees are derived from business parameters of the bidders (see section 5). Moreover, the guarantees are embedded in $Cred_B$. These guarantees create an essence of trustworthiness of the bidders among sellers and auctioneers. The trustworthiness implicitly describes whether the particular bidder is competent enough to carry out a specific transport. The seller defines the auction prerequisites at the start of an auction and bidders

must prove such requirements when they make a bid. However, the seller and, hence, the auction protocol may allow newcomers in exchange for a compensation (see section 6). Furthermore, the protocol also rewards bidders who are willing to prove more attributes about themselves or promise to provide extra services.

(PST3) Accountability. R's signature on $Cred_B$ makes R accountable for the trustworthiness of the embedded *trust values* in $Cred_B$. A bidder B is accountable for its bids and promises, since these are signed with $Cred_B$. The auctioneer returns a signed receipt to the bidder. All auction descriptions and transcripts on the bulletin board are signed by the appropriate parties. Finally, the outcome of a certain completed transport is signed by the seller to ensure authenticity and trustworthiness of the transport's feedback.

(PST4) Selective Disclosure. It is not compulsory to show all attributes of the bidder's $Cred_B$ to participate in an auction. It is sufficient to prove that the attribute values fulfill the auction's prerequisites.

9   Related Work

Many practical electronic auction systems rely on one mediator to maintain the secrecy of bids and to hide the link between bidders and bids. However, bids clearly reveal strategic information about the bidder to the mediator (such as the bidder's economic position, its productivity, ...). Hence, a huge amount of trust in the mediator is typically required. In our solution, bids are anonymous and multiple bids cannot be linked to the same bidder by the auctioneer. Moreover, our system consists of a clear separation of duties and responsibilities. Trust is split among multiple entities, namely the registrar, the auctioneer and the deanonymizer.

Secure multi-party computation is another approach to distribute trust among multiple entities. A lot of research has been performed to solve efficiency problems for special types of applications such as e-voting and e-auctions. Multiple entities are required to reveal the results of the bidding process. Hence, trust is also split among multiple entities. Although a lot of research is invested in secure multi-party computation for auctions, only few practical implementations exist. One prototypical implementation is presented in [24]. The system is used to clear market prices for farmers that produce sugar beets in Denmark. Three servers are involved in the bidding and clearing process. Each server is administered by a different organization. However, that system presents multiple disadvantages compared to our approach. First, although trust is distributed between multiple entities, there is no clear separation of duties and responsibilities. Second, although the secrecy of bids is guaranteed, bidders are not anonymous. Hence, the auctioneer knows in which items bidders are interested (even if the bidder did not win the auction). The system presented in [24] also does not explicitly implement any security measures against cheating bidders.

eBay[6] is a prominent example of a centralized auction system. Bidders are pseudonymous to other bidders during an auction, but the winner of a specific auction can be discovered afterwards by analyzing the seller's profile. eBay allows sellers to restrict

---

[6] eBay Policies: http://pages.ebay.com/help/policies/overview.html

the set of prospective buyers by blocking specific buyers based on personal past experiences, by defining prerequisites (e.g. no buyers from certain countries, only buyers with PayPal,.....) and by canceling the winning bid if the seller cannot verify the true identity of the winner. Also, eBay has a reputation system that is based on feedback given by sellers and buyers. However, it is very difficult for a seller to judge a specific buyer with whom s/he has not dealt before as buyers always get positive feedback. In our paper, we describe a distributed system, in which prospective bidders are completely anonymous towards the auctioneer and the seller (during the auction). Moreover, the winner will remain anonymous towards the auctioneer and other bidders even after the auction has been completed.

Xiong and Liu [2] define a transaction based trust equation as a function of various parameters namely the feedback from peers, the total number of transactions, the credibility of the feedback, and the adaptive transaction context factor. Their trust system does not involve any TTP and lack the essence of accountability. In addition, the trust parameter mainly depend on the feedback instead of the business attributes.

Allen and Merril [6] conduct research by studying and analyzing different trust related aspects on on-line consumers' prospectives. The work includes research methodologies and contributions of such trust aspects. Moreover, they define an abstract trust framework on e-merchant trust beliefs but they do not precisely point out the building blocks of such a concept. It is more like a case study of trust construction where points like trust featured on business attributes and accountability of the attributes are ignored.

Rahman and Hailes [3] illustrate a high level approach of trust in a virtual community. They do not develop a protocol regarding their work and most of the research is based on theories and abstract metrics to calculate transitional trust. Moreover, they ignore how the individual's attributes can deploy trust in the environment.

Research on the usage of context and content based trust mechanisms within semantic web applications has been conducted by Bizer et al. [7]. In their paper they outline a trust architecture which allows the formulation of subjective and task-specific trust policies as a combination of reputation, context and content based trust mechanisms. However, their architecture does not calibrate transaction based trust associations in a SCM platform and it is not an attribute-based trust architecture.

Furthermore, none of these papers including [2,4,18] do address privacy, security, accountability, or anonymity issues.

10 Conclusion and Future Work

This paper presents an anonymous auction protocol, that nevertheless provides guarantees to sellers. These guarantees prove the competence of the bidder in performing a certain transport. The seller may award bonuses to bidders when they agree to provide extra services or prove additional guarantees. Similarly, newcomers may be allowed to take part in an auction if they compensate for their inexperience. The credentials (with embedded trust values) are regularly updated. Privacy policies and preferences should be used during peers' interactions. A *Privacy Policy* states what sort of information a party needs, what it will do with the information, how long it will keep the information, with whom it will share the information and so on. Similarly, a *Privacy Preference* states: what information can be forwarded, how long it can be kept, with whom the information can be shared and so on. For instance, in a bidder ⇌ seller interaction scenario: the seller should send its privacy policy and bidders can check whether these policies match their privacy preferences. The protocol does not include such privacy features and elaborate research is required to determine what policies are required in this context. There is no doubt that the implementation of these features will increase the privacy level of all business parties.

Acknowledgements

This research is partially funded by the Interuniversity Attraction Poles Programme Belgian State, Belgian Science Policy, the Research Fund K.U.Leuven and the IWT-SBO Project (DiCoMAS) "Distributed Collaboration using Multi-Agent System Architectures".

References

1. Layouni, M., Vangheluwe, H.: Anonymous k-Show Credentials. In: Løpez, J., Samarati, P., Ferrer, J.L. (eds.) EuroPKI 2007. LNCS, vol. 4582, pp. 181–192. Springer, Heidelberg (2007)
2. Xiong, L., Liu, L.: A Reputation-Based Trust Model for Peer-to-Peer eCommerce Communities. In: IEEE International Conference on E-Commerce Technology (CEC 2003), p. 275 (2003)
3. Rahman, A.A., Hailes, S.: A Distributed Trust Model. In: Proceedings of the 1997 Workshop on Security Paradigms, pp. 40–68. ACM Press, New York (1998)
4. Kikuchi, H., Harkavy, M., Tygar, J.D.: Multi-round Anonymous Auction Protocol. Institute of Electronics, Information, and Communication Engineers Transactions on Information and Systems, 769–777 (1999)
5. Stajano, F., Anderson, R.: The cocaine auction protocol: On the power of anonymous broadcast. In: Pfitzmann, A. (ed.) IH 1999. LNCS, vol. 1768, pp. 434–447. Springer, Heidelberg (2000)
6. Johnston, A.C., Warkentin, M.: The Online Consumer Trust Construct: A Web Merchant Practitioner Perspective. In: 7th Annual Conference of the Southern Association for Information Systems (2004)
7. Bizer, C., Freie Universitat: Using Context- and Content-Based Trust Policies on the Semantic Web, pp. 228–229. ACM Press, New York (2004)
8. Rivest, R.L., Shamir, A., Tauman, Y.: How to leak a secret. In: Boyd, C. (ed.) ASIACRYPT 2001. LNCS, vol. 2248, pp. 552–567. Springer, Heidelberg (2001)
9. Abdalla, M., Møller, B.: Provably secure password-based authentication in TLS. In: Proceedings of the 1st ACM Symposium on InformAtion, Computer and Communications Security (ASIACCS 2006), pp. 35–45. ACM Press, New York (2006)
10. Camenisch, J., Lysyanskaya, A.: An efficient system for nontransferable anonymous credentials with optional anonymity revocation. In: Pfitzmann, B. (ed.) EUROCRYPT 2001. LNCS, vol. 2045, pp. 93–118. Springer, Heidelberg (2001)
11. Chaum, D.: Security without identification: transaction systems to make big brother obsolete. Commun. ACM 28(10), 1030–1044 (1983/1985)
12. Park, J.S., Ravi, S.: Smart Certificates: Extending X.509 for Secure Attribute Services on the Web. In: Proceedings of 22nd National Information Systems Security Conference (1999)

13. Pedersen, T.: Non-Interactive and Information-Theoretical Secure Verifiable Secret Sharing. In: Feigenbaum, J. (ed.) CRYPTO 1991. LNCS, vol. 576, pp. 129–140. Springer, Heidelberg (1992)

14. Camenisch, J., Damgard, I.: Verifiable encryption, group encryption, and their applications to separable group signatures and signature sharing schemes. In: Okamoto, T. (ed.) ASIACRYPT 2000. LNCS, vol. 1976, pp. 331–345. Springer, Heidelberg (2000)

15. Schutz, S., Eggert, L., Schmid, S., Brunner, M.: Protocol enhancements for intermittently connected hosts. ACM Computer Communications Review 35, 5–18 (2005)

16. Reed, M.G., Syverson, P.F., Goldschlag, D.M.: Anonymous Connections and Onion Routing. IEEE Journal on Selected Areas in Communications 16, 482–494 (1998)

17. Hooks, M., Miles, J.: Onion Routing and Online Anonymity, Final paper for CS182S, Department of Computer Science, Duke University, Durham, NC, USA (2006)

18. Babaioff, M., Nisan, N.: Concurrent Auction across Supply Chain. Journal of Artificial Intelligence Research 21, 595–629 (2004)

19. Thompson, M.R., Essiari, A.: Certificate-based Authorization Policy in a PKI Environment. ACM Transactions on Information and System Security 6, 566–588 (2003)

20. Nelson, R., Aron, G.P.: "p2p Trust Infrastructure", Computer Science Division, University of California

21. Menezes, A.J., Van Oorschot, P.C., Vanstone, S.A., Rivest, R.L.: Handbook of Applied Cryptography (1997)

22. Brands, S.: A technical overview of digital credentials, White Paper (2002)

23. Pedersen, T., Damgard, I., Pfitzmann, B.: Statistical secrecy and multi-bit commitments. IEEE Transactions on Information Theory 44, 1143–1151 (1996)

24. Bogetoft, P., Christensen, D.L., Damgard, I., et al.: Secure Multiparty Computation Goes Live. In: FC 2009, Proc. Thirteenth International Conference on Financial Cryptography and Data Security, Cryptology ePrint Archive: Report 2008/068 (2009)

Realizing Mobile Web Services
for Dynamic Applications*

Sonja Zaplata, Viktor Dreiling, and Winfried Lamersdorf

Distributed Systems and Information Systems
Computer Science Department, University of Hamburg
Vogt-Kölln-Str. 30, 22527 Hamburg, Germany
{zaplata,5dreiling,lamersdorf}@informatik.uni-hamburg.de

Abstract. Use of web services also on mobile devices becomes increasingly relevant. However, realizing such mobile web services based on the standard protocol stack is often inappropriate for resource-restricted mobile devices in dynamic networks. On the other hand, using specialized alternative protocols restricts compatibility with traditional service applications. Thus, existing approaches often do not allow to integrate heterogeneous service instances dynamically, as it is, e.g., required for executing mobile service-based business processes.

In order to adequately support such more complex and dynamic applications, this paper presents a lean and flexible system architecture which supports both mobile web service consumers and providers by allowing to integrate multiple protocols depending on their capabilities and to dynamically access suitable service instances at runtime. As a proof of concept, the paper shows an exemplary combination of practically relevant protocols for resource-limited devices based on WSDL, ASN.1 and overlay transport and presents its integration in a prototype scenario for supporting decentralized mobile business processes.

1 Introduction

Mobile web services currently form one of the most promising approaches to apply well-established service-oriented concepts to mobile environments. Especially the emergence of respective mobile middleware systems leads to a rather ubiquitous availability of information and enables new personalized and context-based services for private consumers as well as for business applications. Considering the provision and consumption of such service functionality in stationary networks, web services have proved to be a successful integration technology. Based on the standardized *Web Service Description Language (WSDL)*, the message encoding format *SOAP* and the *Hypertext Transfer Protocol (HTTP)* as specified by the W3C [4], a web service typically defines an interface between two or more software applications. As web services are self-describing and enable the

---

* The research leading to these results has received funding from the European Communitys Seventh Framework Programme FP7/2007-2013 under grant agreement 215483 (S-Cube).

C. Godart et al. (Eds.): I3E 2009, IFIP AICT 305, pp. 240–254, 2009.

development of loosely-coupled distributed applications, they are - in general - also very well suited to integrate mobile service providers and consumers. Nowadays, standard web service technologies can be applied to several mobile devices almost without any problems, e.g. considering notebooks or the newest generation of mobile phones using relatively reliable wireless networks such as WLAN or UMTS. However, the conventional web service communication framework is mostly inappropriate for small mobile devices in decentralized networks, e.g. for wireless sensors or active RFID tags, which still have very restricted resources with respect to computing power, memory capacity and communication bandwidth (cp. [1]). Several drawbacks of standard web service protocols have already been investigated in previous research works: As the most important point, the textual representation of XML-based descriptions as used in WSDL and SOAP leads to a low information density and thus to an inefficient use of communication bandwidth. As another example, the synchronicity of HTTP results in intolerance to network failures and excludes typical mobile network technologies such as Bluetooth or IrDa. Concerning the discovery of mobile services, centralized systems such as *UDDI (Universal Description, Discovery and Integration)* can hardly be applied in decentralized networks and prove to be inefficient in systems with changing network addresses (cp. [3,14]).

The emergence of manifold and more decentralized applications have therefore triggered the development of alternative web service protocols dealing with some of the before mentioned problems. Being specific to a concrete network or addressing particular drawbacks such as messaging overhead, these protocols focus on the requirements of resource-limited mobile systems and respectively use less complex communication protocols and description languages (e.g. [2,17]). Such alternative protocols enable mobile devices to consume specially adapted web services running on stationary servers, e.g. in order to outsource business logic or tasks which are computationally intensive. Since mobile devices are also able to provide web services themselves, also novel applications such as sharing resources and functionality in mobile ad-hoc networks can be realized. For example, a built-in car navigation system could be used to transfer the current position to a local mobile phone using Bluetooth. Nevertheless, it could also be accessed from remote (e.g. by a desktop PC) to find a stolen car by using a standard HTTP connection. Other application areas involve the provision of context information about the user or its device, or act as a replacement of physical things, e.g. by simulating a wallet by an automatic payment service [3].

Besides such specialized monolithic applications, (mobile) web services can also be part of more complex and dynamic applications, such as, e.g. business processes running on mobile devices (e.g. [8,13]). Due to the prevailing diversity of protocols in the area of mobile web services, most of such distributed applications use rather abstract descriptions of services, avoiding to specify concrete protocols, network addresses and other specific technological details. In contrary to stand-alone applications, the execution of mobile business processes therefore requires a dynamic discovery, selection and binding of available services and thus requires to support more than one specific protocol. At the same time the processes' functionality is provided as an aggregated service itself. This means that there is a need for a dynamic mobile web service architecture embracing functionality for service consumption as well as for service provision, considering heterogeneous devices, networks and protocols.

Addressing such challenges, the following section analyzes existing work in the area of mobile web services and identifies research gaps with respect to dynamism, flexibility and interoperability of mobile service providers and consumers. To overcome the identified restrictions, section 3 introduces a lightweight architecture to both use and provide web services based on arbitrary protocols, as well as to publish, find and bind such services dynamically. Section 4 presents an example combination of protocols suitable for smaller and medium mobile devices. The prototypical implementation is evaluated in section 5, integrating the proposed architecture and its reference configuration into an existing mobile process execution system. The paper concludes with a brief summary and an outlook on future work.

2   Existing and Related Work

Due to the large amount of work in the area of web services and mobile computing, this section abstracts from individual approaches, but classifies them with respect to the strategies used to provide and use web services in heterogeneous mobile environments. Thus in general, respective previous and ongoing research can be distinguished into three main areas: Application and adaptation of standard web service technology; integration of alternative protocols, description languages and registries; and use of additional mediator components.

Adaptation of Standard Web Service Technology. As introduced above, in some cases standard web service technologies (i.e. WSDL, SOAP, HTTP and UDDI) can directly be applied to mobile systems (as e.g. shown by [15]) – assumed that these are relatively powerful, use reliable network connections and are able to provide adequate addressing mechanisms. Smaller and more restricted mobile systems however often omit dynamic components which need a large amount of resources or which cannot be realized due to decentralized infrastructures. Two examples are summarized in the following:

- Considering the consumer side, web services can be bound statically as a fixed part of the mobile application. This relieves mobile devices from service discovery and from generating and integrating web service proxies at runtime. However, this simple approach is very inflexible as services cannot be exchanged at runtime and thus it does not support applications which require to pick service instances dynamically.
- Mobile service providers can optionally abstain from publishing their services in a registry and assume that potential service consumers are aware of the services' existence and syntax. Obviously, this strategy is rather restrictive as service providers can hardly expand the number of users if the service cannot be discovered dynamically.

Alternative Protocols, Description Languages and Registries. As standard web service protocols do not adequately meet the needs of resource-restricted mobile computing infrastructures, alternative technologies have evolved. These address – among others – the overhead of XML in service descriptions and messages, the synchronicity of communication and the centralization of registry information. Examples to exchange (in part or in total) the standard combination of HTTP, SOAP, WSDL and UDDI are sketched in the following:

- Universal (e.g. ZIP) or XML-specific (e.g. XMILL) compression mechanisms can efficiently be used to minimize the size of XML messages (e.g. [17]). Nevertheless such algorithms are quite resource-intensive as they require a relatively large amount of computing power to encode and decode the messages.
- To reduce complexity in another way, the use of XML can be avoided by alternative description languages, such as *JSON (JavaScript Object Notation)* or *ASN.1 (Abstract Syntax Notation Number One)* (cp. [12]).
- A more appropriate asynchronous communication can be realized by using alternative protocols such as SMTP and POP/IMAP, decoupling sender and receiver and thus allowing disconnected operation of web services (cp. [18]).
- The overhead of HTTP can alternatively be eliminated by performing message exchange over TCP or UDP directly (cp. [18]).
- Registries for decentralized infrastructures allow service providers to describe their services locally (e.g. WS-Inspection) or to save service information in a distributed way (e.g. *Konark* presented by [9]).
- The emergence of advanced addressing mechanisms such as *MobileIP* will probably facilitate the access of mobile (web service) resources.

Mobile Web Service Architectures and Use of Mediator Components. While the use of traditional web service technologies does not consider specific characteristics of mobile computing systems, the restriction to specialized alternative approaches leads to an incompatibility with traditional web service applications. Therefore, current research considers the challenges arising from the diversification of above mentioned technologies and protocols. Primarily, approaches which are similar or related to this work focus on the *use of additional mediator components*. The most important examples are presented below:

- In order to address the exclusion of local services and personal area networks, *proxy components* can be applied both to service consumers and providers. As an example, the approach presented by [2], presents an architecture which allows web service invocation over Bluetooth by wrapping SOAP messages to bind them to the Bluetooth transport protocol. More general approaches establish an overlay network to completely abstract from technological details of the underlying transport layer (e.g. [6]).
- To consider limitations of mobile systems and allow proprietary protocols, a *mediation framework* can act as a broker between the mobile device and stationary web service providers or consumers (e.g. [5,7]). In this case, the

mediator is responsible for the transformation and the routing of web service messages. Furthermore, peer-to-peer mediator approaches have also successfully been applied to mobile service providers and consumers [16]. However, if mediators are not accessible, this component represents a hazardous single point of failure in centralized as well as in decentralized infrastructures.

- To integrate alternative transmission protocols dynamically, the preferred message representation can be subject of negotiation. As an example, the *Handheld Flexible Representation (HHFR)* [14] optionally determines which part of a SOAP message is omitted when invoking a service. The approach is characterized by a very flexible architecture and is able to adapt to the requirements of mobile devices dynamically. Considering the repeated invocation of the same service, the following data exchange can be reduced considerably. In case of single service invocations, however, the negotiation itself causes a considerable overhead.

Requirements Summary. As an interim result, it seems that there is no perfect combination of traditional and alternative technologies, but that the use of a specific approach is determined by the capabilities of the mobile system and its applications. Although web services have originally been intended to integrate heterogeneous resources, the diversification of protocols resulting from necessary adaptations leads to another integration problem. On the one hand, heterogeneous capabilities and characteristics of mobile devices with respect to network connection and protocol support have to be considered. On the other hand, interoperability with traditional applications and industry standards should be preserved. Finally, dynamic applications such as ad-hoc mobile business processes require the executing mobile device to adapt to available service instances and protocols at runtime – a system software characteristic which is hardly supported by current mobile web service architectures.

These observations lead to the need of a flexible web service architecture which is able to adapt to the prevailing technology at runtime – provided the respective (mobile) device is able to support one or more (to some extent) established protocols. The next section therefore presents the basic idea of a flexible web service architecture for such dynamic mobile applications.

3   A Flexible Mobile Service Architecture

As presented in the previous section, developers of mobile web service providers and mobile web service clients can select from a large range of protocols and technologies to adjust their application to the requirements and capabilities of the mobile device. To enable a customized design of mobile web service applications, to allow interoperability with more than one service consumer or provider and to access services dynamically, this section presents an adaptable web service architecture for mobile devices.

Figure 1 shows a coarse overview of the *decentralized* mobile service-oriented architecture. It consists of one or more (possibly mobile) service providers and

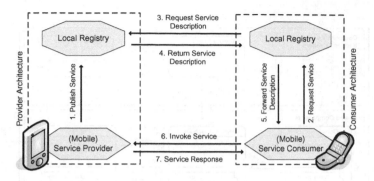

Fig. 1. Overview of the mobile service architecture

consumers which both integrate an individual local registry. In case of the service provider, the registry holds and manages the service descriptions of the service instances provided by the mobile device itself. For the service consumer, the registry is responsible to search for required services by exchanging information with the registries of service providers in the local environment. Because the local registry only acts as a proxy to its environment, also centralized stationary registries (e.g. UDDI) or distributed decentralized registries (e.g. Konark by [9]) can participate if they are in communication range of the mobile service requester.

The detailed architecture for mobile web service consumers and providers is characterized by a modular design. The resulting basic architecture for both roles is depicted in figure 2. Due to potential resource restrictions, basic functionality such as communication, message handling and service registration is shared by consumer and provider components. Functionality exclusive to service providers involves a lightweight service runtime environment which manages respective service instances. Exclusive to the client side, a proxy generator is responsible for generating and assigning local proxies to invoke a mobile web service. The proxy represents a local interface of the remote service, handles the work of mapping parameters to the elements of the description language and prepares the respective message contents to be send over the network.

Depending on the capabilities of the mobile system and on the requirements of the application(s), this abstract architecture can be instantiated with one or more adapters realizing a concrete technology. Alternative technologies can be assigned to service description, to message encoding and to transport protocols. For example, to be compatible to industry standards, services can be described using a WSDL adapter for the local registry and for proxy generation, the message handling can use SOAP format and finally, the communication component can include an HTTP adapter to send the message. To be compatible to resource-restricted mobile devices, alternative configurations can be realized, e.g. as the combination of WSDL, ASN.1 and overlay network transport which is presented in section 4.

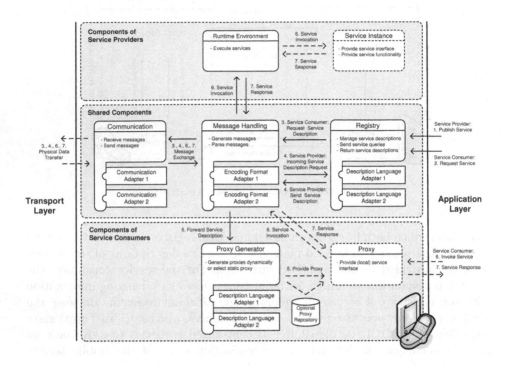

Fig. 2. Mobile service architecture component model

The overall procedure of providing and consuming web services is realized as follows: First, the service provider publishes its services to the local registry (Step 1 in figure 1 and 2). As the deployment of adapters and services is performed at design-time, each published service can be associated with one or more descriptions determined by the configuration of supported protocols.

Potential service consumers are now able to find these services by performing an abstract service request to their local registry (step 2). The abstract service request contains the search parameters of the respective application, e.g. the required functionality of the service and optionally non-functional criteria. The consumer's registry first checks if the required service can be accessed locally, e.g. in case the service is provided by the device itself. Otherwise it forwards the request to other devices in its environment making use of the type(s) of encoding format and communication protocol it supports (step 3). The environment of the device is therefore determined by the capabilities of the communication adapter, e.g. resources on the Internet can be accessed via HTTP, whereas local networks can only be accessed via alternative communication protocols. The resulting request now involves at least the identifier of the service's functionality (e.g. a simple *Uniform Resource Identifier (URI)*, a *Universally Unique Identifier (UUID)* or a link to external semantic resources such as an *Resource Description Framework (RDF)* document) and optionally a list of supported or preferred protocols (cp. figure 3).

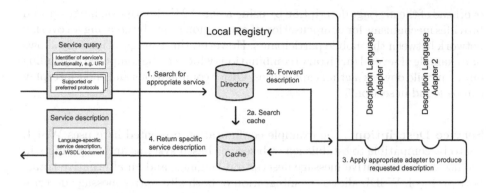

Fig. 3. Service discovery: receiving a remote service request

The potential service provider receives the incoming service request and – assumed it has at least one suitable adapter – forwards it to the registry which picks an adequate format to return the description of the requested service instance (step 4). As the description is received by the consumer, it is forwarded to the proxy generator (step 5). Depending on the implementation, the proxy can either be picked from a proxy repository holding a number of static proxies or can be generated automatically according to the received service description. The service consumer is now able to invoke the service by calling the provided proxy object (step 6). The proxy uses the message format and communication protocol as specified in the service description to send the required input parameters, and if any, receives the service's return values (step 7). If the service is going to be invoked again later, the proxy can optionally be added to the proxy repository.

To address scalability, the presented architecture supports complex applications acting as service providers and service consumers at the same time as well as both roles individually. As the role-specific components are completely optional, unneeded provider/consumer functionality can be omitted to save resources. Furthermore, the type and number of adapter components can be tailored to the capacity and performance of the mobile device. However, if the number of adapters is rather small or the applied protocols are too exotic, the compatibility will be restricted to special application areas and therefore influence the number of suitable service consumers or providers.

4   An Example Configuration for Mobile Web Services

Since actual web service standards WSDL, SOAP and HTTP do not meet the requirements of mobile systems particularly well, alternative technologies for the realization of mobile web services can be considered. This section presents a proposal on technologies that can be integrated into the presented architecture to realize web services on more resource-restricted mobile devices. The configuration reduces the

overhead of the message description by using a non-XML description language and
provides mechanisms for compensation of connection resets by creating an overlay
network between the mobile participants. However, this configuration only shows
one example of several (arbitrary) combinations which can be composed depending
on the mobile devices' actual capabilities. Other combinations and their interplay
can be found in section 5.

Service Description. The example configuration presented here uses WSDL
2.0 to be compatible to established web service based systems and only differs in
the use of an alternative message description language and an alternative transport protocol. WSDL allows the integration of both alternative message description languages and transport protocols without violating the WSDL standards
of W3C (cp. [4]). Listing 1 shows an example of a WSDL binding that contains the URIs associated with the alternative technologies used in this example
configuration.

```
<wsdl:binding name="ExampleConfiguration"
    interface="TestServiceInterface"
    type="http://vsis-www.informatik.uni-hamburg.de/projects/demac/asn1der"
    protocol="http://vsis-www.informatik.uni-hamburg.de/projects/demac/overlay">
    <wsdl:operation ref="testOperation"/>
</wsdl:binding>
```

Listing 1. WSDL Binding

Encoding Format. The example configuration uses ASN.1 and DER encoding
to describe the communication messages containing the payload and the protocol
data. The approach is based on the specifications X.694 [11], X.690 [10] and
X.892 [12] of ITU-T and, in comparison to XML-SOAP, results in a reduced
description overhead, which has also been shown in [12].

The basic idea of the message exchange is to use a predefined set of data types
which are known to all participants (X.694 and X.892) followed by a binary
encoding of the values according to their types (e.g. UTF8 encoding of strings)
and a substitution of the data types by binary constants which are – due to the
standardization – also known to other participants (X.690).

Listing 2 shows an example of an XML schema describing the structure of a
message, whereas listing 3 shows the respective ASN.1 instance. Listing 4 shows
the resulting DER encoding of this instance representing the actual payload of a
communication message. As to see, the encoded value only contains information
about the structure of the original complex value, the values of the elements it
consists of and their types, but it does not contain additional identifiers.

The complete message is encoded similarly to the presented example. The
X.892 specification of ITU-T describes the structure of an ASN.1 SOAP message
and defines the obligatory fields. Among other attributes, each instance representing the payload of the message has an ID attribute to denote the schema of
the instance, particularly its URI (namespace) and its name. Since provider and
client possess the WSDL document of the web service, both can understand the

information that is encoded as an ID, assign the identifiers to the values and interpret the messages correctly.

```
<xsd:complexType name="integerSequence">
    <xsd:sequence>
        <xsd:element name="elem1" type="xsd:integer"/>
        <xsd:element name="elem2" type="xsd:integer"/>
    </xsd:sequence>
</xsd:complexType>
```

Listing 2. Message structure defined in XML Schema

```
integerSequence SEQUENCE ::=
{ elem1 2,
  elem2 3 }
```

Listing 3. Message structure defined in ASN.1

```
00110000 | binary constant associated with a sequence
00000110 | length of the binary representation of
           that sequence (number of octets, 6 in this example)
00000010 | binary constant associated with an integer (elem1)
00000001 | length of the binary representation of that integer
00000010 | value 2
00000010 | binary constant associated with an integer (elem2)
00000001 | length of the binary representation of that integer
00000010 | value 3
```

Listing 4. DER encoding of the example message

Communication Protocol. The communication interface can be realized by one of the individual alternative protocols presented in section 2, e.g. TCP/IP, Bluetooth or IrDA. To also show the applicability for more complex solutions, the communication adapter used in the example configuration abstracts from specific transport protocols, but relies on a peer-to-peer overlay network with its own addressing scheme and an asynchronous message transport (as e.g. proposed in [6]). To detect other devices in the environment, participating devices use their communication adapter to send short broadcast messages in periodic intervals. Within these messages, they encode their UUID – a identifier that is universally unique for every device. When a device receives such a message, it saves the UUID and its source address. This information is updated or complemented in case the same UUID is received with a different source address. As a result, the participating devices have basic up-to-date information about other devices in the (local) environment and the current protocols and addresses that can be used to contact them.

In order to communicate with a particular device, the sender selects an address associated with the UUID of the receiver. This (virtual) address is then translated into a concrete protocol specific address and the message is sent using the respective protocols and endpoint information. If the device is reachable by different protocols, more than one address can be associated with a UUID. The participants are therefore able to select the most appropriate protocol – or change the communication interface in case a connection is temporarily interrupted.

5   Prototype Implementation and Use Case Scenario

In order to demonstrate the feasibility of the approach, the flexible architecture and its example configuration have been prototypically implemented and integrated into the *DEMAC (Distributed Environment for Mobility Aware Computing)* project. DEMAC realizes the idea of mobile (business) processes migrating several stationary and mobile devices in order to share their resources and functionality (cp. [13]). A typical application scenario for such processes is e.g. the context-based collection and processing of information in mobile environments, involving data from wireless sensors, mobile users or traditional web service resources. Since devices which are able to execute mobile processes can be considered to be relatively powerful (e.g. notebooks or PDAs), the presented architecture can be used to aggregate a set of protocols in order to integrate web services from several heterogeneous devices and networks. As required service functionality is specified in a technology-independent way, the process execution engine can use the presented architecture to search for adequate service instances and integrate them at runtime.

The resulting use case scenario is depicted in figure 4. The described example configuration has been applied to a wireless sensor (device 1) which provides temperature data. The application of the example configuration using ASN.1 reduces the size of communication messages considerably (cp. also last row in figure 5) and achieves even better results if the number of long identifiers that occur in the message payload is getting larger. The ASN.1 type library is implemented as a small set of structures which can be combined to create a complete message. The instance of each structure calls the encoding procedure responsible for the associated ASN.1 type and saves its result into a collective output container. Thus the messages do not have to be parsed, but can be encoded directly by passing the respective values to the encoder. In consequence, the implementation is very fast and efficient and can be considered to be quite suitable even for latest technologies such as e.g. active RFID tags which have a very restricted communication bandwidth.

The standard web service configuration is provided by a stationary server (device 2) transforming the temperature data into another representation (e.g. Celsius to Fahrenheit). Device 3 is responsible to execute the mobile process integrating both of these functionalities as a simple sequential service composition. Using adapters for the presented reference configuration addressing small mobile devices (cp. section 4) and adapters for the standard set of web service technologies (i.e. WSDL, SOAP and HTTP), the executing mobile device is able to access the wireless sensor as well as the traditional stationary web service. It is further able to dynamically generate the respective proxies and thus involve the required functionality to fulfill the mobile processes' activities at runtime. The integrated services are re-offered as a composed service functionality using either the example configuration, the standard web service technologies or even another mix of protocols, as exemplary represented by another web service consumer (device 4). However, if the set of supported protocols does not match any other configuration (as indicated by device 5) the required services cannot be

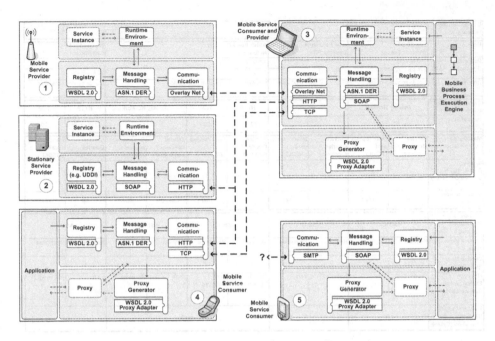

Fig. 4. Mobile web services test configuration

accessed. Due to its mobility, the incompatible device is however still able to potentially find adequate services in another environment.

The number and size of the messages exchanged to execute the presented scenario are depicted in figure 5. To allow a proper comparison of message sizes, all services used in the test share a similar message structure (i.e. a request-response message exchange pattern with one input and one output parameter) as well as a similar service description (in WSDL). The italic font indicates that the respective value is variable and results from the parameters used in the test scenario.

The experimental evaluation of the prototype shows that the load of finding the proper configuration only affects devices which are able to cope with different protocols and adapters - and thus can be regarded to be more powerful. If more than one adapter for communication is available, the device can start service discovery with its preferred protocol and fall back to other protocols in case there is no positive response. For instance, in the worst case, device 3 would have to send the service discovery message over all of its three communication protocols. It is obvious that the more adapters are available on a mobile device, the higher is the probability of finding an adequate service. Less powerful devices will simply ignore the messages which cannot be interpreted and only respond to those which will lead to a correct service invocation. The configuration of adapters and thus protocols can be installed in a way which fits the device's capabilities and performance best, leading to an reduced message description overhead as exemplary shown by the total message size of device 1 in the last row of figure 5: The message overhead is only 138 Bytes, which constitutes only

Device Number in scenario	1		2		3				4	
Device	Sun SPOT Wireless Sensor		Intel Pentium 4 Desktop PC		ASUS Eee PC 1000H Netbook				Nokia 6131 NFC Cell Phone	
Properties (Processor, RAM)	180 MHz / 512 KB RAM		3,2 GHz / 1 GB RAM		1,6 GHz / 1 GB RAM				229 MHz / 26 MB RAM	
Role Type	Mobile service provider		Stationary service provider		Mobile service consumer and provider				Mobile service consumer	
Communication Protocol	Overlay Network		HTTP		HTTP	TCP	Overlay Network		HTTP	TCP
Header Size (Bytes)	86 (+20)		123 (+20)		123 (+20)	20	86 (+20)		123 (+20)	20
Messages for Service Discovery	Service Queries received	Descriptions sent (WSDL)	Service Queries received	Descriptions sent (WSDL)	Service Queries received	Descriptions sent (WSDL)	Service Queries performed	Descriptions received (WSDL)	Service Queries performed	Descriptions received (WSDL)
Message Exchange for Service Discovery	1	1	1	1	1	1	max. 3	1	1	1
Message Size (Bytes)	86	1547	86	1547	86	1547	max. 258	1547	86	1547
Service Message Description Language	ASN.1		SOAP		ASN.1		SOAP		ASN.1	
Service Message Type	Request	Response	Request	Response	Request	Response	Request	Response	Request	Response
Service Message Size (Bytes)	114	24	914	758	114	24	914	758	114	24
Message Exchange for Service Execution	Received: 1	Sent: 1	Received: 1	Sent: 1	Sent: 1 Received: 1	Sent: 1 Received: 1	Sent: 1	Received: 1	Sent: 1	Received: 1
Total Message Size for Service Execution (Bytes)	138		1672		1948				138	

Fig. 5. Overview of message exchange and size within the scenario

8.25 percent of the respective traditional technology (e.g. the message size of device 2: 1672 Bytes).

6   Conclusion and Future Work

Due to the heterogeneity of current mobile systems, it seems that there is no generally applicable combination of web service technologies, but that the use of a specific approach is determined by the capabilities of the specific mobile device. For enabling also more complex and dynamic applications such as ad-hoc mobile business processes, this paper proposes a flexible mobile web service architecture which supports accessing the functionality of multiple heterogeneous devices. By use of a customized configuration of protocols and technologies, this architecture can be tailored according to the requirements of the respective (mobile) application and its users, allowing to preserve interoperability with industry standards while also respecting the restrictions of resource-limited devices.

However, as also to see in figure 5, the exchange of WSDL descriptions takes a significant amount of the overall data transfer. As recommended, a possible solution is to integrate alternative description languages, such as e.g. JSON which reduces the overhead of XML of about 20 percent. If this is still unsatisfying, the presented architecture could be enhanced to optionally provide compression mechanisms for service descriptions and service invocation messages. Furthermore, mobile service requesters capable of carrying multiple adapters may (in the worst case) produce unnecessary messages which could be inadequate for networks with a small bandwidth. This problem can be addressed by an increased network-awareness, enabling the mobile service requester to prioritize more lightweight protocols. Future work therefore involves the integration of context information to adapt not only to the capabilities of mobile devices but also to specific network characteristics.

References

1. Adelstein, F., Gupta, S.K., Richard III, G., Schwiebert, L.: Fundamentals of Mobile and Pervasive Computing. McGraw-Hil, New York (2005)
2. Auletta, V., Blundo, C., Cristofaro, E.D., Raimato, G.: A Lightweight Framework for Web Services Invocation over Bluetooth. In: Proceedings of the IEEE Int. Conf. on Web Services (ICWS 2006), pp. 331–338. IEEE Computer Society, Los Alamitos (2006)
3. Berger, S., McFaddin, S., Narayanaswami, C., Raghunath, M.: Web Services on Mobile Devices – Implementation and Experience. In: IEEE Workshop on Mobile Computing Systems and Applications, p. 100 (2003)
4. Booth, D., Haas, H., McCabe, F., Newcomer, E., Champion, M., Ferris, C., Orchard, D.: Web Services Architecture. Technical report, W3C (2004)
5. Chong, C., Chua, H.-N., Lee, C.-S.: Towards flexible mobile payment via mediator-based service model. In: Proceedings of the 8th Int. Conf. on Electronic Commerce (ICEC 2006), pp. 295–301. ACM, New York (2006)
6. Doval, D., O'Mahony, D.: Overlay Networks: A Scalable Alternative for P2P. IEEE Internet Computing 7(4), 79–82 (2003)
7. Farley, P., Capp, M.: Mobile Web Services. BT Technology Journal 23(3), 202–213 (2005)
8. Hackmann, G., Haitjema, M., Gill, C.D., Roman, G.-C.: Sliver: A BPEL Workflow Process Execution Engine for Mobile Devices. In: Dan, A., Lamersdorf, W. (eds.) ICSOC 2006. LNCS, vol. 4294, pp. 503–508. Springer, Heidelberg (2006)
9. Helal, S., Desai, N., Verma, V., Lee, C.: Konark – A Service Discovery and Delivery Protocol for Ad-hoc Networks, vol. 3, pp. 2107–2113. IEEE Computer Society, Los Alamitos (2003)
10. ITU-T. ASN.1 Encoding Rules: Specification of Basic Encoding Rules (BER), Canonical Encoding Rules (CER) and Distinguished Encoding Rules (DER). Technical report, International Telecommunication Union (2002)
11. ITU-T. ASN.1 Encoding Rules: Mapping W3C XML Schema Definitions into ASN.1. Technical report, International Telecommunication Union (2004)
12. ITU-T. Generic Applications of ASN.1: Fast Web Services. Technical report, International Telecommunication Union (2004)
13. Kunze, C.P., Zaplata, S., Turjalei, M., Lamersdorf, W.: Enabling Context-based Cooperation: A Generic Context Model and Management System. In: Business Information Systems (BIS 2008). Springer, Heidelberg (2008)
14. Oh, S.: Web Service Architecture for Mobile Computing. PhD thesis, Indiana University, Indianapolis, USA (2006)
15. Srirama, S.N., Jarke, M., Prinz, W.: Mobile Web Service Provisioning. In: Proceedings of the AICT and ICIW 2006, p. 120. IEEE Computer Society, Los Alamitos (2006)

16. Srirama, S.N., Jarke, M., Prinz, W.: Mobile Web Services Mediation Framework.
    In: Proceedings of the 2nd Workshop on Middleware for Service Oriented Comput-
    ing (MW4SOC 2007), pp. 6–11. ACM, New York (2007)
17. Tian, M., Voigt, T., Naumowicz, T., Ritter, H., Schiller, J.: Performance Consid-
    erations for Mobile Web Services. Elsevier Computer Communications Journal 27,
    1097–1105 (2004)
18. Werner, C., Buschmann, C., Jacker, T.: Enhanced Transport Bindings for Efficient
    SOAP Messaging. In: Proceedings of the IEEE Int. Conf. on Web Services (ICWS
    2005), pp. 193–200. IEEE Computer Society, Los Alamitos (2005)

Modifying the Balanced Scorecard for a Network Industry

The Case of the Clearing Industry

Michael Chlistalla and Torsten Schaper

Goethe-University Frankfurt, Chair of e-Finance, Grüneburgplatz 1,
60323 Frankfurt, Germany
{Chlistalla,Schaper}@wiwi.uni-frankfurt.de

Abstract. The Balanced Scorecard (BSC) is a well-established framework for the management of a company as it integrates financial and non-financial perspectives. Little attention has been given to its theoretical and conceptual valuation. We illustrate how the stakeholder value theory corresponds with the concept of the BSC and show the importance of underlying cause-and-effect relationships between its perspectives. For the case of clearing in Europe which is currently facing profound changes, we present our three-phased approach how to adjust and to extend Kaplan and Norton's original concept. We modify the generic BSC by adding risk management as a separate perspective and by integrating competition and IT. Based on multiple case studies, we then validate whether the modified BSC is suited to meet the specifics of the clearing industry.

Keywords: Performance Management, Balanced Scorecard, Network Industry.

1 Introduction

Companies use an average of 13 management tools or frameworks at the corporate level. Many of these are tools intended to help measure or monitor the performance of an organization. Within the most popular performance related frameworks (57%) is the BSC [21]. Kaplan and Norton's BSC [13] represents a holistic instrument of corporate management as it integrates a variety of perspectives. The BSC can help the management implement and communicate a strategy within the organization. As the theoretical and conceptual valuation of the BSC in academic literature is rather sparse and any systematic methodology for deriving a tailored BSC is non-existent, the contribution of this paper is twofold: firstly, our aim is to illustrate how the stakeholder value theory corresponds with the concept of the BSC. Secondly, based on our findings and using the European clearing industry as an example, we demonstrate how to derive a BSC for a specific network industry. The European clearing industry is perfectly suited as a research object because it is currently facing enormous challenges and new forms of competition due to new regulatory requirements. We show that the modified BSC is a suitable tool for performance measurement in clearing houses. Our research is also valuable for practitioners as these modifications can serve as a basis for a re-design of current Management Information Systems in this industry. The

C. Godart et al. (Eds.): I3E 2009, IFIP AICT 305, pp. 255–271, 2009.

paper is organized as follows. First, performance measurement with the BSC is introduced, followed by a literature review and a classification of the concept of the BSC into the theories of corporate governance. The next section introduces our approach for modifying a BSC which consists of three phases: initiation, derivation and implementation. The derivation phase is in focus of this paper; it describes the concept of central counterparty (CCP) clearing as well as recent trends in this industry, identifies the relevant stakeholders and analyzes visions of selected clearing houses. On this basis, a holistic BSC for the clearing industry is derived. Subsequently, the research model for the evaluation of this modified BSC and its inherent cause-and-effect relationships is presented. It is followed by the empirical validation via multiple case studies. At last, the main results of this research are summarized.

2   Theoretical Foundations of the BSC

Performance measurement is a way to track performance over time to assess whether goals are met. The management thus involves two key areas: planning and control. Every organization requires plans and a mechanism by which execution against the plan can be controlled [15]. A variety of performance measurement systems exist. The earliest system is the DuPont-System of Financial Control [4]. It is based on an accounting measure, the Return on Investment (ROI), which serves both as an indicator of the efficiency of the firm's operating departments and as the measure of financial performance of the company as a whole [11]. Another method frequently used by organizations to support strategic decisions and to identify process improvement capabilities is Activity-Based Costing (ABC), firstly defined by Kaplan and Cooper [12]. Both approaches are predominantly finance-focused: while ROI focuses on the fact that returns on assets can be expressed in terms of the profit margin and asset turnover, ABC is likewise lopsided as it only provides information on product and customer cost and profitability to the management. In order to obtain a holistic view on corporate performance, the ability of an institution to mobilize and exploit its intangible or invisible assets has become more decisive than investing and managing tangible assets only [13]. An approach that accommodates these needs is the BSC.

2.1   The Balanced Scorecard

The BSC translates the vision of an organization into a comprehensive set of measures and provides the framework for strategic measurement and management. The measures represent a balance between external measures for shareholders and customers, and internal measures of critical business processes, innovation, and learning. By providing explicit links between strategy, goals, performance measures, and outcomes, the BSC helps to achieve high-level performance. The BSC is a powerful tool for communicating strategic intent and motivating performance towards strategic goals [10]. The success of the implementation of a strategy is assessed by four perspectives (see Figure 1) which are described in detail by Kaplan and Norton [13][14].

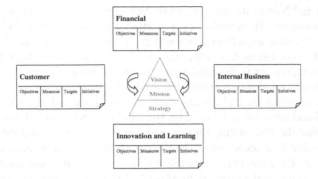

Fig. 1. Four perspectives of the Balanced Scorecard [14]

Cause-and-effect relationships are an essential part of second generation BSCs. These relationships between measures across perspectives were introduced in the mid 1990s, documenting objective-to-objective relationships. Alternatively called strategy maps or strategy linkage models, these relations differentiate performance measurement systems like the BSC from simple key performance indicator lists [14][16], which present an ad-hoc collection of measures to managers but do not allow for a comprehensive view on corporate performance. Instead, performance measurement systems like the BSC try to model the relations of the underlying value chain in cause-and-effect relationships (see Figure 2) to allow prediction of value chain performance measures, communication and realization of the corporate strategy [2].

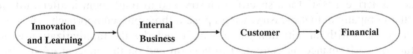

Fig. 2. Cause-and-effect relationships of the BSC [13][25]

2.2 Literature Review

Little attention has been given to the theoretical and conceptual valuation of the BSC, which has only been treated rudimentarily in academic literature [15]. The BSC can be positioned within several concepts of academic theories on corporate governance: The Systems Theory [15], the Shareholder Value Theory [20] and the Stakeholder Value Theory [19]. While the shareholder perspective regards disciplining managers in order to maximize shareholder value as the fundamental goal of the corporation [5], the stakeholder perspective extends this goal to include the stakeholders' welfare rather than concentrating on the shareholder alone [19]. The stakeholder perspective is actually an extension of the shareholder perspective, broadening the purpose of the corporation from maximizing shareholders' wealth to serving wider interests of stakeholders fairly and emphasizing corporate efficiency in a social context. A stakeholder is any group or individual who can affect or is affected by the achievement of the organization's objectives. Thus, two attributes can be defined to identify stakeholders: power to influence the firm and the legitimate claim or interest in the firm [9].

While Kaplan and Norton merely propagate their concept without in-depth discussion or critical assessment [1], Nørreklit [17] is among the first to examine the extent to which there is a cause-and-effect relationship among the four areas of measurement within the BSC. She discusses whether the BSC is able to link strategy to operational metrics that managers can understand and influence, concluding that there is no causal but rather a logical relationship among the areas of the BSC analyzed. Moreover, she suggests some changes to, and development of, the scorecard in order to ensure its organizational and environmental rooting. Blumenberg and Hinz [2], too, focus on the causalities within the BSC stating they are neither thoroughly introduced in theory nor applied in practice in a sound way. Their research is based on Fenton and Neil's [8] conclusions that "Bayesian belief nets (BBNs) were by far the best solution for [handling] genuine cause and effect relationships". In order to support organizations in introducing a BSC, they present BBNs as an approach to model corporate causality relationships within the BSC, acknowledging that – due to the nature of a BBN as a directed acyclic graph – a BSC may not exhibit loops within its underlying cause-and-effect relationships. Considering the usefulness of a sound stakeholder analysis for successful corporate governance, it is advisable and valuable to design the perspectives of a BSC in consideration of the relevant stakeholders. However, the lack of cause-and-effect relationships among the various groups of stakeholders as well as their limited – if not inexistent – effect and foundation on the corporate strategy do not allow for a purely stakeholder-oriented scorecard [15].

3 Deriving a BSC for a Clearing House

In order to derive a BSC for a specific industry and to implement it afterwards for a particular company in that industry, we propose a three-phased approach. The process preferably starts with an initiation phase, which includes the familiarization with the literature on performance measurement in general and on the concept of the BSC in specific. The outcome (milestone) of this phase is a comprehensive understanding of the generic BSC. The second phase is the derivation of the industry-specific BSC, which is in focus of this paper. This phase is subdivided into three steps and can further be structured into a number of consecutive activities:

  — Step 1 (Analysis): Obtain a thorough understanding of the business itself and the challenges that are currently affecting the industry; Identification of relevant stakeholders and development of an understanding of their interests; Analysis of corporate websites, annual reports, organizational charts, and corporate visions, missions and strategies of the specified industry.
  — Step 2 (Design): Deriving the modified perspectives for the specified industry; Model the underlying cause-and-effect relationships.
  — Step 3 (Validation).

Concomitantly, we discussed these steps with selected industry experts and academics. In various feedback loops, their comments inspired our approach. The third phase, which leads to a company-specific BSC, will arguably be structured similarly to phase 2. As the **implementation** of a company-specific BSC, however, requires delving intensely into figures and measures that are proprietary for a single company, this

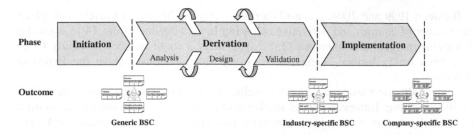

Fig. 3. Approach for deriving a BSC

phase will not be further discussed within this paper. Figure 3 illustrates graphically our approach for deriving a modified BSC. The focus of the outcomes narrows as we move stepwise from left (general BSC) to right (company specific BSC).

3.1 Central Counterparty Clearing

Clearing and settlement cover all processes after a trade has been executed to finalize the transaction. The purpose of clearing is the efficient handling of risks inherent to concluded, but unfulfilled contracts. Clearing confirms the legal obligation from the trade. It involves the calculation of the mutual obligations of market participants and determines what each counterpart receives. Central counterparty (clearing) is not included in the definition of clearing. A central counterparty (CCP) is an entity that interposes itself between the transactions of the counterparties in order to assume their rights and obligations, acting as a buyer to every seller and as a seller to every buyer. The original legal relationship is thus replaced by two new legal relationships. The CCP absorbs the counterparty risk and guarantees clearing and settlement of the trade [26]. A CCP is a service offered by a clearing house. An important driver for the increased use of CCP services in cash markets is the increased use of electronic order books to match trades. The anonymity of the electronic order books complicates the risk management of market participants, as counterparty risk cannot be managed through their choice of counterparty. A CCP is a useful service to clear and settle anonymous trades, since the market participant can manage its counterparty risk towards the CCP. It is important to notice that a CCP takes principal risks and therefore separates itself from the classical post-trade providers, which usually only act as agents. It is essential that the CCP has a functioning risk management system. Besides performing the CCP clearing function, most clearing houses provide further services like collateral management and netting. They enhance the efficiency of clearing and settlement and redistribute the risk between market participants [26].

3.2 The European Clearing Industry

The clearing industry is characterized by network effects and economies of scale and scope [18]. In Europe, the clearing industry used to operate its business facing no competition. Recently, clearing houses are exposed to an increasingly competitive environment. Over time, different governance structures have established: for-profit, not-for-profit, user-owned, and government-owned with hybrid forms existing.

Bctween 1999 and 2004, a consolidation of clearing houses in Europe took place: the number of equities and derivatives clearing houses declined from 14 to eight due to various mergers and alliances [23]. Since then, a small number of equity CCPs have been newly formed. Today, nine equity clearing houses serve the European markets.

Since 2006, the European Code of Conduct for Clearing and Settlement intends to establish a strong European capital market and to allow investors the choice to trade any security within a consistent, coherent, and efficient European framework. The aim of the Code is to offer market participants to choose between their preferred provider of services separately at each layer of the securities trading value chain (trading, clearing and settlement). The Code is a voluntary self-commitment and adheres to a number of principles on the provision of post-trading services for cash equities. The implementation consists of three phases and was finalized by the end of 2007. The guidelines for access and interoperability provide the basis for the development of links between service providers: more than 80 requests for access and interoperability were addressed until today, the majority of which affect clearing houses.

3.3 Stakeholders of a Clearing House

The main stakeholders of a clearing house are identified and described in the following:

- Shareholders have the power to influence the clearing house as they provide the company with capital and have a legitimate interest in the clearing house based on their ownership. As owners of the clearing house, they expect the maximization of their return on investment.
- Suppliers provide the clearing house with necessary infrastructure and services and earn revenues from the clearing house.
- Users can be classified into direct and indirect users. Direct users contribute to the risk capital of the clearing house and pay fees for the services. Thus, they have economic influence over the clearing house and a legitimate claim on the clearing house to apply sound risk management and to provide secure and efficient clearing services at a low price.
- Employees provide the clearing house with human resources and expect to receive adequate compensation and desirable working conditions.
- Community and public authorities provide the regulatory and supervisory framework in which a clearing house conducts its business. They have an interest in the risk management, free and fair competition, and cost-efficiency of the clearing house. Examples are the national banks or the European Central Bank, public authorities at national level and at EU level, and other institutions.
- Regulated Markets and Multilateral Trading Facilities (MTFs) have the capacity to operate a CCP on their own or to appoint one to offer clearing services for the securities traded on their platform. Regulated markets and MTFs have a legitimate interest in the fees as lower clearing fees contribute to the attractiveness of the trading platform because of lower total transaction costs. Netting services and risk management are also important for the safety and efficiency of the regulated market or MTF.

3.4 Company Visions of Clearing Houses

The BSC translates an organization's vision into a comprehensive set of measures and provides the basis for strategic management. A vision is a short, concise, and inspiring statement from the top management of what the organization intends to achieve, often stated in competitive terms. We studied corporate visions of clearing houses, two of which differing in terms of their governance structure are detailed in the following:

— **EMCF** (for profit): In an increasingly complex, yet ever *more convergent world, innovation, speed and agility* will be as crucial as scale, track record and reach. We will stand out as a professional international financial services brand, recognized for our ability to deliver superior and sustainable *stakeholder value* by constantly anticipating and surpassing the needs of *customers, investors, employees, partners and communities* wherever we do business.

— **KELER** (government-owned): KELER shall be an acknowledged clearing house and depository with a *leading position* in the Central Eastern Europe region that *operates in an innovative way*, in the form of a specialized credit institution. It shall be a dominant, active participant of the clearing house systems infrastructure of the region. KELER shall be successful, because its *customers are satisfied* with its services, shall manage to increase its *shareholder's value*, and appreciate and *retain its ambitious team of employees*.

A detailed analysis shows that both clearing houses apparently apply the stakeholder value theory. Elements of the stakeholder theory such as shareholders, customers, and employees are incorporated in both corporate visions emphasizing their importance for the top management. Moreover, further strategic perspectives from Kaplan and Norton's BSC are reflected:

— "needs of investors" / "increase its shareholder's value" → represents the financial perspective;
— "needs of customers" / "customers are satisfied" → represents the customer perspective;
— "needs of employees" / "retain its ambitious team of employees" → represents the innovation and learning perspective;
— "innovation, speed and agility" / "operates in an innovative way" → partially represents the internal business and the innovation and learning perspectives.

However, certain aspects of the corporate visions cannot be mapped to the stakeholder value theory or the traditional perspectives of the BSC:

— "more convergent world" / "leading position in the Central Eastern Europe region" → We interpret this as an indicator for the company's reaction towards the changing competitive European environment.
— "innovation, speed and agility" / "operates in an innovative way" → We interpret this as extension of the internal business and the innovation and learning perspectives by the aspect of IT.

To fit the clearing industry, these extending elements of the corporate visions require a modification of the original BSC.

3.5 The Modified BSC for a Clearing House

Discussions with industry experts and academics revealed that most clearing houses are currently overhauling and institutionalizing their internal performance measurement and management systems. Until recently, these were often rather straightforward tools based on e.g. simple Excel spreadsheets. The recent trends and developments in the European clearing industry and the intensified complexity resulting from increasing volumes and the potential for system risk as well as from competition and the inter-CCP risk management involved were named as reasons. As a result of our analyses, we extend the "Customer" perspective to "Competition and Customer" as Tate [24] argues that competitors should be included in a company's BSC. Additionally, we suggest emphasizing the importance of IT in order to take into account the progressive automation of post-trade processes [6]. Although not included in the corporate visions, we introduce "Risk Management" as a new perspective as it is explicitly considered in the organizational structure of most clearing houses. This extension follows e.g. Ahn [1] who demands that each fundamental goal should be represented by a perspective or Rosemann and Wiese [22] who add a new fifth project perspective to increase completeness and quality of the management report. Extensive discussions with academics and industry representatives indicate support of these modifications. We propose the following modified BSC perspectives for the clearing industry:

Financial Perspective. The financial perspective does not differ from Kaplan and Norton's BSC [14]. This component of the BSC looks at the projects from a financial perspective and discusses financial considerations. We propose to align the financial objectives to the shareholder value theory by introducing value-based measures. In case the clearing house operates on a not-for-profit basis, we recommend focusing on cost-related figures and alignment to the stakeholder value theory.

Competition and Customer Perspective. As stated by Kaplan and Norton [14], customer focus and customer satisfaction are of paramount importance to the success of a company. Due to the newly arising competition, we propose to extend the "Customer" perspective to "Competition and Customer" in order to integrate the monitoring of the strategic actions triggered by the competitive dynamics into the company's BSC. These may include strategies of expansion into new markets or the defense of the established markets.

Process Perspective. We propose to rename the "Internal Business" perspective as introduced by Kaplan and Norton [13] as "Process" perspective. As the original "Internal Business" perspective includes support processes, we suggest focusing on the mission-oriented core processes. Those supporting processes that are essential for a clearing house (such as risk management and IT) are addressed in individual perspectives. The focus of this perspective emphasizes what the clearing house has to do well to meet the customer needs. An appropriate measure could be the rate of straight-through processing.

Risk Management Perspective. A clearing house absorbs the counterparty risk and guarantees clearing and settlement of a trade [26]. The current global financial crisis has shown that markets with an established clearing house were able to handle the systemic risk appropriately. As risk management is the core operation of a clearing house, we propose to consider this core function in an individual perspective. Banks' BSCs often feature such a perspective in order to increase the awareness for operational risks and to facilitate the process of risk management [27]. As measures for this perspective we propose, for instance, the time between margin cycles, the accuracy of margining, the institution's financial rating or the frequency of default funds usage.

Staff and IT Perspective. As stated by Kaplan and Norton [14], "Innovation and Learning" are essential in order to support the critical operations of a clearing house. While the original perspective focuses on staff mainly, we recommend extending this perspective by IT and renaming it to "Staff and IT". The most prominent driver of technological efficiency was the almost complete automation of the post-trade processes by the implementation of innovative IT systems. Continental European markets adopted paperless processes earlier than other markets and are currently marking significant IT investments [6]. As measures for this perspective we propose, for instance, system availability and timeliness of strategic IT projects.

The basic cause-and-effect relationships of the perspectives from Kaplan and Norton [14] remain constant. Adding the risk management perspective, though, requires an adaptation of these relationships. As a clearing house absorbs the counterparty risk of all client trades processed by taking the principal risk (which the client would otherwise need to bear by himself), we are of the opinion that risk management mainly affects the Competition and Customer perspective. Figure 4 represents this in a possible cause-and-effect relationship chain.

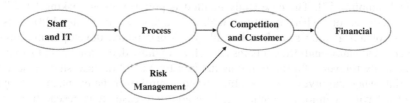

Fig. 4. Possible cause-and-effect relationships of the BSC for a clearing house

4 Validating the BSC

In order to show that the BSC is a suitable steering and monitoring tool for clearing houses in the changing European environment, we test the suitability of the original BSC by means of a case study. In this context, we also validate the traditional perspectives from Kaplan and Norton [14] regarding their applicability for a clearing house. In a second step, we reiterate this process for the modified BSC. In a last step we compare the results for both scorecards. Figure 5 lists our hypotheses, and the stated literature shows their origin. The hypotheses are tested in the following section.

In order to test the hypotheses, an adequate and accepted method would be to conduct a survey among the focus group of market participants. However, the case of clearing houses is very distinctive as their quantity – and hence the viable population for a survey – is very limited. The number of equity clearing houses in Europe

Hypotheses		Literature
H1: The Balanced Scorecard is a suitable tool for performance measurement of a clearing house in the changing environment.		[14]
Kaplan and Norton's BSC	**Modified BSC**	
H2a: The Financial Perspective is important for performance measurement of a clearing house.	**H2b:** The Financial Perspective is important for performance measurement of a clearing house.	[13]
H3a: The Customer Perspective is important for performance measurement of a clearing house.	**H3b:** The Competition and Customer Perspective is important for performance measurement of a clearing house.	[14] [24]
H4a: The Internal Business Perspective is important for performance measurement of a clearing house.	**H4b:** The Process Perspective is important for performance measurement of a clearing house.	[14]
H5a: The Innovation and Learning Perspective is important for performance measurement of a clearing house.	**H5b:** The Staff and IT Perspective is important for performance measurement of a clearing house.	[14] [6]
	H6: The Risk Management Perspective is important for performance measurement of a clearing house.	[26] [27]

H7: The modified Balanced Scorecard is a suitable tool for performance measurement of a clearing house in the changing environment.

Fig. 5. Hypotheses

currently amounts to nine only. We therefore instead decided in favour of the case study as a research strategy, factoring in that such research relies on theoretical, not statistical sampling [7]. The case study method is preferred when asking "how" and "why" questions, or "what" questions with an explanatory character [28]. It is not limited to obtain a static snapshot, but allows to understand developments, process sequences, and cause-and-effect chains as well as to draw data-based conclusions that are practically relevant. Furthermore, as defined by Yin [23], case study research is appropriate when the investigator has little or no control over the events, meaning that relevant behaviors cannot be manipulated. In addition, case study research is appropriate when the focus is on a contemporary phenomenon with real-life context. To achieve the necessary rigor, it is essential to explicitly and properly define the research question and the unit of analysis in the design and preparatory phase. Like field studies, case studies typically utilize questionnaires, coded interviews, or systematic observation as techniques for data gathering [23]. The methods for collecting the data for a case study are not limited to specific methods and are often combined. It is worth mentioning that the expert interview as an applied research methodology differs from qualitative interviews and also allows questioning experts according to their experience and interpretation of relevant research topics [3].

4.1 Case Study

Due to the sensitivity of the requested information in an industry as competitive as clearing in Europe, it is obvious that potential participants are hardly willing to disclose their expert views with their affiliation mentioned. We therefore decided to assure absolute anonymity. We guarantee construct validity during the analysis phase by using multiple sources of evidence (such as academic literature, corporate websites and balance sheets). Our case study consists of interviews with six industry experts from three different clearing houses who each have more than 20 years of experience in the financial industry. With three out of nine clearing houses currently operating through-out Europe, this represents coverage of one third of the market. The open-ended, pre-structured interviews were guided and accompanied, and were conducted by two researchers, with interviewees selected according to their hierarchy and expertise. It must be noted that due to the high level of automation, clearing is not a people-intensive business; accordingly, the number of experts in strategic management positions is limited. Propositions used in the cases are grounded theoretically and explicitly stated [28]. Some interview partners provided additional documentation (such as organizational charts, structure of current PMS, mission statements). The cases were evaluated on the basis of final, written, and mutually agreed interview transcripts.

Case A. The interviewees of Case A are from the senior management of one of the ten largest equity clearing houses worldwide. Formulating hypothesis H1, we intended to find out whether the BSC in its basic form is a suitable tool for performance measurement of a clearing house. Towards this statement, the interviewees were neutral[1]. The intention of the hypotheses H2a to H5a (H2b to H6 respectively) was to find out whether the four perspectives of Kaplan and Norton's original BSC and the five perspectives of our modified BSC respectively are necessary and important for measuring the performance of a clearing house. The following table reflects how, according to the interviewees, the perspectives should ideally be considered for the performance measurement system of a clearing house. The first and fourth columns of the table list the perspectives; the second (fifth) column shows the percentage of each perspective's ideal consideration for performance measurement in clearing houses as attributed by the interviewees. In order to make the figures comparable, we relate in column 3 (column 6) this percentage to the percentage that would be attributed to each perspective assuming equal distribution, that is 25 percent for each original perspective and 20 percent for each modified perspective.

Table 1. View of Case A on ideal consideration of Kaplan and Norton's perspectives versus ideal consideration of the modified perspectives

	Ideally considered	Consideration in relation to equal distribution		Ideally considered	Consideration in relation to equal distribution
Financial	30%	1.2	Financial	15%	0.75
Customer	30%	1.2	Competition and Customer	30%	1.50
Internal Business	20%	0.8	Process	10%	0.50
Innovation and Learning	20%	0.8	Staff and IT	10%	0.50
			Risk Management	35%	1.75

---

[1] Ticking "4" on a 7-item Likert scale (where 1 is "totally disagree", 2 is "strongly disagree", 3 is "disagree", 4 is "neutral", 5 is "agree", 6 is "strongly agree", and 7 is "totally agree").

Columns 1 through 3 of Table 1 display the importance the industry experts attribute to Kaplan and Norton's perspectives for the performance measurement system of a clearing house, illustrating that the financial and the customer perspective are given slightly more weight than the internal business and innovation and learning perspectives. Columns 4 through 6 present the experts' attitude towards our proposed modified perspectives. A clear ranking can be observed, starting with risk management as the most important perspective, followed by competition and customer as second. The remaining perspectives are ranked below average. A clear shift of focus can be observed: Interestingly, the newly introduced risk management perspective is regarded as the most important (35%). At the same time, the financial and the staff and IT perspectives are ranked less significant. Finally, hypothesis H7 aims at documenting whether the modified BSC is better suited than the generic BSC as a performance measurement system for the clearing industry. Here, the interviewees strongly agreed[2]. Compared to the level of acceptance of hypothesis H1, this can be interpreted as evidence for accepting H7 and thus as a support of our modified BSC.

Case B. The interviewees of the second case are from the senior management of an equity clearing house which is not among the ten largest worldwide. The experts agreed[3] to hypothesis H1. The following table 2 reflects how, according to the interviewees, Kaplan and Norton's perspectives should ideally be considered. It illustrates that the customer perspective is most important since the experts allocate as much weight to it (50%) as to all three remaining perspectives. Innovation and learning is also considered important (30%) while interestingly the financial and the internal business perspectives are ranked far below average.

Table 2 also presents the experts' attitude towards our proposed modified perspectives. A clear ranking can be observed, starting with risk management and competition and customer as the most important perspectives, followed by staff and IT as

Table 2. View of Case B on ideal consideration of Kaplan and Norton's perspectives versus ideal consideration of the modified perspectives

	Ideally considered	Consideration in relation to equal distribution		Ideally considered	Consideration in relation to equal distribution
Financial	10%	0.4	Financial	10%	0.5
Customer	50%	2.0	Competition and Customer	30%	1.5
Internal Business	10%	0.4	Process	10%	0.5
Innovation and Learning	30%	1.2	Staff and IT	20%	1.0
			Risk Management	30%	1.5

---

[2] Ticking "6".
[3] Ticking "5".

second most important perspective. The remaining perspectives are ranked below average. A clear shift of focus can be observed: Our newly introduced risk management perspective is regarded most important (30%) while the two perspectives ranked most important previously lose weight. The experts strongly agreed[4] to H7 that the modified scorecard is a suitable tool for performance measurement of a clearing house. Especially compared to the level of acceptance of H1, this can be interpreted as evidence for accepting H7 and thus as a support of our modified BSC.

Case C. The interviewees of the third case are from the middle and senior management of one of the ten largest equity clearing houses worldwide. The experts agreed[5] to hypothesis H1. The following table again reflects how, according to the interviewees, the perspectives should ideally be considered (H2 to H6). Table 3 shows the importance the industry experts attribute to Kaplan and Norton's perspectives and to our proposed modified perspectives, respectively, for the performance measurement system of a clearing house. In both instances, the statement was made that all perspectives are deliberately ranked uniformly and none is prioritized as the interviewees regarded all perspectives as highly connected and interrelated.

Table 3. View of Case C on ideal consideration of Kaplan and Norton's perspectives versus ideal consideration of the modified perspectives

	Ideally considered	Consideration in relation to equal distribution		Ideally considered	Consideration in relation to equal distribution
Financial	25%	1.0	Financial	20%	1.0
Customer	25%	1.0	Competition and Customer	20%	1.0
Internal Business	25%	1.0	Process	20%	1.0
Innovation an Learning	25%	1.0	Staff and IT	20%	1.0
			Risk Management	20%	1.0

The experts strongly agreed[6] to H7 that the modified scorecard is a suitable tool for performance measurement of a clearing house. Compared to the level of acceptance of hypothesis H1, this can again be interpreted as evidence for accepting hypothesis H7 and thus as a support of our modified BSC.

Analysis of the Cases. All three cases do not discard hypothesis H1 that the BSC in its basic form is a suitable tool for performance measurement of a clearing house. In all three cases, the experts strongly agreed to H7 which states that the modified scorecard is a suitable tool for performance measurement of a clearing house. Comparing

---

[4] Ticking "6".
[5] Ticking "5".
[6] Ticking "6".

the levels of acceptance of hypotheses H1 and H7 indicates support for our modified BSC; we therefore conclude that the modified BSC is better suited to fit the needs of a clearing house than the original BSC. The newly introduced risk management perspective finds strong support by the experts from Case A and B. Although Case C does not differentiate the perspectives by weight, the same relative weight is attributed to risk management as to all other perspectives. Also, the extended competition and customer perspective is top-ranked by the experts form Case A and B and equally ranked by the expert from Case C. It is interesting that on inquiry two thirds of the experts interviewed stated to see potential for a new perspective that includes strategic and regulatory issues.

These results show that the concept of the BSC can be adapted to accommodate a specific industry. In order to make it applicable for a particular institution, the industry-specific BSC must be further adapted to the needs of a specific company.

4.2 Cause-and-Effect Relationships within the Modified BSC

Kaplan and Norton [14] point out that good BSCs are more than ad hoc collections of financial and non-financial measures and that the crucial point of the BSC is the linking together of the four areas of measurement in a causal chain that passes through all four perspectives. To accommodate this claim and owing to the fact that during the interviews we were able to observe that all experts are aware of interdependencies between the various perspectives, we further investigated the extent and direction of the cause-and-effect relationships during our case study. We asked the interviewees to state whether in their opinion interdependencies between any of the perspectives existed, and if so, to assess[7] the degree of correlation. This approach was done separately for both the original and the proposed modified BSC perspectives. The interviewees are aware that there are correlations between most perspectives. The following figures, however, only include the stronger correlations. In contrast to figure 2, figure 6 shows an additional linkage between the perspectives "Innovation and Learning" and "Customer". Moreover, the interviewees are aware of a feedback relation between the financial and the customer perspective.

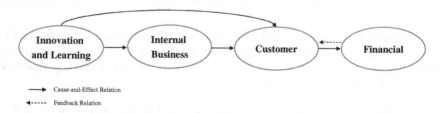

Fig. 6. Cause-and-effect and feedback relations in Kaplan and Norton's perspectives

---

[7] Using a 7-item Likert scale where 1 is "no correlation", 2 is "very weak correlation", 3 is "weak correlation", 4 is "rather weak correlation", 5 is "rather strong correlation", 6 is "strong correlation", and 7 is "very strong correlation".

Concerning the perspectives of the modified BSC, the experts see similar cause-and-effect relations as within the traditional BSC. The main difference can be seen in the cause-and-effects relations of the newly introduced "Risk Management" perspective (see figure 7). Moreover, the experts see feedback relations from the "Financial" perspective to the "Competition and Customer" and "Staff and IT" perspectives.

In case it is intended to model the cause-and-effect relations of the BSC by means of Bayesian Belief Networks (BBN) as proposed by Blumenberg and Hinz [2], the existence of feedback loops must be omitted as the concept of BBNs stipulates that the graph be acyclic. However, the experts emphasize the importance of these feedback loops from the "Financial Perspective" and the usage of the funds for the success of the strategy of the corporation. Therefore, it is essential to model the cause-and-effect relations including the feedback loops.

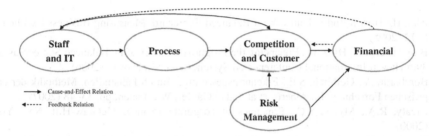

Fig. 7. Cause-and-effect and feedback relations in the modified perspectives

5 Conclusion and Further Research

The BSC is a well-established steering and controlling tool, allowing the management to set up objectives and to communicate these objectives and their performance towards the employees. We introduce the BSC as a funded approach for the management of a company and illustrate how the stakeholder value theory corresponds with the concept of the BSC. Based on our findings and using the European clearing industry as an example, we present a three-phased approach how to adjust and to extend Kaplan and Norton's original concept. Particularly risk management as the core function and key competence of a clearing house requires explicit and detailed consideration. We therefore add risk management as a separate perspective. Moreover, against the background of increasing competition and accounting for the industry's level of automation, we integrate competition and IT into the modified BSC.

In order to show that the BSC is a suitable tool for performance measurement of a clearing house in the changing European environment, we tested the suitability of the original and the modified BSC by means of a case study. The cases lead to two interesting results: firstly, they support the hypothesis that the BSC in general is a suitable tool for performance measurement in the clearing industry; secondly, they indicate that our modified BSC is better suited than the traditional BSC. Especially the introduction of a separate risk management perspective and the extension of the customer perspective by the aspect of competition are supported by the cases. Moreover, we show the existence of underlying cause-and-effect and feedback relations which need to be considered properly upon designing a BSC and choosing the appropriate perspectives. These findings can serve as a basis for the re-design of current Management Information Systems in the clearing industry.

In our further research we plan to analyze the potential of OTC clearing as a growth strategy for single clearing houses and the related chances and risks from their perspective, their users and regulators. Moreover, we plan to analyze the effects of competition and inter-CCP risk management considering systemic risk.

Acknowledgments. The authors gratefully acknowledge the support of the E-Finance Lab, Frankfurt for this work.

References

1. Ahn, H.: How to Individualise Your Balanced Scorecard. Measuring Business Excellence, 5–12 (2005)
2. Blumenberg, S., Hinz, D.: Enhancing the Prognostic Power of IT Balanced Scorecards. In: 39th Hawaii International Conference on System Sciences, Hawaii (2006)
3. Borchardt, A., Göthlich, S.E.: Erkenntnisgewinnung durch Fallstudien, Methodik der empirischen Forschung. In: Alberts, et al. (eds.) Gabler, Wiesbaden, pp. 33–48 (2007)
4. Brealy, R.A., Myers, S.C.: Principles of corporate finance. McGraw-Hill, New York (2000)
5. Copeland, T., Koller, T., Murrin, J.: Valuation: Measuring and Managing the Value of Companies, 2nd edn. Wiley, New York (1994)
6. Börse, D.: The European Post-Trade Market – An Introduction, White Paper (2005)
7. Eisenhardt, K.M.: Building Theories from Case Study Research. The Academy of Management Review 14(4), 557–573 (1989)
8. Fenton, N., Neil, M.: Software Metrics and Risk. In: 2nd European Software Measurement Conference (1999)
9. Freeman, R.E.: Strategic Management: A Stakeholder Approach. Pitman (1984)
10. Ittner, C.D., Larcker, D.E.: Innovations in performance measurement: Trends and research implications. Journal of Management Accounting Research (10), 205–238 (1998)
11. Kaplan, R.: The Evolution of Management Accounting. The Accounting Review 59(3), 390–418 (1984)
12. Kaplan, R., Cooper, R.: How Cost Accounting Systematically Distorts Product Costs. In: Kaplan, R., Bruns, W. (eds.) Accounting and Management: A Field Study Perspective. Harvard Business School Press (1987)
13. Kaplan, R., Norton, D.: The Balanced Scorecard: Measures that drive performance. Harvard Business Review, 77–80 (1992)
14. Kaplan, R., Norton, D.: Balanced Scorecard: Translating Strategy into Action. Harvard School Press (1996)
15. Körnert, J., Wolf, C.: Theoretisch-konzeptionelle Grundlagen zur Balanced Scorecard. University of Greifswald Discussion Paper No. 2 (2006)
16. Lawrie, G., Kalff, D., Andersen, H.: Balanced Scorecard and Result-Based Management: Convergent Performance Management Systems. In: Proceedings of the 3rd Annual Conference on Performance Measurement and Management Control, EIASM, Nice, France (September 2005)
17. Nørreklit, H.: The balance on the balanced scorecard – a critical analysis of some of its assumptions. Management Accounting Research 11(1), 65–88 (2000)

18. Pirrong, C.: The Industrial Organization of Execution, Clearing, and Settlement in Financial Markets. In: CFS, DBAG and EFL Research Conference, Frankfurt (2008)
19. Prabhaker, R.: Governance and Stakeholding: How Different are the Shareholder and Stakeholder Models. New Economy 5(2), 119–122 (1998)
20. Rappaport, A.: Creating Shareholder Value. The new standard for business performance. B&T, New York (1986)
21. Rigby, D., Bilbodeau, B.: Management Tools and Trends. Bain and Company (2005)
22. Rosemann, M., Wiese, J.: Measuring the Performance of ERP Software - a Balanced Scorecard Approach. In: Hope, B., Yoong, P. (eds.) Proceedings of the 10th Australasian Conference on Information Systems (ACIS 1999), Wellington, (with J. Wiese), December 1-3, pp. 773–784 (1999)
23. Schmiedel, H., Schönenberger, A.: Integration of Securities Market Infrastructures in the Euro Area. European Central Bank Occasional Paper No. 33 (July 2005)
24. Tate, D.: Issues involved in implementing a balanced business scorecard in an IT service organization. Total Quality Management & Business Excellence 11(4), 674–679 (2000)
25. Wallenburg, C.M., Weber, J.: Ursache-Wirkungsbeziehungen der Balanced Scorecard – Empirische Erkenntnisse zu ihrer Existenz. WHU Working Paper No. 109 (2006)
26. Wendt, F.: Intraday Margining of Central Counterparties: EU Practice and a Theoretical Evaluation of Benefits and Costs. Netherlands Central Bank, Amsterdam, Netherlands (2006)
27. Wolf, K.: Risikomanagement im Kontext der wertorientierten Unternehmensführung. Deutscher Universitätsverlag, Wiesbaden (2003)
28. Yin, R.K.: Case Study Research: Design and Methods. Sage Publications, Thousand Oaks (2003)

Dynamic Component Selection for SCA Applications

Djamel Belaïd, Hamid Mukhtar, Alain Ozanne, and Samir Tata

Institut TELECOM, TELECOM & Management SudParis
9 rue Charles Fourier, 91011 Evry Cedex
France
{djamel.belaid,hamid.mukhtar,alain.ozanne,samir.tata}@it-sudparis.eu

Abstract. Service Oriented Computing (SOC) has gained maturity and there have been various specifications and frameworks for realization of SOC. One such specification is the Service Component Architecture (SCA), which defines applications as assembly of heterogeneous components. However, such assembly is defined once and remains static for fixed components throughout the application life-cycle.

To address this problem, we have previously proposed an approach for dynamic selection of components in SCA, based on functional semantic matching and non-functional strategic matching using policy descriptions in SCA. In this paper, we extend our existing approach by providing further flexibility in component selection and present the architecture and implementation of our system. An evaluation of the system is also reported.

1 Introduction

In order to provide their services to a large variety of clients, enterprises often manage various contracts with other service providers. One problem faced by such enterprises is the emergence of new competing service providers, with better, cost-effective solutions. Thus, it would be natural that enterprises change partnerships in pursuit of better ones. However, in reality, it is much more different than that.

When inter-enterprise applications are developed on top of the existing Information System, they are created for particular service providers. This results in two major problems. First, if a change of any of the service provider is required, a whole new application needs to developed, which is not always feasible. Second, if only a part of the functionality of the application is required to be reused, again a new application needs to be deployed. Such problems arise due to the fact that most of the time the description of service provider is hard-coded in the application logic instead of the service description itself. Thus, we can rightly call such applications as service-provider-dependent rather than service-dependent.

To overcome such difficulties, Service-Oriented Computing (SOC) has emerged recently. SOC is the computing paradigm that utilizes services as fundamental elements for developing applications/solutions. Services are self-describing,

C. Godart et al. (Eds.): I3E 2009, IFIP AICT 305, pp. 272–286, 2009.
© IFIP International Federation for Information Processing 2009

platform-agnostic computational elements that support rapid, low-cost composition of distributed applications [1]. Services are offered by service providers —organizations that procure the service implementations, supply their service descriptions, and provide related technical and business support.

However, even after arrival of SOC based approaches, the aforementioned problems have not been solved completely. Although the applications have started to become modularized in terms of services, they are still not decoupled from their underlying platforms —the definition of services is still dependent on their implementation. One particular approach for realizing SOC based applications, the Service Component Architecture (SCA), avoids such obstacle by separating the service definition from its implementation. However, as we will explore in this paper, SCA is also limited by the fact that applications defined using SCA are static. Once defined, services and their implementation remain intact afterwards. But in an ideal situation, services can be provided by different providers differently and, hence, will have different implementations. Should a provider changes, the new implementation is to be reused with minimum of effort.

A Motivating Example

Consider a fictitious travel agency based in Paris. The agency provides services such as flight, hotel and car booking as well as arranging for excursions in a specific destination city. To offer its services, the agency relies on a number of other specialized service providers in France. In fact, given the large number of destinations and depending on the time of the year, different destinations are served by different service providers at different time of the year. In order to keep up with so many service providers, the IT personnel at the agency have set up an application that combines the various services from different service providers without letting the travel agent, who is using the application, knows how many and which service providers he is dealing with when making a transaction. The selection of a service provider for a particular service for a particular time period is managed automatically by the application.

Now assume that our agency wants to open a new branch in Madrid. In order to provide their services for various destinations in Spain, the travel agency settles up new agreements with local service providers. Once all the new service providers have been identified, they are registered into the system and the selection of the proper agencies for each type of service is managed automatically, according to the conditions of the agreements and requirements of the travel agency. However, for certain destinations no service provider offers excursion activities. Thanks to the development approach used by IT personnel of the agency, the application will still be able to offer the rest of its services to the travel agent, even though it is missing some of the services for those destinations. This is possible because if the application finds that a service provider is unreachable, it tries to find an alternative service provider. If it does not find any service provider for some service, it continues offering the rest of the services.

As the reader can observe, the above example requires several points: first, the application, whose composition is defined in terms of services, should be deployable at different locations with different service providers. Second, an application designer should be able to make its application work in a kind of degraded mode if some of the service providers required for its full functionalities can not be found. Both of these points formed the basis of our previous approach for service composition in SCA [2]. In this paper, we extend our prior approach to add further flexibility in the composition process. Also, an evaluation of our implemented system is provided in this paper.

The rest of this paper has been organized as following. First, in Sect. 2 we describe the some related work done by others. In Sect. 3 we describe the Service Component Architecture (SCA) upon which we build the rest of the paper. Sect. 4 discusses the notion of abstract and concrete composition and how it can be applied to SCA. Sect. 5 describes the architecture of our system, its implementation and usability while Sect. 6 provides its evaluation. Sect. 7 concludes this paper along with description of the intended future work.

2   Related Work

The idea of describing application as an abstract composition of services, which are resolved into service components dynamically, has been treated previously. However, existing works mostly treat the process from the point of view of a user in a pervasive environment. For example, in the COCOA approach [3], the objective is to find concrete components for abstract services defined in a user task. Their solution builds on semantic Web services (OWL-S) and offers flexibility by enabling semantic matching of interfaces and ad hoc reconstruction of the user tasks conversation from services conversations. Furthermore, COCOA allows meeting QoS requirements of user tasks. For this purpose, they have created COCOA-L, an extension of OWL-S, that allows the specification of both local and global QoS requirements of user tasks. Compared to their approach, our approach also proposes use of semantic matching but instead of being bound to a particular semantic description language such as OWL-S, we propose to use semantic annotations, which are independent of description languages. Also, our approach is more relaxed by providing the possibility to define the different levels of abstraction at different phases of application life-cycle as will be described in the paper.

The Aura project [4] defines an architecture that realizes user tasks in a transparent way. The user tasks defined in Aura are composed of abstract services to be found in the environment. Gaia [5] is a distributed middleware infrastructure that enables the dynamic deployment and execution of software applications. In this middleware, an application is mapped to available resources of a specific active space. This mapping can user-assisted or automatic. Gaia supports the dynamic reconfiguration of applications. For instance, it allows changing the composition of an application dynamically upon a users request (e.g., the user may specify a new device providing a component that should replace a component currently used). Furthermore, Gaia supports the mobility of applications between active spaces by saving the state of the application. Both of the previous platforms introduce advanced middleware to ease the development of pervasive applications composed out of networked resources. However, they are too restrictive when it comes to interoperability between different applications, specifically when they are provided by different parties. Both approaches assume framework-dependent XML-based descriptions for services and tasks. In other words, both approaches assume that services and tasks of the environment are aware of the semantics underlying the employed XML descriptions. However, in it is not reasonable to assume that service developers will describe services with identical terms worldwide. It is for this reason that we base our approach on SCA (Service Component Architecture) which is an open standard, independent of any particular implementation technology or communication protocol.

The subject of semantic service description has also been treated by various research works. Semantic Annotations for WSDL (SAWSDL) [6] defines how to add semantic annotations to various parts of a WSDL [7] document such as input and output message structures, interfaces and operations. For this purpose, SAWSDL defines a new specific namespace *sawsdl* and adds an extension attribute, named *modelReference*, to specify the association between WSDL components and concepts in some semantic model. The matching between a concept and WSDL element is done by using a matching algorithm. One such matching algorithm is proposed in [8]. Following the example of WSDL extension, we have extended SCA to be able to carry out semantic matching for different SCA elements including services, components, interfaces, and properties. As we will describe in the rest of this paper, SCA applications can easily be described at various levels of abstraction and provide a flexible way of extension for supporting semantic descriptions.

There has been some recent work related to the use of policies in SCA. One such approach uses the SCA policy framework [9] for abstract and concrete resource specification [10] which is then used for matching abstract services with their concrete component implementations. However, the approach is based on syntactic matching of SCA artifacts. This approach, together with our current approach, can be used as a component replacement strategy as described in Sect. 5.2. Similarly, in [11] the authors define patterns and roles for applying abstract policies in SCA to their concrete implementations. With an example application they show how their approach can be applied for transactional policies.

3   Service Component Architecture

Service Component Architecture (SCA) [12] provides a programming model for building applications and systems based on a Service Oriented Architecture (SOA). The main idea behind SCA is to be able to build distributed applications, which are independent of implementation technology and protocol. SCA extends and complements prior approaches to implementing services, and builds on open standards such as Web services. The basic unit of deployment of an SCA application is composite. A composite is an assembly of heterogeneous components, which implement particular business functionality. These components offer their functionalities through service-oriented interfaces and may require functions offered by other components, also through service-oriented interfaces.

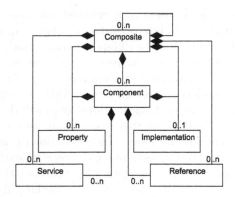

Fig. 1. A basic view of SCA meta model

SCA components can be implemented in Java, C++, COBOL, Web Services or as BPEL processes. Independent of whatever technology is used, every component relies on a common set of abstractions including services, references, properties, and bindings. A service describes what a component provides, i.e. its external interface. A reference specifies what a component needs from the other components or applications of the outside world. Services and references are matched and connected using wires or bindings. A component also defines one or more properties. For example, a component might rely on a property to tell it what part of the world it is running in, letting it customize its behavior appropriately. Figure 1 shows the various SCA elements and their relationships in the SCA meta-model. As shown, the SCA definition of a composite is recursive, i.e., a composite can contain another composite and so on.

SCA allows dependency injection by relieving the developer from writing the code to find the required references and do the appropriate binding [13]. The bindings are taken care of by the SCA runtime and can be specified at the time of deployment. The bindings specify how services and references communicate with each other. Each binding defines a particular protocol that can be used to communicate with a service as well as how to access them. Because bindings separate how a component communicates from what it does, they let the components business logic be largely divorced from the details of communication. A single service or reference can have multiple bindings, allowing different remote software to communicate with it in different ways.

Since SCA already has the notion of services and components and since it allows dynamic binding of services to components, it is an ideal candidate for realization of our proposed approach and, hence, in the rest of the paper we will explain our approach using the SCA artifacts.

3.1   SCA Example Application

First, we show how we can represent our example application in SCA. This has been done schematically in fig. 2(a). The listing below shows how the same SCA application is defined in SCDL (Service Component Description Language), an XML-based description of SCA applications.

```
<composite name="TravelPlanner">

  <service name="TravelBookingService"
    promote="TravelBookingComponent/TravelBookingService"/>

  <component name="TravelBookingComponent">
    <service name="TravelBookingService">
      <interface/>
    </service>
    <implementation.bpel process="BookingProcess"/>
    <reference name="PlaneBookingService"/>
    <reference name="CarBookingService"/>
    <reference name="HotelBookingService"/>
    <reference name="ExcursionBookingService"/>
    <implementation.bpel process="TravelBoooking.bpel"/>
  </component>

  <component name="ExcursionBookingComponent">
    <service name="ExcursionBookingService">
      <interface/>
    </service>
    <implementation.composite name="ExcursionBooking"/>
    <!-- references to coach and restaurant booking components -->
  </component>

  <!--PlaneBooking, CarBooking and HotelBooking components definitions-->

  <wire source="TravelBookingComponent/ExcursionBookingService"
    target="ExcursionBookingComponent/ExcursionBookingService"/>
  <!-- wires between other components of the TravelPlanner composite -->

</composite>
```

The application is described in the composite named TravelPlanner, which offers a single service to the user that is provided by the TravelBooking component. However, the TravelBooking component itself uses services provided by other components namely PlaneBookingCompnent, CarBookingComponent and HotelBookingComponent as well service provided by the ExcusionBooking composite. Finally, the ExcursionBooking composite is also composed of one component namely ExcursionBookingComponent. Note how the services provided by one component are used as references by another component. For example, the ExcursionBookingComponent references are connected to the services provided by the CoachBookingComponent and the RestaurantBookingComponent components.

The TravelPlanner application describes all the services required by the travel agent for a successful trip planning of a client. As mentioned previously, the selection of components implementing these services is made dynamically based

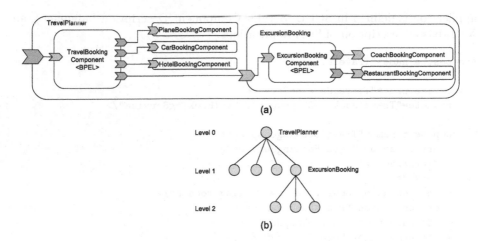

Fig. 2. The TravelPlanner application (a) SCA representation (b) representation as composite tree

on the availability of service provider. However, since the procedure for booking a travel or an excursion is known, such a procedure is already provided in the description of the TravelPlanner composite. Let us assume that this process has been described in BPEL. Our goal is, thus, to find the components that match the references required by the TravelBookingComponent and ExcursionBooking-Component.

4   Abstract and Concrete Composition

As mentioned in the motivating example, an application composition can be described abstractly so that its concretization can be carried out dynamically depending upon the context in which it is used. In general, we say that a composition is abstract when its description lacks some of the information that defines the composition implementation. Such a composition describes the services participating in the composition, but does not tell about how the services are implemented.[1]

When this concept is applied to SCA, we say that an application described in SCA is abstract if its description does not contain complete implementation definition. However, since an SCA composite is defined recursively, we need to distinguish between various levels of abstraction depending on whether all or part of a composite is abstract. This notion can be better explained by using the composition trees.

---

[1] We assume the availability of the technical resources required for instantiating and running such a composition, and hence do not treat such aspects.

4.1 SCA Applications as Composition Trees

The implementation of an SCA composite may be provided by one or more components. However, these components may themselves be defined in terms of other components and so on. This property can be explained easily by a tree structure, where the root is the application itself (i.e., the outermost composite) and its children represent the composites and components enclosed by it. With this tree structure, we observe that the inner nodes of the tree represent the composites and the leaves represent the components. The components, i.e., the leaves of the tree may be found at any level below the root depending on the application composition structure.

Figure 2(b) shows the tree representation of the example SCA application of fig. 2(a). Note that while a composite knows about its contents enclosed by it, it does not have any information about the contents of the composites enclosed by it. For example, in fig. 2(b), the root node (at level 0) knows if its children (at level 1) have known implementations or not, but it does not have this information about the nodes at level 2. To know them, we need to query the composite at level 1.

Bearing such a tree structure in mind, we distinguish between various levels of abstraction for an SCA application:

1) If any of the subcomponents of a composite have no defined implementation, then the composite is *shallow abstract*, e.g., the composite ExcursionBooking at level 1 of the tree in fig. 2(b) is shallow abstract.
2) By recursive definition, if any of the composite enclosed by the root composite is shallow abstract, the composite is called *deep abstract*. However, it is shallow abstract if only the implementation of one of its subcomponents is not defined. For example, the TravelPlanner composite is deep abstract because it encloses the ExcursionBooking composite, which is shallow abstract.
3) If all the subcomponents of a composite have known implementations, then the composite is *shallow concrete*.
4) By recursive definition, if all of the composites enclosed by the root composite are shallow concrete, the root composite is *deep concrete*.

Figure 3 shows these various levels of abstraction diagrammatically.

Our aim is to build a concrete composition tree, which is semantically equivalent to a given (shallow or deep) abstract composition tree. Its fundamental principle is to replace the abstract components of a composition tree by semantically equivalent concrete ones. We assume that a number of concrete components are available in some repository, which is accessible to us and we need to make a selection out of them.

4.2 Transformation of Tree

Our aim is to transform the input abstract application into an equivalent concrete one. This transformation process consists of three intermediate stages:

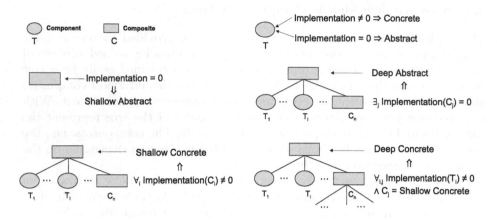

Fig. 3. The different levels of abstraction for SCA applications

1) First, the application is transformed into a composition tree structure as described previously. From the composition tree, a sub-tree is selected that keeps only those branches whose leaves are abstract components. In other words, if some components have well-defined implementations, they are not considered for processing.

2) While walking down the abstract tree, for each component node, we look in the repository for a concrete component, which is semantically equivalent to the abstract one and replace the description of the abstract one by the concrete one.

3) During the second stage, we may find more than one component or no matching components at all for an abstract service. We need to determine a strategy for deciding on what to do in such a case.

   In the second stage of transformation process, semantic matching is used for matching. However, the SCA specifications [12] do not specify any mechanism for matching of services and their implementations (components). Thus, we propose a mechanism for semantic description of services and components for matching purposes.

4.3   Semantic Description

To be able to reason about the functional properties of SCA artifacts, we add semantic descriptions to them, as described in the second stage of the transformation process.

SA-SCA:Semantic Annotations for SCA. We propose Semantic Annotations for SCA (SA-SCA), which suggests how to add semantic annotations to various SCA artifacts like composite, services, components, interfaces, and properties. This extension is similar to the concept of annotations in SAWSDL [6] and is in accordance with the SCA extensibility mechanism [12]. Our proposed SA-SCA defines a new namespace called *sasca* and adds an extension attribute called *modelReference* so that relationships between SCA artifacts and concepts in another semantic model are handled. This choice is motivated by the fact that applications developers can use any ontology language to annotate services rather than be bound to one particular approach. The listing below shows the description of our abstract CoachBookingComponent component:

```
<component name="CoachBookingComponent"
  sasca:modelReference="http://tp.org/booking.owl#CoachBooking">
  <service name="CoachBookingService">
    <interface.java interface="com.example.coachBookingServiceItf"/>
  </service>
</component>
```

Note that the component description now has a reference to an OWL ontology, which contains the definition of the CoachBooking concept. When this abstract component is matched with concrete components, it will be ensured that both of them refer to the same CoachBooking concept. Only if they match, the concrete component description can be used. For example, the coach booking service provided by an agency in Madrid is implemented in Java and described in the following listing:

```
<component name="MadridCoachBookingComponent"
  sasca:modelReference="http://tp.org/booking.owl#CoachBooking">
  <service name="MadridCoachBookingService">
    <interface.java interface="com.example.coachBookingServiceItf"/>
  </service>
  <implementation.java name="spaincoach.madrid.booking.CoachBookingServiceImpl"/>
</component>
```

Since the *modelreference* attribute in both the abstract and concrete descriptions refer to the same CoachBooking concept, they will match.

It is then important to notice that we provide the possibility for both a shallow and a deep transformation of the composite: in the first case, the composite description is brought to a shallow concrete state, while in the second case a deep concrete tree is created. Considering the TravelPlanner composite, its shallow transformation will replace the CarBookingComponent, HotelBookingComponent, and PlaneBookingComponent components with concrete ones, and its deep transformation will, in addition to these, replace the CoachBookingComponent and RestaurantBookingComponent components. This possibility is interesting in the case of a distributed composition. An application composer can process a shallow transformation on a composite located on its hosting computer, and delegate the transformation of the distant subcomposites to the composers located on those hosts.

5   System Architecture and Implementation

So far, we have discussed our approach for abstract and concrete composition. In this section, first we describe the architecture describing the entities involved in

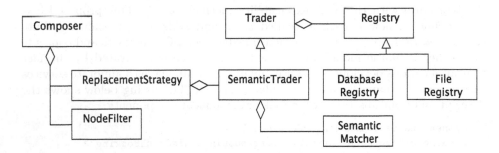

Fig. 4. The Semantic Trader architecture

realizing the abstract-to-concrete composition in Sect. 5.1 and then we provide the details of our implementation, developed as a proof of concept, in Sect. 5.2.

5.1 Architectural Components

Figure 4 describes the architecture of our proposed system. The Composer is the entity in charge of the transformation of the abstract composition description. In order to do so, it uses NodeFilter for selection of nodes in the abstract tree and a particular ReplacementStrategy for replacement of abstract components by concrete ones. Hence, the Composer walks through the abstract tree and when the NodeFilter accepts the current node, the description in the abstract composition is replaced with the one returned by the ReplacementStrategy.

In order to determine what to put in place of an abstract component description, the ReplacementStrategy uses the SemanticTrader which returns the description of a component semantically equivalent but concrete to a given abstract component description.

The SemanticTrader can do this because it specializes the Trader which provides an extensive access to the Registry that contains the concrete components descriptions. A SemanticMatcher is used to compare the abstract component with the concrete ones returned by the Registry.

5.2 Implementation

Currently, our implementation provides two different possibilities for use as a ReplacementStrategy. These strategies actually provide the possibility of replacement of either complete or partial description of abstract component by the concrete one:

- the ImplementationOnlyReplacementStrategy keep the complete description of the abstract component but add to it the implementation field in the description of the concrete component. This strategy is meant to be used when SCA wires refer explicitly to the component and interface names of the abstract component, which are then needed to be kept intact.

- The FullReplacementStrategy replaces the complete description of the abstract component with the complete concrete component. This strategy can be used when SCA wires to the replaced component are automatically generated. It is then possible to import the complete description of the concrete replacement component into the outer composite.

Our implementation also provides three NodeFilters: one that accepts only an abstract component, another that accepts only abstract composite, and the third one that accepts both. So it is possible to apply a specific replacement strategy to each type of abstract components. For example, the FullReplacementStrategy can be used for replacing a full abstract composite, as the concrete replacement composite may promote its subcomponents interfaces.

The Registry can also have various implementations depending on the way the available concrete components are serialized. Currently we provide a database implementation. The DatabaseRegistry uses a MySQL base in which components are stored in a simple table that contains for each component: its name, its XML description, its unique key determined on its registration request, and its provider id.

As we are looking forward to giving a public access to the Composer, the Registry also maintains the list of its authorized users. Indeed each operation on the trader, i.e., component request or publication, requires a user key. There are three kinds of users, each with different rights:

- the customer can request components from the trader,
- the provider can register components but also request them,
- the administrator can register new users, customer or provider.

Usability of Our Approach. By using a service component-oriented model and by dynamically selecting components using semantic description, our approach can be used for service and component bindings both at design time and at runtime. At design time, when the application designer defines the abstract composition, he can select and reuse the concrete components from the component repository —if they are available— and do the bindings at design time, i.e., an early binding is provided. However, if not all components can be found at design time, the designer can leave the choice to the container, which can carry out late binding depending on the available concrete components. This leads to greater flexibility.

6 Evaluation

In order to benchmark our approach we generated various sets of primitive SCA components counting from 100 to 600 elements. We semantically annotated their services and references with concepts taken from the Rosetta ontology (which has 63 classes and 30 subclass relations)[2]. We took care to have a uniform

---

[2] Rosetta is available at
http://www.w3.org/2002/ws/sawsdl/spec/ontology/rosetta.owl

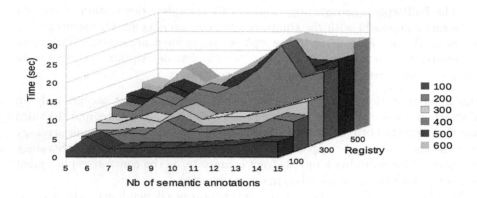

Fig. 5. The time for turning abstract primitive components into concrete ones

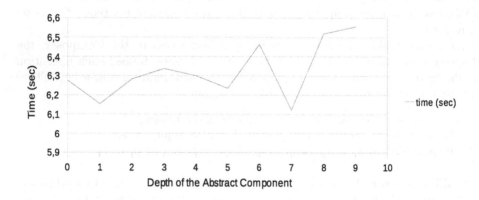

Fig. 6. The cost of the abstract tree building and exploration

distribution of components with respect to the number of semantic annotations they contain. The tests have been done on a 1.86 GHz Pentium M with 1 Gb RAM.

First, we look at how the time to turn an abstract primitive component into a concrete one grows. In order to do so, we took a set of 10 abstract components, holding from 5 to 15 semantic annotations. We measured how long it took to find their concrete equivalents in sets of concrete components varying from 100 to 600 components. What we noticed is that for small number of annotations, the time required to turn an abstract component into a concrete one grows linearly and slowly with the size of the registry. But the slope becomes abrupt for components holding large number of annotations, as shown in figure 5.

Then we look at the impact of the abstract tree building and exploration for the transformation of a deep abstract composite into a deep concrete one. To do so, we took a composite component of ten levels depth. We placed an abstract primitive component to its deepest level and measured the time required for the transformation of the composite. Then we repeat the operation with the abstract component on the other levels of the composite, the result is shown in the figure 6. The additional cost of the building and exploration of the abstract tree is at most 0.25 second, to be compared to the 6.5 seconds took by the matching process. So we shall optimize this latter part of our tool in the future.

7 Conclusions and Future Work

We have presented an approach for dynamic composition of applications whose composition is described in terms of the services provided/required by the application; however, these services are bound to implementations either at design time or dynamically at the time of execution of the application depending on the availability of concrete components in the current context. The service implementations might be distributed and provided by different service providers whose selection is influenced by a particular replacement strategy. The selection of a particular implementation is made on the basis of a matching algorithm. We have discussed an implementation of our system, whose evaluation is also provided.

The applications we consider are described in SCA. To resolve an abstract component, our system looks for the corresponding concrete component. However, it is possible that the implementation of an abstract component may not be provided by any available concrete components; rather we may find more than one component providing the same functionality required by the abstract component. Similarly, if a composition tree requires to resolve several abstract components and instead of providing various concrete components, our system will provide a single concrete composite, which provides the same functionality; this might be either due to unavailability of some of the required concrete components or due to performance reasons.

Currently, we consider only applications whose composition in terms of services is defined statically. In the future, we are looking forward to having such applications created automatically in the pervasive environments in terms of the services available in the environment.

References

1. Papazoglou, M.P.: Service-oriented computing: concepts, characteristics and directions. In: Proceedings of the Fourth International Conference on Web Information Systems Engineering, WISE 2003, December 2003, pp. 3–12 (2003)
2. Belaïd, D., Mukhtar, H., Ozanne, A.: Service Composition Based on Functional and Non-functional Descriptions in SCA. In: Proceedings of The 1st International Workshop on Advanced Techniques for Web Services, AT4WS 2009, Milan, Italy (2009)
3. Ben Mokhtar, S., Georgantas, N., Issarny, V.: COCOA: Conversation-based service composition in pervasive computing environments with qos support. J. Syst. Softw. 80(12), 1941–1955 (2007)

4. Sousa, J., Garlan, D.: Aura: an Architectural Framework for User Mobility in Ubiquitous Vomputing Environments. In: WICSA 3: Proceedings of the IFIP 17th World Computer Congress - TC2 Stream / 3rd IEEE/IFIP Conference on Software Architecture, Deventer, The Netherlands, pp. 29–43. Kluwer, B.V., Dordrecht (2002)
5. Román, M., Campbell, R.H.: A middleware-based application framework for active space applications. In: Endler, M., Schmidt, D.C. (eds.) Middleware 2003. LNCS, vol. 2672, pp. 433–454. Springer, Heidelberg (2003)
6. Akkiraju, R., Sapkota, B.: Semantic annotations for WSDL. Technical report, W3C (September 2006), http://www.w3.org/TR/sawsdl-guide/
7. WSDL 2.0 Home Page: Web Services Description Language (2006), http://www.w3.org/TR/wsdl20/
8. Ould Ahmed M'Bareck, N., Tata, S.: How to consider requester's preferences to enhance web service discovery? In: Second International Conference on Internet and Web Applications and Services, ICIW 2007, May 2007, pp. 59–59 (2007)
9. Open SOA Collaboration: SCA Policy Framework v1.00 specifications (2007), http://www.osoa.org/
10. Mukhtar, H., Belaïd, D., Bernard, G.: A policy-based approach for resource specification in small devices. In: UBICOMM 2008: The Second International Conference on Mobile Ubiquitous Computing, Systems, Services and Technologies. IEEE, Los Alamitos (2008)
11. Satoh, F., Mukhi, N.K., Nakamura, Y., Hirose, S.: Pattern-based Policy Configuration for SOA Applications. In: IEEE International Conference on Services Computing, SCC 2008, July 2008, vol. 1, pp. 13–20 (2008)
12. Open SOA Collaboration: Service Component Architecture (SCA): SCA Assembly Model v1.00 specifications (2007), http://www.osoa.org/
13. Chappel, D.: Introducing Service Component Architecture. White paper (July 2007), http://www.osoa.org

How to Research People's First Impressions of Websites? Eye-Tracking as a Usability Inspection Method and Online Focus Group Research

Csilla Herendy

University of Pécs, Budapest, Hungary

Abstract. The visual surface of the Hungarian governmental portal – magyaror-szag.hu – was inspected in 2007 with two different inspection methods: Eye tacking research and Online focus group research. Both methods help to understand and to chart not only the usability of different websites but also the affective impressions associated with the websites. In this study, an Experimental and a Control-group were tested to assess the usability of the site and the emotional reactions to it. The results reveal that the Hungarian government website is too complicated, dull and difficult to apprehend at a glance.

Keywords: Eye-tracking; online focus-group; website usability.

1 Introduction

In this study, the Hungarian governmental portal, called magyarorszag.hu (in English: hungary.hu) was researched with the use of two different methods, eye tracking research and online focus-groups. The aims of this study were to investigate and assess the usability of the main page of the site and to survey the first impressions and the emotional reactions to the website. The ease (or difficulty) of finding different pieces of information on the site was tested, and users' evaluations of the site as simple or too complicated were investigated. The survey focused on other question as well: the impressions users had of the civil servants who worked at the portal and of the Hungarian administrative sector, after using the site and experiencing the user interface and the visual surface.

The possible uses of different testing methods for websites are highlighted by various studies, such as Usability Inspection Methods [1], F-Shaped Pattern for Reading Web Content [2]. One of the most promising modern tools is eye tracking, as discussed by, for instance, Nielsen [2], Duchowski [3]. These studies concentrate of the eye-movements of the users: how they look at web pages, what they read, what they don't read, what they tend to notice or never see, etc.

Using the eye tracking method, the aim of this survey was to reveal how users find certain information on the site and whether the site meets their general needs and expectations.

In addition to the eye tracking method, online focus groups were used as well. The aim of applying the online focus group method was to obtain information about emotional reactions to the site in an effort to understand why the users liked or disliked

C. Godart et al. (Eds.): I3E 2009, IFIP AICT 305, pp. 287–300, 2009.
© IFIP International Federation for Information Processing 2009

the site, why they judged the site as difficult or simple, how they felt about the people working behind the site (civil servants).

The online focus group completed a range of qualitative and quantitative surveys: semantic differential scale, interviews, collage-making and incomplete sentences test. The users were interviewed about the page, about the results of the eye tracking study, and they were asked to compare the Hungarian portal with the governmental portals of other countries, including those of the USA, Japan, South-Korea and Germany. The countries were selected based on a survey conducted by Waseda University Institute [4].

The present survey could help to understand how users feel about governmental websites, especially about the Hungarian portal. The eye tracking method helps to understand which piece of information is positioned optimally and which is not; the online focus group helps to assess users' opinions. In order to identify possible shifts in attitudes after using the site for practical purposes, our participants were divided into two groups. One group (the experimental group) took part in the eye tracking study, where the users were asked to find some information and some links on the website, while the other group (the Control group) was only exposed to the website for the purposes of focus group tasks.

2 Method

In this study, the Hungarian governmental portal, called magyarorszag.hu (in English: hungary.hu) was researched with the use of two different methods, eye tracking research and online focus groups. The eye-tracking method was used to assess the usability of the website, by measuring speed and tracking eye movement in solving different tasks on print screens from the website.

The online focus group was used to complement and help interpret the results obtained in the quantitative research on the one hand, and to introduce an additional variable for comparing the attitudes of users solving tasks on the site and users viewing the site without any tasks. I was also interested in exploring the general attitudes of users in both groups.

I chose to use online focus groups instead of seating participants together because it makes more accurate data readily available.

First I write about the eye tracking research.

For the research, the eye tracker of the Faculty of arts of the Hungarian Eötvös Loránd University was used. The eye tracker, called "Remote Eye tracking System" was developed by LC Technologies.

This appliance allows a very accurate analysis of the behavior of the users. The appliance is non-obtrusive, which means that there is no need to place it on the head of the user. Eye tracking is the process of measuring either the point of gaze ("where we are looking") or the motion of the pupil relative to the head. An eye tracker is a device for measuring eye positions and eye movements. Eye trackers are used in research on visual surfaces, in psychology, in website-usability or in product design. There are a number of methods for measuring eye movements.

This video-based eye tracker works on the following operating principle: two cameras, placed on a monitor, focus on both eyes and record their movement as the viewer looks at some kind of stimulus. The "Remote Eye tracking System" uses the contrast between the iris and the pupil. The system uses infrared and near-infrared, non-collimated light to create data from the corneal reflection. The vector of these two features can be used to compute gaze intersection with a surface after a simple calibration for an individual.

Using the data, the system makes different overview maps about the eye-movements. Using this map, it is possible to establish clearly how the users watch the visual surface, which part of the surface is more and which is less interesting for the users [5].

The "Scanpath analysis" shows the sequence of the fixations and their exact duration. About saccades and fixations: While drawing a visual information, the eye-movements are mostly not smooth and regular. On the contrary: while watching a visual surface, there are different eye-movements of interest for the present survey. One of them is the saccades – rapid eye movements used in repositioning the fovea to a new location in the visual environment –, the other one is the fixations – eye movements that stabilize the retina over a stationary object of interest [3]. This eye movement is recordable during the eye tracking surveys.

The "Attention level" and the "Hotspot" maps show the length of the fixations, the degree of visual attention. These maps show in a very clear graphic form how the users (part of the experimental group) watched the visual surface. It can be particularly interesting when the users watch websites.

3 Participants

Two groups took part in the research (the Experimental group, 6 users, participating in the eye-tracking research and the Control group, not participating in it).

The average age of the participants was almost identical in both groups (29-30 years). Participants included 6 women and 7 men, 5 from rural areas of Hungary and 8 from Budapest. Two of the subjects had secondary education, 11 had higher education degrees. They had a wide range of interests (information technologies, communication, agility, ceramics, etc.), three of the subjects had young children, and three of them were PhD students.

Table 1. Participants' data

	Number	Average age	Age range
Experimental Group	6	30,2	21-43
Control Group	7	29,9	26-40

4 Eye Tracking and Online Focus Group Research on the Hungarian Governmental Portal

4.1 Eye Tracking Research

The research took place at the Eye tracking Laboratory of the Faculty of Arts of the Hungarian Eötvös Loránd University. The participants arrived after each other. They sat down in front of the screen and were told about the essence of the eye tracking technology and the process of the research. The leader of the research was sitting behind the participants.

The research was conducted in 3 phases:

First, the users were shown unrelated pictures on a computer screen before the test phase of the experiment (family pictures, landscapes, and different websites). This phase was included in order to train the users not to try to influence their gaze.

In the next phase, the users were shown a Print Screen of the test site on the computer screen (only the first page). The Print Screen was made May 17th 2007. (See Fig 1.)

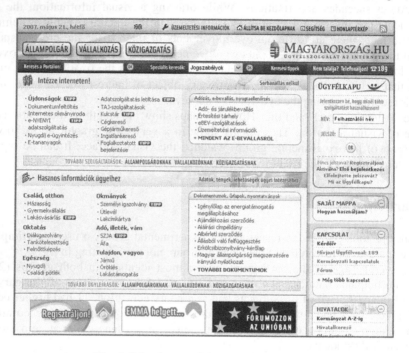

Fig. 1. Print Screen of the site: Magyarorszag.hu

In the third and longest phase of the survey the users were asked to find some information and some links on the site.

These were of two types: basic links (sending an e-mail message, map, search box, back to the main page link) and popular functions (according to official site statistics): "tax and contribution returns", "Home, family" and "Company search" and other specific menus: "Can't find it? Call us!", "Search tips", "The most frequent search topics", "Call us on 198" and the Hungarian national Coat of Arms.

The participants saw the pictures one by one. They walked through the pictures at their own pace, stepping on the next by using the "space" key.

4.2 Results of the Eye Tracking Research

The eye tracking research revealed that the participants found certain functions very easily while others were found only after a long search.

The easy links were: "Date", "the Hungarian national Coat of Arms, "Search tips", and "Ügyfélkapu"; the search for "The most frequent search topics", the "Home, family" and the "Company search" took a long time.

The exact search duration was tracked and listed by the program of the Eye tracker (See Table 2.)

Table 2. Scanpath Duration (ms) – The time of finding the links and functions

No.	Task	Mean	Median
1	Please view the magyarorszag.hu site!	13375,67	13803,00
2	Please find the "Search at the site" link on the Print Screen!	9539,33	7113,50
3	Please find the "Hungarian national Coat of Arms" link on the Print Screen!	1959,33	1198,50
4	Please find the "Map" link on the Print Screen!	6459,00	4308,50
5	Please find the "Tax and contribution return" link on the Print Screen!	14412,83	8103,00
6	Please find the "Home, family" link on the Print Screen!	21033,50	3738,00
7	Please find the "Set as homepage" link on the Print Screen!	12882,50	4008,00
8	Where is the date? ("31st May, 2007. Monday")	1718,33	1846,50
9	Please find the " Can't find it? Call us!" link on the Print Screen!	4478,50	1586,50
10	Please find the "Search tips" link on the Print Screen!	2310,67	2088,00
11	Please find "The most frequent search topics" link on the Print Screen!	19310,33	12677,00
12	Please find the " Call us on 198" box on the Print Screen!	9657,17	8262,50
13	Where would you click to go back to the main page?	11100,33	12648,00
14	Where would you look for the "Write e-mail" possibility?	4647,00	4499,00
15	Where is the "Ügyfélkapu" box?	3374,83	1195,50
15	Please find "Company search" box on the Print Screen!	29601,50	26907,00

4.3 Online Focus Group Research

The Online focus group was organised at the laboratory of the Faculty of Arts of the Hungarian Eötvös Loránd University.

The research leader, the moderator and an IT expert who were responsible for the program were sitting at the laboratory, the participants were at home and they used their own computer. The participants got a link and downloaded the necessary program for taking part in the online focus group research.

Two focus groups were organised: an Experimental group and a Control group. The two focus groups took place on the same day, in the afternoon, about 6 and 7 o'clock.

4.3.1 Warm-Up Phase

The focus group research started with "warming-up": the moderator asked the participants (of both groups) about their internet-use, and whether they use administrative websites or not. The participants said they often use the internet for orientation and for finding information. They also said they know several public administration sites.

The moderator asked the participants to visualize (recall) the website magyaror-szag.hu. The participants of the Experimental group remembered pale colours, white, red and bourdon (ruby). Then they were asked to talk about their impressions of the site; the answers included "boring", "monotonous", "non-functional", "bureaucratic".

At the question "What do the colours suggest?", the participants answered "bland", "boring", "unimaginative", "boring part of a boring system", "there weren't too many colours on it, what I remember is only a white background and some small, grey characters".

They described the structure of the site ("simple or complicated?") as follows: "tangled", "dense", "diffuse". Then the moderator showed a Print Screen about the site and asked the participants for their opinion. They said "so, then I remembered well", "illogical composition", "grey", "it's not too imaginative", "it doesn't look like a professional site, I have problems with it's distribution, the general appearance is more or less OK".

When the Print Screen was shown to the Control group, they described their impressions as follows: "cluttered", "dense", "too much text", "it's simple but a bit confusing, I see suddenly too much text", "it's a little glum", "it's like public admini-stration, greyish, like nothing, cold".

About the structure of the site: "it looks difficult and muddled", "there should be a bit more contrast on it", "it should be a bit more airy', "it looks too difficult at the first sight but if I look it isn't", "it is too much, muddled".

At the warm-up, the participants of the groups were critical about the site's colours and structure. The answers of the groups did not differ too much. Their opinions of the group (and the differences between their opinions) were specified by the semantic differential scale.

4.3.2 Semantic Differential

The semantic differential method is a type of rating scale [6], for measuring the emo-tional charge of concepts, ideas, objects and events. The participants were asked to indicate their position on a 1 to 6 scale between two contrasting words (e.g. cold – warm, friendly – stuffy, strong – weak, formal – casual).

Both groups' participants evaluated the magyarorszag.hu site at the Semantic Dif-ferential. In the whole research, this method showed the biggest difference between the two groups' opinions. The participants of the Experimental group who tried to find different links at the site were much more critical than the participants of the Control group.

The semantic differential is a scale between two contrasting terms. The participants were asked to choose their position on the scale. The biggest divergence between the two groups' opinions was found for:

- How customer-friendly is the site?
- Is the site old-fashioned or innovative?
- I like it / I don't like it
- Is the site formal or casual?
- Is the site complicated or transparent?
- Is the site trustworthy or untrustworthy?
- Is the site cold or friendly?

In both groups the "winning" attributes were: "difficult", "monotonous", "boring". The participants also found the site bureaucratic and too formal, more gloomy than cheerful, more old-fashioned than modern, slow rather than fast, more boring than entertaining, and more monotonous than colourful. Both groups awarded the site the same points for conservative and liberal (1-1), and for superficial and accurate (0 - 0 point), which means that these parameters are not relevant for the site.

On the whole, we can see that the participants of the Experimental group – those who took part in the eye tracking survey – rated the site more negatively on almost all scales than did the participants of the Control group.

These differences point to the fact that the experimental group's opinion is not based on stereotypes but on the difficulties they experienced during the eye-tracking research.

4.3.3 Incomplete Sentences

In the incomplete sentences exercise the participants get unfinished statements and are asked to complete the sentences. An important advantage of this technique is that it may yield spontaneous answers [7].

In this exercise both groups got sentences about the site – about its appearance, about the easiness of orientation, and about the virtual civil servants working "behind" the site.

In this part of the survey, the participants of the Experimental group were again more critical than the participants of the Control group: they didn't use a single positive attribute.

The appearance of the site was described in both groups as "boring", "monotonous", "dreary". The participants of the Control group characterized the site mostly as "boring", "cold", and as one that "needs development"; a single refreshing exception was: "pleasant". The general design and the atmosphere of the site were described as "depressed", "unimaginative", and "too grey".

The Experimental group pictured the "workers of the site" (the civil servants) as "unimaginative", "bureaucrats", "helpful, reacting quickly to questions", "they can't use the site either", "not really thoughtful". The Control group expressed the opinion that the workers of the site are "normal people", "drinking coffee", "no good people", "insipid and have a lot of time", "wearing grey, with a red ribbon only at Christmas".

About orientation on the site ("It is…….. to find your way on the site magyarorszag.hu") both groups had a rather bad opinion, with the Experimental group being more explicitly negative about it. Both groups found that it is hard to find one's way on the site, the site is not effective enough. Some participants thought that there is too much information on the main page and they are not optimally placed.

As to whether the site reflects the Hungarian public administration, most of the participants were of the opinion that it does perfectly. Only a few participants thought otherwise.

About the general impression of the site, the Experimental group was again more critical, which allows us to conclude that their answers are not based on stereotypes. Their general impression of the site was that it is "too difficult", "not good", "more constructive remarks included", "you can use it, but it would be nice if they would do something for better usability" and "less would be more". The members of the Control group were somewhat more tolerant: "not too comfortable", "just acceptable", "dense, hard to get an overview", "world wide waiting?".

It is important to note here that auto-stereotypes may be at work at certain points of the survey ("if something is Hungarian it could only be bad"), therefore it would make sense to control the findings in the future with a bigger survey, containing a blind test with participants who have never seen and used the site, or show the site as the governmental portal of a different country (for example with English, Japanese or German texts).

4.3.4 Collage-Making

Collage making is a rather sophisticated but time-consuming method for assessing emotional attitudes [7].

The most interesting part of the survey was probably the collage-making.

The moderator showed the participants previously hand-picked pictures: various types of cars, office workers of different ages and characters; landscapes, office buildings (old-fashioned as well as ultramodern), offices, queues of people, animals, and cities. He then asked the participants to choose one picture per category which they think represents the general atmosphere of the page magyarorszag.hu. Each participant chose one picture from the nine categories, and placed it into a 3x3 matrix.

In the choice of the pictures there was a clear and interesting difference between the two groups. A few examples: most of the participants of the Experimental group chose the snail from the pictures about animals, while most of the participants of the Control group chose the rabbit, although the difference wasn't too big. From the pictures about offices, most of the participants of the Control group chose a modern office (with Arne Jacobsen's chair in the foreground), while most of the participants of the Experimental group chose a photo about a very old-fashioned office with mountains of paper, old monitors and printers.

There were differences between the pictures of queues: most of the participants of the Control group chose a picture of a man standing in front of a number-dispensing machine. Nobody chose this picture from the Experimental group; they mostly picked the picture showing a long queue.

Since the number of participants in the groups was very low, the differences between the numbers of the chosen pictures are also low. However, even in a small pilot group like this, there are some differences in the attitudes and opinions of the Experimental and the Control group.

The collage-making exercise made a very important feature of the online method apparent: the pictures which were carefully hand-picked beforehand were later easily comparable. Moreover, the time needed for making the collages in this way is very short, whereas in an on-site focus group the participants usually need about half an hour for the same activity.

5   Discussion

The aim of the research, organised in May 2007, was to investigate and assess the usability of the main page of the Hungarian governmental portal magyarorszag.hu and to do a survey about the emotional reactions to the website.

A mixed methodology called triangulation was used for data analysis.

Although the number of the groups (Experimental and Control groups) was relatively low (6 and 7 participants respectively), we can conclude from the results that the visual surface of the main page of the site is complicated, not transparent enough, some of the links are hidden and hard to find. This was confirmed by the Eye tracking research and by the feedbacks from the participants of the online focus group as well.

The eye tracking research also showed that finding some links on the Print Screen of magyarorszag.hu was considerably difficult for the participants. The reasons were the overload of information, the greyish colour of the site, and the way the links are placed on the site.

In addition, the members of the Experimental Group (the participants of which took part in the eye tracking research) were more critical about the magyarorszag.hu site than the members of Control Group.

5.1 The Eye Tracking Research

In the eye tracking research, the participants were asked to find various pieces of information on the Print Screen of the site. They found some of the links very easily (quickly), but in the case of some links they needed 25-30 seconds to find them (see Table 2.)

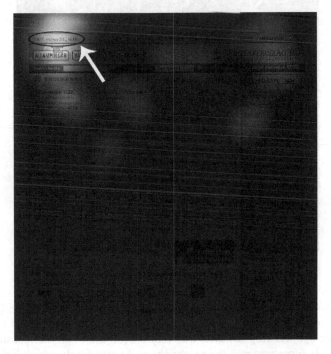

Fig. 2. Attention level map of finding "Date"

The reason for this can be that some of the links are placed on a relatively obvious place, well-known for site-users. For example, the link called "Ügyfélkapu" or the Date was found easily because it is put on a visible, bigger place. The links "Family, home" and "Company search" were placed between the text-links, hidden for the participants, instead of on the usual place, to the right of the header or under the header.

The searching and finding of the information about „Data" and the link "Company search" are shown on the Fig 2-5. As one can see on the Attention-level maps, the whole surface is black, but the participant's eye-movements are shown in white. (The non-black part of a visual surface shows the level of the visual interest.) That is, the links which are easy to find are shown by some clear, bright spots (see Fig 2.), while the links which are difficult to find are shown by bigger, lighter surfaces (see Fig 3.)

The way the participants found these links is shown in the two Figures about Scan-path analysis (see Fig 4-5). The Scanpath analysis pictures show the eye-movements – fixations and saccades – clearly. The fixations are shown with circles of different sizes (the size depends on the time of the fixation), the saccades are shown with lines.

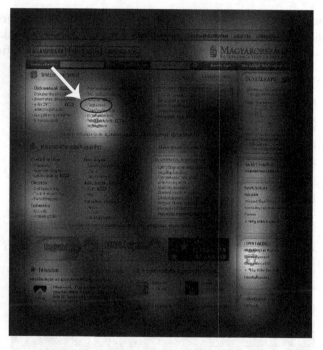

Fig. 3. Attention level map of finding "Company search"

Fig 4 shows how easily the participant found the "Date" link, while Fig 5 shows the difficulty of finding the "Company search" (see the high number of saccades and fixations). The eye tracking research was very useful: although the research was conducted with only 6 participants, the results showed very clearly which links were easy to find, which ones are well placed and which ones are hidden among too much information and in the "wrong" place (not usual on online surfaces).

Fig 4. Scanpath analysis map of the finding "Date"

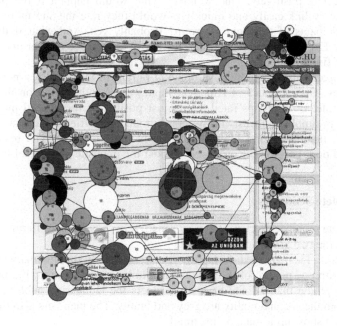

Fig 5. Scanpath analysis map of the finding "Company search"

Generally speaking, it was easy for the participants to find the links that are placed in the same way as it is usual on online surfaces. Based on the eye tracking research we can say the participants get sometimes totally lost and confused while searching for some links on the site.

This result is all the more interesting since the participants are young and well-practiced internet-users. One wonders, then, how the less experienced internet-users manage to find the links they need.

5.2 The Online Focus Group

The most interesting parts of the online focus group were the semantic differential and the incomplete sentences surveys. Both methods showed the attitudes and opinions of the participants very sensitively.

Both the Experimental and the Control groups had basically negative opinion about the site, though the opinion of the Experimental group members was more negative. The reason for the different opinions is probably the negative experience from the eye-tracking research (the members experienced how hard it was is to find some links on the site).

5.3 Semantic Differential

The participants who experienced the difficulty or the easiness of finding the links rated the site less positively. One wonders what would happen if the participants would find every link easily and quickly – would they rate the site more positively than the participants of the Control group? Probably yes. And what if the opinion change of the Experimental group is due to the use of the eye tracker and not to the difficulties of finding the links?

The participants also rated the governmental portals of the countries mentioned before (Germany, United States of America, Japan, and South Korea) on the semantic differential scale. Both groups rated them most positively; they found the sites customer-friendly, simple and trustworthy, non-bureaucratic, friendly, casual, entertaining, cheerful, innovative and liberal, transparent and colourful. The results of the governmental portal of South Korea were almost the opposite of those of the Hungarian portal.

5.4 Incomplete Sentences

The incomplete sentences survey also very sensitively showed the differences of opinions between the two groups.

An interesting idea emerged during the research, namely that the magyarorszag.hu site is some kind of picture of the Hungarian public administration: the participants were of the opinion that the site perfectly reflects the Hungarian public administration, since both the site and reality are grey and heavy. The members also thought that the site doesn't show up-to-date online trends.

I would like to stress that the members of both groups had astonishingly similar opinions about the organisation "behind" the site (the site, obviously, has no employees or officials).

6 Conclusion

The visual surface of the Hungarian governmental portal magyarorszag.hu was examined in 2007 with two different inspection methods: eye-tacking research and online focus group research. The use of these two methods enabled us to understand and to chart the usability of the magyarorszag.hu site as well as the affective impressions associated with the websites on the one hand, and to extract the basic attitudes and the first impressions of the users of the site on the other hand.

The survey showed that the magyarorszag.hu site is poorly usable; the members found it too complicated and grey, dull and difficult to apprehend at a glance and the site is a kind of a reflection of the Hungarian public administration.

If this survey is to be continued it would be worthwhile to ask the participants what they exactly think about the question whether the bad orientation, the information overload, the difficult, non-transparent site and the greyish style reflect the Hungarian public administration. Another possible line of research could raise the question of the obtrusiveness of the eye-tracker as a measurement tool in an online study (that is, actually doing the tasks using a mouse, rather than a print screen) comparing the efficiency and performance of users of the site with and without the eye tracker[1].

An online study using real interaction on the site could yield more sophisticated, realistic and clear results on the same issues.

The survey could also serve as precedent for a bigger, representative survey which could filter out the auto-stereotypes and could help to develop the site into a usable, ergonomic portal.

Acknowledgments

The author would like to thank for István Síklaki for his continuous assistance and suggestions without which this paper would never have been written.

An earlier version of this paper was presented at Párkány, Slovakia, to the students and teachers of the Communication PhD Program of the University of Pécs. The author is grateful for the audience's suggestions and critical remarks.

The eye tracking survey was made at the Laboratory of the Faculty of Arts of the Eötvös Loránd University. The online focus group was made at the virtual studio of Meroving Ltd., with software, called IQON.

The author's participation and presentation at the IFIP I3E 2009 was supported by the NTP TARIPAR3 Project granted by the Hungarian National Office for Research and Technology, via the E-Government Foundation and Research Team.

References

1. Nielsen, J., Mack, R.L.: Usability Inspection Methods. Morgan Kaufmann Publishers Inc., San Francisco (1995)
2. Nielsen, J.: F-Shaped Pattern For Reading Web Content, et al (2006),
   http://www.useit.com/alertbox/reading_pattern.html

---

[1] Thanks to the anonymus rewiever and my professor, Tamás Rudas for this suggestion.

3. Duchowski, A.T.: Eye Tracking Methodology, Theory and practice, pp. 51–52. Springer, London (2007)
4. Waseda University Institute of e-Government, Japan: 2006 World e-Government Ranking by Waseda University Institute of e-Government, Japan, et al (2006), http://www.digitaldivide.net/news/view.php?HeadlineID=955
5. Bodor, P., Illés, A., Síklaki, I.: Eye tracking, Theoretical background, et al (manuscript, 2007)
6. Osgood, C.E., Suci, G.J., Tannenbaum, P.H.: The Measurement of Meaning. Urbana University of Illinois Press (1957)
7. Síklaki, I.: Vélemények mélyén. A fókuszcsoport módszer, a kvalitatív közvélemény-kutatás alapmódszere, pp. 82–101. Kossuth Kiadó, Budapest (2006)

Transforming Collaborative Process Models into Interface Process Models by Applying an MDA Approach

Ivanna M. Lazarte[1], Omar Chiotti[1,2], and Pablo D. Villarreal[1]

[1] CIDISI, Universidad Tecnológica Nacional-FRSF, Lavaise 610, 3000, Santa Fe, Argentina
{pvillarr,ilazarte}@frsf.utn.edu.ar
[2] INGAR-CONICET, Avellaneda 3657, 3000, Santa Fe, Argentina
chiotti@santafe-conicet.gov.ar

Abstract. Collaborative business models among enterprises require defining collaborative business processes. Enterprises implement B2B collaborations to execute these processes. In B2B collaborations the integration and interoperability of processes and systems of the enterprises are required to support the execution of collaborative processes. From a collaborative process model, which describes the global view of the enterprise interactions, each enterprise must define the interface process that represents the role it performs in the collaborative process in order to implement the process in a Business Process Management System. Hence, in this work we propose a method for the automatic generation of the interface process model of each enterprise from a collaborative process model. This method is based on a Model-Driven Architecture to transform collaborative process models into interface process models. By applying this method, interface processes are guaranteed to be interoperable and defined according to a collaborative process.

KeyWords: Business-to-Business, Collaborative Business Process, Interface Business Process, Model-Driven Architecture.

1 Introduction

Enterprises are applying collaborative business models for managing inter-enterprise collaboration with their business partners to improve their performance and competitiveness [1]. Collaborative models can be realized by implementing *Business-to-Business collaborations* that entail a process-oriented integration among heterogeneous and autonomous enterprises. This integration must be achieved at a business level and at a technological level [2].

At the business level, enterprises focus on the design of *collaborative processes* to define and agree on the behavior of the inter-enterprise collaboration. A *collaborative business process* defines the global view of the interactions among enterprises to achieve common business goals [2, 3].

At the technological level, enterprises focus on the integration and interoperability of their B2B systems to execute collaborative processes. This implies the generation of B2B specifications, i.e. interfaces of the partners' systems and business process

C. Godart et al. (Eds.): I3E 2009, IFIP AICT 305, pp. 301–315, 2009.
© IFIP International Federation for Information Processing 2009

specifications required by each enterprise to execute the role performed in a collaborative process and implement it in a *business process management system (BPMS)*.

The design and management of collaborative processes at both levels implies new challenges, mainly the fulfillment of several requirements [2, 3, 4]:

- Autonomy: enterprises behave as autonomous entities, hiding their internal decisions, activities and processes. Information systems, that manage B2B collaborations in each enterprise, have to be independent.
- Decentralized management of collaborative processes jointly managed by the enterprises.
- Peer-to-Peer interactions: the information systems of enterprises interact in a direct way without the mediation of a third party.
- Negotiation: it is required in the management of collaborative processes.
- Alignment between the business solution and the technological solution in order to guarantee that the technological solution provides a full support to the behavior agreed in the collaborative processes.

To fulfill the above issues, we have proposed an MDA-based method for the design, verification, and implementation of collaborative processes [5, 6]. In this method, collaborative processes are modeled with the UP-ColBPIP language [5, 6] from which business process specifications can be generated in technology languages such as BPEL [7] and WS-CDL [2].

B2B collaborations also require the definition of interface and integration processes that each enterprise has to implement to execute collaborative processes. An *interface process* defines the public behavior of the role an enterprise performs in a collaborative process. An *integration process*, which is derived from an interface process, adds the private logic of the enterprise required to support the role it performs in a collaborative process.

The understanding of an interface process by business analysts, at a higher abstraction level, requires the use of process models defined with a high-level modeling language. Furthermore, interface processes must be aligned with the behavior defined in collaborative processes, and hence, they have to be correctly defined in order to guarantee their interoperability and support to the logic of collaborative processes.

To this aim, in this work we propose an MDA-based method for the automatic generation of the interface process model of each enterprise, from a collaborative process model, by applying transformations of business process models. We propose the use of the UP-ColBPIP language (UML Profile for Collaborative Business Processes based on Interaction Protocols) [5, 6] for modeling *collaborative processes* and the use of the BPMN standard language (Business Process Modeling Notation) [8] for modeling *interface processes*.

This paper is organized as follows. Section 2 describes the development process of a B2B collaboration. Section 3 describes the MDA-based method to generate interface process models from a collaborative process model. Section 4 presents an application example of this method. Section 5 discusses related works, and Section 6 presents conclusions and future work.

2   Development of a B2B Collaboration

Two views within the business level and the technological level of a B2B collaboration have to be considered (Figure 1): the *collaboration view*, which refers to the global and public requirements agreed by business partners; and the *partner's view*, which refers to the particular requirements that a partner has to meet to be able to collaborate with other partners.

At the business level, the collaborative view is represented by the collaborative processes that define the inter-enterprise collaboration behavior. A *collaborative business process* defines the message exchange among partners from a global viewpoint [3, 4, 5].

Once partners agree on the *collaboration view*, they define their business requirements in their *partner's view*. The role a partner performs in a collaborative process is depicted in an *interface business process* [4] (also called abstract process [8, 9] or behavioral interface [4]). An interface process defines the public and external visible behavior of a partner in terms of the activities that support the receiving and sending of messages with their partners. This public behavior can be derived from collaborative processes (see section 3). Finally, from interface processes, partners define their *integration business processes* (also called private [8], executable [3, 9] or orchestration processes [4]). An integration process adds the internal business logic required to support the role a partner performs in a collaborative process. The internal business logic includes the activities for producing and processing the exchanged information as well as data transformations and invocations to internal systems.

Although collaborative and interface processes define how partners will coordinate their actions, these processes are not executable. At the technological level, partners have to generate the interfaces of their B2B systems and the executable specifications of integration processes by using a B2B standard process language. Then, these specifications can be interpreted by the partners' BPMSs to execute collaborative processes (see Fig. 1).

To develop B2B collaborations, we have proposed a methodological guide [10] for the modeling and implementation of the above types of business processes as well as a systematic approach to transform conceptual models of collaborative processes into concrete models and specifications of business processes. Our approach involves the following stages:

1. *Analysis and Design of Collaborative Processes* from a business viewpoint to represent the B2B collaboration view.
2. *Derivation of Interface Processes* from collaborative processes in order to define the public view of each partner.
3. *Design of Integration Processes* by incorporating the private logic required to support the message exchange with the other partners in order to define the private view of each partner.
4. *Generation of the Technological Solution* from process models, i.e. the artifacts required to execute collaborative processes: interfaces of the partners' systems and process specifications based on a B2B standard.

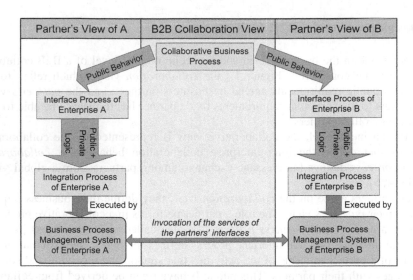

Fig. 1. Business Processes involved in the development of a B2B collaboration

To cope with these issues, we propose the application of the principles of the *model-driven development* (MDD) and the *model-driven architecture* (MDA) [11] to provide a methodological guide for the design and implementation of the business processes required in the development of B2B collaborations. In the MDA, the development process is accomplished through a pattern of transformations that consists of: defining platform-independent models (PIMs), selecting platform-specific models (PSMs) and executing transformations that generate PSMs from PIMs, and finally generating codes by executing transformations of PSMs into Code. A platform refers to the implementation technology. By applying an MDA approach, enterprises can build and transform business process models to generate the code of B2B specifications.

The MDA principles have been exploited in the domain of collaborative processes [6]. An MDA-based approach was proposed to support the conceptual modeling of collaborative processes and the automatic generation of process specifications and partners' system interfaces based on a B2B standard [2, 5, 7]. An MDA-based approach [12] was also proposed to generate formal specifications of collaborative processes and verify if they are well-formed.

In this work we provide a method for the second stage of the development process of B2B Collaborations, which is described below.

3   An MDA-Based Method for Generating Interface Process Models

In this section we propose a method for enabling partners to define an interface process interoperable with the interface processes of their partners and consistent with the global view agreed in a collaborative process.

This method is based on a model-driven architecture to enable the automatic generation of partners' interface process models from collaborative process models. In this method, we propose the use of the UP-ColBPIP language [5, 6] to represent collaborative process models and the BPMN language [8] to represent interface process models.

The UP-ColBPIP language provides suitable abstractions to support the particular features of B2B collaborations and model technology-independent collaborative processes. This language encourages the use of interaction protocols to represent the behavior of collaborative processes. An *interaction protocol* describes a high-level communication pattern through a choreography of business messages between partners.

The modeling of interaction protocols focuses on representing the public global control flow of interactions between partners, as well as on the responsibilities of the roles they fulfill, maintaining the partners' internal logic hidden. This is the main difference with respect to activity-oriented business process languages such as UML2 Activity Diagrams or BPMN [8], which are more suitable to describe interface or private processes from a partner's viewpoint. Although BPMN allows the definition of B2B processes by representing the message exchange among *pools* (partners), it does not provide semantics to define the control flow of the global message exchange.

In addition, coordination and communication aspects of B2B interactions are represented in interaction protocols through the use of speech acts. In an interaction protocol, a business message has an associated speech act, which represents the intention the sender has with respect to the business document exchanged in the message. Thus, the partners' decisions and commitments can be known from the speech acts. This enables the definition of complex negotiations and avoids the ambiguity in the meaning of the business messages of collaborative processes.

BPMN is applied due to the fact that it is a suitable activity-oriented modeling language to represent technology-independent business processes from a partner's viewpoint. BPMN incorporates the concept of interface process through what it calls abstract process, and thus, it allows the representation of the public behavior of the role a partner performs in a collaborative process. Also, BPMN provides suitable concepts to represent the private logic that has to be incorporated into interface processes to define integration processes.

In this way, the proposed MDA-based method focuses on horizontal transformations among business process models defined with these languages (see Fig. 2). The method takes as input a UP-ColBPIP model, containing collaborative processes, represented as interaction protocols. For a selected interaction protocol, a transformation process generates as output BPMN Business Process Diagrams (BPD) corresponding to the partners' interface processes, one BPD for each partner involved in the protocol. In section 4 an example of this transformation process is described.

To carry out the transformation of a UP-ColBPIP interaction protocol into BPMN BPDs, we propose a set of predefined BPMN patterns for each conceptual element of an interaction protocol. Thus, the semantics of each protocol element is represented in terms of the elements and semantics provided by BPMN from one partner's viewpoint.

The model transformation process consists of analyzing each element of a protocol from a partner's viewpoint and generating the corresponding elements in BPMN by applying transformation rules that use predefined BPMN patterns as the output pattern of the rules.

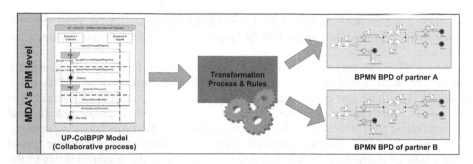

Fig. 2. MDA-based method to transform a collaborative process into interface processes

In Section 3.1 we briefly describe the concepts of the UP-ColBPIP language that are relevant to this work. More details can be found in [2, 5, 6]. In Section 3.2 we describe the MDA-based model transformation process.

3.1 The UP-ColBPIP Modeling Language

A UP-ColBPIP model is expressed by four views: the *B2B Collaboration View*, the *Collaborative Process View*, the *Interaction Protocol View,* and the *Business Interface View*. From the *Interaction Protocol View*, interface process models can be generated. UP-ColBPIP extends the semantics of UML2 Interactions to model interaction protocols in UML2 Sequence Diagrams. The conceptual elements used to define interaction protocols are:

- *Partners* and the *Role* they fulfill are represented through lifelines.
- *Business Message* defines an interaction between two roles. It contains a *business document,* and its semantics is defined by its associated *speech act*, which represents the sender's intention with respect to the exchanged business document. It also indicates that the sender's expectation is that the receptor acts according to the semantics of the speech act.
- *Control Flow Segment (CFS)* represents complex message sequences. It contains a *control flow operator* and one or more interaction paths. An *interaction path* can contain any protocol elements: messages, termination events, protocol references and nested control flow segments. The semantics of a CFS depends on the operator that it used. The *And operator* represents the execution of parallel interaction paths. The *Xor operator* represents that only one path can be executed from a set of alternative paths. A data-based Xor contains conditions on the paths to select the execution path. An event-based Xor is based on the occurrence of the sending and reception events of a message. The *Or operator* represents that two or more alternative paths can be executed in case their condition is evaluated to true. The *If operator* represents a path that is executed when its condition is true. If it is not so, nothing is executed. If it has an else path, it is executed when the condition is false. The *Loop operator* represents that a path can be executed while its condition is satisfied. A loop "Until" with the condition "(1,N)" means that its path must be executed at least once; a loop "While" with the condition "(0,N)" means that its path can be executed zero or N times. The *Exception operator* represents a path to be executed if an exception occurs according

to the path's condition. The *Stop operator* represents a path that manages an exception and requires the abrupt termination of the protocol. The *Cancel operator* represents the path that handles an exception that can occur at any point of the protocol. After executing this path, the protocol ends.

- *Protocol Reference* represents a sub-protocol or nested protocol. When the sub-protocol is called, the protocol waits until the sub-protocol ends.
- *Termination* event represents an explicit end of a protocol. Termination events are: *success*, which implies the successful termination; and *failure*, which implies that the protocol's business logic ends in an unexpected way.
- *Time Constraint* denotes a duration or deadline that can be associated with: messages, control flow segments or protocols. It represents the available time limit for the execution of such element.

Figure 3 shows the sequence diagram of the *Collaborative Demand Forecast* protocol, which describes a collaborative process executed as part of a *Vendor-Managed Inventory* collaborative model. This protocol represents a simple negotiation process between a customer and a supplier to determine a demand forecast. The process begins with the customer, which requests a demand forecast.

The generated request message conveyed the data to be considered in the forecasting (e.g.: products, time-frame). The supplier processes the request and may respond by accepting or rejecting it. If it is accepted, the supplier undertakes to realize the required forecast; otherwise, the process finishes with a failure. If the supplier accepts the request, the customer informs, in parallel, a sales forecast of its points of sales (POS) and its planned sales policies. With this information, the supplier generates a demand forecast and sends it to the customer. Then, the process ends.

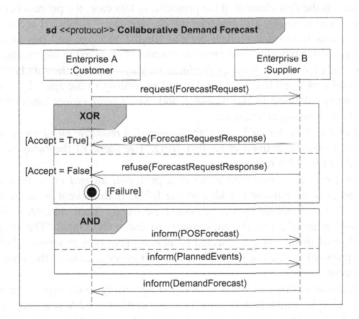

Fig. 3. Collaborative Demand Forecast protocol

3.2   Transformation of a UP-ColBPIP Interaction Protocol into BPMN Business Process Diagrams

The transformation process of a UP-ColBPIP interaction protocol into BPMN Business Process Diagrams (BPDs) of the partners' interface processes consists of:

1. The *lifeline* of each role of the protocol is analyzed and a BPMN BPD is generated, which represents the interface process of the partner that performs such role in the protocol.
2. The BPD is built through the composition of the predefined BPMN patterns by applying the model transformation rules.
3. For each element of a protocol there is a rule that transforms such element into the corresponding BPMN element/s in a BPD.
4. The BPDs of the interface processes and their *embedded sub-processes* begin with a *start event* type *none*, except if the role of the interface process receives the first message (see rule *msgrcv*).
5. An *end event* type *none* models the implicit termination of a protocol.
6. *Reusable* and *reference sub-processes* are modeled in a collapsed form.
7. Embedded sub-processes are modeled in an expanded form. They finish with an *end event* type *none* for each end sequence flow except for an explicit termination (see rule *end*).

Table 1 shows the transformation rules with their BPMN output patterns for each protocol element according to the partner's role in the protocol:

- Rule *msgrcv* (Table 1.a): for each *business message* received by the role being considered in the transformation, an *intermediate event* type *message* is added, except if the message is the first element of the protocol. In this case, the process begins with a *start event* type *message*. *The intermediate or start event* is labeled according to *the speech act* and *business document* defined for the message and has an associated *data object*, which represents the *business document* involved in the message.
- Rule *msgsnd* (Table 1.a): for each *business message* sent by the role being considered, a *send task* is added, which is labeled according to the *speech act* and *business document* defined in the message and has a *data object* associated, which represents such *business document*.
- Rule *ref* (Table 1.b): for each *reference protocol*, a *reusable sub-process* is created to refer to a process defined in another BPD. The name of the *sub-process* is the same as the protocol it refers to.
- Rule *end*: for each *termination event* in a protocol, an *end event* type *terminate* labeled *Success* or *Failure* is added to the BPD. If this event is in an *embedded sub-process*, it is modeled by an *end event* type *signal*. Then, an *intermediate event* type *signal* is attached to the sub-process to catch the signal. The outgoing sequence flow of this *event* is connected to an *end event* type *terminate*. This ensures that the protocol execution ends when the *sub-process* returns the control to the main process.
- Rule *timeconst*: a time constraint is modeled according to the type of protocol element to which it is attached. (1) If it is a *protocol* or a *CFS*, it is mapped into an *embedded sub-process* with an attached *intermediate event* type *timer*. (2) If it is a

message sent by the role or a *reference protocol*, an *intermediate event* type *timer* is attached to the *send task* or *reusable sub-process*, respectively. (3) If it is a *message* received by the role, two mappings are possible. If it is the first received message in a *CFS* with an *Xor* or *If* operator, another *gate* is added to the *exclusive gateway* representing the *CFS*. This *gate* is connected to an *intermediate event* type *timer* indicating the time constraint, unless there is another timer with the same value, in which case the existing one is used. Otherwise, an *event-based exclusive gateway* with two *gates* is defined, one for the *message* and another one with an *intermediate event* type *timer* to represent the time constraint. In all cases, if the protocol has a *CFS Cancel* (Rule *cancel*), which handles time exceptions; the outgoing sequence flow of an *intermediate event* type *timer* is connected to the sub-process that handles the exception. If the protocol does not have a *CFS cancel*, it is connected to an *end event* type *error*.

- Rule *and* (Table 1.c): a *CFS And* is mapped into a *parallel gateway* with a *gate* for each *interaction path*. If two or more *paths* do not have an explicit *termination*, a joining *parallel gateway* is added to synchronize them.
- Rule *xor* (Table 1.d): A *CFS Xor* (either data-based or event-based) is mapped into an *event-based exclusive gateway* if the role receives messages, or it is mapped into a *data-based exclusive gateway* if the role sends the messages in the interaction paths. One *gate* per *interaction path* is added. If two or more *paths* do not have an explicit *termination* event, a *merging exclusive gateway* is added.
- Rule *or* (Table 1.e): a *CFS Or* is mapped into an *inclusive gateway* with a *gate* for each *interaction path*. If two or more *paths* do not have an explicit *termination* event, a joining *inclusive gateway* is added to synchronize them.
- Rule *if*: a *CFS If* is mapped into an *event-based exclusive gateway* if the role receives messages or is mapped into a *data-based exclusive gateway* if the role sends messages. The *gateway* has two *gates*, one for the condition to be satisfied and another one for the *else condition*. The second *gate* is generated if the *else condition* is defined. If it is not, an *intermediate event* type *message* is added if the role receives messages, or a *send task* is added if the role sends messages to indicate that the execution of the protocol should proceed. If two *interaction paths* do not have an explicit *termination* event, the *gates* are joined by a *merging exclusive gateway*.
- Rule *loop*: for each *CFS* with the *Loop* operator, an *embedded sub-process* with a *Loop Marker* is created. The transformation depends on the Loop type. (1) For a "while loop" whose condition is *[(0,n), Var1=True]*, the attribute *LoopCondition* of the embedded sub-process *var1=True* and the attribute *TestTime* with the value *Before* are settled. (2) For a "repeat until loop" whose condition is *[(1, n), Var1=True]*, the attribute *LoopCondition* with the value *not var1* and the attribute *TestTime* with the value *After* are settled.
- Rule *except*: a *CFS Exception* is mapped into an *embedded sub-process* with an attached *intermediate event* type *conditional*. The outgoing sequence flow of this *event* is connected to a *sub-process* that handles the exception. Both *sub-processes* are synchronized by *a merging exclusive gateway* to let the execution continue.

Table 1. Transformation rules of the main elements of an interaction protocol

	Input patterns (UP-ColBPIP)	Output patterns (BPMN)	
		Role A	Role B
a	Enterprise X :Role A — Enterprise Y :Role B SpeechAct(BusinessDocument) **Business Message**	<<send>> SpeechAct BusinessDocument — Business Document Pattern of Rule *msgsnd*	Business Document SpeechAct BusinessDocument Pattern of Rule *msgrcv*
b	Enterprise X :Role A — Enterprise Y :Role B **ref** ProtocolReference **Protocol Reference**	ProtocolReference [+]	SubProcessType: Reusable DiagramRef: BPD Id ProcessRef: Process Name InputMaps: (0-n) Correlations OutputMaps: (0-n) Correlations
c	Enterprise X :Role A — Enterprise Y :Role B SpeechAct(BusinessDocument) **And** SpeechAct(BusinessDocument) SpeechAct(BusinessDocument) **CFS with the *And* operator**		
d	Enterprise X :Role A — Enterprise Y :Role B SpeechAct(BusinessDocument) **Xor** [Var1=True] SpeechAct(BusinessDocument) [Var2=True] SpeechAct(BusinessDocument) **CFS with the *Xor* operator**		
e	Enterprise X :Role A — Enterprise Y :Role B SpeechAct(BusinessDocument) **Or** [Var1=True] SpeechAct(BusinessDocument) [Var2=True] SpeechAct(BusinessDocument) **CFS with the *Or* operator**		

- Rule *stop*: a *CFS Stop* is mapped into an *embedded sub-process* with an attached *intermediate event* type *conditional*. The outgoing sequence flow of this *event* is connected to a *sub-process* that handles the exception. The outgoing sequence flow of this sub-process is connected to an *end event* type *terminate*.
- Rule *cancel*: a *CFS Cancel* is mapped into an *embedded sub-process*. This *sub-process* is triggered by an *intermediate event* type *timer*, if the *interaction path* of the CFS handles a time constraint, or by an *intermediate event* type *conditional* for exceptions related to the protocol logic. The outgoing sequence flow of this *sub-process* is connected to an *end event* type *terminate*.

4 Application of the MDA-Based Method to an Example

The *Collaborative Demand Forecast* interaction protocol described in section 3 is used for exemplifying the model transformation process aforementioned. From this protocol, the supplier's interface process (section 4.1) and the customer's interface process (section 4.2) are generated. These processes are required in order to implement the collaborative process defined by the interaction protocol.

4.1 Generation of the Supplier's Interface Process

The BPMN BPD representing the generated supplier's interface process is shown in Figure 4. In the transformation process all protocol elements are analyzed from a supplier's viewpoint. The first protocol element is the *request(ForecastRequest) business message*, which is received by the supplier. This message is transformed using the rule *msgrcv*, which consists of creating a *start event* type *message*. This event is labeled *Request ForecastRequest* and is associated with the *ForecastRequest data object*, which represents the *business document* interchanged between enterprises.

Then, the *CFS* with the *Xor* operator is transformed by applying the rule *xor*. This rule adds a *data-based exclusive gateway* with two *gates*, one for each *interaction path*. Then, each *path* is analyzed to determine the pattern to be used in the transformation. The first element of the first path is the *agree(ForecastRequestResponse) business message*, which is sent to the customer. The message is transformed by the rule *msgsnd* that generates a *send task*. This *task* is labeled *Agree ForecastRequestResponse* and is associated with the *ForecastRequestResponse data object*, which represents the exchanged *business document*. There are no further elements in this path so the other path is analyzed. The first element of the second path is the *refuse(ForecastRequestResponse) business message*. This *message* is transformed by the rule *msgsnd* that generates a *send task*. The next element is a *termination* event, which is transformed by the rule *end*. Because one path has an explicit *termination*, the two gates are not synchronized and the transformation continues along the path which does not have the explicit termination.

The next protocol element is the *CFS* with the *And* operator that is transformed by the rule *and*. This rule adds a *parallel gateway* with two *gates*, one for each *interaction path*. The first *path* is analyzed and its single element is the *inform(POSForecast) business message*, which is received by the supplier. This message is transformed by applying the

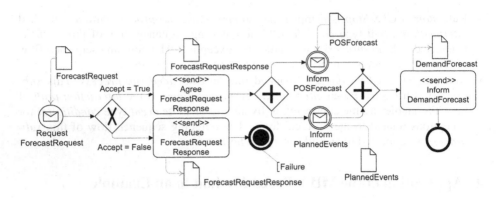

Fig. 4. BPMN Business Process Diagram of the Supplier's interface process

rule *msgrcv*. The second path has one element that is the *inform(PlannedEvents)business message*. This message is also transformed using the rule *msgrcv*. Both path are synchronized by another *parallel gateway* (see rule and) because neither of them has an explicit termination.

After the CFS, the inform(DemandForecast) business message is sent by the supplier to inform the generated demand forecast. This message is transformed by applying the rule msgsnd. Then, the protocol ends with an implicit termination, which is modeled with an end event type none.

4.2   Generation of the Customer's Interface Process

The generation of the BPD representing the customer's interface process is carried out in a similar way to the generation of the BDP of the supplier's interface process. The generated BPD of the customer's interface process is shown in Figure 5.

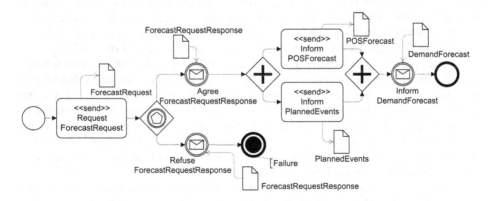

Fig. 5. BPMN Business Process Diagram of the Customer's interface process

5 Related Work

There are several approaches that exploit the benefits of model-driven architectures for B2B processes [13]. A method for modeling cross-organizational processes based on the MDA was proposed [3], which supports the mapping of ARIS models of cross-organizational value chains into BPDM models of abstract (interface) processes. These processes are defined in UML2 activity diagrams. However, the proposed architecture uses a centralized broker to implement and govern B2B interactions. It is different from our approach that encourages the decentralized management of collaborative processes.

Another MDA-based method was proposed to generate BPEL abstract (interface) processes from UP-ColBPIP interaction protocols [7]. Although this method allows generating BPEL specifications, the addition of private logic to BPEL processes has to be done at a technological level. Instead, in this work we provide an approach to elevate the abstraction level of interface processes so that business analysts can use them to generate integration processes. Then, BPEL specifications can be generated from these models.

Also, an approach was proposed to derive local choreographies (interface processes) from UMM global choreographies to register them in a global repository [14]. A UML Profile is proposed to represent local choreographies. It is not based on a model-driven approach. In addition, in this work we use the BPMN standard language so that enterprises can understand and define interface processes, instead of using a particular language.

Another approach is for checking consistency of predefined interface processes [15]. It is a useful method for bottom-up approaches to determine if these processes are interoperable for building a B2B scenario. Instead, our method promotes a top-down approach. Enterprises agree on an interaction global view and the behavioral constraints of each participant are guaranteed by deriving interface processes from a global interaction model.

6 Conclusions and Future Work

In this work we have proposed an MDA-based method for the automatic generation of the interface process model of each enterprise from a collaborative process model. This method enables enterprises to generate interoperable interface processes and in compliance with the global logic of B2B interactions agreed on collaborative processes. This is guaranteed since the partners' interface process models are derived from a collaborative process model by applying a top-down MDA-based approach.

The language UP-ColBPIP is used to define the B2B collaboration view among the partners. It encourages the modeling of interaction protocols to represent the behavior of technology-independent collaborative processes. The use of interaction protocols supports the main features of B2B collaborations: global view of the B2B interactions, enterprise autonomy, decentralized management, peer-to-peer interactions and negotiations.

In addition, this method increases the abstraction level in the design of the partners' view of a B2B collaboration. The BPMN standard language is used to define activity-oriented interface process models. This enables enterprises to understand and focus on the business requirements to fulfill the role they perform in collaborative processes.

Also, it is pretended to integrate this method to the previously proposed MDA-based method for collaborative processes [5, 6, 10], in order to provide a complete methodology that supports the modeling, verification and specification of the business processes required in B2B collaborations.

Finally, the proposed MDA-based transformation process shows that a direct mapping can be applied to derive BPMN Business Process Diagrams of interface processes from an interaction protocol. No intervention is required by a modeler. For each element of the UP-ColBPIP language used to describe interaction protocols, a BPMN pattern is proposed to represent its behavior from the viewpoint of the role a partner performs in the protocol.

Future work will define the transformation rules in ATL languages and implement these process model transformations in an Eclipse-based tool developed for the modeling and verification of collaborative processes [12]. Another work is about the definition of integration processes from interface processes by adding private activity patterns to process or generate the information exchanged between the partners.

References

1. Villarreal, P., Caliusco, M., Zucchini, D., Arredondo, F., Zanel, C., Galli, M.R., Chiotti, O.: Integrated Production Planning and Control in a Collaborative Partner-to-Partner Relationship. In: Sharma, S., Gupta, J. (eds.) Managing E-Business in the 21st Century, pp. 91–110. Heidelberg Press, Australia (2003)
2. Villarreal, P.D., Salomone, E., Chiotti, O.: Transforming Collaborative Business Process Models into Web Services Choreography Specifications. In: Lee, J., Shim, J., Lee, S., Bussler, C., Shim, S. (eds.) DEECS 2006. LNCS, vol. 4055, pp. 50–65. Springer, Heidelberg (2006)
3. Bauer, B., Roser, S., Müller, J.: Adaptive Design of Cross-organizational Business Processes using a Model-driven Architecture. In: Wirtschaftsinformatik 2005, pp. 103–121. Physica-Verlag press (2005)
4. Weske, M.: Business Process Management. Concepts, Languages, Architectures. Springer, Heidelberg (2007)
5. Villarreal, P., Salomone, E., Chiotti, O.: Modeling and Specifications of Collaborative Business Processes using a MDA Approach and a UML Profile. In: Rittgen, P. (ed.) Enterprise Modeling and Computing with UML, pp. 13–45. Idea Group Inc., USA (2007)
6. Villarreal, P.: Method for the Modeling and Specification of Collaborative Business Processes, Ph.D. dissertation. Ceride Press, Santa Fe, Argentina (2005)
7. Villarreal, P., Salomone, E., Chiotti, O.: MDA Approach for Collaborative Business Processes: Generating Technological Solutions based on Web Services Composition. In: 9th Ibero-American Workshop IDEAS, Argentina (2006)
8. OMG. BPMN V1.1 (January 2008), http://www.omg.org/spec/BPMN/1.1/PDF
9. OASIS, Web Services Business Process Execution Language (May 2007), http://www.oasis-open.org/committees/download.php/23964/wsbpel-v2.0-primer.htm

10. Villarreal, P., Roa, J., Chiotti, O., Salomone, E.: Aligning the Business Solution with the Technological Solution in the Development of B2B Collaborations. In: CollECTeR Iberoamérica 2007, Argentina (2007)
11. OMG. MDA Guide V1.0.1 (2003), http://www.omg.org/mda
12. Roa, J., Castañeda, V., Villarreal, P., Chiotti, O.: A Tool for Model-Driven Development of Collaborative Business Processes. In: XXXIV Latin-American Conference on Informatics (CLEI 2008), Santa Fe, Argentina (2008)
13. Folmer, E., Bastiaans, J.: Methods for Design of Semantic Message-Based B2B Interactions Standards. In: Mertins, K., Ruggaber, R., Popplewell, K., Xu, X. (eds.) Enterprise Interoperability III, pp. 183–194. Springer, London (2008)
14. Hofreiter, B.: Registering UML Models for Global and Local Choreographies. In: 10th International Conference on Electronic Commerce. ACM, vol. 342, Art. No. 37, ACM Press, New York (2008)
15. Decker, G., Weske, M.: Behavioral Consistency for B2B Process Integration. In: Krogstie, J., Opdahl, A., Sindre, G. (eds.) CAiSE 2007 and WES 2007. LNCS, vol. 4495, pp. 81–95. Springer, Heidelberg (2007)

The Persuasiveness of Web-Based Alcohol Interventions

Tuomas Lehto and Harri Oinas-Kukkonen

University of Oulu, Department of Information Processing Science
Rakentajantie 3, FIN-90570 Oulu, Finland
{Tuomas.Lehto,Harri.Oinas-Kukkonen}@oulu.fi

Abstract. There are a variety of Web-based alcohol interventions that may reach problem drinkers, who would not otherwise participate in conventional treatment. Web-based alcohol interventions vary greatly in level of finesse: some offer static self-help materials, whereas some sites have highly interactive content and persuasive features embedded. In this study, six Web-based alcohol interventions were evaluated based on a framework for evaluating and designing persuasive systems. This study demonstrates the potential lack of persuasive features on Web-based alcohol interventions sites. Important primary task support elements, such as tailoring and personalization, were used tenuously throughout the sites. The dialogue support demonstrated throughout the sites was average. All evaluated sites successfully demonstrated trustworthiness, expertise, and surface credibility. Many of the evaluated sites were lacking in the social support category. In general, the authors suggest that the persuasive system qualities should be considered concurrently with the feasibility and effectiveness for studying technology-based interventions.

Keywords: Web-based, alcohol, intervention, persuasive technology, PSD model.

1 Introduction

Harm caused by excess alcohol consumption is a major public health concern throughout the developed world [15]. Alcohol is causally related to more than 60 different medical conditions, and 4% of the global burden of disease is estimated to be attributable to alcohol [26]. Heavy and binge drinking is associated with a variety of physical and mental health problems [15].

There are different types of behavioral and pharmacological interventions available for treating alcohol dependence [26]. The terms addiction and dependence are being used interchangeably, and it is unlikely that there is going to be a consensus on the definition of and distinction between these terms [30]. Despite the existence and availability of preventive measures both at the individual and population levels, alcohol problems present a major challenge to medicine and public health [26].

Technology-based interventions related to, for example, nutrition [19], physical exercise [10], [17], smoking [3], [27], alcohol consumption [2], [6], [14], stress management [31], and depression [4], [5] may delay or prevent the onset of a variety of medical problems, and improve the quality of life [11]. A primary goal of self-care interventions is the encouragement of an individual's behavior change, which requires knowledge sharing, education, and understanding of the condition [29].

C. Godart et al. (Eds.): I3E 2009, IFIP AICT 305, pp. 316–327, 2009.

Computer-tailored health interventions vary in terms of level of sophistication. At one end of the scale are computer-assisted risk or health assessments. These are usually brief interventions, providing personalized feedback to the user immediately online or emailed at a later time. At the other end of the scale are longer-term, more complex computer-tailored health programs, which have the potential for covering multiple or difficult-to-influence behaviors. [16]

Relatively few studies have discussed persuasive functionalities in practice. The goal of this study is to contribute to this discussion. Furthermore, the rationale for this study is our concern that the majority of digital interventions may have been developed without a proper insight into what constitutes a successful persuasive system.

The predominant challenge in designing and evaluating technology-enabled interventions, for a variety of health and behavior related issues, is how best to merge theories and approaches from psychology, healthcare, education, software design, and other relevant disciplines [8].

In this study, six Web-based alcohol interventions were evaluated and their persuasiveness was studied utilizing a framework for evaluating and designing persuasive systems. On a more detailed level, we explored how the selected sites used/adhered to the persuasive systems principles and techniques defined in the PSD model [22].

2 Background

There is a growing body of research on the use of the Internet, and the Web, as a means of delivering treatment. Internet interventions are typically focused on behavioral issues, with the goal of instituting behavior change and subsequent symptom improvement. They are usually self-paced, tailored to the user, interactive, and make use of the multimedia. Individuals who use this kind of intervention may overcome many of the obstacles to obtaining traditional care because they can seek such treatments at any time, any place, and often at significantly reduced cost. [25]

In their qualitative review, Copeland and Martin [6] concluded that brief interventions have been the most commonly reported, probably because there is little complexity involved in developing a minimal screener/feedback program in comparison to a fully automated therapy. They also pointed out that the complexity, quality and content of these interventions vary vastly.

There are several important decisions to be made when providing interventions for a variety of alcohol-related problems. For instance, the type, setting, and intensity of the intervention must be tailored to individuals' needs. For some heavy drinkers (without evidence of severe alcohol dependence), an intervention aimed at the reduction of drinking to moderate levels of consumption may suffice. By contrast, the goals of treatment for chronically alcohol-dependent people and high-level drinkers typically include complete abstinence from alcohol, and promotion of long-term recovery. [26]

According to Koski-Jännes et al. [13], there are three groups of problematic drinkers: 1) hazardous or risk drinkers who consume alcohol above recommended limits without any noticeable harm yet, 2) harmful drinkers who have experienced some physical, social or psychological harm without meeting the criteria of dependence, and 3) alcohol abusing or dependent drinkers who meet these criteria and sustain consuming alcohol regardless of substantial negative consequences. Internet-based self-assessments are meant to serve all of these groups, but they are effective mainly in reducing alcohol consumption among hazardous and harmful drinkers. Alcohol-dependent drinkers require a different approach regarding support and treatment. Internet-based self-assessments appear to increase interest in various forms of self-help, especially in Internet-based interactive services for heavy drinkers [12]. There are many advantages in these services: high accessibility, affordability, and discretion. Discretion is a very important factor for individuals wanting to avoid being labeled as problem drinkers or alcoholics. [13]

In their recent systematic review, Bewick et al. [1] found inconsistent evidence on the effectiveness of electronic screening and brief intervention for alcohol use. However, their notion is that Web-based interventions are generally well received. Riper et al. [24] report that the few available evaluation studies of Web-based interventions for problem drinking, most of which involved student populations, have reported promising results.

Digital and fully automated health behavior interventions have the potential of high reach and low cost. A recent meta-analysis of 75 randomized controlled trials provided support for their effectiveness in changing knowledge, attitudes, and behavior in the health promotion area [23]. The benefits of persuasive interventions are crucially dependent on the quality and relevance of the technology and inference algorithms. However, user studies that look at the long-term effectiveness of persuasive technology hardly exist. [11]

3   Evaluating Persuasive Systems

Research on persuasive technology has been introduced relatively recently [9]. Persuasive systems may be defined as computerized software or information systems designed to reinforce, change or shape attitudes or behaviors or both without using coercion or deception [21]. Persuasive technologies can be used in different domains, for example in education, safety and healthcare [9]. Information technology always influences people's attitudes and behavior in one way or another thus all information technology is a persuasive system to some degree [22].

Oinas-Kukkonen and Harjumaa [20], [22] have conceptualized a framework for designing and evaluating persuasive systems, known as the Persuasive Systems Design (PSD) model. The PSD presents a way to analyze and evaluate the persuasion context and related techniques. Persuasion context analysis includes recognizing the intent (persuader, change type) and the event (use context, user context, and technology context) for persuasion, and recognizing the strategies (message, route) in use. In the PSD model, the categories for persuasive system principles are: primary task support (supporting the user's primary task), dialogue support (supporting the interaction between the user and the system), system credibility (the more credible the system is, the more persuasive it is), and social support (the system motivates users by leveraging social influence).

Primary task support. This category addresses the target behaviors. For this category, seven principles are employed: reduction, tunneling, tailoring, personalization, self-monitoring, simulation, and rehearsal.

Dialogue support. This category deals with the feedback that the system offers in guiding the user to reach the intended behavior. Seven design principles are employed for providing dialogue support: praise, rewards, reminders, suggestion, similarity, liking, and social role.

System credibility support. Credibility (or ethos) is a persuasive element. The PSD model describes seven design principles for supporting system credibility: trustworthiness, expertise, surface credibility, real world feel, authority, third party endorsements, and verifiability.

Social support. This category describes how to design the system so that it motivates users by leveraging social influence. The model operates with seven design principles for providing social support: social learning, social comparison, normative influence, social facilitation, cooperation, compensation, and recognition.

In this study, the PSD framework will be applied for identifying the persuasive techniques that have been incorporated into the Web-based alcohol interventions.

4 Research Setting

Web-based alcohol intervention sites were extensively searched (during November 2008– January 2009) from the Internet using public search engines (e.g., Google, Yahoo!), using the following search terms: alcohol(ism), help, stop, quit, recovery, drink(ing), consumption, abstinence, intervention, addiction, dependence, Web, internet, self-help. The search method is by no means exhaustive. For instance, the search phrase "alcoholism recovery" yields tens of thousands of hits on Google alone. In our view, going through all the possible combinations and variations of the search terms is nearly impossible and redundant. We did not limit ourselves to operate solely based on search engines, but also searched relevant literature to find the intervention sites that fell within the scope of this study. The literature was fetched from databases, such as EBSCOhost, Google Scholar, ISI Web of Knowledge, PubMed, and Scopus.

The inclusion criteria for a Web-based intervention portal were:

— it targets reduction of alcohol consumption or supports abstinence from alcohol,
— it is open-access, free of charge (may require registration), ready-to-use,
— it offers interactive functionality, and
— it is in English, Finnish, or Swedish.

An iterative search process (see Figure 1) yielded six Web-based alcohol intervention sites for further evaluation. Four of the intervention portals were in English, one was in Finnish, and one in Swedish. The three languages were chosen based on the authors' language skills.

Alcohol Help Center 2.0 (http://www.alcoholhelpcenter.net, later A1) is intended for individuals who are concerned about their problem drinking and who might want to cut down or quit drinking. The website is produced by Evolution Health (V-CC Systems), which is a privately held corporation.

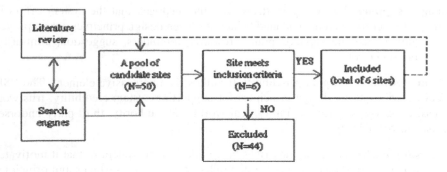

Fig. 1. The search process of the study

Control Your Drinking Online (http://www.acar.net.au/online.asp, A2) is a Web-based self-change program. The website is intended to assist and promote self-change amongst people who drink a lot and wish to reduce their alcohol intake. The Website is produced by the Australian Centre for Addiction Research (ACAR).

Down Your Drink (http://www.downyourdrink.org.uk, A3) has been designed to give people the information they need to make choices about the role alcohol plays in their life. The content of the website has been written by Stuart Linke and Jim McCambridge and produced by Net Impact. The charity Alcohol Concern manages the website.

Sober24 (http://www.sober24.com, A4) is a website for individuals who are recovering from alcohol or drug addiction. The site is also intended for an addicted person's loved ones.

Alkoholhjälpen (http://www.alkoholhjalpen.se, A5) is a website funded by the Swedish National Institute of Public Health. The self-help site divides into two parts; one part is intended for people who are worried about their drinking habits, the other part is for people who are worried about somebody else's drinking (e.g., a friend, a relative, a parent).

Jeppe Juomapäiväkirja (http://www.paihdelinkki.fi/jeppe/index.php, A6) is a Finnish website for people who are willing to reduce or quit drinking. The organization behind the service is the A-Clinic Foundation. The A-Clinic Foundation operates to reduce alcohol, drug and other addiction problems. A6 is a Finnish version of the Dutch MinderDrinken.

The portals were evaluated based on the principles for persuasive system content and functionality presented in the PSD model. The model does not suggest that all systems should always implement all of the features described in it. However, due to the nature of this study, and as the quality of the implemented features varied tremendously, we found it appropriate to use a scoring system. The goal was not to compare the sites against each other since they vary greatly in terms of complexity, content and quality. The aim is to demonstrate this diversity, and pinpoint the possible mutual and individual highlights/shortcomings in persuasive system features on the intervention sites under inspection.

5 Results

5.1 Persuasion Context

5.1.1 The Intent
Persuader
The persuaders behind the interventions appear to be different kinds of organizations. Five of the six sites clearly state the background organization. The persuader behind one of the sites (A4) remains unclear.

Change Type
All of the evaluated sites ultimately aim at individuals' reduced alcohol consumption and/or quitting drinking. Self-help, personal goal-setting, and motivation play an important role in the change process in all of these sites.

The majority of the sites do not explicitly state whether they target change in individuals' behavior or attitude. However, it is relatively safe to assume that the sites favor behavior change over attitude change. In our view, the persuasiveness of the evaluated sites lacks in fostering individuals' long-term behavior change, let alone true attitudinal change, which may be the most difficult to achieve [22].

5.1.2 The Event
Use Context
The use context is described on a very general level on all of the evaluated sites. The intended user groups are hard to identify from such statements as: "Are you concerned about problem drinking? Do you think you might need to cut down or are you thinking about quitting?" (A1), or "If you are someone who wants to think seriously about your level of alcohol consumption – then this website may be for you" (A3). It would appear that the sites fail to recognize different user groups with varying needs, leading to a questionable one-fits-all approach. Tørning and Oinas-Kukkonen [28] argue that systems are often designed to persuade an individual at a system-to-user level to resolve a user-in-society issue.

It seems that Web-based alcohol interventions a) without predefined user groups and b) with minimal tailoring for the groups, cannot offer much more than educational content with minimal effect on users' behavior. For example, differences in gender and culture might also play a role in persuasion [28].

User Context
What is specific to the users of the evaluated Web-based alcohol intervention sites is that they are heavy drinkers or people who are concerned about their drinking. There are possible limitations, e.g. pregnant women and people under 18 should not participate in the interventions. In addition, the interventions are not meant to replace the advice of a physician or other health care provider.

Technology Context
All of the evaluated interventions are Web-based. Most of them work with a basic Web browser, with no additional plug-ins or installations required. Furthermore, the content presented is relatively small in size (except in A5), so that users with lower

bandwidth Internet connections (and/or older computers) can use the sites without great difficulties. Seemingly, the technology context is similar in all of the interventions. Yet, a more detailed inspection reveals differences between the sites.

Alkoholhjälpen (A5) takes advantage of Adobe Flash software. In fact, the majority of the site content is delivered in Flash. This may increase the loading times substantially, thus making the site less usable for users with slower connections. However, some users may favor professionally designed Flash content over traditional HTML-based presentations. There is also some Flash content on Down Your Drink (A3) site. Control Your Drinking Online offers an interesting approach. The self-help material ("Treatment modules") is delivered to the user in printable PDF (Portable Document Format) files. This approach eliminates important persuasive features such as interactivity and tailoring, but still might suit some users. None of the sites seem to be designed for mobile use. Alcohol Help Center has an SMS (text messaging) service providing tips.

5.1.3 The Strategy
The strategy harnessed for persuading the users is very hard to determine from the studied web-based alcohol interventions. Some of the sites state clearly the underpinning methods or procedures, e.g. "The exercises and the information are taken from evidence-based methods such as cognitive behavioral therapy, motivational interviewing and relapse prevention" (A5, translation by the authors).

Message
Presumably, the wider the content the more embedded messages and arguments are likely to be presented to the user. Some of the sites offer a very broad content (A3, A5) whereas others rely on more compact presentation. It has to be noted that the total number of embedded arguments may not necessarily be relevant, compared to the manner in which they are presented.

Route
The embedded arguments seem to try to appeal to users' emotions and logic in all of the sites. All of the sites appear to target the individuals' behavior change through a set of arguments, instead of using one convincingly strong argument only (direct vs. indirect persuasion).

5.2 Persuasion Techniques

5.2.1 Primary Task Support
The sites varied greatly in persuasive system characteristics. Three of the sites (A2, A4 and A6) received a relatively low total score on the primary task support category. Reduction and tunneling were applied in five out of six sites. Surprisingly, tailoring (i.e. different content for different user groups) was applied only in one of the six sites. Furthermore, only low-level personalization was used in all of the sites. All of the sites received low scores on simulation and rehearsal, whereas they all showed self-monitoring (e.g. a drinking diary) functionality. Only one (A5) of the evaluated sites utilized all principles from the primary task support dimension.

Table 1. Primary task support scores

Primary task	A1	A2	A3	A4	A5	A6
Reduction	+	-	+++	++	+++	+
Tunneling	++	+	+++	-	+++	(+)
Tailoring	-	-	-	-	+	-
Personalization	(+)	+	(+)	+	++	(+)
Self-monitoring	+++	(+)	++	++	+++	++
Simulation	-	(+)	+	-	++	-
Rehearsal	+	(+)	++	-	+	(+)

Regardless of the different approaches in each site, it is alarming that many of the users' primary task support did not seem to be utilized fully. The lack of tailoring (and personalization) is a severe shortcoming on a health behavior change website. The interventions that direct participants to relevant, individually tailored materials appear to have longer Web site session times per visit and more visits per person [29].

5.2.2 Dialogue Support

Web-based systems can give immediate feedback, which makes it more likely that the information is matched to the respondent's level of awareness, beliefs and motivations at that particular time. Web-delivered tailored feedback resembles interpersonal counseling, which may enhance the effect of the intervention. [18]

There was variance on the feedback the sites offered in guiding the user to reach the intended behavior. The majority of the interventions demonstrated praise (e.g. user is presented with a positive message upon completing a specific task). However, the praise was usually presented very meagerly. None of the sites offered virtual rewards, such as pictures, sounds, or special content. Half of the intervention sites used reminders (e.g. daily or weekly e-mails). Every site presented suggestions to the user. Since the sites were not directed to a certain demographic, all of them used general language in presenting the information.

Table 2. Dialogue support scores

Dialogue	A1	A2	A3	A4	A5	A6
Praise	(+)	(+)	-	+	++	-
Rewards	(+)	(+)	-	-	-	-
Reminders	+++	-	++	++	-	(+)
Suggestion	+	(+)	+	+	++	+
Similarity	+	+	+	+	+	+
Liking	+	+	++	+	++(+)	+
Social role	+++	-	+	-	++	+

A system that is visually attractive is likely to be more persuasive. All of the sites scored on the liking principle. Most of the systems adopted a social role (e.g. to facilitate communication between users and health specialists). Overall, the dialogue support demonstrated throughout the sites was average.

5.2.3 Credibility Support

All evaluated sites successfully demonstrated trustworthiness (e.g. the presented information is truthful, fair and unbiased) and expertise. In addition, they showed surface credibility (6/6 sites) and low-level real-world feel (5/6 sites).

Table 3. Credibility support scores

Credibility	A1	A2	A3	A4	A5	A6
Trustworthiness	++	++	++	+	++	++
Expertise	++	++	++	+	++	+
Surface credibility	++	+	++	+	++	++
Real-world feel	+	+	+	-	+	+
Authority	-	+	-	-	+++	+
3rd party endorsements	-	-	+	+	-	-
Verifiability	++	-	++	+	+	+

Half of the sites referred to an authority, and two presented third party endorsements. Verifiability was quite low on the majority of the interventions. As a conclusion, none of the six sites had any remarkable problems with credibility issues.

5.2.4 Social Support

The greatest differences between the six Web-based alcohol intervention sites were observed in the social support category. Half of the sites (A1, A4, A5) offered a variety of social support functionality, whereas the other half lacked social support completely. The most versatile sites in terms of social support were A4 and A5, which took advantage of 6 out of 7 principles from the social support category.

Table 4. Social support scores

Social support	A1	A2	A3	A4	A5	A6
Social learning	++	-	-	+++	++	-
Social comparison	+++	-	-	+++	++	-
Normative influence	++	(+)	(+)	+++	++	(+)
Social facilitation	++	-	-	+++	++	-
Cooperation	++	-	-	+++	++	-
Competition	-	-	-	-	-	-
Recognition	-	-	-	+	(+)	-

We agree with Cunningham et al. [7] who state that expert-moderated online social support groups with member-generated content may have the potential to motivate individuals toward seeking treatment.

6 Conclusions and Discussion

This paper provided a qualitative evaluation of the persuasiveness of six Web-based alcohol interventions. The selected sites represent the current state-of-the-art of Web-based alcohol interventions. The results of this study suggest that there is room for improvement in both designing and implementing Web-based interventions for alcohol problems. The evaluation showed that the evaluated Web-based alcohol interventions may not be very persuasive. However, all evaluated sites successfully demonstrated trustworthiness, expertise, and surface credibility.

Primary task support principles were utilized relatively poorly in many of the sites. Interestingly, and perhaps rather worryingly, tailoring was applied in only one of the sites. This finding implies that the interventions may be targeted to too broad an audience. It is reasonable to assume that there should be different approaches for different user groups. In other words, if the user feels the (intervention) content is not designed for her/his needs, there is a high possibility that the user will discontinue using the program.

There were also notable differences between the evaluated intervention sites. For example, some sites placed more emphasis on online social support than others. Many of the sites did not offer any online social support. In our view, providing (expert-moderated) support groups as a part of a technology-based intervention is a very important aspect of such interventions. There are various techniques (e.g. instant messaging, chat rooms, discussion forums, social networking) readily available to facilitate communication between peers. In anonymous online support groups, the participants may overcome the feeling of being stigmatized, and time and location are no longer obstacles for participation. We suggest that Web-based interventions and support groups should not be considered as substitutes, rather as supplements to traditional forms of treatment and peer support.

As a conclusion, the evaluated Web-based alcohol interventions applied the persuasion principles described in the PSD model on a moderate level.

There are some limitations to this study. First, the language of the evaluated sites selected for this study was limited to English, Finnish, and Swedish. Second, no outside evaluators were used, thus the evaluations were at least partially based on the authors' subjective views. Third, the evaluation of persuasiveness of software and information systems may be problematic even with a proper method. The results should be regarded as indicatory for future studies. Finally, the evaluation of the quality of actual information presented in the sites is critical but beyond the scope of this paper.

As technology-enabled self-help interventions for manifold needs and diverse population continue to emerge, there is an apparent need for an understanding of how the persuasiveness of the systems affects users' intended behavior. Effective face-to-face counseling interventions may not be directly translated into the Web environment. Designing persuasive systems requires an interdisciplinary team of professionals with a thorough understanding of the problem domain and the underpinning theories.

Much emphasis has been put on measuring and proving the effectiveness of various digital interventions. However, future research should not limit its focus on validating interventions through randomized controlled trials only. We suggest that the persuasiveness of the system should be considered concurrently with the feasibility and effectiveness of technology-based interventions.

References

1. Bewick, B.M., Trusler, K., Barkham, M., et al.: The Effectiveness of Web-Based Interventions Designed to Decrease Alcohol consumption—A Systematic Review. Preventive Medicine 47, 17–26 (2008)
2. Bewick, B.M., Trusler, K., Mulhern, B., et al.: The Feasibility and Effectiveness of a Web-Based Personalised Feedback and Social Norms Alcohol Intervention in UK University Students: A Randomised Control Trial. Addictive Behaviors 33, 1192–1198 (2008)
3. Brendryen, H., Kraft, P.: Happy Ending: A Randomized Controlled Trial of a Digital Multi-Media Smoking Cessation Intervention. Addiction 103, 478–484 (2008)
4. Christensen, H., Griffiths, K.M., Jorm, A.F.: Delivering Interventions for Depression by using the Internet: Randomised Controlled Trial. British Medical Journal 328, 265 (2004)
5. Clarke, G., Eubanks, D., Reid, C.K., et al.: Overcoming Depression on the Internet (ODIN)(2): A Randomized Trial of a Self-Help Depression Skills Program with Reminders. Journal of Medical Internet Research 7, e16 (2005)
6. Copeland, J., Martin, G.: Web-Based Interventions for Substance use Disorders—A Qualitative Review. Journal of Substance Abuse Treatment 26, 109–116 (2004)
7. Cunningham, J.A., van Mierlo, T., Fournier, R.: An Online Support Group for Problem Drinkers: AlcoholHelpCenter. Net. Patient Education and Counseling 70, 193–198 (2008)
8. Duffett-Leger, L., Lumsden, J.: Interactive Online Health Promotion Interventions: A "health Check". In: IEEE International Symposium on Technology and Society (ISTAS 2008), Fredericton, New Brunswick, June 26-28, pp. 1–8 (2008)
9. Fogg, B.: Persuasive technology: Using computers to change what we think and do. Morgan Kaufmann, San Francisco (2002)
10. Hurling, R., Fairley, B.W., Dias, M.B.: Internet-Based Exercise Intervention Systems: Are More Interactive Designs Better? Psychology & Health 21, 757–772 (2006)
11. IJsselsteijn, W.A., de Kort, Y.A.W., Midden, C., Eggen, B., van den Hoven, E.: Persuasive Technology for Human Well-being: Setting the Scene. In: IJsselsteijn, W., de Kort, Y., Midden, C., Eggen, B., van den Hoven, E. (eds.) PERSUASIVE 2006. LNCS, vol. 3962, pp. 1–5. Springer, Heidelberg (2006)
12. Koski-Jännes, A., Cunningham, J.: Interest in Different Forms of Self-Help in a General Population Sample of Drinkers. Addictive Behaviors 26, 91–99 (2001)
13. Koski-Jännes, A., Cunningham, J.A., Tolonen, K., et al.: Internet-Based Self-Assessment of drinking—3-Month Follow-Up Data. Addictive Behaviors 32, 533–542 (2007)
14. Linke, S., McCambridge, J., Khadjesari, Z., et al.: Development of a Psychologically Enhanced Interactive Online Intervention for Hazardous Drinking. Alcohol and Alcoholism 43, 669–674 (2008)
15. Linke, S., Murray, E., Butler, C., et al.: Internet-Based Interactive Health Intervention for the Promotion of Sensible Drinking: Patterns of use and Potential Impact on Members of the General Public. Journal of Medical Internet Research 9, e10 (2007)
16. Lustria, M.L.A., Cortese, J., Noar, S.M., et al.: Computer-Tailored Health Interventions Delivered Over the Web: Review and Analysis of Key Components. Patient Education and Counseling 74, 156–173 (2009)
17. Napolitano, M.A., Fotheringham, M., Tate, D., et al.: Evaluation of an Internet-Based Physical Intervention: A Preliminary Investigation. Annals of Behavioral Medicine 25, 92–99 (2003)
18. Oenema, A., Brug, J., Lechner, L.: Web-Based Tailored Nutrition Education: Results of a Randomized Controlled Trial. Health Education Research 16, 647–660 (2001)

19. Oenema, A., Tan, F., Brug, J.: Short-Term Efficacy of a Web-Based Computer-Tailored Nutrition Intervention: Main Effects and Mediators. Annals of Behavioral Medicine 29, 54–63 (2005)
20. Oinas-Kukkonen, H., Harjumaa, M.: A Systematic Framework for Designing and Evaluating Persuasive Systems. In: Oinas-Kukkonen, H., Hasle, P., Harjumaa, M., Segerståhl, K. (eds.) PERSUASIVE 2008. LNCS, vol. 5033, pp. 164–176. Springer, Heidelberg (2008)
21. Oinas-Kukkonen, H., Harjumaa, M.: Towards Deeper Understanding of Persuasion in Software and Information Systems. In: The First International Conference on Advances in Human-Computer Interaction (ACHI 2008), Best Paper Award, Sainte Luce, Martinique, February 10-15, pp. 200–205 (2008)
22. Oinas-Kukkonen, H., Harjumaa, M.: Persuasive Systems Design: Key Issues, Process Model, and System Features. Communications of the Association for Information Systems 24, Article 28 (2009)
23. Portnoy, D.B., Scott-Sheldon, L.A.J., Johnson, B.T., et al.: Computer-Delivered Interventions for Health Promotion and Behavioral Risk Reduction: A Meta-Analysis of 75 Randomized Controlled Trials, 1988–2007. Preventive Medicine 47, 3–16 (2008)
24. Riper, H., Kramer, J., Smit, F., et al.: Web-Based Self-Help for Problem Drinkers: A Pragmatic Randomized Trial. Addiction 103, 218–227 (2008)
25. Ritterband, L.M., Gonder-Frederick, L.A., Cox, D.J., et al.: Internet Interventions: In Review, in use, and into the Future. Professional Psychology: Research and Practice 34, 527–534 (2003)
26. Room, R., Babor, T., Rehm, J.: Alcohol and Public Health. The Lancet 365, 519–530 (2005)
27. Strecher, V.J., Shiffman, S., West, R.: Randomized Controlled Trial of a Web-Based Computer-Tailored Smoking Cessation Program as a Supplement to Nicotine Patch Therapy. Addiction 100, 682–688 (2005)
28. Tørning, K., Oinas-Kukkonen, H.: Persuasive System Design: State of Art and Future Directions. In: Proceedings of the Fourth International Conference on Persuasive Technology, Claremont, CA, USA, April 26-29 (2009)
29. Wantland, D.J., Portillo, C.J., Holzemer, W.L., et al.: The Effectiveness of Web-Based Vs. Non-Web-Based Interventions: A Meta-Analysis of Behavioral Change Outcomes. Journal of Medical Internet Research 6, e40 (2004)
30. West, R.: Theory of addiction. Wiley-Blackwell, Oxford (2006)
31. Zetterqvist, K., Maanmies, J., Ström, L., et al.: Randomized Controlled Trial of Internet-Based Stress Management. Cognitive Behaviour Therapy 32, 151–160 (2003)

Analysis of Macro-micro Simulation Models for Service-Oriented Public Platform: Coordination of Networked Services and Measurement of Public Values

Yumiko Kinoshita

Doctorate, Graduate School of Interdisciplinary Informatics, The University of Tokyo,
Research Fellow, Japan Society for the Promotion of Science
7-3-1 Hongo, Bunkyo-ku, Tokyo, 113-0033, Japan
kinoshita.yumiko@iii.u-tokyo.ac.jp

Abstract. When service sectors are a major driver for the growth of the world economy, we are challenged to implement service-oriented infrastructure as e-Gov platform to achieve further growth and innovation for both developed and developing countries. According to recent trends in service industry, it is clarified that main factors for the growth of service sectors are investment into knowledge, trade, and the enhanced capacity of micro, small, and medium-sized enterprises (MSMEs). In addition, the design and deployment of public service platform require appropriate evaluation methodology. Reflecting these observations, this paper proposes macro-micro simulation approach to assess public values (PV) focusing on MSMEs. Linkage aggregate variables (LAVs) are defined to show connection between macro and micro impacts of public services. As a result, the relationship of demography, business environment, macro economy, and socio-economic impact are clarified and their values are quantified from the behavioral perspectives of citizens and firms.

Keywords: Macro-micro simulation models, linkage aggregate variables, e-Gov, service-oriented public infrastructure, public value.

1 Introduction: Service Innovation

1.1 Service Technology and Changing Landscape

A variety of information and communication technologies (ICT) are being developed to implement innovative services so that the needs of today's economy will be met[1, 2]. For an experimental research project for lifestyle related diseases, sensor network is used to collect information so that national healthcare system, medical insurance system, and e-Gov should be designed in an evidence-driven manner[3]. Data for research and development (R&D) are interlinked, indexed, and organized. The practice and management of R&D is refined where a good match of demand and solution is made through web-based database of solution provider. For instance, there is a collaborative information network such as Cancer Biomedical Informatics Grid[1], which promotes

---

[1] https://cabig.nci.nih.gov/

C. Godart et al. (Eds.): I3E 2009, IFIP AICT 305, pp. 328–340, 2009.
© IFIP International Federation for Information Processing 2009

communication related to R&D. These kinds of collaborative activities contribute to the growth of service sectors[1].

ICT has a huge impact on innovativeness, adaptability, and quality of service development[4]. Atkinson and Castro[5] describe a list of benefits, which ICT can bring. Among those is the benefit for developing countries. In 2008, Pfizer and Grameen Health (GH) announced a partnership for healthcare delivery and financing for the exchange of expertise knowledge, and the improvement of micro health insurance, telemedicine and mobile healthcare[6]. It is considered that mobile technologies play a critical role as a low-cost infrastructure. The World Economic Prospect (2008, 2009) summarized by the World Bank[7, 8] articulate that the recent financial turmoil is bringing substantial uncertainty to developing countries due to swings of food and fuel prices, and that demand for commodities is not expected to outstrip supply over the long run. These new services offer channels for financing and commercialization, and access to education, healthcare, and expertise knowledge for micro, small and medium sized enterprises (MSMEs)[2] and people who did not have access to any of those before. To continue to drive such technological innovation and, hence, promote service innovation[1, 2], we may need to focus on the important, dynamic role of MSMEs and third-party to play, and facilitate the co-evolutionary process of ICT with other technological fields[11] i.e. biotechnology and nanotechnology.

In today's socio-economic context, innovation in ICT holds three-faced importance in relation to services: networking of knowledge and expertise, the promotion of business and trade particularly for MSMEs, and a new solution for the development of global economy through service-oriented infrastructure.

1.2 Service Innovation and Macro Economy

The performance of service industry varies widely from sector to sector even in developed countries where service industry already consists 65-75% of the economy. As previously stated, innovation is achieved through networking of knowledge. However, the level of R&D investment in services is still lower than those of the other sectors[12]. The government of the United Kingdom observes that service sectors draw heavily on suppliers and external partners for seeking expertise[4]. Service sector growth led by trade is considered as a vital factor for current and future economic growth. Finland has transformed its economy into service-dominated market by focusing on knowledge intensive services (KIS)[3][13]. KIS influence the business performance of organizations and value chains as they contribute to some types of technological and service innovation directly and form a link of technologies and knowledge beyond sectors[14, 15].

---

[2] One definition of Micro, small and medium-sized enterprises (MSMEs) is 'enterprises which employ fewer than 250 persons and which have an annual turnover not exceeding 50 million euro, and/or an annual balance sheet total not exceeding 43 million euro.' For a detailed description used in Europe, see Article 2 of the Annex of Recommendation 2003/361/EC[9]. Also, refer to Ayyagari, Beck, and Demirguc-Kunt[10] for a summary of various definitions currently used in the world.

[3] Knowledge-intensive services (KIS) are also referred to as 'Knowledge-intensive business services (KIBS)' and 'Knowledge-intensive service activities (KISA).'

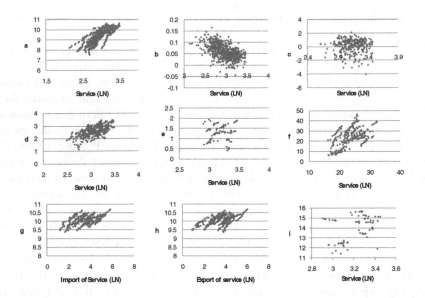

Fig. 1. Commercial Services and Macroeconomic Indicators. *Country: Australia, Austria, Canada, Denmark, Finland, France, Germany, Italy, Ireland, Japan, Netherlands, New Zealand, Portugal, Spain, Sweden, Switzerland, United Kingdom, and United States. **Service (ln): Value added in banks, insurance, real estate and other business services (as percentage of total value added) in 1990-2006; (a) GNI per capita (US dollars, current prices and PPPs); (b) GNI per capita growth rate; (c) MFP (annual growth in percentage); (d) Shares of ICT investment in non-residential gross fixed capital formation (as a percentage of total non-residential gross fixed capital formation); (e) Tertiary attainment for age group 25-64 (as a percentage of the population of that age group); (f) Investment in knowledge (as a percentage of GDP); (g) Gross national income per capita and Imports of services (Bil US dollars); (h) GNI per capita and Exports of services (Bil US dollars); and (i) MSMEs' Participation in the Economy (ln) as a number of companies during 1997-2006. Data source: OECD[18], WTO[16], and IFC[19].

Fig. 1 shows a summary of recent macroeconomic trends regarding service sectors. Service sectors tend to take up a large market share when the following indicators are high: gross national income (GNI) per capita (Fig. 1a), the shares of ICT investment (Fig. 1d), the investment into knowledge (Fig. 1f), and the participation of MSMEs in the economy (Fig. 1i). Also, both export and import tend to increase according to the growth of service industries (Fig. 1g and Fig. 1h). Trade volume is growing particularly in European countries (especially within Europe) and Asian & Pacific countries[16]. On the other hand, either GNI growth rate (Fig. 1b), multi-factor productivity (MFP) (Fig. 1c), or tertiary attainment (Fig. 1e) does not seem to give a substantial influence on the trend of service industry. These data are insufficient to determine a cause-effect relationship although, in general, it is consistent to the observations presented in the previous section.

The following sections of this paper will be dedicated for the analysis of service-oriented e-Gov infrastructure designed for the support of MSMEs. The goal of the analysis is to propose a method to evaluate public values (PV)[15]. This attempt is in response to the needs of today's e-Gov initiative, which is to clarify PV from individual users' perspectives at an organization level[17].

2 Service-Oriented Public Architecture

2.1 e-Gov Platform for the Support of MSMEs

The activity of MSMEs can be supported with public service-oriented infrastructure according to Borresen[20], Stauning[21], and Brun and Lanng[22]. MSMEs and public institutions are linked via a master registry.

According to Ayyagari, Beck, and Demirguc-Kunt[10] who studied SMEs and business environment by country, low entry cost (especially for property registration), easy access to financial capital, and greater information sharing are important for the success of large SMEs in manufacturing sector. The service-oriented infrastructure for MSMEs is designed for lowering barriers to promote the participation of smaller enterprises by optimizing business operation and reducing administration costs through shared infrastructure. The other desired elements are building web-based database on firms for accountability and transparency, promoting peer-to-peer payment mechanisms to meet personal service needs and activity-based service charge, harvesting long-tail of service business, and creating new services through enhanced interaction between vendors and users as well as external professionals. As previously stated, the support of MSMEs has an implication of future inter-governmental e-Gov network, which would facilitate service trade and provide a solution to the global issues.

Based on these preliminary observations, the possible components of the public service-oriented architecture for the support of MSMEs are e-tax, sourcing, cataloging, billing, ordering, data sharing on firm's business profile, and consultation (Fig. 2). The portal for MSMEs is linked to public database and private networks i.e. commercial banks. It is also connected to citizen's one-stop portal so that MSMEs are able to access information of job seekers. These portals are desired to be linked to networks provided by foreign governments to facilitate worker mobility across national borders and firm's entry into the global market. The portal is going to be analyzed according to the definition of PV to be explained in the next section.

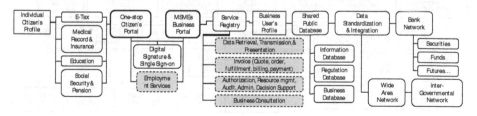

Fig. 2. Open Service-oriented e-Gov Infrastructure for MSMEs. Source: Author's depiction according to Borresen[20], Stauning[21], Yongxiang[23], EURES[24] and Brun et al.[22].

2.2 Analysis of Public Value Chain and Scope of Problem

There are various ways to define PV. One of those is presented by Sudoh, Gotoh, Akatsu, Yoshikawa, Nakagawa, and Kinoshita[25], who defined PV of e-Gov as an aggregate of economic, program, political, societal, and innovative value (Fig. 3).

Economic value refers to gross domestic product (GDP) per capita and external effects. Program value is represented by efficiency, effectiveness, and governance. This category directly and indirectly relates to technical aspects i.e. usability, utilization and scalability. Political value is generated from transparency, participation of citizens, trust, and equality, which are also understood as governance. Societal value is comprised of health, welfare, environment and regional management. Lastly, innovative value refers to industrial growth and creation of new services in both public and private sectors, which would affect national competitiveness.

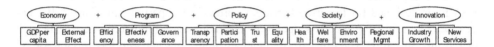

Fig. 3. Public Values (PV) for e-Gov. Source: Sudoh et al.[25].

With regard to the value chain for the portal can be depicted as the next flowchart (Fig. 4). Each box with a solid line is an account of incident in correspondence to possible events occurred. These can be understood further with behavioral approaches. Each box with a dotted line represents either an economic structural framework or qualitative values for the public sector. Both of them must be represented by micro-simulation models with appropriate endogenous and exogenous variables analyzed in logit, probit, linear and logistic regression, and/or Monte Carlo. In the next section, macro and micro simulation models will be discussed in detail.

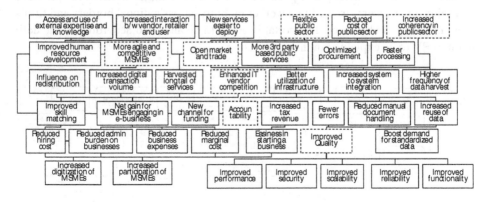

Fig. 4. Value Chain for MSME Business Portal. Source: Author's depiction according to Borresen[20], Stauning[21] and Brun et al.[22].

3 Discussion on Simulation Models

3.1 Macro-micro Simulation Models

The macro-micro simulation is composed of two sets of methodology: one is macro techniques, and the second is micro techniques. Macro and micro models are combined with different degrees of integration[26]. The macro-micro approach allows assessing the micro effects of macroeconomic policy changes.

From macroeconomic perspectives, we need computation models to build structural models with assumptions i.e. utility-maximizing consumer under a budget constraint with tax-benefit system via the one-stop portal. After structural impact is simulated with macro models, results are imputed into micro models (top-down) or vice versa (bottom-up). Micro-simulation models (MSMs) '*allow simulating the effects of a policy on a sample of economic agents at the individual level*'[27]. The approach is useful for the assessment of heterogeneous population over representative approach. It deals with various combinations of social and behavioral characteristics to clarify a mechanism by which individuals are allocated to the policy to receive benefits[28]. Behavioral heterogeneity is observed in source information and exogenous factors[29]. This paper incorporates linkage aggregate variables (LAVs)[26] to find a loop for the feedback between macro and micro models. PV are then clarified as an aggregate of marginal effects on LAVs.

3.2 Application to the Scheme of e-Gov: Structure of Models

This section will discuss the structure and relationship of each component of the methodology as a proposal for the measurement of PV for MSME Business Portal (Fig. 5). In the first step, the service infrastructure is designed according to the trend of macro economy to meet the needs of individuals facing a certain socio-economic environment (top-down loop). The infrastructure is analyzed by using micro models as well as technological assessment models. Consolidating findings makes LAVs, and data is imputed into macro models (bottom-up loop).

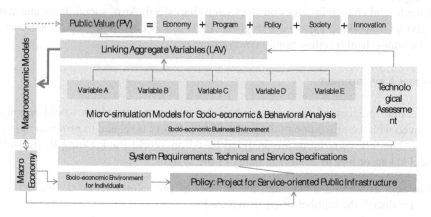

Fig. 5. Assessment Framework for MSME Business Portal (proposed)

In the following sections, the relationship between macro economy and socio-economic environment for individuals will be explained. Then, the micro-simulation models for socio-economic and behavioral analysis will be clarified including the analysis for socio-economic business environment. There is a discussion on technical assessment. Lastly, the relationship of macroeconomic models will be clarified followed by the definition of LAVs.

3.3 Assessment Methodology

Socio-economic Environment for Individuals

Societal value deals with *ex ante* and *ex post* socio-economic conditions to evaluate how the portal will affect individuals and households as a result of linking personal information on tax, healthcare, education, social security, and employment. This category is largely related to the *societal* value. The target population is individuals (N) or of his or her family, who does or has potential to work with MSMEs or who owns a MSME. The outcomes and events below are to be considered[30].

- Education: exit from university, secondary education, or adult education to labor force, entry from labor market to university or adult education, exit from adult education to labor force, occupational training.
- Labor market and status: retirement, unemployment, employment, part-time or full-time, occupation change (compensated sickness days, spouse or other household member's working status).
- Financial and real wealth: housing (own/rent), cost of living, financial wealth inc. pension, interest, dividends, capital gains, other real wealth, debt.
- Tax & Transfers: disposable income, loans, tax, allowance, earnings.
- Noncash benefits: child care, care for elderly, compulsory education, healthcare, medication, take-up of social assistance.

Macroeconomic indicators are given as exogenous variables, for example, annual rate of change in inflation (CPI), annual real general increase in wage rates, net interest rate, dividends, and change in prices on stocks and shares[30]. Also, social index and status are given i.e. working experience, highest education, occupational sector, nationality, marital status, health status, family composition.

Business Environment

The second category of assessment is business environment, which would be greatly improved with the utilization of the portal. This category is related to *program* or *policy* values. The following items are analyzed based on World Bank Doing Business Database[31] according to the functionality of the system.

- Easiness of starting a business: the number of procedures reduced, time reduced, cost reduced, the number of errors reduced.

- Effectiveness in employing workers: skill matching improved, hiring cost reduced, depth of information improved, the number of people using the system increased, time reduced from posting until hiring.
- Effectiveness in getting credit: depth of credit information index improved, extent of disclosure index improved.
- Efficiency in paying taxes: the number of tax payments and procedures reduced, time reduced to prepare, file and pay, cost reduced, the number of errors reduced.
- Increased trading across borders: the number of procedures reduced for export and import, time reduced, cost reduced, the number of errors reduced.
- Effectiveness in closing a business: recovery rate in bankruptcy improved, time reduced, cost reduced, the number of errors reduced.

Covariates are, for example, the number of new regulation, the number of MSMEs participating in the system, industry sector, industry output growth, mobility of workers, wage rate, availability of legal remedies, strength of investor protection, court and attorney's fee, and appreciation and depreciation of assets.

Micro-simulation Models for Socio-economic and Behavioral Analysis

To build micro models for the agent i with characteristics z, we take parameters of preference (β_i), parameters of idiosyncratic preference (ε_i), and the access to business portal system or one-stop portal (γ)[27]. Social welfare function (*SWF*) is:

$$SWF(\gamma) = \sum\nolimits_{i=1}^{n} V[U(z_i, \beta_i, \varepsilon_i; \gamma)] \tag{1}$$

$U(\cdot)$ is the utility function, and $V[\cdot]$ is the social valuation of individual welfare.

The utility function is therefore:

$$\max\ u(c_i, L_i; z_i; \beta_i, \varepsilon_i)\ \text{s.t.}\ c_i \le y_{0i} + w_i L_i + SWF(\gamma), L_i \ge 0 \tag{2}$$

in which consumption (c_i), labor supply (L_i), the initial level of labor income (y_{0i}), wage rate (w_i) are considered. This social welfare function is compared to that of when the portal system is absent.

When we estimate $\hat{\beta}_i$ and $\hat{\varepsilon}_i$, changes in labor supply and consumption are:

$$L_i - L_i^0 = L_i - F(w_i, y_{0i}; z_i; \hat{\beta}_i, \hat{\varepsilon}_i; 0) = F(w_i, y_{0i}; z_i; \hat{\beta}_i, \hat{\varepsilon}_i; \gamma) \tag{3}$$

$$C_i - C_i^0 = w_i(L_i - L_i^0) + SWF(\gamma) - SWF(0) \tag{4}$$

We observe how the portal would affect wage rate due to the reduction of costs for hiring. With regard to industry and firm behavior, we can analyze how the knowledge intensiveness in labor force will improve labor productivity. Therefore, we need to observe how this system would affect capital investment behavior in macro models. The resulting capital-labor ratio (K/L) will influence industry output.

Technological Assessment

Technological factors are generally grouped into performance (*P*), security (*Se*), functionality (*F*), reliability (*R*) and scalability (*Sc*), which directly influence quality and hence the take up of system by the users. In a complex behavioral model, such factors as user's perception, level of satisfaction, and objective/subjective quality should be taken into account. These factors are reactive to the metadata scheme underlining web-based services, which define user groups, a role of agent, interaction sequence and the like. This type of data scheme has been used in, for instance, electronic health record (EHR)[32]. When we study how these aspects would impact and relate to the micro models, the following equation is derived for technological factors for the agent *i* with an attribute set *z*:

$$T(z) = \sum_{i=1}^{n} TI[Q(P, Se, F, R, Sc), D(e_i, z_i; a_i; i, r; \gamma)] \tag{5}$$

in which we take entity (e_i), action (z_i), interaction (*i*), relationship (*r*), and system specific metadata scheme (γ). $Q(P, Se, F, R, Sc)$ is an (objective) quality function, and $D(e_i, z_i; a_i; i, r; \gamma)$ is a data function. $TI[\cdot]$ is the program specific valuation of technological impact. These factors will give an impact on system-to-system integration, data standardization efforts, and hence increased coherency in public sector and the flexibility of public sector. These resulting values are related to *policy* value (in particular, *governance*).

Macroeconomic Models

There are a variety of macroeconomic models, which can be employed for the assessment of MSME Business Portal. Based on the behaviors observed in micro models, it is important to consider how the system influence cost of producing a unit of products, wage rate and labor productivity, profit of firms according to the size of firms and sectors, and export and import of heterogeneous products. Industry and firm behaviors must be modeled properly for both short-term and long-term decisions. As for macroeconomic models, we can take the following equations[33]. The production (*Y*) for country *j* at time *t* is:

$$Y_{jt} = A_t K_{jt}^{\theta} L_{jt}^{1-\theta} \tag{6}$$

where θ is $0 < \theta < 1$ with productivity (*A*), capital (*K*) and labor (*L*). The capital stock is given as:

$$K_{jt+1} = (1 - \delta) K_{jt} + X_{jt} \tag{7}$$

X_{jt} is investment in intermediaries, and δ is depreciation rates. Aggregate output (*Y*) consists of consumption (*C*), government expenditures (*G*), investment (*I*), and the current account (*CA*) surplus.

$$Y_{jt} = C_{jt} + X_{jt} + G_{jt} + CA_{jt} \tag{8}$$

Taxable profits are equal to sales less expenses, which are wage payments, tangible depreciation, and expensed investments on intermediaries. The household utility is

$$\max_{\{c_{jt}, K_{jt+1}\}} \sum_{t=0}^{\infty} \beta^t N_{jt}[\log c_{jt}] \tag{9}$$

in which c_t is per member consumption at time t. β is a parameter. N_t is working-age population. Marginal utility of household is:

$$\frac{c_{jt+1}}{c_{jt}} = \beta[1 + (1 - \tau_K)(r_{t+1} - \delta)] \tag{10}$$

with tax on capital income (τ_K) and r is the rental rate of capital. The budget constraint of the household is:

$$C_{jt} \prec w_{jt}L_{jt} + r_{jt}K_{jt} - \tau_K(r_{jt} - \delta)K_{jt} - \pi_{jt}I_{jt} - X_{jt} \tag{11}$$

where I_{jt} is personal income. We can also analyze cost-disadvantage ratio (CDR) to see if the system reduces fixed cost (FC) relative to total cost (TC), and how investment would be changed accordingly.

Linkage Aggregate Variables (LAVs) and Public Values (PV)

The solution of the micro simulation models provides LAVs. They are fed into macro models, and used for the calculation of PV. PV are measured as a marginal effect of each LAV. Based on all the equations, the following LAVs are defined.

- Economy: output (Y), labor supply (L), technology (A), investment (X), capital (K), household consumption (C), wage rate (w), trade (CA), utility (u) (9 variables)
- Program: easiness of starting a business (4 outcomes), effectiveness in employing workers (5 outcomes), efficiency in paying taxes (5 outcomes), increased trading across borders (4 outcomes), technology/quality (5 parameters, by attributes)
- Policy: effectiveness in getting credit (2 outcomes), effectiveness in closing a business (4 outcomes), quality (5 parameters, by attributes)
- Society: wage rates (by sector, rate, skill level), occupation (by sector), price (% changes, by sector), education (4 outcomes), labor (5 outcomes, 2 complements, by sector), financial and real wealth (3 outcomes, % changes, 5 types), tax (5 outcomes, % changes), noncash benefits (5 outcomes), social welfare (1 outcome)
- Innovation: sector growth (1 outcome), product variety (1 outcome), new entrants (1 outcome), new products and services (1 outcome)

4 Summary and Conclusion

In response to the recent trend of service industry and service-oriented technology, this paper proposes a method of measuring PV in e-Gov infrastructure by taking MSME Business Portal as a case study. This aims to design, implement and utilize service-oriented infrastructure for service innovation in response to today's socio-economic needs. The structure of measurement is structured in five components: socio-economic environment for citizens, business environment, technology, micro simulation, and macro economy. Linkage aggregate variables (LAVs) are specifically introduced so that micro impact of the policy is scaled up to macro perspectives, and that PV are clearly itemized and quantified. With this approach, the citizen's one-stop portal and MSMEs business portal can be analyzed in one sequence, and PV, which are consisted of various kinds of impacts on heterogeneous population, are quantified. The potential inter-governmental coordination in e-Gov initiatives and the role of trade are also incorporated into the model.

For further improvement of the methodology, it is important to test in real scenarios. In this sense, this paper does not comment on the type of data that we need to use. Since micro-level data have not been accumulated well with regard to e-Gov infrastructure, this paper focuses on simulation models rather than empirics. However, to discuss the impact that e-Gov would give to our society and economy, we must increase our efforts to build up firm-level panel data in relation to e-Gov. For future research, the macro-micro models should be tested using actual datasets, find appropriate indices for nonmonetary impact, and optimize methodologies to ameliorate the burden of computation.

Finally, as for a future scenario for the economic growth based on service innovation in line with public innovation, several areas must be considered. One area is an international implication of e-Gov. Currently multi-organizational coordination and business operation reforms are underway so that one-stop services are provided to citizens. For the next stage, international coordination of public services in e-Gov initiatives may be targeted. To solve global issues i.e. poverty, it is crucial to develop of competitive public infrastructure, and to provide better services for citizens to meet the needs of service-oriented economy. Financial, education and healthcare sectors must also orchestrate their efforts within and across countries for a faster economic recovery and growth. This is a collaborative effort to bring service innovation system into our daily life. It is what we need to target as the next stage of public innovation.

Acknowledgment

This work is supported by Grant-in-Aid for JSPS Fellows (No. 21· 166), MEXT, Japan. I appreciate Professor Osamu Sudoh, the University of Tokyo, who has offered deep insights on the concept of measuring innovation. The author is responsible for any possible mistake in this paper.

References

1. Sudoh, O.: The Knowledge Network in the Digital Economy and Sustainable Development. In: Sudoh, O. (ed.) Digital Economy and Social Design, pp. 3–38. Springer, Heidelberg (2005)
2. Council on Competitiveness, Innovate America (2004),
   http://www.compete.org/publications/detail/202/
   innovate-america/

3. Sudoh, O., Inoue, S., Nakashima, N.: eService Innovation and Sensor Based Healthcare. In: Oya, M., Uda, R., Yasunobu, C. (eds.) Towards Sustainable Society on Ubiquitous Networks, pp. 1–14. Springer, Heidelberg (2008)
4. NESTA Policy & Research Unit, Innovation in Services (2008),
   http://www.nesta.org.uk/assets/Uploads/pdf/Policy-Briefing/
   innovation_in_services_policy_briefing_NESTA.pdf
5. Atkinson, R.D., Castro, D.D.: Digital Quality of Life -Understanding the Personal & Social Benefits of the Information Technology Revolution. Information Technology and Innovation Foundation (2008)
6. Bellinghen, D.V.: Grameen Health and Pfizer Announce Novel Partnership To Explore Sustainable Healthcare Delivery Models for The Developing World, Corporate news (September 24, 2008),
   http://www.pfizer.be/Media/Press+bulletins/
   Philantropy/Grameen+Health+and+Pfizer+Partnership.htm
7. The World Bank: Global economic prospects (2008)
8. The World Bank: Global economic prospects (2009)
9. European Commission: The new SME definition (2008),
   http://ec.europa.eu/enterprise/enterprise_policy/
   sme_definition/sme_user_guide.pdf
10. Ayyagari, M., Beck, T., Demirguc-Kunt, A.: Small and Medium Enterprises Across the Globe. Small Business Economics 29, 415–434 (2007)
11. Sudoh, O.: Administrative Evolution and Open Innovation. Journal of Social Informatics Research 1(1), 147–160 (2008)
12. Miles, I.: Innovation in Services. In: Fagerberg, J., Mowery, D.C., Nelson, R.R. (eds.) The Oxford Handbook of Innovation, pp. 433–458. Oxford University Press, Oxford (2006)
13. Finnish Funding Agency for Technology and Innovation (TeKes): Serve -Innovative Internationally competitive business from service innovations (2007),
   http://www.tekes.fi/serve
14. OECD: Innovation and Knowledge-Intensive Service Activities (2006)
15. Service Innovation Research Initiative: Proposal Towards the Establishment of an Informatical Foundation of Services to Realize Innovation. Division of University Corporate Relations, the University of Tokyo (2009),
   http://www.ducr.u-tokyo.ac.jp/service-innovation/pdf/
   090331teigen-en.pdf
16. World Trade Organization, Time Series on International Trade (2009)
17. Kinoshita, Y., Sudoh, O.: Network-driven Context in User-driven Innovation. In: Oya, M., Uda, R., Yasunobu, C. (eds.) Towards Sustainable Society on Ubiquitous Networks, pp. 245–252. Springer, Heidelberg (2008)
18. OECD: Economic, Environmental and Social Statistics. OECD Factbook (2008),
   http://www.oecd.org/publications/factbook
19. International Finance Corporation, the World Bank: Micro, Small, and Medium Enterprises: A Collection of Published Data (2007)
20. Borresen, P.L.: OIOUBL -Case Study of How to Implement a Nationwide Procurement Standard. In: OASIS Symposium (2007)
21. Stauning, S.: Establishing a National Service Oriented eBusiness and eGovernment Infrastructure. In: OASIS Symposium (2007)
22. Brun, M.H., Lanng, C.: Reducing barriers for e-business in SME's through an open service oriented infrastructure. In: Proceedings of the 8th international conference on Electronic commerce, pp. 403–410. ACM, New York (2006)

23. Yongxiang, W.: Information System Integration Project of China Securities Regulatory Commission (CSRC). In: OASIS Symposium (2007)
24. European Commission, EURES, http://www.europa.eu.int/eures/
25. Sudoh, O., Gotoh, R., Akatsu, M., Yoshikawa, H., Nakagawa, T., Kinoshita, Y.: Performance Measurement and Evaluation Framework for e-Government (To Be). e-Government Evaluation Committee's Report for the 2nd meeting, Division of University Corporate Relations, The University of Tokyo, Government report (July 26, 2007)
26. Bourguignon, F., Silva, P.D., Luiz, A.: Evaluating the Poverty and Distributional Impact of Economic Policies: A Compendium of Existing Techniques. In: Bourguignon, F., Silva, P.D., Luiz, A. (eds.) The Impact of. Economic Policies on Poverty and Income Distribution: Evaluation Techniques and Tools, The World Bank (2003)
27. Bourguignon, F., Spadaro, A.: Microsimulation as a tool for evaluating redistribution policies. Journal of Economic Inequality 4(1), 77–106 (2006)
28. Boccanfuso, D., Estache, A., Savard, L.: Electricity Reforms in Mali: A Macro–Micro Analysis of the Effects on Poverty and Distribution. Journal of African Economics 16(4), 629–659 (2007)
29. Essama-Nssah, B.: A Poverty-Focused Evaluation of Commodity Tax Options. World Bank Policy Research Working Paper No. 4245 (2007)
30. Lindgren, B., Klevmarken, A.: Simulating An Ageing Population: A Microsimulation Approach Applied To Sweden. Emerald Group Publishing (2008)
31. The World Bank: Doing Business Database (2009),
http://www.doingbusiness.org/Documents/FullReport/2009/
DB_2009_English.pdf
32. Health Level Seven, Inc.: Health Level Seven (HL7) Meta-Model,
http://www.hl7.org/
33. Hayashi, F., Prescott, E.: The 1990s in Japan: A Lost Decade. Review of Economic Dynamics 5(1), 206–235 (2002)

Enterprise Networks for Competences Exchange: A Simulation Model

Marco Remondino, Marco Pironti, and Paola Pisano

e-Business L@B, University of Turin
10145 Torino, Italy
{remond,pironti,pisano}@di.unito.it

Abstract. A business process is a set of logically related tasks performed to achieve a defined business and related to improving organizational processes. Process innovation can happen at various levels: incrementally, redesign of existing processes, new processes. The knowledge behind process innovation can be shared, acquired, changed and increased by the enterprises inside a network. An enterprise can decide to exploit innovative processes it owns, thus potentially gaining competitive advantage, but risking, in turn, that other players could reach the same technological levels. Or it could decide to share it, in exchange for other competencies or money. These activities could be the basis for a network formation and/or impact the topology of an existing network. In this work an agent based model is introduced (E^3), aiming to explore how a process innovation can facilitate network formation, affect its topology, induce new players to enter the market and spread onto the network by being shared or developed by new players.

Keywords: Process Innovation, Enterprise Management, Network Topology, Business Process, Agent Based Simulation.

1 Introduction

Unlike product innovation, which is targeted towards product engineering, development and commercialization activities, process innovation relates to improving organizational processes. Our understandings of business process innovation come from the growing researches on organizational learning and knowledge management. The transfer and sharing of process innovation is not easy to attain, but information sharing/knowledge transfer (both within and across the boundary of the organization) is seen as an essential element for innovation. The network promote not only the transfer of knowledge (and the possible transfer of process) but also the creation of new knowledge as well, through synergies or competition. Within an organization, cross-unit knowledge transfer can produce "creative abrasion" [3], generate "improvisational sparks" [4] and create new information patterns by rearranging information already in use and incorporating information previously neglected. Enterprises also actively look for external knowledge, for example by expanding their networks to learn new practices and technologies [5]. The process innovation could impact on the network not only by improving the knowledge of the involved enterprises, but also by

C. Godart et al. (Eds.): I3E 2009, IFIP AICT 305, pp. 341–356, 2009.
© IFIP International Federation for Information Processing 20099

changing the number of actors (exit and entry), and changing the numbers and patterns of link information [2]. The network can expand, churn, strengthen or shrink. At the level of a single enterprise, if it is the only one (or among the few) possessing an innovative process, it could become the focal point in a network, attracting others, wishing to link with it. Each network change is brought about by specific combination of changes in tie creation, tie deletion, and by changes in an actor's portfolio size (number of link) and portfolio range (numbers of partners) [2]. While [2] presents four types of network changes, they find that only an expanding network and a churning network are a reflection of a structural change, because new alliances are formed with new partners. An expanding network is brought about by an increase of new alliances without a deletion of old ones (meaning a large average of portfolio), together with an increasing portfolio range (more difference in partners). A churning network reflects the formation of new alliances and the deletion of existing alliances. While the average portfolio remains stable in term of the number of partners, there is a rotation of partners.

In order to empirically study how process innovation can affect an enterprise network, an agent based model is used. Agent based simulation is an effective paradigm for studying complex systems. It allows the creation of virtual societies, in which each agent can interact with others basing on certain rules. In this way, a social system can be observed as if it were a laboratory study, by repeating the experiments all the needed times, and changing just some parameters, by leaving all the others still (*ceteris paribus* analysis), something that would be impossible in the real system. The agents are basic entities, endowed with the capacity of performing certain actions, and with certain variables defining their state. In the model presented here, the agents are reactive, meaning that they simply react to the stimuli coming from the environment and from other agents, without cognitively elaborating their own strategies. An agent based model consists of a multitude of software agents (both homogeneous or heterogeneous), each type being endowed with particular local properties and rules, put together within an environment, formally described as a set of parameters and rules. When the model is formally built and implemented, emergent results can be observed, thus inferring cause-effect relations by simulating different core scenarios.

In the present work, social network theory is briefly analyzed and a definition of process innovation is given. Then, the comprehensive agent based model used is formally introduced, and it is discussed how it can be employed to study how a process innovation affects an enterprise network. Last, some empirical results coming from the model are given and the future work in this direction is discussed.

2   Social Networks

A social network is a social structure made of nodes (which are generally individuals or organizations) that are tied by one or more specific types of interdependency, such as values, visions, ideas, financial exchange, friendship. Social network analysis views social relationships in terms of nodes and ties. Nodes are the individual actors within the networks, and ties are the relationships between the actors. These concepts are often displayed in a social network diagram, where nodes are the points and ties are the lines.

The idea of drawing a picture (called *"sociogram"*) of who is connected to whom for a specific set of people is credited to [6], an early social psychologist who envisioned mapping the entire population of New York City. Cultural anthropologists independently invented the notion of social networks to provide a new way to think about social structure and the concepts of role and position, an approach that culminated in rigorous algebraic treatments of kinship systems. At the same time, in mathematics, the nascent field of graph theory [7] began to grow rapidly, providing the underpinnings for the analytical techniques of modern social network analysis. The strategic network perspective avers that the *embeddedness* of enterprises in networks of external relationships with other organizations holds significant implications for enterprise performance [10].

Specifically, since resources and capabilities such as access to diverse knowledge [11], pooled resources and cooperation, are often acquired through networks of inter-firm ties, and since access to such resources and capabilities influences enterprise performance, it is important from a strategy perspective to examine the effect of network structure on enterprise performance [9]. Relationships between enterprises and their partners affect enterprises' alliance-building, behavior and performance. There is evidence that enterprises' network positions have an impact on their survival, innovativeness, market share [12], and financial returns [18]. However, evidence remains mixed on which particular patterns of inter-organizational relationships are advantageous for enterprises. One of the key ideas currently dominating the literature is [11]) open network perspective, according to which an enterprise can obtain important performance advantages when exploiting relationships to partners that do not maintain direct ties among one another. The absence of direct ties among a firm's partners (the presence of structural holes) indicates that these partners are located in different parts of an industry network, that they are connected to heterogeneous sources of information, and that their invitations to jointly exploit business prospects present the focal enterprise with access to diverse deal-making opportunities [1]. Several studies have shown that enterprises improve their performance as a result of maintaining relationships, whereas other studies have shown negative performance effects of firms' maintaining positions in open networks.

3 Process Innovation

A business process is a set of logically related tasks performed to achieve a defined business outcome [19], e.g.: sequencing of work routines, information flow and so on.

Process innovation is defined as "the introduction of a new method of production, that is, one yet tested by experience in the branch of manufacture concerned a new way of handling a commodity commercially" [16]. Edquist [20] defines process innovation like the result in a decrease in the cost of production. The drives of process innovation are primarily reduction in delivery lead time, lowering of operational costs, and increase in flexibility: process innovations are a firm's new way of design or manufacturing existing or new products. While newness on product innovation is defined at a macro level (market, industry), newness of process innovations is often defined at a micro level (enterprise and business unit).

Meeus and Euist divide process innovations into two categories: technological and organizational innovations: technological process innovations change the way products are produced by introducing change in technology (physical equipment, techniques, system); organizational innovations are innovations in an organization's structure, strategy and administrative processes [16].

Process innovation can and should happen at various levels within the organization as no organization can depend solely upon innovation occurring at one level only. Successful organizations have an innovation process working its way through all levels of the organization.

4 Impact on the Network

Process innovation is a key factor for both competing in a market and creating links with other players. An enterprise owning a proprietary process would in fact exploit it, by gaining a competitive factor over those who do not possess it. On the other hand, it could decide to share it with other enterprises in exchange for money or, even better, in exchange for other competencies it does not know. This is the most important factor behind the creation of what we here define "network for competences exchange", i.e.: a social network of enterprises, where the ties semantically represent a synergy among players exchanging process innovations or, to a more general extent, competences.

Philippen and Riccaboni [13] in their work on "radical innovation and network evolution" focus on the importance of local link formation and the process of distant link formation. Regarding the formation of new linkages [8] finds that the process of new tie creation is heavily embedded in an actor's existing network. This means that new ties are often formed with prior partners or with partners of prior partners, indicating network growth to be a local process. Particularly when considering inter-firm alliances, new link formation is considered "risky business" and actors prefer alliances that are embedded in a dense clique were norms are more likely to be enforceable and opportunistic behavior to be punished ([10]; [2]). Distant link formation implies that new linkages are created with partners whom are not known to the existing partners of an actor. At the level of the enterprise, [11] shows that distant linkage that serve as bridge between dense local clique of enterprises, can provide access to new source of information and favorable strategic negotiation position, which improves the firms' position in the network and industry.

In order to examine and study how a process innovation can spread and affect the network for competences exchange, an agent based model is used. The model is a comprehensive one, showing the network dynamics for enterprises, and is described in detail in the next paragraph.

5 The E³ Agent Based Model

The model has been developed at the e-Business L@B, University of Turin. It is built in pure Java, thus following the Object Oriented paradigm. This is particularly suitable for agent based modeling, since the individual agents can be seen as objects coming from a prototypal class, interacting among them basing on the internal rules (methods). While the reactive nature of the agents may seem a limitation, it's indeed a way to keep track of the aggregate behavior of a large number of entities acting in the same system at the same time. All the numerical parameters can be decided at the beginning of each simulation (e.g.: number of enterprises, and so on).

Everything in the model is seen as an agent; thus we have three kinds of agents: Environment, Enterprises and Emissaries (E^3). This is done since each of them, even the environment, is endowed with some actions to perform.

5.1 Heat Metaphor

In order to represent the advantage of an enterprise in owning different competences, the "heat" metaphor is introduced. In agent based models for Economics, the metaphor based approach [14] is an established way of representing real phenomena through computational and physical metaphors. In this case, a quantum of heat is assigned for each competence at each simulation turn. If the competence is internal (i.e.: developed by the enterprise) this value is higher. If the competence is external (i.e.: borrowed from another enterprise) this value is lower. This is realistic, since in the model we don't have any form of variable cost for competencies, and thus an internal competence is rewarded more. Heat is thus a metaphor not only for the profit that an enterprise can derive from owning many competences, but also for the managing and synergic part (e.g.: economy of scale).

Heat is also expendable in the process of creating new internal competences (internal exploration) and of looking for partner with whom to share them in exchange of external competences (external exploration). At each time-step, a part of the heat is scattered (this can be regarded as a set of costs for the enterprise). If the individual heat gets under a threshold, the enterprise ceases its activity and disappears from the environment. At an aggregate level, average environmental heat is a good and synthetic measure to monitor the state of the system.

5.2 Environment

The environment is regarded as a meta-agent, representing the world in which the proper agents act. It's considered an agent itself, since it can perform some actions on the others and on the heat. If features the following properties: a grid (X,Y), i.e.: a lattice in the form of a matrix, containing cells; a dispersion value, i.e.: a real number used to calculate the dissipated heat at each step; the heat threshold under which an enterprise ceases; a value defining the infrastructure level and quality; a threshold over which new enterprises are introduced; a function polling the average heat (of the whole grid).

The environment affects the heat dispersion over the grid and, based on the parameter described above, allows new enterprises to join the world.

5.3 Enterprise Agents

This is the most important and central type of agent in the model. Its behavior is based on the reactive paradigm, i.e.: stimulus-reaction. The goal for these agents is that of surviving in the environment (i.e.: never go under the minimum allowed heat threshold). They are endowed with a heat level (energy) that will be consumed when performing actions. They feature a unique ID, a coordinate system (to track their position on the lattice), and a real number identifying the heat they own. The most important feature of the enterprise agent is a matrix identifying which competences (processes) it can dispose of. In the first row, each position of the vector identifies a specific competence, and is equal to 1, if disposed of, or to 0 if lacking. A second row is used to identify internal competences or outsourced ones (in that case, the ID of the lender is memorized). A third row is used to store a value to identify the owned competences developed after a phase of internal exploration, to distinguish them from those possessed from the beginning. Besides, an enterprise can be "settled", or "not settled", meaning that it joined the world, but is still looking for the best position on the territory through its emissary. The enterprise features a wired original behavior: internally or externally explorative. This is the default behavior, the one with which an enterprise is born, but it can be changed under certain circumstances. This means that an enterprise can be naturally oriented to internal explorative strategy (preferring to develop new processes internally), but can act the opposite way, if it considers it can be more convenient. Of course, the externally explorative enterprises have a different bias from internally explorative ones, when deciding what strategy to actually take.

Finally, the enterprise keeps track of its collaborators (i.e.: the list of enterprise with whom it is exchanging competencies and making synergies) and has a parameters defining the minimum number of competencies it expects to find, in order to form a joint. The main goal for each enterprise is that of acquiring competences, both through internal (e.g.: research and development) and external exploration (e.g.: forming new links with other enterprises). The enterprises are rewarded with heat based on the number of competences they possess (different, parameterized weights for internal or external ones), that is spread in the surrounding territory, thus slowly evaporating, and is used for internal and external exploration tasks.

5.4 Emissary Agents

These are agents that strictly belong to the enterprises, and are to be seen as probes able to move on the territory and detect information about it. They are used in two different situation: 1) if the enterprise is not settled yet (just appeared on the territory) it's sent out to find the best place where to settle. 2) If the enterprise is already settled and chooses to explore externally, an emissary is sent out to find the best possible partners. In both cases, the emissary, that has a field of vision limited to the surrounding 8 cells, probes the territory for heat and moves following the hottest cells. When it finds an enterprise in a cell, it probes its competencies and compares them to those possessed by its chief enterprise verifying if these are a good complement (according to the parameter described in the previous section). In the first case, the enterprise is settled in a cell which is near the best enterprise found during the movement. In the second case, the enterprise asks the best found for collaboration). While moving, the emissary consumes a quantum of heat, that is directly dependant on the quality of infrastructures of the environment.

5.5 Main Iterations

The main iterations for the simulation model are described in this section.

At step 0, a lattice is created *(X, Y)*. A number n of enterprises are created, *k* of them internally explorative and *n-k* of them externally explorative. X, Y, n, and k are set by the user, before the simulation starts.

At step 1, the environment checks if some enterprise reached the minimum heat threshold; if so, removes it from the world. After that, each enterprise, if idle (not doing anything) decides what behavior to follow.

At step 2, all the enterprises that selected to be EE move their emissary by one cell. All the IE ones work on the R&D cycle (one step at a time).

At step 3, the EE enterprises check if the emissary finished its energy and, in that case, ask the best found enterprise for collaboration (they can receive a positive or negative reply, based on the needs of the other enterprise). The IE enterprises check if R&D process is finished and, in that case, get a competence in a random position (that can be already occupied by an owned competences, thus wasting the work done).

At step 4, the environment scatters the heat according to its parameters. Loop from step 1.

5.6 Parameters in the Model

At the beginning of a simulation, the user can change the core parameters, in order to create a particular scenario to study. In figure 1, the section of the control panel containing the parameters is shown.

Maximum number of steps (0 no limits)	15	
Initial number of Enterprises (0 random)	10	
Initial heat for Enterprises	20	Mean 5 Variance
Number of competences	10	
Competences possessed at startup for each enterprise	6	Mean 2 Variance
Threshold for new Enterprise to enter the market	1 %	
Infrastructure quality	1	
Minimum heat threshold	4	
Minimum percentage of competences to share for link creation	1 %	
Emissary step cost	5 %	
R&D internal exploration duration (steps)	3	
Internal exploration cost (per step)	1 %	
Environment control cycles	5	
Threshold for infrastructure improvement	0 n.a.	
Index for infrastructure improvement	0 n.a.	
Heat dispersion index	9 %	
Lattice dimension	10 x 10	
Initial External Exploration cost	15 %	
Propensity to External Exploration of new Enterprises (average n. of links)	0 . 2	
Number of initial Enterprises doing External Exploration	5	
Propension to Internal Exploration for externally explorative Enterprises	6 %	
Propension to Internal Exploration for internally explorative Enterprises	4 %	
Value of internal competences	1.1 ▼ Value of external competences	1.0 ▼

Fig. 1. The main control panel

Some of the parameters are constituted by a scalar value, others are in percentage, others are used to define stochastic (normal) distributions, given their mean value and their variance. Here follows a synthetic explanation for the individual parameters:

Maximum number of steps: is the number of iterations in the model. 0 sets the unbounded mode.

Initial number of enterprises: is the number of enterprise agents present at start-up (0 is random).

Initial heat for enterprise: a normal distribution setting the initial energy for each enterprise, given the mean and the variance.

Number of competences: the length of the vector, equal for all the enterprises (metaphorically representing the complexity of the sector in which they operate).

Competences possessed at start-up: a normal distribution referring to how many processes an enterprise owns internally, given the mean and the variance.

Threshold for new enterprise to enter the market: a delta in the average heat of the world, after which a new enterprise is attracted in the market.

Infrastructure quality: affects the cost of external exploration.

Minimum heat threshold: level under which an enterprise cease.

Minimum percentage of competences to share for link creation: when asked for a competences exchange, the other enterprise looks at this value to decide whether to create a link or not.

Emissary step cost: percentage of the heat possessed by the enterprise spent for each step of its emissary, during external exploration task.

Internal exploration duration: quantity of steps for internally developing a new competence.

Internal exploration cost: percentage of the heat possessed by the enterprise spent for each step of internal exploration.

Environment control cycles: quantity of steps for sampling the average heat of the environment.

Heat dispersion index: percentage of heat evaporated at each step.

Lattice dimension: the dimension of the grid hosting the enterprise (i.e.: the whole environment).

Internal Exploration cost: "una tantum" cost for setting up an emissary for external exploration.

Propensity to External Exploration for new enterprises: when a new enterprise enters the market, it looks at the average number of links in the network. If more than this value, it behaves as externally explorative, otherwise internally explorative.

Number of initial enterprises doing external exploration: variable to divide the initial behavior.

Value of internal/external competence: reward (heat) given for each internal/external competence possessed.

6 Qualitative Results

While the main object of this paper is to present the model itself as a tool for studying the effects of process innovation on enterprise networks, in the present paragraph some insights will be given about preliminary results obtained from the model itself. The presented ones will be mainly qualitative results, although the model can give many quantitative individual and aggregate results. In particular, a *"computational only"* mode is present in the model, allowing it to perform a *multi-run* batch execution. This is done according to the theory presented in [15]: the model is executed a defined number of times (chosen by the user) and the different outputs are sampled and collected at every n steps (again, n decidable by the user) with the same parameters (in order to overcome sampling effects that could be caused by stochastic distributions) or by changing one parameter at a time by a discrete step, in order to carry on a *ceteris paribus* analysis on the model.

While this kind of analysis will be discussed in detail in future works, here some qualitative and semi-quantitative outputs will be discussed, obtained from the model. The model can give the following different kinds of outputs, when running in *"normal"* mode: 1) a real-time graph, depicting the social network, in which the nodes are the enterprises, whose color represent the behavior they are following at a given step, and the links are the ties indicating two or more enterprises mutually exchanging one or more competences. 2) A set of charts, showing in real time some core parameters, namely: *average heat in the environment, number of links (in the network), number of links (average), number of enterprises doing internal exploration, number of ceased enterprises since the beginning, number of born enterprises since the beginning, number of available competences (overall), total number of skills possessed at the beginning, obtained by external exploration, obtained by internal exploration.*

In figures 2, 3 and 4, the output graph is depicted at times 0 (no links), 100 and 500. These pictures belong to the same simulation, so the parameters are the same for all of them, with the only variation of time, giving a hint about the development of the

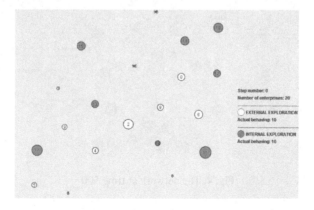

Fig. 2. The network at time 0

enterprise network. In figure 2 the initial state of the network is shown, where no ties have been created, yet. A total of 20 enterprises is on the territory, 10 of which have an internally explorative behavior and the other 10 have an externally explorative mood. Internal competences are rewarded 10% more than external ones, but internal exploration strategy (e.g.: research & development) is 30% more expensive.

After 100 steps (figure 3) some new players have entered the market (an average of 1 new enterprise each 10 steps), meaning that the average heat of the system increased significantly; this can be thought as a starting network, attracting new players thanks to a good overall balance. Some ties have formed and many new competences (the dimension of enterprises) have been internally produced. After the initial steps in which 50% of the enterprise was doing internal exploration, now at the 100th step, only one third (i.e.: 33%) is doing that, since almost all the smaller players are trying to outsource them from the bigger ones, in order to gain some energy.

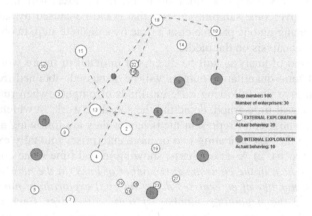

Fig. 3. The network at time 100

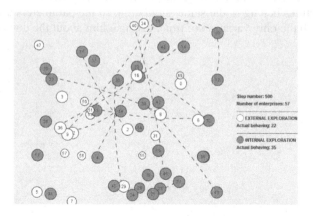

Fig. 4. The network at time 500

Unfortunately, many of these small enterprises have no competence to give to the bigger one in exchange for theirs. They will eventually die (ceased enterprises) or try to change strategy, by starting an internal exploration. That's why at time 500 (figure 4) the total number of players increased again, but at a lower rate (1 every 15 steps, as an average) and now, in percentage, most of the survived enterprises are doing external exploration (62% circa) and have become quite big (many internal competences possessed). Notice that in this experiment the threshold under which an enterprise must cease is a low value, meaning that few of them have to leave the market. This was done intentionally to show how enterprises can react and adapt their behavior even if they are modeled as reactive agents.

6.1 Introduction of Process Innovation

The impact of innovation diffusion on the network depends on the collaboration degree of the system. If the network is collaborative the diffusion of innovation strengthens the ties and increases the number of the links among organizations. The firms are more inclined to exchange competences than to create them inside the organization: they favor an externally explorative behavior that obviously strengthens the network. A feature referred to as *"shock mode"* is used in this section, allowing the user to stop the model at a given step, and change some inner parameter. For example, it is possible to add a specific competence to one enterprise only, so that it's the only one in all the network possessing it. In that way it becomes possible to study how and based on which dynamics this specific competence spreads on the network and which kind of competitive advantage it gives, in terms of central position in the network and bargaining power to obtain other competences not possessed internally.

In particular, here this is used to introduce a process innovation, in the form of a totally new competence; all the enterprises can achieve it, but only one of them possesses it at a starting point.

As shown in figure 5 and figure 6, where some other output graphs obtained from the E³ simulation model are depicted, a collaborative network (A1) is defined by the existence of a large number of strong ties (compared to the number of enterprises). In our example, there are 10 strong ties among the enterprises. In a network structured in this way, the introduction and consequent diffusion of an innovation strengthens the collaborations through:

- An higher number of ties
- Ties that get even stronger (A2). In particular, the existing links get stronger and new ties are created ex novo.

In this case, the "shock effect" defined as the introduction of a process innovation brings effects in the networks that affect the decree of collaboration of the network itself. The introduction of an innovation in the network strengthens the links among the enterprises and the collaboration efficiency increases.

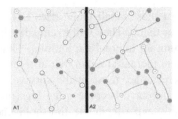

Fig. 5. Collaborative network before (A1) and after (A2) the introduction of an innovation

On the other side, in the case of a network with low propensity to collaboration the strong links do not exist or are a few when compared to the number of enterprises. The introduction of innovation in a network structured in this way can affect the degree of collaboration of the enterprises, according to industry complexity. In this situation (B1), it's possible to notice two different scenarios.

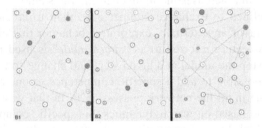

Fig. 6. Non-collaborative network before (B1) the introduction of an innovation. After (B2) in case of non complex industry, and after (B3) in case of complex industry.

If industry complexity is not too high (e.g.: the textile industry), as represented in B2, the number of ties is low and the firms prefer to create innovation inside the organization than receiving it from other organizations: in this case the firms favor internal exploration. So, when the complexity is low, the propensity to collaboration does not change and the enterprises are still loosely connected. The number of links could even increase, but much more slowly compared to the case of a collaborative network (B2 vs A2).

If industry complexity is high (B3), the diffusion of innovation increases the number of ties (but less than in a collaborative network) but the structure of ties is weak: in this case, again, the firms prefer an externally explorative behavior. So, in this case, the propensity to collaborate gets higher than before after the introduction of an innovation, but the links are always weaker when compared to the case of a collaborative network (B3 vs A2).

This qualitative analysis carried on through an agent based model allow to study "in the lab" a social system, like an enterprise network, and to study the effects of an innovation on collaborative and non-collaborative networks. While the purpose of this work is the description of the model itself, the qualitative results in this section show that the innovation diffusion in a network can create new ties among the enterprises (and thus it can be regarded as a driver for links creation in a network). Though, only in a collaborative network, or in a non-collaborative network acting in a complex industry, the number of the links increases significantly, while in non-collaborative networks acting in an industry which is not too complex, the number of links among the enterprises stays more or less the same, even after the introduction of the innovation (the enterprises being more focused on internal explorative behavior).

6.2 An Empirical Evidence

In order to propose an empirical validation of the obtained results two real world scenarios have been considered: Silicon Valley and Route 128. While the former succeeded in adapting to the transformations of the environment, the latter seems to be losing its competitive strength. Despite the similar origins, these regions developed different industrial systems: their different response to the crises happened during the 80s made clear the differences of productive organization whose significance had been underestimated during the quick economic growth of the first decade. During the 70s both Silicon Valley, in Northern California, and Route 128, near Boston, were highly praised by the World for being the leading edges in technological advances in Electronics. Both were honored for their technical vitality, entrepreneurship, and incredible economic growth. The two realities had a similar beginning: university research and post-war financing.

At the beginning of the 80s, the enchant rapidly vanished; the chip producers, located in the Silicon Valley, lost their market to the Japanese competitors, while the producers of mini-computers, located in the Route 128 area, saw the passage of their customers to workstations and personal computers. Notwithstanding the two economies took very different roads; in the Silicon Valley a new generation of enterprises rose, producing semi-conductors and computers, joining the big players already settled. The success of realities like Sun Microsystems, Conner Peripherals and Cypress Semiconductor, along with the dynamism of companies like Intel and Hewlett-Packard proved that Silicon Valley had recovered its previous vitality. On the contrary, Route 128 showed few signs of recovery and, by the end of the decade, most of the producers located there had given away their crown to those settled in Silicon Valley, that became the headquarter of more than one third of the technology societies created after 1965. The market value of these companies increased of 25 billions, when compared to 1 billion of those located in the Route 128 area.

Silicon Valley region features has an industrial system which promotes collective learning and flexible adjustment among the producers specialized in a series of connected activities (collaborative network). The dense social network of this region, along with the open labor market, encourage research and entrepreneurship; the companies compete among them, but at the same time learn from each other and exchange competences to face the market.

On the contrary, the enterprises in the Route 128 region are fewer and independent among them (non-collaborative network), whose industrial system is mainly based on internal competences, not shared with others.

The two scenarios look alike those exemplified in the previous paragraph; while Silicon Valley resembles the example shown in A1-A2, Route 128 is similar to the one seen in B1-B3. Even if in a simplistic way, this real world case constitutes an empirical evidence supporting the qualitative results coming from the E^3 model, and clarifies what kind of analyses can be carried on through this simulation tool.

7 Conclusion and Outlook

Process innovation is characterized by two important aspects: one critical and typical aspect is the ability to gather, develop and transform information and knowledge in a potential competitive advantage. The second aspect regards spending resources like time and money: the development of process innovation is usually time and resource consuming and is difficult to attain, especially when referring to radical cases. Though, process innovation is a key factor for building a network for competences exchange and a very important variable when considering the strategies performed by an enterprise; once possessed, the advantage can be exploited or shared. In the first case, the enterprise can gain customers and money, by being the only one (or among the few ones) possessing it. But it risks to lose its advantage as soon as other players can develop it. Another strategy is that of sharing the process innovation, in exchange for other competencies and/or money.

An agent based model is introduced in this work, aiming at capturing the dynamics behind the creation and the following modifications of an enterprise network for competences exchange, i.e.: a network in which enterprises can internally develop and/or share processes with other players. This is, by the way, one of the focal points behind the creation of industrial districts, enterprise clusters and so on. A well established network of this kind can attract new players, that will probably bring new knowledge and competences in it.

The model is formally discussed in detail, and so the agents composing it and its iterations. While studying quantitative results is beyond the purpose of this work, a qualitative analysis is described, and the network graph, one of the graphical outputs supplied by the model, is analyzed: in order to show how network dynamics emerge from the model and its parameters, settable by the user.

At the beginning, when the enterprises have few competences and high perception of how can be difficult develop and innovation process, they try to link with the enterprises that have already developed innovative processes. That's why, in an initial phase, the number of enterprises doing external exploration tends to increase. After some steps, the number of enterprises choosing external exploration is lower and lower and limited to the smallest players, or the newly arrived ones. The reason is that at the beginning, the enterprise's capability are low and the perception of the effort for developing a process innovation is high. The enterprise at this phase typically try to share and exchange competences with others that have already developed the innovative process, not having to face the risk of inside developing, even if this can be more gainful in the long run. As time passes by, the enterprises start to become bigger and be more conscious about their capabilities and knowledge, thus reducing the perception of the effort to develop innovative processes internally.

Another qualitative example is given, to show the difference among collaborative and non-collaborative networks, depicted by means of simulation, at the introduction of a process innovation; while in the former process innovation proves to be a driver for new link creation, in the latter the impact is quite smaller and almost irrelevant, especially if the sector is not a complex one.

To empirically validate these qualitative results, and in order to connect them to the real world, two cases are quickly analyzed, resembling those depicted in the computational examples: Silicon Valley and Route 128.

The model is comprehensive and its scope is wide. In future works other features will be described in detail, and also quantitative analysis will be carried on in order to study real-world cases (e.g.: existing industrial districts and so on) and the underlying dynamics that lead to their creations. In particular, computational only mode will be used to study the iterative behavior of networks, in ceteris paribus conditions (i.e.: by changing a single parameter at a time).

References

1. Zaheer, A., Bell, G.G.: Benefiting from network position: firm capabilities, structural holes, and performance. Strategic Management Journal (2005)
2. Koka, B.R., Prescott, J.E.: Designing alliance networks: the influence of network position, environmental change, and strategy on firm performance. Strategic Management Journal (2008)
3. Leonard-Barton, D.: Wellsprings of knowledge. Harvard Business School Press, Boston (1995)
4. Brown, J.S., Duguid, P.: Organizational Learning and Communities of Practice: Toward a Unified View of Working, Learning and Innovation. Organization Science 2, 40–57 (1991)
5. Kogut, B.: Joint ventures: theorical and empirical perspectives. Strategic Management Journal (1988)
6. Moreno, J.L., with foreword by White, W.A.: Who shall survive? A new approach to the problem of human interrelations. Nervous and Mental Disease Publishing Co. Psych. Abs., Washington, DC, 8, 5153; (Revised edition published by Beacon House in, Psych. Abs., 28, 4178) (1953)
7. Harary, F.: Mathematical aspect of electrical network analysis (1969)
8. Gulati, R., Gargiulo, M.: Where do interorganizational networks come from? American Journal of Sociology 104(5), 1439–1493 (1999)
9. Gulati, R., Nohria, N., Zaheer, A.: Strategic networks. Strategic Management Journal 21(3), 203–215 (2000)
10. Gulati, R.: Alliances and networks. Strategic Management Journal, Special Issue 19(4), 293–317 (1998)
11. Burt, R.S.: Structural Holes. Harvard University Press, Cambridge (1982)
12. Nohria, N.: The Differentiated Network: Organizing Multinational Corporations for Value Creation (1997)
13. Phlippen, S., Riccaboni, M.: Radical Innovation and Network Evolution (2007)
14. Remondino, M.: Agent Based Process Simulation and Metaphors Based Approach for Enterprise and Social Modeling. In: ABS 4 Proceedings, SCS Europ. Publish. House, pp. 93–97 (2003) ISBN 3-936-150-25-7
15. Remondino, M., Correndo, G.: MABS Validation Through Repeated Execution and Data Mining Analisys. International Journal of SIMULATION: Systems, Science & Technology (IJS3T) 7 (September 2006) ISSN: 1473-8031
16. Sherer, Innovation and Growth: Schumpeterian Perspectives (2007)

17. Srivardhana, T., Pawlowskiv, S.D.: ERP systems as an enabler of sustained business process innovation: A knowledge-based view. Science Direct (2007)
18. Rowley, T., Behrens, D., Krackhardt, D.: Redundant goverance structures: An analysis of structural and relational embeddedness in the steel and semiconductor industries. Strategic Management Journal 21, 369–386 (2000)
19. Davenport, T.H., Short, J.E.: The New Industrial Engineering: Information Technology and Business Process Redesign. Sloan Management Review, 11–27 (Summer 1990)
20. Edquist, C.: The Systems of Innovation Approach and Innovation Policy: An account of the state of the art. Paper presented at DRUID Conference, Aalborg, June 12-15 (2001)

Analyzing Strategic Business Rules through Simulation Modeling

Elena Orta[1], Mercedes Ruiz[1], and Miguel Toro[2]

[1] Department of Computer Languages and Systems,
Escuela Superior de Ingeniería,
C/ Chile, 1,
11003 – Cádiz, Spain
[2] Department of Computer Languages and Systems,
Escuela Técnica Superior de Ingeniería Informática,
Avda. Reina Mercedes, s/n,
41012 – Sevilla, Spain
{elena.orta,mercedes.ruiz}@uca.es, migueltoro@us.es

Abstract. Service Oriented Architecture (SOA) holds promise for business agility since it allows business process to change to meet new customer demands or market needs without causing a cascade effect of changes in the underlying IT systems. Business rules are the instrument chosen to help business and IT to collaborate. In this paper, we propose the utilization of simulation models to model and simulate strategic business rules that are then disaggregated at different levels of an SOA architecture. Our proposal is aimed to help find a good configuration for strategic business objectives and IT parameters. The paper includes a case study where a simulation model is built to help business decision-making in a context where finding a good configuration for different business parameters and performance is too complex to analyze by trial and error.

Keywords: Service-Oriented Development, Business Rules, Simulation Modeling.

1 Introduction

Service-oriented applications are built as a set of business processes and business process flows. Business process flows are in charge of orchestrating the different services, frequently web services, which are used to give response to the business requirements [1]. A very simple definition for a web service defines it as a programming subroutine that happens to be available over the Internet, and that offers a number of advantages such as location independency, standardized access protocol, platform-independency, is highly configurable and easy to evolve to adapt new business needs [2]. In order to achieve the high level of flexibility business applications need, business rules are the instrument chosen to build and link together these dynamic and flexible services. Thus, changes in the business can be translated into the business rules resulting in a new combination of services that respond to the new business requirements without having to change much code.

C. Godart et al. (Eds.): I3E 2009, IFIP AICT 305, pp. 357–368, 2009.
© IFIP International Federation for Information Processing 2009

Understanding and evaluating risks and rewards is now more than ever necessary to manage such flexible architectures to assure that the effect of decisions leads to improvement and benefits. Simulation techniques are known to be useful tools to help evaluate the impact of process changes or help in the design of new ones. As a consequence, the need for simulation and optimization is receiving a growing interest from the service oriented environment and vendors are offering tools to help model and simulate business processes as well as business rules.

In this paper, we propose the utilization of simulation models to model and simulate strategic business rules that are then disaggregated at different levels of a Service Oriented Architecture (SOA). Our proposal is aimed to act as a complementary tool to the available systems. It is aimed to help finding a good configuration for strategic business objectives and IT parameters that can help meet business rules and performance requirements.

This paper is structured as follows: Section 2 provides definitions for the concepts of business agility and business rules and describes a classification for business rules. Section 3, gives an overview of the related works found regarding the application of system dynamics simulation models and SOA. Section 4, describes a case of study to illustrate the application of system dynamics simulation to define strategic managerial business rules. Finally, Section 5 summarizes the paper and draws the conclusions.

2   SOA, Business Agility and Business Rules

Within the SOA approach, it is necessary to distinguish between process logic and decision logic. While process logic is finally supported by means of orchestrated services, decision logic is normally represented by rules that can, or better said should, be finally supported by means of orchestrated decision services. For instance, in a given e-commerce business, a certain set or orchestrated services can support the logic of a business process called *Orders*, responsible for receiving customer orders through the business portal and dispatching the products ordered. To make these actions possible, the business process needs from the decision logic generally provided by the form of business rules that determine how to rule this business process.

Business rules are often referred to be at the border side of business engineering and software engineering. This fact is also highlighted by the Business Rules Group in the definition they provide for the concept of Business Rule, which clearly depends on the perspective one is following [3]: "From the business perspective, a business rule is guidance that there is an obligation concerning conduct, action, practice, or procedure within a particular activity or sphere. From the information system perspective, a business rule is a statement that defines or constrains some aspect of the business. It is intended to assert business structure, or to control or influence the behavior of the business."

There are different kinds of orthogonal classification for business rules. Some of them attend principles of soft or hard coding, or attempt to classify business rules under the information system perspective (e.g., base rules, that can be of one of the following types: derivation, constraint, invariant and script, and classifier rules). However, the former classification does not seem to clearly provide a mechanism for business rules as described from a business perspective.

For the purpose of this study, we part from the classification proposed by Weiden and colleagues [4]. According to their proposal, business rules should be classified attending their semantic properties, that is, the role they play in the business process. Three categories are proposed for the business rules: a) structural, to describe static aspects of a business, b) behavioral, to describe the conditions of execution of tasks, and c) managerial, to define higher-level constraints on the business. In our view, this classification integrates the perspective of business and IT into one comprehensive schema of classification, being the structural and behavioral rules directly related to the IT and the managerial ones to the business perspective. However, these categories are not isolated but interdependent ones. That is, a managerial business rule is often translated into a set of structural and, mostly, behavioral rules.

3 Related Works

This section overviews some of the current contributions that apply simulation modeling techniques in the SOA context.

Jeng and An [5] propose the use of dynamic simulation models in SOA project management. They present a framework for managing SOA projects and how system dynamics simulation can enhance the effectiveness and agility of SOA project management. In [6], the authors present dynamic simulation modeling as a complementary technique for business requirement identification. [7] proposes a collection of heuristics and guidelines for the development of dynamic simulation models based on given business process models. [8] uses the simulation modeling techniques to present a framework for web service management. Finally, [9] presents a business-driven analysis method for business service development in the context of SOA by using the System Dynamics method to model services and simulate their behaviors.

To our knowledge, the originality of our proposal resides in the fact that it is aimed to help join business strategy decision-making with the technical issues of IT implementation. It is not used to test the behavior of decision services as in [9] but to help business management evaluate the fulfillment of strategic decisions and their impact in application performance.

4 Case Study

This section includes a case study that helps to illustrate our proposal. We part from a problem description and a concrete business rule for a company. The simulation model built is aimed to help business decision-making when finding a good configuration for different business and performance parameters is too complex to analyze by trial and error.

4.1 Problem Description

For the purpose of this study let us assume a hypothetical e-commerce company that sells products on the Internet. The company plays a distribution role by buying the products to their manufacturers and selling them to their customers who place orders through the company website.

As it was mentioned before, in SOA projects the main focus is on business needs. These business needs can be expressed in the form of managerial business rules that aggregate different business rules that affect the structure and behavior of the system. One of the most common managerial objectives of service-oriented business is customer satisfaction. Customer satisfaction can be described as a function of many inter-related factors. For our e-commerce company, customer satisfaction can be a function of factors such as the website usability, its functionality, availability and interactivity, the time needed to deliver the products, the system response during customer interaction, and the system capacity for processing orders, among others. It results clear that even though all these factors contribute to the fulfillment of our general business rule, not all of them can be dealt with at the same level of the service-oriented architecture. For the purpose of this paper, we will focus on one of these business rules that lead to customer satisfaction: the ability of the system to process the orders placed by the company's customers. Again, this ability depends of several factors including our in-home database services, the performance and availability of the company's servers and the response of external services, among others.

One of the main features of service-oriented development is that invoked services are platform and location independent. Issues such as performance measurement, priorities, responsibilities and problem resolution, availability, operation or billing model figure in the contract the service provider and a client company subscribe called Service Level Agreement (SLA).

In our case, one of the outsourced services will be the service to validate if the customer's credit card has enough credit to cover the purchase. Estimating the desired performance of this outsourced service is not an easy task since it is highly influenced by the market, the selling policy of the company and its effects on the tendency of customer's orders.

Among the different parameters that help define the service capacity in an SLA, the following are among the most frequent [1]:

- Abandon Rate (ABA): Percentage of calls abandoned while waiting to be answered.
- Average Speed to Answer (ASA): Average time (usually in seconds) it takes for a call to be answered.
- Time Service Factor (TSF): Percentage of calls answered within a definite time-frame, e.g. 80% in 20 seconds.
- First Call Resolution (FCR): Percentage of incoming calls that can be resolved without the use of a callback, or without having the caller call back.

Depending on the values estimates and specified for the former parameters, the billing model and the quantity the company has to pay to the service provider will vary. If these parameters have been under or over-estimated they will have a direct effect not only on the bill but on the application performance, the customer satisfaction and, eventually, on the market position of the company.

With the aim of helping managers in this decision-making process, a simulation model is built to allow *playing* with different service capacities and customer-order tendencies in order to analyze their effects on the fulfillment of our business objective.

4.2 Simulation Model Building

Following Kellner's proposal for describing simulation models [10], this section describes the simulation model built to analyze this problem.

4.2.1 Model Proposal and Scope

The simulation model is built to help analyze on a qualitative manner the fulfillment of one of the business rules that leads to the achievement of customer's satisfaction. This business rule is: *Allow no more than 15% of rejected orders*. The scope of the model is a portion of the life cycle. Its organization breadth is multiple projects and its time span is short, since we are dealing with seconds as a unit. The simulation time-frame is ten minutes.

4.2.2 Result Variables

The main result variable that provides information regarding the simulation model objective is called *Degree of Business Objective Fulfillment*. It expresses the difference between the orders that haven been rejected by the system due to an underestimated credit validation capacity and the maximum rejection rate allowed by the business rule (15% in this case study).

Other result variables can also be helpful to understand what is happening in the system during the simulation timeframe. They are the following:

- *Orders received*: The number of customer's orders received in the website. This number will depend on the tendency of customer's orders.
- *Validated orders*: The number of received orders that have been successfully credit-validated.
- *Rejected orders*: The number of received orders that have been rejected because they have exceeded the waiting time established by the company without being able of getting an answer from the credit validation service. Orders rejected for this reason are due to an underestimation for the credit validation capacity that has been contracted with the service provider.

4.2.3 Input Parameters

Input parameters allow us to configure different scenarios to test the effects of contracting different credit validation capacities in different tendencies of customer's orders. The following input parameters are used to configure the different scenarios for the simulation runs included in this study:

- *Credit Validation Capacity*: It represents the maximum capacity the company has contracted with the credit validation service provider.
- *Waiting Time Allowed*: It holds the value for the maximum time a received order is allowed to wait for the credit validation service response. Once this time is exceeded, the order is rejected.
- *Tendency of customer's orders*: It represents the effect of customer's reaction to the launching of a special order on the number of orders received in the company website.

4.2.4 Process Abstraction

Fig. 1 illustrates the main variables of the model and their interrelationships. It shows that *Customer Satisfaction* depends on the number of *Validated Orders* (the higher, the better), and the number of *Rejected Orders* (the lower, the better). *Validated Orders* depends on the number of *Orders Received* and the *Credit Validation Capacity*. The number of *Orders Received* depends on the current *Tendency of Customer's Orders* which reflects customer's reaction to the presence of, for instance, special offers in the website. Finally, *Rejected Orders* depends on the number of *Orders Received* that has been waiting for more than the maximum *Waiting Time Allowed* as well as the number of *Validated Orders*.

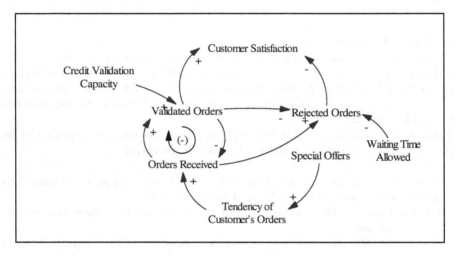

Fig. 1. Causal Diagram with main interrelationships

In the running model, *Orders Received*, *Validated Orders* and *Rejected Orders* are modeled as level variables whose behavior is controlled by the flow variables *Order Rate*, *Validation Rate* and *Order Rejection Rate*. The input parameters of the model are the acting elements upon which the fulfillment of the business rule can be assured.

4.3 Simulation Runs

This section includes different simulation runs resulting from different patterns of behavior of the input variable *OrderRate*.

- CASE 1 (CONST): Assumes that after the launching of a special offer, the mentioned rate experiments a rapid grow and then remains constant at its peak value.
- CASE 2 (RAMP): Assumes a similar behavior for the order rate, but the increment is not step-shaped but gradual, hence it has been modeled as a ramp.
- CASE 3 (PULSE): Assumes that after the launching of a special offer the order rate grows rapidly, stays at its peak value for a while and then descends gradually.

Fig. 2 shows graphically the patterns of behavior considered for this input rate.

CASE 1   CASE 2   CASE 3

Fig. 2. Patterns of behavior for input variable *OrderRate*

The simulation runs shown in this section represent the deviation of the output variable *OrderRejectionRate* respect the initial business objective. It is important to notice that we are focusing only on the rejections due to orders that have been waiting for a credit validation for more than the maximum time allowed by the company. Other reasons for rejections such as server down or incorrect credit card data are not included since they are not affected by the input parameters of this simulation model. The results obtained in the different scenarios follow.

CASE 1: *OrderRate* grows rapidly and then stays constant (CONST)

SCENARIO CONFIGURATION

- **OrderRate (OR):** Table 1 shows the features of the order rate assumed in CASE 1 for the tendency of customer's order.

Table 1. Order Rate behavior in CASE 1

Initial OR	Increment for OR	Pulse Begins at	Pulse Width
500 orders/minute	1000 orders/minute	1 minute	10 minutes

- **CreditValidationCapacity (CVC):** Table 2 shows the different values for this parameter used to configure four different scenarios (named, Const1-Const4).

Table 2. Credit Validation Capacity values for CASE 1

Scenario	Const1	Const2	Const3	Const4
CVC (orders/minute)	500	600	700	900

SIMULATION OUTPUT

Fig. 3 shows the different results obtained for the degree of non-fulfillment for the business objective for each of the scenarios previously described. The variable graphically displayed shows the difference between the *OrderRejectionRate* and the business objective. This figure does not show the results for the scenario *Const4* since in this case the deviation respect the objective is always zero, that is, the business objective is always met during the simulation time frame.

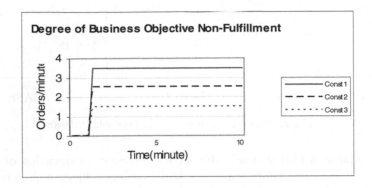

Fig. 3. Simulation output for CASE 1

Looking at the results for the rest of scenarios, the business objective is met in all of them before the increment of the order rate takes place, since OR<=CVC. However, once this increment is achieved, the business objective is only met in scenario Const4 and for that, a CVC=900 orders/minute is needed. Const1 is the scenario with the maximum deviation from the objective (350 orders/minute), while Const2 has a deviation of 250 orders/minute and Const3 presents a deviation of 150 orders/minute.

Therefore, the simulation runs offer the expected results for the given inputs and constraints: the higher the increment of the order rate during the special offer, the higher the capacity needed to validate the credit for incoming orders.

CASE 2. *OrderRate* grows gradually and then stays constant (RAMP)

SCENARIO CONFIGURATION

-   ***OrderRate (OR):*** In this case, the gradual grow of the order rate is modeled by a ramp with a different slope and length in each scenario. Three main groups of simulations have been run (Case21 –Case23) as shown in Table 3.

Table 3. Groups of simulations for CASE 2

	Initial OR (orders/minute)	Ramp Slope	Ramp Length (minutes)
Case21	500	1	2
Case22	500	2	2
Case23	500	1	3

CreditValidationCapacity (CVC):

Table 4 shows the different values for CVC and the former group of simulation leading to the definition of twelve different scenarios.

Table 4. Scenarios simulated for CASE 2

CVC	Case21	Case22	Case23
500 orders/minute	Ramp11	Ramp21	Ramp31
600 orders/minute	Ramp12	Ramp22	Ramp32
700 orders/minute	Ramp13	Ramp23	Ramp33
900 orders/minute	Ramp14	Ramp24	Ramp34

SIMULATION OUTPUT

Fig. 4 shows the different results obtained for the degree of non-fulfillment for the business objective. The outputs for the scenarios Ramp12, Ramp13, Ramp14, Ramp24, Ramp33 and Ramp34 do not appear in this figure since in all of them, the deviation is zero and hence the business objective is always met.

Analyzing the scenarios where a non-fulfillment is found, it can be seen that for a CVC = 500 orders/minute, the business objective is not met at any of the scenarios in which CVC takes that value (Ramp11, Ramp21, and Ramp 31), having Ramp 21 both the largest deviation and the soonest apparition of the deviation. When CVC = 600 orders/minute, the objective is not met at Ramp22 and Ramp32 scenarios, having in this case Ramp22 both the largest deviation and the soonest it appears. When CVC = 700 orders/minute, the only scenario in which the objective is not met is Ramp23. Finally, when CVC=900 orders/minute, the objective is met in every scenario. Therefore, it can be concluded that for a certain CVC, the larger the slope for the order rate and the sooner that growing begins, the larger the deviation respect the business objective is. Besides, the deviation respect the objective grows with the length of the slope for the order rate.

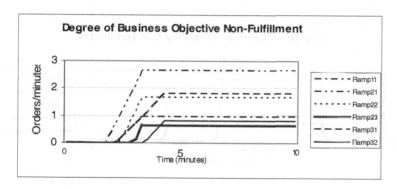

Fig. 4. Simulation output for CASE 2

CASE3: OrderRate grows gradually, stays constant, and then decreases gradually (PULSE)

SCENARIO CONFIGURATION

- *OrderRate (OR)*: In this case, the gradual grow of the order rate is modeled by a pulse with different heights and widths in each scenario. The three main groups of simulations that have been run are shown in Table 5.

Table 5. Groups of simulations for CASE 3

	Initial OR (orders/minute)	Increment (orders/minute)	Step Begins at	Pulse Width (minutes)
Case31	500	1000	1 minute	6
Case32	500	1000	1 minute	4
Case33	500	700	1 minute	6

- *CreditValidationCapacity (CVC)*: Table 6 shows the different values for CVC and the former groups of simulation leading to the definition of nine different scenarios.

Table 6. Scenarios simulated for CASE 3

CVC	Case31	Case32	Case33
500 orders/minute	Pulse11	Pulse21	Pulse31
700 orders/minute	Pulse12	Pulse22	Pulse32
900 orders/minute	Pulse13	Pulse23	Pulse33

SIMULATION OUTPUT

Fig. 5 shows the different results obtained for the degree of non-fulfillment for the business objective. The outputs for the scenarios Pulse13, Pulse23, Pulse32 and Pulse33 do not appear in this figure since in all of them, the deviation is zero and, hence, the business objective is always met.

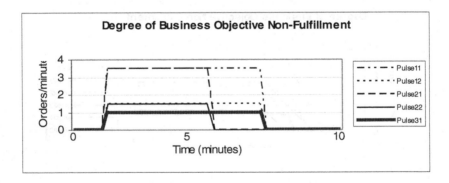

Fig. 5. Simulation output for CASE 3

Analyzing the scenarios where non-fulfillment is found, it can be seen that for a CVC = 500 orders/minute, the objective is not met in scenarios Pulse11, Pulse21 and Pulse31. Pulse11 presents the largest and longest deviation. When CVC=700 orders/minute, the business objective is not met in Pulse12 and Pulse22. Even though the deviation respect the business objective is the same in both scenarios, the deviation is Pulse 12 lasts longer than in Pulse 12. Finally, when CVC=900 orders/minute, the objective can always be met.

Therefore, it can be concluded that for a given CVC, the larger the pulse width, the less time the business objective can be fulfilled. Besides, the larger the pulse height, the larger the deviation respect the business objective.

5 Conclusions and Further Work

In this work we have presented the first results of a research effort aimed at applying simulation modeling in service-oriented architectures. In this paper, a simulation model was developed to help analyze the consequences of under- or overestimation of the capacity of an outsourced service reflected in its SLA on the application perform-ance and hence customer satisfaction. To do that, different scenarios were configured by varying the outsourced service capacity and the tendency of customer's orders that tried to reflect the effect of launching a special offer at a company website.

The simulation model helps mainly to design the suitable combination of service capacity in a customer's demand context to satisfy a business objective (allow no more than 15% order rejection). Other studies can also be made with this simulation model such as sensitivity simulations or optimization studies in the context of deter-mining the suitable billing model.

Our future work is mainly focused on the development of simulation models to help in decision-making in different domains of service-oriented architectures as well as the service-oriented development process. In this sense, new features will be added to the model presented in order to better resemble real life projects and applications. After developing the models, we intend to apply them in real companies to help both calibrate and validate the simulation models and provide the benefits of its usage for their potential users.

Acknowledgments. This research was partly supported by the Spanish Ministry of Education and Science and the European FEDER funds under project TIN2007-67843-C06-04.

References

1. Marks, E.A., Bell, M.: Service-Oriented Architecture: a Planning and Implementation Guide for Business and Technology. John Wiley & Sons, Inc., New Jersey (2006)
2. SOA World Magazine, http://soa.sys-con.com
3. Business Rules Group,
   http://www.businessrulesgroup.org/defnbrg.shtml
4. Weiden, M., Hermans, L., Schreiber, G., van der Zee, S.: Classification and Representation of Business Rules (2002), http://www.omg.org/docs/ad/02-12-18.pdf
5. Jeng, J.J., An, L.: System Dynamics Modeling for SOA Management. In: IEEE Interna-tional Conference on Service-Oriented Computing and Application, pp. 286–294. IEEE Computer Society, Washington (2007)
6. An, L., Jeng, J.J., Gerede, C.E.: On Exploiting System Dynamics Modeling to Identify Service Requirements. In: IEEE International Conference on Services Computing, pp. 277–280. IEEE Computer Society, Washington (2006)

7. An, L., Jeng, J.J.: On Developing System Dynamics Model for Business Process Simulation. In: Winter Simulation Conference, Florida, pp. 2068–2077 (2005)
8. An, L., Jeng, J.J.: Web Service Management Using System Dynamics. In: IEEE International Conference on Web Services, pp. 347–354. IEEE Computer Society, Washington (2005)
9. An, L., Jeng, J.J.: Business-Driven SOA Solution Development. In: IEEE International Conference on e-Business Engineering, pp. 439–444. IEEE Computer Society, Washington (2007)
10. Kellner, M.I., Madachy, R.J., Raffo, D.: Software process simulation modeling: Why? What? How? J. Syst. Software 46(2-3), 91–105 (1999)

Towards E-Society Policy Interoperability

Renato Iannella

NICTA
Level 5, Axon Building #47
Staff House Rd, St Lucia, QLD, 4072, Australia
renato@nicta.com.au

Abstract. The move towards the Policy-Oriented Web is destined to provide support for policy expression and management in the core web layers. One of the most promising areas that can drive this new technology adoption is e-Society communities. With so much user-generated content being shared by these social networks, there is the real danger that the implicit sharing rules that communities have developed over time will be lost in translation in the new digital communities. This will lead to a corresponding loss in confidence in e-Society sites. The Policy-Oriented Web attempts to turn the implicit into the explicit with a common framework for policy language interoperability and awareness. This paper reports on the policy driving factors from the Social Networks experiences using real-world use cases and scenarios. In particular, the key functions of policy-awareness - for privacy, rights, and identity - will be the driving force that enables the e-Society to appreciate new interoperable policy regimes.

Keywords: E-Society, Policy-Oriented Web, Policy Languages, Social Networks, Interoperability, Privacy, Rights.

1 Introduction

The e-Society has been a long term dream that the ICT community, amongst others, have moved towards with new technologies over the past decade. The engagement of citizens in e-Societies has enabled greater participation and opportunities for communities to offer "information commons" [1] for digital interactions. Today, we clearly have this dream realised with Social Networks. Social Networks - via the innovative use of Web 2.0 features - have also taken the ICT community by surprise with such rapid uptake and widespread content sharing.

Social Networks attempt to mimic and support normal society interactions and experiences. In many cases, these seem to be working well, such as keeping friends and family in contact and sharing status information. However, the wide-spread sharing of personal and corporate information within Social Networks (eg photos, documents) have an impact on policy support, such as privacy and rights management decisions. These issues have now become more relevant as Social Networks have empowered the end user to share even more private content with increasing global reach. Additionally, the providers that offer these services have an immense database of personal information at their disposal.

C. Godart et al. (Eds.): I3E 2009, IFIP AICT 305, pp. 369–384, 2009.
© IFIP International Federation for Information Processing 2009

Generally, Social Networks "provide complex and indeterminate mechanisms to specific privacy and other policies for protecting access to personal information, and allow information to be shared that typically would not follow social and professional norms" [2]. There have been numerous attempts to solve this problem in the past but none have been really successful, nor applicable to the Social Networks community. A new approach is required to manage seamless policy interaction for the e-Society masses. The "Policy-Oriented Web" is an emerging idea to bring greater policy management technologies to the core web infrastructure. This will enable polices to interoperate across Social Network service providers.

In this paper we present e-Society use cases from Social Networks to highlight the driver for the adoption of new interoperable policy technologies. We then present an information model for the Policy-Oriented Web and show some example representations. Finally, we look at related works and conclude with how e-Society - via Social Networks - can lead to greater interoperability opportunities for policies across the wider Web.

2 E-Society Use Case: Social Networks

Social Networks, like FaceBook, Flickr, LinkedIn, Xing, YouTube, and MySpace, have been phenomenally successful. They have achieved this by providing simple yet user empowering features that digitally support the online social experience. In particular, the relative ease of sharing content with close colleagues and friends has driven Social Networks participation. However, this experience can have serious repercussions if the implicit arrangements under which content is shared are not known explicitly, or worse, are not respected.

Two recent examples have highlighted these negative experiences. The first was the use of photographs from Flickr in a commercial advertising program [4]. In this case, the image of a person was used by Virgin Mobile in billboard advertising. They had taken the image from Flickr as the photo owner (the person's friend) had selected a Creative Commons license that allowed commercial usage. This highlighted two issues; understanding the implications of commercial usage, and publishing images of your friends on public websites. The photo owner had assumed that commercial usage may have enabled him to participate in the financial rewards (it didn't). His friend who appeared in the photos also had no idea her image was being used, until it was too late (she was not impressed). The lack of understanding the requirement for "model release" permission in the license policy also contributed to this situation.

The second example involved photos from FaceBook being used by the mainstream media to report on the death of a defence force trooper [5]. The media had used his personal photos from his FaceBook profile - including photos of his family - to print in the national newspapers. At no time did they seek permission to reproduce these images. In some of the media responses to this issue, the assumption was stated that since the photos were on the Internet anyway, they were deemed "public domain" and you could basically do whatever you like with the images with little recourse.

Both of these cases involve sharing of photos on Social Networks and highlight challenges to owners and end users on the right level of respect for use of such content. To investigate this issue further, we looked at the processes for sharing photos on Facebook.

Like many Web 2.0 Social Networks, Facebook requires the account owner to certify - implicitly - that they have the right to distribute uploaded photos and that it does not violate the Facebook terms and conditions (see Figure 1). The latter is an eight page document of dense 'legal-ese' wording that not only is unlikely to be read by account owners, but rarely would be understood by the layperson.

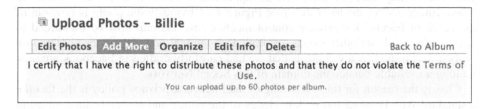

Fig. 1. FaceBook Photo Upload Certification

Facebook allows you to add photos in named Albums to your account. You can then decide on who can see these photo albums with some simple image privacy controls. Figure 2 shows the options available including; Everyone, My Networks and Friends, Friends of Friends, and Only Friends.

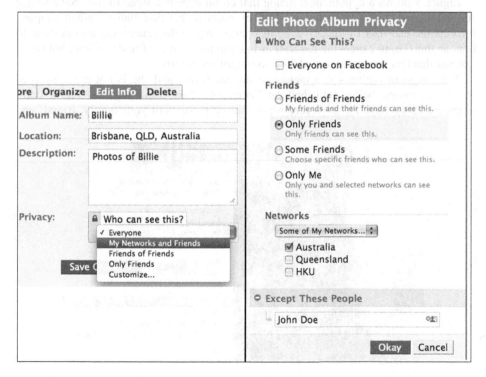

Fig. 2. FaceBook Photo Options   **Fig. 3.** FaceBook Photo Privacy Options

However, when you choose the Customize options, additional detailed privacy controls are available (see Figure 3). Now you can be very specific, such as indicating which individual friends can see the photo ("Some Friends") and who cannot ("Except These People"). You can also specify specific Networks of friends as well.

At this stage, when an end user - be they public, in your network, or a friend - sees your photo, they have the usual file manipulation controls in their web browser to "Save Image As" to the local disk (see Figure 4). Obviously the photo is now out of the reach of Facebook's privacy control mechanisms and can now be forwarded to anyone via email and other means, or printed in national newspapers, or plastered on billboards. So the privacy controls that we had carefully crafted in Facebook are now no longer available outside the domain of this Social Network.

Clearly the reason for this overriding of the Facebook privacy policy is the fact the a standard Web Browser has no knowledge of the policy and any embedded image in a web page can "normally" be saved to local disk. If we could design an enhancement to Facebook - if not all Social Networks - then we would consider a simple mechanism that informs the end user that the photo has some restrictions attached. We don't envisage an "enforcement" mechanism, as this would not be consistent with the ethos of Social Networks, but an "accountability" mechanism would be sufficient and appropriate. This would allow, for example, images to be cached by the browser (for efficiency) but not explicitly saved outside the browser environment.

Figure 5 shows a hypothetical dialog that could appear instead of the "Save Image As" dialog (as shown in Figure 4). The key point is that this dialog - albeit simple - informs the end user of the privacy rules pertaining to the image and allows them to honour this (i.e. to cancel the request) or to continue with the file download, but being warned that this may be recorded for accountability purposes.

The image in Figure 4 is a picture of my cat Billie, and she is not too concerned about her image being published on FaceBook. The issue becomes really compounded, as we have already seen, when sharing pictures of your family, friends and

Fig. 4. Web Browser "Same Image As..." Menu

Fig. 5. New Save Dialog

colleagues. Facebook includes a feature whereby you can annotate photos and indicate the names of the people in the photo. These can be existing Facebook members or non-members. The image would then show their names (with a mouse-over their face) and, for members, would link to their profile.

Figure 6 shows an example of selecting my colleagues faces in a photo and assigning them to their Facebook identity. (Note that the images and names have be deliberately blurred in Figure 6 to protect their privacy). As with the photo of Billie, this photo can also be downloaded and shared bypassing the Facebook privacy policy. It also poses greater threat as my two colleagues in the photo also do not wish their image to be used for any other purpose than a corporate image of the project team.

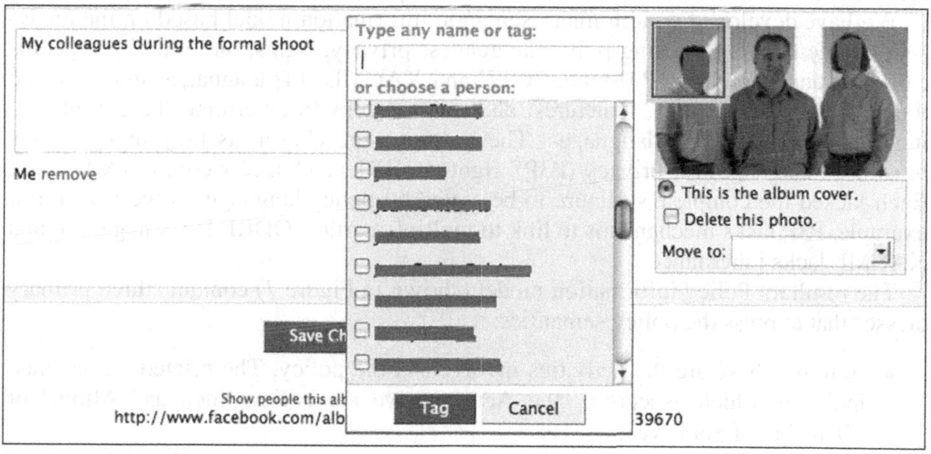

Fig. 6. FaceBook - Photo Friends Tagging

However, we do now have the new possibility of checking the individual's policy needs since we have identified all the people in the photo. We could automatically notify each of them and ask if they would allow their friend (ie me) to publish the photo of them in his photo album and under the privacy policy I have designated. For example, I could allow the photo for complete public access, or limited to a network, or my friends. They could then respond based on this. This "policy negotiation" could also be automated to allow quicker responses, based on an individuals own privacy policy.

To summarise, Social Networks, like Facebook and others, have a tremendous opportunity now to look towards simple, yet powerful, policy support to match the community expectations when sharing content. The emerging Policy-Oriented Web can exploit these use cases as the driver to develop new web infrastructure. Future Web 2.0 services can be built upon this new web infrastructure to provide fair and accountable content sharing services.

3 The Policy–Oriented Web

The Policy-Oriented Web, also sometimes referred to as the Policy-Aware Web, is an emerging field that aims to address the need to manage multiple and conflicting policies in the future distributed service-oriented world. This will increase connectivity across disparate web systems and services as they can achieve a new level of automated interoperability, guided by declarative policies that can adapt to different contexts and environments. In an earlier position paper [6] we outlined the major key strategic challenges posed by the Policy-Oriented Web. This included the need for a unified model that can adequately represent policies. Such a unified model - based on various policy requirements - will capture the core concepts and structures common to all policies. The model should also provide the framework for addressing even deeper policy-specific challenges such as the evaluation, enforcement, and reasoning of policies, and how to deal with inconsistencies across policies.

We have developed a preliminary semantic information model based on the analysis of three types of existing policy languages; privacy, rights, and identity. Specifically, we analysed the P3P [8], ODRL [7] and XACML [14] languages and reviewed their information features, structures, and relationships to determine the commonalities across these policy languages. These three were chosen as they represent the most used languages for privacy (P3P), rights (ODRL) and access control (XACML). Each lacked the complete structure to be a general policy language on their own. For example, P3P lacks mechanisms to link to multiple parties, ODRL lacks negation, and XACML lacks inheritance.

The resultant Policy information model (shown in Figure 7) contains three primary classes that express the policy semantics:

- Action - these are the activities involved in the policy. The related Focus class indicates which aspects of the Action drive the policy, such as "Allow" or "Deny" or "Exclusive".
- Resource - these are the resources/content involved in the policy. The related Target class indicates which aspects of the Resource are relevant to the policy, such as "One" or "Any" or "All".
- Party - these are the people and organisations involved in the policy. The related Role class indicates which role the Party plays in relation to the policy, such as "Licensee" or "Consumer".

These three classes were found to be the core components from the policy languages analysed. Supporting these three classes are the following classes:

- Act - identifies specific acts that can be performed.
- Object - identifies specific entities.
- Function - identifies comparative operators.

A Policy can also include two other classes that modify the behaviour of Actions and Parties:

- Constraint - conditions that will limit an Action of the policy. This can cover a range of options from the fundamental (such as numeric, date ranges, geospatial) to the more complex (such as a particular purpose or domain use).
- Obligation - requirements that must be met by a Party in order to satisfy the policy. This can also cover a wide range from the fundamental (such as payment) to the the the more complex (such as being tracked for usage).

Both the Constraint and Obligation classes are supported by the Operation class. The Operation class links instances of Act, Object, and Function classes to uniquely express the required operation. The Operation will enable reasoning services over policies as it will contain the fundamental data for policy expressions.

We have represented the Policy-Oriented Web Information Model (Figure 7) in RDF and RDF Schema (modeled using the Protégé tool). It was quite challenging in converting a typical information model (such as Figure 7) and mapping it into an RDF model. It some cases it was not clear how to best represent the information artifact, such as Focus and Deny, into the triple-based model of RDF.

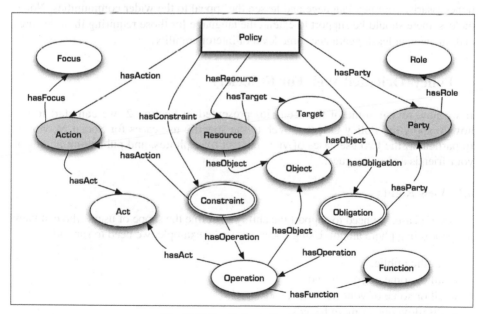

Fig. 7. Policy Information Model

The example RDF Schema snippet below shows the "hasObject" property with "Object" range and domain of "Operation", "Party", and "Resource" classes.

```
<rdf:Property rdf:about="urn:policy:10:hasObject">
    <rdfs:range rdf:resource="urn:policy:10:Object"/>
    <rdfs:domain rdf:resource="urn:policy:10:Operation"/>
    <rdfs:domain rdf:resource="urn:policy:10:Party"/>
    <rdfs:domain rdf:resource="urn:policy:10:Resource"/>
</rdf:Property>
```

We have chosen just RDF and RDF Schema to keep the first iteration of the Policy-Oriented Web as "simple" as possible without over complicating the expression structures. This will be important to meet the technical needs of the Web 2.0 and Social Networks communities. We plan to also use RDFa as another encoding direct into HTML pages.

Others have proposed semantic expression of specific policy languages in the richer OWL language for rights [11, 12] and privacy [13] policies. We envisage the future where use of such advanced semantic web languages will also be supported in the Web 2.0 platform of technologies. In the first iteration of the Policy-Oriented Web, we believe that basing it on the RDF language is the best compromise. The Policy-Oriented Web information model could also be expressed in OWL for more advanced reasoning and ontological features needed by high-end communities. However, this may lead to an unnecessarily complex language and lessen the appeal to the wider communities. Nonetheless, there should be support to extend the language for those requiring these features and this will, at least, guarantee some level of interoperability.

4 Policy–Oriented Web For E-Society

If we now revisit some of the scenarios presented in Section 2, we can start to see how to apply the Policy-Oriented Web to the specific use cases for Social Networks. In particular, the two use cases of view control over photos, and publishing photos of your friends and colleagues.

4.1 View Rights

In this use case, we need to support the ability to define the scope of users who can view the photos in a photo album. Using Facebook, as an example, we need to support:

- all the public,
- all or some of your friends,
- all or some of your networks, and
- disallow one or more friends.

These would be expressed as Constraints in the Policy-Oriented Web model as part of a policy instance. The example below shows the RDF/XML snippet that would express that only people in your "Australia" network can view the photos.

```
<p:Constraint rdf:ID="view-aust-network">
  <p:hasAction rdf:resource="policy:render"/>
  <p:hasOperation rdf:resource="group-australia-network"/>
</p:Constraint>

<p:Operation rdf:ID="group-australia-network">
  <p:hasAct rdf:resource="policy:group"/>
  <p:hasFunction rdf:resource="policy:equal"/>
  <p:hasObject rdf:resource="network-australia"/>
</p:Operation>

<p:Object rdf:ID="network-australia"
  p:hasIdentity="urn:facebook:network:australia"/>
```

These expressions capture the unique identifier for the Facebook Australia Network, and allows viewing (policy:render) for this network (policy:group) using the unique identifiers from the policy model semantics.

4.2 Friend's Privacy

In this use case, we need to allow your friends and colleagues that appear in your photos the ability to state whether they approve their image being published, including the scope of users who can view the photos. Using Facebook, as an example, we need to support the scenario of a friend tagging them on a photo and allow them to opt-out if they do not agree.

This use case is more complex in that it requires negotiation between the owner of the photo and the friends in the photo. We will not discuss the intricacies of policy negotiation [10] in this paper, but highlight this as a requirement for the future Policy-Oriented Web.

Typically, we would see that users would have a default privacy policy as part of their account profile. This policy would express their preferences on how their image can be used in social network photo albums. Their privacy policy would then be compared to the "view rights policy" that one of their friends is proposing. If there is conflict then this would stop the publication (the default action) and the user may be asked to "consider" the policy and confirm/deny it manually.

For example, the below RDF/XML snippet shows a privacy-policy in which the user has denied viewing (render) for any resources containing their image for any Facebook Network.

```
<p:Policy rdf:ID="myPrivacy">
  <p:hasResource rdf:resource="images-of-me"/>
  <p:hasAction rdf:resource="view-deny"/>
  <p:hasOperation rdf:resource="group-network"/>
</p:Policy>

<p:Operation rdf:ID="group-network">
  <p:hasAct rdf:resource="policy:group"/>
  <p:hasFunction rdf:resource="policy:equal"/>
  <p:hasObject rdf:resource="network"/>
</p:Operation>

<p:Object rdf:ID="network"
  p:hasIdentity="urn:facebook:network:all"/>

<p:Action rdf:ID="viewDeny" p:hasFocus="deny" >
  <p:hasAct rdf:resource="policy:render"/>
</p:Action>
```

The same model can be used to deny "public" and "friend" access (with appropriate identifiers from FaceBook). Conversely, if the user was happy to allow access for any network, friend, or public, then the "hasFocus" can simply be changed to "allow".

4.3 Toward Interoperability

Returning to the two real-world use cases described in Section 2, both of these should have been avoided with an appropriate policy expression and accountability across Social Networks and platforms. Today, however, even if the correct rights/privacy/access criteria was selected under the controlled Social Network environment, the lack of policy support at the operating system level (including the web browser) hinders policy conformance. This is one of the greatest challenges for the Policy-Oriented Web; to become pervasive across all platforms and

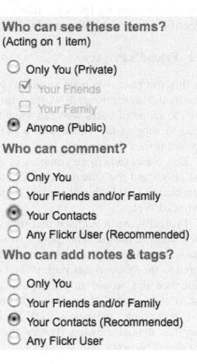

Fig. 8. Flickr Photo Permissions

services to enable any application to depend on open and interoperable policy-support services.

Looking back at the Flickr case, a rights policy could express that "Your Friends" in your photo have not given permission for their image to be reproduced (outside this specific Social Network). Figure 8 shows the permissions from Flickr for photos, which includes these constraints. In the FaceBook case, a similar policy could express that the family photos are not reproducible outside of Facebook.

Notice that the fundamental differences between Flickr (Figure 8) and FaceBook (Figure 3) include some permissions (such as excluding named people and "networks" versus "groups") but are also similar in other respects. This means that at one level interoperability across these two Social Networks is possible if they share (and reuse) some of the core policy constructs. However, if one used "policy:group" and the other defined their own "flickr:family" then there will be some issues to overcome. More significant will be the lack of support for some features (eg exclusion of people) that only one Social Network supports.

The Flickr options (see Figure 8) also includes more permissions than just view (render). Specifically, they also allow for "commenting" and "tagging". However, when you look deeper at the Facebook implementation of "view" it does also allow commenting on photos. This implies that if you translate "view" from Flickr to Facebook then you must not allow "commenting" and "tagging", unless they are also specified. This leads to issues of conflict detection across these policies.

For example, this Act:

```
<p:Act p:hasIdentity="urn:facebook:view"/>
```

is similar to:

```
<p:Act p:hasIdentity="urn:flickr:view"/>
<p:Act p:hasIdentity="urn:flickr:comment"/>
<p:Act p:hasIdentity="urn:flickr:tag"/>
```

However, the reverse is not true.

These two sets of Acts could be in direct conflict if not used correctly. As they currently stand, the process in determining this conflict may involve prior knowledge, most likely via humans mapping the two core parts of the different policy language ontologies, and building the conflict detection into the software application logic.

The longer term aim is to support services for ontology mappings to help automate this process. Ontology mapping is extremely difficult to generalise but significant research efforts are showing early promises [9]. We see this as a key feature of the Policy-Oriented Web and a future research challenge.

The challenges that lay ahead are for the Social Network communities to develop the common vocabularies (ontologies) for the policy expressions. This will enable a policy in Facebook to be supported in Flickr, for example. A greater challenge is the support in different platforms, like web browsers, to be aware that policies are attached to content. This is the long term goal of the Policy-Oriented Web.

5 Related Work

Requirements for any new area of work are always important. A number of research goals in the area of semantic policies include [15]:

- lightweight knowledge representation to reduce the effort for policy-oriented frameworks for specific communities,
- incorporation of controlled natural language syntax for expressing policy rules, and a
- relaxed cooperative policy enforcement regime to not discourage users.

Others [16] indicate that the primary requirement is viewing policies from the privacy and business perspective so as to enable compatibility across the enterprise. Previous international workshops on the Semantic Policies [17] [18] presented many papers on emerging requirements for the policy-oriented web, including trust and negotiation mechanisms. However, very few deal with e-Society and Social Networks as the driver and consider the policy requirements from that context.

There are some efforts now appearing on an initial functional architecture for the policy-oriented web. These include the three basic capabilities of [19]:

- policy transaction logs to enable the assessment of past policy decisions, either in real-time or for post-processing,
- policy language framework that enables a shared policy vocabulary to evolve over time from overlapping communities on the web, and
- policy reasoning tools to enable polices to be evaluated and decisions made to assist the user.

There is also relevant work on privacy and identity management in the PRIME Project [20] and POEM Project [35] that has developed detailed enterprise architectures that could be generalised to support policy management tasks within a Social Networks context.

Some frameworks [21] are grounded on XML technology and define architectures consisting of policy management tools, policy databases, policy decision points, and policy enforcement points. Others follow this idea and extend the policy architecture based on a role-based access control model [22] or view-based access control [23] and a trading services model [24]. Frameworks also classify policies into high-level and low-level [25] to reflect and support different enforcement capabilities.

There is a significant body of work that reviews and compares different Privacy languages (such as as EPAL, P3P, XACML) and supporting frameworks [13] [26] [27] [28] [29]. Their general conclusion is that a common approach in the future will simplify policy analysis and reduce inconsistencies and promote policy reuse across communities and enhance such policy protection on the web. We have found that our Policy information model (see Figure 8) moves towards this goal, and provides more relevant policy-semantics (over existing languages) to express such policies. For example, Parties and roles, and dual-focus Actions provide clearer semantic and functions more relevant to Social Network requirements.

The application of semantic web technologies to structured policy languages (eg XACML) has shown how its expressive power can easily accommodate such transformation and extensions but highlight several aspects for future research [30] and specific needs for a policy language for defining security requirements [31].

Investigation of privacy support in Social Networks has found that third-party access to user information (eg via open APIs such as OpenSocial) as potentially compromising [32] to users as the conformance to the user's policy is solely at the discretion of the third-party. Others found that the user model used for Privacy is not consistent with what is implemented by the Social Network providers [33] nor the way a user's privacy decisions are based on the relationship with the provider as well as other individuals [34].

We have also been working on extending the ODRL rights expression language [36] to accommodate more general policy features. We expect that this will be the basic model that could be widely deployed given its success in the mobile community.

6 Conclusion

We have seen that Social Networks have become an "overnight" phenomenon - backed up by Web 2.0 technologies - and provide rich user experiences. We have also shown that some of these experiences are not socially (or legally) acceptable. This is a golden opportunity for the Policy-Oriented Web to play a more significant role in the e-Society. The core area would be to better express the semantics of policies covering the access to user-generated content, and users personal preferences.

We have also defined the basis for a flexible information model that can underpin the Policy-Oriented Web and promote it as a new platform that will enable pervasive policy management across Web 2.0. We have shown some examples of applying the Policy-Oriented Web language to some use cases from real issues dealing with Social Networks. The current model is not complete and we expect that there will be a number of enhancements that can be applied to this preliminary semantic model with additional use cases, but the key idea is that we can begin to articulate the core concepts, classes, and relationships for a policy language framework. Future research areas will include policy conflict detection and accountability.

These are just the first steps in bringing policy-supportive technologies to the e-Society communities. These communities thrive on "simple" technologies that address their needs. The Policy-Oriented Web - as a semantic policy platform - will need to be integrated into the Web 2.0 style of technologies. This means more work is needed on the user interfaces for policy interactions and the integration with existing Web 2.0 platforms and deployment technologies. The end result should see the Policy-Oriented Web supporting more of the e-Society needs and evolving into a more user-focussed technology platform.

Acknowledgments

NICTA is funded by the Australian Government as represented by the Department of Broadband, Communications and the Digital Economy and the Australian Research Council through the ICT Centre of Excellence program and the Queensland Government.

References

[1] Qui, X.: Citizen Engagement: Driving Force of E-Society Development. In: Wang, W. (ed.) IFIP International Federation for Information Processing. Integration and Innovation Orient to E-Society, Integration and Innovation Orient to E-Society, vol. 252, 2, pp. 540–548. Springer, Boston

[2] Iannella, R.: Industry Challenges for Social and Professional Networks. In: W3C Workshop on the Future of Social Networking, Barcelona (January 15-16, 2009),
http://www.w3.org/2008/09/msnws/papers/
nicta-position-paper.pdf

[3] Weitzner, D.G.: Profiling, and Privacy. IEEE Internet Computing, 95–97 (November/December 2007)

[4] Cohen, N.: Use My Photo? Not Without Permission. New York Times (October 1, 2007),
http://www.nytimes.com/2007/10/01/technology/01link.html?ex=
1348977600&en=182a46901b23f450&ei=5124&partner=permalink&exp
rod=permalink

[5] ABC Media Watch, Filleting Facebook. Australian Broadcasting Corporation (ABC) (October 29, 2007),
http://www.abc.net.au/mediawatch/transcripts/s2074079.htm

[6] Iannella, R., Henricksen, K., Robinson, R.: A Policy Oriented Architecture for the Web: New Infrastructure and New Opportunities. In: W3C Workshop on Languages for Privacy Policy Negotiation and Semantics-Driven Enforcement, Ispra, Italy, October 17-18 (2006)

[7] Iannella, R. (ed.): Open Digital Rights Language, Version 1.1 Specification. ODRL Initiative (September 19, 2002),
http://odrl.net/1.1/ODRL-11.pdf, http://www.w3.org/TR/odrl/

[8] Wenning, R., Schunter, M. (eds.): The Platform for Privacy Preferences 1.1 (P3P1.1) Specification. W3C Working Group Note (November 13, 2006),
http://www.w3.org/TR/P3P11/

[9] Euzenat, J., Shvaiko, P.: Ontology Matching. Springer, Berlin (2007)

[10] Arnab, A., Hutchison, A.: DRM Use License Negotiation using ODRL v2.0. In: Proceedings 5th International Workshop for Technology, Economy, and Legal Aspects of Virtual Goods and the 3rd International ODRL Workshop, Koblenz, Germany, October 11-13 (2007)

[11] Hu, Y.J.: Semantic-Driven Enforcement of Rights Delegation Policies via the Combination of Rules and Ontologies. In: Workshop on Privacy Enforcement and Accountability with Semantics, International Semantic Web Conference 2007, Busan Korea (2007)

[12] García, R., Gil, R.: An OWL Copyright Ontology for Semantic Digital Rights Management. In: IFIP WG 2.12 & WG 12.4 International Workshop on Web Semantics, Montpellier, France (November 2006)

[13] Kolari, P., Ding, L., Shashidhara, G., Joshi, A., Finin, T., Kagal, L.: Enhancing Web privacy protection through declarative policies. In: Sixth IEEE International Workshop on Policies for Distributed Systems and Networks, June 6-8, pp. 57–66 (2005)

[14] OASIS eXtensible Access Control Markup Language (XACML), Version 2.0. OASIS Standard (February 1, 2005),
http://docs.oasis-open.org/xacml/2.0/
XACML-2.0-OS-NORMATIVE.zip

[15] Bonatti, P.A., Duma, C., Fuchs, N., Nejdl, W., Olmedilla, D., Peer, J., Shahmehri, N.: Semantic Web Policies - A Discussion of Requirements and Research Issues. In: Sure, Y., Domingue, J. (eds.) ESWC 2006. LNCS, vol. 4011, pp. 712–724. Springer, Heidelberg (2006)

[16] Kolari, P., Finin, T., Yesha, Y., Lyons, K., Hawkins, J., Perelgut, S.: Policy Management of Enterprise Systems: A Requirements Study. In: Proceedings of the Seventh IEEE International Workshop on Policies for Distributed Systems and Networks, POLICY 2006 (2006)

[17] Semantic Web and Policy Workshop, Galway, Ireland (November 7, 2005)

[18] 2nd International Semantic Web Policy Workshop (SWPW 2006), Athens, GA, USA, November 5-9 (2006)

[19] Weitzner, D.J., Abelson, H., Berners-Lee, T., Feigenbaum, J., Hendler, J., Sus, G.J.: Information Accountability. MIT Computer Science and Artificial Intelligence Laboratory Technical Report MIT-CSAIL-TR-2007-034 (June 13, 2007)

[20] Casassa-Mont, M., Crosta, S., Kriegelstein, T., Sommer, D.: PRIME Architecture V2 (March 29, 2007),
https://www.prime-project.eu/prime_products/reports/arch/
pub_del_D14.2.c_ec_WP14.2_v1_Final.pdf

[21] Clemente, F.J.G., Perez, G.M., Skarmeta, A.F.G.: An XML-Seamless Policy Based Management Framework. In: Gorodetsky, V., Kotenko, I., Skormin, V.A. (eds.) MMM-ACNS 2005. LNCS, vol. 3685, pp. 418–423. Springer, Heidelberg (2005)

[22] Bhatti, R., Ghafoor, A., Bertino, E., Joshi, J.B.D.: X-GTRBAC: an XML-based policy specification framework and architecture for enterprise-wide access control. ACM Transactions on Information and System Security (TISSEC) 8(2), 187–227 (2005)

[23] Koch, M., Parisi-Presicce, F.: UML specification of access control policies and their formal verification. Software and Systems Modeling 5(4), 429–447 (2006)

[24] Lamparter, S., Ankolekar, A., Studer, R., Oberle, D., Weinhardt, C.: A policy framework for trading configurable goods and services in open electronic markets. In: Proceedings of the 8th International Conference on Electronic Commerce, Fredericton, New Brunswick, Canada, August 14-16 (2006)

[25] Pretschner, A., Hilty, M., Basin, D.: Distributed usage control. Commun. ACM 49, 9 (2006)

[26] Tonti, G., Bradshaw, J., Jeffers, R., Montanari, R., Suri, N., Uszok, A.: Semantic Web Languages for Policy Representation and Reasoning: A Comparison of Kaos, Rei, and Ponder. In: Fensel, D., Sycara, K., Mylopoulos, J. (eds.) ISWC 2003. LNCS, vol. 2870, pp. 419–437. Springer, Heidelberg (2003)

[27] Anderson, A.: A comparison of two Privacy Policy Languages: EPAL and XACML. Sun Mircosystems Labs technical report (2005),
http://research.sun.com/techrep/2005/smli_tr-2005-147/

[28] Ardagna, C., Damiani, E., De Capitani di Vimercati, S., Fugazza, C., Samarati, P.: Offline Expansion of XACML Policies Based on P3P Metadata. In: Lowe, D.G., Gaedke, M. (eds.) ICWE 2005. LNCS, vol. 3579, pp. 363–374. Springer, Heidelberg (2005)

[29] Jensen, C., Tullio, J., Potts, C., Mynatt, E.D.: STRAP: A Structured Analysis Framework for Privacy. Georgia Institute of Technology Technical Report GIT-GVU-05-02,
http://hdl.handle.net/1853/4450

[30] Damiani, E., De Capitani di Vimercati, S., Fugazza, C., Samarati, P.: Extending Policy Languages to the Semantic Web. In: Koch, N., Fraternali, P., Wirsing, M. (eds.) ICWE 2004. LNCS, vol. 3140, pp. 330–343. Springer, Heidelberg (2004)

[31] Kagal, L., Finin, T., Joshi, A.: A Policy Based Approach to Security for the Semantic Web. In: Fensel, D., Sycara, K., Mylopoulos, J. (eds.) ISWC 2003. LNCS, vol. 2870, pp. 402–418. Springer, Heidelberg (2003)

[32] Felt, A., Evans, D.: Privacy Protection for Social Networking Platforms. In: Web 2.0 Security and Privacy at the 2008 IEEE Symposium on Security and Privacy, Oakland, California, USA, May 18-21 (2008)

[33] Chew, M., Balfanz, D., Laurie, B.: (Under) Mining Privacy in Social Networks. In: Web 2.0 Security and Privacy at the 2008 IEEE Symposium on Security and Privacy, Oakland, California, USA, May 18-21 (2008)

[34] Grandison, T., Maximilien, E.M.: Towards Privacy Propagation in the Social Web. In: Web 2.0 Security and Privacy at the 2008 IEEE Symposium on Security and Privacy, Oakland, California, USA, May 18-21 (2008)

[35] Kaiser, M.: Toward the Realization of Policy-Oriented Enterprise Management. IEEE Computer, 57–63 (November 2007)

[36] Guth, S., Iannella, R. (eds.): ODRL Version 2.0 Core Model. Draft Specification (March 6, 2009), http://odrl.net/2.0/DS-ODRL-Model.html

Integrating the European Securities Settlement

Torsten Schaper

Goethe-University Frankfurt, Chair of e-Finance, Grüneburgplatz 1,
60323 Frankfurt, Germany
schaper@wiwi.uni-frankfurt.de

Abstract. The cross-border securities settlement in Europe is still said to be highly inefficient. One main reason can be seen in technical barriers between the different domestic settlement systems. Beside efforts to implement industry-specific communication standards an integration of the different settlement systems is necessary. The CSD-link model, the hub and spokes model, and the European CSD model aim to integrate European securities settlement. They have in common that they address the problem of interlinkage of national Central Securities Depositories and differ essentially in the way of achieving integration. These models are evaluated from a macro-economic perspective considering transaction costs, risks, and the integration of the cross-border securities settlement process.

Keywords: Financial Markets, Financial Institutions, Financial Intermediation, Securities Settlement, Integration, Standards.

1 Introduction

Trading on securities markets increases significantly. This means that not only more transactions need to be settled, but more of these transactions need cross-border settlement. Especially due to the increasing use of complex derivatives composed of assets from different trading venues. Trading activity, market liquidity, and capital market growth depend on safe and efficient trading and settlement systems. The importance of an efficient securities settlement system (SSS) lies in the safer transfer of ownership of assets against payment. In context of the financial crisis some of these systems had to handle enormous peaks in volumes: for instance the settlement system of UK (Euroclear) had to handle 1.6 million transactions on 15 October 2008, double the average monthly volume [15]. Such systems have to minimise the risks involved in the securities transactions and generate costs that do not hinder the intention to trade securities. Besides a changing regulatory environment technological innovations are fundamental catalysts behind the past and the future changes in securities settlement. Link Up Markets, the Single Settlement Engine (SSE), and TARGET2-Securities (T2S) are heavily discussed technical platforms that aim to achieve the integration of securities settlement in Europe. Until now little attention has been given to the issue of integration of European cross-border securities settlement.

As far as the author knows, only Kröpfl [19] has evaluated different models for the integration of securities settlement. The aim of this paper is to show the technical

C. Godart et al. (Eds.): I3E 2009, IFIP AICT 305, pp. 385–399, 2009.

barriers in securities settlement, emphasise the importance of an industry specific communication standard, and to introduce models for technical integration. These models are compared using an evaluation framework considering transaction costs, risks, and integration of the settlement process.

The paper is organised as follows. First the status quo of European clearing and settlement is presented. In the following section the technical barriers in the securities settlement are presented. Then the role of communication standards for the interation of securities settlement are stated and different models and recent approaches for the integration of European settlement are introduced and discussed. In the following the presented approaches are evaluated. The paper closes with a conclusion.

2 Clearing and Settlement of Securities Transactions

Clearing and settlement are required after two parties have decided to transfer the ownership of a security. Clearing and settlement services deal with the execution of a trade. The purpose of clearing is the efficient handling of risks inherent to concluded, but still unfulfilled contracts. Clearing confirms the legal obligation from the trade. It involves the calculation of mutual obligations of market participants and determines what each counterpart receives. Central counterparty (clearing) is not included in the definition of clearing. A central counterparty (CCP) is an entity that interposes itself between the transactions of the counterparties in order to assume their rights and obligations, acting as a buyer to every seller and as a seller to every buyer. The original legal relationship between the buyer and the seller is thus replaced by two new legal relationships. The CCP thus absorbs the counterparty risk and guarantees clearing and settlement of the trade [31]. Subsequent to the clearing stage the second operation is settling a trade. Settlement is the exchange of cash or assets in return for other assets or cash and transference of ownership of those assets and cash. A Central Securities Depository (CSD) is the organisation that performs these functions.

Compared with the US, the settlement industry in Europe is fragmented. Settlement in Europe shows its origins in a patchwork of national systems. At the national level, the consolidation has taken place and in most countries only one CSD has prevailed [16]. Domestic settlement systems are efficient within the national boundaries. The costs per transactions in domestic settlement are as expensive as in the United States, but European CSDs realise higher margins [2004]. In contrast, the settlement of cross-border transactions in Europe is not efficient because of various barriers [29]. The main reason for the fragmented European settlement industry is that securities were traded at national level, partly as result of the existence of different currencies. As result, several CSDs at the European level continue to coexist and only recently consolidation has taken place. In the EU the number of settlement engines declined from 23 in 1999 to 18 in 2004 [13].

Recently the European Code of Conduct for Clearing and Settlement is affecting the post-trade industry. The Code is a voluntary self-commitment and follows to a number of principles on the provision of post-trading services for cash equities. The intention is to establish a strong European capital market and to allow investors the choice to trade any European security within a consistent, coherent, and efficient European framework. The aim of the Code of Conduct is to offer market participants the freedom to choose their preferred provider of services separately at each layer of the securities trading value chain and to make the concept of cross-border redundant for transactions between EU member states. The implementation of the Code consists of three phases, implementation of price transparency, access and interoperability, and service unbundling. It was implemented by the end of 2007 [14]. The guidelines defined for access and interoperability provide the basis for the development of links between respective service providers. In total, more than 80 requests for access and interoperability can be counted [28]. Until now these request have not concluded in new connections of post-trade infrastructures.

3 Technical Barriers in Securities Settlement

SSSs are critical components of the infrastructure of global financial markets. A financial or operational problem in any of the institutions that perform critical functions in the settlement process or at a major user of a SSS could result in significant liquidity pressures or credit losses for other participants. Any disruption of securities settlements has the potential to spill over to any payment system used by the SSS or any payment system that uses the SSS to transfer collateral. In the securities markets themselves, market liquidity is critically dependent on confidence in the safety and reliability of the settlement arrangements. Traders will be reluctant to trade if they have significant doubts as to whether the trade will in fact settle or not [3]. In the 27 European countries mainly one domestic CSD has prevailed. Therefore, different channels for the settlement of cross-border transactions coexist and the usage of additional intermediaries is needed for the settlement of these transactions. The usage of intermediaries increases the complexity of the process. These intermediaries increase risks, cause higher transaction costs (due to multiple IT-systems), and generate additional costs in the back-office. The national settlement systems operate on a variety of non standardised platforms. This implies differences in IT and interfaces that add costs to cross-border settlement by requiring a higher level of manual input. Connection and messaging protocols vary from one SSS to another and different rules of transfer and product definitions exist. Differences in reporting requirements between systems also increase the costs. The additional costs arise, because institutions have to invest in understanding the concerning technologies and in multiple back-office interfaces to communicate with all necessary systems, with a need for additional staff to understand and support the various arrangements. On an individual level, the technical difficulties are manageable, but the wish to avoid multiple linkages and the burden of following numerous rules and rule changes are key drivers in the use of local custodians and agents. The European Central Securities Depositories Association (ECSDA) has drafted a set of standards for communication between CSDs to support cross-border settlement [9]. In this context there is also a need for the adoption of an EU-wide protocol, defining message formats between systems and their members [16]. According to the second report on European clearing and settlement, national differences in the IT and interfaces should be eliminated by a protocol defined by SWIFT and the Securities Market Practice Group. Once defined, the protocol should be adopted by the Eurosystem in respect of its operations [17].

4 Technical Integration of European Securities Settlement

The interlinkage of the different SSSs represents a challenge to achieve an efficient and integrated European financial market. The integration can be achieved by the usage of technical standards, industry standards, or by a further going integration via the usage of central services or applications (see figure 1).

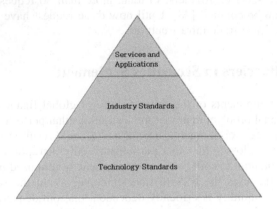

Fig. 1. Levels of integration [2]

4.1 Technology Standards and Industry Standards

Securities messaging and processing arrangements have developed in an uncoordinated fashion, sponsored by particular trading platforms and national arrangements for post-trade processing. Non-electronic trading has been converted into firm-specific order and trading formats for electronic processing. There has been diversity between different electronic platforms, thus equity trades have been recorded using different conventions in different countries. Even within financial centres different conventions for different markets have established. Different providers of security processing services have also developed own procedures [25]. Over recent years, the industry has developed generic procedures that can be used across trading and post-trading, notably the Financial Information eXchange (FIX) protocol and the Message Types (MT) for post-trade messages, promoted by SWIFT. Nonetheless, these formats are not fully standardised. With a large number of local variations they are applied across systems and between firms. Moreover, they are difficult to update. Changes in these standards can require wide-ranging adjustments to computer systems and business processes by financial firms, because implementation varies widely and any change in business relationship, e.g. obtaining transaction management services from a new supplier, involves very substantial IT system costs. The adoption of more fully harmonised and simplified standards will reduce these switching costs [25]. Future development of straight through processing will be facilitated by the use of data formats based on extensible mark up language (XML). XML allows richer message content, supports browser based interaction and communication, and are hence fully software and hardware independent. XML documents are more transparent and human readable. Moreover, XML is well suited to incorporate future changes in technology and processing arrangements [1]. XML standards are well suited to support distributed processing. With XML standards and distributed processing it is not necessary to create centralised processing hubs in order to facilitate EU-wide securities processing. Instead, almost all aspects of securities processing can be handled through a decentralised computing network [25]. XML versions of FIX and the MT message formats have been developed. Specifically, the FIX protocol is contributing its expertise in the pre-trade and trade execution domain while SWIFT is providing post-trade domain expertise. The aim should be to migrate the securities industry to a standardised use of XML, ensuring interoperability across financial industry. In 2005, SWIFT led the industry-wide project to help to define the communication protocol which was identified as the most effective solution for the removal of the national differences in IT. One of the key recommendations was that all securities market infrastructures and participants involved in European clearing and settlement area should support the use of ISO 15022 and 20022 standards. SWIFT is working with the European infrastructural community to identify the processes and activities that they support in the clearing, settlement, and asset servicing market spaces. These activities have been mapped against ISO messages and there is an ongoing process of identifying the gaps [1]. According to the final protocol recommendation it should be mandatory for all infrastructures and participants that are active in European clearing, settlement, and asset servicing of cash equities, fixed income, and listed funds to support the use of ISO 15022 and 20022 standards [1].

The establishment of such an industry standard can be only a first step in the integration of the European financial markets. In the following different models that go further are introduced. These models go back to communication models and general e-Business architectures [2][30] and have in common that such industry standards are essential for further integration.

4.2 CSD-Link Model

The establishment of links between all CSDs is one possibility to improve the settlement of cross-border transactions. These links allow the investor to take ownership of foreign securities through its domestic CSD. Bilateral links could reduce direct and indirect settlement costs, because a participant does not have to pay for the membership in more than one CSD or pay an intermediary to grant access to the foreign market. The resulting network of CSDs is visualised in figure 2.

Such network is difficult to implement completely, given the high costs associated with the establishment of bilateral links and the current low use of most of these links [18]. The total costs of settlement (TC) by this interlinkage are high. Each of the n CSDs has to establish a link (with costs of α_i) to all other CSDs and continue to operate its own SSS (β_i). Besides these fixed costs the variable costs (ε_i) depending on the number of transactions (δ_i) need to be considered.

$$TC = \sum_{i=1}^{n} (n-1) \cdot \alpha_i + \beta_i + \delta_i * \varepsilon_i$$

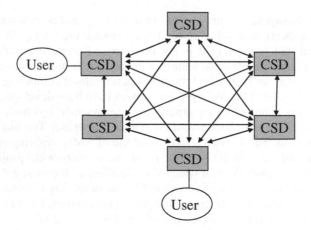

Fig. 2. CSD-link model [19]

The costs for CSD links are stated to range between 500,000 and 10,000,000 Euro [19][24]. Because of the 27 CSDs in Europe 702 links ($n*(n-1)$) would need to be established. This makes an investment of 351 to 7,020 million Euro (depending of assumed link costs) necessary to establish the network. However, the all-in savings are low, because the redundant infrastructure remains in place and the transaction costs would likely be high as each CSD has to open accounts in the CSDs of all counterparties [27].

4.3 Hub and Spokes Model

The hub and spokes model foresees a central hub that has the function to direct transactions to the national CSDs. Each CSD establishes one link to the central hub (see figure 3). The CSD remains the single point of entry for their users.

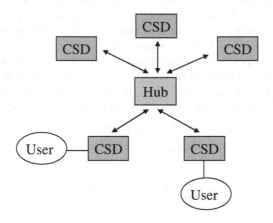

Fig. 3. *Hub and spokes model*

Additional costs arise from the creation of the hub (γ). On the other hand savings are achieved by reducing the number of links to n (one link for each CSD to the hub).

$$TC = \gamma + \sum_{i=1}^{n} \alpha_i + \beta_{i} + \delta_i * \varepsilon_i$$

In the following, two recent approaches related to the hub and spokes model, Link Up Markets and T2S project, are introduced.

4.3.1 Link Up Markets

Link Up Markets is a joint venture by seven CSDs: Clearstream Banking Frankfurt, Hellenic Exchanges, Iberclear, Österreichische Kontrollbank, SIS SegaIntersettle, VP Securities Services and VPS. The aim is to establish a technical platform that is similar to the hub and spokes model. The idea is to overcome the hurdles and inefficiencies in the cross-border equities business by establishing a single cross-border operating organisation. Link Up Markets plans to deliver a central linkage to the national systems. The launch is planned for the first half of 2009. The CSDs still provide the single point of access for domestic and cross-border business [21]. The domestic institutions and infrastructure remain unchanged. The settlement takes place in the issuer CSD, which provides that regulatory requirements are met. Since CSDs are exclusively clients of the Link Up Markets, the CSD of choice is solely responsible for handling the relationship with its customers. The savings are expected to be derived from the fact that only one organisation is to implement and to manage the cross-border network. The market participants will instead continue to settle across borders via their domestic entry into this structure. The need to maintain several different access points stops. Each domestic CSD remains in its current state and function and all access points can still be used. Reduced interconnection costs are expected regarding negotiations, link processing, interfaces, synchronisation of systems, data formats, link contracts, liquidity requirements, and effective use of collateral. In addition, Link Up Markets will achieve network externalities leading to further cost savings shared by the whole community, as centralised linkage will help in standardising processes and practices [21[32]. While a bilateral link is too costly to be justified by the relatively small amount of transactions for a small CSD, a central link does not rule out the possibility of small players benefiting from economies of scale. Although the proposal to link the domestic systems does not lead to a substantial risk concentration in a single system and the safety or stability of systems shown in the domestic environment is not endangered. The platform provides a basis for further consolidation and integration of the European capital market, because the linkage of domestic systems increases the pressure to apply common technical standards, harmonised rules and regulations, identical tax treatment, and handling of country-specific taxes. The vision is to develop common operating standards and principles such as the simplification of cross-border corporate actions and consistent legal frameworks regarding the transfer of securities. This could start an evolutionary process and may spur the consolidation of the European settlement systems, because the platform could help national institutions to agree on uniform standards for securities settlement, rules, and regulations for automated securities lending and borrowing [32]. It also solves the complex bilateral links between all CSDs and thus help to align their work. The project adds another service layer to the settlement process of cross-border-transactions. It achieves integration by providing interoperability to continue the whole system of different national CSDs. The first step to achieve interoperability is to agree on standards, communication protocols, common operation methods, and practices. Link Up Market could act as a catalyst for standardisation.

4.3.2 TARGET2-Securities

On 7th July 2006, the European Central Bank (ECB) issued a press release, stating that the Eurosystem was evaluating opportunities to provide efficient settlement services for transactions in central bank money, leading to the processing of both securities and cash settlement on a single platform through common procedures. The platform, called T2S, is the proposal to the CSDs to transfer their securities accounts to a common technical platform. The main benefits of this platform would be the reduction of settlement engines and therefore the reduction of costs for CSD-infrastructure and for custodians' back offices. Background of T2S is the technical debate about the best way to synchronise the delivery of securities with the cash payment. There is general agreement that the most efficient approach for both security and cash movements is to be managed by the same platform. In some countries this process is managed by the SSS, which determines when settlement takes place. As a result, the CSD effectively controls some payments across the books of the central bank: when the CSD determines that a transaction has settled, this causes the money to move on the books of the central bank. In other countries the central bank is unwilling to outsource control of central bank payments to another organisation. To maintain an integrated system, if the CSD cannot manage the money, the central bank has to manage the securities [28]. Then T2S is the only way to reach the integration of the settlement of securities and cash. The settlement of securities and cash would be realised within a single integrated platform. At the start of every day, participating CSDs would transfer their securities balances and outstanding transactions to T2S. During the day, T2S would settle these transactions and report to the CSDs at the end of the day. One consequence of T2S would be the separation of operation of settlement from the other functions performed by CSDs, such as asset servicing, asset financing, and provision of collateral. These other functions require access to real-time, intraday information on the securities balances held by participants in the systems, and the ability to control those balances. To realise this, a sophisticated linkage between T2S and the systems from the CSDs is required [6].

On 15th January 2007, the ECB presented details on the economic, technical, operational, and legal feasibility of T2S. According to the economic feasibility study of the ECB, T2S could reduce the average costs for domestic and cross-border securities settlement to €0.28 per transaction [7]. According to this study, the costs for domestic settlement in Europe range between €0.45 and €2.30 [7]. For the success of T2S the participation of all relevant CSDs is essential. The economic feasibility report assumes that all CSDs in the Euro area participate. If the participation in T2S is not mandatory, the number of transactions could be significantly lower and the costs per transaction would increase significantly [28]. There are a number of details to be clarified, like supervision of the platform, governance, questions on competition, the effects on the private enterprise infrastructure, and alternatives to integrate the different national infrastructures [20]. On 8th March 2007, the Governing Council of the

ECB has concluded that it is feasible to implement T2S and therefore decided to go ahead with the next phase of the project, namely the definition of user requirements on the basis of market contributions. These requirements were approved by the Governing Council. Most of the CSDs indicated participation and thus the Council decided in July 2008 to go on with the project [8].

4.4 European CSD Model

The European CSD is an integrated model to improve efficiency of the European securities settlement. The European CSD would be the only CSD providing settlement services for the European market (see figure 4).

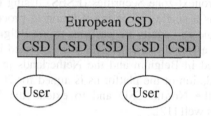

Fig. 4. *European CSD*

Also other operations performed by CSDs would be performed by a single CSD. It would lead to costs reduction, because only one integrated SSS would remain. Furthermore no CSD links would be needed anymore.

$$TC = \beta + \delta * \varepsilon$$

In addition costs reductions in back office of the users would be the result. The European CSD would also lead to an integrated and harmonised securities settlement, because all transaction would be managed within one single system. It must be considered that a central CSD could reduce competition in the settlement industry and could therefore also have adverse effects on market efficiency [29]. A well-known example for such a CSD is the Depository Trust Company (DTC) in the US. The DTC is providing settlement services for different US markets.

In the following, the *Single Settlement Engine* of the Euroclear Group is introduced as an example of an approach similar to an European CSD. Euroclear is forcing an integrated approach. Instead of achieving interoperability of the different national systems in Belgium, France, the Netherlands, Ireland, and the UK, Euroclear is implementing an integrated platform for securities settlement. The SSE is a practical harmonisation project not only providing integrated cash and securities settlement, but also an incorporated system for different European countries [10][5]. The SSE is the first major milestone in accomplishing Euroclear's objective to harmonise services on a consolidated processing platform, merging the five settlement platforms into one. Euroclear plans to save €300 million per year with the consolidation of the different settlement platforms, by market practise harmonisation, and by removing the barriers in the markets served by the Euroclear Group [10]. The users of the SSE operate as if they would act in a domestic market (see figure 4).

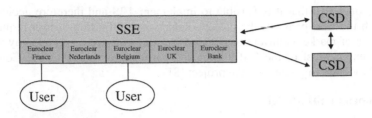

Fig. 5. Integration with the Single Settlement Engine

The next step in Euroclear's migration to a single platform is the launch of Euroclear Settlement for Euronext-zone Securities (ESES). Using the SSE as its foundation, ESES will serve as a single processing solution to process both domestic and cross-border fixed-income and equity transactions in the Belgian, Dutch, and French markets as if they were a single market. ESES was launched in France at the end of 2007, and was launched in Belgium and the Netherlands in the second quarter of 2008. The final consolidation of the platforms is aimed for 2010 [11]. Euroclear has announced to acquire the Nordic CSD and to extend the SSE to these markets (Finland and Sweden) as well [12].

5 Evaluation of Models for Integration

The total costs for settlement services are difficult to determine, because of the large number of factors, fees, risks etc. So far there exists no accepted study on the costs and fees of trading and post-trading in Europe. The European Commission has assigned OXERA [26] to conduct a study on costs and prices in European trading and post-trading. The results are still pending. The costs of the SSSs consist of the total costs of ownership and the processing costs [23]. Due to the large number of European CSDs the costs for the redundant SSSs are high. Furthermore, the processing costs of a transaction crossing different systems are respectively higher than for an inner-system transaction. International technical standards can increase the interoperability of SSSs and thus reduce the costs of cross-border and cross-system transaction [19]. Transaction costs form a very important criterion for the evaluation of the presented models and approaches. However in evaluation of efficiency of securities settlement, transaction costs and settlement risks are often not considered properly. Transaction costs can either arise from the provision or the usage of an institution. The first needs to be considered if institutional arrangements are changed. The focus of the following evaluation lies on these costs. The latter costs consist of the costs of the usage of the institution [19]. Beside transaction costs the risk needs to be considered for the evaluation. Major parts of the transaction risk have nearly been eliminated by the synchronisation of payment and securities delivery, but risk still remains [15]. Risks are often not considered since the respective risks rarely arise [23]. At least it is obvious that these risks need to be considered since the crash in October 1987 [4] and the current global financial crisis [15]. Furthermore, the time for the implementation, the integration of the settlement process, the integration of other post-trade services, and the technical integration have to be taken into consideration. The main difference of the presented models is the interlinkage of the CSDs. These models and current approaches differ essentially. They have in common that they improve the interoperability of SSSs and thus reduce the costs for development, support, mapping, and maintenance of communication.

The CSD-link model reaches integration, but makes investments in infrastructure necessary. The hub and spokes model reaches further integration and reduces the number of CSD-links, but does not reduce the number of national systems. T2S shows an advanced integration of the settlement process by integrating the cash settlement. For market participants these two models mean one more intermediary in the process of cross-border settlement. But the approaches T2S or Link Up Markets could mean a first step towards further consolidation and integration. The model of the European CSD is more comprehensive. By integrating different SSSs into one central platform it aims to reduce the number of SSSs and thus achieves a harmonisation of settlement and custody services. The aim of this model is the creation of a domestic settlement process within Europe. The approaches of T2S and the European CSD have in common that they make fundamental investments in a central IT-platform necessary. The implementation of such complex projects takes a long time. But such a centralised platform could perform an integrated infrastructure and support the process of a harmonised and integrated European securities settlement.

Table 1 shows the key findings of the comparison of the different models and approaches. The comparison was made by giving a score for the single criteria from a macro-economic perspective. The scores range from ++ (very good) to -- (very bad). A more detailed analysis is included in the appendix.

Table 1. Comparison of models and approaches to improve securities settlement in Europe

	CSD-link model	Link Up Markets	T2S	European CSD
Settlement risk	0	0	+(+)	+(+)
Settlement costs	--	-	+	+
Implementation time	+	++	-	--
Technical integration	0	+	++	++
Integration of cross-border settlement	-	0	+	++
Integration of other post-trade services	+	+	-	++
Integration of cash settlement	-	-	++	+

++ very good   + good   0 neutral   - bad   -- very bad

- Due to the settlement within one single integrated platform, the settlement risk on T2S and the European CSD are significantly lower than in the other approaches. T2S integrates cash and securities settlement on one platform. An European CSD could also integrate cash settlement (if the central banks are willing to). This integration reduces the settlement risk essentially.
- The CSD-link model assures interoperability by the interlinkage of the CSDs. The all-in savings are low, because the redundant infrastructure remains in place. The hub and spokes model and the recently discussed approaches T2S and Link Up Markets reach further integration, but do not reduce the number of national systems for settlement. For market participants these concepts mean one more intermediary in the process of cross-border settlement.
- The interlinkage of all CSDs is fastest to realise with Link Up Markets. For T2S or the European CSD the development of a new platform is necessary.
- The best technical integration is achieved by the introduction of one single platform. The integration of cross-border settlement can be achieved best within one platform.
- The integration of other post-trade services can be achieved best if settlement and related custody services are not separated. The only approach that separates these services is T2S. The European CSD provides an integrated European securities settlement in one central SSS. The aim of such a system is the creation of a domestic settlement and custody process for the markets of the European Union.

The presented models show that by improving the interoperability of SSSs cost reductions can be achieved. Centralised approaches share that they make fundamental investments in a central IT-platform necessary and that the implementation of such complex projects takes a long time. Still such a platform could perform an integrated infrastructure and support the process of a harmonised and integrated European securities settlement.

6 Conclusion and Outlook

In the last years integration and consolidation has taken place, but the European settlement is still a fragmented industry, showing inefficiencies in cross-border securities settlement. The introduction of communication standards for improving the interoperability can only be a first step for improving the integration. The interlinkage of the different domestic SSSs represents a challenge in achieving an efficient and integrated European financial market. The CSD-link model assures interoperability by linking the domestic CSDs. The all-in savings are low, as the redundant infrastructure remains in place. The hub and spokes model and the recently discussed approaches T2S and Link Up Markets reach further integration, but do not reduce the number of domestic systems for settlement. For the market participants these concepts mean one more intermediary in the process of cross-border securities settlement. Yet these platforms could mean a first step towards further consolidation and integration. A different approach was chosen by the Euroclear Group with the SSE, integrating different SSSs into one central platform. The advantage of this approach is the reduction of SSSs and the harmonisation of settlement services within the group. The aim of this platform is to create a domestic settlement and custody process for the markets of the group. The main disadvantage is that it is limited to selected markets. The extension to other markets is difficult due to the heterogeneous settlement industry. By improving the interoperability of SSSs a reduction of costs can be achieved. Centralised approaches, as T2S and the European CSD, share that they require fundamental investments in a central IT-platform and that the implementation of such complex projects takes a long time. However, such a centralised system could perform an integrated infrastructure and support the process of a harmonised and integrated European securities settlement. It is interesting that the different central approaches of Link Up Markets, T2S, and SSE are followed at the same time. Euroclear (building up the SSE) and Clearstream Banking (involved in Link Up Markets) as the most important European CSDs have announced to support the further development of T2S.

Acknowledgments. The author gratefully acknowledges the support of the E-Finance Lab, Frankfurt for this work.

References

1. Adams, D.: Elimination of Giovannini Barrier One, SWIFT, Final Protocol recommendation (2006)
2. Albrecht, C., Dean, D., Hansen, J.: Marketplace and technology standards for B2B e-commerce: progress, challenges, and the state of the art. Information & Management 42, 865–875 (2005)
3. BIS. Recommendations for Securities Settlement Systems', Consultative Report (January 2001)
4. Bernanke, B.S.: Clearing and Settlement during the Crash. The Review of Financial Studies, 133–151 (1990)
5. Cox, P., Simpson, H., Jones, L.: The Future of Clearing and Settlement in Europe. Corp. of London City Research Series (7) (2005)
6. ECB, TARGET2-Securities, Frankfurt: European Central Bank (2006)
7. ECB, TARGET2-Securities – Economic Feasibility Study, 2nd TARGET2-Securities meeting with market participants (2007)
8. ECB. Press Release 17.07.2008: Launch of the TARGET2-Securities project (2008), http://www.ecb.int/press/pr/date/2008/html/pr080717.en.html (accessed July 18, 2008)
9. ECSDA, Cross-Border Clearing and Settlement through CSD Links, report by ECSDA WG3 (2006)
10. Euroclear, Delivering domestic market for Europe, Bruessels: Euroclear Group (2002)
11. Euroclear (2007), http://www.euroclear.com (accessed December 10, 2007)
12. Euroclear. Press Release 02.06.2008: Nordic CSD to join the Euroclear Group (2008)
13. European Commission, Draft working document on Post-Trading (2006)
14. FESE, EACH, and ECSDA, The European Code of Conduct for Clearing and Settlement (2006)
15. Francotte, P.: Rising to the challenge of the crisis and change. The view from the CEO of Euroclear (14), 1–8 (2009)
16. Giovannini Group, Cross-Border Clearing and Settlement Arrangements in the EU (2001)
17. Giovannini Group, Second Report on EU Clearing and Settlement Arrangements (2003)
18. Kauko, K.: Interlinking securities settlement systems: A strategic commitment? Journal of Banking & Finance 31, 2962–2977 (2007)

19. Kröpfl, S.: Effizienz in der Abwicklung von Wertpapiergeschäften. Wissenschaftlicher Verlag, Berlin (2003)
20. LIBA, ESF, and ICMA, Letter to the ECB on Securities Sector Representation in T2S Committees (2007), http://www.icma-group.org/market_practice/Advocacy/clearing_and_settlement/target2-securities.html (accessed April 27, 2007)
21. Link Up Markets. Press Conference, Madrid (April 2, 2008), http://www.linkupmarkets.com/pdf/LinkUpMarkets-PressConferencePresentation.pdf (accessed July 3, 2008)
22. NERA Economic Consulting, The direct costs of clearing and settlement: an EU-US comparison, Corporation of London City Research Series, No. 1 (2004)
23. Neumann, D., Lattemann, C.: Clearing and Settlement im Wandel – Eine Perspektive für den europäischen Wertpapierhandel. Zeitschrift für die gesamte Kreditwirtschaft (2002)
24. Norman, P.: The limits to inteoperability. Speed 1, 23–26 (2006)
25. Milne, A.: Standard setting and competition in securities settlement, Bank of Finland, Discussion Paper 2005, No. 23 (2005)
26. Oxera. Methodology for monitoring prices, costs and volumes of trading and post-trading activities (July 2007), http://ec.europa.eu/internal_market/financial-markets/docs/clearing/oxera_study_en.pdf(accessed May 7, 2009)
27. Park, D., Rhee, C.: Building a Settlement Infrastructure for the Asian Bond Markets: Asiasettle. In: Asia's Debt Capital Markets, pp. 291–314. Springer, New York (2006)
28. Schaper, T.: Trends in European Cross-Border Securities Settlement – TARGET2-Securities and the Code of Conduct. In: Veit, D.J. (ed.) FinanceCom 2007. LNBIP, vol. 4, pp. 50–65. Springer, Berlin (2007)
29. Schmiedel, H., Malkamaki, M., Tarkka, J.: Economies of scale and technological development in securities depository and settlement systems. Journal of Banking & Finance 30, 1783–1806 (2006)
30. Weitzel, T., Beimborn, D., König, W.: A Unified Economic Model of Standard Diffusion: The Impact of Standardization Cost, Network Effects, and Network Topology. MIS Quarterly 30, 489–514 (2006)
31. Wendt, F.: Intraday Margining of Central Counterparties: EU Practice and a Theoretical Evaluation of Benefits and Costs. Netherlands Central Bank, Amsterdam (2006)
32. Werner, S.: Interoperability and interlinking: the way forward for the C&S industry. Frankfurt Voice (January 10, 2003)

Appendix

Table 2. Detailed comparison of models and approaches to improve securities settlement

	CSD-link model		Link Up Markets	
	Score	Description	Score	Description
Settlement risk	0	Unchanged. The systemic risk remains low due to the redundant infrastructure.	0	Unchanged. The systemic risk remains low due to the redundant infrastructure.
Settlement costs	--	Redundant infrastructure remains in place, costly links or agents banks are used for cross-border transactions.	-	Costs savings due to reduced inter-linkage costs; the costs for the redundant settlement systems remain; additional costs for the establishment of the hub.

Table 2. (*Continued*)

Implementation time	+	> 1 year.	++	< 1 year.
Technical integration	0	Domestic integration, no integration of cross-border processes.	+	Improved interlinkage of participating entities.
Integration of cross-border settlement	-	No integration.	0	No integration, but harmonisation of processes planed.
Integration of other post-trade services	+	Integration of domestic settlement and custody.	+	Integration of domestic settlement and custody.
Integration of cash settlement	-	No integration.	-	No integration.

	TARGET2-Securities		European CSD	
	Score	Description	Score	Description
Settlement risk	+(+)	Legal and credit risk are reduced significantly due to the integration of cash and securities settlement within one platform; no media breaches in cross-border transactions. The systemic risk is higher due to the concentration in one central platform instead of decentralised platforms.	+(+)	Legal and credit risk are reduced significantly due to the possibility of integration of cash and securities settlement within one platform; no media breaches in cross-border transactions. The systemic risk remains low due to the redundant infrastructure.
Settlement costs	+	Cost saving due to reduction of settlement engines, links, and intermediaries; but additional costs for the new platform.	+	Cost saving due to reduction of settlement engines, links, and intermediaries; but additional costs for the new platform.
Implementation time	-	6 years planed.	--	More than 6 years.
Technical integration	++	One integrated platform for cash and securities for all markets.	++	One integrated platform for all markets.
Integration of cross-border settlement	+	Harmonised almost domestic European settlement process; Custody is not integrated.	++	Harmonised almost domestic European settlement and custody process.
Integration of other post-trade services	-	Separation of settlement and custody.	++	Integration of domestic and cross-border settlement and custody.
Integration of cash settlement	++	Integration of cash and securities settlement on one platform	+	Integration of cash and securities settlement on one platform is possible

Task Delegation Based Access Control Models for Workflow Systems

Khaled Gaaloul[1] and François Charoy[2]

[1] SAP Research
Vincenz-Priessnitz-Strasse 1, 76131 Karlsruhe, Germany
[2] LORIA - INRIA - CNRS - UMR 7503
BP 239, F-54506 Vandœuvre-lès-Nancy Cedex, France
khaled.gaaloul@sap.com, charoy@loria.fr

Abstract. e-Government organisations are facilitated and conducted using workflow management systems. Role-based access control (RBAC) is recognised as an efficient access control model for large organisations. The application of RBAC in workflow systems cannot, however, grant permissions to users dynamically while business processes are being executed. We currently observe a move away from predefined strict workflow modelling towards approaches supporting flexibility on the organisational level. One specific approach is that of task delegation. Task delegation is a mechanism that supports organisational flexibility, and ensures delegation of authority in access control systems. In this paper, we propose a Task-oriented Access Control (TAC) model based on RBAC to address these requirements. We aim to reason about task from organisational perspectives and resources perspectives to analyse and specify authorisation constraints. Moreover, we present a fine grained access control protocol to support delegation based on the TAC model.

Keywords: Workflow, Task, Delegation, Access Control, Authorisation.

1 Introduction

The ongoing prosperity of the "e-" trend such as e-Business, e-Government, and e-Services fosters the ever increasing demand for interactions across organisational boundaries. Electronic government (e-Government) is the civil and political conduct of government, including services provision, using information and communication technologies. The concept of e-Government has been gaining ground from initial isolated to extensive research and applications. The prerequisites for an e-Government enactment strategy are the achievement of a technological interoperability of platforms and a deeper cooperation and security at the organisational level. Those requirements are related with the environment in which the public agencies operate, strictly constrained by norms, regulations, and result-oriented at the same time [1]. Actually, most governmental organisations offer electronic services within a collaborative environment. However, inter-organisational collaboration, especially by means of workflow management systems, is not as widespread.

C. Godart et al. (Eds.): I3E 2009, IFIP AICT 305, pp. 400–414, 2009.
© IFIP International Federation for Information Processing 2009

Currently, we observe a tendency moving away from strict enforcement approaches towards mechanisms supporting exceptions that make it difficult to foresee when modelling a workflow. One specific set of mechanisms ensuring human centric interactions and supporting collaboration cross-organisations is that of task delegation [2].

Security is an essential and integral part of workflow management systems. Protecting application data in workflow systems through access control policies has recently been widely discussed. Sandhu proposed a series of access control models [3,4]: RBAC0, RBAC1, RBAC2, RBAC3, and discussed a variety of constraints and policies including role hierarchy and separation of duties (SoD). These models are called the RBAC96 models. The central idea of this model is that access rights are associated with roles, to which users are assigned in order to get appropriate authorisations. It also involves the role hierarchy that enables the permission heritage. Since the roles in organisations are relatively stable and the number of roles is much smaller then that of users, the work of administrators can be greatly relieved by applying the concept of roles. Thus it is more adaptable to dynamic environments to a certain extent. However, there is no concept of tasks in RBAC, which makes it difficult to satisfy completely the access control requirements in a rapidly-changing dynamic environment [5,6].

In this paper, we propose a task-oriented access control model based on RBAC, thereby addressing the authorisation requirements in workflow management systems. Permissions are authorised both to roles and to tasks. The idea is to leverage the RBAC features regarding permissions assignments based-roles. In addition, users can get permissions through tasks when they execute a process, thereby supporting tasks dynamic constraints. Moreover, we offer a fine grained access control solution to compute delegated privileges.

The remainder of this paper is organised as follows. Section 2 presents a workflow scenario inspired from a governmental use case to motivate our work. In section 3, we give an overview about delegation and present the delegation scenarios. Section 4 defines workflow authorisations constraints and presents our access control model based-task. In section 5, we define a delegation protocol supporting delegation of authority. In Section 6, we discuss and conclude our approach, and outline several topics of potential future work.

2   e-Government Workflow Scenario

We introduce a govermental workflow scenario related to the European administrations collaboration. Europol and Eurojust are two key elements of the European system of international collaboration within the areas of law enforcement and justice. A specific scenario for this collaboration is the Mutual Legal Assistance (MLA) [7].

2.1   Mutual Legal Assistance

Mutual Legal Assistance (MLA) defines a collaborative workflow scenario involving national authorities of two European countries regarding the execution

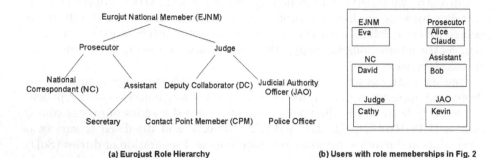

(a) Eurojust Role Hierarchy   (b) Users with role memeberships in Fig. 2

Fig. 1. An example of organisational role hierarchy and users in Eurojust

of measures for protection of a witness in a criminal proceeding. Here we describe the MLA process cross Eurojust organisations A and B, and detail the different business actors and resources models involved in the process. Basically, the two organisations work consists of receiving the request of assistance from the Europol member in order to process it and send it the concerned authority in country B. Eurojust infrastructure integrates systems such as MLA service and CMS (Case management System) to process data on the individual cases on which Eurojust national members are working in temporary work files. Eurojust defines an organisational hierarchy working together to achieve common goals. Figure 1 illustrates the organisational role hierarchy and users role memberships in the Eurojust organisation.

We applied the Business Process Modeling Notation (BPMN) to the MLA process (see Figure 2). BPMN has emerged as a standard notation for capturing business processes, especially at the level of domain analysis and high-level systems design [8]. The notation inherits and combines elements from a number of other proposed notations for business process modeling, including the XML Process Definition Language (XPDL) and the Activity Diagrams component of the Unified Modeling Language (UML).

In our example, we distinguish Prosecutor as the main responsible that collaborates with internal and external employees (Assistant, National Correspondent (NC), Judge and Judicial Authority Officer (JAO)) to process the MLA request. First, Prosecutor A receives the request and checks it in the MLA information service (tasks 1 and 2). If the provided information are correct, the Prosecutor will continue to process the request by asking for the preparation of the request document (task 4). Note that depending on the request context, the application process will differ in the users involved and data that need to be considered. In fact, the specific type of legal document requested will have a direct effect on the involved controls. For instance, the "Translate Request Document" task might be required to carry out the request preparation when exchanged documents are issued in the local language; therefore we need a national correspondent (NC) to translate documents (task 3). After the preparation of the required legal

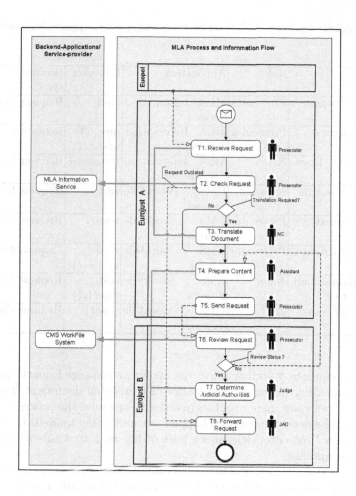

Fig. 2. MLA scenario

documents, the Prosecutor will send the request to his Eurojust colleagues in country B (task 5). The next steps that need to be taken are the review of the request, the determination of the judicial authority in order to forward the request to the concerned authority in country B (Eurojust B) for the final approval (tasks 6, 7 and 8).

The supporting Table 1 summarises the required roles, applications, functions and business objects associated to tasks.

2.2   Problem Statement

Several of the depicted tasks involve human interactions and are possibly time consuming. Tasks taken by the Eurojust organisations can involve several business actors such as Prosecutors, Assistants or Judges. Depending on the current

Table 1. Logistic workflow: Relations between tasks, roles, applications and business objects

Task type	Role	Application	Function	Business Object type
T1. Receive Request	Prosecutor	MLA Information Service	read()	Request Document
T2. Check Request	Prosecutor	MLA Information Service	query(), update()	Request Document
T3. Translate Document	NC	MLA Information Service	translate()	Request Document
T4. Prepare Content	Assistant	CMS WorkFile System	add()	Request Document
T5. Send Request	Prosecutor	CMS WorkFile System	send()	Request File
T6. Review Request	Prosecutor	CMS WorkFile System	read(), update()	Request File
T7. Determine Judicial Authorities	Judge	CMS WorkFile System	add(), modify()	Request File
T8. Forward Request	JAO	CMS WorkFile System	send()	Request File

control-flow sequence, workflow actors can evolve and change from the predefined workflow model. For instance, the absence of translated document (task 3) can lead to a new rearrangement of actors in order to optimise the process execution. In addition, unexpected events can happen without being modelled beforehand. For example, a Prosecutor delegates a part of his work to a subordinate due to emergency situations.

In this scenario, we describe the collaborative work cross-organisations. One of the objectives is to establish a collaboration including information exchange. Those objectives can be achieved using collaborative workflows [9,10]. However, recent works [11,9] presented new requirements such as control and transparency in collaborative workflow systems. What is in many cases described as collaboration appears to be coordination and synchronisation of processes by ignoring human-centric interactions. One type of transparency and control supporting mechanism in human-centric collaboration is that of task delegation. Task delegation is a mechanism supporting organisational flexibility in the human-centric workflow systems, and ensuring delegation of authority in access control systems [12].

3   Delegation in Workflow

In this section, we give a brief overview of delegation in workflows systems. We present the main factors that can motivate delegation and link it to the case study.

3.1   Context and Motivations

Task delegation can be very useful for real-world situations where a user who is authorised to perform a task is either unavailable or too overloaded with work to successfully complete it. This can occur, for example, when certain users are sick or on leave. It is frequently the case that delaying these task executions will violate time constraints on the workflow impairing the entire workflow execution. Delegation is a suitable approach to handle such exceptions and to ensure alternative scenarios by making workflow systems flexible and efficient.

Schaad presented a literature review of the different aspects and motivations for delegation [13]. Generally, delegation is motivated by three main factors: organisational, business process management and resources. In the following, we detail specific factors that can motivate delegation:

1. Lack of resources: The task cannot be achieved due to a lack of resources. The user holding the task misses one or several necessary resources. He has to delegate to another user possessing the required medium. Examples for such resources could be a lack of time or equipments.
2. Specialisation: A user might be sufficiently competent to achieve a goal, but it is more efficient to delegate to users in specialist positions, such that the achievement is optimised. Specialisation is a part of the business process management factor.
3. Organisational policies: Goals may conflict and specific organisational policies such as the separation of duties (SoD) may require a user to delegate. SoD constraint defines exclusive relation between tasks. For instance, tasks t_1 and t_2 can not be assigned to the same user. This defines one of the motivation criteria of the organisational factor.

3.2   Link with the Case Study

During the collaboration between Eurojust organisations A and B, several actors are involved in the MLA process (see Figure 2). We define role-based delegation to support human-centric interactions. We are considering a user-to-user delegation supporting role-based access control model (RBAC) defined in [14]. In the following, we present two scenarios describing both local and global delegation.

Definition 1. *We define a task delegation relation* RD = (T,u_1,u_2,DC), *where* T *is the delegated task,* u_1 *the delegator,* u_2 *the delegatee, and* DC *the delegation constraints. Constraints refer to the condition of delegating accordingly to the global policy.*

Local delegation (DS1): We consider an instance of the process MLA where no intervention is required from the NC member. We denote user *Alice* member of role Prosecutor and user *Bob* member of role Assistant. T5 is assigned to Alice, where Alice needs to send the MLA request to authority B. Alice is overloaded (lack of resources) and need to delegate T5 to one of his assistant. Delegation criteria is based on the role hierarchy (RH) of Eurojust A, where the Assistant Bob is a subordinate to the Prosecutor Alice based on the global policy definition.

The delegation relation (T5,Alice,Bob,(RH,2days)) $\in RD$, where (RH, 2 days) defines the delegation constraints DC regarding the time validity (2 days) and the organisational constraint (RH).

Global delegation (DS2): It defines a delegation cross-organisations. We consider an instance of the process MLA where the MLA request is outdated and exists already in the CMS system of country B. The specialisation of Prosecutor Claude will motivate the prosecutor Alice to delegate T2 for his colleague. Task delegation is defined based on a role mapping (RM) constraint, where distributed resources with external roles are defined in the global policy. The delegation relation (T2,Alice,Claude,RM) $\in RD$.

The next step will be to consider the propagation of authority during delegation. We need to define authorisation requirements with regards to workflow invariants such as task, users and data [6]. To this end, we propose an access control model based on the workflow specifications and user authorisation information (see Section 4.2).

4   Workflow Authorisation Constraints

A workflow comprises various activities that are involved in a business process. Activities that are part of a process are represented as tasks. Authorisation information is given which authorises users to perform tasks. Such authorisation information may be specified using a simple access control list or more complex role-based structures [15].

4.1   Task Execution Model

We define a task execution model using a UML activity diagram composed of three main activities: *Initialisation, Processing* and *Finalisation*. During the initialisation of the task, a task instance is created and then assigned to a user. During task processing, the assigned user can start or delegate the task which gathers all operations and rights over the business objects related to task resources. Finally the task finalisation would notice the workflow management system that the task is terminated, where termination defines completeness, failure or cancellation.

Seeing the task as a block that needs protection against undesired accesses, the activity diagram includes an access control (AC) transition that is in charge with granting or not the access to the task. AC checks defines the transition from the creation of a task to its assignment to a user. This assignment will lead to the processing or the cancellation of the task. Cancellation can be triggered when the assigned user doesn't fulfil the required authorisation to proceed the task instance.

The AC transition defines the on time authorisation supporting task execution. It defines a relationship between user, task instance and authorisation

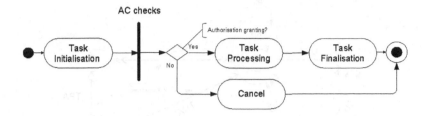

AC checks

Fig. 3. Task execution model

instance. An authorisation instance defines the permission needed to execute operations on business objects to carry out a task.

Definition 2. P *is a set of permissions.* P *defines the right to execute an operation on a resource type. A permission* p *is a pair* (f,o) *where* f *is a function and* o *is a business object:* $p \subseteq f \times o$.

For instance, the task T7 "Determine Judicial Authorities" requires a permission that defines functions *add()* and *modify()* to access the MLA business object (see Table 1). Therefore, the assigned user Cathy member of role Judge needs to be authorised to access T7 task resources.

4.2   Task-Oriented Access Control Model

We propose a Task-oriented Access Control (TAC) model to support authorisation requirements in workflow systems (see Figure 4). Authorisation information will be inferred from access control data structures, such as user-role assignment and task-role assignment relations [16]. We leverage the different task requirements regarding human and material resources and model it in a set of relationships building our model.

Formally, we define sets U, R, OU, T, P, S and TI as a set of users, roles, organisations units, tasks, permissions, subjects and task instances respectively. We define RH (Role Hierarchy), where RH is a partial order on R. $(r_i, r_j) \in R$, RH denotes that r_i is a role superior to r_j, as a result, r_i automatically inherits the permissions of r_j.

We define RM (Role Mapping), where RM is a partial order on R belonging to a set of roles defined in the involved organisations hierarchies (OU). RM defines external roles accessing distributed resources cross-organisations [17]. It provide a decentralised access control mechanism where externally known roles are publicly available, where:

$r_k \in OU_k$ and $r_l \in OU_l$, RM denotes that r_l is a role mapped to r_k, as a result, r_l automatically inherits the permissions of r_k.

Definitions of Map Relations:

– $URA \subseteq U \times R$, the user role assignment relation mapping users to roles they are member of.

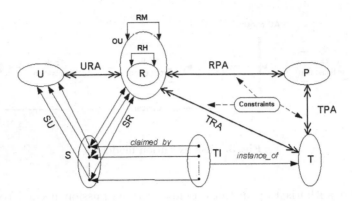

Fig. 4. Task-oriented access control model

- $RPA \subseteq P \times R$, the permission role assignment relation mapping roles to permissions they are authorised to.
- $TPA \subseteq T \times P$, the task permission relation mapping tasks to permissions. This defines the set of permission required to execute a task.
- $TRA \subseteq T \times R$ the task role assignment relation mapping roles to tasks they are assigned to.

Definitions of Functions:

- $SU: S \rightarrow U$ a function mapping a subject to the corresponding user.
- $SR: S \rightarrow 2^R$, a function mapping each subject to a set of roles, where $SR(s_i) \subseteq \{r|(SU(s_i), r) \in URA\}$ and subject s_i has the permissions; $\cup_{\{r \in SR(s_i)\}}\{p|(p, r) \in RPA\}$.
- $instance_of: TI \rightarrow T$, a function mapping a task instance to its task type.
- $claimed_by: TI \rightarrow S$, a function mapping a task instance to a subject to execute it, where:
  $claimed_by(t_i, s_i) = \{t_i|instance_of(t_i, t), (r, u) \in URA|(SR(s_i) = r \bigwedge SU(s_i) = u), (t, r) \in TRA\}$.

Definitions of Constraints:

Here we discuss Separation of duty (SoD) and Binding of duty (BoD) constraints. We define exclusive relation between tasks for SoD, and binding relation between tasks for BoD as follows:

$$TT_{SOD} = \{(t_i, t_j) \in T|t_i \text{ is Exclusive with } t_j\} \subseteq \text{TxT}$$

$$TT_{BOD} = \{(t_i, t_j) \in T|t_i \text{ is Binding with } t_j\} \subseteq \text{TxT}, \text{ where } t_i \leq t_j.$$

If $(t_1, t_2) \in TT_{SOD}$, then t_1 and t_2 can not be assigned to the same subject. For instance, T4 and T6 $\in TT_{SOD}$, where subjects with role Prosecutor must be different.

If $(t_1, t_2) \in TT_{BOD}$, then t_1 and t_2 must be assigned to the same subject.

Contributions and Motivations:

We model permission assignment relations for task and role in order to support both human and material resources. The tuple (P,T,R) specifies TRA, TPA and RPA many-to-many relationships which are specifics to the task execution context. The remaining relations are generic relations based on RBAC model [3].

Definition 3. *A task can only be assigned to a role if and only if* $(t, r) \in TRA \Rightarrow \{p \in P | (t, p) \in TPA\} \subset \{p | (p, r) \in RPA\}$.

The main contribution is to specify the task assignment conditions based on the RPA and TPA requirements (see Definition 3). Actually, two conditions have to be verified to satisfy TRA relation. The first condition is related to task resources requirements. The user's permissions defined in RPA need to satisfy the permissions defined in TPA. If this condition is satisfied, the task is executed if and only if the user is assigned to it. Basically, having permissions to execute a task but not being in the task worklist will not satisfy those conditions and, therefore, deny the access to task resources.

Returning to the example, T2 "Check Request" is assigned a set of permissions (*query()*, *update()*) via TPA in order to carry out this task. Once T2 is claimed, TRA is assigned to roles that are authorised to claim it. On one hand, user Bob with role Assistant is not allowed to claim T2. Bobs permissions (*add()*) do not fulfill T3 requirements. Therefore, the relation for the instance of T2: TRA (T2, Bob) returns false and no authorisation is granted for Bob. On the other hand, user Kevin member of role JAO has the required permissions to carry out T5, however, Kevin does not have the right to claim T2 since the user-task assignments is not defined in the global policy (see Figure 2, Table 1).

5   Context-Aware Delegation for TAC

Delegation is a mechanism that permits a user to assign a subset of his assigned authorisations (privileges) to other users who currently do not possess it. The user who performs a delegation is referred to as a "delegator" and the user who receives a delegation is referred to as a "delegatee". We provide an optimised method to compute the delegated privileges based on the current requirements of the task instances (resources requirements). The TAC model defines the list of potential delegatees (RPA) that may satisfy the delegated task requirements (TPA). For instance, u_1 and u_2 are members of roles r_1 and r_2 respectively; $(t, u_1, u_2, DC) \in RD$ *iff* $(t, r_2) \in TRA \Rightarrow \{p \in P | (t, p) \in TPA\} \subset \{p | (p, r_2) \in RPA\}$.

5.1   Delegation Protocol

We present a fine grained access control protocol to support delegation. Delegation protocol depicts the dialogue between a delegator and a delegatee during a delegation request. We model the protocol using UML sequence diagrams (see Figure 5).

The Authorisation Component supports the access control mechanism to make a policy decision. An access control policy specifies a level of defining access to task resources when starting or delegating a task. The Task Service Manager returns the current task state (started, cancelled, etc.). The Worklist component maintains the user-task assignments during runtime. We detail the basic steps as follows:

1. First the delegator is sending a request for delegation to the Delegation Component (DC) for a specific task and a specific role (Role A).
2. The DC checks with the help of the Authorisation Component (AC) if the delegator can actually delegate based on his policy attributes, then with the Task Service Manager regarding the delegated task status.

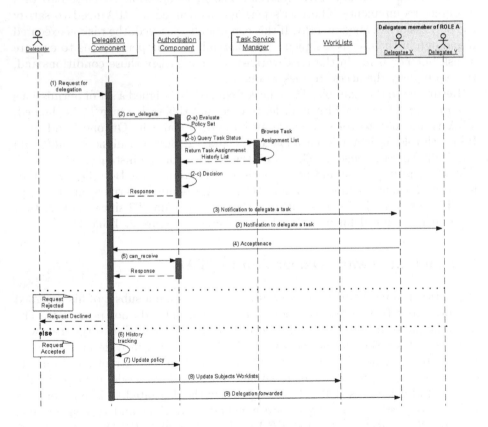

Fig. 5. Task delegation protocol

3. The DC notifies all the delegatees belonging to the role (Role A) of the availability of the task.
4. The first one to respond is allocated with the task.
5. The DC checks with the help of the AC if the delegatee can actually receive the task.
6. The DC then keeps track of the current delegation within internal history records.
7. The DC updates the appropriate policy in the policy repository.
8. The DC updates the appropriate worklists (delegator and delegatee) if the delegation is related to a task instance.
9. Then the delegation is forwarded to the designated delegatee.

Returning to the example, the scenario DS2 can be satisfied. Actually, Prosecutor Alice can delegate T2 "Check Request" to Prosecutor Claude based on their role mapping constraint. In addition, global policy constraints (SoD, BoD) are not specified for T2. Subsequently, Prosecutor Claude will inherit permissions that will authorise him to claim T2 and access its resources afterwards.

5.2 Revocation

Revocation is an important process that must accompany the delegation. It is the subsequent withdrawal of previously delegated objects such as a role or a task. A vast amount of different views on the topic can be found in literature [18] where each author having their own assumptions and opinions on how to model revocation. For simplification, our model of revocation is closely related to the delegation model based user-to-user. Actually, the decision of revocation is issued from the delegator in order to take away the delegated privileges (permissions), or the desire to go back to the state before privileges were delegated.

6   Related Work

Role-based access control (RBAC) is recognised as an efficient access control model for large organisations. Most organisations have some business rules related to access control policy. Delegation of authority is among these rules [19]. In [4], authors extend the RBAC96 model by defining some delegations rules. Barka and Sandhu proposed a role-based delegation model. They deal with user-to-user delegation. The unit of delegation in them is a role. However, users may want to delegate a piece of permission from a role.

Zhang and al. propose a flexible delegation model named Permission-based Delegation Model (PBDM) [20]. PBDM supports user-to-user and role-to-role delegations with features of multi-step delegation and multi-option revocation. It also supports both role and permission level delegation, which provides great flexibility in authority management. However, neither RBAC nor PBDM support the task-based delegation criteria described in the motivated delegation scenarios.

The eXtensible Access Control Markup Language is an XML-based, declarative access control policy language that lets policy editors to specify the rules about who can do what and when. As an OASIS standard, its greatest strength lies in interoperability [21]. Unlike other application-specific, proprietary access-control mechanisms, this standard can be specified once and deployed beyond the boundaries of organisations and countries. The current XACML standard does not provide explicit support for task delegation.

In [22], Rissanen and Firozabadi add new structured data-types to express chains of delegation and constraints on delegation. The main result of their research is an administrative delegation. It is about creating new long-term access control policies by means of delegation in a decentralised organisation. However, this approach does not cover ad-hoc interactions and is not suitable to not support decentralized delegation in the context of heavily human centric collaboration.

7   Conclusion and Future Work

Enormous amounts of data flow cross-organisations along processes and are shared by many different users. Their security must be assured. In this paper, we firstly analyse the relevant authorisation requirements in workflow management systems. Then, based on RBAC model, we propose the task-oriented access control (TAC) model. This model can grant authorisations based on workflow specifications and user authorisation information. The motivation of this direction is inspired from an e-government case study supporting dynamic authorisation changes during delegation. In this context, we proposed a fine grained access control protocol to support delegation based on TAC constraints, thereby ensuring dynamic delegation of authority.

The next stage of our work is the implementation of our approach using the eXtensible Access Control Markup Language (XACML) standard. We propose an extension to XACML specifications supporting task delegation constraints. Future work will look also at enriching our approach with additional delegation constraints supporting historical records. Delegation history will be used to record delegation that have been made to address administrative requirements such as auditing.

References

1. Traunmüller, R., Wimmer, M. (eds.): e-Government at a Decisive Moment: Sketching a Roadmap to Excellence. LNCS, vol. 3183. Springer, Heidelberg (2004)
2. Schaad, A.: A framework for evidence lifecycle management. In: Weske, M., Hacid, M.-S., Godart, C. (eds.) WISE Workshops 2007. LNCS, vol. 4832, pp. 191–200. Springer, Heidelberg (2007)
3. Sandhu, R.S., Coyne, E.J., Feinstein, H.L., Youman, C.E.: Role-based access control models. IEEE Computer 29(2), 38–47 (1996)

4. Barka, E., Sandhu, R.: Framework for role-based delegation models. In: Proceedings of the 16th Annual Computer Security Applications Conference, Washington, DC, USA, pp. 168–176. IEEE Computer Society, Los Alamitos (2000)
5. Liao, X., Zhang, L., Chan, S.C.F.: A task-oriented access control model for wfMS. In: Deng, R.H., Bao, F., Pang, H., Zhou, J. (eds.) ISPEC 2005. LNCS, vol. 3439, pp. 168–177. Springer, Heidelberg (2005)
6. Gaaloul, K., Schaad, A., Flegel, U., Charoy, F.: A secure task delegation model for workflows. In: SECURWARE 2008: Proceedings of the 2008 Second International Conference on Emerging Security Information, Systems and Technologies, Washington, DC, USA, pp. 10–15. IEEE Computer Society, Los Alamitos (2008)
7. R4eGov Technical Annex 1. Towards e-Administration in the large. Sixth Framework Programme, Information Society Technologies (March 2006), http://www.r4egov.info
8. The Workflow Management Coalition. Process Definition Interface – XML Process Definition Language (2005), http://www.wfmc.org.
9. Schulz, K.A., Orlowska, M.E.: Facilitating cross-organisational workflows with a workflow view approach. Data Knowl. Eng. 51(1), 109–147 (2004)
10. Contenti, M., Mecella, M., Termini, A., Baldoni, R.: A Distributed Architecture for Supporting e-Government Cooperative Processes. In: Böhlen, M.H., Gamper, J., Polasek, W., Wimmer, M.A. (eds.) TCGOV 2005. LNCS (LNAI), vol. 3416, pp. 181–192. Springer, Heidelberg (2005)
11. Jensen, C., Scacchi, W.: Collaboration, Leadership, Control, and Conflict Negotiation in the NetBeans.org Community. In: 26th International Software Engineering Conference (2004)
12. Gaaloul, K., Charoy, F., Schaad, A.: Modelling Task Delegation for Human-Centric eGovernment Workflows. To appear in the 10th International Digital Government Research Conference (dg.o 2009).
13. Schaad, A.: A Framework for Organisational Control Principles. PhD thesis, The University of York, England (2003)
14. Zhang, L., Ahn, G.-J., Chu, B.-T.: A rule-based framework for role-based delegation and revocation. ACM Transactions on Information and System Security 6(3), 404–441 (2003)
15. Crampton, J., Khambhammettu, H.: Delegation and satisfiability in workflow systems. In: SACMAT 2008: Proceedings of the 13th ACM symposium on Access control models and technologies, pp. 31–40. ACM, New York (2008)
16. Kandala, S., Sandhu, R., Savith, K., Savith, K., Ravi, S., Ravi, S.: Secure role-based workflow models. In: Metal Detection, vol. II, Technical Proposal, FETC Contract DE-AR2195MC32089, pp. 45–58. Kluwer, Dordrecht (2002)
17. Freudenthal, E., Pesin, T., Port, L., Keenan, E., Karamcheti, V.: drbac: Distributed role-based access control for dynamic coalition environments. In: ICDCS 2002: Proceedings of the 22 nd International Conference on Distributed Computing Systems (ICDCS 2002), Washington, DC, USA, p. 411. IEEE Computer Society, Los Alamitos (2002)
18. Hagstrom, A., Jajodia, S., Parisi-Presicce, F., Wijesekera, D.: Revocations-A Classification. In: CSFW 2001: Proceedings of the 14th IEEE workshop on Computer Security Foundations, Washington, DC, USA, p. 44. IEEE Computer Society, Los Alamitos (2001)
19. Belokosztolszki, A., Eyers, D.M., Moody, K.: Policy Contexts: Controlling Information Flow in Parameterised RBAC. In: POLICY 2003: Proceedings of the 4th IEEE International Workshop on Policies for Distributed Systems and Networks, Washington, DC, USA, p. 99. IEEE Computer Society, Los Alamitos (2003)

20. Zhang, X., Oh, S., Sandhu, R.: PBDM: a flexible delegation model in RBAC. In: SACMAT 2003: Proceedings of the eighth ACM symposium on Access control models and technologies, pp. 149–157. ACM Press, New York (2003)
21. eXtensible Access Control Markup Language (XACML v2.0). Standard, Organization for the Advancement of Structured Information Standards (OASIS) (February 2005),
http://docs.oasis-open.org/xacml/2.0/access-control-xacml-2.0-core-spec-os.pdf
22. Rissanen, E., Firozabadi, B.S.: Administrative Delegation in XACML. Swedish Institute of Computer Science, Kista-Sweden

Data Refining for Text Mining Process in Aviation Safety Data

Olli Sjöblom

Turku School of Economics, Rehtorinpellonkatu 3, 20500 Turku, Finland

Abstract. Successful data mining is an iterative process during which data will be refined and adjusted to achieve more accurate mining results. Most important tools in the text mining context are list of stop words and list of synonyms. The size and richness of the lists mentioned depend on the structure of the language used in the text to be mined. English, for example, is an "easy" language for search technologies, because with a couple of exceptions, the stem of the word is not conjugated and terms are formed using several words instead of creating compounds. This requires special attention to definitions when processing morphologically rich languages like Finnish. This chapter introduces the need and realisation of refining the source data for a successful data mining process based onto the results achieved from first mining round.

Keywords: Data Mining, Text Mining, Flight Safety.

1 Introduction

Air transport is among the safest modes of transport. However, although the global rate of accidents is stabilising and the situation is somehow satisfactory, the growth in air traffic will increase the absolute number of fatal accidents per year and therefore new ways of improving air safety need to be explored [3].

Therefore the newest research resources and data processing techniques are unavoidable. The focal point in this context is analysis. Fundamental to every Safety Management System is the principle of collecting and analysing operational data [5]. The only way to process narrative data with computing has till the end of the 1990s been to utilise query tools for specific issues of data base systems relying on the skills and experiences as well as the memory of the safety officer [13]. The idea to apply data mining and especially text mining as investigation and analysis tool for flight safety reports was created by the author of this article when he worked as inspector in Investigation and analysis unit in Finnish Civil Aviation Authority (FCAA).

2 Data Mining

A data mining system cannot be described easily, because it can use several of these methods as a combination. A rather good definition among many of them is that by Parsaye who regards data mining as *"a decision support process in which we search for patterns of information in data"* [14]. Simply expressed, the goal of data mining process is extracting high-level knowledge from low-level data. That is to search for relationships and global patterns that exist in large databases but are *hidden* in the vast amounts of data, which might take years to find with conventional techniques [18]. The significant development in database and software technologies, i.e., warehousing of transaction data has enabled the organisations to build the foundation for knowledge discovery in databases (KDD) which consists of such phases as selection, pre-processing, transformation, data mining and interpretation/evaluation [1].

The data mining process contains several steps or phases which chain from data to knowledge is presented in Figure 1. The first results of data mining process after representing the discovered patterns need to be evaluated carefully by consolidating them with the existing domain knowledge, which is more a combination of art and common sense than science [8]. Discovery process often begins with making a hypothesis, but using data mining this is not necessary. Text mining, that this article is about, is one subclass of data mining [19].

Usually the data accumulates in organisations faster than it can be processed [17]. The need for automated means to process the data is also increasing rapidly [2]. Skilled analytical and technical specialists are still required, because data mining process does not give straight answer to questions. Its role is purely a decision support system [10]. When used by professionals, data mining can discover patterns and anomalies that have not been thought before [13]. The main target of data mining in aviation safety is to find hazardous trends and patterns in collected flight safety data. Despite of a couple of successful projects, the volume of using data mining is at a very moderate level. As a bottom line these projects produced a statement: "Very encouraging and very promising; more work to be done" [12].

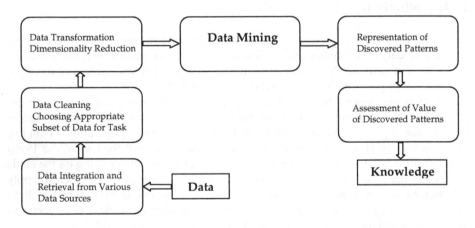

Fig. 1. The Knowledge Discovery in Database process [4], [6]

The structured data can be analysed easily using queries from databases and running their results through graphic tools but there have not been tools to analyse textual data before text mining. It is estimated that the main part (over 80%) of the information in reporting is written in the unstructured and textual format. Narrative text mining is demanding because of the multiplicity of languages spoken in the world.

2.1 Data Mining in Finnish

The Finnish language is a compound rich and very inflectional language having an inflectional and derivational morphology. As English has only two, there are 15 cases in Finnish. Finnish case endings correspond to prepositions or postpositions in other languages (cf. ilma/an, ilma/ssa, ilma/sta, in English to the air, in the air, from the air) [7]. In Finnish, a noun may have some 2,000 forms, an adjective 6,000, and a verb 12,000 forms. If the effect of derivation is also taken into account, the figures will be increased roughly by a factor of 10 [9].

The FCAA has used "normal" tools like Excel and report generators of database systems lacking a tool that could process safety report narratives. Using flight safety reports as test material text mining was tested. The study can be considered as a jump to the unknown, because, as far as the authors' knowledge, text mining in Finnish has been generally made only to some extent and nobody has applied text mining to Finnish flight safety reports before.

2.2 Research Process

The research process was planned to follow the process presented in Figure 1. As the first phase, flight safety reports from years 1994-1996, about 1200 cases, were chosen. All the test data was extracted from one Microsoft Access database in .csv form. Taking the narratives only for final test material can be regarded as phase two, choosing appropriate subset of data. The cleaning process, in this case correcting misspelled words and expanding acronyms, happened through creating list of synonyms. As for the third phase, choosing narratives can be seen as dimensionality reduction and due to source, no data transformation was needed. Using complex mining techniques, data needs to be cleaned frequently from inaccuracies like duplicate records, anomalous data points and human errors [15].

Three different systems seemed to be appropriate enough for comparing the expected results as benchmarking. The author was aware of one prototype and one commercial product with Finnish module prototype as well as one commercial system with encouraging results mining Spanish, which seemed worth testing Finnish.

The processing systems are normally built to recognise formal language only. This requires a list of words that the system does not recognise. Stop words list includes words that will be ignored. These are the ones that do not provide any insight, like: a, about, above, across, after, almost, although, always, etc.

Stop words list was created manually using the filtered list of words. From the total amount of more than 8000 filtered words 446 stop words were listed. The verb 'to be' in all its forms was defined as a stop word, because it appears rather often in the reports and it can freely be ignored without losing any information.

List of synonyms is mapping multiple synonyms to one word including misspellings and abbreviations. Optionally, non-alphabet and non-number characters are mapped to 'blank', and numbers are mapped to 'delete'. Some examples of these are:

- "   <blank>
- `   <blank>
- '   <delete>

- a/c   aircraft
- apparent   appear
- apparently   appear
- kts   knots
- rwy   runway
- taxied   taxi
- taxiing   taxi

The list of synonyms, like stop words, was created manually from filtered list of words and it contained 2048 words, a rather high amount because of the characteristics of Finnish.

3   Evaluation of the Tools

Clustering was chosen to be used, because the main target especially was to find similar cases from a vast amount of report data without having any presumption whether these exist or not. The length of the reports in the basic data varied remarkably. Therefore, the question about data quality that means data accuracy and completeness emerges as one of the biggest challenges for data mining. before.

3.1   Tool #1

The Tool #1 is primarily from Xerox laboratories, America, but now developed and represented by Text Mining Solutions, TEMIS, in France. The Value-Added Reseller for TEMIS products in Scandinavian is Lingsoft Oy in Turku, Finland [11]. Testing this system was prototyping, because the module for processing Finnish was quite new and there were no experiences in a wider range.

TEMIS decided to create 26 clusters leaving out 8 reports as unclassified documents, as which system handled each report. Their size varied from 109 to 21, and due to mining rules the biggest cluster was divided into two sub clusters with 58 and 50 documents. Every document is listed with its percentage explaining the cluster, the highest being 27 which be regarded significant in this context. The smallest clusters produced some applicable information. However, although the new Finnish module worked properly, a list of special synonyms and acronyms depending on the context might be needed because they do not exist in the thesaurus of the mining system.

3.2   Tool #2

The tool #2 is developed at Tampere Technical University, Signal Processing Laboratory as one of the results of the project called GILTA (manaGIng Large Text mAsses) between 1999 and 2003. The scientific objective is to find out if it is possible to find the desired things in a mass of documents by using self-organising maps (SOM) or similar methods combined with linguistic sentence analysis. Simply expressed, the documents are converted into vector form. The vectors determine the similarity of the documents through using Euclidean distance. The shorter the distance, the more similar the documents are. This method provides total language independence. Using systems training the methodology can easily be adapted to any application field [16].

The system itself decided to share the data into 100 clusters when the amount of most significant words was chosen to be 9. The size of the clusters varied between 158 and 1. The amount of the clusters can be considered to be appropriate in this context, but the distribution of reports should be more uniform.

3.3 Tool #3

The tool #3 is a commercial product of American origin called PolyVista. The company is located in Houston, Texas. It is a full-capable data mining system with several components and technologies built-in having ability for mining both numerical and text data. Also with this tool only clustering was performed using different amounts of clusters that could be determined by the user. This was the first time when Finnish text was mined. The tool is built to be used in English context, but tests had been made with Spanish achieved good and encouraging results and that is why the company dared to test its applicability for Finnish. This seemed to be successful as well.

The results were returned to the researcher in form of pictures taken from the Cluster Browser window. The first run was kind of a preliminary one made without any pre-processing and determining 15 as the amount of clusters by a guess. After using stop words the results looked different and the process was continued by taking synonyms with. The data was processed determining the number of clusters first to be 6 and then raising it up to 20 with step of 2. All the research phases in the process of estimating this tool have produced some kind of good and applicable results, especially when the smallest clusters are observed. The scores of most important words are high and quickly estimated the words seem to be of significant character.

4 Preparation of the Test Material for the Second Round

The first results proved an obvious need for tuning the test material, especially the definition of stop words and synonyms. This was seen through the mining results of GILTA system, because they were listed in a clear form of Excel datasheet.

The search technologies are often confronted by great challenges in conjugation forms and compounds. In Finnish, for example, the words may have thousands of conjugation forms and in addition to that, they can be parts of compounds in almost countless amounts. In average, every seventh word can be found in its basic form in fluent Finnish texts. For search technologies English is an "easy" language. With a couple of exceptions, the stem of the word is not conjugated and instead of compounds, terms are formed using several words. Because in most of the information systems used search technologies are constructed onto English, the conjugated forms of compounds are often not found. This happens especially in processing large amounts of documentation in morphologically rich languages like Finnish.

If the mining system contains language tools, like TEMIS, there is generally no significant need for defining words. When processing short texts including special terminology there is. As an example can be taken the words 'gear' and 'landing gear (one compound in Finnish)', as well in English as Finnish, which are pure synonyms in this context, but not necessarily in general language.

It was a pure mistake, that one of the most common stop words '*jälkeen*' (after) was forgotten from its list. The consequences were clear in its frequent appearance in the most significant words of the clusters. These kinds of mistakes are worthy to correct, because the word mentioned appears 304 times totally. Despite of its characteristics of an obvious stop word, its frequency in this size of data is significant, which would anyway require paying special attention onto it. Another obvious mistake was that some tenses were not taken into account when list of synonyms was created.

One of the most remarkable problems in this study appeared due to the high frequency of the word '*kone*' (plane). This caused the class #11 to contain 158 reports, which makes no sense, at least in this test data context, where the appropriate cluster size should be at most about 25 reports. The word appeared among the nine most significant words in 42 classes and as the most significant word in 5 classes.

What to do with a word that causes the enormous size of one cluster but which is among the most important if not even one of the really most important words? The first idea would not be just to ignore it, and that is why it required careful analysing its role in the data. This problem acting as an efficient accelerator, quantitative data analysis application called NVivo was taken into use to get deeper analysis information. This move appeared to be a very successful one, because using Excel and Word alone would not have led to a satisfactory goal in understanding the relations between the concepts in test data.

The first test with using NVivo was a simple query which had the definitions for searching all words in different forms meaning aeroplane, so, text search criteria were (in English) plane OR aeroplane OR aircraft OR a/c. Although Finnish is a rather complicated language, using wildcard – any characters (*) after the stem of the word, all forms were taken into the result of the query, because all forms of this word in this context, according to the list of words, do not make changes to its stem. NVivo takes into account all the words defined in the query options and determines their relevance in the data mass. GILTA counts the word only once if it can be found in the report although would appear several times. This causes differences when distributions of words and their significances are estimated in this research process. NVivo counted 67 classes including word 'kone' its relevance varying between 34% and 1% as GILTA has taken 42 classes into account. The word 'kone' (plane) has a total of 680 appearances in all its case forms. At the first round, its synonym 'lentokone' (airplane) with 51 appearances was taken into account, but 'ilma-alus' (aircraft), 20 appearances, was kept separate, although it means the same thing. Aircraft can, of course, have several meanings (e.g., helicopter, glider, etc.), but in this context there is practically no difference between these concepts, especially as its usage in the reports is almost nil which can be seen from its frequency in the data, too. However, the English abbreviation a/c with total of only three appearances had been added to the synonyms of 'kone' (plane), which brought one report to class 11, in which it appeared two times. Combining 'plane' and 'airplane' raised the amount of the concept from 680 to 731, only about eight per cent. Adding the word 'aircraft' to the synonyms would increase the number by less than three per cent, so the latter can be seen not having any effect to the final results, although, as mentioned before, it caused one more report to belong to the class 11.

Class 34 must be mentioned separately, as being rather well-formed and homogenous, because it contains reports written about crossing border without permission. It will be interesting to see during the second round how this will change because the frequencies of the expressions 'without permission (24)' and 'plane (22)' are so close to each other. Speculatively scanned, ignoring the word 'plane' would not seem to change the core information of the class.

During the process of analysing how this word possibly affects the results, it was noticed that this word was found in the most important words 454 times, so, the rest 297, close to the half of the whole amount, stayed beyond the significant words.

The further this special problem was studied the cleared was noticed that from the point of view of the whole study it really makes sense to solve this basic seeming question very carefully. In the final test the query definitions included all the different forms and synonyms of the word were taken into account. It appeared in 45 classes with its relevance varying between 4.9 and 1.0 per cent. The four highest had their relevance between 4.0 and 4.9, the next four between 2.1 and 3.3, and the rest having less than 2.0, among which the relevance of the last 14 classes was exactly 1.0%.

This result gave a slight presumption to ignore the word in mining process. Because there were no more than those 45 classes mentioned, it was simple to manually go through all the classes. This investigation resulted to the finding that the word can very obviously be added to the list of stop words, because it could have been ignored in the reports without losing relevant information in them. With this manual check the results achieved from using NVivo were confirmed.

All the airfield abbreviations for airports and airfields in Finland (EF+ which stands for Europe - Finland + two characters for the place name, for example EFTU = Turku airport), were removed. These were 141 different expressions, one abbreviation alone or a combination of two or more abbreviations describing for example the route, making together 363 'words'. This was done because the place, in a small country like Finland, does not contain information value in mining process, considering the uneven distribution of especially the airline traffic which concentrates into Helsinki. From the mining results it could be easy to draw the conclusion that Helsinki is the most dangerous airport in Finland with large marginal to others, which is not the case, indeed. If the place has any significance to the mining process, it will surely be discovered through other deviations during the deeper analysis of the mining results.

Helsinki as a name can be found 103 times in different forms in the data, being the most significant word with 24 appearances in class 51 that contains 24 reports. Interesting point in this class is that the next important word with 18 exemplars is *to return*. In this class the most cases are about returning to the airport because of some reason and it can be stated that the airport does not have any significance, it just happens to be Helsinki because of the traffic volume. It does not appear in any other class among the nine most significant words, so it could be added to the stop words. In case something happens especially at or close to a certain airfield or airport, the possible place causing problems will certainly be found as one of the findings when the cases concerning the problem are examined more minutely.

Due to the same reason, *Finnair* with its abbreviations (together 92 words in six different forms) was removed, because of the multiple volume of traffic compared with the total of the other operators together. It is worth noticing that it was the most significant word with frequency of 15 in class 40, which contained 17 reports.

Generally, what happened and for which reason is more important than to whom it happened, which can be as well derived from the reports in case it would be important. This is on view very clear in this class also. A special attraction was focused onto class 40, where the two most significant words were 'Finnair' (or FIN) and 'kone'. It is worth noticing that in this case the conjugation forms and cases only of the word are taken into account, not its synonyms. This combination produced the relevance of 42.5% to the class mentioned. The next classes were 11 with relevance of 25.8%, 82 with 11.7%, 4 with 10.5%, and 78 with 10.1% the rest 22 classes with their relevance varying from 9.9% till 2.2%. In different contexts, however, these kinds of removals could not have been done, because bigger countries even in Europe have several air traffic hubs and big companies, in which case the company and the place might play an important role in report analysis.

Another significant discovery that formed a bit complicated situation was the rather important concept *Flight Level* and especially its abbreviation, *FL*, because in this process could be stated that 'everything depends on everything'. It figured 50 times which brought it to the class of rather frequent words and thus its impact should be decreased. When the written expressions for it with all synonyms and case forms are counted, the total amount will moderately exceed 150.

General overview showed that it has a significant frequency only in class 22 in which it was the most describing word with frequency of 12. The size of this class is 12 reports and the abbreviation can be seen separately 26 times and five times written together with the numbers (for example FL220, that means an altitude of 22 000 feet). The same abbreviation was available the second time only in class 10 as the last significant, the ninth, word with frequency of two (relevance 1.5%). This class contains seven reports of which the two most significant words have the frequency of six and for the third one the correspondent value is five. The analysis using NVivo confirmed the discovery, because in the class 22 the relevance of the abbreviation was 33%, but decreased beyond this class dramatically being between 2.5% and 1.2% in the remaining 13 classes in which it appeared.

It is, however, worth noticing that the criteria of NVivo differ from the correspondent of GILTA. This can clearly be seen in the query results of this special word, in which the most relevant matches with GILTA, but between the two classes GILTA has taken into account mentioned above, NVivo has put four classes with their relevance varying between 2.5 and 1.6. The same difference can be discovered from the query results of the synonyms. This discovery could cause somewhat confusion, but because the results are rather close to each other, it can be stated that accuracy achieved with these arrangements can be considered as sufficient taken into account the fact that all these results are preliminary and only leading the mining process further.

The impact of its synonyms, that means in this context, the words 'lentopinta (flight level)' or 'pinta (level), seems to be somewhat similar. The first one is the most describing word in class 42 with nine occurrences, the same number as class size. The same appears another time in class 22, where it is the least significant word with three occurrences. As for the relevance, there is class 48 with percentage of 11.7 between these two. The second one, 'pinta (level)' is distributed as presented in Table 1.

Table 1. Distribution of word 'pinta (level)'

Class #	Reports in class	Significance (9-1)	Number of appearances	Relevance %
48	11	9	7	6.2
92	4	7	2	4.0
24	2	1	1	2.3
42	9	5	3	2.1

NVivo has found together 17 classes including the word mentioned and given slightly different distribution compared with GILTA. The relevancies vary between 6.2 and 1.4 but the four classes in table can be found in top-eight, which proves that compared to the amount of classes, the results are not far away from each other.

If both synonyms with their different forms are combined, the results look as presented in Table 2. As seen from the two separate tables, one class might include both synonyms, which makes the situation slightly different. Number of appearances can be combined using the same pattern as GILTA (=in how many reports the word appears), but significance should be ignored, because counting them together or taking average does not make any sense in this context.

Table 2. Distribution of combined synonyms

Class #	Reports in class	Significance (9-1)	Number of appearances	Relevance %
42	9	9	9	32.3
48	11	9	7	10.8
22	9	5	3	5.0
92	4	7	2	2.6
24	2	1	1	1.6

Query for only synonyms mentioned before brought a list of 25 classes in which the relevance varied between 32.3% and 1.1% but the distribution was rather clear which can be seen also from the table. All classes in the table are among the 11 highest ranked by NVivo.

This case generally revealed the mistake that synonyms were not taken into account sufficiently because the abbreviation with the explicit words 'lentopinta (flight level)' and 'pinta (level)' were not combined to mean the same concept although case forms of both were returned their basic forms. All these observations prove that the concept Flight Level in its different forms cause distortion to mining results enough to be eliminated, that is to be put into stop words. This is grounded on accurate manual analysis of reports in clusters, where the word has significant meaning.

The next problem was caused by abbreviation of *foot* or *feet*, ft. It is a useful and common term and abbreviation in air traffic, but its role and significance in this context should be estimated again. It appears 87 times alone and once combined with / and /min. It is the most significant 'word' in class 82, where it appears in all 26 reports with total amount of 41 times. Carefully inspected it can be stated, that none of them has any significant contribution to the report primarily. For example, six reports have been written due to bird strike, in which case the most important point of view are the conditions and the phase if flight. This can primarily be analysed on basis of other information than altitude of the occurrence that could be of greater importance later. As for the appearance beyond class 82, the abbreviation ft is displayed only twice in the clustering results of GILTA, three times in one cluster as the last significant word and two times in another as the second last important. Thus, from the total number of 87, about half, 46 are counted into the most significant words, so, according to its distribution, the affect of this abbreviation can easily be removed from the data by adding it into stop words.

The English word *'gear'* (seven appearances) was added to its Finnish translation 'laskuteline' which was forgotten to do before. This mistake led to the discovery of another, as the synonyms 'teline (gear)' and 'laskuteline (landing gear)' were kept as separated words, which mistake surely affects significantly the mining results. The first word mentioned has 62 appearances and the second 57 which makes the total of 119, which amount can be considered as significant.

The word *route, 'reitti'*, appears in its different forms not less than 234 times, being the most significant word in four classes and among the nine most significant words in 26 other classes. This observation is in line with the test made with NVivo which found the word in 46 classes its relevance varying between 13.3 and 1.9 per cent. The high frequency might cause the ignorance of the word, but its distribution is so even that it cannot be expected to cause any skewed impact onto the clustering.

To *declare, 'ilmoittaa'* with its total 98 appearances in different case forms and tenses is an interesting piece of testing, because the verb with its forms was left out from synonyms list during the first round, although the synonyms of a correspondent noun, declaration, 'ilmoitus' was put onto the list. As a verb it appears only two times in the most significant words being the sixth with two appearances in class 63, the size of which is six reports, and in the similar way but with three appearances in the class 88, and according to the query performed using NVivo, the verb appears in 37 classes its relevance varied between 9.2 and 1.2 per cent. On the basis of this, it cannot be considered to be significant at all. It is, however, worth to add to the synonyms list, because in this amount of test data, 98 appearances might change the distribution of classes. These both words might be ignored totally after having the results of the second round, because the most important thing is that something has happened and not that somebody declared something to be happened. As a general observation in the test data, the relevant information can be achieved from the reports leaving out the expression about declaration, but this has to be examined carefully.

Almost one hundred checking procedures were made with synonyms and stop words. After careful estimation about the impact of possible changes, no major ones were made, only the most obvious tunings in case forms which does not change the process but make the results to be more accurate. As a total, after this process, the list of stop words contained 569 words when 124 new words were added to it. The list of synonyms contained 2045 word definitions for the first round and it was changed slightly, when 74 new definitions were added, 25 were changed and 57 words were moved from this list to the stop words list, the total of definitions being 2062 for round two.

One essential point in this context was to keep the data as untouched as possible to keep the impacts of the changes as measurable as possible. The main purpose of this refinement is to correct the obvious mistakes, which include both evident mistakes, like forgotten values as well as consequential ones, like wrong estimations of words as for their role and impact to mining results. After the second results the data can be more refined and especially fine tuned, if and when the corrections can be proven to have been successful in the mining process.

5 Conclusions

Despite of the big amount of work to be done when analysing carefully the first results to refine the data for reaching better mining, the results of the first round were encouraging to develop the study further. According to them the direction is correct. The aim of the researcher was already at the very beginning not to stop after the first round but to continue the process and achieve more accurate and usable results. This was both because of the theory which, clearly states that iterations are normal, as well as the increasing interest to the research and its possibilities. All the tested system confirmed the fact that data mining and especially text mining should be an iterative process.

When this article was written, the refined lists were delivered to the operators for the second round. As these are processed, the research will continue by analysing the results carefully. This analysis will reveal whether the research has gone to the right direction or not, that is, the clusters contain more accurate information as for their size and content. However, all the time it should be taken into consideration that data mining tools are "only" decision support systems not giving straight answers to questions but they can well be utilised in scarce retrieval of information.

References

1. Blake, M.B., Singh, L., et al.: A Component-Based Data Management and Knowledge Discovery Framework for Aviation Studies. International Journal of Technology and Web Engineering 1(1) (2006)
2. Delen, D., Crossland, M.D.: Seeding the survey and analysis of research literature with text mining. Expert Systems with Applications: An International Journal 34(3), 1707–1720 (2008)
3. European Commission: Proposal for a Directive of the European Parliament and of the Council on occurrence reporting in civil aviation. Commission of the European Communities. Brussels (2000)
4. Fayyad, U., Piatetsky-Shapiro, G., et al.: Knowledge Discovery and Data Mining: Towards a Unifying Framework. In: Second International Conference on Knowledge History and Data Mining (KDD 1996), Portland, Oregon. AAAI Press, Menlo Park (1996)
5. GAIN Working Group B: Role of Analytical Tools in Airline Flight Safety Management Systems, Global Aviation Information Network (2004)
6. Han, J., Kamber, M.: Data Mining: Concepts and Techniques. Morgan Kaufmann Publishers, San Francisco (2001)
7. Karlsson, F.: Finnish grammar. Porvoo, WSOY (1987)
8. Kloptchenko, A.: Text Mining Based on the Prototype Matching Method. Turku Centre for Computer Science. Turku, Åbo Akademi University: 117 plus additional pages including original papers (2003)

9. Koskenniemi, K.: An application of the two-level model to Finnish. Computational morphosyntax: Report on research 1981-84. Helsinki, Department of General Linguistics (1985)
10. Kutais, B.G. (ed.): Focus on the Internet. Nova Science Publishers, Inc. (2006)
11. Lingsoft and TEMIS Announce Partnership to Expand Text Mining Coverage to Northern European languages and countries,
    http://www.lingsoft.fi/news/2005/temis.html
12. Muir, A.: Fundamentals of Data and Text Mining. In: Seventh GAIN World Conference, Montreal, Canada, Global Aviation Information Network (2004)
13. Nazeri, Z.: Application of Aviation Safety Data Mining Workbench at American Airlines. Proof-of-Concept Demonstration of Data and Text Mining. McLean, Virginia, US, Center for Advanced Aviation Systems Development, MITRE Corporation Inc. (2003)
14. Parsaye, K.: A Characterization of Data Mining Technologies and Processes. Journal of Data Warehousing 2(3), 2–15 (1997)
15. Seifert, J.W.: Data Mining: An Overview. In: Kutais, B.G. (ed.) Focus on the Internet. Nova Science Publishers, Inc. (2006)
16. Toivonen, J., Visa, A., et al.: Prototype Based Information Retrieval in Multilanguage Bibles. In: WIAMIS 2001 (2001)
17. Wang, X., Huang, S., Cao, L., Shi, D., Shu, P.: LSSVM with fuzzy pre-processing model based aero engine data mining technology. In: Alhajj, R., Gao, H., Li, X., Li, J., Zaïane, O.R. (eds.) ADMA 2007. LNCS (LNAI), vol. 4632, pp. 100–109. Springer, Heidelberg (2007)
18. Watson, R.T.: Data Management: Databases and Organizations. John Wiley & Sons, Chichester (1999)
19. Visa, A., Toivonen, J., et al.: Data mining of text as a tool in authorship attribution. In: Data Mining and Knowledge Discovery: Theory, Tools and Technology III, Orlando, USA. SPIE-The International Society for Optical Engineering (2001)

A 360° Vision for Virtual Organizations Characterization and Modelling: Two Intentional Level Aspects

Luz-María Priego-Roche, Dominique Rieu, and Agnès Front

LIG Laboratory, SIGMA Team, BP 72, 38402 Saint Martin d'Héres, Cedex France
{Luz-Maria.Priego-Roche,Dominique.Rieu,Agnes.Front}@imag.fr

Abstract. Nowadays, organizations aiming to be successful in an increasingly competitive market tend to group together into virtual organizations. Designing the information system (IS) of such virtual organizations on the basis of the IS of those participating is a real challenge. The IS of a virtual organization plays an important role in the collaboration and cooperation of the participants organizations and in reaching the common goal. This article proposes criteria allowing virtual organizations to be identified and classified at an intentional level, as well as the information necessary for designing the organizations' IS. Instantiation of criteria for a specific virtual organization and its participants, will allow simple graphical models to be generated in a modelling tool. The models will be used as bases for the IS design at organizational and operational levels. The approach is illustrated by the example of the virtual organization UGRT (a regional stockbreeders union in Tabasco, Mexico).

1 Introduction

Nowadays most organizations are subject to many events which affect their working methods: new competitors, new customer requirements, new technologies, etc. Globalization has accelerated these changes; consequently, companies seek new strategies to survive. Moreover, organizations do not work alone; they are conscious that they are no longer isolated entities and that they must have collaborate with other organizations in various ways in this changing environment. One way to deal with ever changing business opportunities is to form a Virtual Organization (VO). According to several authors [15][4][27][38][50], a VO could be considered as "An alliance for integrating competences and resources from several independent real companies, that are geographically dispersed. This integration is possible throughout the layout of an information systems infrastructure to satisfy customer's requirements, or to seize a business opportunity without having to form a new legal entity".

The organizational unit concept has changed through time starting from individual and group based structures [35], passing by organizational based functional departments [45], evolving to virtual organizations [15][1] and virtual organization networks.

C. Godart et al. (Eds.): I3E 2009, IFIP AICT 305, pp. 427–442, 2009.
© IFIP International Federation for Information Processing 2009

Many researchers agree that information and communication technologies play a fundamental role in a VO [18][12][14][32]. Thus, information systems facilitate cooperation, communication and collaboration of the VO's members. They support sharing resources and new working modes while preserving their individual administrative structures.

Information Systems (IS) have a dominating influence in the organization's ability to adapt to these changes; a company's agility strongly depends on the agility on its IS [44]. To function, a VO requires integrated IS, allowing services, collaboration and cooperation among the Participant Organizations (PO).

VO's information system development involves methodological and technical problems. The identification and representation of requirements are difficult for a "traditional" organization. Such tasks require more effort for a VO due to the large number of organizations and the differing backgrounds and cultures of the people involved.

This article proposes a framework for analyzing a VO based on a 360° vision: intra-organizational (PO's individual properties), inter-organizational (collective properties) and extra-organizational (environmental properties). It particularly covers a set of aspects for characterizing a VO and its PO at an intentional level where collaboration definition and common objectives are emphasized. The aspects are taken from previous research on business management [18][24][26][16][20][10][2] and are intended to support the modelling of a VO allowing various actors (shareholder, user, project manager, business analyst) to obtain all necessary knowledge to conceive collaborative information systems through a VO IS methodology. More precisely, this work aims to facilitate:

– setting up agreements among the different POs by identifying the set of properties linked to their alliance (identification of PO, compromises, objectives, etc.),
– formalizing requirements, a necessary step for defining organizational processes and consequently the adapted collaborative IS.

For doing so, we identify, classify and formalize [36] the intentional characteristics of the VO, to represent them in the form of simple graphic and textual models, and to provide a software platform to capture and manage the characteristics as much as the models. These two approaches have proved to be effective means in helping actors to understand and communicate that understanding among them [5][43][28][17] in various scientific fields [34][37]. Properties formalization is carried out with UML diagrams, an accepted standard for covering conceptual elements [3].

Our research method is strongly based on a case study, the Tabasco's Regional Stockbreeders Union's case study (UGRT)[1], based on one of the authors (Priego) working experience in this organization. The UGRT gathers several companies working in the cattle industry. It offers multiple services and products to its members in a strong cooperation atmosphere in order to increase the economic revenue of cattle production. It is formed by several enterprises (a slaughter-house, a

---

[1] Union Ganadera Regional de Tabasco (http://www.ugrtab.com)

packing facility, a retail store, etc) illustrated in Figure 1. Among them, the stock-breeders are regarded as members of the organization and have the right to use the services offered by the companies, they are grouped in Local Stockbreeders Associations.

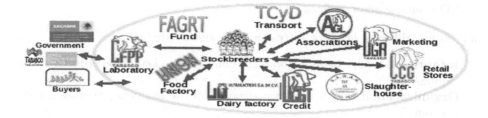

Fig. 1. Case study: the VO UGRT

Thereafter, we specify a 360° vision for the VO (section 2). A description of the relevant aspects to study for a VO at the intentional level is presented in section 3. Two of these aspects are detailed in sections 4 and 5, each of them is broken down, formalized in a UML diagram and illustrated with a graphic model. The illustrations are based on our case study and on a prototype tool for managing the aspects and their representation in graphic models generated automatically from the seized data. Section 6 summarizes our proposals and prospects for future study.

2   A 360° Vision for a VO

Different points of view are needed to ease IS requirement elicitation of the VO. We propose to characterize the VO's requirements across three levels covering a 360° vision that allow us to analyse the VO from different angles and complement other visions [33][13] (Figure 2):

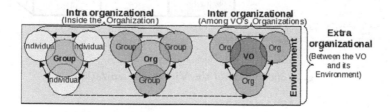

Fig. 2. Intra, Inter and Extra Organizational levels

– **Intra-organizational** level: it has an internal orientation focusing on the relationships among the functional actors (individuals and groups) of the participant organizations (POs) of the VO. This level involves the traditional structure of an organization.

- **Inter-organizational** level: it focuses on the relationships among the POs forming the VO. This level involves a new collaborative strategy among several organizations.
- **Extra-organizational** level: it has an external orientation focusing on the relationship between the VO and its macro environment. This level involves VO's outside actors influences.

In addition, different levels of abstraction are also needed [40]:

- **Intentional** level, where collaboration definition and common objectives are emphasized.
- **Organizational** level, where formalization of the business processes is carried out.
- **Operational** level, where the actions for executing the proposed business processes are detailled, describing the structure and the operation of the IS.

Figure 3 represents the proposed 360° vision that combines the extra, inter and intra organizational points of view and the intentional, organizational and operational abstraction levels. The work presented in this article focuses on the intentional level whose major aspects are described in the following section.

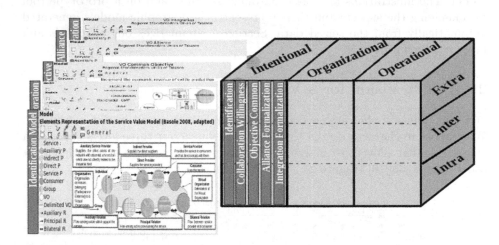

Fig. 3. 360° vision of the Virtual Organization

3   Intentional Level

The intentional characterization is an essential starting point for organizational and operational modelling of a collaborative IS for a VO. Many research work have highlighted the properties that characterize a virtual organization. Some of these approaches are interested in the collaborative aspects ([26],[32]), others emphasize business processes ([38], [47]), or identifying the common benefits [31], or the physical dispersion [1]. Specific works dedicated to small and medium-size companies (SME Collaborate[2], ECOLEAD[3] for example), offer methods and technological infrastructures dedicated to supporting collaboration among these companies. Several modelling languages dedicated to requirement engineering have been proposed to represent organizations: i* framework [21], KAOS [46], CREWS [30], MAP [8], e3 VALUE [19], Service Value Networks [37], etc. The charts used in this article are inspired by the Service Value Networks modelling language [37].

According to [23] a VO life-cycle is composed by identification, formation, operation/evolution and dissolution/termination, we suggest analyzing the VO according to five relevant aspects that support the formation phase of a VO through collaboration alliance [33] (Figure 4):

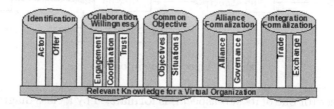

Fig. 4. Major aspects for studying a Virtual Organization

- **Identification:** it characterizes the VO and its composition in terms of organizations and offered services (described in detailed in section 4).
- **Collaboration Willingness:** it characterizes the compromises among the Participant Organizations (PO) to establish the alliance and to work together (described in detailed in section 5)
- **Common Objective:** it characterizes the shared goal and the directions to be followed for reaching it. The latter could answer customer's needs (integral services), satisfy companies' objectives (to share costs, benefits, to create more effective processes)[22], make new business (new markets, new products or services), confront difficulties (absence of knowledge). Usually, objectives emerge from situations that could be classified in opportunities (circumstances favoring the alliance) or problems (difficulties that justify exploring the alliance).
- **Alliance Formalization:** it characterizes the way the alliance is built, more often on agreements or contracts than on mergers and/or acquisitions. Dynamism of the VO is linked to the short or long term alliance established [33]. Moreover, it defines the strenght each organization has in the VO: strong-weak (one leader PO defining the rules, procedures for achieving the objective) or equal (each PO has the same power for making decisions).

---

[2] Small and Medium Enterprise Collaborate, [http://www.smecollaborate.com/]
[3] European Collaborative Networked Organisations Leadership Initiative, [http://ecolead.vtt.fi/]

– **Integration Formalization:** it characterizes the elements the organizations agree to share as part of their competencies and their resources. It defines the POs business processes offered to the VO and their impact in the service value generation. Each PO determines the resources willing to give and expecting to receive from the alliance, it requires defining the mechanisms to ease the electronic integration patterns: information (data, text, messages, images, voice) and communication (connection, access, transfer) [10][50].

To define the VO more precisely, we propose to identify from each aspect, a set of sub-aspects, criteria and sub-criteria (Figure 5). Some of these criteria relate to the VO in general (generic criterion), other criteria are specific to the PO.

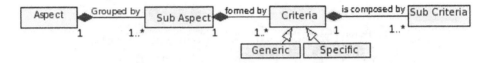

Fig. 5. Aspects decomposition

Each aspect (or one of its sub-aspects) is formalized by a class diagram (example Figure 6). A criterion is represented by a stereotyped class. Sub-criteria are represented either by simple attributes, or by associations linking the criterion class to the value class, describing the sub-criterion possible values. An instance example of these models, resulting from our case study, is represented in the form of prototype screens which are in process of development (example Figure 7). From this instantiation it is possible to deduce automatically simple graphic models (example Figure 8). The next two sections detail the Identification and Collaboration Willingness aspects.

4   Identification Aspect

The Identification Aspect is composed of two sub-aspects detailed below and formalized in Figure 6.

– The **Actor**'s goal is to identify and characterize the organizations (independently of their participation in the VO) as well as the VO. It is composed of two criteria.

- *Organizations.* Each organization is characterized by a *name*, a *description*, a *size*, a *location* (city, state, country), a *constitution* (individual organization or group) and an *activity sector*. The *size* is given based on a scale from Small to Large, while taking into account the number of employees, the turnover, the market share and the organization peculiarities. The peculiarities describe common properties to consider (e.g. "Manual Work for small stockbreeders"). An individual organization is not composed of other organizations. A group organization is a subsidiary of a holding organization which controls or guides the groups' activities. *Activity sectors* (*specific and general*) characterize the organization in its business context; we use those proposed by NAICS[4]. The sectors are characterized by a *code*, a *name* and a *description*; they are related to activities (example of specific activity: Livestock production; examples of general activities: Agriculture, Forestry and Fishing).

- *Virtual Organization.* A VO has a *name*, a *description*, a *creation date* and a *specific activity sector*. The VO is composed of organizations (at least two), each of whom plays a role in the VO: either as a Participant Organization (PO) in the alliance or as an External Organization (EO); the latter is not part of the alliance but it interacts directly with the VO either soliciting or rendering services. The roles have fixed durations set by starting and termination dates.

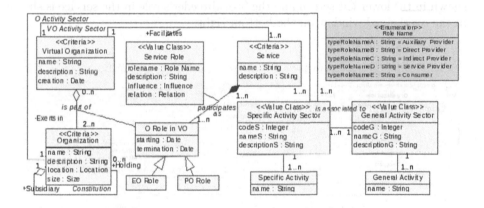

Fig. 6. Identification model

- The ***Offer***'s aim is to identify and characterize the services offered by the organizations and the roles the organizations play to produce these services. It is composed of two criteria.

  - *Services.* A VO provides one or more services without making a distinction between a physical product (like the meat for example) or a service (like the distribution of the meat) [41]. A Service has a *name* and a *description*.
  - *Role.* Each PO or EO has a role in the achievement or the consumption of the service. It can be a role of provisioning or using the service (this means the relationship of the PO or the EO to the service). This role can be essential or secondary for the achievement of the service, meaning the influence on the activity by the PO or EO. The identified roles come from the work of [37]:

---

[4] North American Industry Classification System,
[http://www.census.gov/epcd/naics02/naicod02.htm]

     * an *auxiliary service provider* supplies the other actors of the net-
      work with essential services but which are not directly related to the
      industrial field,
     * an *indirect provider* supplies the direct suppliers,
     * a *direct provider* supplies the service providers,
     * a *service provider* provides the service to consumers and has direct
      contact with them,
     * a *consumer* uses the service.

Figure 7 illustrates an instance of this aspect. The top left screen allows users
to assign organizations to a VO (here the Regional Stockbreeders Union of
Tabasco), either as a PO or an EO. The top right screen characterizes each
organization (size, location, etc.), for example Stockbreeder, and the bottom
right screen lets users associate its activity sectors. Finally, the VO service is
shown in the lower left screen and the Stockbreeder's role in the service is shown
in the overlapped window on the bottom right.

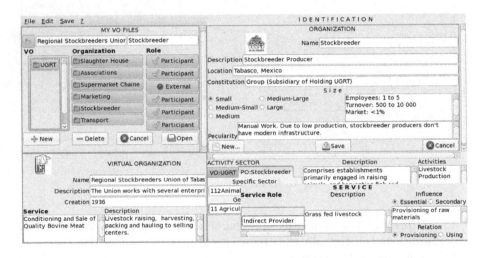

Fig. 7. Identification instance

From these properties, graphic representations can be generated in the form
of models. For example, Figure 8 shows the set of organizations which form
the VO of our case study based on an adaptation of [37]'s modelling language:
the POs (Stockbreeder, Associations, Slaughter-house, Transport, Marketing)
and the EOs (Supermarket Chains, Government Regulators, Meat Consumers)
which compose the service "Conditioning and Sale of Quality Bovine Meat". The
roles of each organization or organization groups and their relationships are also
illustrated.

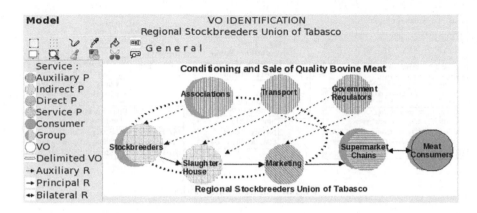

Fig. 8. Graphic representation of the Regional Stockbreeders Union VO

5 Collaboration Willingness Aspect

The Collaboration Willingness aspect is composed of three sub-aspects detailed below:

- **Engagement** qualifies the availabilities and the investments which the participant organizations are ready to engage (see Figure 9).
  - The *availability* that the PO is ready to give is described by a *time* reserved for the relationship, a *priority* the PO assigns to this project compared to other projects and the PO's *adaptability* to changes. All these attributes can have a value estimated by a scale from Low, Medium-Low, Medium, Medium-High, to High.
  - The *investments* concern the elements that each PO devotes to the VO, for example financial or material assets, human, relational or organizational capital. This typology is suggested by [20]. An *investment* thus has a *type* (for example financial credit), a *frequency* which can be constant, sporadic or event-triggered, and an *impact* (direct or indirect). Investments are described by sentences such as *Give a contribution for each slaughtered cattle* and by measurement objects (calculations and constraints).

In Figure 9, the availability criterion is represented in UML, the class "PO Role" has three attributes: time, priority and adaptability. We point out that the class "PO Role" is an association class characterizing the role of a PO in a VO (cf Figure 6 "PO Role'" sub class of '"O Role in VO"). Each instance of this class is related to investments which are related to measurements.

Figure 10 illustrates an instance of the Engagement Model for the PO "Stockbreeder" in terms of *availability* (top left screen), investment (in this case a financial type in the form of a "contribution evaluated by average costs"). This contribution is event-triggered (when the cattle is slaughtered) and has a direct

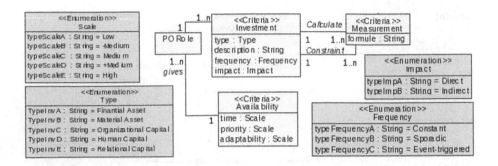

Fig. 9. Engagement model

impact on the VO. The bottom right screen shows a chart for the Engagement.
The arcs bind the Stockbreeder PO with the VO; the squares delineated by continuous lines represent availabilities; the squares delineated by dotted lines do
so for investments. For the latter, an icon inside the square illustrates its type.

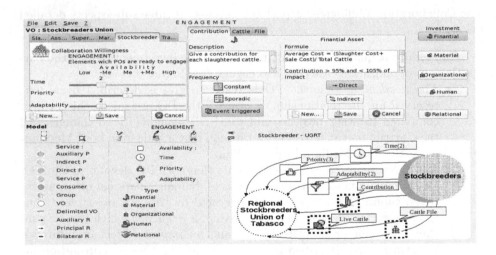

Fig. 10. Engagement instance

— **Coordination** characterizes the way the POs are organized to work together (see Figure 11). This is based on the work of [48], [15], [11], [49],
  to characterize inter-organizational coordination which is composed of the
  following two criteria:

  • *Elements* involved that must be coordinated. Contrary to an invest-
    ment, the coordinated elements remain the property of its organization.
    Each *Element* has a *description* and a *dependence* (coupled, uncoupled).
    An element can be a person or a process. The coordination of people

requires knowing their profiles (preferences, personal information) and their work team (size, role). Process coordination implies specifying the task to carry out (planning, design) by characterizing its execution type (routine, non routine) and the information concerned (data, texts, messages, images, voice).

- *Communication* of each element is characterized based on CSCW[5] [29] and Denver [42] models. We describe *communication* through answering the questions *where, when* and *how* in terms of space, time and movement. Space includes a place (remote or local) and a state of presence (physical or virtual). Time includes a frequency (it can be constant, recurring, sporadic or event-triggered) and a moment (synchronous or asynchronous). Movement includes accessibility (mobile or fixed) and a direction (transmission, interaction, reception). This characterization determines the specific IS that offers the necessary functions of electronic communication to organize the interacting elements.

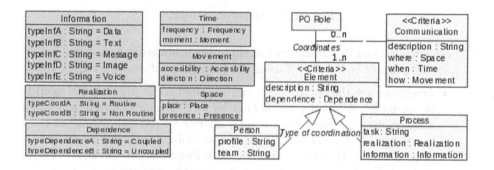

Fig. 11. Coordination model

Figure 11 proposes a coordination model where the criterion element is represented by a class. A PO can have one or more *elements* (people or process) to coordinate. Each element coordinated by a PO is characterized in terms of space, time and movement by an instance of the Communication class. Figure 12 illustrates an instance of the coordination model. The "Stockbreeder" has two elements to coordinate: a person type, manager and a process type, inventory (in top right screen). A graphic instance inspired from Basole's model is proposed in the bottom screen. The element types to coordinate are framed by pentagons, continuous sides for people and dotted sides for processes; they are attached to legends describing the attributes using icons.

- **Trust** among partners plays a decisive role in the alliance [6][26] from group [39] to virtual organization perspective [7][25]. In [9] Sauders *et al* conceptualizes it as Benevolence (acting in good will), Integrity (adherence to an accepted moral code), Competence (expectation of technically competent role

---

[5] Computer Supported Cooperative Work.

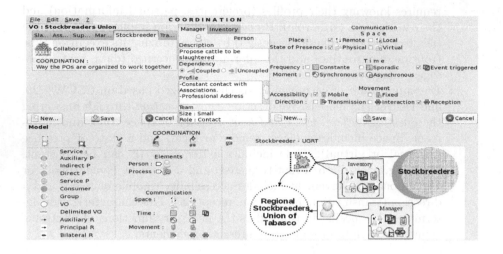

Fig. 12. Coordination instance

performance) and Predictability (acting in accordance to an expected behavior). We propose to describe it using the following criteria (see Figure 13):

- *Functions* are the control activities required to be vigilant and need to be regulated. A function carried out by a PO is characterized by a *name*, a *description*, an *agreement* among all PO on the importance of these functions, an *achievement* (optional or obligatory) and an *execution*. According to [16], the execution of these functions can be done either by giving entire freedom of action (indicating the independence of each PO to achieve its responsibilities), or by controlling them.
- *Regulation* of the functions ensures the good performance of the VO. A regulation is characterized by the *type* of element to control (for example active material) and its *description* (for example cattle), a *visibility* (if the PO supervises the execution of its proper functions, we talk about self-regulation; if it must debrief to other PO, we talk about surveillance), a *control frequency* (constant, sporadic, event-triggered) and *penalization* in case of violating the control function (penalty, no penalty, warning). Regulation is quantified through a set of calculations and constraints.

Figure 13 represents the Trust model. Each PO (through its various roles played in a VO) can have or not functions to control. The function criterion is represented by a class formed by the attributes: name, description, agreement, achievement and execution. The regulation function is characterized in terms of type, description, visibility, frequency and penalization. Figure 14 proposes an instance of the PO "Stockbreeder" and its function "Cattle weight control and evaluation". This function is controlled by a material asset ("weight standard per cattle type") in the top right screen. The bottom right screen shows the Trust's graphic representation. The functions to be controlled are represented by rectangles with rounded corners attached to legends describing them ("Classification" and "Meat").

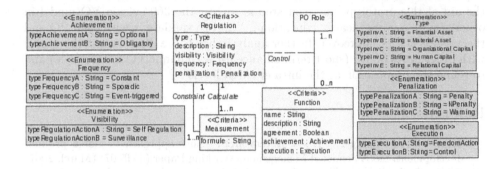

Fig. 13. Trust model

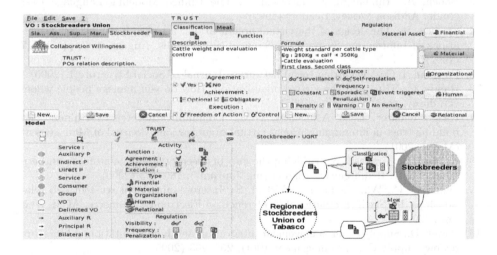

Fig. 14. Trust instance

6   Conclusion and Perspectives

This article proposes a collection of criteria to characterize at an intentional level the various participants' organizations within the VO and their interrelationships. These criteria, resulting in particular from work in the management field, are gathered in five aspects. The first two aspects, Identification and Collaboration Willingness are formalized in UML models. The instances come from our case study the Regional Stockbreeders Union of Tabasco in Mexico. The three other aspects (Common Objective, Alliance Formalization and Integration Formalization), are not described in this article because space constraints.

In addition to this formalization, a modelling prototype tool is under development that will allow the automatic generation of simple graphic models from captured instances. These models are the base for identifying and modelling the requirements that the VO's IS should conform on the basis of the PO's IS. Whith the aid of this prototype the next step is to test the 360° vision VO model in other service sectors (health, education ...) and to validate it with each PO and the various actors. Moreover, further analysis has to be done to test the model with other types of VO (short term alliance for a Dynamic VO for example) and to refine the proposition at the intra et extra levels.

References

1. Tripathy, A., Eppinger, S.D.: A system architecture approach to global product development. Sloan School of Management Working Paper (4645-07) (March 2007)
2. White, A., Daniel, M.: Electronique marketplace to marketplace alliances: Emerging trends and strategic rationales. In: ACM Second International Conference on Entertainment Computing, Pittsburgh PA, May 3-10 (2003)
3. Booch, B., Rumbaugh, J., Jacobsen, I.: The Unified Modeling Language User Guide. Addison-Wesley, Reading (1999)
4. Travica, B.: The design of the virtual organisation.: a research model. In: Associations of Information Systems Conference, Indianapolis, August 1997, pp. 15–17 (1997)
5. Freeman, L.C.: Visualizing social networks. Journal of Social Structure 1 (2000)
6. Handy, C.: Trust and the virtual organization: How do you manage people whom you do not see? (May/June 1995)
7. Kasper-Fuehrer, E.C., Ashkanasy, N.M.: Communicating trustworthiness and building trust in interorganizational virtual organizations. Journal of Management (May 1, 2001)
8. Rolland, C., Prakash, N.: Bridging the gap between organisational needs and erp functionality. Requirements Engineering Journal 5, 180–193 (2000)
9. Saunders, C., Wu, Y., Li, Y., Weisfeld, S.: Interorganizational trust in b2b relationships. In: Sixth International Conference on Electronic Commerce. ACM, New York (2004)
10. Power, D.: Supply chain management integration and implementation: a literature review. Supply Chain Management 10(4), 252–263 (2005)
11. den Hengst, M., Sol, G.: The impact of information and communication technology on interorganizational coordination: Guidelines from theory. Special Series on Information Exchange in Electronic Markets 4(3) (2001)
12. Porter, M.E.: Strategy and the internet. Harvard Business Review, 62–78 (March 2001)
13. Barki, H., Pinsonneault, A.: A model of organizational integration, implementation effort, and performance. Institute for Operations Research and the Management Sciences 16(2), 165–179 (2005)
14. Bouarfa, H., Abed, M.: Acquisition of tacit knowledge in virtual organizations. In: CIMCA/IAWTIC, pp. 383–388 (2005)
15. Davidow, Z.H., Malone, M.S.: The virtual corporation: Structuring and revitalizing the corporation for the 21stcentury. T. Harper Business, NY (1992)
16. Fenneteau, H., Naro, G.: Controle et confiance dans l'entreprise virtuelle, illustrations logistiques. IBM Systems Journal, 203–219 (May-June 2005)

17. Grönniger, H., Krahn, H., Rumpe, B., Schindler, M., Völkel, S.: Text-based modeling. In: Proceedings of the 4th International Workshop on Software Language Engineering (ateM 2007), Nashville, TN, USA (2007)
18. Burn, J., Marshall, P., Wild, M.: Managing knowledge for strategic advantage in the virtual organisation. In: Proceedings of the ACM SIGPR Conference on Computer Personnel Research, New Orleans, USA, April 8-10, pp. 19–26 (1999)
19. Gordjin, J.: Value-based Requirements Engineering: Exploring Innovative e-Commerce Ideas. PhD thesis, Vrije Universiteit Amsterdam (2002)
20. Parung, J., Bititci, U.S.: A conceptual metric for managing collaborative networks. Journal of Modellling in Management 1(2), 116–136 (2006)
21. Yu, E.S.K.: Towards modeling and reasoning support from early-phase requirements engineering. In: IEEE 3rd International Symposium on Requirements Engineering, Annapolis MD, January 5-8, vol. 235, pp. 226–235 (1997)
22. Goldman, S.L., Nagel, R.N., Preiss, K.: Agile competitors and virtual organizations: Strategies for enriching the customer. Van Nostrand Reinhold (1995)
23. Camarinha-Matos, L.M., Afsarmanesh, H.: A roadmap for strategic research on virtual organizations. In: Proceedings of IFIP Working Conference on Virtual Enterprises - PRO-VE 2003, Lugano, Switzerland, pp. 33–46 (2003)
24. Brandenbuger, A.M., Nalebuff, B.J.: The right game: use game theory to shape strategy. Harvard Business Review, 57–71 (July-August 1995)
25. Ibrahim, M., Ribbers, P.: Trust, dependence and global interorganizational systems. In: Proceedings of the 39th Hawaii International Conference on System Sciences. IEEE, Los Alamitos (2006)
26. Kanter, R.M.: Collaborative advantage: The art of alliances. Harvard Business Review, 96–108 (July-August 1994)
27. Mazzeschi, M.: The virtual organisation. In: 7th International Conference on Concurrent Enterprising. Bremen, vol. 24(11), June 27-29, pp. 331–335 (2001)
28. Petre, M.: Why looking isn't always seeing: Readership skills and graphical programming. Communications of the ACM 38(6) (June 1995)
29. Roseman, M., Greenberg, S.: Groupkit: A groupware toolkit for building real-time. Conferencing applications. In: CSCW 1992 (1992)
30. Maiden, N.A.M.: Crews-savre: Scenarios for acquiring and validating requirements. Journal for Automate Software Engineering 5(4), 419–446 (1998)
31. Marshal, P., McKay, J., Burn, J.: The tree s's of virtual organisations: Structure, strategy and success factors. School of Management Information Systems, Edith Cowan University (1999)
32. Robinson, P., Karabulut, Y., Haller, J.: Dynamic virtual organization management service oriented enterprise applications. In: IEEE International Conference on Collaborative Computing: Networking, Applications and Worksharing (2005)
33. ECOLEAD Project. Characterization of key components, features, and operating principles of the virtual breeding environment. Afsarmanesh UvA, H. (ed.) D21.1:8 (March 2005)
34. Albert, R., Barabasi, A.L.: Statistical mechanics of complex networks. Reviews of Modern Physics 74 (January 30, 2002)
35. Shani, R., Grant, R.M., Krishnan, R., Thompson, E.: Advanced manufacturing systems and organizational choice: Sociotechnical system approach. California Management Review 34(4), 91–111 (Summer 1992)
36. Sousa, R., Putnik, G.: A formal theory of bm virtual enterprises structures. In: IFIP International Federation for Information Processing, vol. 159 (2005)
37. Basole, R.C., Rouse, W.B.: Complexity of service value networks: Conceptualisation and empirical investigation. IBM Systems Journal 47(1), 53–70 (2008)

38. Cheng, S., Xu, X., Wang, G., Li, Q.: An agile method of modeling business process simulation for virtual enterprises. In: IEEE International Conference on e-Business Engineering (2005)
39. Iacono, C.S., Weisband, S.: Developing trust in virtual teams. In: Proceedings of the Thirtieth Hawaii International Conference on System Sciences, vol. 2, pp. 412–420. IEEE, Los Alamitos (1997)
40. Nurcan, S., Barrios, J., Rolland, C.: Une methode pour la definition de l'impact organisationnel du changement. In: XXème Congrès INFORSID, Nantes, June 4-7 (2002)
41. Levitt, T.: Production line-approach to service. Harvard Business Review 50(5), 41–52 (1972)
42. Salvador, T., Scholtz, J., Larson, J.: The denver model for groupware design 5yeeeeee haaaaaa! Conferencing applications. In: CSCW 1992, CHI 1995, Denver Colorado, vol. 28(1), pp. 52–58 (1996)
43. Brandes, U., Raab, J., Wagner, D.: Exploratory network visualization: Simultaneous display of actor status and connection. Journal of Social Structure 2(4) (October 19, 2001)
44. Sambamurthy, V., Bharadwaj, A., Grover, V.: Shaping agility through digital options: Reconceptualizing the role of information technology in contemporary firms. MIS Quarterly 2(27), 237–263 (2003)
45. Tatikonda, M.V., MontoyaWeiss, M.M.: Integrating operations and marketing perspectives of product innovation: The influence of organizational process factors and capabilities on development performance. Management Science INFORMS 47(1), 151–172 (2001)
46. van Lamsweerde, A., Darimont, R., Letier, E.: Managing conflicts in goal-driven requirements engineering. IEEE Transactions on Software Engineering 24(11), 908–926 (1998)
47. Barnett, W., Presley, A., Johnson, M., Liles, D.H.: An architecture for the virtual enterprise. In: IEEE International Conference on Systems, Man, and Cybernetics, Humans, Information and Technology, October 1994, vol. 1(2-5), pp. 506–511 (1994)
48. Malone, T.W.: What is coordination theory? In: National Science Foundation Coordination Theory Workshop (February 19, 1988)
49. Laurillau, Y.: Conception et realisation logicielles pour les collecticiels centrees sur l'activite de groupe: le modele et la plate-forme Clover. PhD thesis, Universite Joseph-Fourier Grenoble I (2002)
50. Yang, Z., Zhang, J.B., Low, C.P.: Towards dynamic integration on collaborative virtual enterprise using semantic web services. In: IEEE International Conference on Industrial Informatics (2006)

Author Index